Dynamic Physical Education for Elementary School Children

Fourth Edition

Victor P. Dauer

Washington State University
Pullman, Washington

Burgess Publishing Company

426 South Sixth Street • Minneapolis, Minn. 55415

Preface to the Fourth Edition

In presenting the fourth edition of *Dynamic Physical Education for Elementary School Children,* the author has attempted to weld together newer elements and approaches with older concepts and directions of value into a functional program of physical education. It is believed that the book represents a rational, proportional emphasis on skill development, fitness elements, basic movement (movement education), and perceptual-motor concepts. In addition, personal and educational values for the student have been incorporated throughout.

Following an extensive tour of elementary school programs in selected countries of Europe in 1965-66, the author in conjunction with the Pullman, Washington, Schools was awarded a three-year Title III, ESEA, study to develop a specially designed elementary school physical education program by combining selected European ideas with chosen American approaches. This program is now in operation in the Pullman Schools following the completion of the federally funded study. The present edition reflects the results of this program and can be regarded as a thoroughly child-tested curriculum.

A number of convictions which prompted the original authorship of the book still have relevance. Additionally, several other concepts have expanded its educational emphasis.

First, a broad program of physical education should be the right of each child, with emphasis on rugged and demanding activities. Children need to be challenged if they are to move along the path of development. Enough physical education materials are available in this text so that a variety of learning experiences can be presented on each grade level. New and exciting experiences should face the children as they progress from grade to grade.

A second conviction is that a successful program for children occurs only through careful planning. The curriculum must be blocked out in enough detail that the year's work is outlined. Superimposed on the year's outline is the vital element of progression, progression from grade to grade, within grades, and within activities. A major purpose of this text is to present learning experiences either allocated by grade level or in progression within the activity descriptions. In some instances, the basic elements of an activity or area are presented in chart form to make apparent the progressions.

The third belief is that the learning environment involving the teacher, the learner, and the activity will suggest the most appropriate method of approach to attain the expected outcomes. At times experiences can be presented with a structured and directed approach, while at other times basic movement methodology will offer better results. Teachers differ in aptitude, personality, and background. To ask a teacher to restrict his efforts to one type of methodology is not sound. On the other hand, teachers must become familiar with basic movement techniques as these widen and broaden the learning potential of the material. Problem-solving, exploratory, and creative approaches enhance and enrich the movement experiences of children.

A fourth conviction is that physical fitness values for children come primarily from a program which is planned and administered with that end in view. The attainment and maintenance of suitable levels of physical fitness are neither happenstance nor casual. The child must be placed in a program in which the development and maintenance of fitness are regarded as important goals. Caution must be observed so that the emphasis on fitness does not become the dominant or overriding consideration.

i

Lastly, the conduct of the program must give consideration to the development of personal values (self-image) and make important contributions to the overall educational progress of the child. The key to this lies both in the kinds of learning experiences which are selected and in the manner in which they are conducted.

The author would like to give recognition to Mr. Robert Pangrazi, Supervisor of Elementary Physical Education for the Pullman Schools, who served as an associate in the Title III study and collaborated with the author in this revision. Many of the sequences and approaches presented in this edition were developed under Mr. Pangrazi's direction.

The illustration with regard to good and poor posture was adapted by permission from one of the curriculum guides of the Seattle Public Schools. The material on Rope Jumping is also from the Seattle Public Schools and was developed by Dennis Meyer. This was adapted from original material compiled by Paul Smith, Director of Physical Education for Shoreline Public Schools, Seattle, Washington. The author is also indebted to many other teachers and supervisors too numerous to mention for the many ideas incorporated into the book.

The teachers and children of the Pullman Schools, particularly Jefferson School, merit our heartfelt thanks for their cooperation and efforts as subjects for the many illustrations in the text.

Photography credits go to Robert Bullis, staff photographer, Washington State University, Pullman, Washington. Credits for selected drawings and illustrations go to Ron Smith, Pullman, Washington. Action sequences were drawn by Bruce Frederick, University of Wisconsin at Superior.

The assistance of Dr. James M. Sweeney, The Ohio State University, in previous revisions is gratefully acknowledged.

Pullman, Washington   Victor P. Dauer
March, 1971

Contents

iii

1

The Child and Physical Education

What Is Physical Education?
Educational and Cultural Forces Affecting Physical Education
Modern-Day Educational and Sociological Trends
The Approach to Physical Education

The results of good physical education are not limited to the body alone, but they extend even to the soul itself.
—ARISTOTLE, 350 B.C.

The general goal of education *and* physical education is two-fold: (1) the greatest possible development of each individual, and (2) education for responsible democratic citizenship. Physical education provides an important educational medium which can make a significant contribution toward this goal. Basically, it makes use of the activity drive of children who, even the most timid, enjoy movement. The principal aim of physical education, then, should be to satisfy this insatiable appetite for movement, help them to enjoy it more, and guide them so that they may build lasting values. The aim of each teacher should be to assist in attaining the maximum development possible for each child.

These broad values can be achieved only if children like, enjoy, and appreciate physical education. A child will derive little value from the program if he has learned from traumatic experiences to detest his physical education classes and physical activity. The dignity of the individual must be preserved in his physical experiences, and each child must meet some measure of success in his own activities and activities with his peers. From this base, the full potential of physical education as an educational tool can be realized. To achieve high success in personal development, children need to become totally involved in the program and what they are doing.

The Elementary School Physical Education Position Paper* expresses this so adequately:

> In a very real measure, the degree of success the elementary child experiences in his work and play is influenced by his ability to execute movement patterns effectively and efficiently. For the child, movement is one of the most used means of non-verbal communication and expression. It is one of the most important avenues through which he forms impressions about himself and his environment.

To make important contributions to the growth and development of children, a quality program, well-planned and well-taught, is needed in our elementary schools. Physical education must be an integral part of the total education program for the child.

WHAT IS PHYSICAL EDUCATION?

Physical education, then, is education of, by, and through human movement. It is that phase of general education which contributes

*_Essentials of a Quality Elementary School Physical Education Program—A Position Paper_ (Washington, D. C.: AAHPER, 1970).

1

to the total growth and development of the child primarily through selected movement experiences and physical activities.

Today's emphasis on physical education centers on its educational potential, its power to contribute to more than just the development of physical fitness, skills, or desirable social qualities. Educators are looking to physical education for more than just lip service to total child development. Increasing evidence appears to demonstrate that physical education can effectively expand its function as an educational tool by focusing on exploration, creativity, thought and problem-solving processes, concept formation, and concomitant learnings, leading to self-confidence and the establishment of a good self-concept and self-image.

That physical education can make significant contributions to total child development and learning is becoming increasingly more evident. Nevertheless, the concept of total development must include adequate attention to physical fitness and neuromuscular skills, which are the unique contributions of physical education to the child's well-being.

Health, vitality, and vigor are a basis for excellence in living. Physical education should be concerned with contributing to physical welfare and vigor, which are basic to a balanced life. If physical education does not provide the child with experiences to realize these attributes, no other area of the school curriculum will compensate for this loss.

Important too are basic skills and perceptual-motor competencies, which evidently have a bearing on academic progress in the lower grades. Studies by Kephart* and others have revealed that these competencies are of critical importance in the primary grades, particularly with respect to reading readiness and achievement. It is reasoned that as children learn to move effectively, handle their bodies in a variety of situations and challenges, and react favorably to their physical environment, a competency base is built upon which academic concepts and learnings can function more effectively.

*Newell C. Kephart, *The Slow Learner in the Classroom* (Columbus, Ohio: Charles C. Merrill Co., Inc., 1960).

EDUCATIONAL AND CULTURAL FORCES AFFECTING PHYSICAL EDUCATION

It is important that all educators recognize and appreciate the quality and depth of the changes which have taken place in elementary school physical education under the impact of educational and cultural forces, particularly during the last decade. In a sense, the emphasis in physical education curriculums has been cycloidal in that educators have embraced new ideas and approaches enthusiastically when they first appeared, subsequently retaining only their best features as the glamor of the "New Look" wore off.

The Foreign Influence — Prior to World War I

Up to the outbreak of World War I, no single strong movement in physical education held dominance in the United States. A number of European systems, particularly German and Swedish, had their advocates, with no strong American system appearing to challenge these imports. European programs were rigid and militaristic in nature, with mind and body considered separate entities. This dichotomy, labeled "dualism," spawned a program which was pointed primarily toward the physical aspects of an individual.

The emphasis was largely on an exercise program, with dissenting voices from advocates of the German system favoring a gymnastic approach. In many of our schools, the physical education program consisted primarily of a series of exercises which could be done in the classroom while each student stood alongside his desk.

The Games and Sports Emphasis — World War I to 1930

Early in World War I it was determined that physical training programs for soldiers based on the prevailing calisthenic approach were unsuitable for military purposes, and a shift toward the utilization of games and sports for developmental purposes occurred. Dualism also continued in the new programs with mind and body still separated, but physical educators slowly became aware of the educational possibilities of physical education and its contributions to total development of the individual. The games and sports program appeared to be appropriate for the development not only of the physical goals, but also for the attainment of desirable social qualities.

On the elementary level, the program centered on the games and sports, strongly influenced by the athletic emphasis of the secondary and college sports programs. Literally, it was a program which could be described by answering the question, "What games are we going to play today?"

The Depression Years — 1930 to 1940

While physical education received strong impetus from the games and sports emphasis during the Roaring Twenties, it sank to a low level during the depression years. This was particularly true in the elementary schools, where the "frills" in education, i.e., art, music, home economics, shop, and physical education, were relegated to secondary roles, or in many cases eliminated entirely.

Gradually, dualism was being rejected and physical education began to center on the development of the total individual. Concern was still given to the physical aspects, but only within the concept of the total development of the child; physically, mentally, socially, and emotionally.

The Reawakening — World War II

Men and women accepted in the Armed Services in World War II were subjected to rigorous training programs, particularly in flyer and commando corps. The cream of American physical educators labored in both physical fitness developmental and hospital reconditioning programs, which provided an opportunity for much experimentation in methodology and new approaches.

The new approaches would argue that an improvement in the quality of American physical education might have been expected after the war, but little effect was evident in the quality of elementary school programs. It seemed that American physical education on the elementary level reverted back to "business as usual" routines, with emphasis on simple games with some sports added for good measure.

The Surge of Physical Fitness — 1954 to Present

Although physical fitness has always been considered an important goal in physical edu-

cation, at times a renewal of the emphasis has occurred, dependent upon the social forces dominant at the time. Such a renewal occurred in 1954 following the publication of the comparative fitness levels of American and European children, based on the Kraus-Weber Tests. A study by Dr. Hans Kraus, comparing certain strength and flexibility measurements of 4000 New York area school children with a comparable sample of Central European children, had far-reaching results. The American press became aroused concerning the comparative weaknesses of American children, and with this concern, the present fitness movement was born.

One result of the furor over physical fitness was the establishment of the President's Council on Physical Fitness, a potent force in promoting good physical fitness not only among school children, but also among citizens of all ages. The President's Council on Physical Fitness and Sports, as it is now named, through its many publications, services, and promotions, has had a major influence on school programs leading to the development of better levels of physical fitness among children.

The results of this new emphasis on fitness have been evident in the elementary schools. Programs are of improved quality, and many have been established where none existed formerly. Administrators have become increasingly aware of the contributions which physical education can make to the growth and development of children. Other apparent effects are increased time allotment for physical education, better facilities and equipment, and provision for consultant service and specialized teachers. The Council's national seven-item physical fitness test has widespread acceptance and affords fitness comparisons on a country-wide basis.

Movement Education — 1960 to Present

Movement education brought a fresh new approach, a new methodology, and a new way of providing learning experiences for children. With its emphasis on the individual child, it features the problem-solving and exploratory approach.

Movement education has its origins in England and reached this country directly or through Canadian programs. At present it has become an indispensable and fully accepted part of American physical education. Movement education centers on the indirect (exploratory) method of teaching as opposed to the direct (command) approach. In practice, the degree to which indirect teaching is employed varies, giving rise to many choices of methodology.

There is confusion concerning the meaning of terms and definitions in movement. These will be clarified in later discussions.

Perceptual-Motor Competency — 1960 to Present

Based on the theories of Montessori, Luria, Piaget, and others, the importance of motor experiences in the normal learning process of children was recognized. Delacato and Kephart were among the leaders in developing a practical school approach based on the theory that children deficient in certain academic competencies could be helped with a structured perceptual-motor program, so as to achieve better in their academic pursuits.

Perceptual-motor theory holds that each child normally must pass successively through stages of neuromuscular development during childhood. If one or more of these stages is omitted or underdeveloped, then the child will have trouble with appropriate motor reponses, which may cause him difficulty in normal academic progress, specifically with reading, speech, spelling, and writing. The theory is that a program of selected perceptual-motor activities can help develop the missed stages, thus providing a better basis for normal academic achievement.

Evidence is strong that a certain stage of neuromuscular development is necessary for optimum academic development. Research is lacking pertaining to identification of the perceptual-motor qualities, and a good scientific basis for programs is not available. However, it is established that the thinking mind is rooted in the physical being, and all cognitive learning is based on physical and sensory input.

MODERN-DAY EDUCATIONAL AND SOCIOLOGICAL TRENDS

A number of trends and influences, some from education in general, are having and will have a profound effect on elementary school physical education. Their full impact has not yet been manifest, but they merit attention.

Education now centers on the individual, with instruction and progress determined by how fast each child can absorb what the school has to offer. In physical education, more attention is focused on individual activities, with less on competition between teams or individuals. A child should be allowed to progress at his own rate.

In keeping with educational individualism, the development by each child of a proper self-image and self-concept is of vital importance. It is necessary to offer the type of programs where each child can meet success and not be discouraged by failure.

Conceptual understanding, i.e., the application of abstract ideas drawn from experience, also plays an important part in physical education today. Thus in the process of movement the child learns to distinguish between near and far, strong and weak, light and heavy, high and low. He should be given the opportunity to experiment and thereby establish an understanding of such other terms as curve, stretch, twist, turn, balance, and bounce, and so on. He should also be enabled to learn to work purposefully toward a designated goal or to be self-critical. Thus the learning environment of physical education becomes an extension of the educational activities of the classroom.

The role of physical education in working with disadvantaged and culturally deprived children needs to be re-evaluated. While the problems and relationships are complicated and deep, physical education can nevertheless help youngsters achieve status, enjoy respect, and succeed through improved peer regard.

There is a trend toward extending education downward and upward. The downward aspects are of importance to the elementary school physical educator with the appearance of preschool education and child care centers. It is necessary to revise our thinking downward to provide movement experiences for these children. Head Start programs are another extension of the educational system. Since much of the instruction is motor and physical, there must be concern with providing appropriate and effective movement experiences for preschool children.

A potent influence for educational experimentation and dissemination of results is found in the many research programs sponsored by the U. S. Office of Education under the legal provisions of such vehicles as the Elementary and Secondary Education Act and the Education Professions Development Act.

Modern international travel and interchange of educational personnel have provided fruitful exchanges of program ideas and equipment, broadening and enriching American programs. Such items as the balance-beam bench, climbing ropes on tracks, wall-attached climbing frames, and floor apparatus have now found their way from European programs into American schools.

An event of far-reaching importance affecting elementary school physical education programs was the establishment in the AAHPER of a consultant in elementary school physical education. This reflects a trend to recognize elementary school physical education as an entity in itself rather than as hanging on to the coattails of secondary school physical education. The consultant at the time of this manuscript, Dr. Margie Hanson, has been able to weld together many varied factions working toward common goals by scheduling national institutes and regional workshops, forming commissions, and publishing philosophical and explanatory material in the field.

Another trend appearing is toward the employment of the specialist in physical education on the elementary level. Where previously classroom teachers handled the physical education instructional chores, there is recognition that quality programs are possible only with quality teaching by specially trained instructors. Since this involves some added expense to school districts, total acceptance of specialist teaching has not yet arrived.

With the increased employment of specialists, a necessary adjustment of college teacher-training programs is indicated to provide a product that can function effectively in the elementary school physical education environment. Where formerly education of the elementary teacher was merely an extension of secondary training in physical education, appropriate programs in teacher education are now being structured, with particular emphasis on movement theory.

A type of school organization which will have implications for elementary school programs is the nongraded school. To fit into this philosophy, a physical education program will need to have many alternatives so that individual differences can be met. No longer will intact classes be scheduled for physical education. Groups of students will appear for physical education experiences, or children may even come and go as individuals on a varied schedule. This may mean chronological age differences greater than seen in the present program geared to the classroom schedule.

More attention is being centered on programs for special students, which include both the physically and the educationally handicapped. Federal funding has generated much interest and experimentation in programs labeled "Special Education."

It is interesting to note, too, that the American Medical Association, representing the entire medical profession, has recognized the value of physical education in a statement adopted at its national convention in 1960.

> Resolved, That the American Medical Association through its various divisions and departments and its constituent and component medical societies do everything feasible to encourage effective instruction in physical education for all students in our schools and colleges.*

The 1960 resolution was reaffirmed in 1969, strongly supported by the AMA Committee on Exercise and Physical Fitness, a body which was not in existence at the time of the 1960 resolution.

In the final analysis, the great change has been in the kinds of learning experiences now being provided for children in physical education. Programs have been expanded and broadened to include activities and experiences which were unknown a decade ago. Administration of such a program demands not only skilled instructors, familiar with a broad range of activity, but also sufficient supplies and equipment to conduct such a program. School boards must assume the responsibility for providing administrative support to finance and staff a modern program.

*Proceedings, The 1960 Annual Convention, (Chicago: American Medical Association, 1960).

Another educational trend which some physical educators favor is the expression of expected outcomes in behavioral terms. A behavioral objective is expressed in terms of observable human behavior, is predictable, and is measurable. But not all elements of movement can be reduced to easy mathematical terms. Thus, reducing the accepted physical education objective that each child should demonstrate the ability to manage his body effectively in all situations to measurable mathematical terms would be a formidable task, and differentiating between the performance standards expected from different grade and age levels would be difficult.

Another variable is the instructional dimension. Who is directing the learning experiences, the specialist or the classroom teacher? If it can be reasoned that the physical education specialist should be able to accomplish more in terms of pupil progress, then two levels of performance outcomes must be considered to take care of the instructional dimensions.

The mere task of setting valid behavioral objectives is complex, and they are of value only if they are measured. For the teacher to evaluate all the pertinent cognitive, affective, and psychomotor variables after a period of instruction would demand an inordinate amount of teaching-learning time.

The physical fitness objective is actually the one most easily expressed in terms of pupil performance. Projected goals are available for all fitness tests. But some have objected that set standards in physical fitness do not consider individual differences, i.e., since each child should progress at his own rate, one standard for all is unsound. This raises the question of how this principle of consideration for individual differences could be incorporated effectively into behavorial objectives. Flexible standards would be necessary, further complicating the procedure. While behavioral objectives stated in precise performance expectations are undoubtedly of value to the teacher, their application presents difficulties which need solution before it can be effectively implemented.

THE APPROACH TO PHYSICAL EDUCATION

Some physical education people hold that modern educational theory has relegated the traditional approach to elementary school physical education to the sidelines. The rigid traditional (sometimes called the direct) approach, specifying conformance of all children to the same manner, is now considered by some to be an inferior approach. Little attention was given to creative aspects, the varied interests of children, the difference in capacity, and the opportunities for movement exploration.

On the other hand, in the opinion of the author, the pendulum has swung too far the other way *in some cases* in complete use of what is termed the indirect approach. This is a fresh approach to child-centered education in which the child has opportunity to explore, create, and move according to his desires and capacities. There are those who feel the term "Physical Education" is no longer apt and should be replaced by "Movement Education," since movement is the key to the new methodology. It takes a skilled and resourceful teacher to make the most of the indirect approach so that objectives are met, and the result is not merely a variety of free play.

It can be reasoned that if the present program has achieved something good, we must be doing some things right. The problem is to retain from our programs what has value and to prune some of the out-of-date ideas and deadwood from our methodology. Movement education has much to offer, and we should adopt those learning experiences which offer a better potential than what we now have to achieve optimum development of the child. Development is the key to the learning situation, and the teacher should employ those learning experiences which he feels offer the best chance of achieving this development. Prudent teachers will examine new ideas and try them out, rejecting those which are impractical, and retaining those which are found successful.

On a scientific basis, changes in methodology should be based only on appropriate research. Caution is indicated not to make abrupt and sweeping changes without an adequate basis. Empirical experiences, however, are providing some indications and direction for physical education in the wake of changing concepts. The right of the teacher to employ the approach he considers the most appropriate is affirmed.

2

The Basis for
the Program

In selecting the purposes and content of the program for elementary school children, the characteristics, capacities, needs, interests, and basic urges of children should be given utmost consideration. The broad concept of basic urges applies to all age groups and is relevant to most children from kindergarten to sixth grade. A basic urge is an intense drive, which the child seems to have in his natural makeup, toward certain goals or levels of achievement. A good program will provide opportunity so that these basic urges can be satisfied.

BASIC URGES OF CHILDREN

Basic urges will vary somewhat among children, but for most are important reasons for living and being. It is difficult to rank them in importance, and no attempt is made to do so here, as children will evaluate them differently.

The Urge for Success and Approval. Children not only like to achieve, but also desire recognition of this achievement. They wilt under criticism and disapproval, whereas encouragement and friendly support promote growth and maximum development. Failure can lead to frustration, lack of interest, and inefficient learning. In extreme cases, failure can lead to an antipathy to physical education which can have a profound effect on later physical participation.

The Urge for Physical Fitness and Attractiveness. Every teacher should understand how eager boys and girls are to be physically fit and possess bodies that are agile and attractive. To be strong is both a joy and a glory. It gives dignity and confidence. Teachers should understand the humiliation suffered by the youngster who is weak, fat, crippled, or abnormal in any way.

The Urge to Contest. This is tied up with the first urge and refers to the child's desire to match physical skill and strength with his fellows. It means the urge to wrestle, to hit a ball, to pit one's skill, to overcome the other, to take joy in competition, and to be successful in situations of stress.

The Urge for Social Competence. The child would like to be accepted, respected, and liked by others. He doesn't want to feel awkward or embarrassed at games or contests. He wishes to appear to an advantage not only with his peers, but also in the world of adults.

The Urge for Adventure. This is the urge to participate in something different, romantic, or unusual. The child desires to climb to the heights, to be able to do something different, and to participate in activities which of themselves are interesting. It means a change from the "old stuff" to something new and exciting.

The Urge for Creative Satisfaction. Children like to try out different ways, experiment with

7

different materials, and see what they can do creatively. Finding different ways of expressing themselves physically satisfies the urge for creative action.

The Urge for Rhythmic Expression. Every boy and girl basically likes rhythm. The program should offer a variety of rhythmic activities which every boy and girl should learn well enough to give them many pleasant, satisfying hours. Rhythm is movement and children like to move. Dancing, rhythmic movements, rope jumping skills, ball bouncing and dribbling routines, and similar activities are pleasing and exciting experiences under competent leadership.

The Urge To Know. Young people live in a world of curiosity. They are interested not only in what they are doing, but they want to know why. The "why" is a great motivator. Lasting habits are established only if the individual is convinced they are worthwhile.

CHARACTERISTICS, INTERESTS, AND NEEDS IMPORTANT IN PROGRAM PLANNING

KINDERGARTEN AND FIRST GRADE

Characteristics	Program Needs and Implications
Noisy, constantly active, egocentric, exhibitionist. Imitative and imaginative. Wants attention.	Vigorous games and stunts. Games with individual roles — hunting, dramatic activities, story plays. Few team games or relays.
Large muscles more developed, game skills not developed.	Basic movement. Fundamental skills of throwing, catching, bouncing balls.
Naturally rhythmical.	Music and rhythm with skills. Creative rhythms, folk dances, singing games.
No sex differences in interest.	Same activities for both boys and girls.
Short attention span. May become suddenly tired, but soon recovers.	Change activity often. Short explanations. Use activities of brief duration. Provide short rest periods or include activities of moderate vigor.
Sensitive and individualistic. The "I" concept is very important. Accepts defeat poorly.	Needs to learn to take turns, share with others. Learn to win, lose, or be caught gracefully.
Is interested in what his body can do. Curious.	Movement experiences. Attention to basic movement.
Eye-hand coordination developing.	Needs opportunity to handle objects such as balls, beanbags, hoops, etc.
Perceptual-motor areas important.	Needs practice in balance, unilateral, bilateral, and cross-lateral movements.
Likes small group activity.	Use entire class grouping sparingly. Break into small groups.
Sensitive to feelings of adults.	Needs praise and encouragement.
Can be reckless.	Stress sane approaches.
Enjoys rough-and-tumble activity.	Include rolling, dropping to the floor, etc., in both introductory and program activities. Stress simple stunts and tumbling.
Pelvic tilt can be pronounced.	Give some attention to posture problems.

SECOND AND THIRD GRADES

Characteristics	Program Needs and Implications
Still active but attention span longer. More interest in group play.	Active big muscle program, including more group activity. Begin team concept in activity and relays.
Like physical contact and belligerent games.	Dodgeball games and other active games. Rolling stunts.
Enjoy rhythm.	Continue creative rhythms, singing games, and folk dances.
Developing more skills and interest in skills. Want to excel.	Organized practice in a variety of throwing, catching, moving, and other skills. Basic movement work.
Improved hand-eye and perceptual-motor coordination.	Opportunity for handling hand apparatus. Movement experiences. Practice in perceptual-motor skills — right and left, unilateral, bilateral, and cross-lateral movements.
Becoming more social-conscious.	Learn to abide by rules and play fair. Learn social customs and courtesy in rhythmic areas.
Becoming more sports interested.	Introduce sports skills and simple lead-up activities.
Are curious to see what they can do. Love to be challenged.	Various challenges with movement problems. More critical demands in stunts, tumbling, and apparatus work.
Like to do things well and be admired for it.	Begin to stress quality somewhat. Provide opportunity to achieve.
Essentially honest and truthful.	Accept their word. Give opportunity for trust in game and relay situations.

FOURTH, FIFTH, AND SIXTH GRADES

Characteristics	Program Needs and Implications
Steady growth — girls more rapidly than boys. Boys better in game skills.	Continue vigorous program. Separate sexes for some activities. Stress correct movement fundamentals and posture.
Enjoy team and group activity. Competitive spirit.	Include many team games, relays, combatives.
Sports interests.	Sports in season with emphasis on lead-up games. Good variety.
Muscular coordination improving and skills are better. Want to know how and why. Interested in detailed techniques.	Continued emphasis on the teaching of skills through drills and practice. Emphasis on correct form.
Little interest in opposite sex. Some develop sex antagonisms.	Need coeducational activity. Stress social customs and courtesy through folk and square dances.

Characteristics	Program Needs and Implications
More acceptance of self-responsibility.	Need safety controls. Need leadership and followership opportunity. Include students in evaluation procedures.
Differences in capacity.	Flexible program and standards so all may succeed.
Great desire to excel both in skill and physical capacity.	Stress physical fitness. Include fitness and skill tests both to provide motivation and check progress.
Sportsmanship a factor.	Establish and enforce fair rules for activity.
Posture problems can appear.	Posture correction in activity. Special posture instruction.
Girls (Sixth) may show maturity characteristics. May not wish to participate as fully.	Need to have consideration for their particular problems. Encourage to participate.

THE PURPOSES OF PHYSICAL EDUCATION

While the general goal of physical education, and, for that matter, all education — well-rounded development of our children and youth as responsible citizens — is of a general nature, learning experiences should be provided to help the child attain more definable purposes or objectives. To be judged effective as an educational tool, physical education should help each child to:

1. Develop and maintain a suitable level of physical fitness.

2. Become competent in management of the body and acquire useful physical skills.

3. Acquire desirable social standards and ethical concepts.

4. Acquire needed safety skills and habits.

5. Enjoy wholesome recreation.

6. Acquire a desirable self-concept and an effective self-image.

7. Derive personal and educational benefits from the program.

An examination of basic urges and characteristics of children will show that each of the above objectives contributing to total development can be substantiated as meeting some portion of the basic growth and development needs of children.

PHYSICAL FITNESS

Purpose: *The physical education program should provide each child with the opportunity to develop and maintain a level of physical fitness commensurate with his individual needs.*

While physical education must be a means of expression through movement, it must be more than that. Physical education in our society must provide a developmental experience. Call it what you will — "physical fitness," "physical development," "organic development," — the name is not important, but the concept is. The physical education program must provide a planned, progressive environment of activity which will make sufficient physical demands on an individual during the seven growth years of the kindergarten and elementary school. In fact, this principle extends back even into the preschool years.

The child must have vigorous physical activity based on good physiological principles as a part of his regimen to assure proper development. This activity should be of sufficient intensity to make these demands on the body. Development occurs when the child has worked harder and longer than he has previously. Bones become stronger, musculature improves, and ligaments and tendons are strengthened to meet the demands of activity. The cardiorespiratory system, as well as other body systems, derives benefit from activity demands. The benefit from regular and systematic exercise in relation to the prevention of heart disease is a concept that should be established early in the child's education.

Physical fitness is a unique and important contribution which *can* be made by physical education as contrasted to other subject matter fields in the curriculum. If physical education cannot or does not provide fitness development, no other area of the curriculum will. A child who is deprived of, or who has an insufficient amount of, activity fails to reach his growth potential.

Fitness has other values. There is evidence that peer status and relationships, particularly for boys, are better for those possessing suitable levels of physical fitness. Desirable fitness levels seem to lead to better social adjustment and a more buoyant, action-minded, optimistic personality.

A more detailed analysis of physical fitness and its implementation in the school program is found in Chapters 9 and 10.

MOVEMENT EXCELLENCE — USEFUL PHYSICAL SKILLS

Purpose: *The physical education program should be so structured that each child can become competent in management of his body and acquire useful physical skills.*

More and more we are becoming a nation of skill seekers. Every elementary school boy and girl should have an opportunity to develop excellence in many kinds of movement and useful skills, so that they can enjoy activities and develop a desire to participate in them. This includes:

Competency in Management of the Body. Management of the body refers to physical control of the body in a variety of movement situations in relation to environmental demands. Basically, proper management of the body is needed to counteract the forces of gravity in normal activity. This is the maintenance of good posture. The child should understand, appreciate, and employ simple postural skills.

Other concerns in body management are control and balance of the body in different positions, rhythm of movement, coordination, and efficient movement. A child should be able to manage his body effectively on the floor (as in balance or flexibility stunts), moving across the floor, in the air (off the floor), and suspended on apparatus. Also, body management includes efficient use of force in such tasks as pushing and pulling, as well as weight-support tasks.

Perceptual-motor competency is an important body management goal. Included is the concept of laterality, which has a correlation with children having learning difficulties. The ability to control the two sides of the body separately and simultaneously must be developed. Good body management implies that the child can make unilateral, bilateral, and cross-lateral movements with ease and in good balance.

Basic Movement Skills and Patterns. These are the fundamental skills relating to body movement which are useful for the basic activities of living and playing. A child should become proficient in locomotor skills (walking, running, jumping), nonlocomotor skills (twisting, turning, forming shapes), and manipulative skills (throwing, catching, striking, kicking).

Special and Sports Skills. Included here are the more specialized skills of rhythmics, sports, stunts and tumbling, and similar activities.

The relationship of the elements of physical fitness and motor learning must be understood. The common elements of physical fitness—strength, endurance, and power, among others—are needed for optimum development of physical skills.

Grade Level Emphasis

Movement competency and basic skills are the emphasis on the primary level. More precise skills are acquired through learning experience centered in the intermediate grades. Management of the body is stressed throughout with experiences which give opportunity for the child to use his body in a variety of situations.

THE SOCIAL GOAL

Purpose: *The physical education environment should be such that children can acquire desirable social standards and ethical concepts.*

Physical education is concerned with the development of desirable standards of ethical behavior and social and moral conduct. Many terms, such as good citizenship and sportsmanship, can be used to describe this goal. A child needs to be able to get along with others, to take turns, to win and lose gracefully, to work for the common good, and to respect the personality of his fellows. He should learn to exercise self-control in activities which are often emotionally intense. He can be helped to act wisely with courage and resourcefulness in situations of stress.

Since successful living demands the ability and willingness to lead skillfully and to follow intelligently, the child should be afforded opportunities to develop these capacities. One can develop the powers of judgment, observation, analysis, and decision through the medium of complex physical activities.

Physical education can aid the child in developing respect for facilities and equipment and an appreciation of the opportunity that is his through physical education. He needs to learn to be at ease in a variety of social situations and to accept the consequences of his own actions. He can learn to appreciate the concept of competition as life itself is competition.

Nowhere in the curriculum are the opportunities for give and take as high as they are in physical education. As life is governed by social rules, customs, and traditions, so are the activities on the playfield and gymnasium floor. Fair play, honesty, and conformance with the rules can be stressed through physical activities.

A respect for the "spirit" as well as for the letter of the rules should be developed. Physical education stresses the sportsmanship viewpoint of sharing with the officials the responsibility for seeing to it that contests are played according to the spirit of the rule.

Basically, the teacher's task is to help children to discover the difference between acceptable and unacceptable ways of expressing feelings, and to guide behavior on this basis. This should include establishing and enforcing limits of acceptable behavior.

Proper attitudes of boy-girl relationships can be furthered through properly conducted coeducational activities. Courtesy and consideration between opposite sexes can be promoted in rhythmic activities. The group method, so often used in physical education, provides numerous opportunities for social and emotional growth.

In addition, peer relationships indicate that physical skills are of such importance that much social interaction centers around them, particularly in the intermediate grades. The child who does not possess the movement competencies to participate successfully in play activities which occupy and interest his classmates is likely to have a lonely time.

It must now be concluded that skill achievement is a much more important factor in personal and social adjustment than we have been led to believe. Teachers should strive to provide learning experiences for and give attention to those low-skilled and inept children who are in need of help to improve their skills. Giving them a better basis for peer relationships is important in good social and emotional health.

The school is an agent for establishing an attitude complex. The children may forget facts, but will retain values, concepts, and behavior patterns. Children need to learn how to live effectively and harmoniously in our society.

SAFETY SKILLS AND ATTITUDES

Purpose: In physical education, each child should have the opportunity to acquire safety skills and habits and to develop a high degree of awareness regarding safety for himself and for others.

In the child's world today, attention to safety factors is of utmost importance. The capacity for safe living is not an automatic value but must be sought. The ability to use equipment safely, to consider oneself and fellow students in the light of safety, and to handle one's body efficiently in times of stress are attributes which are important for safe living. The teacher needs to explain the techniques of an activity in the light of the consequences from unsafe procedures. While all necessary precautions should be taken to develop habits of safety, consideration also must be given to avoiding fear and overcautiousness in activity. Rules are needed to eliminate unsafe procedures, and children need to understand and recognize the importance of these practices.

It needs to be emphasized that the teacher should be so familiar with the activities that the program can be carried out in a safe environment, and that the youngsters will learn safe procedures.

Water safety is an important facet of physical education. Although few elementary schools provide opportunity for aquatic instruction, students should be encouraged to seek swimming instruction. Communities should look for cooperation among the various agencies to see that a swimming and water safety program is a part of the educational opportunities for the child. This can be done variously and not necessarily as a part of the school physical education program. Each child of elementary school age should have the opportunity to participate in such a program, and communities should take steps to see that this is realized.

WHOLESOME RECREATION

Purpose: Through physical education, each child should be stimulated to seek participation in and derive enjoyment from wholesome recreation during his leisure.

Since children will play many hours beyond the opportunity afforded them in physical education, the program should aim at making this a fruitful experience. Part of this preparation can be met by teaching a variety of skills *well enough* so that the child has the tools for his leisure-time activities. In addition, the youngster should develop knowledge, attitudes, and appreciations which will guide him in his free play. Some of the ways physical education can contribute to the recreational ideal are:

1. Give the child an understanding of physical fitness and its importance, and show how to develop and maintain this important body attribute. This would imply an appreciation of the values of physical activities for healthful living.

2. Provide him a wide variety of activities which are of use to him in his play time. This should include active games and movement experiences suitable for the home and backyard.

3. See that he knows the rules, regulations, and strategies of various games, together with ways of modifying and improvising these for use with small groups and spaces.

4. Give the child experience in playing with and accepting other children in physical activities. Children should seek the company of other children of their ages and interests and not play alone.

5. Permit him to study the sources and origins of activities. In the rhythmic program, for example, a dance becomes more meaningful if the children know the origin and can acquire an appreciation of the culture of the people.

A second approach would be the effect of the program on the leisure-time activity in his future years. While few adult activities of carry-over value are taught in the elementary program, habits and interest in purposeful activity can be established. An appreciation of beauty in physical skills and in the human form can be motivating factors for further participation.

THE SELF-IMAGE AND SELF-CONCEPT

Purpose: Each child should acquire a realistic self-image and develop a desirable self-concept through relevant physical education experiences.

Not only is it essential to understand the learner, but it is important for the learner to understand himself. Each child brings into the world his own basic characteristics, limits of intelligence, body structure, energy drive, and sensitivity to external stimuli. He needs to make some assessment of what his abilities are and how they can be utilized to achieve what he is capable of.

This means that he must have an opportunity in physical education to expand, to extend, to develop, to create, and to mature. To express himself and seek self-enhancement are important goals for the individual. To become a fuller self and a more complete individual stimulates learning.

The concept of himself which a child develops is vital in the learning process, as it can make it possible for him to learn or it may prevent or block his ability to learn. If a child can feel he "belongs," that he is loved and respected, and that his successes outweigh his failures, then he is well on the way to establishing a desirable self-concept. Nothing succeeds with a child like success. Security gives him a basis for the development of a healthy personality.

The urge to grow must not become lost in personal problems and concerns. It must not become buried under layers of psychological defenses. The candle of learning must not be smothered under a blanket of emotional blocks.

Physical education can do much to bring out the child and give him an opportunity to express himself, be creative, and achieve success, stressing comfortable physical experiences well within the emotional, physical, and intellectual limits of the child. Children will retain substance from those experiences which hold personal significance and personal value. Each child needs to consider that in the educational process he is of value, worthy in his own right.

While certainly some competition in educational circles is essential, physical education can provide individual experiences where the child can work at his own rate without pressure of peer performances or competition. Children naturally compete against their peers, as they would like to do as well as, if not better than, their classmates. Each child should achieve success within himself and not be judged according to whether or not he can come up to the performance of his peers.

On the other hand, life itself is competition and children need to recognize this fact. Much of what is learned does take place in group situations, even if its emphasis is purportedly individual. Children do learn from each other and fundamental values are involved in group learning experiences. Achieving success in a learning situation is basically not determined on whether the approach is individual or group, but that progress is evaluated on an individual basis, with recognition, acceptance, and utilization of individual differences an important feature of the instructional process.

Physical education can not only be a medium for some measure of success for all children; it can also be particularly valuable to the child who performs at a lower level academically but can achieve his higher measure of success in physical activities. This may be the place where he blossoms.

PERSONAL AND EDUCATIONAL VALUES

Purpose: *Each child should be able to acquire personal and educational values which are within the developmental potential of a quality physical education program.*

There are many values of personal adjustment which can be gained from a sound program of physical education. It is often said that a school with a good physical education program is a happy school. The simple ability to have fun and take part freely and joyously in physical activities has high value in adjustment for the child. The relief from tension and anxiety through activity is important to his future well-being. Finding satisfaction and release in play is a goal for each child.

Developing creativeness and imaginative play should be an outgrowth of activity experiences. Development of reasoning powers can be furthered if the child is challenged with movement problems which reach a satisfactory and adequate solution. Such qualities as self-confidence, initiative, and perseverance can be given opportunity for development through problem-solving experiences.

Physical education should also tap levels of the child's conceptual thinking. Good teaching should concern itself with conceptual understandings, as these are the ingredients for thinking. Selected concepts as they relate to movement are important inclusions in the teaching process in physical education. Guidance should be given to the child in his concept growth and in the personalized interpretations which he has made along the way. The child should show not only versatility in movement, but also that he has established basic understandings of his movement.

A sound program, particularly on the primary level, will emphasize movement factors known to have relevance to perceptual-motor competency. Children should have opportunities for a broad range of movement in which activities stressing balance, coordination, identification of body parts, spatial judgments, and laterality are stressed. While valid evidence is lacking, there is indication that activities of the nature described can help some children achieve a level of movement competence which will contribute to their achievement in the classroom.

PHYSICAL EDUCATION AS A TOOL IN THE EDUCATION OF THE DISADVANTAGED

In addition to the aforementioned basic purposes, physical education can function as a tool of education and social relevance in the education of disadvantaged children. First of all, a physical education program can give the disadvantaged child a chance to achieve and a chance to compete with his peers. This may be the area in which he can first attain a measure of success and gain the respect of his peers. To gain in self-concept and in self-image is an important goal for the disadvantaged child. He needs to be brought out of the devastating feeling of uselessness.

A second line of attack can be made through the social relationships manifest in a physical education program. This is a two-way street. The disadvantaged child can be given opportunities to act in his own interests while avoiding intrusion on the rights of others. The peer group, on the other hand, can through properly structured approaches accept the child on his own personal worth as an individual and minimize racial, class, or ethnic bias.

A corollary to this is an opportunity for each child to share in democratic decisions in group associations and be a participant in leader-follower situations.

Basically, the disadvantaged must be kept academically alive. In today's society, career choice is vital for survival. Most positions require years of formal training, and there is little place for the drop-out or low achiever. Physical education and the related programs of intramurals and athletics can provide some measure of attraction and motivation for better school attendance and perhaps lead to a greater interest in academic work. In a larger sense, many disadvantaged youths have been able to attend colleges and universities on athletic scholarships, an opportunity which would have been denied them otherwise. And for some, professional athletics have provided a quick road to economic stability and respect.

Physical education in no sense is to be regarded as a panacea for the ills of society, nor is it assumed that any of the above approaches can be easily and effectively implemented. Because of the uniqueness of the physical approach, teachers who are sensitive and perceptive can capitalize on the inherent potential of physical education for the betterment of human relations and recognition of the dignity of the individual.

HOW CAN THESE PURPOSES BE ATTAINED?

Basically, to attain these purposes and objectives, physical education must be a planned developmental program which takes into consideration the needs and interests of each child in the school. The following attributes characterize such a program:

1. There must be movement. There must be something happening. Movement is the basis of physical education, and one way to judge the quality of a physical education program is to evaluate the degree of movement which each child experiences. Children learn by doing and skills are taught by repetition. If there is practice, for example, in bouncing a ball, a child profits in direct relationship to how many times he is able to handle and bounce the ball. What the child does to the ball is important, but what the ball does to the child is more important.

Physical education implies activity. The child profits little from an experience which is characterized by too much standing around waiting for equipment to be arranged, lengthy explanations by the teacher, and domination of activity by one or two children.

2. The selection of the activities must be based upon the needs and interest of the youngsters and geared to their level. This means preplanning and not just a "what-shall-we-do-today" type of program. If desirable learnings are to result, the activities must be suited to the developmental level of the child.

3. The activities need to be directed and conducted in such a manner that the purposes of physical education will be attained. The values of physical education are not gained automatically or accidentally. Physical activities need to be skillfully taught by understanding teachers who like children and have faith in their own ability to help children develop through this medium. This implies the application of educationally sound methods of teaching and the evaluation of the teaching process in terms of progress to the goals. Values in activity are not inherent in the activity but rather in the method of presentation. If a child is to achieve his potential in skilled movement, he must have quality teaching.

Mere participation does not mean that the child will attain the developmental level he should. The activities must be planned and directed by qualified leadership. This cannot be stressed too strongly. If quality of movement is to result, the learning process must be directed toward this end.

stop

The Physical Education Program

Basically, a school- or district-wide approach in planning the program of physical education is needed. A practical curriculum guide which will give good direction but at the same time permit some flexibility should be developed. The following guidelines are important in establishing an educationally sound physical education program.

GUIDELINES FOR PROGRAM PLANNING

1. The basic goal of planning is the formulation of a program which will serve as the basis of a school curriculum guide. The program should be outlined in sufficient detail to provide necessary direction.

2. The program should be based on the needs, characteristics, abilities, and basic urges of children. It should allow the child to be a child and not rob him of his childhood.

3. A balanced and varied program covering many experiences should be presented. It should be balanced with proportional emphasis on basic movement, rhythmics, physical developmental activities, stunts and tumbling, games and relays, and selected sports. It should be varied in that children meet with a variety of experiences, approaches, and activities. Childhood is a time for experimenting, sampling, and choosing. A broad range of activity opportunity makes this possible.

4. Program content should be based on the concept of value for *all* children — the highly skilled, the moderately skilled, and the low achiever. In addition, appropriate consideration for exceptional children and other special needs must be included in the program planning.

5. The selection of program activities should relate to the basic purposes of physical education, i.e. it should cover (1) vigorous physical activity which will promote growth and development and the attainment of an appropriate level of physical fitness; (2) the development of a broad range of movement competency and motor skills; (3) a variety of activities useful in leisure play; and (4) safety attitudes and practices as associated with the selected activities.

6. The program content should be constructed so that it can serve as a vehicle for the achievement of desirable behavioral changes, associated educational values, and personal benefits. It is true that many of the desirable changes in children and the values they receive from participation are determined more by instructional procedures than by the program *per se*. However, the selection of activities should be such that the aforementioned changes and values *can* be achieved with appropriate methodology. For example, a program relying chiefly on exercises, games, sports, and relays will do little for the individual child in terms of self-direction, creativity, self-reliance, and individual level of progress.

7. Program content should rest on a foundation of efficient body management and basic movement skills, geared to the developmental needs of the child. This implies an instructionally oriented program, leading toward a goal of reasonable skill and concept acquisition. The program should set aside sufficient time for skill instruction and practice. Practice should be systematically organized and based on good concepts of motor learning. The emphasis on instruction should be intense enough to lead to reasonable mastery of skills.

8. Progression is an essential element in program planning. The program must reflect progression from grade to grade, within each grade, and within activities. It is a major purpose of this guide to provide orderly learning sequences upon which instructional procedures can be based.

9. The learning experiences at any one grade level should be planned on a year's program outline, with consideration for seasonal activities. Such planning gives unity to the experiences and allows the teacher to center attention with proportional emphasis on the more important aspects of the program.

10. An extended physical activity interest program, the basis of which is provided by physical education, should be established within the school. The broad program should include an intramural program for both boys and girls, and may include educationally sound interschool competition. Sports days, play days, and special interest clubs round out the possibilities. In addition, cooperative municipal recreation departments may provide extended opportunity with scheduled recreation programs after school, on Saturdays, or during holiday periods.

11. The physical education program must have appropriate administrative support if it is to achieve its educational goals for children. The administration has an obligation to provide:

  a. Competent instruction
  b. Adequate indoor and outdoor facilities to permit adequate time allotment and scheduling of classes
  c. Adequate budget for the purchase of supplies and equipment
  d. Appropriate storage space for supplies and equipment
  e. Dressing rooms and showering facilities

The degree of administrative support will have a profound effect on the program. The above points are treated in discussions found in later sections of this guide.

Climatic and Geographical Factors

It is recognized that the weather is an important factor in planning. Whereas physical education should be an outdoor experience when possible, the vagaries of the weather in some sections of the country have a profound effect on the planning of an adequate program. Where the weather is consistent, few alternate programs are needed. Where the weather is uncertain, teachers must modify their overall plans from day to day.

The length of the seasons determines the emphasis within the program. In temperate climates, children can play outdoors well into December and are able to be on the playground again in late February. This means an indoor program of only eight to ten school weeks as contrasted with the possibility of perhaps double this figure in other localities.

Considerations by the administration for adequate facilities would involve such items as covered outside areas (shed types) and hard-surfaced areas which dry quickly. Where the climate permits, thought should be given to the installation of basketball goals and volleyball standards in areas large enough to sustain a wide number of children.

For those who lack facilities, inclement weather means that the teacher must provide physical experiences in the classroom setting, with its attendant problems.

The practice of teaching health instead of physical education during inclement weather when the children cannot go outside leaves a bad taste for health instruction. The motivation to better health is doubtful when taught under these circumstances.

PLANNING IN TERMS OF BROAD PROGRAM AREAS

A varied physical education program can help provide the interest and motivation to encourage lifelong habits of vigorous exercise. The time allocated to the various broad categories of activities appropriate to the interests and needs of the children at each level should be carefully balanced, and one way to accomplish this is on a percentage basis. This is the first step. This method will provide an answer to the questions of parents and administrators relative to the activity emphasis of the program.

The suggested percentages in the chart below should be regarded only as approximate and a starting point for planning. However, each area must have its proportionate share of emphasis, and too much shifting of material will destroy the factor of balance.

ELEMENTARY SCHOOL PHYSICAL EDUCATION PROGRAMS
Grade Level Emphasis and Suggested Yearly Percentages

Primary Grades	Grades			
	K	1	2	3
Movement Experiences and Body Mechanics.........	40	35	35	20
Fitness Routines, Activities				10
Rhythmic Activities	30	25	25	20
Apparatus, Stunts, Tumbling	15	20	20	20
Simple Game Activities and Relays	15	20	20	20
Sports Skills and Activities				10
Swimming and Water Safety				(a)
Intermediate Grades		4	5	6
Movement Experiences and Body Mechanics		5	5	5
Fitness Routines, Activities, Testing		20	20	20
Rhythmic Activities		15	15	15
Apparatus, Stunts, Tumbling, Combatives		15	15	15
Simple Game Activities and Relays		20	15	10
Sports Skills and Activities		25	30	35
Swimming and Water Safety		(a)	(a)	(a)

(a) Swimming and Water Safety is a recommended area of instruction for elementary school children. The amount allocated to this area would depend upon the facilities and instruction available. If swimming is included in the school program, it should proportionately reduce the percentage of time allotted to other activities.

THE ALLOCATION OF SPECIFIC ACTIVITIES TO GRADE LEVEL

After the broad categories have been determined, the activities within each should be designated. Grade level placement of the specific activities within the broad categories is somewhat regulated by arbitrary selection. Adjustment upward or downward with respect to grade level should be made on an empirical basis, after a period of class trial.

Another factor enters the picture. A skilled specialist usually has more success in achieving higher skills at a lower grade level than does a classroom teacher with a more limited background. However, as a starting point for program planning, the following chart is presented. What it says is simply that a certain activity should be part of a particular grade level program. The elements to be included, the approaches to be followed, and the instructional procedures to be utilized are discussed in later sections of this guide.

SUGGESTED ALLOCATION OF SPECIFIC ACTIVITIES
ACCORDING TO GRADE LEVEL

Activity	K	1	2	3	4	5	6
Movement Experiences and Body Mechanics	K	1	2	3	4	5	6
Basic Movement — Locomotor, Nonlocomotor	K	1	2	3			
Stretch Ropes				3	4	5	6
Basic Movement — Manipulative	K	1	2	3	4	5	6
Beanbags	K	1	2	3	4	5	6
Yarn or Fleece Balls	K	1	2	3			
Playground Balls (8½")	K	1	2	3	4	5	6
Small Balls (sponge, softball size)				3	4	5	6
Paddles and Balls				3	4	5	6
Hoops	K	1	2	3	4	5	6
Jump Ropes	K	1	2	3	4	5	6
Parachutes	K	1	2	3	4	5	6
Wands				3	4	5	6
Rhythmics (see chart page 318)	K	1	2	3	4	5	6
Rope Jumping to Music				3	4	5	6
Apparatus	K	1	2	3	4	5	6
Bounding Boards	K	1	2				
Balance Boards	K	1	2	3	4	5	6
Balance Beams	K	1	2	3	4	5	6
Benches			2	3	4	5	6
Climbing Ropes	K	1	2	3	4	5	6
Climbing Frames	K	1	2	3	4	5	6
Individual Mats	K	1	2	3			
Ladders and Bars		1	2	3	4	5	6
Stunts and Tumbling	K	1	2	3	4	5	6
Pyramids					4	5	6
Combatives					4	5	6
Simple Games	K	1	2	3	4	5	6
Relays			2	3	4	5	6
Story Games, Poems, Quiet Play	K	1	2				
Sports Skills and Activities				3	4	5	6
Basketball				3	4	5	6
Flag Football-Speedball					4	5	6
Soccer				3	4	5	6
Softball (mostly skills)				3	4	5	6
Track and Field					4	5	6
Volleyball					4	5	6

On examining the chart it will be noted that no breakdown (except for rope jumping) has been presented for the rhythmic activities. Rope jumping has been shown here because this activity (without music) is listed under the manipulative area and its inclusion under rhythmics serves to clarify its place in the recommended allocations. Apart from this, an explanation of all aspects of the rhythmic program would demand too much space at this point and be out of context. The program breakdown for rhythmic activities is included in Chapter 19, and for that reason does not appear here.

PHYSICAL EDUCATION PROGRAMS FOR EACH GRADE LEVEL

The material which follows will present descriptions of the type of program recommended for each grade level. Correlation should be evident between the recommended programs and (1) the needs of children, (2) program guidelines, (3) broad category percentages, and (4) grade placement of specific activities.

The Physical Education Program — Lower Grades

Some general comments can be made on the program in the lower grades, but the bulk of program description is presented in discussions under each grade level. The greatest change today is found in the program of the lower grades, featuring individualism, self-direction, exploration, creativity, and movement theory. Perceptual-motor theory also has strong application up to the third grade. A suggested kindergarten program is presented, but if there is no kindergarten its function as an introduction to physical education needs to be shifted to the first grade.

One great change in today's programs is that the games program is now the "frosting on the cake," and is no longer the "main dish." This is reflected in lower allocations to games programs and also in the format of the daily lesson plan, where the game becomes more of an added feature than the center of instructional procedures.

The increase in the number of recommended activities is apparent, broadening the program to the point where it is difficult to include all desirable activities to the extent of developing a reasonable level of competence.

The Kindergarten Program

There is a greater awareness of the characteristics of the learner at this level, resulting in more attention being focused on the learning process and the child. Play type activities are highly important in the kindergarten program, as young children are naturally active and learn best when they enjoy what they are doing. For some, kindergarten is a medium of adjustment, an attempt to ease the difficult transition from the security of the home to the uncertainty of the educational world. A child comes from a home where he is the center of attention to the classroom, where he is just one of a group of children his own age.

The large majority of suggested activities for kindergarten children are individual in nature, centering on movement experiences (40%) and rhythmics (35%). Some emphasis is given to simple stunts (15%) and to simple games (15%). While there is accent on cooperation with others, there is little emphasis on group or team play. The types of activities are such that the child has good opportunity to explore, try out, and create. He learns to express himself through movement and continues to develop the skills of verbal communication — speaking and listening.

In movement, he begins to lay the foundation of body management and basic skills, with attention to laterality, directionality, balance, and coordination. He seeks to further eye-hand coordination with simple manipulative activities. His fitness needs are taken care of within his movement experiences. Perceptual-motor competency theory has strong application to methodology on the kindergarten level.

The First Grade Program

The first grade program embraces the same four general areas as the kindergarten program, with some shift of emphasis to the apparatus, stunts, and tumbling areas. The largest portion of the first grade program is devoted to movement experiences (35%), which includes attention to physical development through selected movement. As in kindergarten, there is emphasis on basic skills and efficient management of the body, stimulated through challenges to elicit a wide variety of movement. Locomotor skills are of prime importance, with some application to non-locomotor movements. Manipulative skills are stressed, with a foundation being laid for the important play skills of throwing and catching. Beanbags, yarn balls, and playground balls (8½"), are important tools for experimentation. Hoops and jump ropes also are included.

Good body mechanics and posture are important, with attention to specific movements leading to the development of the arm-shoulder girdle and the abdominal region. Emphasis should be on both the how and why of activity. Perceptual-motor factors are an important consideration in conducting activities for the first grade child.

The rhythmic program (25%) should provide an extension of movement to rhythm, reinforcing and relating to basic movement experiences. The creative aspects of rhythmic activities have a prominent place in the first grade. In more structured numbers, singing games are stressed more than folk dance, although both are in included.

The apparatus, tumbling, and stunts program is of material import (20%). Each school should possess apparatus in sufficient numbers to have a rounded program in this area, including climbing ropes, climbing frames, fixed or moveable ladders, balance beams, bounding boards, benches, and individual mats. Floor and mat stunts give the children an opportunity to react to directions and achieve a specific movement pattern. Methodology in apparatus, stunts, and tumbling should be based on basic movement principles, seeking a wide and flexible response to the tasks.

The games program (20%) has its proportional place in the program, but has yielded its traditional importance to movement experiences. In addition to the usual gymnasium-playground games for this level, story games, poems, and dramatic play have a place.

The Second Grade Program

In essence, the second grade program follows the pattern of the first grade, with the exception of the introduction of simple relays based primarily on locomotor skills. Children are still encouraged to move in their own way, to experiment, and to explore, but specific patterns of coordination begin to appear. Continued practice in the basic locomotor, non-locomotor, and manipulative skills (35%) is provided. Children should also be made aware of and encouraged to develop good posture. A few simple forms of systematic exercise may be introduced, but not to the extent of the more formal fitness routines.

The rhythmic area (25%) moves toward more emphasis on folk dances, but singing games, creative rhythms, and basic rhythms receive good coverage. Ball bouncing and dribbling skills to rhythm are well accepted on this level, as the children begin to improve their manipulative competency.

Apparatus, stunts, and tumbling (20%) as an area receives continued attention. Youngsters begin to take pride in achievement and lay the basis for future activities.

Play is increasingly structured into some forms of group games (20%). The basic locomotor and ball handling skills are combined with lines, circles, and other patterns to provide group experiences and an introduction to team play. This concept is furthered by the introduction of simple relays. The seeds of sports interest, which comes into its own in the third and fourth grades, are found in the late second grade program.

The Third Grade Program

Movement experiences (20%) still have an important function on this grade level. However, the emphasis on body management is secondary to improvement of basic skills, particularly of the manipulative type. It is here the child begins to find himself in skills. The third grade program provides a transition between the simplified activity program of the lower grades and the sports interests and more advanced emphasis of the intermediate level.

The third grade level is suggested for the introduction of the more precise fitness routines (10%), such as exercise programs, circuit training, and the like. It is here the child begins to absorb the concept of needed work if he is to realize good dividends from his fitness potential.

In the rhythmics (20%), a transition from the casually organized dances of the previous grades to the concept of dancing with a partner is now stressed, as the children have opportunity to coordinate their own movements more precisely with those of a partner. The application of rhythm to ball skills and rope jumping is an important outlet for creativity, in addition to the retention of some emphasis on basic locomotor skills done to rhythm.

The stunt area (20%) becomes more complicated and more precise with increased demands on balance, strength, and coordination. There is a shift toward more inclusion of what are regarded as the standard tumbling stunts. Apparatus work should stress a wide variety of movements, built upon the foundation of the previous grades.

Simple games and relays (20%) become increasingly important to challenge the child with his newly acquired skills.

A major difference in activity for the third grade is the introduction of simple sports skills and activities (10%). Balls are rolled, bounced, kicked, batted, dribbled, thrown, and caught using reasonable technique. Attention is directed to specific sports skills in softball, basketball, and soccer. Selected lead-up games provide a useful laboratory for the evaluation of the achievement of these simple skills.

If swimming and water safety are to be included in the school program, the third grade is a likely level for this introduction. Ten percent of the allotted yearly time should probably be apportioned to this activity, with the time spent in the other activities reduced proportionately.

The Physical Education Program — Intermediate Level

Some basic differences are apparent in the intermediate program as compared with the program of the lower grades. More emphasis is now placed on physical fitness and special developmental activities. Physical fitness testing is introduced, with most authorities agreeing that the fourth grade is the proper level where testing should begin. This is borne out by fitness tests of both the President's Council and the American Association for Health,

Physical Education and Recreation, for which the norms begin at the fourth grade level. The allocation (20%) to fitness allows each class period to devote the first 5 to 6 minutes to fitness routines.

Lesser emphasis is placed on movement experiences; the bulk of what emphasis there is is concentrated on manipulative activity. While the perceptual-motor competency emphasis is centered primarily in the lower grades, some attention to the concepts should be given in the intermediate grades. Skills and movements can be accomplished on both the right and left sides to emphasize laterality. However, concentration should be on the dominant side (arm or leg), so that a functional skill for a sport — pitching for example — can be developed.

Basic movement principles are to be incorporated throughout the program, particularly in the teaching of skills. While the teaching of specialized skills will probably rely heavily on direct teaching, exploration and creativity should be encouraged wherever applicable.

Certain category percentages are stabilized throughout the three grades: movement experiences (5%); fitness routines (20%); rhythmic activities (15%); and apparatus, stunts, and tumbling (15%). However, the percentages for simple games and relays decrease (20%, 15%, to 10%), while those for the sports skills and activity area increase (25%, 30%, to 35%), moving from grade 4 to 6. Combatives, a new activity, are introduced in the fourth grade.

The Fourth Grade Program

The fourth grade sets the basis for the two grades which follow. Progression is the key word for the intermediate level, and the suggested program for the fourth grade must be the basis of the progressions on the fifth and sixth grade levels.

The first full experience with fitness activities (20%), including a testing program, begins here, although some routines were introduced in the third grade.

More specialized skills are taught in all areas, particularly the selected sports (25%). A gradual involvement in the sports program is possible as the student learns the needed skills and participates in lead-up games in the fourth grade to the point in later grades where he takes part in the sport itself, perhaps modified for the elementary grades.

In rhythmics (15%), a beginning in dance steps is made. Most of the dances specify partners, and social factors become important. Rope jumping to music becomes increasingly emphasized.

The apparatus, tumbling, and stunts program (15%), continues the progressions of earlier grades. There is a strong shift to the standard tumbling items. Combatives are new.

Simple games and relays (20%) become more challenging in serving as a laboratory of the learned skills. Selected games show a balance between individual and team emphasis.

Swimming and water safety can be an inclusion on this level. Some movement experiences (5%) are retained, primarily in the manipulative area.

The Fifth Grade Program

The fifth grade program is much like that of the fourth grade, except for a slightly increased percentage allotment for the sports program (30%), taken from the allotment for simple games and relays (15%). Increased interest in the sports program should be evident, as fifth graders generally have become eligible for participation in the intramural program.

Both movement experiences (5%) and fitness activities (20%) are continued at about the same pace as in the fourth grade. In rhythmics (15%), additional dance steps are introduced and dances become more intricate.

There is little change in the area of apparatus, stunts, and tumbling (15%). Stunts, naturally, become more challenging and are more difficult to achieve. More emphasis is centered on form.

The Sixth Grade Program

Sports (35%) now become the largest increment in the sixth grade program. When the child finishes his sixth grade program, he should have had experiences in regular or modified versions of basketball, softball, soccer, volleyball, flag football (boys), speedball, and track and field. He should have an extended opportunity in these in the intramural and interschool programs.

In rhythmics (15%), the waltz and square dance are new endeavors. More of an adult touch to the rhythmic program is apparent. Jumping ropes are still important as rhythmic tools.

Other areas are continued, with lesser emphasis on simple games (10%). Swimming is a consideration, dependent upon the overall school plan.

The sixth grade program can be viewed as a curriculum transitional to the junior high school program.

Special Programs

Several programs merit special discussion to bring out their relationships to the overall curriculum in physical education. Considered here will be the program of swimming and water safety, the adapted program, and the program for the physically underdeveloped child.

Swimming and Water Safety

Swimming and water safety form a most important area of instruction, one which should be made available to each child. A community-wide approach is needed, in which the school may or may not have a part. The crux of the matter is that someone must get the job done. If the responsibility falls to the schools, then a number of decisions need to be made.

The first is to seek facilities. Cooperation can generally be secured from the municipal recreation department or the YMCA for the use of a pool. In some cases the program can utilize recreation facilities during the month of May, before the heavy use of summer. Weather is of course a factor. The pool should have a means of raising the water temperature to comfortable levels.

Portable pools are another possible solution. Commercially built pools which can be set up by a crew in one day are now available. Pool size varies, but a great deal can be accomplished so far as water skills are concerned in a pool 24' by 24' with a depth of 3'. The pool can be placed in one location for four to six weeks and then moved to another school. Some states are recognizing the utility of the pool by authorizing the installation of both water valves and a drainhole connected with the sewage system in new construction.

Portable Swimming Pool. Courtesy Port-A-Pool (Universal Bleacher Co.) and Los Angeles City Schools.

Certified instruction is needed, and the instructional procedures of the Red Cross can be followed. It is suggested that the school swimming instructional program begin in the third grade, with a second program scheduled in either the fifth or sixth grade. Much attention should be directed toward helping the nonswimmer.

The Adapted Program

In many classrooms there will be children who cannot participate fully in the regular program in physical education. Frail children, those often absent due to illness, and others with identified handicaps need special consideration. The restriction may be permanent or it can be on a temporary basis as for children who have not fully recovered from injury or recent illness. It needs to be emphasized that a physician should be the determining factor in the recommendation for limited activity. Parents sometimes tend to be overly protective and set restrictions which are not in the best interests of the child.

A basic principle for children with restrictions is that they participate in the regular program within the limits of the restrictions. They need to be included in the group so that the concept that they are "different" is minimized. They need to be urged to become more self-directive with limitations rather than constantly having prescribed activity. In much of the activity program, the disabled or less able can profit by being in the regular program. Goals for them need to be adjusted and are not the same goals as for the rest of the children.

In the physical fitness elements, the physically handicapped child should develop an optimum degree of physical fitness for his condition. This means a selection of individual activities which the child can do on his own or with the aid of another student. It is important that the child learn to live with and within his physical condition. There is a great need to have the handicapped child gain status. If some accomplishment or knowledge can be achieved, this will be an important factor in creating a better self-image.

The teacher should give personal attention to the problems of the handicapped child. The practice of "excusing" him or shunting him to one side is no longer tenable. In some instances he can be utilized as a monitor, official, or scorekeeper in activities which are beyond him. However, this should not be overworked, as the other children may not react favorably to these appointments. He should have his turn and perhaps some special consideration.

If the school has a developmental program for the low-fit child, the handicapped person can take part in this. Homework and special tasks within his capacity are meaningful to him.

Unless the school has unusual facilities, the teacher will probably need to develop some special activities which can be carried on while other children are in the regular program.

Suggested activities from which selection can be made are listed below:

Aerial Darts
Archery (suction cup arrows)
Beanbag Tossing
Bowling Games
Box Hockey
Croquet
Darts (suction cup)
Horseshoes (rubber for indoors)
Lawn Bowling
Shuffleboard
Table Tennis

If the restriction is major, then quiet games should be utilized. Chess, checkers, and other table games are available.

The attitude of the other children toward those with handicaps is important. Children should invite and urge the handicapped child to participate within the limits of his handicap. They can take turns working with him in special activities. Tolerance and understanding are excellent social values which can be an outgrowth of such a program.

Teachers need to remember that physical education has values for everyone, not just the skilled or the so-called normal child. The wants and desires of the restricted child are the same as those of the normal child. His needs are realized in different ways.

The Special Program for the Physically Underdeveloped Child

Test scores will reveal that a number of children have fitness levels indicating a need for special attention, which is not possible in the regular class setting. A special program for the physically underdeveloped child (sometimes called the "low-fit" child) should be administered if these children can be identified. Further discussion of this subject and the means of implementing such a program will be found in Chapter 9.

TRANSLATING THE PROGRAM INTO YEARLY, WEEKLY, AND DAILY PROGRAMS

After activity categories have been determined, the next step is to formulate a sequential program of activities for the school year for each grade level. The purpose of this is to provide a schedule which gives the day-to-day program of activities.

Some decisions need to be made regarding a weekly schedule. Should the same schedule be carried on throughout each day of the week, or should some other combination be employed?

The recent experience of the author with an experimental program has convinced him that weekly units of activities are superior to a schedule where different activities are done on different days. In a weekly unit, an activity is carried on during the entire week. There can be combinations of activity, games for diversion, and flexible programs on the last day of the week.

The advantages of the weekly plan are several. First, the teacher needs only one lesson plan for the week. The lesson plan should include sufficient material for the week. The teacher's objective in the lesson is to move the children along the path of learning at a comfortable rate. In a sense, what we don't quite cover today can wait until tomorrow.

A second point is that little orientation is needed after the first day. Safety factors, instructional techniques, stress points, and concepts need only brief review in the day-to-day plan during a week. Equipment needs are quite similar from day to day.

The third advantage is that progression and learning sequences are quite evident, as both the teacher and the children can see progress. The teacher can begin a unit with the basics of an activity and progress along to a point where instruction and skill practice are again indicated. This procedure provides needed review and adapts the activity to the group. The sequence of activity for each day is built upon that of the prior lesson. If the teacher has difficulty or needs to investigate an approach, he has time between lessons to clear up questionable points. Children may also be referred to resource material to study the activities for the next day or to clarify a point of difficulty from the past lesson.

The objection some have to a weekly unit program is that it does not have enough variety, and children tend to become tired of the same activities over a protracted period of time. Activities should be spaced so not more than two or three weeks at the most of the same type of activity are practiced in successive weeks. The games and relay area can provide a change of pace when this seems to be indicated.

Some other combinations in weekly planning are in vogue. One is to have one type of activity on Monday, Wednesday, and Friday of a week, and another type on Tuesday and Thursday. Another is to reserve the games and relays for Friday of each week, utilizing the first four days for more sequential material. Both of these arrangements will show good elements of progression.

The least desirable plan is to have a different program each day of the week, burdening the teacher with five different lesson plans each week. Also, this plan does not favor good elements of progression or allow ample time for practice.

Developing Weekly and Daily Programs

How does the teacher begin to translate the suggested emphasis from the percentage chart into an effective program in physical education? A step by step procedure is presented by which this can be accomplished.

Step 1. Take from the chart the activities and percentages for the grade level involved. Thus, the year's activities have been selected, and the proportionate amount of time to be devoted to each has been determined.

Step 2. The second step is to calculate the number of minutes per year which would be devoted to an activity category, based on the round figure of 5400 minutes for the total program. This is based on a school year of 36 weeks (180 days) and a daily class of 30 minutes, totaling 150 minutes for the week. An illustration will help clarify this procedure. The example is a fourth grade plan. Steps 1 and 2 have been accomplished.

FOURTH GRADE PROGRAM

Activity Category	Percentage (year)	Total Minutes (year)
Movement Experiences and Body Mechanics	5%	270
Fitness Routines, Activities	20%	1080
Rhythmic Activities	15%	810
Apparatus, Stunts, Tumbling, Combatives	15%	810
Simple Game Activities and Relays	20%	1080
Sports Skills and Activities	25%	1350
Totals	100%	5400 minutes

Step 3. The third step is determining the number of weeks for an activity or combination of activities by first making an estimate of the number of days and then combining the days into weeks. One might ask, why not translate the percentages directly into weekly programs? The difficulty with this is that this kind of planning does not suit fitness routines and activities. Fitness activities are a part of each day's lesson and cannot be viewed in terms of a program of so many weeks. Fitness activities are allotted 6 minutes of each day's

lesson, generally at the beginning of the lesson. This leaves a total of 24 minutes for the remainder of the lesson on any one day.

Having disposed of fitness activities into this niche, we can now turn our attention to the other activities in order to form schedules. The figures will be given in both days and weeks so a planner may have a choice of a weekly program or a program of varied days. The place of simple game activities and relays should be explained. These are used in two ways, first to finish up lessons involving other activities, and second, as the main focus of a lesson.

Movement Experiences — 270 Minutes

Movement experiences in the fourth grade should consist mainly of manipulative activities. The daily lesson plan for movement experiences can be standardized in this fashion by combining it with a related game activity. If we arbitrarily divide the movement allotment into 15 days (3 weeks), we have 18 minutes per day for these experiences. The remaining 6 minutes can be given over to related game activities or relays. In the computations which follow, fitness activities can be disregarded as they are consistent throughout the year.

Lesson (30 minutes)

Fitness Activities
    6 minutes

Movement Experiences
    18 minutes x 15 days = 270 minutes

Game or Relay
    6 minutes x 15 days = 90 minutes

Rhythmic Activities — 810 Minutes

Assuming that the rhythmic program will be all that is scheduled for any one lesson, to find out the number of days divide the total (810 minutes) by the number of minutes available in each day's lesson (24 minutes). This makes a total of 33 days for the rhythmic program.

Apparatus, Tumbling, Stunts, Combatives — 810 Minutes

As in the rhythmic program, the entire class period (24 minutes) will be devoted to this area. Result — 33 days.

Simple Games and Relays — 1080 Minutes

Subtracting the amount already allotted in the movement area (90 minutes), we have 990 minutes for games and relays. When this figure is divided by 24, the result is 40 days for games and relays, beyond that allotted to the combined lessons with movement experiences.

Sports Skills and Activities — 1350 Minutes

Sports skills will take the largest block of days. Based on the available 24 minutes per day, sports skills and activities will cover 56 days or 11 weeks.

Step 4. The chart under Step 2 is now realigned to add the days and weeks. Two other allocations need to be made. One day at the beginning of the year is for organization. Two days need to be included for fitness testing. In presenting the following chart, it must be remembered that the computation and figures need not be precise and a shift can take place according to preference. Keep in mind that fitness routines (6 minutes) are a part of each day's lesson.

FOURTH GRADE PROGRAM

	Designated Days	Weeks
Movement Experiences and Body Mechanics — Games ..	15	3
Rhythmic Activities	33	6.6
Apparatus, Tumbling, Stunts, Combatives	34	7
Simple Games and Relays	40	8
Sports Skills and Activities	55	11
Organization	1	0
Fitness Testing	2	.4
Total	180 Days	36.0 Weeks

Step 5. The next choice to be made involves activities within a category. The most convenient illustration is in the sports area, where definite subdivisions (sports) make a further breakdown necessary. The allocation of 55 days or 11 weeks in the sports area can be spread in the following fashion:

Soccer	10 days	2 weeks
Touch Football	10 days	2 weeks
Basketball	10 days	2 weeks
Volleyball	5 days	1 week
Track and Field	10 days	2 weeks
Softball Skills	10 days	2 weeks

The allocation to sports is arbitrary and subject to choice. The same procedure must be followed with the other areas to pinpoint specific activities.

Step 6. A yearly schedule is now made, with the program for each of the 180 days of the year specified. Since each of the activity areas has its allotted number of days or weeks, the sequence of activities can be arranged in weekly order or in any other fashion desired by the planner. A sample year's program is presented with planning on a weekly basis.

Illustration of a Year's Program by Weekly Scheduling

To formulate a year's schedule, some breakdown under other categories, similar to that presented in Step 5 for sports, is necessary. Remember that fitness activities are given daily, and so a 36-week schedule is needed for the various routines. The order and selection are similar to that presented on page 101.

The inclusion of games and relays in daily lessons presents a slightly different aspect. This area is implemented in the year's program in two ways. First, games and relays may be presented as the focal point of a lesson in much the same manner as other activities. Secondly, these may be included in a lesson with other activities as the finishing touch of the day's work to utilize the learned skills of the lesson or to provide a change of pace or a diversion. In the plan which follows, games and relays are included in lessons with movement experiences (manipulative activities) and rhythmics. This means that the allotment of time in these lessons devoted to games and relays must come out of the total time which is allocated to them in the year's plan. The time remaining is devoted to full lessons of games and relays.

Games lessons provide flexibility in the program, particularly when the scheduled outdoor activity is not possible because of weather conditions. A games lesson can serve as a substitute indoor lesson.

The games area, however, consists of activities of the low-organized type, not the lead-up games found within the sports units. Lead-up games for sports units are a part of the time allotment for sports activities.

The weekly activity allocations are presented under each of the categories, some of which are given entire lessons (24 minutes) while others are in combination with another activity. The first 6 minutes of each lesson are given over to fitness activity.

Fitness Routines — 36 Weeks

Exercises (6), exercises to music (6), circuit training (12), astronaut drills (6), grass drills (3), continuity drills (3).

Manipulative Activities (Movement) — 3 Weeks (includes about 1-week allocation of games)

Wands and hoops, games (1), playground balls — 8½" — and games (1), paddles and balls, games (1).

Apparatus, Stunts, Tumbling, Combatives — 7 Weeks

Climbing ropes - ladders - climbing frames and benches (2), balance beams and combatives (2), stunts and tumbling (3).

Rhythmic Activities — 7 Weeks (includes .4 Weeks of Games)

Rope jumping and rhythmic activities (4), ball skills to music and rhythmic activities (2), rhythmic activities and simple games (1).

Sports Skills and Activities — 12 Weeks (includes 1-week allocation of simple games and relays)

Basketball and related games (3), soccer (2), touch football (2), volleyball (1), track and field (2), softball skills (2).

Administrative and Testing — .6 Week

This includes the first day (organization) and two days of testing.

**Simple Games Activities and Relays —
6.4 Weeks**

The remainder of the time allocation for the year is designated for simple games and relays, affording the factor of flexibility. If any one particular area seems not to have enough time allotment, the games allocation can be reduced.

SUGGESTED YEAR'S PHYSICAL EDUCATION PROGRAM BY WEEKS
Fourth Grade Level

Week 1 Orientation (1 day) Exercises Games and relays Fitness test (1 day)	**Week 2** Exercises Soccer	**Week 3** Exercises Soccer	**Week 4** Exercises Games and relays
Week 5 Exercises Touch football Soccer — Girls	**Week 6** Exercises Touch football Soccer — Girls	**Week 7** Circuit training Games and relays	**Week 8** Circuit training Manipulative — Playground balls Game

Week 9
Circuit training
Rope jumping
Rhythms
	Week 10
	Circuit training
	Rope jumping
	Rhythms
		Week 11
		Circuit training
		Manipulative — Wands
		  and hoops
		Game
			Week 12
			Circuit training
			Climbing ropes-
			  ladders-frames
			Benches

Week 13 Astronaut drills Balance beam Combatives	**Week 14** Astronaut drills Basketball Related game or relay	**Week 15** Astronaut drills Basketball Related game or relay	**Week 16** Grass drills Basketball
Week 17 Grass drills Balls to rhythm Rhythms	**Week 18** Grass drills Balls to rhythm Rhythms	**Week 19** Exercises to music Stunts and tumbling	**Week 20** Exercises to music Stunts and tumbling
Week 21 Exercises to music Stunts and tumbling	**Week 22** Exercises to music Volleyball	**Week 23** Exercises to music Games and relays	**Week 24** Exercises to music Climbing ropes-ladders- frames Benches
Week 25 Circuit training Balance beam Combatives	**Week 26** Circuit training Rope jumping Rhythms	**Week 27** Circuit training Rope jumping Rhythms	**Week 28** Circuit training Rhythms Games and relays
Week 29 Circuit training Games and relays	**Week 30** Circuit training Manipulative — Paddles and balls	**Week 31** Continuity drills Softball Skills	**Week 32** Continuity drills Softball skills
Week 33 Continuity drills Games and relays	**Week 34** Astronaut drills Track and field	**Week 35** Astronaut drills Track and field Fitness testing (1 day)	**Week 36** Astronaut drills Track and field (1 day) Junior Olympics (1 day) Games and relays

Step 7. The final step is to make up lesson plans for the weeks, based on instructional units. Discussion of lesson planning is found in Chapter 8.

Proportional Weekly Scheduling

A simpler plan of scheduling may be more appropriate for the kindergarten, first, or second grade, where the activities are more general in nature, and the scheduling is not complicated by special fitness activities. In this plan, the overall percentages for the broad categories are maintained in a weekly schedule. Each week then conforms in percentages to the overall pattern. As an illustration, let us take the first grade program and base the calculations on a minimum of 150 minutes per week.

FIRST GRADE PROGRAM

Activity Category	Percentage (Yearly)	Total Minutes (Weekly)	
Movement Experiences	35	52.5	
Rhythmic Activities	25	37.5	
Apparatus, Stunts, and Tumbling	20	30	
Simple Games	20	30	
Totals	100%	150	Minutes

ILLUSTRATIVE PROPORTIONAL FIRST GRADE WEEKLY PROGRAM

Day	Monday	Tuesday	Wednesday	Thursday	Friday
Activity	Movement 18 Min.	Rhythms 18 Min.	Movement 18 Min.	Rhythms 18 Min.	Movement 18 Min.
	Games 12 Min.	App.-Tumb. 12 Min.	Games 12 Min.	App.-Tumb. 12 Min.	Choice Games and/or App-Tumb. 12 Min.

This does not come out to the *precise* percentages listed above, but the percentages are at best an approximation. Adherence to this weekly schedule does assure a broad, balanced inclusion of activity content. Step 7 is the same for this as for the other plan, the stipulation of the activities for selected time blocks.

Within activity categories, allowance can be made for the short attention span. The teacher can vary the time schedule on any one day, dependent upon the response of the children to the instructional sequences.

UNIT PLANNING

A unit is a planned sequence of learning experiences based on an activity area. It has purpose for the children and is directed toward certain valid program goals. It involves the concept of time, since a period is established during which the unit is to be completed. It should encompass a meaningful whole, a body of material which it is to cover.

There are a number of possible subdivisions into which a unit may be broken up, depending on the activity area suggested. These divisions should include the basic goals and the specific goals which the unit seeks to accomplish.

1. General Purposes or Objectives of the Unit. Included here should be a statement in broad terms of what the unit is attempting to accomplish.

2. Specific Goals.

a. *Knowledge and Understandings.* These items are in terms of the children, listing knowledge and understandings to be acquired by them through the unit.

b. *Habits and Attitudes.* What social and

ethical concepts are to be an outgrowth of the learning experiences of the unit?

c. *Skills to be Acquired.* Skills to be included as a part of the learning experiences should be listed in proper progression as they appear in the unit.

d. *Activity Experiences.* Lead-up games, races, forms of competition, and other ways that selected area experiences will be presented to the children should be listed.

A focal game or outcome can be designated toward which the unit is directed, the achievement of which can be used as a basis of evaluation.

3. Facilities and Equipment Needed.

a. List the items needed.

4. Approximate Time Allotments for Various Parts of the Unit.

a. Orientation. Background, rules, etc.

b. Skill Drills and Instruction.

c. Lead-Up Activities.

d. Competitive Play — Tourney, Meet, Roundrobin Play, etc.

e. Evaluative procedures.

5. Weekly Schedule.

a. *General Schedule for the First Week.* If the unit is presented for only one week or less, the entire schedule can be planned. If the unit is more than one week in length, the schedule beyond the first week should be withheld until the first week's schedule has been completed. A lesson plan covering the first week's work is based on the suggested schedule. The progress during the first week will largely determine what is to follow.

6. Instructional Procedures.

Critical instructional procedures should be listed, centering attention on the important approaches not to be overlooked.

7. Instructional Materials Sources.

a. Bibliography.

b. Audio-visual aids.

THE LESSON PLAN

Following a determination of program elements and the establishment of units for the separate activities, lesson plans can be formulated. Directions for making lesson plans are found in Chapter 8.

4

Facilities, Equipment and Supplies

It is essential that sufficient facilities and adequate equipment and supplies be present so that an effective program can be operated. Standards should be established and adhered to. In setting up a building program, it is important to decide first the type of program desired and then plan the play facilities to meet the needs. In building, be sure to build the gymnasium large enough for maximum enrollment, as physical education facilities are difficult to enlarge. Planning may also need to consider community use during non-school hours.

FACILITIES

 Facility planning must consider climate and geographical conditions with respect to both indoor and outdoor play space. In geographic areas where weather conditions require adequate indoor facilities a minimum of one indoor teaching station for each ten classrooms is needed. Beyond ten and up to twenty classrooms, a second teaching station is needed.

All children should change to play clothing, including gym shoes. Provision must be made for the storage of play clothing. Such storage space for the kindergarten and first and second grades can probably be arranged in the classroom, thus enabling the teacher to make sure that each child has the necessary items when the class starts for the play area.

For grades 3 to 6 dressing rooms and shower facilities large enough to take care of peak loads should be available.

Since it is advisable to have children from grades 3 through 6 change to play clothing and shower after activity, different provisions for clothing storage should be made. A storage system away from the regular classroom will remove the odor problem present when play clothing (particularly gym shoes) is stored there.

Adequate storage room should be planned for supplies and portable equipment. In view of the trend toward employment of the physical education specialist, it is desirable to have an office in the facility, since often no assigned space is available elsewhere in the school. Such an office should contain a shower and a toilet.

The combination gymnasium - auditorium - cafeteria facility leaves much to be desired, creating more problems than it solves. Labeled a "multipurpose room," a better term probably would be "multiuseless." The cafeteria is a particular problem. The gymnasium must be vacated prior to the lunch hour for setting up chairs and tables, and is not available for activity until the facility has been cleaned, which usually involves mopping. This eliminates any noon-hour recreational use, leaving little play area for children during inclement weather. In extreme cases, the lack of help takes the gymnasium out of use during the early part of the afternoon until the custodian has completed his cleaning chores.

Play and special event practice is hardly compatible with the free atmosphere of physical education activities. Special programs, movies, and other events necessitating chairs also complicate the situation.

The indoor facility should be planned as a physical education facility in which athletic contests may be scheduled at times, not predominantly as an athletic facility with consideration for spectators. The latter approach is not in error if the physical education needs do not suffer.

Outdoor planning should include provision for sufficient field space, hard-surfaced areas, apparatus areas, and other needed space. Play area standards should meet the minimum of 5 acres, with one additional acre for each 100 pupils. Automobile and bicycle parking areas should be in addition to play space standards.

Outdoor areas should be suitably turfed, surfaced, leveled, and drained. An automatic sprinkler system is desirable, but the sprinkler heads should not prove to be safety hazards. The hardtop surface should be suitably marked for movement patterns and games. Areas for court games are also desirable. Separate areas should be established where various groups of children may play in safety without interference from other groups of children. Good standards of maintenance and sanitation should prevail in both indoor and outdoor facilities.

EQUIPMENT AND SUPPLIES

Equipment refers to those items of a more or less fixed nature. Supplies include those nondurable materials which have a limited time of use. To illustrate the difference — a softball is listed under supplies while the longer-lasting softball backstop comes under the category of equipment. Equipment needs periodic replacement, and budgetary planning must consider the usable life span of each piece of equipment. Supplies are generally purchased on a yearly basis.

It is important not only to have adequate financing for equipment and supplies, but also to expend funds wisely.

If the objectives of physical education are to be fulfilled, there must be an adequate amount of equipment and supplies. It is difficult to envision children learning skills or acquiring physical fitness when they handle objects only infrequently or are limited to an occasional turn on the mat. Since physical education is activity, there must be sufficient materials to keep the children active. Special attention to policies involving purchase, storage, issue, care and maintenance records, and inventory are necessary if maximum use and return from the allotted budget is to be realized. It is important to decide what the boys and girls need in the program, and then base the purchasing plan upon this list.

Purchasing Policies

The purchase of supplies and equipment involves careful study of needs, prevailing prices, the quality of workmanship, and satisfactory materials. Safety and protection of the participants are also of vital concern.

Quantity buying by pooling the needs of the entire school system generally results in better use of the tax dollar. However, there may need to be compromise on the type and brand of materials in order to satisfy different users within a school system. If bids are asked, there is need to make careful specifications for materials. Bids should be asked only on those items specified, and "just as good" merchandise should not be permitted as substitutes.

One individual within a school should be designated as responsible for the keeping of records of equipment and supplies and for the purchase of these items. Needs vary from school to school, and it becomes practical for the school district authorities to deal with a single individual within a school. Prompt attention to repair and replacement of supplies is more likely under this system.

Constructed or home-made equipment should receive strong consideration. However, quality must not be sacrificed. Articles from home such as empty plastic jugs, old tires, milk cartons, and the like should be regarded as supplementary and enrichment materials. Care must be taken that administrators do not look for the cheap, no-cost route for supplies and sacrifice valuable learning experiences if an appreciable cost is indicated.

Recommended Equipment

Two criteria are important in selecting equipment for the outdoor setting for physical education. The first is that the piece of equipment must contribute to the development of the child. For this reason items which involve only "sit and ride" experiences such as swings, teeters, and merry-go-rounds are not recommended. In addition, the slide is questionable, but some feel that there is value in the climbing part, and that the slide is a challenge to overcome fear. The second criterion is the safety factor. Many of the circular, hanging types like the giant stride are prone to cause accidents.

Outdoor Equipment

Climbing Structures. There are many names and many good varieties. Various types such as jungle gyms, castle towers, and similar items have value in physical fitness.

Horizontal Ladders. Horizontal ladders are valuable pieces of equipment on the playground. They come in a variety of combinations and forms. Arched ladders are quite popular, as they allow children to reach the rungs easily. Uniladders, consisting of a single beam with pegs on each side, offer good challenge for children. A set comprising two arched ladders, crossing each other at the center at right angles, offers the potential for many types of movement experiences.

Arched Ladders

Climbing Ropes. In some climates where the weather is not too severe, schools are installing climbing ropes outside. These should not be over 12' to 14' in height and should be equipped with a circular stop at the top.

Balance Beams. Beams made from 4" x 4" beams can be put in permanent installations. These can be arranged in various patterns as indicated, but should not be more than 12" to 18" above the surface. Outdoor balance beams provide an extension of the instructional activities of the program.

Turning Bars. Turning bars made from 3" galvanized pipe offer exciting possibilities for children. The bars can be from 6' to 10' in length and positioned 30" to 36" above the ground.

Horizontal Bar Combinations. The set of three horizontal bars together at different heights is a valuable piece of apparatus for physical education.

Basketball Goals. These may or may not be combined with a court. Youngsters play a great deal of one-goal basketball, and a regulation court is not needed for this game. These should be in a surfaced area, however.

Volleyball Standards. Volleyball standards should have flexible height adjustments, including a low height of 30" for use with paddle ball.

Softball Backstops. Softball backstops can be either fixed or portable.

Tetherball Courts. Tetherball courts should have fastening devices for the cord and ball so that these can be removed from the post for safe keeping.

Track and Field Equipment. Jumping standards, bars, and pits should be available. These must be properly maintained.

Obstacle Courses. Considerable choice is available in setting up outdoor obstacle

Outdoor Obstacle Course

courses, a new development on the equipment market. Many interesting and challenging obstacles can be put together in an effective course.

Indoor Equipment

A shortcoming of many schools is the lack of suitable developmental equipment in the indoor physical education facility. As the basis for a good program, it is imperative that the gymnasium be equipped with overhead support equipment, climbing structures, climbing ropes, balance beams, and mats, in addition to the usual basketball goals and volleyball standards. Boxes for jumping and vaulting should also receive strong consideration in planning. Overhead support equipment includes horizontal ladder sets, exercise (horizontal) bars, and chinning bars. Climbing sets may be fixed or portable. Climbing ropes are particularly valuable tools for physical education. Suggested items for consideration in equipping an indoor facility follow.

Balance Beam Benches. This item has a double use. It can be used as a regular bench for the many types of bench activities, or when turned over becomes a balance beam. It should be of sturdy construction to stand up under the various demands. Wooden horses or other supports can be used to provide inclined benches. Six benches are a minimum for class activity.

Balance Beams. A wide beam (4") is recommended for the kindergarten and the first grade. Otherwise, the usual 2" beam should be used. Balance beams with alternate surfaces (2" or 4") can be constructed of normal building materials. Construction details are found in the appendix.

Chinning Bar. The chinning bar is especially useful in the testing program for physical fitness, as well as providing body support activities. The portable chinning bar to be used in the doorway of the gymnasium is a substitute.

Tumbling Mats. Mats are basic to any physical education program and at least six should be present. Enough mats must be available to provide safety flooring for climbing apparatus. Mats should be 4' wide and 6' to 8' long. Light folding mats, while not as soft as some of the others, have the advantage that the children

can handle them with ease. Folded mats also stack better. Mats should have fasteners so that at least two may be coupled together. Plastic covers are more suitable, as the old canvas mats are most difficult to keep clean.

Climbing Ropes. Climbing ropes are essential to the program. At least eight should be present, but more allow for better group instruction. Climbing rope sets on tracks are the most efficient method of handling these pieces of equipment. With little effort and loss of time, the ropes are ready for activity. Ropes are available in a variety of materials, but good quality manila hemp seems to be the most practical. Ropes should be either 1¼" or 1½" in diameter.

Climbing Ropes on Tracks

Volleyball Standards. The standards should allow for various heights for different grades and also for other games.

Portable Climbing Structures. These are portable sets usually based on wooden or metal horses and include supported bars, ladders, and other equipment for climbing. (See diagram in the appendix.)

Bounding Boards. These are 2' by 6', generally made of ¾" marine plywood. Knots in poor plywood will cause the boards to break. Useful in the primary program, four boards should be constructed. (See appendix.)

Balance Boards. Four to six balance boards of different types are a desirable extension of apparatus experiences. (See appendix.)

Types of Balance Boards

Record Player. A good record player with a variable speed control is a must for the program. Pause control is also helpful. The physical education program should have its own record player, as there is enough demand to justify this. Access to a tape recorder is also helpful.

Supply Cart. A cart to hold supplies is quite desirable.

Jumping Boxes. Small boxes used for jumping and allied locomotor movements have good value in extending the opportunities for basic movement skills. For kindergarten and first grade, boxes should be 8" and 16" in height. For the older children, boxes of 12" and 24" offer sufficient challenge. The box with the lesser height can be 16" by 16" while the taller box can be 18" by 18" in size. The smaller box can be stored inside the larger box.

The top of the box should be padded with carpet padding and covered with leather or durable plastic. Holes drilled through the sides will provide finger holds for ease of handling. Eight boxes, four of each, are a minimum number for the average size class.

Horizontal Ladder Sets. Horizontal ladders which fold against the wall make an excellent addition to indoor equipment. The ladder may be combined with other pieces of apparatus in a folding set.

Climbing Frames. Climbing frames, mostly of European origin, are becoming increasingly popular and available in this country. The author has found excellent success in his program with a particular type of frame popular in Holland.

Another type of frame which has good

First Grade Children Using 16" Jumping Boxes

Klimraam — Holland Climbing Frame

acceptance in this country is the Hampton Frame, a type popular in England.

English Climbing Frame — The Hampton Frame

Supplies

The basic rule for supplies is that they should be in sufficient amount so that no child has to wait too long for a turn because there is insufficient quantity. For some items there should be one for each child. The list is divided into two sections: basic items and additional supplies.

Basic Items

Jump ropes (one for each child). Length: Primary, 7' or 8'; intermediate, 8' or 9'.
Beanbags, assorted color (2 for each child).
Long jump ropes, 14'-16' (1 for each five children).
Small balls, assorted colors (1 for each child).
Yarn or fleece balls (for K-1, 1 for each child).
Rubber playground balls (mostly 8½", but have variety. One for each child).
Sports balls (football, volleyball, basketball, soccer; 6 of each).
Wooden paddles for paddle tennis and similar games (1 for each child).
Softball equipment, including masks.
Batting tees for softball (4).
Indian clubs (12 or more).
Wands, 36" or 42" (1 for each child).
Pinnies or other team markers (1 for each two children).
Cageballs, 24" (2).

Gym scooters (4 for relays, or 1 for each two children).
Rubber beach balls, 12"-15" (2).
Stopwatches, 1/5 second (2).
Measuring tape, 50' (1).
Jump-the-shot ropes (3).
Volleyball nets (2).
Rubber traffic cones for boundary markers, 12" (24).
Records.
Tom-tom or drum with striker (1).
Hoops, 36" (1 for each child).
Wire baskets for storage (6 or more).
Ball inflator with gauge (1).
Eyeglass protectors (4).
Whistles (6).
Individuals mats, 18" x 36" or 20" x 40" (1 for each child).
Magic or stretch ropes (8).
Parachute, 24'-28' (1).
Tetherball sets.

Additional Supplies

In addition to the items specified as basic, a number of the following should be considered:
Deck tennis rings.
Rubber horseshoes.
Shuffleboard equipment.
Bongo boards.
Microphone for record player.
Wooden blocks, 1" x 1", for relay races (24).
Large tug-of-war rope, 60' or more in length.
Stilts (6 pair).
Table tennis equipment.
Pogo sticks.
Lummi sticks.
Broom handles (8).
Dry liner and marking lime.
Target for pitching.
Bicycle or auto tires.
Oversize inner tubes.
Rubber balloons (12).
Plastic floor hockey set.
Large pushball, 48" (1).

Storage Plans

When a teacher takes a class into the gymnasium for physical education, he has the right to expect and be assured of sufficient supplies to conduct his class. A master list stipulating the kinds and quantities of supplies which should be in storage should be established. A reasonable turnover should be expected, and supply procedures should reflect this. One teacher should be placed in charge of the supply room, with responsibility for maintenance and replacement. The supplies from this source should be used for physical education and after-school events. It should not be a source of recreational issue for recess or free play periods. Each classroom should have its own supplies, marked for classroom identification, for this purpose.

Available supplies should be arranged in such a fashion that an easy count can be made. There should be a particular spot or bin to which the supplies should be returned. Off-season items should be removed to a "dead" storage area. Good housekeeping procedures should be followed and the supply room kept orderly. Selected students or squad leaders could take some responsibility for helping to maintain a tidy storage area.

Some schools have found it helpful to use small supply carts of the type pictured below.

Equipment Cart — Home Constructed

The cart holds the articles in more frequent use. It does take up space, but it is quite a time-saver. Carts can be built inexpensively to a personal plan or an equipment carrier can be purchased. A second cart to hold the record player and records is also suggested.

The principal or physical education supervisor should inspect storage areas at regular intervals. An established routine of taking care of repairs and replacement of supplies must also be instituted.

A few schools dispense with a central storage area and place the responsibility for supplies in each classroom.

This plan keeps a sufficient supply of physical education materials in each classroom for participation of that class. Advantages of the plan are:

(1) Less time is wasted. (2) The supplies available are known. (3) Definite responsibility may be fixed for loss or damage. (4) Children have a sense of responsibility for "their" materials. (5) There is no competition or overlap in demands for supplies by different classes.

Disadvantages given for this plan are that it is initially expensive, storage facilities are needed for each classroom, and equipment must be marked carefully to ensure its being returned to the right classroom.

Recommendations for Supplies

Some supplies are designed especially for children in the intermediate grades. Junior-size footballs and basketballs are available and should be used. Rubber-covered balls generally prove more satisfactory than the leather variety for use in the elementary school, particularly during wet weather.

Smaller children can use rubber playground balls for volleyball-type games. When playground balls are used for soccer skills, they work more satisfactorily when slightly deflated.

When children are working on simple bouncing skills, it is desirable for each child to have a ball. The supply of balls can be augmented by tennis or sponge balls. Discarded tennis balls from the high school tennis team are a good source. Sponge balls are inexpensive and with care last indefinitely.

For jump ropes, ⅜" sash core is suitable. The ends should be whipped or dipped in some type of hardening solution in order to prevent unraveling. Adhesive tape may also be used to bind the ends of the ropes. The new plastic link jumping ropes are particularly attractive and should be considered. With care, these last indefinitely.

Another good source for jump ropes is ⅜" yellow plastic (not nylon) rope of a *hard weave* variety. The ends can be melted with a match or burner.

Beanbags can be made easily. Good quality, bright colored muslin is suitable. Some prefer a beanbag with an outer liner which snaps in place to allow for washing. Another idea is to sew three sides of the beanbag permanently. The fourth side is used for filling and has an independent stitch. The beans can be removed through the side when the bag is washed. Beanbags should be about 6" by 6" and can be filled with dried beans, peas, wheat, rice, or even building sand.

Batting tees can be constructed using a wooden or metal base, similar to a high jump standard, and a piece of radiator hose. If it is to be adjustable, then two pieces of hose can be used so that one will slide (adjust) for different heights. However, this adjustment takes time and isn't always satisfactory. An alternate suggestion would be to make tees of various sizes.

For games requiring boundary markers, pieces of rubber matting can be used. In addition, small sticks or boards, painted white, are excellent. A board 1" by 2", 3' or 4' in length makes a satisfactory marker.

Empty gallon plastic jugs filled halfway with sand and recapped, make fine boundary markers. Clorox or similar plastic jugs can be cut down to make ball catchers.

Tetherballs should have a snap-on fastener for easy removal.

Softballs can be purchased without stitching (concealed stitch) which eliminates the problem of broken stitches and consequent repair.

A jump-the-shot rope can be made by using an old, completely deflated volleyball tied on the end of a rope.

Old tires, even those from bicycles, can be used for throwing targets.

Schools in and near ski areas may contact lift proprietors for discarded tow ropes. These make excellent tug-of-war ropes.

Indian clubs can be turned in the school woodshops. However, many substitutes can be made. Lumber of size 2" by 2" cut off in short pieces (6" to 10" long) will stand satisfactorily. Lumber companies generally also have available round poles from 1" to 1½" in diameter. Sections of these make satisfactory Indian clubs. Broken bats also can be made into good substitute clubs.

Bases can be constructed from heavy canvas. The canvas should be folded over three or four times and then stitched together. Bases may be made from outdoor plywood and should be painted. Heavy rubber matting also is suitable material for bases.

Handles from old brooms or mops can provide the needed wands and sticks. These come in various diameters, but this is not an important factor.

Deck tennis rings can be made from heavy rope by splicing.

Deck tennis rings and hoops can also be made from plastic water pipe. However, the color selection is limited and uninspiring. (See appendix.) Garden hose can also be used to make deck rings.

White shoe polish has numerous uses and will come off the floor with a little scrubbing. Marking lines and making designs are some of the uses for this marking device.

Individual mats can be made from indoor-outdoor carpeting that has a rubber backing. Mats of this type can be washed readily.

Coffee cans (3 lb.) can be used as targets.

Empty half-gallon milk cartons also have a variety of uses.

Paddles can be made from ⅜" to ½" plywood. Handles can be augmented with the use of plastic tape. (See appendix.)

Inner tubes can be cut into strips to provide resistive pieces of exercise equipment. Cut across the tube in strips about 1½" wide.

Play scooters can be constructed, but care must be exercised in selecting swivel wheels which will not mark the floor.

Magic or stretch ropes can be made by stringing together twenty-five to thirty large size rubber bands. Common clothing elastic, ½" or ¾", also makes excellent stretch ropes. (See appendix.)

Yarn balls can be made by older children or by the PTA. Wool yarn has the advantage of shrinking after washing, tightening into an effective ball. (See appendix.)

Blocks with a groove on the top and one of the sides are excellent for forming hurdles with wands. A 4" x 4" timber cut into various lengths, 6", 12", and 18", gives a variety of hurdles. Grooves can be cut with a dado or a regular table saw. Grooves should be ¾″ wide and about ½″ deep. (See appendix.)

Old bowling pins can be obtained from most bowling alleys free of charge. Since they are too large for the children to handle easily, cut off the top 6″ to 8″. Parallel cuts through the body of the pin will provide hockey pucks and shuffle board disks. Bowling pins can be turned down on a lathe in the woodshop to resemble Indian clubs.

Care and Repair. There must be a definite system established for repair of supplies and equipment. If the central storage system is used, the repair materials can be kept in this location. Children and teachers tend to become discouraged if the repair process is lengthy and, rather than be deprived of an item, may continue to use it until it is no longer worth salvaging.

An important social objective for children is respect for and care of school property. Proper development of attitudes and habits in the care of physical education materials will help achieve this goal.

Balls need to be inflated to proper pressures. This means an accurate gauge and periodic checking. The needle should be moistened before it is inserted into the valve. Children should not sit on balls and should kick balls made specifically for kicking (soccers, footballs, and playground balls).

Softball bats and wooden paddles should not be used for hitting rocks, stones, or other hard materials. Neither should bats be knocked against fences, posts, or other objects that will cause damage. Broken bats should be discarded, as they are unsafe even if taped around the break. Children should learn to keep the trademark up when batting. Bats should be taped to prevent slippage.

Cuts, abrasions, and breaks in rubber balls should be immediately repaired. In some cases this repair can be handled by means of a vulcanizing patch as used for tire tube repairs. In others, the use of a hard-setting rubber preparation is of value. However, some repairs are beyond the scope of the school, and the ball should be sent away for repair.

Storage and Marking.

A systematic procedure should be estab-

lished for the storage of equipment and supplies. A place for everything and everything in its place is the key to good housekeeping. A principal certainly is more favorably inclined toward purchase requests when he observes the good care that the supplies are receiving.

Mats are expensive and care is needed if they are to last. A place where they can be stacked properly should be provided or there should be handles for hanging them up. A mat truck is another solution, provided there is space for storing the truck. The newer plastic or plastic-covered mats should be cleaned with a damp, soapy cloth.

For off-season storage, balls should be deflated somewhat, leaving enough air in them to keep their shape. Leather balls should be cleaned with an approved ball conditioner.

For small items, clean ice cream containers (2-gallon) make adequate storage receptacles. Most school cafeterias have these and other containers which may be used in the storage room to provide order. Small wire baskets also make good containers for small physical education materials.

An area should be established for the equipment needing repair so that the articles for repair are evident at a glance.

Equipment that will warp should be laid in a flat place.

All equipment and supplies should be marked. This is particularly important for equipment issued to different classrooms. Marking can be done with indelible pencils, paint, or stencil ink. However, few marking systems are permanent and re-marking at regular intervals is necessary. Sporting goods establishments have marking sets available for this purpose.

An electric burning pencil or stamp is also useful but must be used with caution so as not to damage the equipment being marked.

Rubber playground balls come in different colors, and an assignment to a classroom can be made on the basis of color. A code scheme can also be used with different color paints. It is possible to devise a color system by which the year of issue can be designated. This offers opportunities for research into equipment use.

5

Organizing for Effective Teaching

The Community, the Administration, and the School
Patterns of Teaching Responsibility
Consultant and Supervisory Services
Scheduling
Policies for Health and Safety
Safety Procedures
Operational Policies
The Extended Activity Program
Promotional Ideas and Public Relations
Pageants, Demonstrations, and Assembly Programs

THE COMMUNITY, THE ADMINISTRATION, AND THE SCHOOL

With physical education fast approaching the milestone of acceptance as a partner in education, school administrators are now more concerned with the type and quality of their overall school programs. This program in turn will reflect the degree of confidence which the school administration has in physical education as an educational tool. A quality physical education program will convince school officials that physical education is worthy of the effort and support it requires.

It is vital that the administration accept the fundamental concepts that physical education is a developmental and instructional program which is an important part of the child's educational experience, and that this teaching area merits suitable consideration in planning. It is also important for the administration to understand the relationship which exists between perceptual-motor competency and certain academic skills. Whether or not physical education is a teaching period or a glorified recess period, where the chief purpose seems to be for youngsters to let off steam, is largely determined by the administrative approach.

The community climate for physical education must be positive. If parents are made aware of the existence of a quality physical education program and know what it can do for their children, pressures on schools to provide better physical education experiences will result. PTAs can become effective lobbies. Physical educators should never underestimate the power of parents and should welcome every opportunity to work with parent groups through displays and effective dissemination of informational materials.

Two administrative decisions with regard to personnel must be made at the beginning to set the basis for the program. The first is the decision as to who is to teach the classes — specialist, regular teacher, or other pattern. The second specifies the kind of consultant or supervisory aid to help the teacher.

PATTERNS OF TEACHING RESPONSIBILITY

The patterns of teaching physical education vary with respect to staff assignments from school district to school district. Larger school districts have more flexibility in selecting an appropriate pattern, but many small districts have solved the problem of providing quality teaching. Some of the plans by which physical education teaching is organized today are as follows:

1. Full Responsibility by the Classroom Teacher with No Consultant or Supervisory Services. Often in this administrative arrangement no curriculum guide is available. This kind of format does not generally result in a quality program. In many cases the program becomes no more than a supervised play period. This is not a recommended teaching pattern for physical education.

2. Specialist Teaching in Physical Education. This plan produces the best results in terms of child progress toward the objectives of physical education. A major objection to specialist teaching is that it requires extra teachers. A second reservation about this program is that the classroom teacher loses contact with the students during the physical education classes and thus misses a valuable opportunity to work with and observe the children in this setting. Some of this objection can be overcome by having the classroom teacher present during the physical education lesson.

The most prevalent practice is to assign the specialist the responsibility for the intermediate level classes and have the classroom teacher handle the kindergarten and primary grades. On the intermediate level, the charac-

ter of physical education changes into a more specialized program of activities, demanding a higher degree of skill proficiency for teaching than that needed for the lower grades.

3. Departmentalized Teaching. The advantage of this plan is specialist teaching or teaching by personnel with good background without the need for additional teaching personnel.

This plan involves a rotation of teachers and subject matter fields among classes on much the same plan as used in high school scheduling. The teachers usually work with the self-contained classroom during the morning (or afternoon), and the other half of the day is given over to departmentalized teaching by the same teachers on a rotating class schedule. Here is one way such a plan could work utilizing two fifth and two sixth grade classes and subject matter fields of music, social studies, language arts, and physical education.

Periods	5th — 1	5th — 2	6th — 1	6th — 2
1st	Teacher A Music	Teacher B Social Studies	Teacher C Language Arts	Teacher D Physical Educ.
2nd	Teacher D Physical Educ.	Teacher A Music	Teacher B Social Studies	Teacher C Language Arts
3rd	Teacher C Language Arts	Teacher D Physical Educ.	Teacher A Music	Teacher B Social Studies
4th	Teacher B Social Studies	Teacher C Language Arts	Teacher D Physical Educ.	Teacher A Music

This plan could also be adapted to separating the sexes for activity. The plan could work equally well with two or three classes. Since this plan demands only a time arrangement, it represents no additional staff expense to the administration.

4. Teaching Responsibilities Shared by the Classroom Teacher and the Special Teacher. This must be a partnership of effort between the two teachers or it will fail. The ideal arrangement is to have the special teacher introduce units and teach the more difficult elements, with the classroom teacher providing follow-up lessons. The logistics of this

arrangement are difficult. In some instances, the specialist teaches only one day per week and the classroom teacher the remainder. When the special teacher comes the following week, he has little knowledge of what has transpired between his visits. The special teacher has a difficult time learning personality characteristics of the children; in fact, he may not even be able to learn their names from his meager contacts.

5. Teaching by the Classroom Teacher With Consultant Aid. To implement this plan, it is necessary to have a program of inservice education. The classroom teacher basically does the teaching, but there could be demonstration teaching by the consultant. Curricular materials and lesson plan formats need to be provided. Classroom teachers generally are willing to follow a prescribed curriculum if the demands of paper work are not excessive.

6. Trading or Combining Classes. A practice which has merit is to have a man and a woman teacher combine two classes for physical education, usually on the intermediate level. With two sixth grade classes and two teaching stations available, the male teacher could take the boys of both classes, and the woman teacher instruct the girls. This arrangement should not rule out coeducational activity, but is a convenience in activities where the sexes should be separated.

Irrespective of the selected pattern of organization, the teacher responsible for physical education instruction should endeavor to develop and maintain his proficiency and background in the field. This means welcoming and utilizing consultant service, acquiring a personal library and accumulation of related materials, seeking additional training in course work and graduate courses, and participating in professional meetings.

CONSULTANT AND SUPERVISORY SERVICES

In the era of rapid change, with new ideas, activities, and teaching approaches coming to the fore, some plan for consultant or supervisory services is essential. Careful selection of the individual who is to function as a consultant or supervisor is important. Not only should he be qualified, but he should possess the confidence and enthusiasm to work successfully with teachers. He must be a superior teacher himself.

Working relationships with the principal and the teachers must be clarified. The pattern of inservice meetings, the frequency of consultant visits, and other relevant working procedures must be established.

He must be both knowledgeable and available. His office should be a center for resource materials, and he should produce instructional aids for the teacher as needed and requested. Paper work for teachers must be kept to a minimum.

The human relationships with his educational community are also of high importance. A "help" attitude based on constructive criticism is much more effective than a posture of supervision. A good rapport with the teaching staff is important.

A sound philosophy and an effective and functioning curriculum, based on good educational standards, serve as the basis for this type of program. A curriculum guide should be in the hands of all teachers working in the program. The practice of placing one or two curriculum manuals in the principal's office means that little use will be made of them.

The importance of the principal in the educational scheme must be recognized in the relationships the supervisor maintains with the school. The principal should be kept informed and should be consulted as indicated. He should receive a copy of all announcements and directives for his teachers. An effective procedure is to route all equipment and supplies through his office, so that he will know what has been received.

The consultant should be a participating member of local, state, regional, and national professional associations. As a function of this professional involvement, he should interpret new trends to his school community and incorporate into his program desirable changes and additions which are of proven value.

SCHEDULING

A definite schedule for physical education classes should be established at each school, based on instructional time of at least 150 minutes per week, exclusive of recess or other supervised play. The standard is for instructional time and does not include time needed for moving to and from class, changing to gym clothing, visiting the washroom, and cleaning up.

The recommendation by most national bodies is that physical education be scheduled on a daily basis. However, some consideration should be given on the intermediate level to another plan if the children change clothing and also shower after activity. A weekly schedule of three class sessions of a longer period of activity (45 to 50 minutes) would tend to alleviate some of the dressing and shower-ing problems yet still meet the standard for time. Some teachers regard this as superior to the daily plan as more efficient instruction is possible with emphasis on progression.

Where sufficient teaching stations exist, the scheduling problem is minimized. Caution is urged with outdoor scheduling where equip-ment is to be shared and conflicts can arise with limited supplies. Problems occur when too many classes are scheduled using the physical education materials available.

Class size should not exceed the normal limits of one class. The practice of sending out two or more classes with one teacher for physical education results in little more than a supervised play period.

The substitution of band, chorus, play prac-tice, and athletic programs for physical educa-tion is not a recommended procedure. Teachers too frequently take the physical education period to practice special events for part or all of the children. Neither should health instruction be counted as a part of the physical education requirement. Health in-struction is an important area in its own right and should be so treated. Confusion exists because often the terms health and physical education are coupled in literature.

POLICIES FOR HEALTH AND SAFETY

The school has both a moral and a legal responsibility toward its students. The moral responsibility is part of the school's broad educational purposes, namely to provide a school setting in which each child may devel-op an optimum level of personal health. The legal responsibility arises out of the public's assumption that the school cannot escape the legal obligation to provide a healthful and safe environment for the child.

Periodic Health Examination

A first concern for the student is the provi-sion of a periodic health examination. This should determine, among other things, the extent of a child's participation in physical education. Ideally this examination would be held yearly and would include all health factors having a bearing on the child's educa-tional experience. In practice, however, exam-inations are given about every third year and

can be scheduled on entrance into school, in fourth grade, in seventh grade, and in the ninth or tenth grades, depending somewhat on the basic organizational plan of the school district.

The examination should classify students in one of three categories: (1) normal partici-pation in physical education; (2) participation subject to certain adaptations or restrictions; and (3) severe limitations or nonparticipation. The teacher must have access to the results of the examination in order that each student may receive the consideration stipulated in the examination.

An examination form approved by the local medical society makes for more consistent information. Agreement can also be reached with the local medical society with respect to a standard fee for the examination.

Excuses and Readmittance

If a child is to be excused from physical education for a day or two for health reasons, the teacher can accept a note from the par-ent. If the excuse involves a significant length of time, it should be accepted only on the recommendation of a physician. Readmittance of children who have been out for a period of time should also be subject to a physician's recommendation. If there is a school nurse, excuse and readmittance cases should be routed through her and she will in turn discuss the problem with the physical education teacher. In the absence of recommendations from both physician and nurse, consultation with the principal and the parent is probably the best solution.

Students who have been absent because of illness or some other condition should be ob-served closely for signs which might suggest that they are not ready to participate in unlim-ited physical activity. Girls should not be required to take part in vigorous activity dur-ing the early part of their menstrual periods.

Good rapport between the physicians and the schools is important in handling the health problems related to excuses and readmit-tance. One physician from the medical society should be designated to provide liaison among those responsible for physical educa-tion and the medical profession.

Screening by the Teacher

Periodic health examinations will not uncover every health problem related to physical activity participation. Some conditions may appear only after exercise. In other instances, the condition may develop between examinations or even shortly after an examination and have an important bearing on the health status of the individual.

The task of screening children who respond poorly to exercise is not difficult, as it involves primarily noting certain observable conditions which are an indication of an abnormality. The Committee on Exercise and Fitness of the American Medical Association lists these observable signs which may accompany or follow exercise and which are indications for referral and further investigation:

Excessive Breathlessness. Some breathlessness is normal with exercise, but breathlessness that persists long after exercise is cause for medical referral.

Bluing of the Lips. Except in a cold wet environment, bluing of the lips or nailbeds is an unnatural reaction to exercise. Its occurrence in the ordinary exercise setting is cause for medical referral.

Pale or Clammy Skin. Pale or clammy skin or cold sweating following or during exercise is not a normal reaction to physical activity within the usual temperature ranges of the gymnasium or playing field. Again, medical referral is recommended.

Unusual Fatigue. Excessive fatigue, as evidenced by unusual lack of endurance or early failure to maintain moderate activity, also suggests the need for medical referral. It is dangerous to attribute such reactions to malingering until possible organic causes have been ruled out.

Persistent Shakiness. Unusual weakness or shakiness that continues for more than ten minutes following vigorous exercise is cause for medical referral. Normally, recovery will be reasonably prompt.

Muscle Twitching or Tetany. Muscular contractions such as twitching or tetany, whether localized or generalized, sometimes occur as an unusual reaction to exercise. It may be abnormal and warrants medical investigation.

In addition, such medical symptoms as headache, dizziness, fainting, broken sleep at night, digestive upset, pain not associated with injury, undue pounding or uneven heartbeat, disorientation, or personality changes are contraindications of normal functioning. The Committee cautions that an occasional episode need not alarm the instructor, but recurring or persisting patterns of any of these symptoms, particularly when related to activity, indicate the need for medical review.

The instructor needs to be sensitive to these possible reactions of the children and note them in stride. He is further cautioned to remind himself that *unusual* reactions are not necessarily *abnormal* reactions.

The specialist, with his scientific and health background, is in a better position to assess such health indications than is the classroom teacher. However, with concentration and practice the classroom teacher can make effective use of the physical education period as a part of the daily health screening of the children.

Healthful Environment for Physical Education

A healthful environment for physical education requires attention to standards for school safety, hygiene, and sanitation. In addition, the physical education setting should emphasize good standards in cleanliness, ventilation, and heating. Ventilation should be sufficient to remove objectionable odors. Temperatures, depending upon the extent of the activity, should range from 65 to 68 degrees. Generally, a temperature comfortable for an elderly teacher is too high for active youngsters.

Healthful environment also includes attention to mental hygiene factors. Proper student-teacher relationships in activity areas are important. Students should be able to relieve tensions through activity. Physical education should be a period where students lose rather than acquire tensions.

Cleanliness of the gymnasium floor is particularly important in the present-day physical education program, as many of the movements require the children to place their hands or bodies on the floor. The floor should be swept in the morning just prior to the classes. In addition, it should be swept as often as needed between classes. A wide dust mop should be handy for this purpose, as children can perform this chore.

Ideally, all children should change to gym clothing for physical education classes, and children from the third grade on up should shower after activity. Even if showers are not available, a better physical education class can be conducted if appropriate clothing is worn. It is particularly important that girls wear something other than dresses.

The solution to the problem of changing clothing for class is not easily found. Some teachers find it practical to have youngsters change when convenient, wearing the play clothing during class sessions. Changing in washrooms has drawbacks, but at least accomplishes the task.

The problem of storing the children's play clothing if lockers are not available needs a positive approach. The cooperation of the classroom teacher must be gained to establish some kind of a system. The system should preserve the ownership of each child's things, not be time-consuming, and be a child-handled system.

As a basic minimum, children should wear gym shoes during the physical education class. The practice of having children "skate" around in stockinged feet limits the children greatly in their responses to activity challenges. It would be better to have the children in bare feet, rather than in stocking feet. The teacher should also be in appropriate clothing and footwear.

Adequate facilities should be available for cleaning-up after class, and enough time should be allowed for the finishing-up procedure.

SAFETY PROCEDURES

It is often said that proper safety is no accident. Safety education should be positive in terms of what approaches and considerations are needed and not based on the "scare" approach. A school safety committee is desirable to set safety regulations, policies, and procedures. The committee should be composed of students, faculty, the school nurse, and perhaps representatives of the PTA. A school safety code should be established and a written compilation, including all policies, regulations and procedures,

should be in the hands of all teachers. Regulations affecting the students should be posted. The committee should be open-minded and receptive to safety suggestions from students, faculty, and others. An important function would be to review accidents for the purpose of determining appropriate preventive measures to be taken.

The school safety program consists of three aspects: (1) a safe school environment; (2) safety education; and (3) safety services. Each is discussed in turn.

Safe Environment

The school must be certain that the school environment meets all the criteria for safety. This involves a number of aspects.

1. Health Status.

As previously discussed, the health status of the children must be ascertained through a health examination so no child may be placed in a physical environment beyond his capacity.

2. Provision for a Safe Teaching Place.

This is both quantitative and qualitative. There must be sufficient room for the activity, and the area must be suitable for the intended purpose. The character of the activity will determine the amount of space needed for safe play, including sufficient boundary clearance from walls, fences, and other obstructions. The area should be free from posts, wires, holes, and other hazards. The presence of broken glass, along with miscellaneous junk, is a source of accidents. Sprinkler heads and pools of water can also cause serious injury.

3. Safety in Equipment and Supplies.

The equipment and supplies provided must be suitable for the level of the children and the selected activity. The equipment should be in good functioning condition or removed from use.

4. Regular Inspection of Facilities and Equipment.

Inspection of facilities should be made on a regular basis, perhaps monthly. This can be a shared experience by the principal, custodian, and physical education specialist. Items needing attention should be noted. Where indicated, equipment should be taken out of service until properly repaired.

5. Supervision of Activities and Play Periods.

All school-sponsored activities must be supervised, including recess, noon-hour recreation, and after-school play. Much of this can be assigned to qualified teacher aides, releasing the teacher for instructional duties. Under the law, a class may not be turned over to high school students or cadet teachers, as supervision must be supplied by a certified individual.

6. Proper Selection of Activities

The selected activity must stand up under scrutiny as a proper educational medium for the group involved. Teachers should avoid highly specialized or difficult games beyond the ability of the children. The scheduling of tackle football, for example, is a questionable procedure for the elementary level. The principal who sets rules for snowball fighting is encouraging an activity which is questionable and may cause injury.

Safety Education

The term *safety education* as it relates to instructional procedures will be used in a limited sense in this discussion. The physical education teacher has a responsibility to instruct children in the skills needed in an activity so that they may take part in it safely. The instruction should cover the basic essentials in sequential order.

A second phase of safety education involves considering the inherent safety hazards of each activity and taking whatever measures are necessary to meet the challenge. The teacher must provide the leadership in seeing that the safety precautions for each activity have been met. An instance of this is the placement of mats under climbing ropes. The children must be made aware of safety practices and taught them along with the instruction. They must be motivated to accept responsibility for their own safety and that of others. They should ask for and be willing to provide help as needed.

Safety Services — Emergency Care

In spite of all precautions, accidents will occur in various phases of the school program. The school has a responsibility to arrange a system of emergency care; so that prompt and appropriate measures will be taken to protect the child who has been injured. Emergency care procedures should follow this sequence:

1. The administration of first aid is the first step. The problem of proper care is solved if a school nurse is present. If not, at least one person in the school should have first aid certification. Some principals like to have the school secretary with such certification, because she is readily available. If a teacher has first aid responsibilities, proper supervision must be supplied for his class when he is called to the scene of the incident. First aid procedures will indicate if the child can be moved and in what fashion.

2. Unless the injury is such that the child needs to be taken to a doctor without delay, the parents should be notified. The school should have on hand sufficient information pertaining to each student to give direction in case of an emergency. This would include telephone numbers of the parents, both at home and at place of employment. In addition, it is well to have written permission from parents to refer the child to the family doctor for treatment. Sometimes the name of a neighbor or close friend to whom the child can be taken in case the parents cannot be contacted is helpful.

3. The third step is to release the child to his parents or other person designated by them. Policies for transportation should be established.

4. A report of the accident should be filled out promptly, generally on a form adopted by the school system. The teacher and the principal should each retain copies, the additional specified copies being forwarded to the administration. The report should contain all necessary details with respect to full names of the child and witnesses; details of the accident including place, time, activity, circumstances, and possible causes; and disposition of the child.

5. Follow-up procedures should be instituted to eliminate the causes of the accident and prevent future occurrences.

The Medicine Chest

Whether or not to have a medicine chest is a debatable point. The medical association for the area (local or county) should help make such a decision. Only those medications and materials approved by the association should be in the medicine chest and approved directions for use of the contents should be prominently posted.

Student Insurance

The school should make available accident insurance providing compensation in case of accident to a child. If a parent rejects the option of school accident insurance, in case of an accident he has little basis for objection to expenses which could have been partially or fully covered by insurance.

Other Safety Considerations

Dogs and other animals should be kept from the schoolyards. Children can trip over the animals and the possibility of being bitten is always present. Whenever the skin is broken from an animal bite, the possibility of rabies must *always* be considered. The animal must be caught and held for the authorities. Only by observing the animal for a period of two weeks or so can the possibility of rabies be rejected.

The rubbish burning area should be protected from the children. Children are naturally attracted to fire, and they love to handle burning materials.

Throwing stones and snow balls needs to be controlled. Other habits of rowdyism having possibilities of injuries need to be controlled also.

Special rules need to be established for procedures in various areas, particularly in the use of various pieces of apparatus on the playground. These should be discussed with the children and posted.

Legal Responsibility

Since the child is subject to compulsory attendance laws, the school has the legal responsibility of providing a safe environment. Teachers, as individuals, share this responsibility. While the teacher cannot be held responsible for all accidental occurrences in activities under his supervision, he can be held legally responsible for the consequences of his negligence which has proven injurious to one of the children.

Liability occurs when the teacher is held responsible for a given situation. It is always a court action, and negligence by the teacher

must be established. Negligence is a basic factor involved in all liability. A person is deemed negligent when he has failed to act as a reasonably prudent person would act under the circumstances. Foreseeability is the key to whether or not there is negligence. If the teacher could have foreseen the causes leading to the injury, and failed to take action as a prudent person would, then the ruling of negligence can result.

Each teacher needs to ascertain that the child is in an environment that meets all the criteria of safety. In addition, it would be well to consider liability insurance, which is available quite reasonably in conjunction with memberships in some educational societies. However, schools should have liability insurance to cover adequately all teachers and other staff members.

OPERATIONAL POLICIES

Coeducational Activity

Coeducational activity is activity in which boys and girls participate together. If the social and emotional objectives of physical education are to be realized fully, boys and girls should have the opportunity to play together in some activities on each grade level. In today's physical education programs it is becoming less and less necessary to separate sexes. In fact, some schools operate the entire program on a coeducational basis.

On the primary level, there is little need for separation of sexes in any activity. Boys and girls of these ages are very much alike in development and almost all activities may include both sexes. However, schools should consider separating boys and girls in some activities beginning in either the fourth or fifth grade. The types of activity where separation is recommended are the contact and rougher sports. Certain other activities must make due allowance for modesty. If stunts and tumbling classes are coeducational, children must be properly attired.

In intermediate classes, a solution found practical at times is to have the entire class working on similar activities, but divided according to sex. Basketball and soccer are sports that lend themselves to this approach.

The Supervised Play Period

Commonly called recess, the supervised

play period provides a time for relaxation and relief from tensions for youngsters. Adequate supervision is necessary to insure that safety practices are being followed and that youngsters have proper consideration for each other. Children must be reminded that they are under self-discipline and must follow established rules.

Supervision should be positive and in terms of helping youngsters make the most of their free play. Intermediates can develop and carry out their own plans of organization based on equal opportunities for all and on good standards of play conduct. Teachers must recognize that supervisory duties of this type are a regular and important part of the teaching duties. Assignments are generally handled on a rotation basis.

The Noon-Hour Play Period

The noon-hour period can be both educational and recreative. The first part must be devoted to a supervised, happy, restful lunch. After this, the children should be allowed to play, in the main, in quiet games. There should be plenty of time allowed for attending to personal needs.

Each child should have an opportunity to enjoy an activity of his interest. Individual games, quiet games, table-type activities, and semiactive sports are recommended. While some adult supervision is needed, older children can plan and carry out an adequate noon-hour program.

Children who eat lunch at home should not return to school before the designated time for afternoon classes.

THE EXTENDED ACTIVITY PROGRAM

The competitive urge is strong in children, and the school should supply opportunities to satisfy this strong feeling. Participation in a sound sports program can contribute materially to the objectives of physical education. Competition should be an extension of the physical education program, which itself must be a quality program to provide a functional basis. That such a program has value is expressed by the AAHPER position paper* on elementary school physical education:

> Competition at the elementary school level is a vital and forceful

educational tool. Properly used it can stimulate a keen desire for self-improvement as well as create environments in which children, motivated by common purpose, unite in an effort to accomplish goals in a manner not unlike the roles they will play as adults in a democratic, competitive society.

Two programs can satisfy this competitive urge. An intramural program, defined as a program operated within a school, should have priority. An extramural program, defined as interschool competition, comes next. The extramural program should not operate unless there is an intramural program.

Playdays and sports days have a slightly different purpose in the program. They are interesting to children as the emphasis is on fun.

The Intramural Program

The intramural program should be an outgrowth of a sound physical education program, that is, it should provide an opportunity to extend and expand the skills and knowledges gained from the physical education program and supply the element of competition. The emphasis in the program should be on competing and participating and not the determination of champions. Generally, the program is carried on after school, but some schools find it feasible to use other times. Adult leadership is an essential ingredient, but students should have an important part in the planning and execution of the program.

Teams may be chosen on the basis of classrooms, by a classification system, or by lot. Equitable competition is needed to maintain interest. The program should be an opportunity for all boys and girls and not just the more skilled. Since the program is for the intermediate level, competition should be separate for boys and girls. This does not rule out the possibility of suitable coeducational activities, but these should be minimal.

The teacher directing the program should receive special compensation. To ask a teacher to assume this responsibility without remuneration in addition to regular duties seldom produces the desired results.

*Essentials of a Quality Elementary School Education Program, A Position Paper. (Washington, D.C.: AAHPER, 1970), p. 8.

Club work can be encouraged. Clubs for tumbling, hiking, swimming, skiing, skating, and other activities increase the motivation for activity. Opportunities for informal physical recreation in the school should be encouraged and sponsored.

Extramurals

The term "Extramural Program" is more appropriate than other terms connoting interschool activities. While there is value in competition between schools, the competition should be of an informal type and should not involve the common high school pattern with its concentration on a few highly-skilled individuals. Such other attributes of interscholastic athletics as yell squads, pep rallies, distant travel, emotional partisanship, ornate uniforms, emphasis on the winning team through district and league championships, publicity exalting individual performances, and all-star teams have little place in the elementary program.

The question today is not whether to have interschool competition, but rather how to develop a program with educationally sound policies. The school should have complete control of the program and supply efficient leadership.

One acceptable way to function is to coordinate the program directly with the intramural operation. Competition would be held first on an intramural basis, and selected players later would participate in interschool competition. This introduction to competition should be in a relaxed low-pressure program, which hopefully will stimulate further development. It is admittedly difficult to escape the fact that the purpose of competition is to win, but — "Win with the code and your head and your honor held high."

Playdays

A playday is a festival-type setting where children of a school or different schools meet to take part in physical education activities. The emphasis is on the social values rather than competition. Yet competition is important in that teams made up from different participating schools can play against each other.

A playday may be entirely within a particular school. However, the usual pattern is for a playday between schools. It may be carried on during the school day, after school, or on a Saturday.

The program may be made of sports-type activities or it may include the more simple games, relays, and contests. Stunts, individual athletic events, and even rhythms are the basis of activities in some meets. The programs vary according to the size of the schools and the grade level of the children. They usually involve both boys and girls and may include some coeducational activities on the intermediate level.

Playdays which attempt to emphasize champions or which glorify the star performers from each school are undesirable. The real purpose of a playday is to have "everyone on a team and a team for everyone."

Children should have a large part in the planning, and the experience gives them a fruitful opportunity to act as hosts or as guests in a social situation. The program emphasis may be on activities which have been previously practiced or rehearsed, or it may include new and unique events broadening the scope of the physical education experience.

PROMOTIONAL IDEAS AND PUBLIC RELATIONS

The marked changes in physical education over the last decade create a necessity for public understanding if the physical education program is to receive its measure of support. In the minds of some, physical education means a sports program. Others regard it as simply a time to play games. Since the philosophy, educational approach, instructional methods, and content differ markedly from what was the experience of the adult population, a positive program of public relations, primarily informative, should be instituted so school patrons can be made fully aware of the education possibilities of physical education. Such measures should include a variety of approaches.

A Quality Program

The most effective public relations instrument for physical education is a quality program. The informal reports of the children to the parents on the satisfaction, interest, and value the program holds for them is a most effective means of creating a climate of parental regard for the program.

Parent Involvement

Parents can be involved actively as participants or in a passive manner as spectators. One approach is to schedule a Parents' Night, which may take the following directions: (1) parents participating along with the children in regular class work; (2) parents observing a regular schedule of classes; (3) Achievement Night to show special attainments; (4) demonstrations interpreting the main features of the year-round physical education program.

The PTA should serve as a vehicle for interpreting the program. Discussions, panel presentations, outside experts, and selected visual presentations are effective program elements. Parents should be given the opportunity to ask questions and resolve debatable points.

School-Affiliated Methods

Many promotional ideas can utilize elements of the school program. The physical education program can contribute to assembly programs. Demonstrations can be used as half-time programs at athletic events. Sportsdays or playdays can be scheduled. Special events involving some competition, such as Junior Olympics, free throw contests, gymnastic-type competition, demonstrations, and the like have value.

Community-Oriented Informational Measures

Public informational media should be utilized. Newspapers should be supplied with articles of special interest or action. Pictures are important. At times, feature articles or sections can be assembled.

Television and, to a lesser extent, radio should be exploited. Events of special interest provide a second jolt of publicity through television coverage. Radio panel discussions have good value also.

The support of service clubs should be enlisted through speeches, films, demonstrations, and other approaches. Service clubs are often anxious to provide material support in the form of sponsorship of some special event or the purchase of a special piece of equipment, beyond the fiscal capacity of the school.

Brochures covering yearly summaries, program descriptions, philosophy, and educa-tional values are effective instruments toward better understanding.

The physical educator should take part in community affairs, joining such clubs and groups as feasible. He should be willing to help groups seeking the kind of school services for which he is responsible.

PAGEANTS, DEMONSTRATIONS, AND ASSEMBLY PROGRAMS

Classroom teachers are asked at times to organize demonstrations for assembly programs, parents, and other groups. These are excellent mediums of public relations and dispel some of the false notions regarding physical education. If such programs are requested, the following may be helpful:

1. The activities should grow out of and be typical of the physical education program.

2. The activities should not require a long period of preparation so that the physical education period becomes a training period for the demonstration.

3. Children should be properly dressed for the activity, but elaborate and intricate costuming should be avoided. Simple costumes that can be made by the children are most acceptable.

4. The demonstration should generally include numbers of children. Programs can be designed so that all children participate in some phase of the exhibition. However, recognition can be given to superior ability by specialty numbers.

5. It is important to avoid tests of strength and skill which would lead to embarrassment of those defeated.

6. While a high degree of performance is not needed, the activities should be done reasonably well within the level of the children.

7. The program should be fast-moving and contain activities of good audience appeal. Music is indispensable, and a well-balanced program will contain several numbers with music.

8. The program should call attention to physical fitness, and some elements should be devoted to this area. A demonstration of physical fitness testing is always well-received.

9. Some part of the program can include a demonstration of instructional procedures rather than centering all attention on accomplishments.

6

Movement Education

Movement education as a term is a fairly recent addition to the conceptual framework of physical education. In the past, physical educators spoke about each child having the opportunity to develop skills. Today, we think more in broader terms of helping an individual acquire movement competency. The process by which the child is helped to acquire movement competency is called movement education.

MOVEMENT COMPETENCY

A better understanding of movement education can be achieved if one can look ahead at the behavioral changes in children which are its goals. Traditionally, physical education directed its efforts in motor learning toward two skill goals, namely, basic skills and specialized skills. Basic skills refer to those simple skills which relate to a broad spectrum of activity, important to the child's play and daily living. They have wide application to many situations.

Specialized skills is a term reserved for skills having application to a particular sport or activity. Many are intricate and specific, with clear-cut points of technique.

Added to these traditional concepts is the human capacity known as competency in the management of the body. Recognition of the area of body management competency as important in elementary school physical education has provided new educational signifi-

cance to programs. A deeper look into body management competency, basic skills, and specialized skills will serve to pinpoint the place of each in movement competency and demonstrate the interrelationships among them.

Competency in Body Management

Body management involves the body as a whole. Learning to manage the body leads to greater control and skill over gross movements. The child controls his body in a non-locomotor or fixed location, in movements across the floor, through space, or when suspended on apparatus. To secure good body management skill is to acquire, expand, and integrate elements of general motor control through wide experience in movement, based on an exploratory and creative approach. The child needs to learn what his body can do and how he can manage his body effectively in a variety of movement situations and challenges.

Good body management practices are also related to the body's resistance to the forces of gravity. We want children not only to be able to manage the body with efficiency and ease of movement, but also to accept good standards of posture and body mechanics as meaningful constituents of their movement patterns.

In addition to posture and body mechanics, another consideration in body management skill is perceptual-motor competency. The principles and concepts basic to perceptual-motor competency have strong relationship and application to the area of body management. Good motor control requires sufficent neurological control and development, which can be aided by attention to perceptual-motor approaches and activities. Perceptual-motor approaches which are considered relevant to physical education include those which give attention to balance, coordination, laterality, directionality, awareness of space, and knowledge of one's own body and body parts.

Basic Skills

Basic skills can be divided into three categories, each of which can be considered separately for clarification. It is possible for a child to isolate and perform a selected skill from a category. On the other hand, a movement pattern may include a number of skills from different categories. For example, a child may shake his body (a nonlocomotor activity) while running across the floor (a locomotor skill). Or, he may combine throwing and catching a beanbag (a manipulative skill) while hopping in various directions (a locomotor skill).

Locomotor Skills

Locomotor skills are those used to move the body from one place to another, or project the body upward, as in jumping or hopping. In addition to jumping and hopping, locomotor skills include walking, running, skipping, leaping, sliding, and galloping.

Nonlocomotor Skills

Nonlocomotor skills include those which the child does in place or without appreciable movement from place to place. Nonlocomotor skills are of a wider variety and not as clearly defined as locomotor skills. Nonlocomotor skills include bending and stretching, pushing and pulling, raising and lowering, twisting and turning, shaking, bouncing, circling, and others.

Manipulative Skills

Manipulative skills are defined as those skills employed when the child handles some kind of a play object. Most of these involve the hands and feet, but other parts of the body can be used also. Manipulative objects lead to better hand-eye and foot-eye coordination. Propulsion (throwing, batting, kicking) and receipt (catching) of objects are important elements to be developed using beanbags and a variety of balls.

Control of an object such as a wand or hoop also has a place in manipulative activity. Manipulative activities are the basis of the related game skills, so important in the lives of children.

Specialized Skills

These are the skills related to the various sports and other physical education areas such as apparatus, tumbling, dance, and specific games. In the development of specialized skills, progression is obtained through planned instruction and drills. Many of the specialized skills have critical points of technique, with a heavy emphasis on conformance.

DEFINING MOVEMENT EDUCATION

The term "movement education" is subject to different interpretations and definitions. Some people hold that the term refers to the newer methodology employing problem-solving techniques emphasizing individual response and stressing exploration, choice, and creativity. Such terms as "basic movement," "movement education," "movement exploration," and "educational movement" can, therefore, be used interchangeably. Others hold that "movement education" has a broader meaning. The author agrees with those who define movement education broadly, as the sum of all the child's experiences in movement.

Movement education has also been defined as learning to move and moving to learn. This makes it somewhat synonymous with the term "physical education."

If one accepts the broad concept of movement education, then another term must be applied to the problem-solving approach or the "indirect method," as it is sometimes called, since this can now be regarded as a part of the overall concept of movement education. While the designation "the indirect method" has some acceptance, a better and more appropriate term would be "basic movement."

What, then, is included in the "sum of all the child's experiences in movement"? What instructional approaches can be effectively utilized in helping a child attain movement competency as defined earlier? What can each approach contribute to the functional whole of movement education?

Movement education can be divided into four instructional approaches, each of which has a unique and important function in the attainment of overall movement competency. These are:

1. Basic Movement.
2. The Skills Instructional Program.
3. Posture and Body Mechanics.
4. Perceptual-Motor Competency.

Each has its place in the program of physical education, depending upon the particular kind of skill or type of body management competency to be developed. In practice, the methods are often combined to arrive at the most effective instructional procedure. The following analysis of the purposes of each will indicate how each relates to the whole of movement education:

Basic Movement

Provide opportunity for the child to explore, create, and consolidate.

Structure an environment which stimulates the child to think. Develop the child's versatility in movement, including the development of good body management skills.

Allow each child the element of self-direction so he can work at his own pace governed by the limits of his own potential. Provide a foundation of basic movement skills, upon which specialized skills of later years are built.

The Skills Instructional Program

Provide sequential instructional procedures with drills and repetition of movement leading to the acquisition of both basic and specialized skills.

Provide a means by which children can learn critical skills of sports and games with emphasis on the "how" and "why" of known techniques.

Posture and Body Mechanics

Stimulate the child to the achievement of good body alignment and carriage.

Give opportunity for correct body mechanics as the child goes about his daily living tasks.

Perceptual-Motor Competency

Provide consideration in the physical education program for such perceptual-motor competencies as balance, laterality, directionality, and others considered important qualities for children.

Further discussion of each of the above four terms follows.

BASIC MOVEMENT

The key to the entire approach of basic movement is the incorporation somewhere in the methodology of the factor of self-selection, the opportunity for the child to be creative. If choice is eliminated, then the process becomes direct teaching, the traditional approach to teaching. The degree of choice, the degree of opportunity for self-discovery, indicates the extent to which basic movement concepts are employed in the learning experiences for the child. True and pure basic movement would permit the child to select for himself the activity in which he would like to participate, the apparatus (hand or large) he would like to use, and the movement experiences he would like to undergo.

At times this approach of broad choice may be of value, but for more practical purposes the teacher must place certain limitations on the type of activity the child experiences. While in movement language this is termed as "setting a limitation" for the problem to be solved, in actuality this is a direct command (direct teaching) establishing the extent to which the child may move. Within the limitation so set, the child has the opportunity for self-discovery, self-education, exploration, and problem-solving. Within the goal of the teacher to assist each child attain the maximum development possible for that child, the teacher may use methods ranging throughout the entire spectrum of direct to indirect teaching. The question for the teacher is not whether or not basic movement should be employed, but the degree to which learning experiences should be so organized. Whenever possible, the child should be encouraged to experiment, create, and explore. He should be directed to apply his knowledge in many different situations in movement.

Characteristics of Basic Movement

The element of self-selection is paramount in basic movement. An opportunity for experimentation, exploration, and self-discovery must be included. This ranges from exploration within precise and narrow limitations to opportunity for children to make choices of activity and the approach they wish to follow. It is the responsibility of the teacher to set the stage and create situations which challenge the child to develop his resources of movement. The teacher no longer dominates the lesson, but stimulates the children to use their ideas to plan different ways to carry out the movement experiences. Each child is encouraged to make what contributions he can to the whole. Since children have a desire to express themselves physically, as well as in other ways, satisfaction of this desire can only be obtained if the children have a measure of choice and an opportunity to exercise individuality.

Because the child expresses himself individually in movement, he can achieve a satisfactory measure of success *for himself as* opposed to teacher-dominated or group standards. The child progresses according to his innate abilities, stimulated by the teacher and the learning situation. No child need feel awkward or self-conscious because he doesn't measure up to predetermined standards. The fact that children differ in size, shape, maturity, and motor ability does not preclude success and satisfaction. The child makes progress according to his own rate and to his satisfaction.

There is deeper aim in basic movement in that it seeks to develop the child's awareness not only of *what* he is doing, but also of *how* he is moving to do it. By this it is hoped to have the children appreciate their own ability and make better interpretation of their movement patterns. The process then becomes the acquisition of movement experiences rather than an accumulation of knowledge or subject matter. Each child should be given the opportunity to succeed in his own way according to his own capacity. There is value not only in the accomplishment of the child, but also in the manner by which he reaches this accomplishment. The teacher attempts to establish a learning experience by which the child is stimulated to think.

Basic movement methodology is presented in Chapter 11 on page 125 together with suggested movement experiences.

Some Observations About Basic Movement

It should be emphasized that a great deal of the teacher must go into the process of basic movement. To make movement purposeful and guide children toward maximum growth and development so that desirable progress can be made requires a knowledge of children and of the learning process. The teacher who labors under the misconception that he can retire into the background after the children have chosen the activity has completely missed the point of movement methodology. This practice will not bring out good variety, let alone quality in movement. It is necessary for the teacher to approach the lesson with a plan concerning the kinds of things which are to be done; the tasks, problems, or approaches to be used; and the methods of guidance, together with stress factors of importance to be considered. The lesson plan should include consideration not only for providing variety of responses, but procedures for improving the quality in movement.

Another point of contention in movement methodology is the question of how much direction should precede the introduction of a movement pattern. Some hold that every child must *first* have a chance to try out the movement pattern or skill in his own way until he has gotten the feeling of it and has experienced the difficulties and the challenges. How strictly this rule might be applied probably should be governed by the type of activity or skill. A blanket rule is not educationally sound because it deprives the teacher of his right of individual approach.

Today so much emphasis is placed on the basic movement method as the "educational method" and on the benefits of choice, self-discovery, and exploration that some teachers feel they are out-of-date and wrong if they are not employing basic movement, at least in part. Emphasis should be placed upon the right of the teacher to *determine* the best approach.

A question arises about the relationship of basic movement to the development of physical fitness. When a child chooses his activity and how he will carry out the problem, how can it be assured that there will be sufficient vigorous big-muscle activity so that the major elements of physical fitness (strength, power, and endurance) will receive proper attention? In addition, how can it be assured that all areas of the body, particularly the arm-shoulder girdle and the abdominal wall, will receive proper development? It is unsound to substitute movement exploration with its stress on choice, variety, and educational concepts for developmental activities pointed toward the physical development of the child. *Both* developmental activities and basic movement can and should be included in the program.

One problem in the guidance and directive process leading to quality in movement is that group instruction becomes difficult if the children are engaged in different activities or on different pieces of apparatus. With a variety of activities, instruction becomes an individual process, limiting the effectiveness of the teacher. He can hardly center his attention on one or two children when all should be considered. This becomes even more difficult when the teacher feels that he must center his efforts on the one piece of apparatus which needs attention because of potential safety hazards.

An element of basic movement which is of concern to a number of educators is the premise that children are free to choose and free to respond in the manner they wish and at their own rate. It is postulated that allowing children to do only those things they choose and in the manner they choose is not desirable social training. Few real life situations are based on this premise. To counterbalance this attitude, the teacher can include certain required activities regardless of whether or not the children approve. Children from homes where they are permitted considerable freedom often meet with problems in the school situation where more conformance is required.

Movement Exploration

Some clarification of the term "Movement Exploration" is needed. Exploration implies a degree of choice of response, experimentation, and exploration. It refers to a type of methodology and not to an area of content in physical education. The employment of exploratory activity is most important in basic movement. It has an application even in direct teaching techniques when an appropriate opportunity is used for experimentation and exploration. The idea of trying out this or that to discover which is more valuable or useful is an excellent reinforcement of learning.

Some physical educators tend to regard movement exploration as a different kind of physical education, while in reality it provides another valuable method of attaining the goals of physical education. Within the framework of instruction, it is important that children have an opportunity to try out different ways and approaches to learning skills.

THE SKILLS INSTRUCTIONAL PROGRAM

The skills instruction program provides instruction in both basic and specialized skills. The approach is more concerned with direct (command) teaching, with predetermined goals in mind as a result of the teaching process. This does not rule out exploratory activity, as experimentation and exploration should be utilized within the concept of good technique.

The emphasis is on the "how" and "why" of the known techniques, with drills and repetition of specific movements as the basis of the learning process. Skills should be based on sound techniques. It is important to avoid simply exposing the child to a skill and trusting to providence for results. Instructors need to know well the skills they are teaching. Demonstration is important in the teaching process, in contrast to basic movement, where the ideas originate mostly from the children.

A sound instructional program will, no doubt, have a positive effect on strengthening and consolidating good body management generally, although this must be regarded as a concomitant value. Naturally, skill instruction will include regard for good body management practices as related to the skill being taught. The child should receive instruction on how to handle himself and how to move effectively while developing a particular skill.

Instructional procedures with respect to motor learning and the acquisition of skills are given treatment in two areas of this guide. Along with other general instructional procedures, skill instructional principles and guides of a general nature are presented in Chapter 7. The approach for skills of a special activity, like basketball, for example, is found under the material for that particular activity.

POSTURE AND BODY MECHANICS

Posture and Body Mechanics have an important part in movement education.

Posture refers to the habitual or assumed alignment and balance of the body segments while standing, walking, sitting, or lying. In good posture, these parts are in proper relation to each other, and their good balance is reflected in ease, gracefulness, poise, and efficiency of carriage and bearing.

Correct use of the body is called good body mechanics and has its basis in good posture. How to lift and carry objects, open windows, go up and down stairs, climb ladders, and pull or push are examples of simple activities which need application of good principles of body mechanics.

Consideration of posture and body mechanics in movement education should be from two standpoints. First, direct instruction in posture and body mechanics should at times be included in the program. Secondly, good standards of posture and body mechanics should be an overriding concern for all physical activity and movement. No matter how the child moves, postural considerations should be a guiding factor.

Posture is dependent primarily upon the strength of the muscles which hold the body in balance against the force of gravity. These muscles work continually and require sufficient strength and energy to hold the body in correct alignment.

However, in good posture from a mechanical standpoint, the musculature must be balanced and hold the bones and joints in proper position and provide a basis for efficient movement. Faulty alignment can cause undue strain on supporting muscles and ligaments, leading to early fatigue, muscle strain, and progressive displacement of postural support. In extreme cases, pain may result and the position and function of vital organs, primarily abdominal, can be impaired.

It needs to be recognized early by the teacher *and* child that the maintenance of good posture is a positive act and has its basis primarily in the practice of good postural habits. The teacher needs to be concerned not only with faulty posture, but also with the causes underlying this condition. Physical abnormalities such as poor vision and hearing, deformities, and even disease cause postural problems. Children who lack energy and fatigue easily become prone to postural slumps. Proper clothing and shoes are a consideration for good carriage. Emotional factors are important, as the bearing of an individual reflects his emotional outlook.

Anatomical and Physiological Principles Affecting Posture

A better understanding of postural conditions can be established with an examination of some basic physiological facts which have bearing on posture problems.

The body, the wonderful mechanism it is, adjusts to the exterior forces applied to it. Unfortunately, this is true with regard to poor posture. With elementary school children, poor posture may just be a habitual position. But, as the child matures, this becomes a growth characteristic. The result is that the muscles which activate the joints, of necessity, adapt both in length and function to the faulty positions of the body segments.

Further breakdown occurs when the body is slumped continuously. The vital organs are compressed and crowded out of position and bones are forced out of alignment. Postural conditions which were once remediable in the elementary school now become structural, with more difficult correction. Early attention to posture will yield large dividends.

For every set of muscles having a specific movement, there is another group with an opposite action. There must be balance to the power of these antagonistic muscle groups, particularly in those keeping the body in alignment. If one set of muscles is markedly stronger than the other, the resultant elastic pull and possible shortening causes an imbalance at the joint concerned. An example of this is in the muscle groups governing the position of the shoulders. The chest muscles exert force to pull the shoulder blades forward, tending to round shoulders, and the upper back postural muscles must counteract this influence with sufficient development. A second example concerns the lower back curve which can be kept in check with a strong abdominal wall working against the lower back muscles.

In addition to the opposing muscle pull, the postural muscles have the force of gravity to overcome. If posture is poor, this gravitational force becomes stronger, and, coupled with the opposing muscle pull, causes the muscles holding body alignment to weaken and stretch.

Flexibility should be sufficient to permit the child to assume good postural positioning without excessive effort or strain. A short, tight muscle group, lacking enough flexibility, can exert sufficient pull at a joint to make it difficult for the child to assume good posture.

Muscles exhibit another characteristic important in postural considerations. This is the development of muscle tone, defined as a slight degree of tension or contraction. Muscle tone is important because it aids in holding the body in correct skeletal alignment. If muscles are weak, flabby, and underdeveloped, tone is lacking and posture suffers. Good tone is a characteristic of a healthy, conditioned muscle.

From the standpoint of body structure, the slope or tilt of the pelvis is a critical point. The vertebral column is composed of small bones, called vertebrae, which form a number of natural curves governing body contour. The foundation of the vertebral column rests on the pelvis, forming a joint with very little movement. With correct tilt of the pelvis, the body contours can be natural and graceful. If the front of the pelvis is tilted down, the lower back curve becomes exaggerated, causing swayback which can vary from slight to pronounced. A slight curve in the lumbar region (lower back) is natural. Correct tilt will aid in flattening both a protruding abdomen and a prominent seat. Incorrect tilt in the standing position of an individual has a tendency to force the upper legs back, with attendant hyperextension of the knee joint.

What the Teacher Can Do

Teachers must include in their lesson plans and administrative practices specific attention to good body mechanics and posture. Careful planning is needed if good posture is to result. But, in this area, teachers are not to regard themselves as corrective specialists. They can, however, help children form desirable postural patterns and acquire good habits in the many postures assumed. There are a number of factors to which the teacher can give attention in working with youngsters for better posture and body mechanics.

1. The first and most important objective is to provide motivation for good posture. There must be a development of understanding and appreciation of good posture through pictures, posters, demonstrations, and other media so that the youngster consciously develops within himself the desire for a body in good alignment.

2. A program of vigorous physical activities to strengthen muscles that hold the body correctly is needed. The program should include especially designed muscular development (fitness) activities and broad movement experiences, as well as rugged, demanding games, sports, stunts and tumbling, and rhythmics.

3. A planned program of instruction in the basic skills of locomotion, work, and play should be instituted as a part of the physical education program with definite time apportionment and definite goals on each grade level.

4. A healthful school environment is needed with particular attention to proper seating, good lighting, avoidance of overfatigue, and elimination of tension.

5. The removal and correction of health conditions which contribute to poor posture are a necessity. Cooperation between home, school, and physician in this program is essential.

6. The teacher must give attention to such emotional factors as discouragement, feelings of inferiority, consciousness of an unattractive appearance beyond the power of the individual to change, and severe acne. Children with fears, timidities, and other feelings of insecurity often reflect these inner states in postural positions. Another factor to be considered in the intermediate grades is the girl who feels that she is "overly tall." Since girls reach their growth more quickly than boys, there will be girls who are as tall or taller than any boy in the class. Feeling that they are conspicuous in their tallness, some girls react by slumping and trying to make themselves smaller. In contrast, boys want to be tall and usually are proud of their growth attainments.

7. The teacher needs to accept the concept that good posture is a practice and not a subject. Even in the most simple movements and position, postural problems are continuously present. The teacher should introduce and teach good postural habits, particularly as related to activities the children are learning. Children should be given a word of encouragement or advice as reminders for good practice. The teacher needs to be able to recognize good posture and deviations from the normal.

8. The rigid military type of posture is not the goal of normal living. While the service academies at West Point, Annapolis, and Colorado Springs find this useful, it has little part in the posture picture of the elementary school child.

9. The teacher should be an example of good body mechanics and posture. It is important not only that the children have a good example to follow, but also that the teacher be able to endure the demands of classroom teaching with less fatigue.

10. The teacher should refer the student to the nurse, physical education specialist, principal, or other appropriate agencies for help in problem posture cases. After a corrective program has been set up, the teacher's part is in cooperating with the program and guiding the youngster in fulfilling his prescribed corrective work.

What Is Good Posture?

Posture varies with the individual's sex and body type, and what is proper posture for one individual may not be suitable for another. However, the basic components for posture are much the same for all children. These are illustrated by the following chart.

GOOD POSTURE   FAIR POSTURE   POOR POSTURE

Good Posture	Fair Posture	Poor Posture
Head up, chin in, head balanced above the shoulders with the tip of the ear directly above the point of the shoulders	Head forward slightly	Head noticeably forward, eyes generally down
Shoulders back and easy with the chest up	Chest lowered slightly	Chest flat or depressed
Lower abdomen in and flat	Lower abdomen in but not flat	Shoulder blades show winged effects
Slight and normal curves in the upper and lower back	Back curves increased slightly	Abdomen relaxed and prominent
Knees easy	Knees back slightly	Back curves exaggerated
Weight properly placed with toes pointed forward	Weight a little too far back on heels	Knees forced back in back-kneed position
		Pelvis noticeably tilted down
		Weight improperly distributed

Directions for Assuming Good Posture in Standing Position

Feet. Toes are pointed straight ahead, weight evenly distributed on balls of feet and the heels. Cue by saying "Feet forward! Point feet straight ahead! Feet parallel! Weight off heels!" The feet should be parallel and from 2" to 4" apart.

Knees. Knees should be relaxed and easy. Avoid the back-kneed position where the knee joint is held forcibly back as far as it can go. Remind the children: "Knees easy! Knees relaxed!"

Lower Back and Abdomen. The abdominal wall should be flattened but relaxed. The lower back curve should be natural and not exaggerated. Children can be told: "Tuck your seat under! Flatten your tummy! Push the body up, tummy in! Flatten lower back! Hips under!"

Upper Body. The shoulders should be back and relaxed and the shoulder blades flat. Chest should be up and raised. Give them directions like: "Shoulders easy! Shoulder blades flat! Lift chest! Chest high!"

Neck and Head. The head should be up and chin in. Neck should be back. The ear should be directly over the point of the shoulder. Say: "Chin in! Head high! Stand tall! Stretch tall! Chin easy!"

Lateral Deviations in Posture

The discussion of posture to this point has been concerned mostly with the forward-backward plane of movement. The body must also be in balance in the lateral plane. From a structural standpoint, when viewed from the front or rear, a perpendicular line should divide the body into two symmetrical or equal halves. If parts of one-half of the body cross over this line, there is an unnatural curvature. Again, habit plays a part. The position may be due to faulty practices. A shift of the head may be caused by either visual or hearing problems or both. Uneven shape or size of the bones, particularly the leg bones, will cause the pelvis to tilt laterally, with a compensating curvature of the spinal column.

The presence of lateral curvature can be determined by a check on the level of the pelvis, whether or not the shoulders are even, or if the head has a tilt to either side. It is estimated that about 50 per cent of the population have a lateral tilt to some degree. The teacher needs to be observant to screen for referral those cases requiring attention.

Faulty habits contributing to this condition are standing on one leg, leaning against a support, and sitting improperly.

Good Walking Posture

Good walking posture begins with proper use of the feet. It is vitally important that the feet point forward and stay nearly parallel for best functional use. A person who walks with toes pointed out is subject to considerable strain in the arch and lower ankle, leading to a breakdown of the arch and lower leg structure. The heel should touch first in a step, with the weight transferred quickly to the balls of the feet and to the toes for a push-off.

The legs should swing freely from the hips with the knees bent enough to clear the feet from the floor.

The arms should swing in opposition to the legs, the body should retain the properties of good standing posture, and the eyes should be focused on a point on the floor 50' to 60' ahead.

Proper Sitting Posture

The knee joint should form a right angle, the feet flat on the floor and pointed generally forward. The hips should be back against the chair and the body erect. Forward movement in a working position should occur mostly from the hip joint, with the head, upper body, and pelvis remaining in good balance.

Evaluating Posture

Since it is a responsibility of the elementary school teacher to detect and refer bodily conditions needing attention, some program of posture evaluation must be established. Evaluation can be done through observation, both formal and informal, and measurement devices. The discussion will cover only those methods which classroom teachers can find practical and usable.

Formal Observation. Posture screening can be accomplished through a rating device which allows the teacher to check segments of the body and note the condition with respect to postural standards. The following simplified rating sheet is useful for making checks.

POSTURE CHECK SHEET

Name_____ Grade_____ School_____

Date_____ _____Check made by_____

SIDE VIEW
Head

    Erect, chin in_____Somewhat forward_____Markedly forward_____

Upper Back

    Shoulders back_____Slightly rounded_____Round shoulders_____

Lower Back

    Slight natural curve_____Moderate curve_____Hollow back_____

Abdomen

    Flat_____Slight protrusion_____Protruding_____

Knees

    Relaxed_____Slightly back_____Hyperextended_____

Feet

    Pointed ahead_____Somewhat out_____Pointed out_____

FRONT AND BACK VIEW
Shoulders

    Level_____Slightly uneven_____ Considerably uneven_____

Hips

    Level_____Slightly uneven_____ Considerably uneven_____

Back of Ankles and Feet

    Heel and ankle straight_____ Turned out somewhat_____Pronated_____

Remarks

The teacher may prefer a single sheet including all of the class. Such a sheet could be organized as follows.

POSTURE CHECK

Class_____ School_____

Date_____ Teacher_____

Code			Side View						Front and Back View			
			Head and Neck	Upper Back	Lower Back	Abdomen	Knees	Feet	Level of Shoulders	Level of Hips	Feet and Ankles	Remarks
Meets good postural standards	1											
Slight but definite deviation	2											
Marked deviation	3											
Name												
1.												
2.												
3.												

The individual form lends itself better to interpretation by parents and administrators. The class form is more adaptable for class analysis and comparisons. Each item can be rated 1, 2, and 3 on an ascending scale. By averaging the rating numbers, it is possible to come out with a mean rating for each child.

Some formal type of organization is needed. Children can be examined five or six at a time. While it does present some difficulties, a better posture evaluation can be made if the children are in gym clothing or swim suits. Any formal posture evaluation is an analysis of an assumed posture and not necessarily the one the child uses in daily living.

Informal Observation. Postural checks can be made of young people when they are participating in classroom and physical education activities. How does he walk, stand, or sit when he is not conscious of an observer? The teacher can make notes and supplement the formal posture check.

The Plumb Line Method. A plumb line can be used for a practical check of body alignment. The plumb line should hang freely. The student stands so the plumb line is between him and the observer, positioned so the line bisects the instep. The plumb line should go through the tip of the ear, the point of the shoulder, the point of the hip, just back of the knee cap, and the middle of the instep. Divergencies from the line can be checked and noted.

The Ear-Shoulder Method. The ear-shoulder method is based on the plumb line method and the principle that if one part of the body is out of line, another part compensates in the opposite direction to provide body balance. This would mean then that if the head were forward, there would be other parts of the body protruding to counterbalance the first poor alignment. If we measure the degree the head is forward, then we have an estimate of general posture.

Other Methods. The use of pictures or silhouettes to check posture is expensive and time-consuming, but is effective. It has more use on the high school and college level because of the availability of specialized physical education personnel and facilities.

The Feeling of Good Posture

Every child needs to "feel" when he is in good posture. The wall or door method provides an easy check which the child can use at home. The child places himself with his heels against a flat wall which has no floor molding. A flat door can also be used. The child stands with his heels, calves of the legs, seat, elbows, shoulders, and back of the head touching the surfaces. He walks away maintaining this position without tenseness or strain. The wall position is exaggerated but has value in aiding the child in getting the feeling of proper alignment.

A posture walk can be done by using the wall position. A tom-tom can give the signals. When the tom-tom begins to beat, the children walk away from the wall in good walking posture. On a loud thump the children abruptly change direction, continuing the walk. When the beat is changed to a fast beat, the children shuffle rapidly to the nearest wall and stand in the wall posture position.

A second method of providing a kinesthetic feel is to have the child take a deep breath, lifting up his chest while at the same time tucking the pelvis under. Have him release the air but maintain the lifted position without tenseness.

A method to aid the shoulders to be back in proper position is to rotate the thumbs outward (arms at the sides) as far as they will go, at the same time bringing the shoulders back and flattening out the abdominal wall. Release the contraction in the arms but keep the shoulders back and the abdomen flat.

Exercises for Posture

A rounded program of vigorous activities coupled with hanging, climbing, and other activities which use the arms to support the body weight is helpful in strengthening the antigravity muscles of the body. However, at times, the teacher may wish to use special exercises, strengthening areas which generally need attention from the standpoint of body alignment.

HEAD-SHOULDER-UPPER BACK DEVELOPMENT

HOOK LYING
Position: Lie on back with the feet flat on the

floor, knees bent, and arms out in wing position, palms up.

Movement: Press elbows and head against the floor, keeping chin in. Hold for 4 to 6 counts. Repeat 6 to 8 times.

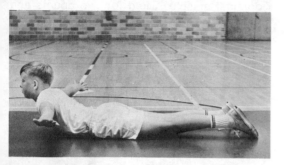

SWAN EXERCISE

Position: Prone lying (face down), arms extended sideward with palms down.

Movement: Raise upper back, head, and arms in an exaggerated swan dive position. The chin is kept in and the movement is limited to the upper back. Hold for two counts. Repeat 8 or 10 times. Confine movement to upper back *only*.

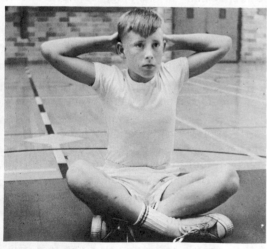

TAILOR EXERCISE

Position: Sit tailor fashion (cross-legged) with trunk erect and locked fingers on middle of back of head, elbows out.

Movement: Force head and elbows back slowly against pressure. Repeat 10 to 15 times. Be sure that there is no change in the erect body position.

ABDOMINAL MUSCLES
PARTIAL CURL-UP

Position: On back with feet flat and knees bent, with hands flat down on top of thighs.

Movement: Leading with the chin, slide the hands forward until the fingers touch the kneecaps, lifting the head, shoulders, and upper body from the floor. Hold for two counts and then return to position. Repeat 10 to 15 times.

CURL-UP

Position: On back with feet flat and knees bent. Instep should be held by a helper. Hands are placed at side with palms down.

Movement: Rise to sitting position with arms extended at shoulder height. Keep head well back. Hold for four counts. Repeat 10 to 15 times.

ROWING

Position: Lie on back with arms overhead.

Movement: Sit up, bringing knees to chest and holding firm. Arms are parallel to the floor and pointing beyond the knees. Repeat 10 to 15 times. Use slow rhythm.

CURL-UP WITH TWIST

Position: On back with feet flat and knees bent. Toes should be held by a helper. Fingers are clasped behind the head.

Movement: Curl-up and touch the right knee with the left elbow. Repeat, alternating elbows. Repeat 10 to 15 times. The movement should be in the abdominal region.

THE MAD CAT

Position: On hands and knees with the back somewhat sagging.

Movement: Arch the back as rounded as possible with a forcible contraction of the abdominal muscles. Hold for two counts and return to position. Repeat 6 to 10 times.

FEET

FLOOR SCRATCHING (Sand Scraping)

Position: Sitting or standing, feet flat on floor.

Movement: Using the toes, scratch the floor by bringing the toes toward you forcibly on the floor. Repeat 10 to 15 times.

MARBLE TRANSFER

Position: Sitting on a chair or bench. A marble or a wadded piece of paper is needed.

Movement: Pick up the marble with the right foot and bring it up to the left hand. Transfer the marble to the right hand and bring up the left foot to put the marble back on the ground. Repeat 8 to 12 times.

KNOT TYING WITH FEET

Position: Standing.

Movement: Lay a jumping rope on the floor. Tie a knot in the rope using one foot only. Repeat with the other foot.

FOOT CARRY

Position: Standing.

Movement: A piece of rope or narrow felt tied in a loop about 1' in diameter is to be carried. The child grasps the loop with the toes of one foot and hops a short distance. He repeats changing the loop to the other foot.

Perceptual-Motor Competency and the Slow Learner

During the last decade, the growth of perceptual-motor programs for the slow learner has made an important impact on physical education programs. The programs were originally for the slow learner and the neurologically handicapped, but, if the theories are valid, they have value for all children, whether or not they have learning disabilities.

Good scientific basis for the perceptual-motor programs has not been forthcoming, but substantiation of program effectiveness comes from empirical judgments and observation. However, there is enough indication from current programs to warrant consideration of perceptual-motor principles as they affect the physical education program.

It is not the purpose of this guide to discuss perceptual-motor programs as separate programs or entities. Discussion will concern only how physical education programs can benefit from accepted perceptual-motor principles and activities. This discussion is found in Chapter 12.

Movement Competency and Skills in the Total Program

The following chart presents diagramatically the continuum of skills throughout the total program, from the development of body management competency to the ultimate of higher skill attainment. Not all children will go through the entire range of skills, but this is to be expected.

CONTINUUM OF PROGRAM DEVELOPMENT BASED ON SKILL DEVELOPMENT AND ATTAINMENT

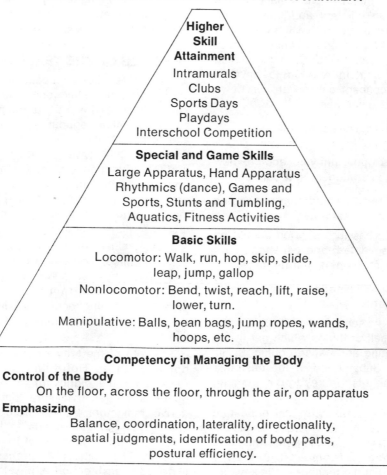

Higher Skill Attainment
Intramurals
Clubs
Sports Days
Playdays
Interschool Competition

Special and Game Skills
Large Apparatus, Hand Apparatus
Rhythmics (dance), Games and
Sports, Stunts and Tumbling,
Aquatics, Fitness Activities

Basic Skills
Locomotor: Walk, run, hop, skip, slide,
leap, jump, gallop
Nonlocomotor: Bend, twist, reach, lift, raise,
lower, turn.
Manipulative: Balls, bean bags, jump ropes, wands,
hoops, etc.

Competency in Managing the Body
Control of the Body
On the floor, across the floor, through the air, on apparatus
Emphasizing
Balance, coordination, laterality, directionality,
spatial judgments, identification of body parts,
postural efficiency.

7

Effective Class Management

The purpose of effective class management is to structure an efficient and effective instructional environment so that the child may realize his potential in educational progress and achieve educational outcomes deemed appropriate for him. In relation to physical education, this concept can be broken down into three broad outcomes.

The Acquisition of New Elements of Learning

The child has opportunity to acquire new skills, knowledges, attitudes, and concepts.

Improvement and Consolidation of Learned Elements Deemed Desirable

What the child has that is good should be reinforced, consolidated, and expanded so it becomes a part of his personal heritage.

Lessening and Elimination of Undesirable Learned Elements

In this area, the teacher needs to aid the child to rid himself of things which get in the way of his learning and cause conflict in his personal living. Substitution of the desirable for the undesirable is the key to this learning situation.

It is quite obvious that physical education activity not only is an end in itself, but also is a learning environment for the achievement of other educational outcomes. It is equally apparent, then, that the teacher is the key factor in implementing the achievement of a broad range of objectives now thought to be within the potential of physical education.

THE ROLE OF THE TEACHER

It is the teacher's responsibility to develop an instructional atmosphere that will be in keeping with the stated purposes of the school physical education curriculum. First and foremost, the teacher must possess the conviction that physical education is an important educational medium for the child's optimum development not only in the physical area, but also in many other aspects of learning. To believe in physical education is the first essential for successful teaching.

Closely allied to this viewpoint is a second basic premise. The teacher needs to recognize that physical education is largely an instructional program and as such needs planning. A well-executed lesson is a joy for the children and a source of pleasure for the teacher.

The role of the teacher is that of a leader, not a dictator. Helpfulness, friendliness, respect for the dignity of the individual are qualities needed to assure that children will derive maximum benefit from their experiences. The teacher needs to talk with and listen to children in contrast to merely talking to them. The democratic process can be an instrument of direction in physical education.

This is even more true in today's physical education with its "new look," where the teacher teaches the child and not the activity. Children demonstrate much variation in their rates of progress and derive different sets of values from activity. However, in some ways they are very much the same and travel a common path of growth and development. This allows the teacher to select activities of a central core for the class, but consideration for individual differences remains important. It is not a sound practice to set the same standards for all children.

The interaction of children with their peers in an activity situation provides a fruitful opportunity to observe them in the interchanges with each other in a social setting. Helpful knowledge can be garnered about children. Intelligent observation is also needed to assess the learning situation and inject hints, suggestions, and guidelines, stimulating the child to greater variety and better quality of movement.

The teacher can learn from the students. Rather than attempting to provide all the guidelines for activity development, the teacher should seek the aid of the children to expand development in an activity area or help provide direction for the lesson.

The teacher should be a reasonable example of the health and physical fitness dictums that the school is attempting to promote. Elderly teachers may feel that this would be a difficult standard to meet. However, the teacher should be free of glaring departures from what are considered good healthful practices.

Children tend to imitate those whom they admire and respect. The teacher needs to be certain that his personal example will not lay the basis for improper habits or attitudes. Teachers should be appropriately dressed for physical education teaching, at least to the extent of having proper footwear.

The teacher is the key to the learning situation. The degree of control, the quality of the instructional procedures, and the response of the children are inherent in the personality of the teacher. Whether physical education is a quality educational experience or just glorified free play is determined by the teacher's approach.

GUIDING THE LEARNING PROCESS

Having elaborated on the elements of learning, the role of the teacher, and other physical education conceptual factors, we can now turn our attention to the task of teaching the child. This will involve a discussion first of general principles of education designed to promote optimum learning, and then of more class-related instructional procedures in physical education, categorized into a number of subdivisions.

General Educational Considerations

Three requisites are important in the learning process. The first is that the child be capable of learning what is presented. The second is that the child have the level of motivation necessary so learning can be accomplished. The third is that the environment be so structured that learning can follow an orderly process and take place.

Capability

Capability simply means that the learning task is within the capacity of the child, that he is capable of doing what he is expected to do. Many factors affect capability, among them maturation level, physique, state of physical fitness, previous experience, and personality factors. The physical and neural levels of competency should be such that the child can achieve a good measure of success in performing the tasks with which he is presented.

Capability can be modified by appropriate experience in movement. A child should move from one grade to another with experiences which are consistent and progressive. It is not educationally sound to teach children softball when their throwing and catching skills are not up to the level required for the game.

Good body management skills lead to good basic skills, which in turn are the basis of specialized skills. The teacher may need to "back up" in the activity until a point is reached where the children can handle the prescribed chores. Expansion *within activity* may be the indicated approach rather than too much progression up the ladder of challenge. The teacher must start at the children's level of competence and move forward from that point. If the lowest level of the activity does not meet this criterion of capability, then the activity is not a suitable educational experience.

If a child can handle the activity and meet with success, he is capable of progress. If he experiences intense frustration, learning will either move in undesirable channels or be cut off almost entirely. It is frustrating and a waste of effort to attempt to teach children on a level which is beyond their capacity.

Motivation and Readiness to Learn

Capability infers that the child can learn. Being motivated means that he wants to and is ready to learn. Capability has both a physical and neural basis, while motivation centers on psychological drives. The learner must have a need, some kind of a drive to action, or little learning will take place. Children must want to learn.

Motivation comes from within. The task must hold personal significance for the child; he must have a "stake" in it. He must feel the necessity to become involved, and that involvement must be of sufficient depth.

Physical education itself carries motivation for the child. The teacher can see the faces of the children light up when he tells them it is time for physical education period. They go to the activity area with an aura of expectancy. To satisfy this drive for activity and skim off some of the energy, introductory activities (Chapter 8) are educationally sound.

Another critical motivational factor is the teacher-image projected to the children. If the teacher is prepared, enthusiastic, and positive in his approach, some of this feeling is bound to rub off on the children. The teacher needs to demonstrate in his behavior many of the characteristics he expects from the children. The process of identification with an appropriate model, in this case the teacher, is a mechanism of high importance.

The children should be included, at times, in the planning, capitalizing on the premise that those who participate in the planning are more likely to support the activities. This forms a preset-in expectancy, as they know what they will receive in the lesson which follows. This, however, can cause children to react negatively, as they may reject a program prematurely which they feel they will not like.

The eagerness and expectancy that our young people have for physical education should be exploited. This initial motivation and readiness should be maintained through appropriate reinforcement and feedback.

Maintaining Readiness to Learn — Feedback and Reinforcement

Feedback and reinforcement can be effective in modifying the learning process and maintaining receptiveness to learning. Unfortunately, detrimental effects can appear if feedback is unpleasant or negative. Feedback refers to the impressions, feelings, or concepts a child derives from the learning experiences in which he engages. Reinforcement implies a strengthening, a consolidation, a shoring-up of learning, as a result of feedback.

First of all, children should find enjoyment and pleasure from participation in physical education. Learning is facilitated when children enjoy what they are doing.

The child should experience the consequence of his actions, that is, accomplish something. The learner builds confidence when he meets with success and is ready to move to higher achievements. The learning situation should be such that each child can attain a measure of success. Success should vary with children, as they progress at different rates and attain success differently.

A related postulate is that reasonable goals should be set for the child which are within his power to reach. Children are stimulated when they have a target goal which is both challenging and attainable. Somewhere the child needs to get the feeling that he has met the challenge and "I did it!"

Include in instruction the reason for doing things; teach not only the "how" but also the "why." Children learn more readily when they know the "why" of an activity. This attaches significance to the procedure and gives it a personal value to the learner.

Children thrive on praise and encouragement, as the positive approach is more meaningful to them than negative comments. With students who have problems involving confidence, this becomes increasingly important. The feedback comes from the child's urge to seek status through approval, which is reflected in the comments of the teacher. Encouragement can help the child to progress by indicating to him that he is on the right track. It can overcome fear of failure.

From a negative viewpoint, children sometimes react violently to a traumatic experience in physical education to the point of strong antipathy or even withdrawal. Deep psychological hurt can be caused by sarcasm, biting comments, slurs, and embarrassing situations.

INSTRUCTIONAL PROCEDURES

Some reference has been made to teaching procedures in the preceding material, particularly with respect to feedback and reinforcement. Instructional procedures applicable to a broad range of activities are presented here. Procedures relevant to specific activity areas are treated in the respective sections for each activity area.

Working with Children

1. See that each child has an opportunity to be active in the learning situation. Self-activity is the basis of physical learning and — for that matter — all learning. There should be sufficient equipment so that there can be individual activity. In group work, the children should be divided into small enough groups so there is little waiting for turns. Standing, watching, and waiting should be kept to a minimum.

2. Involve all children in the program, including the handicapped, the overweight, and the unskilled.

3. The child who does not participate, who is not accepted by the group, or whose ineptness does not allow him much success needs special consideration to help him find himself. Give him tasks in which he can succeed or can achieve status in the eyes of his fellow students.

4. Beware of activities which tend to eliminate slow or unskilled children. Those eliminated usually are the ones who need the activity the most. Get eliminated children back into activity fast. Use this type of organization sparingly.

5. Give children opportunity for exploratory and creative activity. Children need an opportunity to try out their own ideas, solve some of their own movement problems, and bring forth movement of their own origin. Teachers need to take advantage of this drive by providing opportunity for the child to come up with his own movement ideas.

6. Get primary children into activity as quickly as possible.

7. Children love to run at times for the sheer zest of activity. Provide time in the program for this basic drive.

8. If children are assigned as leaders, give them an actual opportunity to lead. Give children all the responsibility they can assume.

9. A class should be organized into squads, each with a leader. These are convenient groups to use for activity. Change squad composition and leaders frequently, giving all children a chance to lead if possible.

10. In selecting squads or groups, use methods of selection which will not embarrass a child chosen last. In no case should this be a "slave market" type of selection, where the leaders look over the group and visibly pick whom they wish.

11. Have a designated place and formation for squad assembly. When the teacher says, "Get into squad formation," four squad columns are formed with the leader in front of his squad, and the assistant leader next. The children should be seated cross-legged with the columns far enough apart so children cannot reach each other. The formation is convenient for instruction and strengthens the concept of squad organization.

12. Teach respect for equipment. Children should take care of equipment as if it were their own.

13. Have a system for issuing and returning equipment. Children should handle this whenever possible.

14. Teach children to wait for instruction before using equipment they have been issued. They should receive this instruction promptly. In some cases it is well to tell the child what to get and what to do with it at the same time so that he can immediately begin to practice.

15. Devise ways of moving children easily and efficiently from one activity to another.

16. Have respect for the dignity of the child. Avoid laying hands on him, or pushing or placing him in position when he does not understand the directions.

17. Avoid overstimulation with children, especially those in the lower grades.

18. If facilities permit, children should change to gym clothing for activity. Better

health practices result when children can also shower and clean up properly.

19. Rubber-soled shoes or sneakers should be a requirement for indoor play. Children in kindergarten and first grades may need instruction and practice in tying shoe laces. Shoes may also have to be marked so that children can distinguish right and left. One suggestion is to place the shoes flat on the floor with the inside edges together. A mark can be placed on each shoe so that the marks will come together when the shoes are placed alongside each other. This avoids the right shoe being on the left foot and vice versa.

20. Consideration for proper storage of the gym shoes is important. The child's name should be on the shoes, preferably on the outside where it can be read easily. Also, a routine for orderly arrangement of street shoes should be established, so that after the class the child can find his own shoes quickly without unnecessary scrambling.

The cooperation of the classroom teacher should be sought in helping to solve the shoe storage problem.

21. Each child should be expected to work at or near his potential. It is important that children gain the concept that success can be achieved only through good effort. The child that doesn't "put out" is selling himself short. If a teacher expects poor effort and work from a child, he will certainly get them. Children should learn to "give it a good try."

22. Have some kind of predetermined means of selecting partners, when such is indicated. Partners can be set for a period of time, with children matched according to size or some other factors.

Directing Activities

1. The teacher should use the daily lesson plan as the basis of the instruction. For the experienced teacher this can be brief. Proper coverage of material is assured only through planned lessons.

2. A major technique to be acquired is the ability to change and vary an activity so that the most value can be secured from what is chosen for learning experiences. The various ways of securing variety in movement experiences are important. Basic movement provides many ideas for extending the potential of activity. Games, relays, combatives, and stunts are activities which can be enhanced by an enterprising teacher with changes and modifications offering additional challenge to the children. Teachers should be alert for changes which can increase interest and make more physical demands of the children. The children should be a source of suggestions for change and variations.

3. Use the whistle sparingly. Give one sharp blast and insist on the courtesy of attention. Early attention to this will pay off later in the dividends of time saved.

The whistle should be used only to halt activity. Starting commands for activities can be given with verbal signals. The whistle should mean, "Stop, Look (at the teacher), and Listen."

4. Whether to teach by the whole or part method must be decided. The whole method is the process of learning the entire skill or activity in one dosage. The part method is to learn parts separately until all parts are learned and can be combined into a unified whole. The choice of the whole or part method depends upon the complexity of the skill or activity. The teacher needs to decide whether or not the activity is simple enough to be taught wholly or if it should be broken down into parts.

5. Use the more formal methods of organization only when needed. Stunts and tumbling are examples of activities in which good selection of formations is needed for safety and good teaching.

6. A sanitation problem is present when children share whistles for officiating. Enough whistles are needed so that each referee may have one to himself. Provisions for washing and sanitizing whistles emphasize good health procedures. Thorough washing and immersion in alcohol is one method.

7. Techniques of evaluation should be a part of the program. Only through evaluative procedures can the degree of progress toward the objectives of the program be ascertained.

8. At times, allow choice of activity.

9. If the classroom teacher has the responsibility for the physical education instruction, maximum use of activity time can be derived by giving time-consuming explanations in the

classroom prior to the scheduled time for going to the play area. Rules can be explained, procedures and responsibilities outlined, and formations illustrated on the blackboard.

10. Teachers should analyze each activity from the standpoint of how maximum movement can be a part of the activity. Teachers must realize that activities are a means of development through movement and that as much movement must be coaxed from them as possible.

11. Avoid too rigid an approach. At times allow for experimentation and exploration by the children. The teacher may find it appropriate to give basic instruction in the topic or skill and then allow for exploration and creative activity based upon the material just presented.

12. When giving instructions in activity, be explicit. If there are different, acceptable ways to perform, show these and discuss with the children the reasoning behind the various difference in technique. Explain enough to get the activity underway successfully.

13. Set up your procedures so that when the explanation is completed, the activity will begin.

14. Know and emphasize the stress points in an activity. These are the critical points which are important to success in an activity.

15. The prevention of fear in young children in handling play objects should be a consideration. Use a soft ball or beanbag in introductory phases. When the children work as partners, begin with short distances, using the simplest activity first. Begin in a stationary position before progressing to moving skills.

16. A physical education class needs to be a happy medium between quiet and boisterousness. Youngsters should be able to let off steam but be under control. Two types of noise should be differentiated. The first is the noise growing out of purposeful activity, interest, and enjoyment. The second is noise that springs from disorder, disinterest, rowdyism, and lack of control.

17. The teachers need to use caution so that their own interests do not rule the program. Generally, adults drift toward those activities which they know and can do successfully.

18. While desirable learnings can result in a proper learning atmosphere, these are not automatic for activities but are the result of planning. Relays can be used as an example. In a good learning atmosphere, a child can learn to cooperate, to observe rules, and to abide with the capacities of his teammates. On the other hand, in a poorly conducted class, he can learn to cheat, to become intolerant of the shortcomings of the members of his team, and to put winning over all other goals.

19. The development of courtesy, fair play, and honesty are important goals to be achieved by elementary children. In discussion and evaluation, children need to bring out what constitutes proper conduct in various situations.

Teachers should note in their lesson plans where opportunities exist for introduction of these social concepts. Their development must not be left to chance.

The Vocal Side of Teaching

1. When there is instruction, the teacher should have the attention of the students. Be brief and to the point. Avoid excessive verbalization.

2. Speak in terms consistent with the maturity of the children. Gradually develop the child's vocabulary, but avoid technical terms which will not be understood. In working with disadvantaged children, be sure the terms are appropriate and relevant to the group.

3. Use a voice with enough "carry" to cover the group, but do not shout.

4. Stand where you can see all the children. Avoid the center of the circle. Position the children so you, the teacher, are facing the sun or the light source.

5. In phrasing instructional points of the lesson, accent the positive. Instead of saying, "Don't land so hard," say rather, "Land lightly."

6. Avoid excessive repetition and reliance on certain words and phrases, such as "OK," "All Right," and that irritating "and-uh."

7. Avoid rhetorical questions which in reality are meant to be commands, such as "Shall we go in now?" or "Would you like to . . . ?"

8. Use appropriate methodology for questions and answers.

a. Phrase questions in such a manner that they stimulate a child to a thoughtful answer and not just a "yes" or "no" response.

b. In asking questions, select an individual child, as a question thrown at a group will get a chorus of responses. The teacher will then need to designate a child to be heard, a procedure which should have been instituted in the first place.

c. Children should wait to be recognized before answering, usually by raising a hand.

d. Try to stimulate a free flow of ideas by expanding the answer with probing phrases, such as, "What are other points?" and "Let's have another reason."

9. If a child does not respond to directions, an assessment needs to be made as to whether the difficulty is in communication or a lack of ability.

Disciplinary Factors

Several points are important in maintaining a good instructional climate. If disciplinary trouble develops, one must look first at the teacher and the program, that is, is there any reason for the deviant behavior? After this has been determined, attention can be turned to the children. With children, some aggression is normal, but it must be channeled into proper outlets.

The selection of membership for squads offers an opportunity to minimize certain problems of association. It offers a chance to separate children who might cause trouble by being in too close association.

The class clown is a nuisance and sometimes a disturbing problem. His chief aim in life is to get the other children to laugh. Care should be used in asking such an individual to demonstrate. His antics should receive no support from the teacher. Acceptable response should be encouraged.

Because of the attractiveness of physical participation, classroom teachers on occasion use the exclusion from physical education as a disciplinary measure for breaches of conduct not related to physical education. This cannot be regarded as a sound educational practice, as the child has a right to the learning experience. However, within the physical education class framework, temporary exclusion is effectively practiced by some teachers. Children who do something naughty are told, "You go over to the sidelines and sit down.

You tell us when you are ready to come back and play according to the rules."

The best antidote for discipline problems is a teaching climate of warmth, understanding, friendliness, **and** firmness.

Principles Important in Skills

Skill includes both basic and specialized skills. Specialized skills need more precise and definitive approaches than basic skills, which can be taught through the exploratory approach of basic movement. For this reason, the instructional procedures for skill learning are more applicable to the specialized skills, but still have a firm place in basic movement methodology.

To move more effectively and reach a better level of skill performance, the elementary school child should apply certain established principles to his movement patterns and skills. First of all, he should be made aware that there are such principles; and, secondly, he should learn how to apply these in his learning experiences. It is also important that the teacher utilize the principles in coaching and helping youngsters with their skills.

If effective patterns and correct techniques are established early in the learning process, the child will have little need to make a difficult adjustment later from an undesirable habit which has been allowed to be established in his skill patterns.

The principles are mostly general in nature, covering a variety of skills. A few, however, are specific and refer to certain types of skills. For elementary school children, the following principles in the performance of skills should be considered.

Basic Principles Important in Movement Experiences and Skill Performance

Body Position

In a normal, ready position for an activity, the feet should be at shoulder width. For some skills one foot may be forward of the other. The knees are loose, toes pointed forward, and weight carried on the balls of the feet. There is a readiness so that the legs may move easily in any direction as desired. The back should be reasonably straight, the head up, and the hands ready for action (as in catching).

If a fast start is needed, the feet are brought together more (less than shoulder width), and a body lean in the direction of the proposed movement should be made. The center of gravity is lowered somewhat by the body lean and more bend at the knees.

For the powerful movements of pulling or pushing, the base (the feet) should be widened, the knees bent, and the center of gravity dropped with the lower base.

Visual Concentration

Visually, the eyes should be focused on some fixed or moving point in keeping with the skill. In catching, the child should watch the ball. In shooting a basket or bowling, the fixation should be on the target. In kicking, he should keep his head down and watch the ball.

Follow-Through

Follow-through refers to a smooth projection of the already-initiated movement. The principle is vitally important in throwing, striking, batting, and kicking skills. In kicking, the movement is to kick through the ball, not at it. In batting, the normal swing must be fully completed, not arrested.

Relaxation

The child should be relaxed in his movements. To be relaxed means to use just enough muscular effort to perform the skill, but avoid an overuse, generally called "tightening up," causing a distortion of the skill. This principle has particular application to target skills such as shooting baskets or pitching.

Opposition

Opposition refers to the coordinated use of the arms and legs. In throwing right-handed, the forward step should be made with the left foot. In walking or running, the movement of a leg is coordinated with that of the arm on the other side of the body. A step with the left foot means a forward swing with the right arm.

Total Body Coordination

Many skills require the entire body to be brought into play to perform the skill effectively. A child who throws primarily with his arm should be taught to bring his whole body into play.

Development of Torque

Torque means to bring to bear together a combination of body forces employing twisting and rotating motions. It is related to the foregoing point of total body coordination. In throwing or batting, the child should start with a forward motion of the hip and rotation of the body, thus adding force to the throw or batted ball.

Weight Transfer

A transfer of weight from the back to the front foot is a critical element in throwing, batting, striking, and rolling skills. The initial weight of the body is on the back foot, with the transfer occurring during the execution of the skill.

Visualization

The mental review of a skill with emphasis on the key points to be done in sequential fashion is called visualization. A performer thinks through the execution of the skill with a mental performance before actually performing the skill. The value comes in concentrating on the key points which make for better success in the skill. Visualization has application mostly to the more complex skills.

Pads of the Fingers

The pads of the fingers are the controlling elements in many manipulative skills, particularly in ball skills. A ball should be handled with the pads of the fingers.

Effective Motor Learning

Methods of teaching depend upon the level of the children and the skill being taught. Some considerations are given in motor learning on the elementary level.

1. There must be sufficient repetition to establish good retention. This involves the principle of overlearning. Correct form must be practiced until it becomes fixed. The more complex the skill and the higher the performance level, the more need for practice to maintain the level. Repetition is effective only if it does something beyond what it did previously.

2. Provide effective demonstration and visual aids. Children learn by example, and effective demonstrations can show youngsters how to perform skills. Many techniques lend themselves to slow motion demonstrations. Select-

ed children, properly directed, can provide suitable demonstrations. In addition, slides, film strips, motion pictures, pamphlets, posters, and other visual aids can be obtained from different sources. Loop films are of particular value in teaching skills.

3. Teachers should be able to verbalize skills.This means to break a skill down verbally into its component parts so the children can follow the pattern of instruction.

4. Skills should be practiced with as small a group as possible consistent with the skill and the equipment available. Whenever possible and practical, *each* child should have a piece of equipment.

5. Relatively short practices (in time or in number of repetitions) make for more efficient learning than do longer practices.

6. Older children can derive more benefit with longer practice than is possible with younger children.

7. The "start-and-expand" technique should be the basis for skill learning. This means that the skill level is started low enough so that all children meet with success and then expanded to more challenging skill performance.

8. Children should follow sound mechanical principles, but to expect all to perform skills in an identical manner is an error, not in keeping with the principle of individual differences.

9. A teacher should emphasize the "best" way to do things and what constitutes correct technique in a specific skill. However, he should point out to the student that there are performers who are successful even when using what is considered poor form. Such performances should be regarded as exceptions developed only after a long period of practice and participation.

10. A child must participate to learn. He should have an opportunity to explore, try out, and experiment with different ways of performing skills as opposed to the autocratic "this is the way you do it" teaching.

11. Mimetics have a place in skill teaching. Students can be in mass formation and follow the directions of the leader. Many can practice at one time, good form is emphasized in a short time, questions can be answered, and gross errors can be discovered at the earliest period. Since the student can concentrate on

the skill without the implement (ball, bat, or object), kinesthetic feeling for the skill can be acquired. The child gets the feel of the movement.

12. Teachers need to be able to coach youngsters to good levels of skill, by analyzing and making corrections. Students expect an intelligent answer to the question, "What am I doing wrong?" Coaching depends on good powers of observation and the development of keen recognition ability. Coaching involves two aspects. The first is the application of the basic principles important in movement and skill performance. The second involves items of technique which are important to the skill itself.

13. After a period of skill practice, the teacher may hold a critique with the students for discussion of the stress and critical points of the skill. It can be based on a question such as, "What are the important things we must remember to do this skill efficiently?"

14. Speed in relation to performance has several aspects. Children learn well at a speed which is just slightly less than the normal speed of a skill, moving up to normal speed as soon as feasible. In other cases, too much speed in a game or relay before the child has absorbed the skill hardly helps learning.

15. Competition can enhance learning and performance. However, when competition becomes too heated, performance deteriorates. When excessive emotions are involved, learning ability goes down.

16. Teachers should not assume that the youngsters will learn the skill elsewhere. While some may learn from parents, brothers, sisters, and older children, repetition and practice will improve the level of performance. If errors in execution are present, the skill session can establish correct form.

Patterns of Skill Organization

There are a number of ways a class may be organized for learning and practicing skills.

Each Child Practices the Same Skill. This lends itself to mass teaching and group control. It demands adequate facilities and sufficient supplies so that each child has a piece of equipment, or at least does not have to wait unnecessarily for a turn. The instruction must be broad and challenging enough to cover the range of varying skill. It is not incorrect to teach every child the same thing if there is consideration for different levels of ability.

Children Are Divided into Groups According to Skill. Children can be given more meaningful and challenging learning experiences if they work with peers of similar ability. Groups could be assigned similar or different tasks. The teacher should be concerned with all students, but should give a good share of attention to the low-skilled.

Children Work in Pairs. Generally, this means one piece of equipment for each pair. Throwing and catching lends itself well to this means of organizing children.

The Class is Divided into Halves; Each Half Works on a Different Skill. When there is a shortage of equipment, instead of having some of the children wait for a turn, divide the class into two equal groups, one of which works with one type of skill and the other half with another.

A Class in Squad Formation

Each Squad Practices a Different Skill and Squads are Rotated on Signal. With different skill activities being practiced, considerable reliance on squad leaders is necessary. The teacher cannot feasibly provide explanations and directions for the different activities at the same time. The skills practiced also must have a similarity in accomplishment with respect to the time limit. It would be a poor learning situation for the rotation signal to be given when one group was "just getting started" and another "finished a long time ago."

Different Activity Stations are Set Up and the Child Goes to the One Where He Feels the Greatest Need. In softball, the teacher could set up four stations, batting, bunting, pitching, and fielding grounders. A leader would direct the activities at each station, which requires

prior planning and instruction. Individual choice may result in an imbalance of groups, so it may be necessary to establish more than one for the same skill.

In considering the different types of formations, if too many activities or approaches are involved, the instruction is diluted. The teacher must move from one group to another, making coaching and correctional instruction difficult.

Formations Useful in Skill Instruction and Conducting Relays

Whether the teacher has organized skill instruction by individuals, couples, small groups, or squads, a number of formations are suggested for instructional purposes. The majority of these formations can be adapted to relays, which makes for a convenient change from serious practice to a fun relay. Other formations more relevant to a specialized activity are found in the separate activity areas.

1. Mass or Scattered

```
X     X X   X X X

   X   X X X   X X

 X X   X   X X X
```

2. Small Group

```
 X   X   X   X   X
XX  XX  XX  XX  XX    (by 3s)

XX  XX  XX  XX  XX
XX  XX  XX  XX  XX    (by 4s)
```

3. Lane or File

```
X   X   X   X
X   X   X   X
X   X   X   X
X   X   X   X
X   X   X   X
X   X   X   X
```

4. Squad with Leader (or plus one)

```
X   X   X   X
X   X   X   X
X   X   X   X
X   X   X   X
X   X   X   X
X   X   X   X
―   ―   ―   ―
L   L   L   L
```

5. Spoke

```
X               X
   X         X
      X   X
      X   X
   X         X
X               X
```

6. Line and Leader

```
X   X   X   X   X   X
            L
```

7. Semicircle and Leader

```
      X   X
   X         X
 X             X
      L
```

8. Circle

```
   X   X
 X         X
 X         X
   X   X
```

9. Circle and Leader

```
   X   X
 X         X
      L
 X         X
   X   X
```

10. Double Line (also Partner Practice)

```
X   X   X   X   X
X   X   X   X   X
```

11. Zigzag Double Line

```
X   X   X   X   X
  X   X   X   X   X
```

12. Shuttle

13. Shuttle Turn-back

```
→ X X X X⌐   ⌐X X X X ←
```

The Teacher Who Cannot Demonstrate

There are teachers who, because of physical limitations, cannot demonstrate effectively. Few teachers, who are not physical education specialists, can do all physical activities well. Even the relatively skilled teacher will, at times, need to devise substitutions for an effective demonstration. For the teacher who has difficulty in demonstrating activities, the following suggestions should prove helpful.

1. Through reading, study, analysis of movement, and other devices, arm yourself with an understanding and knowledge of the activities which you have difficulty demonstrating. Even

if you cannot perform, know how the activity is to be done.

2. Select skillful children to help demonstrate.

3. Be able to verbalize the skill so you can coach the students and correct their errors.

4. Secure and use effective visual aids at appropriate points in the unit of teaching.

5. Place more reliance on the squad leaders and use the squad formation in skill drills.

Safety in the Instructional Program

Policies for health and safety have been introduced in Chapter 5 as they relate to administrative responsibility. Additional safety suggestions of instructional nature are offered here. Safety precautions and considerations with respect to the various activity areas are presented with the instructional sequences and procedures of the separate activities. For example, softball has definite need for safety rules such as not throwing the bat, and having the waiting batters stand in a safe area. These items relate only to softball and are discussed under that unit.

There is nothing automatic about establishing a good safety climate. Instruction in safety must be taught along with the other elements of the activity, and the lesson plan should reflect appropriate emphasis. The positive approach should be stressed with emphasis on how we can play safely, in contrast with the scare approach of possible injury.

Once the rules have been established, good supervision and observation are needed to insist on correct and safe application of the rules. Some important general considerations for safety are as follows:

1. The first responsibility is to see that the playing area is a suitable and safe environment. A quick assessment by the teacher will note the presence of obstructions and articles which might prove hazardous and merit removal. The area should be of sufficient size.

2. Next, the teacher *must* consider the forthcoming activity and what is needed for safe participation. The children should know the basic and lead-up skills well enough for safe participation. They should be instructed in needed safety procedures and rules. The teacher needs to make sure the safety regulations are followed.

3. Where the children are in two or more groups, leave sufficient space between them. The activity should not demand that the children of different groups run toward each other, as nasty collisions can occur. Also, where throws are employed, as in dodgeball, distances should be such that the throw has lost its force or hits the ground before entering the territory of another group.

4. In ball activities, teach children to keep eyes on the ball, not to throw the ball to another child unless he is watching.

5. Traffic rules in games and drills are important. Children should pass to the right when coming toward each other in games. Establish the time or distance when children follow each other, such as consecutive turns on a mat, high jumping or the obstacle course. One-way patterns should be established for other activities.

6. Set up rules about recovering balls. One child only should go after a ball. Have stringent rules regarding procedure in recovering balls that go into streets, areas of other groups, apparatus areas, etc. A stop-and-look pause should precede any action for recovery.

7. Shoelaces should remain tied. Stop the play and see that this is done. Children should be required to wear shoes for outside activity. In some races and contests, children like to remove shoes because they feel they can travel faster, but this should not be permitted.

8. Maintain the instructional climate by not permitting horseplay and unnecessary roughness. Viciousness, such as vindictive tagging, has no place in physical education.

9. Children should be cautioned against bringing pencils or pens to the physical education class, nor should they be allowed to chew gum or munch on suckers.

10. For rough activity, glasses should be removed or glass guards made available. If glasses are removed, establish a safe place for them to protect against breakage.

11. Rules governing different activities and pieces of apparatus should be developed among the teachers as a whole, so the children have uniformity in direction. It is well to have regulations posted.

12. Teach children to keep their hands off other children, as this not only is annoying, but can lead to trouble.

In no sense is this meant to be an all-inclusive list of safety considerations for all activity. The teacher is referred to the specific activity section for others.

Leadership Experiences

If the goals of leadership and followership are to be realized, the program must provide social situations wherein the students have real opportunities to lead. The very nature of the physical education program provides many jobs which can be distributed among students to give them real opportunities to assume responsibility. This training results on the one hand in an understanding of the nature of authority and responsibility, and on the other in an acceptance by the children of the leadership authority so designated.

Guides for the Leadership Program

1. The leadership program is not to be regarded as a time-saving device for the teacher. Furthermore, it is unfair to ask children to assume responsibilities without adequate guidance. The teacher must give due consideration to the training of the leaders and provide sufficient supervision. This takes both time and effort.

2. The jobs assigned should be realistic and definite, and should be assigned over a designated time period. Job descriptions aid in orienting the child to the proper performance of duties. A list of duties avoids overlapping and designates definite areas of responsibility.

3. If leadership is considered a fine developmental opportunity, then it follows that it is good for all children. Jobs should be rotated at specified periods so that all children are given some type of responsibility during the year. It is recognized that jobs require different levels of ability and that the teacher must assign carefully on the basis of the child's capacity.

4. The student should be held to a reasonable standard of job performance. He should be brought to the realization that to be a leader requires planning, and he must allot sufficient time to plan and discharge his duties.

5. The use of leaders should actually improve the efficiency of the class. The important element is not leadership, but the quality of the physical education experience. A class should not suffer through an inferior experience because of the emphasis on leadership training.

Types of Leadership Experiences

1. **Equipment Manager.** He obtains, arranges, and returns equipment for the day's activities.

2. **Area Supervisor.** The duties of this individual include marking fields, setting up boundaries, and, in general, seeing that the area is ready for the activity. Indoors, this would entail duties like setting up mats or getting the public address system ready.

3. **Squad Leaders.** The possibilities in this area are numerous. Responsibilities vary from simple tasks like keeping the squad in proper order for relays or taking turns in stunt activities, to supervisory responsibilities in the teaching of skills. Routine record-keeping of individual performance and in test scores can be a part of the duties.

4. **Officials.** Officials need to have a thorough knowledge of the rules of the game. Enough officials can be assigned so that each one will get a chance to play in the activity and still hold his responsibilities.

5. **Game Leader, Demonstrator, Exercise Leader.** Children can be assigned to choose and lead a game. If the activity or situation makes pupil demonstration desirable, the teacher can assign these duties to selected and properly-directed students. Trained students may also lead exercises.

6. **Monitors.** Special responsibilities can be assigned to monitors. Turning lights on and off, supervising the washup after class, and making safety inspections are duties which can be assumed.

Some consideration can be given to a leaders' club which would include all the leaders for a given period. Such a club can be organized in a class or on an all-school basis. Leaders' clubs can meet during the club period in the regular curriculum or be scheduled for an after-school session or on Saturday morning. The club organization provides for good discussion of duties, an improved *esprit d corps,* and definite discharge of duties.

While children gain from leadership experiences, care must be taken that the leaders are not kept too busy to participate in the regular program. Also, assistant leaders might be appointed, assuming head duties during the next period. Continuity can be preserved in this manner.

Evaluation

Evaluation is the process of determining the extent to which the program in physical education meets its stated objectives. It would provide more valid information if all evaluative techniques could be based on measurement procedures, but not all objectives lend themselves to measurement. Physical educators are attempting to build greater precision into the evaluative process by zeroing in on behavioral objectives. These objectives attempt to specify in more precise and definite terms, for example, discarding "acquiring a satisfactory level of skill" in favor of the more limited measurable and precise behavioral objective of "attaining a distance of 72" in the standing long jump."

Until behavioral objectives have been fully developed and refined to the point of practicability, the available objective means of assessment must be employed. These include fitness, posture, skill or achievement, and knowledge tests. But many of the outcomes deemed important in physical education cannot be measured by such devices. Reliance on other means of assessment is needed. For the purpose of discussion, evaluation is divided into four areas: (1) general standards for the program; (2) accepted tests; (3) teacher observation; and (4) pupil expression and opinion.

General Standards

General standards set the pace for the entire program, and because of this are examined first:

Evidence of Planning. The program should be based on good planning procedures. Available as evidence should be an overall year's program from which the weekly and daily programs are drawn. Instruction should be based on lesson plans.

Time Element. Is there a daily program totaling at least 150 minutes per week?

Facilities, Equipment, and Supplies. Are these sufficient for the particular situation so that they do not provide detrimental limitations in the experiences for children?

The Program. Does the program meet good education standards? Is it geared to the needs, interests, and capacities of the children?

The Direction. Is the instruction in the capable hands of a trained and interested teacher? Does the teacher keep up-to-date through current literature and inservice or college workshops or courses?

Health and Safety. Are there good standards of health and safety? Is the participation based upon a regular medical examination? Is there proper provision for emergency care?

Is there consideration for the child who cannot participate fully?

Testing

Measurement is important in physical education because it provides an objective means by which a student can be made aware of his progress. Children like to know their standing compared to other students and standards.

Tests can point out the strengths and weaknesses in terms of achievement toward standards or specified goals. The measurement program can re-emphasize to the school administration and parents the importance of the goals of physical education and the children's progress toward those outcomes.

The tests should be used in counseling and can be a part of the child's periodic report to the parents.

Measurement in physical education on the elementary level should consist of physical fitness, skill, and pencil and paper tests on knowledge and attitudes.

Tests covering knowledge have a place in the program as they emphasize the importance of these learnings to both children and parents. Attitude tests are not frequently used in the elementary program in physical education.

Skill tests are many and varied. Discussion in this text of skill tests has been placed with the activity in which the skill occurs. Testing in physical fitness is covered in the appendix.

Observation by the Teacher

The teacher can make reasonable judgments of the progress toward the goals of physical education by observing certain signs of desirable progress.

Physical Fitness. How well does a youngster meet the strength and endurance demands of activity?

How smoothly and adequately can he handle his body?

How does he respond physiologically to the demands of activity? Is there dizziness, nausea, shortness of breath, unusual paleness or redness, weakness, depressed mental or emotional states, or anxiety states?

How well does the child recover from activity? After ten minutes, does the pulse return to normal? Is he still overly tired? Is there marked stiffness or soreness that evening or the next day? Has he recovered the next day from the activity?

Is his posture and bearing satisfactory?

What about arm and shoulder girdle development? Can he perform on the ladder and horizontal bar with reasonable success?

Does he enjoy and thrive on vigorous activity?

Competency in Body Management. Can he manage his body in a variety of movement situations? Does he move with ease? Can he go over, around, and under apparatus and obstacles?

Useful Skills. Has he mastered the basic skills of locomotion? Can he do these successfully to rhythm?

Does he show good form in specialized skills? Is he making satisfactory progress for his size and maturity?

Has he mastered throwing, kicking, and batting skills well enough to take part successfully in game type activities.

Can he perform on apparatus the activities appropriate for his age?

On the intermediate level, can he integrate dance steps into dances?

Does he know and apply the appropriate mechanical principles to skill learning? Does he have the desire to practice for better performance?

Does he have a wide appreciation of skills rather than concentration in a narrow area?

Social Learnings. Does he act democratically by entering wholeheartedly into activities chosen by group process?

Do children play together well and comfortably as boys and girls with wholesome boy-girl relationships? Are social graces the rule in the rhythmic program?

Is there evidence of good leadership and followership patterns? Do the children accept the proper decisions of the leader?

In competitive games, is there evidence of good sportsmanship in observing the rules, accepting the decisions of officials, and following the captain's suggestions? Can the youngsters win or lose in a sportsmanlike manner?

Can the child share with others and not try to dominate the play?

Safety. Have the children developed a safety consciousness?

Are they considerate of other children in safety situations?

Do they spot hazards and unsafe conditions and tend to correct them?

Recreational Objective. During free play, can the child organize his own play either individually or with other children?

Does he learn the rules of activities so he can enjoy these on his own time?

Can he play with assurance on various pieces of apparatus?

Does he know modifications of rules so that he can adapt games to small-group play and places?

Is he motivated to take part in activity for activity's sake — that is, the maintenance of fitness?

Developing a Realistic Self-Image and Acquiring a Desirable Self-Concept. Does he "belong" to the group? Is he accepted by his peers? Is he achieving success in his play activities? Does he seem secure in his physical education experiences? Does he have a realistic self-image in terms of his capabilities.

Personal and Educational Values. Does he take part joyously in play and find satisfaction in movement experiences? Can he react creatively when the call is for free rein to the imagination?

Does he approach problems with assurance and confidence? Does he give evidence of reasoning powers during problem-solving situations?

Is he learning terminology, acquiring understandings, and learning concepts as he participates in movement experiences? Does he understand the reasons behind what he is doing?

Student Opinion and Discussion

After a class period or the completion of a unit, the teacher can organize an evaluating session with the children for the purpose of critical discussion of the merits of the experience. Discussion should be in terms of what was accomplished and how well they enjoyed the activity. Suggestions can be made on what needs to be done and how it can be accomplished.

A technique that can be used with intermediate children is the Buzz Group procedure. The class is divided into four to six small groups, each with a chairman and a recorder. The questions for discussion should be written on the board, and each group assigned to a section of the room to discuss them. The procedure gets its name from the buzzing that goes on while groups are discussing values. After a specified period (there should be a preliminary warning), the class is brought together again for the reports from the recorders. Further discussion can be expanded on the class level.

TEACHING AIDS IN PHYSICAL EDUCATION

Film Strips, Motion Pictures, Slides

In addition to the regular class work in physical education, the teacher should consider enriching the program demonstration with the use of loop films, motion pictures, film strips, slides, and opaque projector. Good audio-visual procedures need to be followed.

The visual aid should fit in with the learning situation and be appropriate for the level of the children. Since the rental charge covers the use of the film for a period of time, coordination with other classes should be arranged for additional showings. Programs ought to be projected far enough ahead so films may be scheduled for correct placement in the program.

Visual aids emphasizing skill techniques should be shown early in a skill learning unit. Those illustrating strategies and game situation probably can come later.

Loop films have become an important medium of instruction. A wide variety of topics is available, including basic movement techniques. New projectors utilizing plastic cart-ridges have made this an effective aid for instruction. Schools can make their own loop films using Super 8 film and a tourist type camera.

Sound films and sound strips generally need to be shown completely through without interruption. Discussion can be permitted in a slide presentation or with a film strip without sound.

Teachers should give some thought to the use of the 35 mm slide as a teaching tool. Critical skills probably cannot be too well illustrated, but formations, game boundaries, and field layouts lend themselves to the home slide projector.

The Opaque Projector

Another useful tool to consider is the opaque projector. This device, like the old magic lantern, will throw on the screen an enlarged version of the material. A teacher who uses a card system for games, rhythms, or other activities will find this an effective and useful time-saver. If a new game is scheduled, the teacher can flash the card on the screen or blackboard and go over the details with the children.

Bulletin Boards

The class bulletin board should devote a proportionate space to physical education. It is well to select a theme for the board and change it often. A theme could illustrate fitness, a unit, a sport, physical education in other areas, posture, or health practices. A particular skill can be selected for illustration. Pictures from magazines, newspapers, and other sources can be used for illustrations.

The board can be constructed of wall board or beaver board which will hold thumb tacks or staples. A backdrop made of colored paper or colored muslin makes a nice display. The color scheme can be tied up with the theme and changed with the display. Some materials that can be used are listed:

1. Pictures and diagrams lend life to the display. Snapshots also can be included. Newspaper materials should be pasted or stapled to sturdy paper for better display.

2. Colored paper of all kinds and colors is needed. Construction paper provides an excellent source for these materials.

3. Stickmen can be made from pipe clean-

ers. These are interesting and provide an outlet for creative talent.

4. Yarn or string can make field outlines or provide borders for the displays.

The character of the bulletin board is limited only by the imagination of the children. The responsibility for the board could be assigned to groups of children on a rotative basis. An interesting bulletin board program also offers possibilities for integration with other subject matter fields.

Displays

Displays offer possibilities similar to bulletin boards. However, the display is generally done in three dimensions. The display should have the material organized around a theme.

A display may be put in a showcase in the school hall. It could be arranged on a table in the classroom.

Bibliographical Materials

Physical education is not static and the collective written materials provide a wealth of ideas for enriching a program. Materials can be classified as follows:

1. **Texts in Elementary School Physical Education.** Works offering an overall treatment of physical education in the elementary school are available in considerable number. It seems that each year one or two new manuscripts are offered. While there is considerable duplication among texts in the basic material presented, each text emphasizes certain ideas and activities.

2. **Curriculum Guides in Physical Education.** Curriculum guides have been assembled on a number of different levels. Many states, counties, cities, and school systems have developed guides for their own situations. The guides are not generally advertised but are available reasonably from the various agencies.

3. **Specialized Subject Area Books.** For more intensive treatment in a particular area of physical education, a number of good books are on the market. These treat only a portion of the physical education program, but develop the area to a much greater extent than the written works covering the entire program. Books dealing with games, sports, rhythmics, posture, classroom activties, testing, and similar topics are available from publishers.

4. **Magazines and Periodicals.** There are magazines devoted to physical education in general, but no periodical which gives its entire emphasis to the elementary school physical education program is on the market. The *Journal of the American Association for Health, Physical Education and Recreation* is probably the one best source for up-to-date materials in physical education on the elementary level.

5. **Card Files.** Available today are card files for various physical education activities. Card files* can be secured in the area of games, rhythmics, relays, and stunts. These are convenient teaching aids and good time-savers. Cards include the description of the activity, teaching suggestions, safety considerations, and variations.

6. **Miscellaneous Materials.** Posters, pamphlets, mimeographed material, convention reports, and research reports are indicative of the vast amount of material which is available to the teacher today. Some system of filing is necessary for the teacher. Materials can be filed under the general topic (like rhythmics) and be available for handy reference.

A successful and enterprising teacher will keep up-to-date in his materials.

---

*Card files are obtainable from Burgess Publishing Company, 426 South Sixth Street, Minneapolis, Minnesota 55415.

Lesson Planning and Introductory Activity

THE PHYSICAL EDUCATION LESSON

The physical education lesson for a particular class period should grow out of a unit of instruction, which in turn is a part of the year's plan. Each lesson should be a part of a sequence based on the work of previous lessons. It is most important that each lesson follow a written plan, especially for a beginning teacher. A written lesson plan will vary in form and length dependent upon the activity and the background of the teacher. A written lesson plan ensures that thought has been given to the lesson before the children enter the activity area. It avoids spur-of-the-moment decisions, losing unity and progression of the material. This does not mean that a teacher cannot modify the lesson as needed, but it does keep the central core and purpose of the lesson intact.

Progression is more likely to occur in the forthcoming lesson if the teacher has the previous lesson plan for a guide. In future years, the teacher can also refer to his collection of lesson plans for suggestion and improvement.

A lesson can be divided into the following parts, each of which is discussed:

1. Introductory Activities (1-3 minutes)
2. Developmental Activities (4-8 minutes)
3. The Lesson Core
   a. Review of Previously-Presented Material
   b. New Learning Experiences
4. Closing Activity (2-5 minutes)

Except for the lesson core, any of the parts can be omitted as indicated by a particular lesson. In some cases, developmental activities serve as introductory work.

Introductory Activity

Introductory activity accomplishes in the lesson just what the designation implies. Children come to the physical education class eager for movement, and the first part of the lesson is designed to meet this sheer appetite for movement. Once this is satisfied, the lesson can proceed toward the achievement of its specific objectives. A secondary purpose of introductory activity is to serve as warm-up activity, preparing the body for the movements which are to follow.

Generally, some type of gross, unstructured movement is used for introductory activity, usually based on locomotor movements. An enterprising teacher can employ many different activities and variations effectively as introductory activity. Examples are found later in this chapter.

Developmental Activities

Developmental activities are defined as those activities which have as a major objective the development of the various qualities of physical fitness — strength, power, endurance, agility, and flexibility, among others.

Some activities, such as circuit training and the obstacle course, involve the entire body. Others, such as exercises and gross movement, involve development of a specific part of the body. Rope jumping, grass drills, guerrilla exercises, and other general fitness activities can also be used.

The developmental activities should show a progression of increasing demands. The work demands must be gradually and consistently increased as the program develops.

The development of physical fitness is presented in Chapters 9 and 10.

The Lesson Core

The lesson core is the heart, the meat of the lesson. Presented here are the learning experiences growing out of the overall instructional unit. The first consideration is to review and work with the activities of the previous lesson, until a satisfactory level of learning has been reached. In some instances the entire lesson core would be taken up with a repeat of the work of the previous lesson.

After sufficient time has been given to the review, the new learning experiences are presented. Skill instruction, participation in a rhythmic activity, or a progression of stunts and tumbling are the kinds of things which are in the lesson core.

The amount of time to be devoted to the lesson core is determined by the time demands of the other three parts of the lesson. After introductory and developmental activities have been done, the remainder of the time, less that needed for the closing activity, can be devoted to the lesson core.

The Closing Activity

Closing activity can take many different forms. The lesson can be completed with a game or other fun activity for the purpose of finishing up with something the children know and enjoy. The game should be simple in nature and one in which all the children have a vigorous part, so that a pleasurable feeling is taken away to the next class after the physical education class.

A consideration in closing the lesson is returning equipment, apparatus, and supplies to their proper storage places. This should utilize student responsibility with definite as-

signments. Squads under the direction of leaders can assume this responsibility.

The closing activity could take the form of group evaluation, with suggestions for future procedure. This is reinforcement of learning and contributes to a better learning climate.

In some lessons, the closing activity may be minimal or deleted entirely. This might be the case when a game or other activity as the core of the lesson demands as much time as possible.

THE DESIGN OF THE WRITTEN LESSON PLAN

A written lesson plan should be made out for each physical education lesson. The plan should contain all information needed for the teacher to ensure progression, unity, and completeness. Some teachers find it helpful to have a form which saves time and effort and includes all necessary information. The format given as an example provides the following data:

General Information

Name of school, classroom or class involved, date, activity.

Specific Objectives of the Lesson

A short description of the specific things the lesson is trying to accomplish.

Supplies and Equipment Needed and the Initial Arrangement of These

A list of the materials needed, indicating the specific number of each item.

The Lesson Description

This should be divided into the four parts of the lesson — introductory activities, developmental activities, the lesson core, and the closing activity. Under each should be listed the time allotment for the activity, the specific learning experiences, and the organizational and teaching procedures. Under the heading of "content" should be included hints for performance or form, points to be stressed as important to the activity or skill, safety factors and concepts to be brought out. Organizational and teaching procedures specify how the children will be arranged for the various learning experiences and how the teaching process is to proceed.

The Evaluation

During and after the lesson, the teacher should note what was covered and with what success. The teacher should make notes to himself for directions for future lessons.

Some teachers may question the feasibility of writing out lesson plans, saying that it takes too much time and effort, and is not really needed. From the standpoint of length, a lesson plan should be precise enough to be an effective guide for the learning experiences. The length of a lesson plan would depend upon the background of each instructor. Beginning teachers necessarily will need to provide more detail than a more experienced instructor. A lesson plan should be understandable as a functional tool. Some teachers may need only a word or a phrase to suggest an idea or a procedure, while others may need more written directions. This understanding should be apparent at the time of teaching and also when it is necessary to refer to a lesson already given.

A specimen lesson plan is detailed for a lesson in simple ball skills on the third grade level. The plan illustrates the four parts of the lesson.

LESSON PLAN FOR PHYSICAL EDUCATION

School: __Washington__   Classroom: __3rd — Jones__   Date: __10/3/71__   Teacher: __Sweeney__

Activity: __Bowling at Pins — Gym__

Objectives of This Lesson

Introduce bowling at clubs.
Learn reasonable form.

Materials Needed

8 playground balls — 8½"
8 Indian clubs

Initial Arrangement of Equipment

None

Time Min.	Specific Activity	Organization and Teaching Procedures	Content — Hints, Stress Points, Safety
2	Introductory Activity	One-half scattered, down on hands and knees. Change on whistle. If time, change to second activity.	Go over the down person — hop, jump, etc. Use any order. Watch out for others. Stress being high enough and landing lightly. Down people form high bridge. Change to going under. Stress low crawling in alligator fashion.
5	Developmental Activity	Scattered at their floor places. Bent-over position.	Practice swimming strokes: Crawl, breast, dolphin, back. Change time factors: Slow, fast, slow to fast, fast to slow. Change levels, raising and lowering.
		Face down on floor. Change to supine position.	Repeat above. Try each movement slowly and then fast. Bring up same foot and hand. Bring up opposite foot and hand.

Time Min.	Specific Activity	Organization and Teaching Procedures	Content — Hints, Stress Points, Safety
			Bring both feet up and hands. Bring both feet, touch with crossed hands. Touch one foot as far out to the side as possible. Other foot. Reach high with one foot. Make figures, write words and name. Other foot.
2	Lecture and Demonstration	Group seated in semicircle. Get ball.	Explain bowling: Face forward, feet together. Right hand under, left hand over ball. Bring both hands back, slight twist at waist. Weight change on delivery. Good follow-through, ball off fingers. Lower body with knee bend. Eyes forward on target. Demonstrate.
4	Dry Run Practice	Scattered at home positions.	Repeat the directions. Each done slowly. Use "Ready, back, roll" (3 counts).
5	Practice	Squad divided, each half in shuttle formation across the floor. Use one squad for demonstration. All squads participate.	Squad leaders get 2 balls. Roll back and forth. Stress accurate rolling.
5	Bowl at Clubs	Same as above, but 2 students at club, one to handle ball and one the club.	Each squad leader gets 2 clubs. Practice bowling at the club. Right and left. Change club to other end.
5	Game — Bowling One-Step	Need club setter, ball chaser. Child stands 5 yards back.	Each child takes a turn at bowling. He keeps going as long as he hits the club. Each time he does, he takes one step backward, until he reaches the line. Rotate to setter and chaser.
2	Evaluation and Closing	Seated in semicircle.	Questions: What are the important things to remember about bowling? What makes a ball curve? What do we mean by "follow-through?" What foot do we step with?

INTRODUCTORY ACTIVITY

The chief characteristic of introductory activity is its vigorous nature. Gross movements, generally locomotor activity, are employed, but the activity can take many forms. It should challenge every student with movement, should not be rigidly structured, and should allow considerable freedom of movement.

Introductory activity should require only brief instructions, as its purpose is to get the children into activity quickly. Abrupt changes in direction, in the kinds of movements, and in the pace of activities predominate. Moving and stopping is another pattern often used. The first activity presented is European Rhythmic Running, which represents a strong bias of the author for inclusion.

European Rhythmic Running

Some type of rhythmic running is done in many countries of Europe to open the daily lesson. Essentially, this is light, rhythmic running to the accompaniment of some type of percussion, usually a drum or tom-tom. Skilled runners do not need accompaniment, but merely keep time with a leader.

Much of the running follows a circular path, but it can follow other patterns. To introduce a group of children to rhythmic running, have them stand in circular formation and clap to the beat of the drum. Next, as they clap, they can shuffle their feet in place, keeping time. Following this, have them run in place, omitting the clapping. The children should now be ready to move in a prescribed path with the run. It is essential that the run be light, bouncy, and rhythmic, keeping strict time with the beat.

A number of movement ideas can be combined with the rhythmic running pattern.

1. On signal (whistle or double beat on the drum), runners freeze in place. Resume running when the regular beat begins again.

2. On signal, make a running full turn in four running steps. Lift knees high while turning.

3. Have children clap hands every fourth beat as they run. Instead of clapping, sound a brisk "hey" on the fourth beat, raising one arm and fist on the sound.

4. Run in squad formation. Follow the path set by the squad leader.

Rhythmic Running, Circular Fashion

Gross Locomotor Movements and Changes

Most of these patterns involve either a change from one locomotor movement to another, a change in direction, or a stop in a specified position. Some examples of variations in free locomotor movements are:

1. Free running. Run in any direction, changing direction at will. Or, run and do giant leaps as you wish.

2. Running and changing direction. Run in any direction, changing direction abruptly on signal. Change levels on signal.

3. Running and changing the type of movements. On signal, change to a different type

of locomotion. The change could be free choice or specified. Change of direction and a change of the locomotor movement could be combined.

4. Running and stopping. Run and, on signal, freeze.

5. Running and assuming a specified position or pose. Run and on signal assume a pose such as push-up position, a balance task, or a specified shape.

6. Running, stopping, and doing a task. Run and on signal stop and do a specified task such as exercises, jumping in place, or a stunt.

7. Different locomotor movements to the beat of the drum. Most of the above ideas can be incorporated with rhythmic accompaniment.

8. Tortoise and Hare. Run in place slowly (tortoise), and on signal change to a very rapid run (hare), but still in place.

9. Combinations of movements. A flow of several movements can be specified, such as run, skip, and roll. Or, jump, twist, and shake.

Most of the routines use two signals. The first signals the change, and the second tells the children to revert to the original pattern (running). Running has been used in most of the routines, but other locomotor movements can be substituted.

Partner or Group Activities

Partner or group activities offer excellent opportunities for introductory work.

1. Marking. The children can do what the English call "marking." Each child has a partner, somewhat equal in ability. One partner runs, dodges, and tries to lose the other partner, who must stay within one yard of him. On signal, both stop. The chaser must be able to touch his partner to say he has "marked" him.

2. Follow Activity. One partner leads and performs various kinds of movements. The other partner must move in the same fashion. This idea can also be extended to squad organization.

3. Partner Carry. One partner carries the other. On signal, reverse positions.

4. Group Over and Under. One-half the children are scattered. Each is in a curled position. The other children leap or jump over the down children. On signal, reverse the groups quickly. Instead of being curled, the down children form arches or bridges, then the moving children should go under these. A further extension is to have the children on the floor alternate between curled and bridge positions. If a moving child goes over the curled position, the floor child immediately changes to a bridge. The moving children react accordingly.

5. New Leader. Squads run around the area, following a leader. When the change is signaled, the last person goes to the head of the line and becomes the leader.

6. Manipulative Activity. Each child has a beanbag. The children move around the area, tossing the bags upwards and catching them as they move. On signal, they drop the bags to the floor and jump, hop, or leap over as many bags as possible. On the next signal, they pick up any convenient bag and resume tossing to themselves. One less beanbag than children adds to the fun. Hoops can also be used in this manner. Children begin by using hoops in rope jumping style. On signal, the hoops are placed on the floor, and the children jump in and out of as many hoops as they can. Next, they pick up a near hoop and resume jumping. The activity can also be done with jumping ropes.

Tambourine-Directed Activity

The tambourine can signal changes of movement because of its ability to produce two different kinds of sounds. The first sound is a tinny noise made by vigorous shaking. The second is a percussion sound made by striking the tambourine as a drum, either with the knuckles or the elbow. Movement changes are signaled by changing from one tambourine sound to the other. Suggestions are listed according to the types of sound:

Shaking Sound

1. Children remain in one spot but shake all over. These should be gross movements.

2. Same movement, but children gradually drop to the floor (level change).

3. Children scurry in every direction.

4. Children run very lightly with tiny steps.

Drum Sound

1. Jerky movements to the drumbeat.
2. Jumping in place or covering space.
3. Locomotor movements in keeping with the drumbeat.
4. Using three beats of the drum — collapse (beat one), roll (beat two), and form a shape (beat three).

To form a combination of movements, select one from each category. When the shaking sound is made, the children perform that movement. When the change is made to the drum sound, the children react accordingly.

Games

Selected games are quite suitable for introductory activity, provided they keep all children active, are simple, and require little teaching. A familiar game saves organization time. Some appropriate games are listed:

Addition Tag, page 296.

Loose Caboose, page 301.

Stop and Start, page 285.

Circus Master, page 276.

One, Two, Button My Shoe, page 278.

Squad Tag, page 302.

Miscellaneous Approaches

Children can run laps around a field or gymnasium for warm-up.

Certain pieces of manipulative equipment, such as jump ropes, balls, hoops, and wands can be put out. Children can be directed to practice as they wish for a few minutes.

Climbing ropes, climbing structures, mats, boxes, balance beams and/or benches can be arranged so the children may have practice on a selected piece of equipment as they wish.

9

The Physical Development Goal

What Is Physical Fitness?
Guidelines for Achieving Physical Fitness
Fitness Elements of the School Physical
    Education Program
Motivation in Physical Fitness

Few children, left to their own devices, will engage in systematic and demanding exercise sufficient to satisfy the body's basic need for physical activity. It is granted that some children are quite active and seem to be in perpetual motion. But what about the masses of children whose living habits have been influenced by the ease of modern living and the benefits of modern technology? Gone now are the chores and the physical demands of the homes of the past. The school literally and actually has inherited the task of keeping America's children physically fit.

The discussions which follow stress physical fitness as an important goal in physical education. In no sense do we imply that it is the only goal worth seeking, nor is it the most important goal. Some American programs can be justly criticized for going overboard on fitness. The viewpoint that should be established is that physical fitness is an important goal of physical education, and that a positive approach in action must be taken or the goal will not be realized. On the other side of the picture, it should also not be regarded as a concomitant goal growing out of a program employing a particular kind of methodology or approach. Some strong proponents of educational movement regard physical fitness developmental activities as unsuitable learning experiences because of the direct teaching

approach, labeling them as "training activities" rather than educational experiences.

WHAT IS PHYSICAL FITNESS?

A person who is physically fit possesses the strength and stamina to carry out his daily tasks without undue fatigue and still has enough energy to enjoy leisure and to meet unforeseen emergencies. The definition can be broken down into a number of concepts:

1. A person should possess enough strength, power, endurance, flexibility, agility, coordination, balance, and speed to do easily and effectively the routine duties and maximum tasks that the day may bring.

2. He should be free from disease and removable handicapping disorders.

3. He should possess a sturdy physique, which means a well-developed body with proper proportions of bone, muscle, and fat tissue. His posture should be acceptable and evidence of good nutritional habits should be present

4. At the end of the day he should be sleepy, but not overly tired. He should be able to sleep well and feel recovered in the morning from the activities of the preceding day.

The Health Appraisal and Physical Fitness

The first step in establishing a firm foundation for physical fitness is the identification of pupils with correctable orthopedic and other health problems and subsequent referral to medical authorities. A child's health status is determined by medical evaluation in the form of a periodic health appraisal. Correctable defects and health problems should be referred for professional attention. After such measures have been taken to bring up the level of the child's health to the highest standard possible, the child can then effectively benefit from the school physical education program. The appraisal may also uncover in a few children certain permanent health conditions or handicaps which demand special consideration in the form of adapted programs tailored to the child's difficulty.

An ideal, but not practical, standard is that each child undergo a health appraisal each and every year of his school career. A more practical standard is to have the child examined at the beginning of different stages of his school career, i.e., kindergarten-primary, intermediate school, junior high school, high school, and college. In addition, health appraisals should be scheduled when health conditions need clarification.

The health appraisal becomes a meaningful procedure under two conditions. The first is that information from the health appraisal is available to and utilized effectively by the teacher to consider appropriate measures for the physical limitations of certain children. The second is that referral is made for health conditions needing attention. A large majority of the children will have no restrictions placed on participation. A few may need special consideration in their activities. These special considerations must be known and followed.

GUIDELINES FOR ACHIEVING PHYSICAL FITNESS

An important guideline for conducting the physical education program is recognition that physical fitness can be acquired only through the medium of muscular effort and is maintained only through continued activity. A second guideline, closely related to the first, is that, to raise levels of fitness, the child must exercise regularly and must participate in a progressive program. Motivation is important and progression must be incorporated so students will be taxed at the level of effort necessary for development. A third guideline is that the type of activity must be geared to the age, sex, and physical condition of the child. Flexibility must be built into the program, to take care of the needs of all children.

A fourth guideline involves viewing physical fitness in the light of its components. If each of the respective components is given emphasis, then collectively the development of physical fitness will be accomplished. The most important measurable components of physical fitness are strength, power, and cardiorespiratory endurance. Agility and flexibility rate only slightly less in importance, followed by such qualities as speed, balance, and coordination. It should be noted that balance and coordination, while of secondary importance *as components* of physical fitness, are of high importance in the perceptual-motor competency area. These are related more to movement competency than to physical fitness, but still are considered a part of fitness.

The development of each of the components of physical fitness is discussed in turn.

1. Strength. Strength refers to the ability of a muscle or muscle group to exert force. Among the child's learning experiences in physical education, there must be sufficient big muscle activity over a wide range of activities done regularly and with enough intensity to develop strength. The improvement of strength is a basic necessity to the development of physical fitness. Muscles can be developed only through stress and the tension applied during exercise. A physiological principle important in this process is that of loading the muscle. This principle holds that as the limits of the demand (load) for muscular work are increased, strength also increases. We need to make our children work progressively harder if strength is to be developed.

Strength is necessary in skill performance, since without strength a low standard of performance can be expected, as muscles give out before they can reach their skill potential.

2. Power. Power implies the process of using strength to apply force for effective movement. Power is based on strength and its application to movement. Teaching youngsters how to move effectively in situations demanding an application of force will develop the ability to apply powerful movements when needed.

3. Endurance. Endurance refers to the ability to carry on muscular effort over a period of time. It has a basis in strength in that the stronger person is able to keep up muscular effort longer than one without adequate strength. However, there are other involvements in the body. Primarily, this is a postponement of the stages of fatigue so that muscular work can be carried on. A person with good endurance has a conditioning involving the cardiorespiratory system and other deep body mechanisms.

4. Agility. Agility refers to the ability to change direction swiftly, easily, and under good control. A particularly agile person is one who is hard to catch in a tag game. He can dodge and change direction well.

Agility is a needed safety quality. Many persons today are alive and free from injury because they were agile enough to get out of the way of a moving object.

5. Flexibility. Flexibility is a person's range of movement at the joints. A flexible child can stretch farther, touch his toes, bend farther, etc. He has more freedom of movement and can adjust his body to various movement challenges more readily. Youngsters need movement experiences where they can stretch, reach, bend, hang, and otherwise force the joints into maximum ranges of movement.

6. Speed. The ability to move quickly and rapidly is a needed skill in many physical activities. While there are inherent limitations of ultimate speed, each youngster should have the opportunity to develop efficient speed with respect to his potential. Among fitness qualities, speed has a high prestige factor, as illustrated by track stars and the ultimate Olympic winners.

7. Balance. Balance is the ability to maintain control of the equilibrium in a variety of positions and movements. The control of balance is of particular importance in kindergarten and first and second grades, but has value at all levels. Program elements should cover three aspects of balance: (1) *Static Balance,* the ability to maintain equilibrium in a fixed position; (2) *Dynamic Balance,* maintaining balance while moving or engaging in

action; and (3) *Rotational Balance,* the ability to maintain or regain balance after turning, rolling, or other maneuvers while not in contact with the floor or apparatus.

8. Coordination. Coordination refers to the harmonious functioning of muscles in producing complex movements. Generally, a movement of high skill well done demands a high degree of coordination. A characteristic of many people with high levels of physical fitness is their graceful carriage, fluidity of motion, and ability to meet the challenge of more complex movements.

FITNESS — ELEMENTS OF THE SCHOOL PHYSICAL EDUCATION PROGRAM

To accomplish the physical fitness objective, the physical education program can channel its emphasis into five major elements of an overall program.

1. Developmental Activities.
2. Program Activities.
3. The Testing Program.
4. The Program for the Physically-Underdeveloped Child.
5. The Extended Program.

Physical Developmental Activities

Developmental activities are those carried on primarily to develop physical fitness with little consideration for the other goals of physical education. Included in this category are exercises (calisthenics), circuit training, grass drills, astronaut drills, jogging, and the like. Isometric exercises and individual tug-of-war ropes are also valuable.

Probably the most appropriate place to begin formal fitness work of these types is in the third grade. However, some instructors have found first and second grade children quite receptive to these drills. For children in kindergarten through the second grade, effective use can be made of the basic movement methodology, with emphasis on gross body movements, leading to the total body development.

No matter what the approach, specific attention should be centered on strengthening the traditionally weak areas of the abdominal wall and arm-shoulder girdle.

In Chapter 10, the implementation of a for

mal physical developmental program is presented, together with procedures for the recommended physical fitness routines.

Program Activities and Physical Fitness

The types of activities included in the physical education program should be selected *and* conducted with the physical fitness goal in mind. There should be a rugged and demanding program, measured by the criterion of how much physical work the individual child receives during the lesson. Children should be kept active.

Many of the usual physical education activities involve primarily the use of the legs, lower back, hands, and arms. A good program will include hanging and arm-support activities, which are generally used insufficiently in programs. The inclusion of rope climbing, ladder work, horizontal bar stunts, and similar hanging activities is important in making sure that the upper torso is developed proportionately to other parts of the body.

Another approach to upper body development, which has particular relevance to the kindergarten and primary levels, is the principle of including activities during which the children get down on the floor in movements and positions where the body is partially supported by the arms. Care must be taken to include a variety of positions, including the crab position, where the body is supported by the hands and feet, but faces the ceiling.

The trend toward more stunts and tumbling activities in the program will pay off in total body development. These activities also provide ample opportunity for the exercise of balance control.

To achieve endurance, the program must make demands on the individual in the form of muscular effort which causes accelerated breathing. Generally, this involves activities including running or other sustained movement. No activity should be carried on to the point where the participants are breathless. However, the children need to push themselves beyond the first inclination to cease.

The conditioning for endurance connotes increased dosages. Many athletic coaches adhere to this principle by gradually increasing the dosages of activity until the athletes can participate in a full-length game. Teachers are cautioned that a process of this nature takes time. If the children are to play an active game (like soccer), they must be brought up gradually to the level of endurance through increased dosages of activity.

Rope skipping to music, rhythmic running (European style), and similar movements contribute to the development of endurance.

Agility can be developed in many games, relays, and similar activities. The development is not automatic, however, and children need to be taught how to stop, start, and change direction properly.

Flexibility can be furthered by stimulating children to extend the limits of joint movement in twisting, bending, and rotational movements, particularly in the stunts and tumbling program. Children need to be urged to extremes in joint movements by such directives as, "See how far you can stretch," or "How far can you bend?"

Relays, simple games, and sports provide opportunities to practice speedy movement. Chase and tag games are particularly valuable in this respect, as well as for reinforcing agility. Track and field activities provide instruction in proper running techniques.

Testing for Physical Fitness

A testing program is essential to the fitness program. Testing should uncover low-fitness students, measure the status of the remainder, determine needed areas for improvement, create motivation for the students, and provide material for public relations. Certainly, much of the effectiveness of the physical education program can be measured with respect to how it meets the challenge of fitness.

As a minimum, testing should take place at the beginning and end of the school year. Another testing period may be administered at the middle of the year to check progress at the half-way point. The progress of low-fitness children should be checked more often.

A valid, reliable, and accepted test should be employed. A widely used test, and one which this source recommends for consideration, is that from the *Blue Book* of the President's Council on Physical Fitness. This test was patterned by a national committee after an earlier California test, and has national norms interpreted either in the form of categories or in percentiles. (See Appendix for directions and norms for the test.)

Another recommended test, which is simpler and less time-consuming, has been developed and adopted in Oregon. (See Appendix.) An advantage of this test is that it can be administered during one regular class period. In contrast, the national test takes at least two periods and usually more. The Oregon test provides an overall fitness score, while the national test stresses only individual item analysis.

The President's Council on Physical Fitness and Sports has also developed a screening test which has value for quick identification of physically underdeveloped children. The test consists of three items, and sets basic minimums for strength, flexibility, and agility. Directions and norms for the test are included in the Appendix.

A screening test generally establishes basic minimums which must be met, or the child is screened out for further investigation. It is not to be regarded as a diagnostic tool, but merely a device to identify quickly the more deficient children. In some cases, the borderline student can meet the basic physical minimums and is not so identified. However, children with serious deficiencies can be readily identified by a screening test. The regular physical fitness test gives more detailed and relative information about fitness levels of all children, including those who are physically underdeveloped.

Teachers should note that few tests are considered feasible below the fourth grade, and most test norms begin with that grade level.

Test results for each individual should be a matter of school record and a consideration in his overall school evaluation. Since fitness is a good indication of the child's health, his fitness scores should be a part of his health record, to follow him throughout his school career.

The Program for the Physically Underdeveloped Child

After the physically underdeveloped pupils have been identified, the next step is a determination of possible causes of underdevelopment. A professional approach to the diagnosis is needed. An examination of the child's health status should be made through available health records. If indicated, an examination by a physician should be scheduled. Next, through consultation with the child and his parents, the health habits of the child should be evaluated.

Steps should be taken to correct any unsatisfactory health conditions. If health habits also need adjustment, changes toward improved healthful living are in order. It would be futile to prescribe an increased physical work load when the causes of the underdevelopment lay elsewhere.

After the areas of personal health and health habits have received appropriate consideration, it becomes a matter of prescribing an individualized program so that the child may increase in those qualities of physical fitness in which he is deficient. An excellent approach to the problem of the underdeveloped child is on a committee basis. Such a committee can be composed of the school nurse, a physician, the school principal, the physical education supervisor or teacher, and elementary school teachers. Each case can be reviewed and remedial measures prescribed.

The measures can be extra and specialized work in the regular class period, extra periods beyond the regular class schedule, afterschool or Saturday work, or special summer instruction.

The burden of raising the fitness level must be on the child. The goal of the low-fitness program is not only to help the child achieve independence in raising his level of fitness but also to provide him with procedures and motivation with which he can maintain an acceptable level of fitness.

Cooperation with the home is also essential. Corrective and developmental measures will succeed only if there is cooperation from the parents. It is advantageous to assign homework in the form of physical activities which the student is able to do at home. Both the parent and the child should understand why the child is in the low-fitness group and what direction their efforts should take to have the child reach a desirable level of fitness. Some schools find it helpful to have printed material with appropriate activities as homework. The particular activities to be stressed by the child can be checked, providing a more scientific approach than a word-of-mouth method. The directive should include not only the activities to be done, but also directions and illustrations for proper execution.

As the child works toward better fitness, period retesting is important. Besides providing an indication of progress, the testing provides motivation in itself.

Working with underdeveloped children is a rewarding experience. For many of these children, it is the first time that someone has paid particular attention to them and attempted to help them with their problems. Both the underdeveloped child and his parents usually take pride in his evident progress.

The Extended Fitness Program

The school physical education program alone cannot provide all necessary physical activity for proper development. It must provide, however, a good beginning and the necessary motivation toward improved fitness. The school can extend program experiences into other areas.

The school playground should provide suitable play space and be equipped with appropriate apparatus so that it can function as a laboratory for the learning experiences of the physical education program. Climbing structures, monkey rings, horizontal ladder types, and exercise bars are examples of the kinds of playground equipment which have good fitness development potential.

An obstacle course can be a part of the school's outdoor opportunities. Obstacle courses can be set up compactly or arranged on an extended layout. Schools have also found it profitable to lay out jogging courses on the school grounds.

For both boys and girls, an intramural program, growing out of the experiences of the physical education activities, should be operated. Saturday morning recreational programs can also extend the opportunities. A sound interschool competitive program is a further extension, mostly for the benefit of the more skilled. Special clubs such as a sports group or tumbling club provide outlets for special interests.

Municipal recreation programs, particularly during summer vacation months, can take up some of the slack when schools are not in session. Recreation groups can also cooperate with the schools in making the facilities available during the long Christmas and Spring vacations.

The interest in and motivation for physical activity will often carry over into the home. Basketball goals and badminton courts are sometimes constructed. Climbing frames and chinning bars of home design can be made. More important than just providing equipment is the moral support and push that parents can provide to stimulate youngsters to become eager participants in regular activity.

MOTIVATION IN PHYSICAL FITNESS

The physical education program can provide strong motivation, which is important in the fitness picture if the child is to be stimulated to good effort. Since fitness values are in proportion to the effort expended relative to the present status of physical fitness, educationally sound drives and incentives can provide reinforcement of the learning experiences of the gymnasium and playground. Some considerations for motivation follow:

1. The school can adopt the award system promoted nationally by the President's Council (see appendix) to recognize commendable levels of physical fitness as measured by the national physical fitness test of the Council. However, the school system may wish to base its award system on another accepted test and can establish achievement levels similarly, using the 85th percentile as the basic minimum award standard. In the norms, a student must achieve the 85th percentile in all testing items to qualify for the award.

2. A second type of award is for commendable progress. This would stimulate and serve to reward low achievers in physical development to attain satisfactory levels. The system would also enable the school to recognize good achievement in terms of progress which would be short of the higher standards set for awards like those of the President's Council.

3. The bulletin board in the gymnasium and in the classroom can be utilized for items of interest and stimulation with regard to fitness. The material should be up-to-date and changed periodically.

4. Although a fallacy exists in trying to get

"everyone over the average," the publication of school norms and records gives the students a goal.

5. The use of visual aids should be exploited. A number of good films dealing with fitness are available.

6. An excellent motivation for fitness is an understanding by each child concerning the values of physical fitness and how, physiologically, fitness can be developed and maintained.

7. As previously mentioned, cooperation by the home is essential. Children are more likely to be fit if their parents are concerned about fitness.

8. School demonstrations for parents and physical education exhibitions can feature the topic of fitness.

9. The level of fitness should be an item on the periodic school report of the child's progress to the parent.

10. Some caution is urged in the use of contests between classes and/or schools based on fitness statistics. This can place undue pressure on low-fitness children, and can lead to undesirable peer relationships.

10

Implementing the School Physical Fitness Program

In planning a fitness program for the school year, it is well to establish variety in activities and include a number of different approaches or means of fitness development. Reliance on a single approach to develop fitness is not sound, as children get tired of "the same old stuff" and lose motivation, an all-important factor in stimulating children to good effort. Variety is educational, promotes interest, and assures a broader approach to body development. This approach also tends to minimize any inherent weaknesses or lacks in any one routine.

No matter what the selection of developmental activity, sound criteria governing good fitness methodology and theory need to be considered. The criteria need to provide answers to the major concerns of a fitness program:

1. How can we structure a physical environment so that the physical developmental needs of the child are met?

2. How does the child feel (react) to these experiences?

3. What will be his concern in the future with respect to his obligation to himself to maintain a fitness level commensurate with his needs and interests?

CRITERIA FOR FITNESS DRILLS AND ROUTINES

Certain criteria are important in the selection and conduct of activities for the development of physical fitness.

1. The activity be capable of developing physical fitness and should lend itself to progressive doses.

2. It should not involve danger and should demand only simple skills.

3. It should require a minimum of equipment and be appropriate to the space demands of the modern school.

4. It should require only a small expenditure of time.

5. It should consider individual differences.

6. It should provide carry-over value to the child's daily living program.

7. It should allow opportunity for student leadership in conducting the drills.

8. In every drill or routine, there should be at least one activity centered on abdominal wall development, and one pointed toward the arm-shoulder girdle.

9. The activity should be interesting so that the child will be motivated toward all-out effort.

10. Planning should consider two separate groups of children: (1) kindergarten through grade 2, and (2) grades 3 through 6. The needs, characteristics, and capacities of younger children indicate a more informal approach for them in contrast to a more rigid fitness program for the older children to in-

clude the more formal fitness routines and drills.

PLANNING A YEAR'S PROGRAM FOR GRADES K-2

Each lesson should begin with introductory activity, which also has fitness implications. This is generally, but not necessarily, some type of gross locomotor activity. Much of this involves heavy demands on the lower limbs and serves as an introductory and warm-up activity for the fitness activities to follow.

Movement experiences, selected according to kind and conducted toward fitness outcomes, seem to be the best fitness approach for younger children. The patterns are based upon the principles of basic movement, but more emphasis is centered on direct teaching methodology and gross body movements. At times, the teacher may wish to employ some of the more formal fitness routines explained in the fitness program for grades 3 through 6. These must, of course, be modified to fit younger children. Exercises and a simplified form of circuit training seem to offer the best opportunity. However, movement experiences are flexible enough to induce a wide variety of movement, which can include many of the exercises.

Movement Experiences for Fitness (K-2)

Many big-muscle experiences can be structured for children, assuring demands on all, or at least most parts of the body. To assure that the various areas of the body receive attention and that several elements of fitness (strength, flexibility, agility, etc.) are considered, the following sequence is suggested. The sequence is based on successive attention to various parts of the body.

Trunk Development

Included in this category are bending, twisting, stretching, and similar movements. While the movements will necessarily include the limbs, the emphasis is on gross body movements, which include movements making demands on the abdominal region.

Arm-Shoulder Girdle Emphasis

The key to developmental possibilities in this area is to have the children take the weight of the body partially or wholly on the hands. This means getting them down on the floor on hands and feet.

Leg Development

Activities which make demands on the legs will include movements in flight (locomotor) and movements in place (nonlocomotor). Running should be included at times.

Methodology

In working with the three movement categories, it is recognized that many movements will contribute to more than one body area, and in some cases to all three divisions. This is understandable, but the emphasis on gross movement fitness work during any one daily lesson must be such that all three body areas receive appropriate work demands.

In all three categories, movements can be locomotor or they can be in place. If the movement is locomotor, the children must be directed to move in such a fashion that the desired area of the body will be exercised.

If the movements are done in place (nonlocomotor), generally two elements are necessary. The first is to put the student into some kind of a position and proceed from this base. The second is to provide a number of challenges or directives so movements having fitness values for that area of the body will occur. Inventiveness and imagination on the part of the teacher or leader are essential ingredients to successful movement work.

The formations for basic movement (page 136) can be employed for locomotor movements. Nonlocomotor movements are generally done with the children scattered or in extended squad formation.

Trunk Development

Movements which include bending, stretching, swaying, twisting, reaching, and forming shapes are important inclusions here. No particular continuity exists, except that a specified approach should move from the simple to the more complex.

The most logical approach is to select one or more of the above movements and use it or them as the theme for the day. Vary the position the child is to take — standing, lying, kneeling, sitting, etc. From the selected position, stimulate the child to varied movement based on the theme for the day. Examples follow with regard to how the different types of trunk movements can become both fitness and learning experiences for youngsters.

Bending

Bend in different ways.

Bend as many parts of the body as you can.

Make different shapes by bending two, three, and four parts of the body.

Bend the arms, knees in different ways and on different levels.

Try different ways of bending the fingers and wrist of one hand with the other. Use some resistance. Add body bends.

Stretching

Keeping one foot in place, stretch your arms in different directions, stepping as you move with the free foot. Stretch at different levels.

On the floor, stretch one leg different ways in space. Stretch one leg in one direction and the other leg in another direction.

Stretch slowly as you wish and then snap back to original position.

Stretch with different arm-leg combinations in diverse directions.

See how much space on the floor you can cover by stretching. Show us how big your space is.

Combine bending and stretching movements.

Swaying and Twisting

Sway your body back and forth in different directions. Change the position of the arms.

Sway your body bending over.

Sway your head from side to side.

Select a part of the body, twist as far as you can in opposite directions.

Twist your body at different levels.

Twist two or more parts of the body at the same time.

Twist one part of the body while untwisting another.

Twist your head to see as far back as you can.

Twist like a spring; like a screwdriver.

Stand on one foot and twist your body. Untwist.

From a seated position, make different shapes by twisting.

Forming Shapes

Children love to form different shapes with their bodies, and this interest should be utilized to aid in trunk development. Shapes can be formed in most any position—standing, sitting, lying, balancing on parts of the body, and moving. Shapes can be curled or stretched, narrow or wide, big or little, symmetrical or asymmetrical, twisted or straight.

Abdominal Emphasis

The best position to ensure exercise of the abdominal muscles is to have the child lying supine on the floor or mat. Challenges should direct him to lift the upper and lower portions of the body from the floor either singly or together. The following are examples of directives to a child lying on his back on the floor:

Sit up and touch both toes with your hands.

Sit up and touch the right toe with the left hand. The other way.

Bring up your toes to touch behind your head.

With hands to the side, bring your feet up straight and then touch them by the right hand. By the left hand.

Lift your feet up slowly an inch at a time. Without bending your knees.

Pick up your heels about 6" from the floor and swing them back and forth. Cross them and twist them.

Lift your head from the floor and look at your toes. Wink with your right eye and wiggle your left foot. Reverse.

Arm-Shoulder Girdle Development Activity

Movement experiences contributing to arm-shoulder girdle development can be divided roughly into two groups of activities. The first includes movements where the arms are free of any body support function. In the second the arms support the body weight either wholly or in part.

In the first group, where the arms are free, movements such as swinging, pulling, pushing, lifting, and reaching can be exploited for development.

Swinging and Circling

Swing one limb (arm or leg) at a time, different directions and levels.

Combine two limb movements (arm-arm, leg-leg, or arm-leg combinations) in the same direction and in opposite directions. Vary levels.

Swing arms or legs back and forth and go into giant circles.

Swing arms as if swimming—bent-over position. Try a backstroke or a breaststroke. What does a sidestroke look like?

Make the arms go like a windmill. Go in different directions.

How else can you circle your arms?

Pretend a swarm of bees are around your head. Brush them off and keep them away.

Reaching and Pulling

Reach high into the sky and pull stars toward you.

Using both hands, pull something high, pull something low. Pull from different directions.

Reach out and grab snowflakes. Did you get one?

Pull from different positions — kneeling, sitting, lying.

Reach out in one direction as far as you can and then reach out with the same hand in the opposite direction. Reach out high in one direction and low in another.

With your hands clasped behind your head, pull your head forward. See if you can make wind by waving your elbows back and forth.

From a sitting position, pull on your knees and legs. Can you pull your big toe up to your nose? Try it with the other foot.

Reach up and climb a ladder to the sky. See how high you can reach.

Pushing

Pretend to push something heavy with both hands. Push it at a high level. Push it at a low level.

Push up the sky slowly. Hold it up with your feet on tiptoes.

Push with one hand then the other. Alternate hands back and forth.

From a kneeling position, push yourself up to a stand.

Lie on your tummy. Push yourself backwards with your hands. Push yourself right and left.

Sit on the floor with legs outstretched. Place your hands alongside your seat and lift your seat off the floor.

Lifting

Lift your arms as high as you can. Extend them out wide. Bring them close.

Kneel down. Start your arms low and lift them high. See how many different ways you can lift them.

Pretend you are lifting and throwing logs. Throw in different directions. How high can you lift your log?

Developmental Activities Based on the Push-Up Position

Each child is asked to assume the push-up position, which he uses as a base of operation. The challenges require a movement and then a return to the original push-up position.

PUSH-UP POSITION

From this position we ask the children if they can —

Lift one foot high. Now the other foot.

Bounce both feet up and down. Move the feet out from each other while bouncing.

Inch the feet up to the hands and go back again. Inch the feet up to the hands and then inch the hands out to return to the push-up position.

Reach up with one hand and touch the other shoulder behind the back.

Lift both hands from the floor. Try clapping the hands.

Bounce from the floor with both hands and feet off the floor at the same time.

Turn over so the back is to the floor. Complete the turn to push-up position.

Lower the body an inch at a time until the chest touches the floor. Return.

Inch the hands (one at a time at first) out to the sides. Return.

There is value in maintaining the push-up position for a length of time. The various tasks to be done provide interest and challenge to the youngsters. The informal and individual approach stimulates the child to good effort in muscular work.

The crab position should also be utilized in a similar fashion. The side leaning rest postion is another which may be employed. Many of the same directives listed above for the push-up position can be used with modification for that position.

PLANNING A YEAR'S PROGRAM FOR GRADES 3-6

In contrast to the program for the lower grades, the emphasis in fitness shifts to more formalized drills and routines, with less stress on exploratory movement. A well-executed exercise program should be the basis for the fitness activities for grades 3-6. Exercises must be learned and learned well, as they are basic to other routines. Exercises should be given in both the regular fashion and to music. Other routines which are effective and add variety to fitness work are isometrics, circuit training, continuity exercises, grass drills, astronaut drills, obstacle course, jogging, and a number of miscellaneous activities. How a selection of these can be incorporated into a year's program is illustrated. Following the year's program, each of the fitness routines is discussed in turn.

Illustration of a Year's Program for Grades 3-6

The following is an example of a year's program for grades 3-6, including six different fitness routines, scheduled over a 36-week period. Some adaptation to school schedules may need to be made depending upon vacations and open days.

Week	Fitness Routine or Drill
1-6	Exercises (Calisthenics)
7-12	Circuit Training
13-15	Astronaut Drills
15-18	Grass Drills
19-24	Exercises: to music
25-30	Circuit Training
31-33	Continuity Drills
34-36	Astronaut Drills

A similar version of this plan could be structured using a program of drills to cover one-half the year (18 weeks), and then repeating it. Student interest remains higher in a varied program, and if the drills are employed from year to year, little instructional time is needed when change to another activity occurs.

FITNESS ROUTINES AND DRILLS

A program of fitness for the year should lead off with exercises, as these provide the basis for many of the other drills. The drills are quite flexible and subject to many variations. The criteria for fitness routines and drills should apply to all. Most of the drills and routines provide a total body workout, but some do not and need to be supplemented. This is indicated in the discussions which follow.

Exercises

Exercises, or calisthenics, as they are sometimes termed, have much to offer and can make the following contributions to the physical education program:

1. Developing and Maintaining Specific Muscle Groups. Emphasis should be on those muscle groups which give support to the body in the matter of posture. The important muscle groups include those of the feet, the abdominal wall, the back muscles, and those holding the shoulders and head in normal position of good posture.

2. General Overall Physical Activity. Vigorous exercises involving most or many of the large muscle groups in the body are used for this purpose.

3. Carry-Over Activity. Providing exercises in the program enables the youngsters to learn their value and develop the basis for desirable activity in later life when the vigorous games and activities are not recommended.

4. Loosening and Stretching Muscles. Preliminary to such activity areas as stunts and tumbling, apparatus, and track and field, the children can be put through a series of stretching exercises to loosen and prepare muscles for the activities which follow. Bending, stretching, and twisting exercises are the most commonly used for this purpose.

5. Particular Attention to Selected Fitness Components. Exercises can be selected to contribute particular fitness attributes such as flexibility, coordination, power, strength, and agility. Endurance is not developed through an exercise program to a great degree, nor is balance. No categories for endurance or balance are included in overall exercise groups.

Cautions in Giving Exercises

Certain cautions should be observed in giving exercises. These also apply to other physical education activities.

1. Good postural alignment should be maintained. In exercises where the arms are held in front, to the side, or overhead, the abdominal wall needs to be tensed and flattened to maintain proper position of the pelvis. In most activities, the feet should be pointed reasonably straight ahead. The chest should be kept up, and the head and shoulders kept in good postural position.

2. Some care should be taken in using exercises requiring a straight leg position with no bending at the knee joint, such as forward-bending exercises. These activities tend to force the knee back in a hyperextended position, which contributes to posture faults. Some stretching of the leg muscles is excellent for flexibility, but the knee joint should be relaxed slightly rather than forced back to a back-kneed position.

3. Repeated deep knee bending (full squats) is regarded by some as injurious to the knee joint. While an exercise or activity which demands an occasional deep knee bend causes little harm, an activity which calls for repeated full knee joint bending should be avoided. It is interesting to note that Japanese physical educators dispute the danger element of deep knee bending. Their claim is that the Japanese people have sound and strong knees, in spite of the many squatting positions which are assumed as part of their living habits.

4. The activity known as the "Bicycle Ride" or the "Bicycle" should be used only if there is no overstretching of the muscles in the back of the neck. In the "Bicycle" the child is on the back of his neck and shoulders with his feet going in circles as in riding a bicycle. The exercise should be done with the weight mostly on the back of the shoulders, not high on the back of the neck.

5. In each set of exercises, there should be an exercise for the arm-shoulder girdle and one for the abdominal wall.

6. The Curl-up, with the legs in a bent-knee position and feet flat on the floor, should be used in preference to the sit-up, where the legs are extended on the floor with the knees straight. The Curl-up tends to isolate the abdominal muscle group from the psoas muscle group. The straight leg sit-up develops the psoas muscle group, which can lead to increased lower back curve, the opposite of the desired effect of strong abdominal muscles.

In addition, when the upper part of the body comes up, as in the Curl-up, the movement should begin as a roll-up, with the chin moving to touch or come close to the chest as the initial movement. This also helps to flatten out the lower back curve.

7. In exercises using leg raising, such as marching in place or running in place, the knees should be lifted to the point where the thigh is parallel to the floor. By lifting the knees high, more and different muscles are brought into play, which ordinarily would not be true with a moderate knee lift.

8. Exercises in themselves do little to develop endurance. Additional activity in the form of running, rope jumping, or other such vigorous activity is needed to round out fitness development and take care of this component.

9. The tempo with which an exercise is done is important. Most exercises have an effective rhythm which should be employed. Experimentation is needed to determine which speed of cadence is best for a particular exercise.

Setting Formation

In giving exercises to a class, the first task is to get the students into an appropriate formation quickly. This can be done in a number of ways:

1. In an early session of the class, set up a formation for the exercise program. Upon a signal, the students take their places in this prearranged formation. Spots or numbers can be painted on the floor.

2. Have the students simply scatter, allowing sufficient room for the activity.

3. Use squad formation and extend the formation to the rear, with the students far

enough apart so as not to interfere with each other.

4. Using a line formation, have the students count off by fours, and then have each student double his number and take that many steps forward.

Introducing Exercises

Once the students are in formation, the instructor proceeds with a description of the exercise. He can follow the procedure outlined below:

1. "The first exercise we are going to do is the Side Straddle Hop."

2. "Starting position is the position of attention. It is a two-count exercise."

3. "On count one, jump to a side straddle position with arms overhead." (Illustrate.)

4. "On count two, recover to starting position." (Illustrate.)

The instructor now has the class go through the exercise slowly (by the numbers) with him until he is satisfied that he can put them through the activity in cadence. Exercises are usually performed in four or eight-count rhythm. The number of repetitions will vary according to the fitness level of the group.

After the instructor has given his description and has had the group go through the exercises slowly, he is ready for class activity. This introductory procedure is satisfactory for most exercises.

Leading Exercises

1. After the exercise has been named or described (if necessary), the leader can emphasize the stress or critical execution points. For example, he can say for the Rowing Exercise, "Remember to squeeze tight with the knees and point the arms out level to the front." Attention to proper execution is important in exercises, particularly in new exercises, so that the purpose of the exercise can be realized.

2. Put the group in starting position. This can be done informally by simply directing the children to assume the starting position, or it can be done by a command such as, "Starting position—TAKE." The emphasis is on the last word with a hesitation between the preliminary part and the command word "TAKE."

3. The next command gets the group off together in rhythmic execution. The starting command can be "Ready — exercise," or "In time — exercise." This should be given in approximately the same cadence as the exercise rhythm.

4. The count now continues and the exercise should be done in unison. The count goes (for example) "1-2-3-4, 1-2-3-4." To halt the group together, slow down the count, change the tone of the voice, and command "1-2-and halt."

5. The number of repetitions is a consideration. Begin the program with around five repetitions for each exercise. The counting can include the repetitions in this fashion: "1-2-3-1, 1-2-3-2, 1-2-3-3," etc. Or, it could be: "1-2-3-4, 2-2-3-4, 3-2-3-4," etc.

6. The exercise should be followed by a brief period of relaxation. Give the group, "At ease" or "In place — rest."

There are times when it is best to allow the students to set their own limits informally. This works well with Curl-ups, Push-ups, and similar exercises where the limits can be based on individual capacity. The instructor simply requests the child to do as many repetitions as he can.

Another method of counting can be employed for such two-count exercises as the Curl-up and Push-up, where a specified number of repetitions is desired. For the Curl-up, the cadence count can go, "Up — one, Up — two, Up — three," etc. For the Push-up, it can go, "Down — one, Down — two, Down — three," etc. This allows an accurate count so the specified number can be administered. The children can be involved in the counting by having the leader give the initiating command, "Down" or "Up" and the children count in unison as they complete each movement.

Securing Progression

Progression is essential in the exercise program, and each lesson plan should specify the number of repetitions. If development is to occur, what is known in physical education as the overload principle must be applied so that the child works harder each exercise period.

Increasing the number of repetitions is only one way of providing progression by means of the overload principle. A second way is to change to a more demanding type of exercise of a similar nature. A third method is to increase the speed of the repetitions, and a fourth is to lessen the resting time between the exercises. Combinations of the above may also be used to increase the work load.

Student Leaders

At times, selected students should lead exercises — either single exercises or an entire routine. Careful instruction is needed, and students should realize that prior practice is essential to lead their peers effectively in a stimulating exercise session. Probably the greatest difficulty comes in maintaining a steady, even, and appropriate cadence. Starting and stopping the exercise are also sources of difficulty. The student leader should have directions concerning the number of repetitions and should use a counting system which keeps track of the progress. One should ask for volunteers or make assignments so students can practice ahead of time. No child should be forced to lead, as this can result in a disastrous failure, both for the child and for the class. A unique formation, which requires four student leaders, can be arranged in the following manner:

```
                    O
              LEADER No. 3
              X   X   X   X

              X   X   X   X

   O          X   X   X   X          O
LEADER No. 2  X   X   X   X   LEADER No. 4

              X   X   X   X

              X   X   X   X

                    O
              LEADER No. 1
```

A student leader stands on each of the four sides of the formation. The sequence of leaders is generally clockwise, but could be otherwise. The first leader, after he finishes his exercise, gives the command, "Right — face." The children are now facing the second leader who repeats the process. Two more exercises and changes bring the children back facing the original leader. This formation could be adjusted to employ only two leaders, positioned on opposite sides of the formation. The

command after the exercise led by the first leader would be "About — face."

Squad organization is also valuable for providing students with opportunities to lead exercises. Each leader takes his squad to a designated area and puts his members through the exercises. The procedure works best as a planned activity with prior announcement to the squad leader rather than as a spur-of-the-moment approach. It is helpful if the squad leader has a card on which is specified the sequence of the exercises and the number of repetitions. The squad leader, if he wishes, can assign various members of his squad to lead exercises.

Combined Exercise Routine

An interesting fitness activity can be fashioned by combining exercises in the following manner: make it a rule that after an exercise is given (in the normal way) the child immediately does a prescribed floor exercise, such as Push-ups or Curl-ups. A teacher's direction could be: "We are going to do a series of exercises. Just as soon as you finish an exercise, you will immediately do five push-ups without waiting for any direction from me." This system works better if the directed exercises are given from a standing position, so that either the Push-ups or Curl-ups are a definite change. After the child has completed his floor exercise (on his own), he immediately stands and awaits the next directed exercise from the teacher.

Other combinations can be put together. Exercises can be alternated with running, jumping, or hopping in place.

Unison Cadence Counting

Children enjoy group cadence counting in unison, as it involves them in the instructional process. The counting should be clipped and sharp and moderate in intensity. Avoid shouting while counting.

The leader names or describes the exercise, specifies the number of repetitions, and puts the group in starting position. The following dialogue exchange then takes place:

Leader: "Ready — Command."

Group Response: "Ready — Exercise."

Group Cadence: "1-2-3-4, 2-2-3-4," etc. (in unison).

At the start of the last sequence of counting, the leader raises an arm high overhead to indicate the completion of the desired number of repetitions. If eight repetitions are the desired number, the group stop themselves thus:

Group Response: "8-2-and-Halt."

The leader may put the group at ease, or a response pattern can be used in the following manner:

Leader: "Ready — Command."

Group Response: "At ease."

Adding Isometric Principles

The developmental potential of certain exercises can be enhanced by incorporating positions which are held as in isometric exercises; that is to say, a position of the exercise is held for a period of time (4 to 8 seconds) with a near maximal contraction.

Exercises to Music

Exercises to music add another dimension to developmental experiences. While there are many commercial record sets with "canned" exercise programs available, the most effective approach is to rely on the tape recorder. The teacher has control over the selection, sequence, and number of repetitions, and the routine can be adapted to the needs and characteristics of the group. The usual starting and halting procedures are easily incorporated into tape sequences.

Appropriate music for taping can be found in basic movement record sets, polkas, waltzes, marches, jazz music, and other selections from the wide variety of records available today. It is also possible to use a skilled pianist, a practice which is in vogue in some European countries.

A record player can be used in place of a tape recorder with someone designated to change the selection for each exercise. This presents difficulties as speeds must be changed, and initiating and halting each exercise creates a problem. The tape recorder remains the best solution.

SELECTED EXERCISES

The recommended exercises in this section are presented under the following categories.
1. Flexibility.

2. Arm-Shoulder Girdle
3. Abdominal
4. Leg Agility
5. Trunk Twisting and Bending

In any one class session, the number of exercises employed should be from six to ten. Included in each lesson should be two exercises from the Arm-Shoulder Girdle Group and at least one from each of the other categories. Specific exercises should be changed at times, and a minimum of twelve to fifteen exercises should be included in the overall year's experiences.

Several approaches are used to insure a variety in exercise selection. One system is to select a basic or fundamental group of exercises. Let's assume that twelve exercises are selected. These could be divided into two sets of six each, with the selection meeting the standards of category coverage as previously discussed. Some teachers like to alternate the sets day by day. Others prefer to have one set in effect for a week or two before changing.

As a timesaver, teachers can make up sets of exercises on cards, using a different colored card for each of the categories. In this manner, the teacher can be assured of full developmental coverage by selecting a card from each color, with the stipulation of two from the Arm-Shoulder Girdle group.

Variety in exercise selection is desirable. It is not sound to stay with a narrow, inflexible set of exercises through the entire year.

Recommended exercises are presented under each of the five categories, Stress points or points critical to execution are presented where appropriate under the exercises. Teachers can supplement the listed exercises with those of their own choice, provided the exercises are fundamentally sound. Some exercises which have value as corrective activities in posture work have already been presented and reference is made to them in the exercise program.

FLEXIBILITY EXERCISES

Many exercises in general can contribute to the development of flexibility. However, the main goal of those included in this section is the development of flexibility. Flexibility exercises feature forceful stretching of joints or muscle groups well toward their limits. The exercises may be accompanied by a rhythmic cadence or not, at the option of the teacher.

BEND AND STRETCH

Starting Position: Standing erect, hands on hips, feet shoulder width apart and pointing forward.

Cadence: Slow.

Movement:

1. Bend forward, touch the knuckles to the floor three times.

2. Return to starting position.

The knees should be relaxed slightly, if needed, to prevent a hyperextended knee position.

SITTING STRETCH

Starting Position: Sitting on the floor with legs extended forward and feet about a yard apart. Hands are clasped behind the neck, with the elbows pointed forward and kept close together.

Cadence: Slow.

Movement:

1. Bounce down with the upper body, bringing the elbows as close to the floor as possible.

2. Recover slightly and bounce again.

3. Repeat (2).

4. Recover to sitting position.

Variation: Instead of bouncing straight forward, bounce first toward the left knee, then straight forward, then toward the right knee, and recover to sitting position on the fourth count. Next sequence, reverse the direction.

Stress Points: Because the legs are against the floor, there is little chance for a hyperextended knee position, so the bouncing can be quite forceful.

KNEE HUG

Starting Position: Standing erect, hands at the side.

Cadence: Slow.

Movement:

1. Raise the left knee up to the chest, at the same time pulling in to the chest with the left hand on the knee and the right hand just above the ankle.

2. Return to starting position.

3. Raise the right knee, pulling it in with the right hand on the knee and the left hand just above the ankle.

4. Return to starting position.

Stress Points: When lifting the legs alternately to the chest, be sure to maintain the erect position of the chest, shoulders, and the head. The knee and leg should be brought up to the chest, and not the chest down to the knee.

HURDLE STRETCH

Starting Position: One leg is pointed forward and fully extended. The other thigh is to the side, with the knee bent and the leg pointing to the rear. The position resembles that of a hurdler going over a hurdle. Both arms are pointed forward toward the extended foot.

Movement:

1. Bounce forward with the upper body and reach the hands toward the forward foot.

2. Recover slightly and bounce forward again.

3. Recover slightly and bounce again.

4. Recover to original position.

Stress Points: Attempt to keep the movements in an erect forward-backward movement, avoiding a tendency to lean away from the side of the back leg. The leg position should be reversed after about four exercise patterns (4 counts each).

ARM-SHOULDER GIRDLE EXERCISES

PUSH-UPS

Starting Position: Front leaning rest. The body is straight from head to heels.

Cadence: Moderate or at will.

Movement:
keeping body straight.

1. Bend elbows and touch chest to ground,

2. Straighten elbows, raising body in straight line.

Modification: If student is unable to perform the activity as mentioned above, have him start with knees or hips in contact with the floor.

Stress Points: The only movement should be in the arms. The head should be up and the eyes looking ahead. The chest should touch the floor lightly without receiving the weight of the body. The body should remain in a straight line throughout, without sagging or humping.

Variations: (1) After the children have some competence in doing push-ups, have them try the following four-count sequence:

(a) Halfway down

(b) All the way down

(c) Halfway up

(d) Up to starting position

2. For kindergarten classes, this can be called a "Flat Tire." The teacher can start the movement with a "bang," and the children can lower themselves slowly to the accompaniment of the sound of air escaping from a tire.

RECLINING PULL-UPS

Starting Position: One pupil lies on his back. His partner stands astride him, looking face to face, with his feet alongside the reclining partner's chest. Partners grasp hands with fingers interlocked.

Cadence: Moderate to slow.

Movement:

1. Partner on floor pulls up with arms until his chest touches partner's thighs. His body remains straight, with the weight resting on the heels.

2. Return to position.

Variation: A variation which should be used is the wrist grip, in which each grasps the other's wrist. The reclining pull-up is one of the means, short of using hanging type apparatus, by which the arm flexor muscle can be exercised.

Stress Points: Body should be kept straight throughout. The up movement should go as high between partner's thighs as possible.

 ARM CIRCLING

Starting Position: Erect, feet apart, arms to the side with palms up.

Cadence: Moderate.

Movement:

1. Five forward 12″ circles, moving both arms simultaneously, palms up.

2. Five backward 12″ circles, moving both arms simultaneously, palms down.

The number of circles to be made before changing to the opposite direction can be varied.

Stress Points: Good posture position should be maintained with the abdominal wall flat and the head and shoulders held back.

CRAB KICKING

Starting Position: Crab position — the body is supported on hands and feet with the back to the floor. The knees are at right angles.

Cadence: Moderate.

Movement:

1. Kick as high as possible toward the ceiling, alternating the feet.

2. Extend one leg forward so the heel touches the floor. Alternate the legs.

3. Begin with both feet flat on the floor with knees bent in normal crab position. Thrust both feet forward so the legs are straight and the weight is on both heels. Recover.

4. Have the children move forward, backward, sideward on all fours, maintaining crab position. Turn in a small circle, right and left.

Stress Points: Children must maintain a high hip position. The tendency is to drop the seat. A method of getting children to maintain proper body position is to have them watch the ceiling.

WING STRETCHER—

Starting Position: Stand erect; raise elbows to shoulder height, fists clenched, palms down in front of the chest.

Cadence: Moderate.

Movement:

1. Thrust elbows backward vigorously. Be sure to keep the abdominal wall flat and the head erect. Keep elbows at shoulder height.

2. Return to position.

Variation: Alternate the backward elbow thrust with a full backward swing of the arms. This makes it a four-count exercise.

Stress Points: The abdominal wall should be kept flat and the head and shoulders held in good postural position.

Other Exercises

In addition to the preceding five exercises, the following exercises included with the discussion of posture development should be considered:

6. The Swan (page 63)
7. Hook Lying (page 62)
8. Tailor Exercise (page 63)

ABDOMINAL EXERCISES

For most exercises stressing abdominal de-velopment, the child lies on his back on the floor or mat (supine position) as a basic start-ing position. To secure abdominal muscle in-volvement from this position, the child can brings his legs up, his upper body up, or both the legs and upper body up at the same time. If the upper body is brought up, the movement should begin with a roll-up by moving the head first so that the chin makes contact or near contact with the chest, thus flattening and stabilizing the lower back curve. The bent-knee position of the legs, either originally or in the execution of the movement, places more demands specifically on the abdominal muscles.

Isometric principles of utilizing held posi-tion can be applied efficiently to abdominal exercises. The position should be held with-out movement for 4 to 8 seconds at the point of the greatest contraction specified for the particular exercise.

Two excellent exercises for abdominal de-velopment which do not use the supine posi-tion are the *Leg Extension* and the *Mad Cat.*

HEAD AND SHOULDER CURL

Starting Position: On back with hands clasped, palms down, behind the small of the back. Knees and soles of the feet flat on the floor.

Cadence: Moderate.

Movement:

1. Lift the head and pull the shoulders and elbows off the floor.

2. Hold the tensed position for 5 counts.

3. Return to starting position.

The verbal count for the exercise can be: "Up (lift), 2-3-4-5 (hold), down (return)."

Variation: The arms are extended so the hands are palms down on the thighs. When the upward lift of the shoulders is made, the hands slide to the knees.

KNEE RAISE (Single and Double)

Starting Position: On back with knees slightly flexed, feet flat on the floor, and arms out to the side.

Cadence: Moderate.

Movement:

1. Raise one knee as close to the chest as possible.
2. Return.
3. Raise the other knee.
4. Return.

The exercise should be done later with both knees coming up at once and returning.

TOE TOUCHER

Starting Position: Flat on back, feet about 2′ apart, arms extended overhead.

Cadence: Slow.

Movement:

1. Roll up, thrust arms forward and touch toes keeping knees straight.
2. Roll back to original position.
3. Raise legs, swinging them over head, keep knees straight, touch toes to ground behind head.
4. Lower legs to starting position, slowly.

This exercise strengthens the muscles of the abdomen, thighs, and hips. It also stretches

the hamstring muscles which aid in the development of suppleness and flexibility. The massaging effect on the abdominal viscera is beneficial.

Other Exercises

Abdominal exercises included under the discussion of posture should also be included here.

5. Curl-Up (page 63)
6. Rowing (page 64)
7. Curl-Up with Twist (page 64)
8. Mad Cat (page 64)

LEG EXTENSION

Starting Position: Sitting on floor with legs extended and hands on hips.

Cadence: Moderate.

Movement:

1. With a quick, vigorous action, raise the knees and bring both heels as close to the seat as possible. The movement is a drag with the toes touching lightly.
2. Return to position.

LEG-AGILITY EXERCISES

Leg-Agility exercises should feature rhythmic, graceful motion with emphasis on control. Cadence should be regular and even.

RUNNING IN PLACE

Starting Position: Standing with arms in loose thrust position.

Cadence: Slow, fast, slow.

Movement: Stationary run. Begin slowly (counting only on left foot). Speed up somewhat, raising knees to height of hips, then run at full speed, raising knees hard, then slow down. Run should be on the toes.

Variations:

1. *Tortoise and Hare.* Jog slowly in place. On the command, "Hare," double the speed. On the command, "Tortoise," slow the tempo to original jogging speed.

2. March in place, lifting knees high and swinging the arms well up.

SIDE STRADDLE HOP

Jump Jack

Starting Position: At attention.

Cadence: Moderate.

Movement:

1. On count one, jump to a straddle position with arms overhead.

2. On count two, recover to starting position.

Side Straddle Hop is also a coordination exercise.

Variations:

1. Begin with the feet in a stride position (forward and back). Change feet with the overhead movement.

2. Instead of bringing the feet together when the arms come down, cross the feet each time, alternating the cross.

3. On the completion of each set of 8 counts, do a quarter turn right. After four sets, the child will again be facing in his original direction.

THE SQUAT THRUST

Starting Position: Attention.

Cadence: Moderate.

1. Bend slightly at the knees and sharply at the hips; place hands on the ground in front of the feet in a squat position with the knees inside the elbows.

2. Thrust feet and legs backward to a front leaning rest position with body straight from shoulders to feet, weight supported on hands and toes.

3. Return to the squat position.

4. Resume standing position.

The *Squat Thrust* is one of the best exercises to develop agility. It reaches and strengthens primarily the muscles of the trunk, thighs, and hips.

Stress Points: On the thrust to the rear, the body must be straight and the head up. On the completion of one full cycle of 4 counts, come back to a full standing position.

THE TREADMILL

Starting Position: Push-up position except that one leg is brought forward so that the knee is under the chest.

Cadence: Moderate.

Movement:

1. Reverse position of the feet, bringing the other leg forward.

2. Change back with original foot forward. The exercise is continued rhythmically with feet alternating. The *Treadmill* is one of the test items in the New York State Physical Fitness Test.

Stress Points: Head should be kept up. A full exchange of the legs should be made with the forward knee coming well under the chest each time.

TRUNK EXERCISES

These activities are primarily twisting and bending exercises which cover a variety of movements with emphasis on trunk development. Some involve either bending or twisting movements. A few include both twisting and bending motions. Twisting and bending should be done to forceful limits. Movements should be large and vigorous.

THE BEAR HUG

Starting Position: Standing, feet comfortably spread, hands on hips.

Cadence: Slow.

Movement:

1. Take a long step diagonally right, keeping the left foot anchored in place; tackle the right leg around the thigh by encircling the thigh with both arms. Squeeze and stretch.
2. Return to position.
3. Tackle the left leg.
4. Return to position.

The value in flexibility comes from forcing a good stretch.

SIDE FLEX

Starting Position: Lie on side, lower arm extended overhead. The head rests on the lower arm. Legs are extended fully, one on top of the other.

Cadence: Moderate.

Movement:

1. With a brisk action, raise the upper arm and leg vertically. Attempt to make contact with hand and foot, without bending elbow or knee.
2. Repeat for several counts and change to the other side.

BODY CIRCLES

Starting Position: Feet shoulder-width apart, hands clasped behind the head, body bent forward.

Cadence: Moderate.

Movement: The movement is a complete circle done by the upper body in 4 counts. A specified number of circles should be made to the right and the same number to the left. The right circle is described:

1. Circle upper body a quarter turn to the right.
2. Another quarter turn to the back.
3. Another quarter turn to the left.
4. A final quarter turn ending in original position.

This exercise can be done in free movement by directing the children to circle in one direction until told to stop. Direction is then reversed.

TRUNK TWISTER

Starting Position: Standing with feet about 2′

apart sideward, hands clasped behind head, elbows held backward, chin in.

Cadence: Slow.

Movement:

1. Bend and bounce downward, knees straight. Recover slightly. Do this vigorously.

2. Bounce downward, but simultaneously rotate trunk sharply to left.

3. Same to the right.

4. Return to original position, pulling head back and chin in strongly.

The *Trunk Twister* reaches and strengthens all muscles of the trunk. It has excellent postural benefits. It results in greater flexibility of the lower back region.

TURN AND BOUNCE

Starting Position: Erect, with feet shoulder width apart and arms out to the side, level, with palms down.

Cadence: Moderate.

Movement:

1. Using the lower body as a fixed base, twist the upper body as far as possible in one direction, carrying one arm as far backward as possible.

2. Recover slightly and twist again (bounce).

3. Recover and bounce again.

4. Recover to original position.

Repeat to the opposite side.

Stress Points: Abdominal wall should be kept flat and upper body in good postural position throughout. The hips must be kept in place, with the vigorous twist on the hips as a base.

ISOMETRIC CONDITIONING EXERCISES

An isometric exercise is characterized by having virtually no movement of the body part, but a high degree of muscular tension. In this type of activity, the muscles should undergo a holding contraction of eight slow counts. To prevent movement, the pulling, pushing, or twisting action is braced against some external stabilizing force. This can be against a wall, the floor, the sides of a door frame, or a special isometric apparatus. Or, an individual could work one set of muscles against another so that there is no movement. In addition, iso-metric exercise can be done with partners, with one partner providing the stabilizing action.

In the regular classroom, where the narrow confines and furniture limit activity, an isometric program has value because of the "no movement" feature. Furthermore, many of the activities can be done by children seated at desks, with the desks themselves used as braces to prevent movement.

Isometric exercises are useful for building strength, *but only strength.* Other activities where movement occurs, particularly endurance-type activities which contribute to the development of the cardiorespiratory system, are needed to round out the program. Isometrics have value in the posture program in strengthening the antigravity muscles, thus contributing to better postural habits.

The exercises are simple, and there is little, if any, danger of injury. Children can use these activities as "homework," particularly in the program for the low fitness group. The exercises have good carry-over value as they can be used on any age level.

It should be stressed that maximum or near-maximum tension of the muscle group to be developed must be achieved and held for approximately 8 seconds, hence the eight slow counts. There is no need for repetition of an exercise at any one session, as maximum strength development is gained from one contraction at an exercise session. Contractions should be repeated three or four times per week.

INDIVIDUAL ISOMETRIC EXERCISES

1. Arms. Standing or seated. With the left palm up and the right palm down, clasp the hands in front of the body, chest high. Press down with the right hand, resisting with the left. Reverse.

2. Fingers and Grip. Seated. Two ordinary books are needed so that together the thickness is 1". Grasp the books in an opposed thumb grip. Squeeze hard with the fingers of both hands.

3. Arm and Shoulders. Standing or seated. Clasp the fingers together in front of the chest with the forearms held level to the floor (elbows out). Pull against the fingers to force the elbows out. Be sure to keep the chest up, shoulders back, and the head erect.

4. Arm and Shoulders. Standing or seated. Using a grip with the palms together, the fingers interlocked (knuckles upward), push the palms together. Be sure the elbows are up and out.

5. Legs. Seated. With the right foot on the floor, move the left foot on top of it, with the heel about halfway to the ankle. Lift the right foot, resist with the left. Reverse. The same exercise can be done by crossing the feet so the pressure is ankle against ankle.

6. Legs, Arms, Abdominals. Seated. Place hands, palms down, with fingers extended, on the lower portion of the top of the thighs. Press down with the hands and up with the legs.

7. Arms and Shoulders. Seated. Drop the hands to the sides so that they are straight down. Curl the fingers under the seat. Pull up with the shoulders, keeping the body erect.

8. Neck and Arms. Standing or seated. Clasp the hands behind the back of the head. Keeping the elbows well out, force the head back against the pressure of the hands.

9. Back, Arms, Thighs. Seated. Sitting as erect as possible, place both hands under the thighs close to the knees. Pull up with the hands against downward pressure of the thighs.

10. Legs. Against a wall. This is called the Skier's Sit. With the heels about 12″ away from the wall, go into a sitting position (no chair or bench) so that back is against the wall, the thighs are parallel to the floor. A right angle is formed by the thighs and the body, and again at the knee joint. Hold for 30 seconds. The arms are folded across the chest. The head and shoulders are up and maintain contact against the wall.

11. Abdominals. Hook Lying Position. Hook the feet under a mat or have a partner hold. With the hands clasped behind the neck, knees bent, come up to a halfway position of the sit-up. Hold for 30 seconds. In this position, try to keep the back straight and the abdominal wall flat.

12. Back and Shoulders. Lying on the back. The hands are placed alongside the buttocks, palms down. Lift the body from the floor so that only the heels, hands, and head touch.

If the hands are placed out to the sides, a more demanding exercise can be given.

13. Arms, Abdominals, General Body. Stand about 3′ behind a chair. Bend forward at the waist until the hands can be put on the back of the chair (elbows are straight). With a strong downward pull from the abdominal wall and the arms, pull down against the chair.

14. Flexed Arm Hang. A chinning bar is needed. This can be done also with a horizontal ladder or climbing rope. Hang from a bar so that the mouth is just even with the hands (palms away grip). Hang for 15 seconds or more.

PARTNER ISOMETRIC EXERCISES

The exercises which can be done by partners are innumerable. Most of the exercises described in the previous section as individual isometrics can be adapted as partner activities. A partner can keep arms or legs from being lifted or forced down, moved together or apart, raised or lowered, etc. A few partner exercises will serve as illustrations.

1. Push-up Position. One partner in push-up position with arms bent so that the body is about halfway up from the floor. The other partner straddles his head and puts pressure on top of his shoulders, forcing down. The amount of pressure takes judgment by the

partner as too much will simply cause the bottom man to collapse. This can also be done as a resistive exercise where the push-up is actually done with the top man supplying resistance.

2. Neck. On hands and knees. One partner is down on hands and bent knees, the other standing immediately in front of the head. Pressure is down against the back of the head. A second exercise is to apply pressure

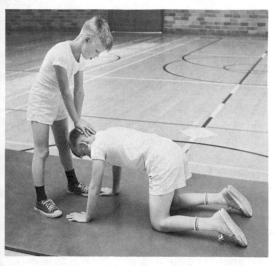

by a lift with the clasped hands, which are positioned under the forehead.

3. Legs. Prone position. One partner is in face down position with his hands overhead, palms down. His legs are lifted so that the soles of the feet are toward the ceiling, with a right angle bend at the knee joint. Partner kneels near the feet and pulls back on one

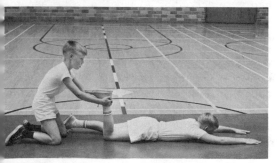

heel. The bottom man tries to flex his leg against the resistance. Change to the other leg. Both legs can be done at once, but it is a little awkward to hold both legs at the same time.

ISOMETRIC EXERCISES WITH EQUIPMENT

Wands and individual tug-of-war ropes are also useful as the basis for isometric exer-
cises. The suggestions for exercises are included under the progressions for those pieces of equipment. See page 161 for wand exercises and page 266 for exercises utilizing ropes.

CIRCUIT TRAINING

Circuit training is an exercise program consisting of a number of stations arranged in the form of a circuit. Each of the stations demands an exercise task from the child, as he moves from station to station in sequential order.

Basic Theory

The exercise tasks composing the circuit should contribute to the development of all parts of the body. In addition, the activities should contribute to the various components of physical fitness, i.e., strength, power, endurance, agility, flexibility, and others. Thus, circuit training can be a valuable tool in the development of physical fitness.

Methodology

Each station should provide an exercise task which is within the capacity of the children. The type of activity at each station should be one that the child can learn and do without the aid of another child. As the child moves from one station to the next, the exercises which directly follow each other should make demands on different parts of the body. In this way the performance at any one station does not cause local fatigue which could affect the ability to perform the next task.

It is important that sufficient instruction in the activities be given so that the children can perform correctly at each station. The children should be taught to count the number of repetitions correctly, if a system of counting is employed.

The class can be divided so that some start at each station. From the standpoint of supplying necessary equipment at each station, this method keeps the demands low. For example, if there are thirty children for a circuit of six stations, five children would start at each spot. The maximum equipment at each station in this case would be that necessary for five children.

Timing and Dosage

In general, a fixed time limit at each station seems to offer the best plan for circuit training on the elementary level. Each child attempts to complete as many repetitions as he can during the time limit at each station. Increased work load can be accomplished by increasing the number of repetitions (by the child) and increasing the amount of time at each station. A suggested progressive time schedule to be used as a guide for timing the circuit is as follows:

Introduction	15 seconds at each station
First 2 weeks	20 seconds at each station
Second 2 weeks	25 seconds at each station
After 4 weeks	30 seconds at each station

Keeping in mind that children must be challenged, the above schedule should be modified accordingly. Children need to be "pushed" and the time limit is adjusted to accomplish this. A circuit that is too easy will contribute little to the development of fitness.

A 15-second interval should be established to allow children to move from one station to the next. Later, this can be lowered to 10 seconds or even 5 seconds. Students may start at any station as designated, but must follow the established order of stations.

A second method of timing is to sound only one signal for the change to the next station. Under this plan, the child ceases his activity at one station, moves to the next, and *immediately* begins the task at that station without awaiting another signal.

Another means of increasing the activity demands of the circuit is to change the individual activities to more demanding types. For example, a station could specify knee or bench push-ups and later change these to regular push-ups, a more demanding exercise.

Red, White, and Blue Circuits

This method of operating the circuit employs definite dosages at each of the stations. The repetitions at each of the stations are established under this kind of a formula:

Red: Modest challenge. Most children can do these.

White: Moderate challenge.

Blue: Considerable challenge.

Under this system, for example, the following could be established for the push-ups.

Red: 10   White: 15   Blue: 20

Naturally, the number of repetitions and the progression would depend on the capacity of the children and their fitness level. Some experimentation is needed to set the repetition progressions at each of the stations.

Since the children progress at individual rates from station to station, the problem of sufficient equipment and space at each station is an important consideration. Signs at each station are valuable to designate the number of repetitions for each of the colors.

Another valuable suggestion is to have super circuits labeled silver and gold. These could be award type of circuits combining the repetitions and a time to do them. Thus, to qualify, the student would do the specified dosages at each station and complete the circuit within a designated time. The silver and gold circuits would be special events and not part of the regular program of activities. Specially designed emblems could be awarded. It should be emphasized that awards of this type should be enough of a challenge to make them respected. The gold award, especially, should be difficult enough so as to be within the range of only the top fitness students. Standards should be set for different grade levels and be different for boys and girls.

The Stations

The manner in which a circuit is organized can vary according to what is to be accomplished. Equipment needed is also a consideration, and it is recommended that exercise tasks at the different stations be selected from those requiring a minimum of equipment. Exercise programs can include weight-lifting activities, but this is hardly feasible for the average elementary school.

The number of stations can vary, but probably should be not less than six and not more than eight. Activities should be selected so that consecutive stations do not make demands on the same section of the body. The exercise activities for circuit training designated at any station will be either for general body conditioning or for a particular section of the body.

Signs designating the different stations are of considerable help. The sign can contain the name of the activity and the necessary cautions or stress points for execution. Where children move between lines as limits as in the *Agility Run,* traffic cones or beanbags can be used to mark the designated boundary lines.

A circuit should always include activities for exercising the arm and shoulder girdle and for strengthening the abdominal wall. A wide variety of activities are available for the circuit. The following are suggested and are put into classifications, from each of which one activity may be selected.

General Body Activity

Rope Jumping
Use single-time speed.

Side Straddle Hop
This two-count exercise is also called the *Jumping Jack* (page 111).

Jump and Reach (against a wall)
This is the same as *Jump and Reach Test,* except that the child touches as high as he can with his right hand for five times and then works with the left hand for five.

Running in Place
Be sure the knees are lifted to a point on each step where the thighs are up parallel to the floor.

Push-up Types — Arm and Shoulder Girdle

Push-ups — knee or regular (page 107).
Squat Thrusts — 4-count exercise (page 111).

Agility Runs — Legs (Endurance)

Agility Run — Touch With the Toes.
Two lines are established 15' apart. The child moves between the two lines as rapidly as possible touching one line with the right foot, and the other with the left.

Agility Run — Touch With the Hand.
The same as above except that the lines are touched with the respective hand instead of the foot.

Arm Circles — Arm and Shoulders

Standing Arm Circling (page 108).

Lying Arm Circling
The child lies face down, with the arms out to the side. Alternate forward and backward arm circling, changing after five circles in each direction. The head and shoulders are lifted from the ground during the exercise.

Abdominal Exercises

Rowing (page 64).
Curl-ups (page 63).

Alternate Toe Touching
The child begins flat on his back with hands extended overhead. He alternates by touching the right toe with the left hand and vice versa. He should bring both the foot and the arm up at the same time and return to the flat position each time.

For curl-ups, some means of anchoring the feet may be desirable. Mats can be used so that the child can hook his feet under the edge to provide support which ordinarily is given by another person holding his feet.

Crab Position — Arm and Shoulder Girdle

Crab Walk (see page 201 for description).
Two parallel lines are drawn 6' to 8' apart. The child starts with his hands on one line and his feet in the direction of the other. He moves back and forth between the lines in crab position, touching one line with his heels and the other with his hands.

Crab Kicking (page 108).
The child is in crab position and alternates with right and left foot kicking toward the ceiling.

Leg Exercises

Step-ups
A bench is needed for each three children who are at this station. The child begins in front of the bench, stepping up on the bench with the left foot, then up with the right foot.

The child now steps down in rhythm left and then right. The next class period the child does the step-ups he should begin with the right foot to secure comparable development. The legs should be fully extended and the body erect when he is on the top of the bench.

Treadmill (page 111).

Straddle Bench Jumps
The child straddles a bench. He alternates jumping to the top of the bench and back to the floor. The activity is quite strenuous. Since the degree of effort is dependent upon the height of the bench, benches of shorter height should be considered. These can be constructed in the form of small elongated boxes 4' long, 10" wide, and different heights of 8", 10", 12", and 15". A 4' box will accommodate two children at one time.

Squat Jumps

The child crouches to about a three-quarter bend with his hands on the floor, slightly to the front and side of his feet. One foot is slightly in front of the other. He springs into the air about 4″, changing the position of his feet. Each time he uses his hands to absorb some of the shock of the returning position. The full knee bend should be avoided.

Bend and Stretch — Flexibility and Back

Bend and Stretch (page 106).

Windmill

The position is similar to the previous exercise except the hands and arms are out to the side with palms facing forward. The child bends over touching the left toe with the right hand, and then returns to erect position.

Trunk Twister (page 112).

Others

Many other exercises, stunts, or movements can be used. Some can be used in combination. In leg exercises, for example, the task can be designated as 25 steps running in place and then 5 pogo jumps into the air. This is repeated.

If chinning bars, horizontal ladders, and climbing ropes are present, circuits can make use of these. Chinning, climbing, and traveling activities may be prescribed for tasks at stations.

SAMPLE CIRCUIT TRAINING COURSES

Six Station Course

1 Running in Place	2 Curl-ups	3 Arm Circling
6 Crab Walk	5 Trunk Twister	4 Agility Run

Supplies and Equipment: Mats for curl-ups (to hook toes).

Time Needed: 4 minutes — based on 30-second activity limit, 10 seconds to move between stations.

Eight Station Course

1 Rope Jumping	2 Push-ups	3 Agility Run	4 Arm Circling
8 Bend and Stretch	7 Step-ups	6 Crab Walk	5 Rowing

Supplies and Equipment: Jumping ropes, mats for knee push-ups (if used), benches or first row of portable bleachers.

Time Needed: 5½ minutes — based on 30-second activity limit, 10 seconds to move between stations.

A tape recorder can be used effectively to give directions for the circuit. Music, whistle signals, and even verbal directions can be prerecorded to give direction. The tape provides a rigid time control and gives a measure of consistency to the circuit. Tape also frees the teacher for supervisory duties, allowing him to give attention to performance rather than the circuit routine.

CONTINUITY EXERCISES

Continuity drills had their origin in Europe. They are sometimes directed by a tape recorder, however, the drill described here can be controlled by a whistle or verbal commands.

The children are in an extended squad exercise formation. Each has a jumping rope. The children alternate between rope jumping and four exercises. A specified time period governs the length of the rope jumping, which should be done in fast time (single jumps). At the signal to stop the rope jumping, the children drop the rope and immediately take the position for the selected exercise. The exercises all demand a down body position and are in a two-count cadence.

When the children are positioned for the exercise, the leader says, "Ready!" All children do one repetition of the exercise, counting out loud the two-count cadence with, "One, two." For *each* repetition, then, the children wait until the leader initiates the repetition with a "Ready," and each child replies with the action and the cadence count, "One, Two."

The sequence of rope jumping and the selected exercises forms this pattern.

1st Signal: Children begin rope jumping.

2nd Signal: Children drop ropes and take push-up position. (See page 100.) On each command of "Ready," one push-up is done to a two-count cadence.

3rd Signal: Children resume rope jumping.

4th Signal: Children drop ropes and go into a supine position with arms overhead along the floor, preparatory to doing the rowing exercise. (See page 64.) The command "Ready" is given and each child performs the exercise to the two-count cadence.

5th Signal: Children resume jumping.

6th Signal: Children drop ropes and take a crab position, preparatory to doing a crab kick. On the signal "Ready," both feet are thrust forward to an extended leg position with the weight momentarily on the heels and then back to the crab position, in a fast two-count cadence.

7th Signal: Children resume rope jumping.

8th Signal: Children go into a side-lying position on the left side for the side flex exercise. (See page 112.) On the "Ready," each performs a Side Flex in a two-count cadence. After performing one repetition, the child immediately rolls over to a right-side position. On the next command, he performs a Side Flex on the right side and again rolls back to the left position.

9th Signal: Finish, or one more session of rope jumping can be taken.

Continuity exercises done snappily and with vigor are enjoyable experiences for youngsters. Having them reply with a repetition *and* the cadence count involves them in the drill more than just as passive participants. The cadence count should be pert, bitten off, and not overly loud, somewhat in military fashion.

The leader of the drill should make a note beforehand of the number of repetitions he wishes for each of the exercises. This will depend upon the age and physical condition of the group. Some experimentation may be necessary to determine the length of the rope jumping periods.

As in circuit training, a tape recorder can signal changes of movement and can also supply appropriate music for rope jumping. The tape conserves time and allows the teacher to concentrate on the responses of the children.

GRASS DRILLS

Grass drills have been with us for a long time, having been used for many decades in the development of football teams. They are strenuous, since they are performed in quick succession and at top speed. Progression is gained by gradually increasing the length of the work periods. The drills are executed in place. A circle formation or regular exercise formation can be used.

Grass drills involve moving rapidly from one of three basic positions to another, using command words, "Go," "Front," and "Back."
1. "Go" — run in place at top speed on the toes, knees raised high, arms pumping, and body bent forward slightly at the waist.
2. "Front" — drop to the floor in prone position with hands underneath the body, ready to push off to change position. Head should point toward the center of the circle or front of the room. Feet are extended back and kept together.
3. "Back" — the position is flat on the back, arms lying alongside the body with the palms down. The head-leg direction is opposite to the "Front" position.

There are two ways to operate grass drills. The choice is after the "Go" signal, which starts the children running in place.
1. *Continuous Motion:* In this method, when the command "Front" is given, the child immediately goes to the prone position and comes back up to the running position without a second command. This also occurs when the "Back" command is given.
2. *Interrupted Motion:* With this, instead of coming automatically back to the running position, the child stays in position (running, prone, or supine), until a change is called.

Instead of running in place on "Go," fast stepping can be substituted. In this, the children move their feet as rapidly as possible with tiny steps in place. Arms are held out diagonally.

Abdominal exercises should be added after the drills as there is little abdominal development potential in grass drills.

ASTRONAUT DRILLS

The children form a large circle and are spaced about 6' apart. The basic movement is a walk around the circle, not necessarily in step. The teacher gives various commands designating the activity to be performed. Most of these are locomotor movements which the children do while moving in the circle. The teacher may, however, direct the circle to stop and do certain exercises. After the task has been done, the children continue the walk around the circle.

The following movements and tasks can be incorporated into the routine.

1. Various locomotor movements such as hopping, jumping, running, sliding, skipping, giant steps, high on toes, etc.
2. On all fours, moving in the line of direction forward, backward, and sideward. Repeat backward and forward using crab position.
3. Stunt movements like the *Seal Walk, Gorilla Walk, Bunny Jump,* etc.
4. Upper torso movements and exercises that can be done while walking, such as arm circles, bending right and left, body twists, etc.
5. Various exercises in place. Always include an abdominal development activity.

Children who lag can move toward the inner part of the circle and allow more active children to pass them on the outside.

THE OBSTACLE COURSE

The obstacle course, so familiar to men in the Service during World War II, is becoming increasingly popular as a tool for fitness development in the elementary school. Obstacle courses can roughly be divided into two types: the outdoor (generally permanent) and the indoor (portable).

The courses can be run against a time standard or can be done just for the exercise values. A course should be designed to exercise all parts of the body through a variety of activities. By including running, vaulting, agility, climbing, hanging, crawling, and other activities, good fitness demands are present when the child moves through the course as rapidly as he can.

Such physical education equipment as mats, parallel bars, horizontal ladder, high-jump standards, benches, and vaulting boxes make effective obstacle courses. A great variety of courses can be designed, depending upon the length and the different tasks to be included. Indoors, the space available would be an important factor. Some schools, fortunate enough to have a suitable wooded area, have established permanent courses.

An illustration of an indoor course is given; it is based on the assumption that a horizontal ladder is available. The list of items needed is:
   3 benches (16" to 18")
   3 tumbling mats (4' by 8')
   1 folding card table
   1 set of high-jump standards (2) with cross bar

OBSTACLE COURSE — INDOOR

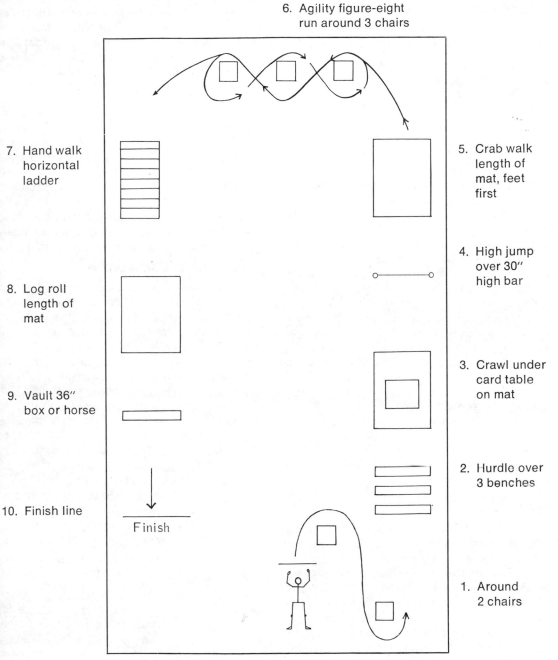

6. Agility figure-eight run around 3 chairs

7. Hand walk horizontal ladder

5. Crab walk length of mat, feet first

4. High jump over 30″ high bar

8. Log roll length of mat

3. Crawl under card table on mat

9. Vault 36″ box or horse

2. Hurdle over 3 benches

10. Finish line

Finish

1. Around 2 chairs

Start, lying face down with palms braced on the floor.

1 horizontal ladder
1 36" vaulting box or wooden horse
5 chairs

COURSE CONTINUITY

Start: Lying face down with hands, palms down, near the chest ready to get up.

1. Run forward, around the first chair and back around the second.

2. Three benches are placed about 5' apart. The runner hurdles or jumps over them.

3. This station consists of a mat with a card table placed on it to form a tunnel for the runner. The runner goes under the card table on hands and knees.

4. The bar on this station is placed between the two high-jump standards. The bar is 30" above the ground. Runner does a scissors jump.

5. The task here is a crab walk across the length of the mat. He should begin with his feet pointed in the direction he is to go. He finishes when his feet are off the mat at the far end.

6. The run is made in a figure-eight manner in and around the chairs. He goes in figure-eight fashion down to the end of the three chairs, back to the first chair, and down to the end once more.

7. Station 7 is a hand walk on the horizontal ladder. The runner should use the side rails to hand walk the length of the ladder.

8. The runner does a log roll the length of the mat.

9. A vault over a vaulting box or wooden horse 36" high is made.

10. Cross finish line where time can be checked.

The starting and finish lines are close enough together to be convenient for the timers. Timing can be systematized in having runners leave the starting line at ten-second intervals. The faster children should run first to avoid conflict at any one station if the course is such that only one child can be at any one station at a time. However, timing is not an important aspect of the activity for elementary children. The run can be made just for the values of the activity.

The course can be shortened or lengthened and the stations changed with respect to order. Also, children can run the course making more than one circuit at a time.

MISCELLANEOUS ROUTINES

A number of other activities can be utilized to aid in the development of fitness. Many are quite simple and make only a partial contribution to overall development. This means that they must be supplemented.

Walk, Trot, Sprint

Children are scattered around the circumference of the room, all facing counterclockwise. The signals are given with a whistle. On the first whistle, the children begin to walk around the room in good posture. The next whistle signals a change to a trotting run. On the next whistle, the children run as rapidly as they can. Another whistle signals for them to walk again. The cycle is repeated as many times as the instructor feels is necessary.

The Basketball Slide Drill

The children are scattered on the floor or playground, with each assuming a guarding stance as in basketball. One foot is ahead of the other, and the hands are out as if guarding. The movements forward and backward should be made using a shuffle step with the feet retaining their approximate position. Movements to the side should be a slide.

The leader stands in front with a whistle. He points in a direction and immediately the players move that way (forward, backward, or to either side). When the whistle is blown again, all stop. Other signals, such as "Go" or "Stop," could be used in lieu of a whistle.

Another method to move the children is to station a player in front of the group with a basketball. He dribbles rapidly in any direction, and the players move in relative position with him.

Fast Stepping

Each child does very fast stepping in place just as rapidly as he can. This is kept up for ten seconds and then there is a ten-second rest. The cycle is repeated. This is quite strenuous and the children should be checked carefully to determine dosage.

Timed Activities

Children are stimulated to good effort if

they know that they are being timed and are competing against other children. Timing can be done for 30, 45, 60 seconds, or some other interval. The following should be considered.

1. *Rope jumping for time.* The object is to turn the rope as fast as possible during the time limit. The number of successful jumps is counted.

2. *Agility run between lines.* Two lines are selected, any convenient distance between 10' to 20', just so all children are faced with the same distance. The child touches the lines alternately with the hands. He should touch one line with the left hand and the other with the right.

3. *Potato relays for time.* A potato-type relay can be organized in the following fashion.

Start   Box

(all distances between the start, box, and blocks — 10')

A box is placed 10' in front of the starting line, with four blocks in individual circles the same distance apart. The runner begins behind the starting line. He puts the blocks one at a time in the box and finishes across the original line. He can bring the blocks back one at a time to the box in any order he wishes. All blocks must be put inside the box. The box should be 12" by 12" with a depth of 3" to 6". Blocks must be placed, not thrown, in the box.

Movement Experiences

Movement experiences, previously described in the program for younger children, (pages 98-101) can be adapted effectively for older children. They are a welcome change of pace from other routines.

JOGGING FOR FUN AND FITNESS

Jogging, a fitness program for young and old, should be started in the intermediate grades. It can provide a strong carry-over activity in the way of a personal jogging program. It has value in the general fitness program as it develops endurance and can lead to habits of regular activity.

Jogging is defined as easy, relaxed running at a pace which the person feels he can keep up for long distances without undue fatigue or strain. It is the first level above a walk.

The school should provide instruction in jogging techniques and planning a progressive program. Instruction can be offered during physical education time, but the activity itself should be done primarily during recess, the noon hour, after school, or at other free times.

Jogging is unique in that it takes no special equipment, can be done most anywhere, can be an individual activity, consumes relatively little time, and is not geared to any particular time of the day. For most people, it is an exercise in personal discipline. *For children* it can enhance the self-image and raise confidence levels.

Three types of jogging can be considered. The first is the jog-walk-jog method, which is generally employed during early or introductory phases of jogging. One way to apply this system is for the child to cover a selected distance by a combination of jogging and walking. The child jogs until he feels the need to walk and walks until he feels like jogging again. Progression is realized in eliminating as much of the walking as possible while maintaining the selected distance.

Another way to use the jog-walk-jog method is to divide the selected distance in specified increments of jogging and walking. For example, the jogger, to cover a quarter of a mile, could jog 110 yards, walk 55 yards, jog 110 yards, walk 55 yards, and jog the remaining 110 yards.

A second method of jogging is to jog all the way over a set distance by increasing or decreasing pace in keeping with body reaction to the demands. Obviously, better endurance conditioning is needed for this procedure than in the jog-walk-jog method.

A third method is to maintain the pace but increase the distance. Combinations of the three methods are also possible.

Generally, authorities recommend that jogging be done on alternate days, to allow for recovery from the effects of the day's workout. Some joggers, however, like to run each day, alternating between heavy and light workouts.

The teacher should not be concerned much with foot action, as the child will select the means which is most comfortable for him.

Arms should be easy, with elbows bent and the head and upper body in good postural position. Eyes should look ahead, and the body position in jogging should generally be erect but relaxed.

Beginning distances for elementary school children should offer sufficient challenge, but not to the point of causing distress and undue fatigue. A suggested beginning distance is 220 yards, with the stipulation that the child can adjust to his individual requirements. Children should gradually increase the distance until they are running a mile or more.

Many schools have sufficient room and suitable terrain for a jogging course. Checkpoints of known distances should be placed around the course.

A number of devices can be used to stimulate jogging. Record sheets can be kept by the teacher to record total distances jogged by individuals. Each student reports his jogging progress to the teacher and records on his record form the mileage covered. The individual mileage sheet could have a total of 100 miles, recorded in increments of quarter miles. Certificates of commendation could be given for totals of 50 or 100 miles of jogging.

Another stimulator is the cross country contest, where one class may challenge others to "run" a set distance. The first class to total the mileage is the winner. A United States map on which the children keep track of their class program helps to keep the contest alive.

Children need instruction in estimating distance by pacing so that each child can lay out his own course near his home and have a reasonably accurate estimate of distance. To do this, stake out 50 yards and have the child count the number of normal walking steps he takes to cover the distance. It is then possible to determine the length of the child's normal walking step so that he can use this to calculate the length of any selected course.

Another way is to "chain" the course distance by using a length of rope. Two children using a nonstretch rope 100' long can walk around a course and count the number of lengths of the measuring rope necessary to cover the distance.

Student art work and posters illustrating such catchy phrases as "Jog a bit and keep fit," "Get the beat — use your feet," and "Jogging is Tops" add interest to the activity.

Two cautions must be observed. Children with certain types of handicaps such as cardiac abnormalities, asthma, and diabetes should jog within stipulated medical limitations, if at all. Also, progression in jogging programs should be slow. The development of endurance for jogging is the result of a deep, systemic capacity, which changes slowly in response to demands.

11

Basic Movement

Basic movement is movement carried on for its own sake, for increased awareness and understanding of movement possibilities of the body, and for the acquisition of a good vocabulary of movement skills. The child, through guidance, uses basic movement as a way of expressing, exploring, and interpreting himself and of developing his capabilities. The experiences should be organized so that the child can learn about his movement possibilities.

Basic movements must be guided. Teachers must be prepared to introduce originality and something of their own personality into the teaching process. Invention is the key to the movement experiences. The problems are set up with instruction and demonstration kept to a minimum, to be used only as needed.

The emphasis in basic movement is on activity and movement of a *purposeful* nature. The teacher must be interested in promoting within the child *both* quantity and quality of movement. Only then does movement become an educational experience. Too often the children undergo movement experiences without guidance or insistence on their doing things as well as possible. Learning takes place primarily when a child reinforces a desirable motor pattern or concept, or acquires a new pattern or concept. Creativity means coming up with something worth saving, either because of its own intrinsic value or because it can be the basis for another movement pattern.

PURPOSES OF BASIC MOVEMENT

What are the objectives of the basic movement program? The following are considered basic and important:

1. Basic movement must structure a learning environment so that children learn to think for themselves and accept responsibility in a large measure for their own learning.

2. The program should offer a wide experience in movement, so that children will move with ease, coordination, fluency, and versatility to the limit of the body's potential.

3. The program should seek individual *creative* responses and should be structured so that the children have the opportunity to be creative and participate in self-learning.

4. The children should be made aware of their movement possibilities, so that in time they can move skillfully with sureness and confidence in a variety of situations, with emphasis on more efficient management of the body.

5. The children should develop a "movement vocabulary" of basic skills to serve as a foundation for the more complicated sports and dance skills.

6. The movement experiences should include gross movements so that developmental

125

demands will be made on the body. A variety of big-muscle activities should be a part of the program so fitness values can accrue for each child. (Page 98.)

7. The learning situation recognizes individual differences and allows each child to improve at his own rate and reach a measure of satisfaction in achievement.

8. It is postulated that a safer atmosphere is provided because children are not forced or urged to perform movements beyond their own capacity. They are led to a particular performance only when they themselves have established appropriate readiness.

9. The program should develop an awareness of the concepts of space, time, qualities of movement, flow, and body factors and their relationship and influence in movement.

10. Children should be able not only to move efficiently, but also to analyze critically their own movements and those of others.

PROCESSES IN BASIC MOVEMENT

Basic movement can be viewed as the summation of four different processes which cannot be taught in isolation but must be related.

What can the body do?

The teacher looks to basic movement to aid in four areas of movement competency, which in essence involves most human movement. Movements and skills can be selected from any of these areas.

a. *Efficient body management.* Body management involves the body as a whole. The child should gain body awareness, i.e., he must be aware of each part of the body as related to other parts or to the whole. This is an awareness of the individual (self) in the total physical environment.

b. *Basic skills.* Basic skills include specified locomotor movements (as opposed to general locomotor movements), nonlocomotor movements, and manipulative skills. In today's programs, manipulative skills have been broadened in number and scope so that they can be regarded as an entity in themselves. Manipulative skills are discussed in Chapter 13.

c. *Specialized skills.* These are the skills of the sports, specialized rhythmic activities, stunts and tumbling, and fitness. While most of the skills have techniques of a specific nature, their development can be enhanced through the application of basic movement instructional procedures.

d. *Apparatus skills.* Apparatus skills make up a special category, as they can serve as important tools of basic movement, particularly to develop body management competency. Like manipulative skills, apparatus activities have increased in number. They are presented in Chapter 14.

The kind of movement competency specified as the goal for a basic movement program will determine the approach. More freedom and exploration are required when the goal is good body management competencies, more specific instruction is needed to develop basic skills, and still more individual and specific instruction is demanded for specialized skills.

With what or with whom does he move?

The concerns here are the relation of the child and his movements to the physical environment (gymnasium, classroom, playground, or other area) in which he moves, whether large or hand apparatus is involved, and whether he works alone or with other children.

a. *Individual work.* The child first learns to move with competency and to manage himself and his piece of apparatus without interfering with other children.

b. *Partner work.* After he has learned to handle himself reasonably well as an individual, he can learn to work with another child.

c. *Participating in a group situation.* The child can develop sensitivity to others and learn to work effectively as a member of a group through this type of organization. Sharing experiences and judgments in a give-and-take situation leads to better social maturity.

Where can the body move?

This concerns the use of space. Spatial factors have two aspects, general and personal. In general space, the child moves with consideration for others in locomotor movements. In personal space, the child is concerned only with *self* in his movements. Spatial factors are direction, level, patterns, size, and plane of movement.

How can the body move?

Included in this concept are: time factors,

qualities of movement, flow, and the body factors involved in the movement. Time includes variation in speed, acceleration and deceleration, and rhythm. Qualities of movement, which some term *force,* include force of the movement and expressive movement. Flow can be either sustained (free) flow or interrupted (bound) flow. Body factors describe the body and its parts in relation to the prescribed movement problem.

FACTORS FOR SECURING VARIETY OF RESPONSE

The various factors of space, time, qualities of movement, flow, and body factors merit increased discussion and expansion, as they are most important in instructional procedures in basic movement. A thorough understanding of the factors is essential if the teacher is to stimulate the children to potential limits of variety and depth of movement.

Space — Space factors involve level, direction, size, plane of movement, and patterns.

Level — low, high, or in-between.

Direction — straight, zigzag, circular, curved, forward, backward, sideward, upward, and downward.

Size — large or small movements.

Plane of movement — horizontal, vertical, or diagonal.

Patterns — forming squares, diamonds, triangles, circles, figure eights, and other patterns.

Time — The time factor may be varied as follows:

Different speeds — slow, moderate, or fast.

Acceleration or deceleration—increasing or decreasing the speed of movement.

Even or uneven time — sudden, jerky, smooth, or even movement; variation in rhythm.

Flow — Establishing continuity of movement.

Interrupted flow (bound flow)—stopping at the end of a movement or part of a movement.

Sustained flow (free flow) — linking together smoothly different movements or parts of a movement.

Qualities of Movement

Force — light or heavy, strong or weak.

Climbing Frames Combined with Benches

Expressive movement — happy or sad, gay or restrained, angry, rough.

Imitative — imitating animals, personalities, machines, fictitious characters.

Body Factors — A number of considerations in the use of the body can add variety to movement.

Shape — can be long or short, wide or narrow, straight or twisted, stretched or curled, symmetrical or asymmetrical.

Weight bearing — different parts of the body supporting the weight, or receiving the weight; different number of body parts involved in a movement.

Execution — the movement may be done unilaterally (one-sided), bilaterally (both sides together), or cross-laterally (each side independently), performing with a different part of the body.

Body center-oriented — leading with different parts of the body, movements away from and toward the center of the body.

Variations Working on Apparatus

In addition to the variations just presented, variety in movement as the children work on large apparatus can be stimulated by the following considerations:

1. Apparatus can be arranged in different sequences, combinations, and numbers. Benches and balance beams, for example, can be placed on an incline, suspended higher than normal, or placed in combination with other equipment.

2. Variety can be promoted by viewing apparatus as a three-step process, and each step can be varied. Various ways to get on or mount the apparatus can be stipulated. Things to do on or with apparatus can be outlined. Different means of dismounting or getting down from apparatus can be specified.

3. Things to do on apparatus can be varied. The child can be challenged to go over, under, around, or through apparatus. He can support himself in different fashions, using a variety of body factors.

INSTRUCTIONAL PROCEDURES

The impression sometimes exists that we either have basic movement or we have direct instruction. This is a common misconception, as there are many shades or combinations of the two. There can be a heavy emphasis on command teaching with some exploratory activity included, or there might be a movement-centered approach with a modicum of direct teaching. The following diagram of methods of teaching* illustrates the range of teaching approaches.

METHODS OF TEACHING

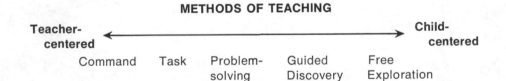

Teacher-centered				Child-centered
Command	Task	Problem-solving	Guided Discovery	Free Exploration

Command methodology allows for no individualization. Children are told what to do and how to do it. *Task* approaches set up a type of task to do, but allow little variety in the method of doing it. *Problem-Solving* sets up a problem and guides the students toward the solution. There can be freedom of choice, but guided toward a desired solution. *Guided Discovery* is more open-ended than problem-solving and accepts more individualization of

response. *Problem-Solving* can be used more for the development of skills, while *Guided Discovery* is more applicable to general body movement (body management) activities. *Free Exploration* without restrictions from the teacher is usually employed after a level of competency and background have been established to provide the child with sufficient experience on which to base his exploratory movements.

In this guide, the terms "problem-solving" and "guided discovery" are included under the broad term of problem-solving, with the recognition that problem-solving has broad

---

*Tillotson, Joan and Staff, "Questions and Answers about Movement Education." *Selected Readings in Movement Education,* Robert T. Sweeney, Editor. (Reading, Mass.; Addison-Wesley Publishing Co., 1970), p. 168

ranges of application and at times can permit a wide and individualistic solution to the problem.

Movement patterns, however, can be roughly divided into two broad categories, depending upon the desired outcomes. The first is unstructured movements with the goal of body management competency. The second is structured movements, with the objective of the development of certain skills.

Unstructured Movement

Unstructured movement aims toward the development of body awareness and efficient management of the body in a variety of situations. The emphasis is on exploration, repetition, and creation. Movement tasks of this nature specify certain factors of movement to be included in the problem, but do not specify a precise skill or movement. For example, the child may be asked to move about the room using a quick, low movement in alternation with a slow, high movement. Or, the directive might be, "Find a way to make your ball travel around the floor." There is no right or wrong answer as long as the child solves the problem. The choice is the child's, and the teacher should accept the solution. Unstructured movement will elicit a wider response of movement than problems for structured movement. The instructional emphasis focuses on versatility and breadth of response.

Another approach, which is occasionally used in unstructured movement, is expressive and imitative movement. Expressive movement relies on feelings such as being happy, gay, sad, angry, contrite, etc. Imitative movement mimics animals, personalities, and other elements. Expressive and imitative movement add breadth to the movement possibilities, but should not be regarded as the main objective.

Unstructured movement can be based on broad themes which give meaning to the movement patterns. An entire lesson can be based on a theme which provides the central idea for movement or two or more themes can be combined in a day's lesson. Many themes can be used. Here are some examples:

1. Learning to receive and transfer the weight.
2. Learning to take the weight on the hands (or other part of the body).
3. Shapes in the air.
4. Curling and stretching.
5. Leg work.
6. Over and under things.
7. Flight.
8. Lifting and lowering.
9. Symmetry and asymmetry.
10. Leading with different parts of the body.

Developing the theme 6, over and under things, using wands and cones.

Many other themes, some broad and some narrow, can be used. Additional themes can be established using equipment and hand apparatus.

Structured Movement

Structured movement involves a specific skill which can be named and identified as opposed to general movements of a wide choice under unstructured movement. Children may practice such structured movements as walking, batting, bouncing, jumping, and pitching. A structured movement can be identified by the fact that it usually ends in the suffix "-ing." Included in structured movement are the basic skills, specialized skills, and the more precise skills on apparatus. Structured activity implies a limitation; the child must conform to the specified activity, but the activity can be accomplished or interpreted by various responses. The emphasis is on the development of a particular skill, which includes a concept of right and wrong with respect to technique, but the child should be allowed to arrive at or discover the best way or ways for him to do the skill, within reasonable limits.

The more precise the skill, the more critical the need to establish good techniques. Good techniques should prevail even if the child feels more comfortable with a known departure from accepted form. A child who throws right-handed and steps with his right foot as he throws should be induced to change to a left foot step, as the right hand, right foot throwing technique will establish an undesirable habit pattern which would need to be changed later. He should be encouraged to change, even if after exploration and experimentation he feels more comfortable in the right hand, right foot throw.

When dealing with structured movement, a different instructional approach than with unstructured movement is necessary. For structured movement, the range of acceptable technique needs to be known and adhered to. In some cases this can be broad, but in others, it can be quite narrow. The solution is to establish the basis in technique and then proceed with exploration, repetition, and creativity on this fundamental basis.

Organizing the Class

The objectives and nature of the movement experiences will indicate to the teacher how a class should be organized for activity. The amount and type of equipment and supplies will affect the approach.

There are many variations and subdivisions of the three basic schemes. In each case, the children may work as individuals, with a partner, or as a member of a group.

The Single-Activity Organization

All children are reacting to the same challenge, whether as individuals, partners, or with groups. The plan of organization is excellent for introductory work, because the children are all at approximately the same starting point. The plan allows the teacher to conduct the class with a planned lesson and the elements of progression. It is convenient for providing guidance (coaching), demonstrations, and evaluation at the completion of a segment of the lesson.

Multiple Groups

The class is divided into two or more groups, each working with a different movement problem, which could involve different large or hand apparatus.

Dividing the groups for work with different movement patterns is of value at times, particularly when supplies and apparatus are insufficient for the entire class to participate in the same activity at one time. In this way, equipment can be better utilized and waiting for turns is minimized. Some means of rotation should be established, either by signal or at will. Class control and guidance become more of a problem as it is not practical to stop the class to give instruction and guidance. The teacher must move from group to group, providing help as needed.

Another problem is the time element. Each group, ideally, should have sufficient opportunity in the activity for full development. In some activities, children may finish and run out of things to do, while in others the opposite may be true.

For effective movement the children should have some basis on which to superimpose new experiences if they are to be given a number of activities in rotation. Dividing into groups should be done usually after the children have had experience in the kinds of movement experiences designated for the groups. Introductory and initial work can best be accomplished through single activity organization.

Individual Choice

Children select the movement experiences with which they choose to work and rotate at will. They can get their own equipment out, or can choose from selected pieces already placed. This should be done after the children have a good basis for further exploration and creativity. They should be encouraged to practice on needed areas or create beyond their present level. It should be a period of creativity, not just supervised free play.

Some teachers have found this effective as the introductory activity to a daily lesson. Occasionally, the teacher can give the following directions to a class upon entrance into the gymnasium. "For the first few minutes of our class period today, you may select and practice the movement pattern you wish." The teacher can qualify this by enumerating the possibilities with: "You may practice movements without equipment; you may select from the available balls, beanbags, wands, or hoops; or you may work on the climbing ropes, balance beams, or mats."

A choice period could also be used to finish up a daily lesson or a unit of work. The choice could be limited to the activities and movements of the lesson or unit.

PROBLEM DEVELOPMENT

The Approach to Problem Development

A number of guidelines should be considered in developing a problem with children.

Repetition. Repetition is the basis for learning, and sufficient repetition in particular patterns is necessary. The teacher must develop the sensitivity to determine when sufficient exploration and repetition have occurred at a particular stage so that children may move to the next progression.

Experimentation. Each child must be permitted free expression of movement within the limitations of the problem. His energies are to be directed toward the solution of the problem, and he must be allowed sufficient time to accomplish this goal working at his own rate according to his own ability.

Creative Opportunity. The child should have the opportunity to create and come up with movement patterns arising within himself, based on experimentation and exploration pointed toward the solution of the problem. His creativity should show that the movement patterns and concepts of the lesson have been absorbed, and that he can put to his use the factors from the movement experiences. Creativity in this instance would mean coming up with something relevant and worth saving.

Focus on Potential. To help each child reach his full potential, high standards and a full effort should be demanded from each child.

Principles of Movement. Principles of movement governing the development of skills have strong application to movement work and should be an integral part of guidance and coaching. At times, they can be embodied in the instruction. (Page 72.)

Challenging Quality. As soon as children have responded and succeeded in meeting the demands of the problem in the introductory stage, they should be stimulated toward more efficient movement. Inept or sloppy performance should not be tolerated beyond the initial stages.

Perceptive Guidance. For the teacher, the lesson period is one of observation, analysis, and perceptive guidance.

Demonstrations. Demonstrations are important in basic movement procedures. They serve the purpose of illustrating variety or depth of movement, showing something unique or different, pointing out items of good technique or approach, illustrating different acceptable styles, and showing progress or accomplishments.

Demonstrations should be used only infrequently at the beginning of the lesson, as children should be given opportunity to develop individual approaches rather than imitating the style of another child. However, a few basics indicating the problem limits might be presented early in the lesson, or even in the introductory phases, to give direction to the activity.

The demonstration should be directed toward increasing the child's understanding and movement potential. A child needs to observe critically and analyze rather than just be entertained by the presented movements. In order that he may profit by what he has just viewed, the demonstration should be followed by a period of practice.

The demonstration may include an entire movement pattern or just some portion of it. The children selected for demonstration should be capable of presenting a reasonable model of what is desired. The teacher can ask for volunteers, or can pinpoint children who have proved capable of demonstrating what is wanted. The selection should be varied so that the chore of demonstrating does not fall too frequently on a few children. During the course of lessons, all children should be given the opportunity to demonstrate, with the caution that their self-concept and peer regard must be preserved.

The pattern of demonstrations may take several forms:

1. **The Single Demonstration.** In this pattern, one demonstration is presented at a time. It may be limited to one presentation, but it is well to have more than one individual successively provide demonstration, so that children may see varied approaches. If partner or small group work is undertaken, the same principle holds.

2. **The Multiple Demonstration.** In this a number of children (individually, by partners, or in small groups) are providing demonstrations simultaneously. One convenient way to organize this is to have squads demonstrate. In utilizing squads, the teacher may select one of the squads to demonstrate and then direct the children to return to activity. Other squads could have turns later. The teacher might even use this as a motivational device by telling the children: "After a period of time, I am going to select the squad which I feel has made the best progress to demonstrate."

Another means is to have one-half the class demonstrate, while the other half watches.

3. **The Achievement Demonstration.** This may use either of the two previous patterns, but is more likely to take the multiple method. At the end of a unit or sizeable portion thereof a demonstration is held to show what has been accomplished. The squad provides a desirable unit for this purpose.

The question-and-answer technique has a place in the demonstration process, but must not dominate it. Questions can be directed toward such learning elements as what was good, what factors are important, and what directions the efforts should take. Care must be taken so that the demonstration period does not become too protracted due to a lengthy question and answer period.

Steps in Developing the Problem

After the initial, introductory activity, the development of the movement lesson can follow these steps:

1. Set the original problem, sometimes called the central problem. This follows the process of basic movement. The directives given to the child can be answers to these questions:

What is the child to do? (Jump, run, move to a certain spot, balance, etc.) How is he to work? (Individually, with a partner, or with a group.) On or with what apparatus? (A ball, wand, or hoop: on a balance beam, bench, or rope?)

Where is he to move? (What direction, level, or other factor?)

How is he to move?

On, off, or across the floor?

What body parts are used to execute the movement and how?

What quality factors are involved?

On apparatus, where does the body go?

An example of an unstructured problem following this format is: "Let's see you move across the floor, changing directions, with a quick movement on one foot and a slow movement on the other."

An example of a structured movement is: "Let's see you run across the floor in any direction you wish, changing the levels of the arms frequently." For structured movement, hints for technique may be added such as: "Remember to run lightly on your toes with a slight body lean."

The children are now introduced to the problem and initial movements occur.

2. The second step in the progression is to extend and challenge the creativity of the children, seeking to enhance their movement, to give depth to movement experiences around the problem, to encourage a variety of response, and to give attention to qualities of movement.

Securing a variety of response means that the teacher should be familiar with the factors which can elicit variation. These factors are time, space, flow, qualities of movement, and body factors and have been previously discussed.

3. After the children have exhausted the possibilities of variety, attention should be turned toward developing quality in move-

ment. Have the children select and practice a movement with the objective of securing quality, doing it as well as it can be done under the circumstances. They may work on several movements, emphasizing good form and techniques, and such qualities as smoothness, lightness, coordination, and rhythm.

For structured movement and proper development of skills, this step should include stress on critical points of technique, which are important to the skill being practiced. This can be accomplished in a number of ways, such as by demonstration, discussion, or a question-and-answer period.

4. The fourth step is to put the movement patterns in sequence and combination, emphasizing sustained flow from one movement pattern to another. The child can select certain movements from those which have been practiced and put them together in sequence, with good transition from one movement pattern to the other. For example, he may be instructed to "put together a light run, a heavy run, and a body turn."

Practice can be extended to include different types of movement which demand from the child the ability to think how he might put these together most effectively. The problem emphasizing different movements could be: "As you dribble the ball, move with different locomotor movements in various directions. Select some definite combinations, and repeat several times before changing to a new combination."

5. The fifth step, which may or may not be employed, is to use the movement pattern in a relay or a game. This demonstrates the utility of the movement or skill and shows the child the practical application of what he has practiced.

Another way to extend the experience is to have the child work with a partner or as a member of a group.

Working with a Partner

In partner work, the learning experiences should be the type which the child cannot do alone. Working with a partner is generally confined to later stages of movement patterns after practice has occurred on an individual basis. Teaching cooperation to children is an important social goal. It is generally better, depending upon the activity, to pair children

of reasonably equal achievement, but at other times, size and weight might be governing factors.

How may children work together? A number of suggestions follow:

1. One child may be used as an obstacle and his partner devises ways of getting over, under, and around the "obstacle."
2. One child may support the weight of the other in part or wholly.
3. There can be matching, contrasting, or following movements.
4. Sequence building can be undertaken.
5. There can be critique of movement, with one child moving and the other providing the correction and critique.

Working as a Member of a Group

Group work in movement education is generally confined to small groups. This is not to be interpreted as a group of children working individually on similar movements, but a group of children working together on a movement task. The task of the group should be definite so that the interests are directed toward a common end. Examples of group work are finding different ways of making a human tower or finding different ways two children can bear the weight of two other children.

There is some difficulty in coordinating this type of activity, because activities are not balanced in length and interest and one group may finish before another. If the groups are too scattered, it is difficult for the teacher to provide proper help and guidance for each.

Phrasing the Challenge or Question

Stimulating an effective movement response from the children depends upon the manner in which the problems are phrased. Problems can be presented in the form of questions or statements, both of which should be of a nature to elicit and encourage variety, depth, and extent of movement. The teacher can secure ideas from the following directives, but will no doubt develop his own style and approach. The form is given first, and a specific application of the form follows. The directives are divided into those which initially define the problem to be solved and those which have value in stimulating variety or imposing a particular limitation.

Presenting a Problem

1. Show me how a . . . moves, or Show me . . . Show me how an alligator moves along the ground.
2. Have you seen a . . . ?
   Have you seen a kangaroo jump?
3. What ways can you . . . ?
   What ways can you hop over the jump rope?
4. How would you . . . ?, or How can you . . . ?
   How would you dribble a ball changing hands frequently?
5. See how many different ways you can . . .
   See how many different ways you can hang from a ladder.
6. What can you do with a . . . ?, or, What kinds of things can you . . . ?
   What can you do with a hoop?
7. Can you portray a . . . ?
   Can you portray an automobile with a flat tire?
8. Discover different ways you can . . .
   Discover different ways you can volley a ball against a wall.
9. Can you . . . ?
   Can you keep one foot up when you bounce the ball?
10. Who can . . . a . . . in such a way that . . . ?
    Who can bounce a ball in such a way that it keeps time with the tom-tom?
11. What does a . . . ?
    What does a cat do when he is wet?

Securing Variety or Setting a Limitation

1. Try it again another way, or, Try to . . .
   Try to jump higher.
2. See how far (many times, high, close, low, etc.) . . .
   See how far you can reach with your arms.
3. Find a way to . . . or, Find a new way to . . . Find a new way to jump over the bench.
4. Apply . . . to . . .
   Apply a heavy movement to your run.
5. How else can you . . . ?
   How else can you roll your hoop?
6. Make up a sequence . . .
   Make up a sequence of previous movements, changing smoothly from one movement to the other.
7. Now try to combine a . . . with . . .
   Now try to combine a locomotor movement with your catching.
8. Alternate . . . and . . .
   Alternate walking and hopping.
9. Repeat the last movement but add . . .
   Repeat the last movement but add a body twist as you move.
10. See if you can . . .
    See if you can do the movement with a partner.
11. Trace (or draw) a . . . with . . .
    Trace a circle with your hopping pattern.
12. Find another part of the body to . . . , or, Find other ways to . . .
    Find another part of the body to take the weight.
13. Combine the . . . with . . .
    Combine the hopping with a body movement.
14. In how many different positions can you . . . ?
    In how many different positions can you carry your arms while walking the balance beam?
15. How do you think the . . . would change if . . . ?
    How do you think the balance we are doing would change if our eyes were closed?
16. On signal . . .
    On signal, speed up your movements.

Stimulating Effort

While stimulating variation will in a sense stimulate the children to better effort, it is important that the children extend themselves within the movement itself. This is the idea of including in the establishment of the movement problem incentives such as asking them to carry out tasks "as far as possible" or "with abrupt or definite changes." Although competition between individuals is not an accepted concept in movement education, some goals like "How far can you reach?" or "How far can you jump?" lend themselves to measurement. The number of floor boards covered or reached could be counted. There is also the idea of using beanbags or other markers and placing them "as far as you can." The device of having children stretch or reach until they pull themselves from their base makes them extend their limits.

STRESSING QUALITY IN MOVEMENT

Establishing quality is the vital part of movement education. Without this aspect, movement is mere activity. If the educational process can be viewed as experimentation, selection, modification, clarification, and repetition, guidance and direction fall into their proper perspective. If desirable learning is to occur, the child must be supplied with the basis to select from the many experiences those which he wishes to retain and develop. Thus retained and repeated, the movement pattern becomes a part of his being.

The guidance process of movement experiences first centers on securing a variety of response. The teacher must, however, be able to assess the child's performance in terms of suitability and quality. It is axiomatic that the teacher, in order to improve the quality of performance, must develop the ability to analyze movement and suggest the necessary adjustments to the children so that desirable learning proceeds toward the goal of individual development. The element of demonstration, primarily by the student, is also brought in. In the case of more precise skills, teaching aids would also be of value.

Guidance in movement can be roughly divided into two aspects. The first is in general terms of the quality of movement and the application of what is termed "Principles Important in Movement and Skill Performance." This is discussed in the text on pages 72-73. The principles are applicable to basic movement patterns as well as to skills.

In unstructured movement, where there is no "right" way to respond with a movement pattern, the concentration in guidance can be centered on general qualities of movement, lightness, smoothness, and coordination.

The second aspect of guidance occurs where structured movement is the basis of the lesson. There can be, and is in many cases, a correct way to perform the skill; and there also are certain undesirable elements which should be avoided. In a lesson emphasizing or including walking, stress should be placed on the feet being pointed reasonably forward. Children should not be permitted to walk with their toes pointed out *even if they so choose*. Teachers must know the basic elements of skills so that proper techniques can be inculcated and undesirable habits avoided in the learning process. This means that the more precise and demanding the skill, the less room for movement education methodology and the more emphasis on direct instruction. Systematic progression is needed if skill is to improve. An increasingly difficult challenge must be presented, and effective repetition must be introduced. However, experimentation and exploration always have a place in the learning experiences for establishing skills. Often the performer will need to select the pattern he wishes to adopt by experimentation from among a number of good or accepted ways.

The question of how much form should be stressed is raised. Few elementary school children will reach perfection in form in any activity. On the primary level, form should be considered in a minor sense but should be consistent with the development of the child. Necessarily, the child should not be permitted to acquire a poor habit which will cause him difficulty later. For intermediate children, the quality in movement is of greater importance than quantity of movement. Emphasis should be on doing things as well as possible, but this must not become an overriding consideration.

Proper postural habits must be emphasized throughout movement education, since these are related in many cases to quality of performance. Within the concept of maximum growth and development of the child, there should be stress on the possession of reasonable body alignment and the establishment of good postural habits. These also become factors in the guidance and directive process of movement education.

FORMATIONS FOR MOVEMENT

Instruction involving nonlocomotor movement involves little problem with the children, as they can take a place on the floor and undergo the movement experiences. In locomotor movement, however, a different situation presents itself with regard to the manner in which the children can be organized for movement. The number of the children, the space available, and the type of activity are factors which influence the choice of formation for effective teaching. The following formations can be considered for locomotor movement:

1. Individual movement in every direction. The children must be cautioned about collisions and the need to be courteous. Children should be directed to use all the available space and to move in various directions.

2. Around the area in a circular fashion. The objection to this is that it creates competition and generates conformity. However, collisions are not likely, and the teacher can observe the children effectively.

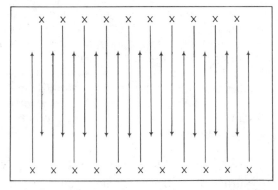

3. On opposite sides of the room, exchanging position. The children on signal cross to the opposite side of the area, passing through the opposite line.

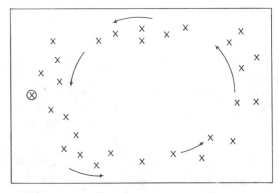

4. On opposite sides of the room, moving to the center and back. A line can be formed with ropes, wands, or cones to mark the center limit. Children move to the center of the area and then return to place.

5. On opposite sides of the room, one line moving across and back. The two sides alternate in their turns. The line of children from one side crosses to a point near the other line

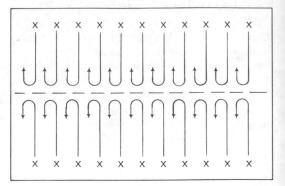

and then makes a turn, returning to place. After these children have completed the movement, the other group takes a turn.

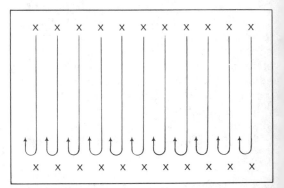

6. Squad formation, re-forming at the other end of the space. The leading child in each squad begins his movement across the floor. When he is about halfway, the next child starts. The squads re-form at the other end and get ready for another movement.

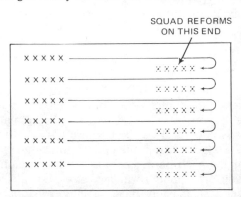

SQUAD REFORMS ON THIS END

7. Squads in crisscross formation. Squads form as indicated, with two opposite squads moving at a time. In effect, they exchange places. Members of each squad move in turn

when the child in front is far enough ahead. After the first two squads have performed, the other squads move similarly.

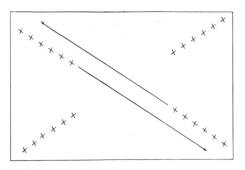

8. Children on four sides of the area, exchanging position. The children on one pair of opposite sides exchange first, and then the others exchange. They alternate back and forth in this manner.

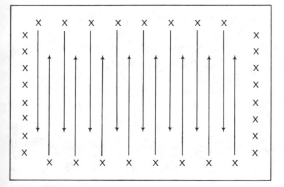

DEVELOPING IDEAS FOR UNSTRUCTURED MOVEMENT

The challenge to the child gives him the general directions of movement, but does not specify the precise skill or movement by which he meets the challenge or question. It should lead to a variety of response, which can later be refined or altered. The examples as given are stated as tasks to be done, but should be properly phrased using the guidelines for phrasing questions as previously discussed (page 133). These are divided into locomotor and nonlocomotor challenges, but could be combined in some cases.

Locomotor Challenges

1. Move about the room and in every direction with a rapid, low movement followed by a slow, high movement. Various other combinations can be specified.

2. Do a movement at regular speed, followed by the same movement in slow motion.

3. Use big, wide movements to imitate an elephant. Other animals can be imitated.

4. Be a giant, a dwarf, or a witch.

5. Go over (or along, or under) the benches using different movements and body shapes.

6. Move around the room using different swimming strokes.

7. Move around the room using any movement you wish. On signal, freeze. On the next signal try another movement.

8. One-half of the children are on hands and knees (or face down, or in curled position). The other half on signal go over all the other children, using various locomotor movements. Other factors can be added. After a period of movement, reverse the children.

9. Home base activities can be used. Each child has a home spot on the floor. He is given tasks to do and returns each time back to his home base. Have him (1) pick out another spot, do a stunt, and return; (2) touch a wall or walls and return; (3) trace a particular pattern on the floor with his movement and return; (4) other tasks can be set.

10. Move so one foot is always off the ground.

11. Move around the room with a selected high locomotor movement, gradually lowering your body until you can do some kind of a roll. Begin anew.

12. Move around the room beginning with a low position, gradually raising until you propel yourself into the air. Drop to a low position and repeat.

13. Move around the room taking the weight on different parts of the body.

14. Travel around the room using bilateral movement of the hands and feet.

15. Travel around the room with your head lower than your waist.

16. Carry a wand around the room as you move. On signal, place the wand on the floor and jump or hop back and forth over it. Repeat using a beanbag, hoop, jumping rope, or other piece of hand apparatus.

17. Carry a piece of hand apparatus as you move around the room. On the first signal, place the piece of apparatus on the floor and

move over and around the pieces of apparatus on the floor. On signal #2, pick up the piece nearest you and again move around the room.

18. Move around the room in various directions touching different walls. After you touch a wall, try a new movement.

19. Each child has a partner. On signal #1, one of the two partners moves around the room with a movement of his choice, the other child imitating the movement. On signal #2, the other child leads with a new movement.

20. Move around the room, stressing taking the weight on different parts of the feet.

21. Practice different ways of moving the feet — singly, crossing, alternately, together, one foot leading.

22. Move around the room using movements like the different track and field events.

23. Move around the room making right angle turns. Each time you turn, change your type of movement.

24. Pick a sport and pretend you are playing that sport.

25. Choose a piece of small apparatus (ball, beanbag, etc.) and practice with that apparatus piece, sometimes standing still and sometimes moving.

26. Demonstrate different ways of rolling, utilizing different shapes, directions, and parts of the body.

27. Move sideways (backwards, or forwards) in as many different ways as you can.

28. Move around the room in different directions, experimenting with different parts of the body leading.

Nonlocomotor Challenges

1. Balance on one, two, or three parts of the body, or on a particular part of the body.

2. Stretch your body to full limits in different directions.

3. Make different body shapes to represent kinds of buildings, autos, trains, machines, etc.

4. Make different kinds of bridges with the body.

5. Show different ways and combinations in which you can twist the body to its limits.

6. Keeping one foot in place, show how far you can reach in different directions.

7. Alternate curling and stretching movements.

8. Make yourself big and small with various shapes.

9. Using various positions such as push-up, crab, sitting, lying (prone or supine), on hands and knees, on all fours, side-leaning rest, and others, react to challenges like these:

Lift various parts of the body off the floor.

With a part of the body, make a pattern, or write a letter or word in the air.

Draw a picture.

Reach out as far as possible in different directions with various limbs. Touch the floor.

Change positions of the limbs in various manners and combinations. Use unilateral, bilateral, and cross-lateral patterns.

10. Make big circles with various parts of the body. Use different planes — horizontal, vertical, and diagonal.

11. Show in different positions the different kinds of swimming movements that can be made.

12. From a wide straddle position, bend and twist in various directions, touching the floor as far out as possible. Touch with the hand out to the opposite side.

13. Practice different balances on one foot. On the one hand and one foot.

14. With a partner, practice different ways of supporting each other wholly or in part.

15. Make one hand follow the other hand around the body.

16. Experiment with the different joints of the body and see what movements each can do.

17. Make different parts of the body move in patterned movements or tracing designs. This has wide application. The children can be standing, sitting, or in any of the various body positions. One, two, or even three of the body parts can move in tracing different designs. Geometrical designs, letters, words, and other ways of moving can be explored.

DEVELOPING IDEAS FOR STRUCTURED MOVEMENT

Locomotor Challenges

These include walking, running, jumping, galloping, sliding, hopping, skipping, and leaping. Some general directions for all movements of this type can be made to secure variety of response.

1. Changes in speed — slow to fast, accelerate or decelerate.

2. Weight bearing on different parts of the foot — on the toes, heels, sides of the foot.

3. The length of the stride or jump — tiny to large.

4. Varied actions of the feet — pointed out or in, following (one foot catching the other), crossing front or behind, changing leading foot.

5. Changing directions.

6. Moving forwards, sidewards, backwards. Using turns.

7. Tracing different patterns — squares, triangles, figure eights.

8. On and over objects.

9. Putting together sequences of various locomotor movements.

In addition, space, body, flow, and movement quality factors as previously discussed can be employed.

While variety is important, quality in movement is essential and must be sought in the instructional process. Each child should be encouraged toward the highest quality movement of which he is capable.

An Example of an Exploratory Approach in Structured Movement, Emphasizing Running, Leaping, and Stopping Techniques

The following routine illustrates how a locomotor movement like running can be combined with leaping and stopping to provide meaningful experiences for children. Although the approach is primarily direct instruction, children have the opportunity to respond in individual patterns within the tasks as set. There is good control and opportunity for instruction in having the movement performed by squads in squad column formation with the stipulation that each squad member follows when the member in front of him is halfway across the area. The children run across an area 20 to 30 yards in width, depending on their age level. When they have completed a run across the area, the squads re-form on the other side, awaiting directions to come back.

Cross your feet over each time as you run.

Run low, touching the ground on either side alternately.

Run low, touching the ground with both hands as you go along.

Run forward, looking back over your right shoulder.

The same, except look back over the left shoulder.

Run zigzag, that is — changing direction every few steps.

Run to the center, stop, and continue.

Run forward, stop with the right side forward, then another stop with the left side forward.

Run forward and stop. Come back three steps and stop again. Continue in original direction.

Try a two-count stop with a definite "one, two" slap on the ground with the feet.

Try a hop, step, and a jump and then continue.

Run sideways, leading the first time with one side. Next time, reverse the position.

The children can devise other combinations to try out. Be sure that the children understand and use good running form. Skipping, galloping, and other locomotor movements can be included in the combinations.

The following running variations can be done as the children run across the area:

Run as lightly as possible.

Run high on the toes.

Run on the heels.

As you run, bounce as high as you can.

Run with tiny, fast steps.

Run with giant strides.

Run with high knee action.

Mix in giant leaps with your run.

Run backward.

Run forward halfway and backward the rest.

Run backward halfway and forward the rest.

As you run across, turn around (right) completely and continue across.

The same, but turn to the left.

Run slowly and then suddenly change to running fast.

Run with an exaggerated arm movement.

Run with a goose step movement.

Additional Suggestions for Jumping and Hopping Activities

Jumping and hopping activities should develop spring, lightness, balance, coordination, and control in activity. Some ideas for activities are presented.

1. Jump or hop in and out of various patterns and designs on the floor made by jump-

ing ropes, hoops, wands, benches, or balance beams.

2. Specific floor patterns can be marked on the floor or on sheets of vinyl or plastic by painting footprints on them. Right and left are marked and the children follow as indicated. Lines in different kinds of geometric figures and mazes can be painted on blacktop surfaces. Many basic locomotor movements can be done on these patterns.

Nonlocomotor Movements

Nonlocomotor movements include bending, twisting, turning (in place), movements toward and away from the center of the body, raising and lowering the parts or the body as a whole, and other body movements done in place. Nonlocomotor movements do not lend themselves as well to the distinction between unstructured and structured movement as do the locomotor and manipulative skills. Gross body movements to the limits of flexibility are important. Good control and a variety of body movement leading to effective body management are also important goals. Balance is another factor which should receive attention.

Structured movements have a place in the program when the teacher wishes to emphasize a particular movement and have the children explore this to its extent. Here are examples of structured problems:

1. "Take a comfortable position with your feet about shoulder width apart and pointed ahead. Bend forward without bending the knees, and see how far you can touch down in front of you, between your legs, and to the sides. Try it now with a wider position of the feet."

2. "From a wide straddle position with the arms out to the sides at shoulder level, twist as far as you can to the right and determine how far you can see around behind you, using a full twist of the body. Try it to the left side. See if it helps if you bounce the twist. Try it with your arms in other positions."

These are examples of a specific kind of a movement which the teacher wishes to have the children explore to the full extent of the body's range of movement. This increases their awareness of what the body can do. Similar challenges can be applied to other particular kinds of movement.

Combinations of Movement

The foregoing illustrations and suggestions of movement possibilities have generally been directed toward a single movement with little thought of combinations. Combining different kinds of movement opens extensive possibilities. Both locomotor and nonlocomotor movements can be put together in various combinations and sequences, such as the following:

1. Run, leap, and roll.
2. Run, collapse, and roll.
3. Twist and lift.
4. Twist and smile.
5. Lift and grin.
6. Hop, turn around, and shake.
7. Run, change direction, and collapse.
8. Hop, make a shape in the air, and balance.
9. Rock, jump high, and sit down.
10. Rock and twist.
11. Curl, roll, and jump.
12. Twirl and make a statue.
13. Make different letters of the alphabet.
14. Show us how waves come in on an ocean beach.
15. Kneel and balance.
16. Kneel and sway.
17. Stretch like a rubber band. Snap back to position.
18. Blow up like a balloon. Let the air out.
19. Blow up like a balloon. Let the balloon burst.
20. Squat and do a jump turn.
21. Twist and untwist. Slow one way and fast the other.
22. Click heels different ways. Add various kinds of hand claps.

Attention should be centered on following directions and doing movements as well as possible.

THE MOVEMENT SUGGESTION BOX

An idea which has been received enthusiastically by children is the Movement Suggestion Box. This box, which should contain enough cards for the whole class, can be used in two ways.

The first approach is to have movement challenges on the cards. Each child takes a card and responds to the challenge. This activity can be used well at the beginning of a lesson.

In the second approach the child is offered some choice of the type of movement he may select. Cards covering three or more areas can be in different compartments. Suggested are:

Mat Activities

Locomotor Movement

Nonlocomotor Movement

A Manipulative Activity

The child may choose a second area if he has finished his first task and there is still time left.

PERCEPTUAL-MOTOR ACTIVITIES, MANIPULATIVE ACTIVITIES, AND APPARATUS ACTIVITIES

The teacher is referred to the next three chapters for additional material on movement experiences. The focus in the present chapter was on locomotor and nonlocomotor activities. Manipulative and apparatus activities should be a strong part of basic movement. Perceptual-motor activities also have value, but some are in a different context. While some of these activities involve exploration to a degree, many are inflexible because they are a response to a command. They can serve to supplement activities of basic movement.

12

Perceptual-Motor Competency

Characteristics of the Underachiever or
   Slow Learner
How Are These Individuals Discovered?
Implications for Physical Education Programs

There is increasing evidence that an association exists between perceptual-motor competency and certain academic skills, primarily reading readiness and achievement. Some children, often normal or above normal in intelligence, fail to achieve satisfactorily because of a learning disability. Many of these children, who are classed as underachievers or slow learners, can be helped with a program of specific movements leading to perceptual-motor competency. A slow learner may possess such characteristics as poor balance, mixed or no lateral dominance, visual-motor problems, poor hand-eye coordination, and poor spatial body image.

The perceptual-motor educational concept is based on the theory that correlation of movement is centered in the brain stem and that reading, writing, spelling, and speech are controlled by this area of the neurological system. If the child has good perceptual-motor skills, then the motor-neural system has matured and developed to the point where it is not a negative factor in the learning process. Conversely, the theory holds that a child with deficient perceptual-motor development will exhibit disability or fail to reach the proper potential in one or more of the areas of reading, writing, spelling, and speech.

While the main emphasis to this point has been the correction of deficiencies, it can be postulated that a program of activities stressing good perceptual-motor training would also be of benefit to children with apparently satisfactory levels of achievement. If a program of perceptual-motor training can help raise the level of deficient children, then it should be of value in increasing the academic achievement potential of the so-called normal child.

CHARACTERISTICS OF THE UNDERACHIEVER OR SLOW LEARNER

What characteristics does a child with poor or deficient perceptual-motor development exhibit? The child may have trouble holding or maintaining his balance. He appears clumsy and cannot carry himself well in motion. He may appear to be generally awkward in activities requiring coordination.

He may show signs of dysfunction in lateral dominance. He can do things well or better with one side or one limb of the body. He does not know right from left readily and may have to hesitate or think carefully before being able to come up with a definite movement or answer to a direction. In locomotor skills, he does movements much more efficiently on one side than the other. He may reverse with regularity when such a reversal is not indicated.

Kindergarten or first-grade children may not be able to hop or skip properly. They have difficulty making changes in or combinations of movement. After learning after a fashion to hop or skip, they cannot then hop or skip backwards, nor can they hop well for a period of time.

Spatial orientation is another area in which indications can appear. The child has difficulty in gauging space with respect to his body, and bumps and collides with objects and other children. He may be accident-prone. Hand-eye coordination may be poor. He has trouble handling the simple tools of physical education — beanbags, balls, and other objects that involve a visual-motor-perceptual relationship.

HOW ARE THESE INDIVIDUALS DISCOVERED?

While the teacher may believe from indications that a child has a perceptual-motor disability, definite testing measures can be employed to make this determination. A Perceptual Rating Scale has been devised by Newell V. Kephart and is presented in his book, *The Purdue Perceptual-Motor Survey.** Testing involves two aspects. The first is whether or not the child can do the task as specified, and the second is the assurance and confidence with which he does the task. The test includes not only physical skills, but also hand-eye skills in using the chalkboard. Two areas only from the test are presented for purposes of illustration.

Testing for Balance and Laterality

A walking board, on the balance beam principle, is made up of a 2″ x 4″ board 12′ long. The 4″ side is used for the test. The child is asked to walk forward, backward, and sideward (each way) without losing balance. Children should be able to move forward, backward, and sideward with ease and assurance. A child with a laterality problem will have difficulty moving one of the ways sideward, usually from left to right.

Skill Movements and Combinations

Combinations of hopping, jumping, and skipping movements on the floor are used in this part of the test. The child is given commands to demonstrate the following movements:

1. Put both feet together and jump forward one step.

2. Hop forward one step using the right foot only.

3. Hop forward one step using the left foot only.

4. Skip across the room.

5. Hop in place, first on the right foot and then on the left, continuing this pattern.

6. Same as the foregoing, but twice on the right and twice on the left.

7. Same procedure, but twice on the right and once on the left.

8. Same as (7) but twice on the left and once on the right.

The child is carefully observed to see that he can make the movements and the changes with a smooth, rhythmical motion and with ease and assurance. Failure indications would be a stiff, jerky motion, with pauses indicating that he has taken time to think before moving.

IMPLICATIONS FOR PHYSICAL EDUCATION PROGRAMS

Testing and specialized remedial work in perceptual-motor training are within the province of specialists. Classroom teachers can cooperate with these programs, but generally the work is outside of the normal physical education program. If a child is low in reading readiness and reading achievement, testing should be accomplished to determine the possibility of perceptual-motor deficiency.

Since perceptual-motor development is located in the early primary years, activities which have the potential of development in this area should be stressed. The following guides are important:

1. Children should be given opportunity and practice in hand-eye and foot-eye coordination by frequent use of activities where they can handle balls, beanbags, hoops, ropes, rings, and the like.

2. The balance beam and its activities should be a part of the program.

3. A program emphasizing the development of basic locomotor skills should be

*Roach and Kephart. *The Purdue Perceptual Motor Survey* (Columbus, Ohio: Charles E. Merrill Books, Inc. 1966).

instituted. This should be an instructional program.

4. Opportunity for management of the body in a variety of situations should be a part of the curriculum. Children should have activities on the floor, off the floor, across the floor, and on apparatus.

5. The concept of laterality should be included in all movement. The child should counter a move to the right with a similar move to the left. If he moves forward, stress a backward movement. No one side of the body nor direction of movement should dominate.

6. Movements should be further considered from the standpoint of unilateral, bilateral, or cross-lateral approach. Wherever possible, all should be used. A unilateral movement is one done by a single part or side of the body. Moving one arm forward would be a unilateral movement. A bilateral movement occurs when both arms or legs make corresponding movements. Moving both arms forward in a similar fashion is an example of a bilateral movement. A cross-lateral movement demands that parts of the body move in a different manner. Moving one arm forward and one backward at the same time would be a cross-lateral movement. This movement, however, is an opposed cross-lateral movement. An unrelated cross-lateral movement occurs when two corresponding parts move without relationship to each other. Lifting one arm up and the other arm forward would be unrelated movements.

7. A variety of movement and movement combinations should be presented as challenges to the child. The teacher needs the imagination and ability to take a simple movement and exhaust it completely with variety and combinations, thus giving play to many perceptual-motor-neural pathways.

8. Specialized activities designated particularly for perceptual-motor training should be included. These are the bounding board, Angels in the Snow, specialized movement sequences, cross-lateral crawling and movements, touching and naming body parts, left-right discrimination activities, and rope jumping.

There is evidence that perceptual-motor training can help deficient and mentally retarded children. Whether or not such training can help regular students in increasing their academic potential has not been resolved. However, the application of the movement principles of perceptual-motor work can enhance and give breadth to children's movement competencies. It is a new and exciting approach toward the concept of education for the whole child.

The movement experiences should begin simply, but increase progressively in complexity, offering more challenge. Throwing and catching to self, for example, should start with an "in place" practice. Later, the teacher should add locomotor movements and other requirements to the task. The basic tasks should allow success so that progress can be made from this base.

In discussing the inclusion of perceptual-motor considerations in the program for *all* children, two types of activities are presented. The first group is from the "normal" type of physical education activities which are part of a recommended program. The second group of activities are those which can be regarded as designed particularly for perceptual-motor objectives.

Regular Physical Education Activities Having Value in Perceptual-Motor Development

1. Ball skills stressing throwing, catching, bouncing, dribbling, volleying, striking, and others, using all sizes and varieties of balls in as many combinations as possible.

2. Individual rope jumping, using both feet, right and left feet in various combinations. Stress rhythm and timing.

3. Balance beam work.

4. Simple tumbling stunts.

5. Handling objects, such as beanbags, hoops, wands, and rings.

6. Climbing up, over, and around ropes and apparatus.

7. Fundamental skills to rhythm.

8. Basic movement competency.

Specialized Perceptual-Motor Activities
Crawling and Creeping Patterns

1. Unilateral crawling — Crawl forward on hands and knees, using the arm and leg on the same side together.

2. Bilateral movement — Move forward,

reaching out with both hands and then bringing the feet up to the hands (Bunny Jump).

3. Cross-lateral crawling — Crawl forward, moving the right arm and the left leg at the same time, and vice versa.

Variations:

1. Move forward, backward, sideward, make quarter turns right and left.

2. Add turning the head first toward the leading hand and then opposite to it, coordinating with each step.

Command Movements Involving Jumping, Hopping, and Turning

1. Jump forward, backward, sideward. Jump in patterns.

2. Hop forward, backward, and sideward, stressing right and left.

3. Hop in various combinations: R-1, L-1; L-1, R-1; R-2, L-2; L-2, R-2; R-2, L-1; L-2, R-1. (The notation R-1, L-1 means to hop once on the right and once on the left.) In addition to the combinations listed, others can be devised.

4. Jump with quarter turns right and left, half turns, right and left.

5. Establish the directions (east, south, west, north) and call out directions with the children making jump turns.

Angels in the Snow—Command Movements

Children are on their backs with hands at the sides and feet together. On any command, the arms and legs as designated move out and then back along the floor. The directions are given as follows:

"Right arm, left leg — MOVE," (pause) "BACK."

Then alternate the words "Out" and "Back," repeating each movement 6-10 times. The following movements are suggested:

Bilateral — both arms, both legs, both arms and both legs together.

Unilateral — right (or left) arm, right (or left) leg, right arm and right leg together, left arm and left leg together.

Cross-Lateral — right arm and left leg, left arm and right leg.

NOTE. The Angels in the Snow exercises were originally designed to be given by the examiner pointing to an arm or leg and saying,

"Move that arm (or leg)." This, however, is individual activity and not suitable generally for group work. Children, conceivably, could work in pairs, and this type of Angels work could be done.

Command Movements — Standing

These movements follow the same command pattern as Angels in the Snow with the directive given first, followed by the execution command "Move." The position is held until the leader says "Back." Children should learn to exercise good control in waiting without preliminary movement until the command "Move" is given, at which time they make the prescribed movement. The initial movement is held until the teacher can check the accuracy of the response. Two approaches can be used. The first is to change from one pattern into another, without repetition of any pattern. The other is to repeat a pattern as when giving exercises. Repeat 6-10 times.

Types of movements which are effective are:

Right arm, right leg forward (unilateral).

Left arm, right leg forward (cross-lateral).

Both arms forward (bilateral).

Both feet forward — a jump (bilateral).

Add the turn of the head to the movements. The head is usually turned toward the arm which is moved forward, but can vary. Such a command would be, "Right arm and left foot forward, head right — MOVE."

Side steps left and right can be used, with arms still moving forward and head turning as directed.

Imitation of Movements

The children stand facing the teacher so that all can see the teacher. Feet are apart enough (6"-12") for good balance and arms are at the sides. The teacher makes definite movements with the arms first in various movements. Arm and leg movements in combinations are also to be imitated. Children imitate the movements on the same side (right for the teacher, left for the children). There should be emphasis on all three types of movement — unilateral, bilateral, and cross-lateral. A mixture of movements should be made. All movements are to the side first. Later, forward movements of the arms can be added.

Some games using imitation of movement are useful and fun for the children. *Do This, Do That* has its basis of fun in that the child imitates the movement as done when the leader says, "Do this!" When the leader says, "Do that!" no one is to move. Those caught can have points scored against them. The game, *Simon Says,* follows the same principles, with the children moving when the command is preceded by "Simon says."

Another similar game is that the leader attempts to confuse the children by giving directions, which they are to follow, and making a different movement. For example, he can say, "Touch your shoulders," and at the same time put his hands on his hips. The children are to follow the verbal directions.

Bounding Board (see appendix for diagram)

Bounding high on the bounding board.

1. Simple bouncing — both feet, right foot, left foot, combinations.

2. Bouncing with quarter and half turns.

3. Begin at one end, jump along the board. Repeat using right or left leg only. Jump forward, backward, and sideward.

4. Sight fixation targets should be established so that the child fixes his gaze on a point and maintains the pattern of movement.

The Balance Board (see appendix for diagram)

The child stands on the board with his feet

Balancing beanbags while on balance boards.

separated and attempts to keep his balance. Try with one foot. Sight fixation targets should be used with the balance board. Pick spots high and low, right and left, and have the child hold this visually.

Obstacles

Wands and chairs can be used as obstacles. A wand over the top of two chairs makes an obstacle under which the children move. Move underneath without touching, backward or sideward as well as frontward. Another obstacle can be made by having a wand over the seats of two low chairs or over 12" hurdle blocks. The children step over this without touching. A hoop can be held by a partner, allowing the child to crawl through without touching.

The Perceptual-Motor Team

Although the emphasis in previous discussions is on incorporating perceptual-motor principles and instructional procedures into the *regular* physical education program, the physical education instructor should be a member of the perceptual-motor team which considers student problems of deficiency in this area. He can cooperate with special perceptual-motor programs and can also give encouragement and special help in the regular physical education program to individuals identified as needing such aid.

13

Manipulative Activities

Activities Utilizing Beanbags
Basic Ball Skills
Bowling
Paddle and Ball Activities
Parachute Play
Wands
Hoops

A manipulative activity is one in which a child handles some kind of a play object, usually with the hands, but it can involve the feet and other parts of the body. As basic skills, manipulative activities invite strong application of basic movement methodology, adding an important dimension to movement experiences. Manipulative activities can strengthen both hand-eye and foot-eye coordination, as well as develop dexterity in handling a variety of play objects. Activities utilizing beanbags, balls of various kinds, hoops, wands, paddles and balls, and a parachute round out a basic program. Deck tennis rings, toss items like rubber horseshoes, lummi sticks, and floor hockey equipment can enrich the offerings. Individual rope jumping is in a sense a manipulative activity, but is usually classed among individual and dual activities, where it has been placed in this guide (Chapter 20).

The supply factor is critical to a program of manipulative activities. For individual work, one item should be on hand for each child. In partner work, one item should be present for each two children. The demands for group work are less. However, most activity consists of individual and partner work, except, of course, for parachute play. One parachute is sufficient for a normal size class.

Beanbags and yarn balls provide the first throwing and catching skills for younger chil-

dren. A softer object instills confidence and tends to eliminate the fear younger children have of catching a hard or unyielding object. After these introductory skills, other types of balls are added and more demanding skills are brought in.

Since early competency in handling objects provides a basis for later or specialized skills, basic principles of skill performance (page 72) should have strong application, particularly as related to throwing and catching skills.

The Start-and-Expand approach is sound for manipulative activities. Start the children at a low level of challenge so all can achieve success, and expand the skills and experiences from that base. In progression, most activities begin with the individual approach and later move to partner activity. Partners should be of comparable ability.

ACTIVITIES UTILIZING BEANBAGS

Activities based on beanbags provide valuable learning experiences for children at all levels in the elementary school. They provide a good introduction for throwing and catching skills for kindergarten and primary children and should precede instruction with inflated balls. All parts of the body can be brought into play with beanbag activity.

Instructional Procedures

1. Smaller beanbags (4″) are suitable for K-2 grades. A larger beanbag (6″) should be

used with older children. The larger beanbag balances and can be controlled better on various parts of the body, offering a greater measure of success for intermediate children.

2. Throwing and catching skills involve many intricate elements. Emphasize the skill performance principles of opposition, eye focus, weight transfer, and follow-through. It is important that children keep an eye on the object being caught and on the target when throwing.

3. Stress laterality and directionality, and work at different levels.

4. Give some attention to targets when throwing. Children should throw about chest high to a partner, unless a different type of throw is specified. Teach all types of returns — low, medium, high, left, and right.

5. In early practice, stress a soft receipt of the beanbag when catching by "giving" with the hands, arms, and legs. Softness is created by having the hands go out toward the incoming beanbag and bring it in for a soft landing.

6. In partner work, keep distances between partners reasonable, especially in introductory phases. Fifteen feet or so seems to be a reasonable starting distance.

7. In partner work, emphasize skillful throwing, catching, and handling of the beanbag. Hard and difficult throwing, the purpose of which is to cause the partner to miss, should be avoided.

Recommended Activities with Beanbags

Activities are generally classified into individual and partner activities. A few activities are done in groups of three or more.

Individual Activities

1. In place, tossing to self. Toss with both hands, right hand, left hand. Catch the same way. Catch with back of the hands.

Toss from side to side, right to left, (reverse), front to back, back to front, around various parts of the body, different combinations.

Toss and catch at different levels. Toss and catch from seated position.

2. In place, adding stunts. Toss overhead to the rear, turn around and catch. Toss and do a full turn and catch.

Toss, clap hands, and catch. Clap hands more than once. Clap hands around different parts of the body and catch.

Toss, kneel on one knee, and catch. Try this going to a seated or lying position. Reverse the order, coming from lying or sitting position to a standing position to catch.

Toss, touch the floor and catch. Explore with other challenges. Use heel clicks, or balance positions.

3. Locomotor movements. Toss to self, moving to another spot to catch. Toss forward, run, and catch. Move from side to side. Toss overhead to the rear, run back, and catch. Add various stunts and challenges previously described.

Vary with different locomotor movements.

4. Balancing beanbag on various parts of the body. Balance on head. Move around, maintaining balance of beanbag. Sit down, lie down, turn around, etc.

Balance the beanbag on various parts of the body and move around in this fashion. Balance on top of instep, between knees, on shoulders, on elbows, etc.

Use more than one beanbag for balancing.

5. Propelling beanbag with various parts of the body. Toss to self from various parts of the body — elbow, instep, between feet, between heels, knees, shoulders.

Sit and toss bag from the feet to self. Practice from a supine position. From a supine position, pick up the bag between the toes, place it behind the head, using a full curl position. Go back and pick it up, returning it to original place.

6. Manipulating with bare feet. The children are barefooted. The bag should be picked up by curling the toes. This has value in strengthening the muscles supporting the arch.

Pick up with one foot. Hop to another spot. Change feet.

Toss to self from either foot. Using a target (hoop), toss the beanbag into the target.

7. Juggling. Begin with two bags and keep them in the air alternately. Juggle three bags.

8. Other activities.

a. From a wide straddle position, push the beanbag between the legs as far back as possible. Jump into the air with a half turn and repeat.

b. Take the same position as in (a). Push the bag back as far as possible between the legs, bending the knees. Without moving the legs, turn to the right and pick up the bag. Repeat the maneuver, turning to the left the next time.

c. Stand with feet apart, holding the beanbag with both hands. Reach up as high as possible (both hands), bend over backwards, and drop the bag. Reach between the legs and pick up the bag.

d. Get down on all fours in kneeling position and put the bag in the small of the back. Wiggle and force the bag off the back without moving the hands and knees from place.

Partner Activities

1. Tossing back and forth. Begin with various kinds of two-handed throws — underhand, overhead, side, and over-shoulder. Change to one-handed tossing and throwing.

Throw at different levels, also at different targets — right and left.

Throw under leg, around the body. Center as in football. Try imitating the shot put and the discus throw. Try the softball windmill (full arc) throw.

Have partners sit tailor (cross-legged) fashion about 10' apart. Throw and catch in various styles seated in this fashion.

Use follow activities, where one partner leads with a throw and the other follows with the same kind of a throw.

Toss in various directions to make partner move and catch.

With one partner standing still, have the other partner run around him in a circle as the bag is tossed back and forth.

Propel two beanbags back and forth. Each partner has a bag and the bags go in opposite directions at the same time. Try tossing both bags at once in the same direction, using various types of throws. Try to keep three bags going at the same time.

2. Propelling back and forth with different parts of the body. Toss bag to partner with foot, toe, both feet (on top and held between), elbow, shoulder, head, and any other part of the body that can be used. Use a sitting position.

With back to partner, take a *Bunny Jump* position. With bag held between the feet, kick bag back to partner. Try from a standing position.

Partners lie supine on floor with heads pointing toward each other, heads about 3' apart. One partner has a beanbag between his feet and deposits it in back of his head. The other partner picks up the bag with his feet (his feet are over his head) and returns the bag to the floor after returning to a lying position. Try to transfer the bag directly from one partner to the other with the feet with both partners in backward curl position.

Group Activities and Games

1. Split Vision Drill. A split vision drill from basketball can be adapted to beanbags. An active player faces two partners about 15' away. They are standing side by side, a short distance apart, in this fashion:

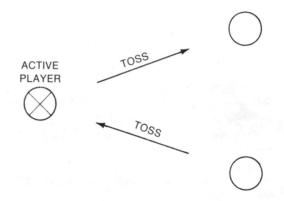

Two beanbags, one in the hands of the active player and one with one of the partners, are needed for the drill. The active player tosses his bag to the open partner, and *at the same time* receives the other bag from the other partner. The two bags move back and forth together between the active player and the two others, alternately. After a period of time, change positions.

2. Target Games. Wastebaskets, hoops, circles drawn on the floor, and other devices can provide targets for beanbag tossing. Target boards with cutout holes are available on the commercial market. Holes can be triangles, circles, squares, and rectangles, stressing form concepts.

3. Beanbag Quoits. The game is played in the same way as horseshoes. A court is drawn with two spots on the floor about 20' apart.

Spots can be made from masking tape and should be 1" in diameter. Each competitor gets two bags, a different color for each player. Tosses are made from behind one spot to the other. The object is to get one or both bags closer to the mark than the opponent. If the bag completely blocks out the spot, as viewed from directly overhead, this bag scores three points. Otherwise any bag nearer to the spot than the opponent's nearer bag scores one point. Game can be a predetermined score — 11, 15, or 21 points. The player winning the previous point tosses first.

4. Other Games and Relay Races. The following games or relay races can be used as the culmination of a lesson in beanbags.

One step — page 295
Teacher Ball — page 279

BASIC BALL SKILLS

Included in this section are the basic ball skills in which the child handles balls without the aid of other equipment such as a bat or paddle. Ball skills are mostly of two types:

Hand-eye Skills: throwing, catching, bouncing, dribbling (as in basketball), batting (as in volleyball), and rolling (bowling).

Foot-eye Skills: kicking, trapping, and dribbling (as in soccer).

Other parts of the body are used on occasion, but the main emphasis centers on ball handling with the hands and feet.

Ball skills are of vital importance to children in their play experiences. A good basis for these skills must be laid in the lower grades, with continued development in the upper grades. Not only should the children acquire skill through varied experiences in handling balls, but they should also gain knowledge of skill principles essential to competency in ball-handling skills.

Type of Ball

Yarn and fleece balls are excellent for introductory skills on the kindergarten and first grade level, as they help overcome the fear factor. Some teachers have found success with balls made from crumbled-up newspaper. A design for yarn ball construction is in the appendix. Another type of ball that has value is a soft softball, a much softer version of the regular softball. It has advan-

tages in catching thrown balls and fielding grounders but does not hold up well if batted.

The inflated rubber playground ball (8½") should be the predominant ball for most of the children's ball-handling experiences. Skill work should start with this size ball and move to smaller items later. Balls should be moderately inflated so that they will bounce well, but not to the point of overinflation, which causes difficulty in catching. Overinflation can also distort the spherical shape.

Individual, Partner and Group Organization

Instruction in lower grades should begin with individual work and progress to partner and group activities. After the children have acquired some skill, a lesson can include both individual and partner activity.

In propelling the ball back and forth between partners, children can progress from rolling the ball to throwing the ball on first bounce, to throwing the ball on the fly. Be sure a disparity in skill between partners does not cause a problem for either partner. A skilled child can aid a less skilled child to better performance, but the more skilled individual may resent being restricted in more complex skills by an inept child.

Group work should be confined to small groups (3-6), so that each child can be actively involved. Group work should include activities and approaches which are not possible in individual or partner activity.

Other Factors

Distance between partners should be short and gradually lengthened. The concept of targets is introduced by directing the children to throw the ball to specific points. Later, a change from a stationary target to a moving target maintains progression. Relays are useful in reinforcing skill learning, but caution is suggested that the skills are reasonably learned before being applied in a relay.

Instructional Procedures

1. The principles of skill performance (page 72) have strong application to ball skills, particularly visual concentration, follow-through, arm-leg opposition, weight transfer, and total body coordination. These principles should be incorporated into the instructional se-

quences and, in addition, be an important part of the coaching process. Balls should be handled with the pads of the fingers and should not be "palmed."

2. In catching, a soft receipt of the ball should be created by a "giving" movement with the hands and arms. Hands should reach out somewhat to receive the ball, and then cushion the impact by bringing the ball in toward the body with loose and relaxed hands.

3. In catching a throw above the waist, the hands should be positioned so the thumbs are together. To receive a throw below the waist, the catch is made by the hands with the little fingers toward each other and the thumbs out.

4. When throwing to a partner, unless otherwise specified, the throw should reach the partner about chest high. At times, a variety of target points should be specified — high, low, right, left, knee-high, etc.

5. A lesson should begin with simple basic skills within the reach of all children and progress to more challenging activities.

6. Laterality is an important consideration. Right and left members of the body should be given practice in turn in somewhat equal time allotments.

7. Practice in split vision should be incorporated into bouncing and dribbling skills. Children should learn to look somewhat forward, not at the ball, in bouncing and dribbling work. A split-vision drill (page 149) is of value in throwing patterns.

8. Tactile senses can be brought into play by having the children dribble or bounce the ball with eyes closed, allowing practice in getting the "feel" of the ball.

9. Rhythmic accompaniment, particularly for bouncing and dribbling activities, adds another dimension to ball skills.

10. It is desirable that enough balls be present so each child may have a ball. However, in case there are only enough balls present so that two children need to share a ball, the first child does the prescribed routine and then bounces, tosses, or passes the ball as prescribed to the second child, who repeats the designated routine.

Recommended Ball Activities

Activities with balls are presented with the larger rubber playground ball (8½" or larger) in mind. Some modification is needed if the balls are smaller or are of the type which does not bounce, as in the case of yarn or fleece balls. Activities are presented under four headings: (1) individual activities, (2) partner activities, (3) group activities, and (4) bowling.

Individual Activities

Each child has a ball and practices by himself. In the first group of individual activities the child remains in the same spot. Next, he utilizes a wall to rebound the ball to himself. In the third group of activities he is performing alone while on the move.

In-Place Activities

1. Controlled Rolling. The child assumes a wide straddle position, places the ball on the floor, and rolls it with constant hand guidance between and around the legs. Other positions are: seated with legs outstretched, cross-legged sitting, and push-up position.

2. Bounce and Catch. Beginning with two hands, bounce and catch. Bounce a given number of times. Bounce at different levels. Bounce one-handed in a variety of fashions. Bounce under the legs. Close eyes, bounce and catch.

3. Toss and Catch. Toss and catch, increasing height gradually. Toss from side to side. Toss underneath the legs, around the body, from behind. Add challenges while tossing and catching: clap hands one or more times, make body turns (quarter, half, or full), touch the floor, click heels, sit down, lie down, etc.

Toss upward and let bounce. Add various challenges as above.

Toss upward and catch the descending ball at as high a level as possible; at a low level. Work out other levels and put into combinations.

From a seated position, toss ball to self from various directions. Lie down and do the same.

4. Bat the Ball (As In Volleyball) to Self. Bat the ball, using the fist, open hand, or side of hand.

Bat and let ball bounce. Catch in different fashions.

Rebound the ball upward using different parts of the body. Let it bounce. Practice serving to self.

5. Foot Skills. Put toe on top of ball. Roll it in different directions, keeping the other foot in place and retaining control of the ball.

Use two-footed pick-up, front and back.

From a sitting position with the legs extended, toss the ball with the feet to the hands.

6. Dribbling Skills. Dribble the ball first with both hands, then with the right and the left. Emphasize that the dribble is a push with good wrist action. Children should not bat the ball downward. Use various number combinations with the right and left hands. Dribble under the legs in turn, back around the body. Kneel and dribble. Go from standing to lying position, maintaining a dribble. Return to standing position.

Against a Wall

The wall should be reasonably free of projections and irregular surfaces, so the ball may return directly to the student. If the ball is to bounce after contact with the wall, the children can stand back farther than if they are to handle the return on the fly.

1. Throwing Practice, Catching on the First Bounce. Throw the ball against the wall and catch the return after a bounce. Practice various kinds of throws — two-handed, one-handed, overhead, side, baseball, chest-pass, etc.

2. Throwing Practice, Catching on the Fly. Repeat the throws used in #1, but catch the return on the fly. It may be necessary to move closer and have the ball contact the wall higher.

3. Batting and Handball Skills. Drop the ball and bat it after it bounces. Keep the ball going, as in handball. Serve the ball against the wall as in volleyball. Experiment with different means of serving.

4. Kicking and Trapping — Foot-Eye Skills. Practice different ways of controlled kicking against the wall and stopping (trapping) the ball on the return. Try keeping the ball going with the foot on the bounce against the wall.

Activities While Moving

1. Rolling. Roll the ball, guide it with the hands in different directions. Roll the ball forward, run and catch up with it.

2. Toss and Catch. Toss ball upward and forward. Run forward and catch after a bounce. Toss ball upward in various directions — forward, sideward, backward — run under ball and catch on fly. Add various stunts and challenges such as touching the floor, heel clicks, turning around, etc.

3. Batting the Ball. Bat the ball with the hand upward in different directions, catch ball on first bounce or on fly.

4. Foot Skills — Soccer Dribble. Dribble ball forward, backward, and in other directions. Dribble around an imaginary point. Make various patterns while dribbling, such as a circle, square, triangle, figure eight, etc.

5. Dribbling as in Basketball. Dribble forward using one hand and back to place with the other. Change directions on whistle. Dribble in various directions, describing different pathways. Dribble in and around cones, milk cartons, or chairs.

Partner Activities
In-Place Activities
(Both Partners Are Stationary)

1. Rolling. Roll the ball back and forth to partner. Begin with two-handed rolls and proceed to one-handed rolls.

2. Throwing and Catching. Toss ball to partner on first bounce, using various kinds of tosses. Practice various kinds of throws and passes to partner. Throw to specific points — high, low, right, left, knee-high, etc. Try various odd throws such as under leg, around the body, backward tosses, centering as in football. Throw and catch over a volleyball net.

3. Batting and Volleyball Skills. Serve as in volleyball. Serve to partner who catches. Toss to partner and have him make a volleyball return. Keep distances short and the ball under good control. Bat back and forth on first bounce. Bat back and forth over a line or over a bench.

4. Kicking. Practice different ways of controlled kicking between partners and different ways of stopping the ball (trapping). Practice a controlled punt, preceding the kick with a step from the nonkicking foot. Place ball between feet and propel forward or backward to partner. Practice foot pickups. One partner rolls the ball and the other hoists ball to self with extended toe.

5. Throwing from Various Positions. Prac

tice different throws from a kneeling, sitting, or lying position. Allow the children freedom for creativity in selecting positions.

6. Two-Ball Activities. Using two balls, pass back and forth with balls going in opposite directions.

Against a Wall

Alternate throwing and catching against a wall. Alternate returning the ball after a bounce as in handball.

Throwing on the Move

Spatial judgments must be good to anticipate where the moving child will be to receive the ball. Moderate distances should be maintained between children.

1. One Child Stationary. One child remains in place and tosses to the other child, who changes position. The moving child can trace different patterns such as back and forth between two spots and in a circle around the stationary child.

2. Both Children Moving. Practice different kinds of throws and passes as children move in different patterns. Considerable space is needed for this type of class work. Practice foot skills of dribbling and passing.

Group Activities

Groups should be kept small and there should be attention to rotation so that all children are included. Group activities include group drills, relays, and games.

1. Drills
    a. Split vision drill (see explanation un-

der Group Activities and Games for Beanbag Activities on page 149).
    b. Additional drills
       Additional drills are found in the sports units of basketball, softball, and soccer.

2. Relays
    a. Selected ball relays (Chapter 16) add interest to the instruction.

3. Target Practice
Many targets can be devised for throwing skills. Targets with concentric circles painted on the wall are good. Targets can be mounted on the wall. Rolling hoops are challenging targets.

Throwing at a Wall Mounted Target

For large yarn balls, wastebaskets serve for targets. Smaller targets can be empty 3-pound coffee cans. The principle of One-Step (page 295) can be used. With the can upright, stand with the toes touching the can. Take one step backward. Holding the arm out straight, shoulder-high, drop the yarn ball into the can. Back up one step and throw underhanded. Repeat several steps. A second child may need to hold the can to avoid tipping.

4. Scoop Ball
Using the 3-pound coffee can, one child throws and the other, holding the can, catches the ball in it. Scoops for catching might be made out of Clorox plastic containers or something similar. Children can throw and catch with the scoops (see appendix).

5. Games
Selected ball games are listed in the games section of this guide.

Split Vision Drill. The boy on left is passing to the girl, while receiving the ball from the boy on right.

BOWLING

Children in the kindergarten and lower two grades should practice informal rolling. In about the third grade, the emphasis should change from informal rolling to bowling skills, continuing through the sixth grade.

Bowling skills should begin with a two-handed roll and progress to one-handed rolls, using both right and left hands. Various targets can be utilized, including Indian clubs, milk cartons, small cones, blocks, and human targets.

The regular (8½″) rubber playground ball is excellent for bowling skills. Volleyballs and soccer balls can also be used. Stress moderate speed in the moving ball.

Bowling activities are organized mostly into partner or group work. When targets are being used, two children on the target end are desirable. One child resets the target, while the other recovers the ball.

The ball should roll off the tips of the fingers with good follow-through.

BOWLING SKILLS — PARTNER ACTIVITY UNLESS OTHERWISE NOTED

1. Begin with two-handed rolls from between the legs, employing a wide straddle stance.

2. Roll the ball right handed and left handed. Receiver can employ the foot pickup, done by hoisting the ball to self (hands) with the extended toe.

3. Practice different kinds of spin (English) on the ball. For a right-handed bowler, a curve to the left is called a "hook ball" and a curve to the right is a "backup ball."

4. Employ human straddle targets. Organize children in groups of four, two on each end. One child on each end becomes the target and the other the ball chaser. Using a stick 2′ long, make chalk marks on the floor. The target child straddles the chalk marks so that the marks are on the inside edges of his shoes, making a space of 2′ between his feet. Stress moderate bowling distances (15′-20′) at first and adjust as the children become more proficient. Scoring can be based on two points scored for a ball that goes through the legs without touching, and one point scored for a ball that goes through, but touches the leg.

5. Indian clubs, milk cartons, or even regular bowling pins can be used as targets. Begin with one and move up to two, or three. Plastic bowling pins are available for this purpose. Other targets can be made by laying a wastebasket on its side and rolling into it or using the 3-pound coffee can for the smaller ball.

6. Four-Step Approach

The four-step approach is the accepted form for ten-pin bowling and its basis can be set in class work. The teacher is referred to bowling manuals for more details, but here is the technique in a brief form for a right-handed bowler.

Position: Stand with both feet together and the ball held in both hands comfortably in front of the body.

Step 1: Step forward with the right foot and at the same time push the ball directly forward and a little to the right.

Step 2: Step with the left foot and allow the ball to swing down alongside the leg on its way into the back swing.

Step 3: Step with the right foot. The ball reaches the height of the back swing with this step.

Step 4: Step with the left foot and bowl the ball forward.

As cues, the teacher can call out the following sequence for the four steps: (1) "Out," (2) "Down," (3) "Back," (4) "Roll."

7. A fine game to round off the activities is Bowling One-Step (page 286).

PADDLE AND BALL ACTIVITIES

Paddle and ball activities are an important part of the program as they are closely related to paddle and ball sports such as tennis, badminton, squash, and table tennis. The suggested level for instruction is from the third grade upward, as younger children have difficulty holding the commercial wooden paddle made for paddle sports. Sponge balls and old tennis balls are excellent, provided they are not too lively.

For those who wish to introduce the activity below the third grade level, a lighter paddle is needed. The regular table tennis paddle can be used for younger children.

Instructional Procedures

1. All paddles should have leather wris

thongs. The hand should go through the leather loop before grasping the paddle. No play should be permitted without this safety precaution. (See appendix.)

2. Proper grip must be emphasized, and to see that children maintain this is a constant battle. The easiest method of teaching the proper grip is to advise the student to hold his paddle perpendicular to the floor and then shake hands with it. Young people tend to revert to the inefficient "hammer" grip, which is similar to the grip used on a hammer when pounding nails.

from individual to partner work as quickly as feasible, since this is the basic reality of the racquet sports.

Individual Activities

1. Place ball on paddle and attempt to ballance it to prevent it from falling off. As skill increases, attempt to roll the ball around the edges of the paddle.

2. Bounce the ball in the air using the paddle:

    a. See how many times it can be bounced without touching the floor.

Holding the Paddle Properly — the Handshake Grip

Incorrectly Holding the Paddle — the Hammer Grip

3. Accuracy and control should be goals of this activity, and the children should not be concerned with force or distance.

4. The wrist should be held reasonably stiff and the arm action should be a stroking motion. The body should be turned sideways in stroking.

5. Early activities can be attempted with both right and left hands, but the dominant hand should be developed in critical skills.

6. During a lesson, related information about racquet sports may be quite relevant.

7. Practice in racquet work should move

    b. Bounce it off the paddle into the air, and catch it with the other hand.

    c. Increase the height of the bounce.

3. Dribble the ball with the paddle:

    a. From a stationary position.

    b. Moving.

4. Alternate bouncing the ball in the air and on the floor.

5. Bounce the ball off the paddle into the air and "catch" it with the paddle. This requires one to "give" with the paddle and create a soft home for the ball.

6. Bounce the ball off the paddle into the air:
   a. While the ball is in the air turn the paddle on edge and attempt to bounce the ball on the edge.
   b. Alternate sides of the paddle to bounce the ball.
7. Bounce the ball into the air and perform the following stunts while the ball is in the air:
   a. Touch the floor.
   b. Heel click (single and double).
   c. Clap hands.
   d. Turn completely around.
   e. Various combinations of the above.
8. Stroke the ball against the wall. This is a good lead-up to tennis and paddleball. Have the children practice both the forehand and backhand strokes.

Partner Activities

All partner activity should begin with controlled throwing (feeding) by one partner and the designated stroke return by the other. In this way, the child concentrates on his stroke without worry about the competitive aspects.

1. Forehand
Toss and return stroke.
Stroking back and forth with partner.

2. Backhand
Toss and return stroke.
Stroking back and forth with partner.

3. Continuous Play
Back and forth play over a "net." Improvised "nets" can be set up by laying a jumping rope on the floor crosswise to the field of play, also by supporting a wand on blocks or cones, or utilizing a bench for the barrier.

4. Volleying
Toss and return stroke.
Volley back and forth.
In the volley, the ball does not touch the floor. The volley is a punching type of stroke, with the racquet remaining faced against the ball.

5. Partner Play
This is doubles play. Partners on each side alternate turns returning the ball.

PARACHUTE PLAY

Parachute play can be enjoyed by all children from the first through sixth grades. Activities must be carefully selected for the younger children, however, since some of the skills presented in the recommended list will be difficult for them. One parachute is sufficient for the normal size class of thirty children.

Parachutes come in different sizes, depending upon whether their use was for personnel or cargo. Personnel parachutes are the most suitable for parachute play as cargo parachutes are usually large and cumbersome.

Each parachute has an opening near the top to allow trapped air to escape and keep the parachute properly shaped. Modern personnel parachutes are generally constructed of nylon.

Values of Parachute Play

Parachutes provide a new and interesting medium of accomplishing physical fitness goals, with good development of strength, agility, coordination, and endurance. Strength development is especially centered on the arms, hands, and shoulder girdle. However, at times strength demands are made on the entire body.

A wide variety of movement possibilities, some of which are rhythmic, can be employed in parachute play. Locomotor skills while manipulating the parachute are much in evidence. Rhythmic beats of the tom-tom or appropriate music can guide locomotor movements.

Parachute play provides many excellent group learning experiences, as individuality disappears in much of this type of play.

Terminology

As the activities unfold, certain terms peculiar to the activity must be carefully explained. Terms such as inflate, deflate, float, dome, mushroom, and others need to be clarified when introduced.

Grips

The grips used in handling the parachute are comparable to those employed in hanging activities on apparatus. Grips may be with one or two hands, overhand (palms facing away), underhand (palms facing), or mixed, a combination of underhand and overhand grip. They should be varied.

Instructional Procedures

1. For preliminary explanations, the parachute can be stretched out on the ground in

its circular pattern with the children seated back just far enough so they cannot touch the parachute during instructions. During explanations when the parachute is held by the children, they should retain their hold lightly, letting the center of the parachute drop to the ground. Children must be taught to exercise control so that they do not manipulate the parachute while explanations are in progress.

2. The teacher explains the forthcoming activity, demonstrating as needed. If there are no questions, he initiates the activity with a command such as: "Ready — BEGIN!" Best success occurs when children start together on signal. At times, the teacher may wish to have the children lay the parachute down, back off a step or two, and sit down for further instructions or for a short rest.

3. Squads can be used in forming the parachute circle. Each squad occupies one-quarter of the parachute circumference. Squads are useful for competitive units in game activity.

Activities

Activities are presented according to type, with variations and suggestions for supplementary activity included. Unless otherwise specified, activities begin and halt on signal. Pupil suggestions can broaden the scope of activity.

1. Exercise-type Activities

Exercises should be done vigorously and with enough repetitions to challenge the children. In addition to the exercises presented, others can be adapted to parachute play.

a. **Toe Toucher.** Sit with feet extended under the parachute and the chute held taut with a two-hand grip, drawn up to the chin. Bend forward and touch the grip to the toes. Return to stretched parachute.

b. **Curl-Ups.** Extend the body under the parachute in curl-up position so that the stretched parachute comes up to the chin when held taut. Perform Curl-ups, each time returning to tight parachute.

c. **Dorsal Lifts.** Lie prone, head toward the parachute, and feet pointed back away from Grip the chute and slide backwards until there is some tension on it. Raise the chute off the ground by a vigorous lift of the arms,

with the head and chest off the ground. Return.

d. **V-Sit.** Lie in a position similar to that for dorsal lifts, but supine. Do a V-Up by raising both the upper and lower parts of the body simultaneously to form the "V" position. Knees should be kept straight.

e. **Backward Pulls.** Backward pulls are made facing the parachute and pulling back, away from its center. Pulls can be made from sitting, kneeling, or standing positions.

f. **Other Pulls.** Side pulls using a flexed-arm position can be structured. Other variations of pulling can be devised.

g. **Hip Walk and Scooter.** Begin with the parachute taut. Move forward with the *Scooter* (page 213), and the *Hip Walk* (page 212). Move back to place with the same movement until the chute is taut again.

2. Circular Movements

Circular movements, where the center hole in the parachute remains above the same spot, offer many opportunities for locomotor movements either free or to the beat of a tom-tom. Rhythmic running, European style, is particularly appropriate. Holds can be one- or two-handed.

Many basic movements can be utilized while children move in a circular fashion, such as walking, running, hopping, skipping, galloping, sliding, draw steps, grapevine steps, and others. The parachute can be held at different levels.

3. Shaking the Rug and Making Waves

Shaking the Rug involves rapid movements, either light or heavy. Making Waves are large movements to send billows of cloth up and down like waves. Waves can be small, medium, or high. Children can alternate turns to see who can make the best waves.

4. Making a Dome

Begin with the parachute on the floor, children holding with two hands and kneeling on one knee. To trap the air under the chute and make a dome shape, each child stands up quickly, thrusting arms above the head and returning to starting position. Vary by having all or part of the children change to the inside of the chute on the down movement, as in a cave. Domes can also be made while moving in a circle.

Forming a Dome

The Dome

5. Stunts Under the Chute

a. **Number Exchange.** Children are numbered from 1 to 4. The teacher calls a number as the dome is made, and those with the number called must exchange positions before the chute comes down. Locomotor movements can be varied. Tasks under the chute can be specified, such as turning a certain number of turns with a jump rope, throwing and catching a beanbag, bouncing a ball a number of times, etc. The needed objects are under the chute before the dome is made.

b. **Chute Crawl.** One-half the class, either standing or kneeling, stretches the chute out level with the floor. The remaining children crawl under the chute to the opposite side from their starting position.

6. Mushroom Activities

With the chute on the floor and students on one knee holding with two hands, stand up quickly, thrusting arms overhead. Keeping the arms overhead, each walks forward three or four steps toward the center. The arms are held overhead until the chute is deflated.

a. **Mushroom Release.** All children release at the peak of inflation and either run out from under the chute, or move to the center and sit down, with the chute descending on top of them.

b. **Mushroom Run.** Children make a mushroom, move into the center, and without further delay, release holds and run once around the inside dome of the chute, counterclockwise, back to place.

7. Kite Run

One-half the class holds the chute on one side with one hand. The leader points in the direction they are to run and they do so, holding the chute aloft as a kite.

8. Activities with Balls and Beanbags

a. **Ball Circle.** Place a basketball or cage ball on the raised chute. Make the ball roll around the chute in a large circle, controlling it by raising or lowering the chute. Try the same with two balls.

b. **Popcorn.** Place a number of beanbags (6-10) on the chute. Shake the chute to make them rise like popping corn.

c. **Team Ball.** Divide the chute players in half, so each team defends one-half the chute. Using two to six balls, any variety, try to bounce the balls off the opponents' side, scoring one point for the attacking side.

d. **Poison Snake.** Place four to six Olympic jump ropes on the chute. By shaking the chute, try to make them hit players on the other side, who have a point scored against them for each touch. Players with the lowest score are the winners.

e. **Circular Dribble.** Each child has a ball suitable for dribbling. The object is to run in circular fashion counterclockwise, holding to the chute with the left hand and dribbling with the right hand, retaining control of the ball. This is the preferred direction for right-handers, but is more difficult for left-handers. As an equalizer, try the dribbling clockwise.

The dribble should be started first. Then on signal, each starts to run. If a ball is lost, the child must recover the ball and try to hook on at his original place.

9. Other Activities

a. **Running Number Game.** Have the children around the chute count off by fours. Start them running lightly circular fashion, holding the chute in one hand. Call out one of the numbers (1-4). Children holding the number immediately release their grip on the chute and run forward to the next vacated place. This means that they must put on a burst of speed to move ahead to the next vacated place.

b. **Routines to Music.** Like other routines, parachute activities can be adapted to music.

Popping Popcorn (Beanbags) in the Chute

A sequence should be based on eight counts, with the routine made up of an appropriate number of sequences.

WANDS

Wands are made from ¾" doweling and come in two lengths, 36" and 42". If the school purchases one size only, it should be the longer wand. Those with assorted bright colors have a special appeal for children.

Wands serve the physical education program in three ways; (1) wand stunts, (2) exercises using wands, and (3) combative activities. Wand stunts and exercises are presented here, and combatives are found in the section under that title (page 215).

Wands are noisy when they hit the floor. Putting rubber crutch tips on each end of the wand alleviates most of this and makes it easier to pick up from the floor. The tips should be put on with mucilage.

The year's supply of wands should include five or six extra beyond the number needed to have one for each child. There will be some breakage.

The recommended level of introduction for wands stunts is the third grade.

Beginning the Grapevine

Instructional Procedures

1. Since wands are noisy, it is helpful to have the child hold his wand with both hands during instruction or lay it on the floor.

2. Many wand activities require great flexibility, which means that not all children will be able to do them. Girls usually perform flexibility stunts better than boys.

3. An adequate amount of space is needed for each individual, as wand stunts demand room.

4. Wands are not to be used as fencing foils. Stop this nonsense at once.

Individual Stunts

1. Wand Catch. Stand a wand on one end and hold it in place with the fingers on top. Bring the foot quickly over the stick, letting it go and catching the stick with the fingers before it falls. Do this right and left, inward and outward for a complete set. Try to catch it with just the index finger.

2. Thread the Needle — V Seat. Maintaining a V seat position, with the wand held in front of the body with both hands, bend the knees

Grapevine — Second Stage. Head ducks under and wand is passed down the back.

between the arms and pass the wand over them and return, *without touching* the wand to the legs.

3. Thread the Needle — Standing. Holding wand in both hands, step through stick one leg at a time and return without touching stick. Step through again, but this time bring the wand up the back, over the head, and around in front. Reverse. Try from side to side with the stick held front and back.

4. Grapevine. Holding wand near the ends, step with right foot *around* right arm and over wand inward towards body. Pass the wand backwards over head and right shoulder until you are standing erect with wand between legs. Reverse back to original position. Try with the left foot leading.

5. Back Scratcher. Hold wand with under grip (palms up) with arms crossed in front of the body. Bend the elbows so that the wand can go over and behind the head. Attempt to pass the wand down the length of the body from the back of the shoulders to the heels. Do not release grip on wand. The wand is worked down behind the back, while the arms stay in front of the body.

Back Scratcher. Wand has been passed overhead and is now being forced down the back.

6. Wand Whirl. Stand wand upright in front of you. Turn around quickly and grasp wand before it falls. Do it right and left. Try making two full turns and catch the wand.

7. Twist Under. Grasp upright-standing wand with right hand. Twist around under the right arm without letting go of wand, taking it off the floor, or touching knee to floor. Repeat using left arm.

8. Jump Stick. Holding the wand in front with both hands, jump over the wand. Jump back. The wand passes under the body during the jumps. Hold the wand with the tips of of the fingers. (A rope or towel may be substituted for children having difficulty.)

9. Wand Juggle. Balance wand with one hand or on one finger, keeping it upright. Walk forward and back. Sit down, lie down, or move into other positions keeping the wand balanced.

Partner Stunts

1. Partner Catch. Partners face each other a short distance (5′) apart, each holding his wand in his right hand. On signal each throws his wand to the partner with his right hand and catches the incoming wand with his left.

2. Partner Change. Partners face each other a short distance (5′) apart, each with his wand standing upright, held by the right hand on top. On signal, each runs to the other's wand to catch it before it falls. This can also be done in the same way as the *Wand Whirl,* with each whirling to the other's wand. Proper positioning will need to be determined.

Isometric Exercises

Isometric exercises have been discussed in general on page 113 and these principles should be followed. The isometric exercises with wands presented here are mainly grip exercises.

A variety of grips should be employed. With the wand level, use either the overhand or underhand grips. With the wand in vertical position, a grip can be taken so the thumbs are pointed up, pointed down, or pointed toward each other. Repeat each exercise with a different grip. The exercise can be repeated with the wand in different positions: in front of the body, held level, overhead, behind the back, or in front of the body, held vertical.

1. Pull the Wand Apart. Place the hands 6" apart near the center of the wand. With a tight grip to prevent slippage, and the arms extended, pull the hands apart. Change grips and position.

2. Push the Wand Together. Same as the previous exercise, except push the hands together.

3. Wand Twist. Same hand positioning. Twist the hands in opposite direction.

4. Bicycle. With the wand level throughout and using an overhand grip, extend the wand out and downward. Bring it upward near the body, completing a circular movement. On the downward movement, push the wand together, and on the upward movement, pull the wand apart.

Stretching Exercises

Physical educators have been using wands for a long time for stretching, bending, and twisting movements.

1. Side Bender. Grip wand and extend arms overhead. Feet are apart. Bend sideways as far as possible, maintaining straight arms and legs. Recover and bend to the other side.

Slave Twist to Knee

2. Slave Twist. Place the wand behind the neck with the arms draped over the wand from behind, forming the slave position. Rotate the upper body first right as far as possible and then left. Both feet and hips should remain in position. The twist is at the waist.

3. Slave Twist to Knee. Same position as above. Bend the trunk forward and twist so the right end of the wand touches the left knee. Recover and touch the left to the right knee.

HOOPS

Most American hoops are made from plastic, but Europeans use some made from wood. The plastic variety is less durable, but is more versatile. Extra hoops are needed as there will be breakage. The standard hoop is 36" in diameter, but it is desirable to have smaller hoops for younger children (30"). The hoop with the lead shot inside is of no advantage.

Instructional Procedures

1. Hoops are a noisy activity. The teacher might find it helpful to have the children lay the hoops on the floor when they are to listen.

2. Hoops can be a medium of creativity for children. Allow them some free time to explore their own ideas.

3. Allow the children an adequate amount of space in which to perform, as hoops require much movement.

4. In activities which require children to jump through hoops, instruct the child holding the hoop to grasp it lightly so that if the performer hits the hoop it will not cause an awkward fall.

5. Hoops can serve as a "home" for various activities. For instance, the children might leave their hoops to gallop in all directions and then quickly return to them upon command.

6. Hoops make good targets. They can be made to stand by placing an individual mat through the hoop and over its base (see appendix).

Hoop Activities

1. Place the hoops on the floor to create various patterns. Have the children perform various locomotor movements in, out of, and between the hoops.

2. **Hula Hoop** using various body parts such as:

    a. Waist   c. Arms
    b. Legs   d. Fingers

While hula hooping on the arms, try and change the hoop from one arm to the other.

3. Jump or hop through a hoop held by a partner. Further challenge can be added by varying the height and angle of the hoop.

4. Roll the hoop and run alongside it. Change directions when a command is given.

5. Use the hoop like a jump rope. Jump forward, backward, and sideward.

6. Roll the hoop with a reverse spin to make it return to the thrower. The key to the reverse spin is to pull down (toward the floor) on the hoop as it is released.

7. Roll the hoop with a reverse spin and jump over the hoop and catch it as it returns.

8. Roll the hoop with a reverse spin and as it returns, kick it up and catch it.

9. Many partner stunts can be performed such as:

    a. Play catch with a partner.

    b. Play catch with two or more hoops.

    c. Hula hoop and attempt to change the hoops from one partner to another.

    d. One partner rolls the hoop with a reverse (comeback) spin, and the other attempts to crawl through the hoop. This is done most easily just after the hoop reverses direction and begins to return to the spinner. Some children can go in and out of the hoop twice.

Hoop Floor Patterns for Exploratory Activity

1.
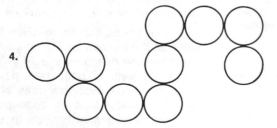

2.
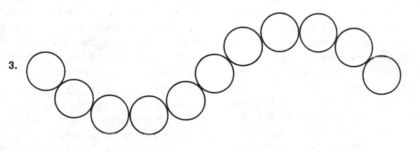

3.

4.
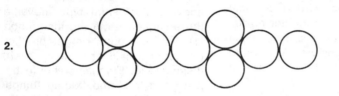

14

Apparatus Activities

Activities on apparatus have an important part in physical education programs. A wider variety of apparatus than ever before is now available from commercial sources or through school construction. Exercising on overhead and climbing apparatus has strong physical effects on the grip, arm, and shoulder girdle. Flexibility and stretching effects have value in the maintenance of posture. The child learns to manage his body free of ground support.

Equipment placed on the floor provides important extensions for basic movement. Exploratory and creative activity, as well as wide experience in body management, should characterize the approach to instructional procedures. Individual response in movement should be stressed, with the emphasis on doing but not on conformity. Variety in apparatus activity can be enhanced by the addition of hand apparatus such as beanbags, balls, wands, hoops, blocks, and other items. Individual or partner manipulative activities as the children perform and move on apparatus add another dimension to the movement possibilities.

Traffic rules should be established, stipulating when the child next in turn starts. His return route to the starting point can be established.

The children should set up and store the equipment. Mats should be placed where needed for safety and to cushion dismounts. In addition, children should be instructed in spotting techniques along with the performance items.

Attention to form is relative to the types of activity. Most stunt type movements involve three sequences in the instructional process: (1) how to mount, or get on the apparatus; (2) doing a skill or meeting a challenge; (3) dismounting. Emphasis should be on "giving it a good try," and "doing things as well as we can." The teacher can think in terms of minimal and maximal performance standards, taking individual differences into consideration. On the lower end of the skill scale, children like to know "did I do it?" On the upper end, they like to know that they achieved marked success.

The Start-and-Expand technique reinforces this kind of an approach by starting at a low point on the progression of skills. Achieving some measure of success is important. Serious enjoyment and fun should keynote the instructional climate in apparatus activities.

Some attention should be given to the dismount as determined by the character of the apparatus. The dismount should be controlled by landing with a bent-knee position and weight balanced over the balls of the feet. The child should land in good control and hold the position momentarily to show control. Many challenges, such as shapes through the air, turns, stunts following the landing, and others, can be structured into dismounts.

Return Activity

The employment of return activity can increase the movement potential of mat work, balance beams, benches, and other selected pieces of apparatus. In this technique, the child performs some kind of movement task on his way back (return) to his place in line. The return activity is usually something different, a change of pace, from the instructional emphasis. The instructional concentration is centered on the lesson activities, so the return movements should demand little supervision. Choice and exploration should characterize return activities.

An illustration of return activity in combination with the balance-beam bench follows. In this, the child performs on the bench, accomplishes his dismount, and does a forward roll on the way back to place. Three children are in place, illustrating the three aspects of the activity. One child is performing, another is dismounting, and the third child is rolling.

Return Activity

GROUP ACTIVITY

Group organization can be effectively employed utilizing apparatus. Groups should be small enough with respect to the amount of available apparatus so that little standing or waiting occurs. The method is effective for squad organization if each squad is provided with enough equipment.

Group activity works best if there has been some preliminary instruction or orientation with regard to the apparatus. Children at each station should have specified things to do or challenges to meet, otherwise the activity is merely a type of supervised free play. Rotation is usually by signal, but can be by choice. The latter approach can teach youngsters to share. The teacher circulates around, helping, encouraging, and suggesting.

Group activity leaders can be designated to be responsible for activity at a station. Manipulative activities can be combined with apparatus activities in the group plan.

APPARATUS TYPES

The following types of apparatus are included in the instructional material which follows:

Climbing and Hanging (Body Support) Types

Climbing ropes, horizontal ladders, climbiing frames, the exercise bar.

Apparatus Placed on the Floor

Balance beam, benches, jumping boxes, magic ropes, individual mats, balance boards, bounding boards, gym scooters, combination sets.

ROPE CLIMBING

Rope climbing offers high developmental possibilities for the upper trunk and arms, as well as good training in coordination of the different parts of the body. Adequate grip and arm strength are necessary prerequisites to climbing. Becoming accustomed to the rope and gaining in confidence are important goals in early work on the ropes. Many children need to overcome a natural fear of height.

Instructional Procedures

1. Mats should be under all ropes.

2. The hand-over-hand method should be used for climbing and the hand-under-hand method for descending.

3. Children should be cautioned not to slide, or they may get rope burns on the hands and skinned places on the leg.

4. If a climber becomes tired, he should

Rope Climbing on a 10-Rope Set

stop and rest. Proper resting stops should be taught with the climbing.

5. Always leave enough margin to descend safely. No child should go higher than his strength will allow.

6. Spotters should be used where the body is inverted in stunts. Spotters may hold the rope steady while the child climbs.

7. Resin in powdered form and magnesium chalk are aids to better gripping. It is particularly important that they be used when the rope becomes slippery after use.

8. Children swinging on the ropes should make sure the other children are out of the way.

9. Marks to limit the climb can be put on the rope with adhesive tape. A mark 8' to 10' above the floor is the limit for all children until they can demonstrate sufficient proficiency to be allowed to climb higher.

Preliminary Sequences

Progression is important in rope climbing and the basic skill progressions should be followed.

Supported Pull-Ups

In these activities, a part of the body remains in contact with the floor. Pull up hand-over-hand and return hand-under-hand.

1. Kneel directly under the rope. Pull up until on tiptoes.

2. Sitting position. Pull up; legs are supported on the heels.

3. Standing position. Grasp rope, rock back on heels and lower body to floor. Keep a straight body. Return to the standing position.

Hangs

In a hang, the child pulls himself up in one motion and holds the position for a length of time — 5, 10, or 20 seconds. Stress progression.

1. From a seated position, reach up as high as possible and pull the body from the floor except for the heels. Hold.

2. Same as previous stunt, except pull the body completely free of the floor and hold.

3. From a standing position, jump up, grasp, and hang. This should be a bent-arm hang with the hands about even with the mouth. Hold.

4. Repeat previous stunt, but add leg movements:

> One or both knees up
>
> Bicycling movement of the legs
>
> Half lever — leg (one or both) comes up parallel to the floor
>
> Full lever — bring feet up to face

Pull-Ups

In the pull-up, the child raises and lowers his body repeatedly.

Repeat all activities under *Hangs,* except substitute the pull-up for the hang. Pull up each time till the chin touches the hands.

Inverted Hang

Reach up high with both hands. Keep the rope to one side. Jump to a bent-arm position and at the same time bring the knees to the nose, inverting the body, which is in a curled position. In a continuation of the motion, bring the feet higher than the hands and lock the legs around the rope. Body should now be straight and upside down. In learning phases, the teacher should spot.

Swinging and Jumping

Use a bench, box, or stool for a take-off point. To take off, the child should reach high and jump to a bent-arm position while swinging. Landing should be done in a bent knee drop.

1. Swing and jump. Add half and full turns.

2. Swing and return to perch. Add single and double knee bends.

3. Jump for distance, over a high jump bar, or through a hoop.

4. Carry articles — beanbags, balls, deck tennis rings. Partner stands on side away from take-off bench and puts articles between knees or feet to be carried back to perch.

5. Not using take-off devices, children can run toward a swinging rope, grasp it high up and secure momentum for swinging.

Climbing the Rope

1. Scissors Grip. Approach the rope and reach as high as possible, standing with the right leg forward of the left. Raise the back leg, bend at the knee, and place the rope *inside* of the knee and *outside* the foot. Cross the forward leg over the back leg and straighten the legs out with the toes pointed down. This should give a secure hold. The teacher should check the position.

The Scissors Grip

Climbing Using the Scissors Grip. From the scissors grip position, raise the knees up close to the chest with the rope sliding between them while supporting the body with the hand grip. Now lock the rope between the legs and climb up with the hand-over-hand method as high as the hands can reach. Bring the knees up to the chest and repeat

the process until the following goals are reached:

   a. Climb halfway.

   b. Climb three-fourths of the way.

   c. Climb to the top mark.

A top mark should be established beyond which the children should not be permitted to climb.

2. Leg-Around Rest. Using the left leg and keeping the rope between the thighs, wrap the left leg completely around the rope. The bottom of the rope now crosses over the instep of the left foot *from the outside*. The right foot stands on the rope as it crosses over the instep, providing pressure to prevent slippage. To provide additional pressure, release the hands and wrap the arms around the rope, leaning from the rope at the same time. If the right leg is used, the above instructions should be reversed.

The Leg-Around Rest

Climbing Using the Leg-Around Rest. Climbing with the leg-around rest is similar to climbing with the scissors grip, except that the leg-around rest grip needs to be loosened each time and re-formed higher up on the rope.

Descending

There are four methods of descending the rope. The only differences are in the use of the leg locks, as the hand-under-hand is used for all descents.

1. Reverse of the Scissors Climb. From an extended position, lock the legs and lower the body with hands until the knees are against the chest. Hold with the hands and lower the legs to a new position.

2. Using the Leg-Around Rest. From the leg-around rest, lower hand-under-hand until the knees are against the chest. Lift the top foot and let the rope slide loosely to a lower position. Again secure with the top foot. Repeat until down.

3. Instep Squeeze. The rope is squeezed between the insteps by keeping the heels together. The hand-under-hand movement lowers the body while the rope slides between the insteps.

4. Stirrup Descent. The rope is on the outside of the right foot and is carried under the instep of the foot and over the toe of the left foot. Pressure from the left foot holds the position. To get into position, let the rope trail along the right leg, reach under, and hook it with the left toe. When the force of the left leg is varied, the rope can slide smoothly while the descent is made with the hands.

Other Climbing Activities

1. Climbing for Time. A stopwatch and a definite mark on the rope are needed. The height of the mark will depend upon the children's skill and capacity. Each child should have three trials (not in succession, however) and the best time is recorded as his score. He should start from a standing position with hands reaching as high as he wishes. The descent should not be included in the timing, as too much emphasis on speed in the descent causes children to drop from too great a height or promotes rope burns on the hands and other parts of the body.

2. Climbing Without Using the Feet. This strenuous activity should be attempted only by the more skillful. During early sessions the mark set should not be too high. Start from a sitting position. This can also be timed.

3. Organize a Tarzan Club. Put a marker at the top limit of the rope and make each child who can climb and touch the marker a member of the Tarzan Club. Form a Super Tarzan Club for those who can climb to the marker without using the feet. The climber must start from a sitting position on the floor.

Stunts Using Two Ropes

Two ropes, hanging close together, are needed for these activities.

1. Straight Arm Hang. Jump up, grasp one rope with each hand, and hang with the arms straight.

2. Bent Arm Hang. Same as above except that the arms are bent at the elbows.

3. Arm Hangs With Different Leg Positions.
   a. Single and double knee lifts.
   b. Half Lever — bring feet up parallel to floor, toes pointed.
   c. Full Lever — bring feet up to face and keep knees straight.
   d. Bicycle — pedal like a bicycle.

4. Pull-Ups. Same as a pull-up on a single rope.

5. Inverted Hangs.
   a. With the feet wrapped around the rope
   b. With the feet against the inside of the ropes
   c. With the toes pointed and the feet not touching the ropes

Spotting for Inverted Hangs on Double Ropes. Holding the performer's hands on the rope gives confidence in learning stages.

6. Skin the Cat. From a bent-arm position, kick feet overhead and continue the roll until the feet touch the mat. Return to the starting position. A more difficult stunt is to start from a higher position so the feet do not touch the mat. Reverse to original position.

7. Climbing.

a. Climb up one rope, transfer to another, and descend.

b. Climb halfway up one rope, cross over to another rope and continue to climb to the top.

c. Climb both ropes together without legs. This is difficult and requires the climber to slide one hand at a time up the ropes without completely releasing the grip.

HORIZONTAL LADDER AND CLIMBING FRAMES

Horizontal ladders and climbing frames are manufactured in a variety of models. The most usable ladder is one that can be stored against the wall out of the way. If the ladder can be adjusted so it is inclined, the movement possibilities are extended.

The climbing frame pictured below is from Holland, where it is called the *Klimraam.* It stores out of the way against the wall and can be moved into place by children. The frame has two positions, vertical and inclined. In the author's program, three *Klimraams* are combined with climbing ropes for instructional purposes, with half the class on each type of apparatus.

Another effective wall-attached climbing

Exploring on Climbing Frames

frame is the Hampton Frame, made in England but available now in the United States. It offers a wider choice of activity than the *Klimraam,* but does not lend itself as easily to group instruction (page 37).

Instructional Procedures

1. The opposed-thumb grip, in which the thumb goes around the bar, is important. In most activities, the back of the hands should face the child. Vary the grip, however, using other holds. Use other grips, such as the lower grip (palms toward the face) and the mixed grip (one hand facing one way and one the other) for variety.

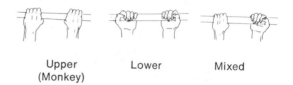

Upper   Lower   Mixed
(Monkey)

2. Whenever the child is doing an inverted hang, spotters should be present.

3. Speed is not the goal of this activity. In fact, the longer the child is hanging from the ladder, the more beneficial the activity will be. There is value in just hanging.

4. In activities involving movement across the ladder, all children should travel in the same direction.

5. Mats should always be placed under the climbing apparatus when they are in use.

6. When dismounting from ladders, the child should be instructed to land in a bent-leg position, on the balls of the feet.

7. Don't force children to climb the wall-attached climbing frames. Many children have a natural fear of height and need much reassurance before they will climb. If necessary, climb the frame with the child until he is confident of his ability.

8. Bars placed out-of-doors should not be used when wet, as they become slippery.

Horizontal Ladder Activities

Hangs. The hangs should be performed with the opposed thumb grip and with straight arms. Encourage the children to hang in a bent-arm position, however, to involve more muscles in the upper arms. The following hang variations are suggested:

1. Straight leg. Keep legs straight and point toes toward ground.

2. Knees up. Lift the knees as high as possible toward the chest.

3. Bicycle. Lift the knees and pedal the bicycle.

4. Half Lever. Bring the legs up parallel to the ground with the knees straight and the toes pointed.

5. Inverted. Hang with the hands on a rung. Bring the feet up and over the next rung and hook the toes under a second rung. Release the hand grip, and hang in an inverted position.

Note: A spotter should be present during the child's first few attempts at inverted stunts.

6. Flexed Arm. Stand on a box if necessary to get in position. Hang as long as possible with the chin even with the hands.

7. Swinging. Hang from a rung with both hands and swing the body back and forth.

8. Swing back and forth and jump as far as possible. Vary with turns.

Moving Activities on the Horizontal Ladder

1. Travel the length of the ladder using the rungs. Start by traveling one rung at a time and then skip one or more rungs to add challenge.

2. Travel the length of the ladder using both side rails; also use just one rail to travel the ladder.

3. Hang with both hands on the side rails. Progress the length of the ladder by jumping both hands forward at once.

4. Travel along the ladder with both hands on the same rung. Progress by jumping forward with both hands simultaneously from one rung to the next.

5. Travel underneath the ladder in a monkey crawl position with both hands and feet on the rungs. Try with the feet on the side rails.

6. Travel the length of the ladder carrying a beanbag, ball, or any other similar object.

Wall-Attached Climbing Frame Activities

Hangs. All the hangs possible on the horizontal ladder may be used with the wall-attached climbing frames.

Moving Activities on the Wall-Attached Climbing Frame

1. Climb to the top of the frame on the back side using the hands and the feet. Descend in the same manner.

2. Climb the back side of the frame to the top and descend using only the arms and hands.

3. Climb the front side of the frame, transfer to the back side and descend to the bottom using only the hands.

4. Climb the back side of the frame to the top using only the hands.

5. Climb the frame, transfer *through* the frame from one side to the other.

6. Follow-the-leader activity is excellent for climbing frames.

EXERCISE BAR (LOW HORIZONTAL BAR)

Horizontal bars should be installed on the playground in series of at least three at different heights. The primary program should be limited to simple hangs and climbs. To perform many of the more complicated stunts on the bar, it is necessary to have sufficient arm strength to pull the body up and over the bar. Some of the youngsters in the third grade will begin to have this capacity, but the emphasis in the primary grades should be on a more limited program.

In the intermediate program, attention should be turned toward the more gymnastic type of stunt. However, the advanced skills are difficult and the teacher should not be discouraged by apparent lack of progress.

Instructional Procedures

1. Only one child should be on a bar at a time.

2. Do not use the bar when it is wet.

3. The basic grip is the opposed-thumb grip, upper style (see page 169) for grip description). The lower and mixed grips should also be used.

Sequence of Activities

1. Hangs. Feet pointed, one or both knee up, half or full lever.

2. Swings. Swing back and forth, propelling the body forward to a stand.

3. Moving Along the Bar. Begin at one side

and move hand against hand to the other end of the bar. Move with crossed hands.

4. Sloth Travel. Face end of bar, standing underneath. Grasp bar with both hands and hook the legs over the bar at the knees. In this position, move along the bar to the other end. Return by reversing the movement.

5. Arm and Leg Hang. Grasp bar with upper grip. Bring one of the legs between the arms and hook the knee over the bar.

6. Double Leg Hang. Same as #5, but bring both legs between the hands and hook the knees over the bar. Release the hands and hang in the inverted position. If the hands touch or are near the ground, a dismount can be made by releasing the legs and dropping to a crouched position on the ground.

7. Skin the Cat. Bring both knees up between the arms as in the previous stunt, but continue the direction of the knees until the body is turned over backward. Release grip and drop to ground.

8. Skin the Cat Return. Same as #7, except do not release the hands. Bring the legs back through the hands to original position.

9. Front Support. Grasp the bar with an upper grip and jump to a straight arm support on the bar. Jump down.

10. Front Support Push-Off. Mount the bar in the same way as in #9. In returning to the ground, push off straight with the arms and jump as far back as possible.

11. Tumble Over. Jump to a front support position. Change the grip to an under grip. Bend forward and roll over to a standing position under the bar.

12. Single Knee Swing. Using the upper grip, swing one leg forward so that there is a single knee hang. Using the free leg to gain momentum, swing back and forth.

13. Side Arc. Sit on the bar with one leg on each side of the bar, both hands gripping the bar in front of the body. Lock the legs and fall sideways. Try to make a complete circle back to position. Good momentum is needed.

14. Single Leg Rise. Using the position in #12, on the back (up)swing, rise to the top of the bar. The down leg must be kept straight. Swing forward (down) first and on the back (up)swing push down hard with straight arms.

A spotter can assist by pushing down on the straight leg with one hand and lifting on the back with the other.

BALANCE BEAM

Balance beam activities are valuable in contributing to the control of balance in both static (stationary) and dynamic (moving) balance situations. The balance-beam side of a balance-beam bench is ideal for this activity, with its 2″ wide and about 12′ long beam. However, balance beams come in many sizes

The Balance-Beam Bench

and can be constructed from common lumber materials (see appendix). Some teachers prefer a wider beam for kindergarten and first grade children and, in particular, special education children. Children should graduate to the narrower beam as soon as the activities on the wider beam no longer seem to challenge them.

Learning good control of balance demands a considerable amount of practice and concentration. The teacher should not be discouraged by apparent slow progress. Proper practice will in time greatly increase the children's proficiency.

Instructional Procedures

1. Children should move with controlled, deliberate movements. Speedy movement is

not a goal. Advise the performer to recover his balance before taking another step or making another movement.

2. In keeping with the principle of control, children should step slowly on the beam, pause momentarily in good balance at the end of the activity, and dismount with a small, controlled jump from the end of the beam when the routine is completed.

3. Mats can be placed at the end of the bench to cushion the dismount and allow for selected rolls and stunts after the dismount.

4. Visual fixation is important. Children should look ahead at eye level, rather than down at the feet. Eye targets can be marked or attached to walls to assist them in visual fixation. Visual fixation allows balance controls other than vision to function more effectively. From time to time, movements can be done with the eyes closed, entirely eliminating visual control of balance.

5. Children should step off the beam if they lose balance, rather than teeter and fall off awkwardly. Allow the performer to step back on the beam and continue his routine.

6. Success early in a balance-beam activity can be based on two levels. The lower level allows the performer to step off the beam once during his routine. The higher level demands that he remain on the beam throughout. In both levels, he must pause at the end of the beam *in good balance* before dismounting.

7. Both laterality and directionality are important. Corresponding parts of the body (right and left feet), should be given reasonably equal treatment. For example, if the performer does follow steps leading with the right foot, the next effort should be made leading with the left foot. Directions right and left should be given equal weight. A child will naturally use his dominant side and direction with which he feels more skillful and confident, but must be encouraged to perform otherwise.

8. The child next in turn begins when the performer ahead is about three-quarters distance across the beam.

9. Return activities should be a consideration to enhance the breadth of activity. (See page 165 for explanation of return activity.)

Balance Beam Activities

Activities are presented in categories. Generally, each category should be fully exploited and exhausted before proceeding to the next.

Moving Across the Full Length of the Beam

Walk, follow steps, heel and toe, side (draw) steps, tiptoes, step behind, grapevine (step behind, step across), etc.

Different directions — forward, backward, sideward.

Different arm positions — on hips, on head, behind back, out to the sides, pointing to the ceiling, folded across chest, etc.

Balance objects (beanbags or erasers) on various parts of the body — one, two or three on the head, back of hands, shoulders.

Half and Half Movements

These repeat the movements, arm positions, and balance objects as previously described, except that the performer goes halfway across the beam using a selected movement, then changes to another type of movement at the center, and does this on the second half of the beam.

Challenge Tasks or Stunts

The performer moves along the beam to the center with a selected movement, performs a particular challenge or stunt at the center, and finishes out his movements on the second half of the beam. Examples of challenges or stunts which can be performed at the center of the beam are:

Balances — Front Balance, Back Layout, Stork Stand, Seat Balance, Knee Balance, Side Leaning Rest.

Stunts — Knee Dip, Heel Sit, Forward Leg Extension, Back Finger Touch.

Challenges — Full Turn, pick up beanbag at center, pick up paper at center with teeth, do a push-up.

More Difficult Movements Across the Beam

Hop the length of the beam forward, sideward, and backward.

Cat Walk (page 196), Rabbit Jump (page 197), Lame Dog Walk (page 199), Seal Crawl (page 201), Crab Walk (page 201).

Do various locomotor movements with eyes closed.

Using Wands and Hoops

Carry wand or hoop. Step over wand or through hoop – various fashions.

Step over or go under wands held by partner. Same with hoop.

Use the hula hoop twirling on arms or around the body while moving across the beam.

Manipulative Activities to Self

Using one or two beanbags, toss to self in various fashions — around the body, under the legs, etc.

Using a ball, toss to self. Circle ball around body, under the legs.

Bounce ball on the floor and on the beam. Dribble on floor.

Roll ball along the beam.

Manipulative Activities with a Partner

With partner standing beyond far end of beam — toss and throw a beanbag or ball back and forth. Have partner toss to performer for a volleyball return. Bat ball (as in volleyball serve) to partner.

Partner Stunts

Regular and reverse wheelbarrows (page 233), with support performer keeping feet on floor.

Partners start on opposite end of beam, moving toward each other with the same kind of movement, do a balance pose together in the center, and return to respective ends of the beam.

ACTIVITIES ON BENCHES

The balance-beam bench is an effective piece of apparatus of dual use. Bench activities are interesting and challenging to children, and offer a variety of movement possibilities.

Instructional Procedures

1. All activities on the benches should contain three distinct parts: the approach and lead up to the bench, the actual activity on the bench, and, lastly, the dismount off the bench.

2. Mats should be placed at the end of the benches to facilitate the dismount and allow for various rolls and stunts after the dismount.

3. Benches may be positioned horizontally,

A Class in Bench Activities

inclined, or in combination with other equipment for variation and greater challenge.

4. Four to five children assigned to a bench for activity should be the maximum number assigned to one bench.

5. The child next in turn begins when the performer ahead has reached about the three-quarters distance on the bench.

6. Return activities for the child to perform as he returns to his place in line add to the activity potential.

7. Speed is *not* a goal in bench activities. Movements should be done deliberately and carefully with attention given to good body control and management.

8. Attention should be given to use of corresponding parts of the body and directional movements. For example, if a child hops on the right foot, the next effort should be made on the left foot. In jump turns, both right and left movements should be utilized. A child naturally uses the stronger or preferred part of his body. See that he has a balance in the demands.

Bench Activities

1. Animal Walks on the Bench. Perform various animal walks on the bench, such as:
   a. Seal Walk (page 201).
   b. Cat Walk (page 196).
   c. Lame Dog Walk (page 199).
   d. Rabbit Jump (page 197).

2. Locomotor Movements. Perform various locomotor movements on the bench, such as:

a. Step on and off.

b. Jump on and off.

c. Hop on and off.

d. Skip on the bench.

e. Gallop on the bench.

3. Pulls. Pull the body along the bench in the various following combinations:

a. Prone Position—head first and feet first.

b. Supine Position—head first and feet first.

c. Side Position—head first and feet first.

Note: Various leg positions such as legs up in a half lever position, knees bent, etc., should be used while performing pulls and pushes.

4. Pushes. Push the body along the bench using the following positions.

a. Prone Position—head first and feet first.

b. Supine Position—head first and feet first.

c. Side Position—head first and feet first.

5. Movements Along the Side of the Bench. Proceed alongside the bench in the following positions. (Keep the limbs on the floor as far from the bench as possible.)

a. Prone Position — hands on bench.

b. Supine Position — hands on bench.

c. Turnover — proceed along the bench changing from prone to supine positions, hands on bench.

d. All of the above positions performed with the feet on the bench.

6. Scooter Movements. Sit on the bench and proceed along the bench without using hands.

a. Regular Scooter — proceed with the feet leading the body. Try to pull the body along with the feet.

b. Reverse Scooter — proceed as above but with the legs trailing and pushing the body along the bench.

c. Seat Walk — proceed forward by walking on the buttocks. Use the legs as little as possible.

7. Crouch Jumps. Place both hands on the bench and jump back and forth over the bench. Progress the length of the bench by moving the hands forward a few inches after each jump.

a. Straddle Jump—a variation of the crouch jump. Straddle the bench with the legs. Take the weight on the hands and jump the legs as high as possible.

b. Regular — use both hands and both feet. Jump as high as possible.

c. One Hand and Two Feet—same as above except eliminate the use of one hand.

d. One Hand and One Foot — perform the crouch jump using only one hand and one foot.

8. Basic Tumbling Stunts on the Bench. Basic tumbling stunts can be incorporated into bench activities.

a. Back Roller (page 194).

b. Backward Curl (page 207).

c. Forward Roll (page 200).

d. Backward Roll (page 207).

e. Cartwheel (page 230).

Dismounts

As stated earlier, all bench activities in which one moves from one end of the bench to the other should end with a dismount. The following are suggested dismounts that may be used:

1. Jump Dismounts

a. Single Jump — forward or backward.

b. Jump with Turns — half, three-quarters or full turn.

c. Jackknife — jump, kick legs up, and touch toes with the fingertips. Keep feet together.

d. Jackknife Split — same as above except spread legs as far as possible.

2. Jump Dismounts followed by a Stunt on the Mat

a. Jump to a Forward Roll

b. Backward Jump to a Back Roll

c. Side Jump to a Side Roll

d. Shoulder Roll

e. Jump with combinations of the above stunts.

Many other stunts can be utilized.

Prone Movements — Head First

Supine Movements — Feet First

Crouch Jumps

A Forward Roll

A Balancing Stunt

Dismounting from an Inclined Bench

Additional Experiences for Expanding Bench Activities

1. The range of activities can be extended with the addition of balls, beanbags, hoops, and wands. Wands and hoops can be used as obstacles to go over, under, around or through. Basic balance and manipulative skills can be incorporated into the activity with balls and beanbags.

2. Different balance positions on the benches can be done. Two children should perform at a time, each near one end of the bench.

3. Children love to go over and under a series of benches in a row, in a kind of obstacle course. Some of the benches can be supported on jumping boxes, making them excellent for vaulting activities.

4. Benches can be placed in a hollow square formation, with children moving around the sequence of the square, doing a different movement on each bench.

5. Place one end of the bench on a jumping box or other bench. Children can secure good jumping practice by running up the incline and going for good height at the end of the bench.

6. Benches are appropriate for some partner activities. Children can start on each end and pass through or around each other, reversing original position. Wheelbarrow walks are quite suitable.

ACTIVITIES ON JUMPING BOXES

Jumping boxes can be constructed or purchased. They provide opportunities for the children to do the natural activities of running, jumping, and propelling the body through the air. Boxes should be made in two heights; 12" and 24" are suggested. They are usually square in shape, about 18" by 18" for the larger height. The smaller box should be about 16" by 16", so as to fit inside the larger box for storage. The top should be padded and covered with durable leather or plastic cloth. A rubber floor pad can be placed under the box to offer good floor protection. Commercially constructed boxes have sloped sides for better stability (see appendix).

Instructional Procedures

1. Attention should be given to "meeting the ground" in proper form, stressing lightness, bent-knee action, balance, and body control.

2. Mats should be used to cushion the landing.

3. The exploratory and creative approach is important as there are few "standard" stunts in jumping box activities.

4. A group of not more than four or five children should be assigned to each series of boxes.

5. Additional challenge can be incorporated into the activity by the use of hoops, wands, balls, etc. In addition, rolling stunts after the dismount extend the possibilities of movement.

6. Return activities work well with boxes.

7. Children should strive for height and learn to relax as they go through space.

8. The suggested activities which follow can be augmented with a little imagination. Let the children help expand the breadth of the activity.

Jumping Box Activities

1. Mounting the Box. Use combinations of the following locomotor movements to get on the box:

a. Step

b. Jump

c. Leap

d. Hop

An example of the above activity might be to step on the box and jump off or to hop on the box and leap off.

2. Dismounting. The following dismounts can be used to develop body control:

a. Jump off with a quarter, half, or full turn.

b. Jump off with different body shapes such as stretch, curl up into a ball, jackknife, etc.

c. Jump over, under, or through various objects.

d. Jump off followed by a forward or backward roll.

e. Change the above dismounts by substituting a hop or leap in place of the jump.

3. Various Approaches to the Boxes. The approach to the box can be varied by performing various movements, such as:

Jump Dismounts from a 16" Box

Through the Hoop!

a. Run

b. Gallop

c. Skip

d. Hop

e. Many animal walks, such as bear walk, crab walk, etc.

4. Addition of Equipment. Use various pieces of equipment to enhance the box activities. The following are some suggestions:

a. Beanbags — throw them up while dismounting or try to keep them on your head while mounting or dismounting the box.

b. Balls — try to dribble a playground ball while performing the box routine.

c. Hoops — jump through a stationary hoop (held by a partner) while dismounting, or use the hoop as a jump rope and see how many times you can jump it while dismounting.

d. Wands — jump over or under the wand.

5. Box Combinations. Boxes can be arranged in a straight line or other pattern. The child does a different movement over each box as though running an obstacle course.

MAGIC ROPES

Magic ropes come from Germany. Each rope is similar to a long rubber band. Ropes can be made by knitting wide rubber bands together or can be constructed from ordinary ¾" white elastic tape, available in most clothing stores. Loops on each end enable the child to thrust his hand through and grasp the rope. Ropes should be long enough to stretch to between 30' and 40' (see appendix).

A major advantage of the magic rope is its flexibility; children have no fear of hitting or tripping on it while they are performing. Ropes should be stretched tight enough so there is little sag.

Instructional Procedures

1. Two or more children need to be rope holders while the others are jumping. Develop some type of rotation plan so that all children participate.

2. Many variations can be achieved with the magic ropes by varying their height and by raising and lowering opposite ends of the rope.

3. The jumping activities are strenuous, therefore alternate between jumping activities and those activities that involve crawling under the ropes, etc.

4. Emphasize to the class that they should

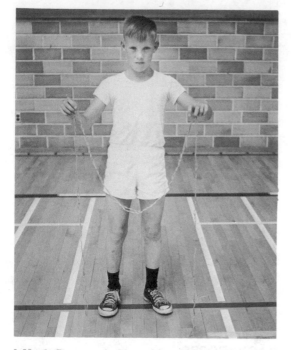

A Magic Rope made from wide rubber bands knitted together.

Over a Single Magic Rope

concentrate on *not* touching the rope. The magic ropes can help develop the child's perception of his body in space if he regards the rope as an obstacle to be avoided.

5. Better use can be made of the ropes using an oblique approach, which involves starting at one end of the rope and progressing to the other end using jumping and hopping activities, etc. By comparison, the straight-on approach allows the child to jump the rope only once.

6. A total of eight ropes is needed for a class, two to each squad. Squads make excellent groups for this activity, as the leader can control the rotation of the ropeholders.

7. The child next in turn should begin his movements when the child ahead is almost to the end of the rope.

Magic Rope Activities

Single Rope Activities. Start the ropes at a 6″ height and progressively raise them to add challenge.

1. Jump the rope.
2. Hop the rope.
3. Jump the rope and perform various body turns while jumping.

4. Change body shapes and sizes while jumping.
5. Crawl or slide under the rope.
6. Alternate going over and under the rope.
7. Crouch jump over the rope.

Double Ropes. Vary the height and spread of the ropes.

1. *Ropes parallel to each other*
   a. Jump in one side and out the other.
   b. Hop in one side and out the other.
   c. Crouch-jump in and out.

Over Double Magic Ropes

d. Perform various animal walks in and out of the ropes.

2. *Ropes crossed at right angles to each other*

   a. Perform various movements from one area to the next.

   b. Jump into one area and crawl out of that area into another.

3. *One rope above the other to create a "barbed wire fence" effect*

   a. Step through the ropes without touching.

   b. Crouch-jump through.

   c. Vary the height and the distance apart at which the ropes are placed. This will add much excitement to the activity as children are challenged not to touch the ropes.

4. *Miscellaneous*

   a. Perform the various activities with a beanbag balanced on the head or bouncing a ball.

   b. Use four or more ropes to create various floor patterns.

   c. Use a "follow the leader" plan to add variety to the activity.

   d. Create an obstacle course with many ropes for a relay.

INDIVIDUAL MATS

Individual mats are English in origin and are the basis for many exploratory and creative movements. Essentially, the mat serves the child as a home base of operation and as an obstacle which he goes over or around.

Mats can vary in size, but 18" by 36" or 20" by 40" seem to be the most popular. In thickness, the ¾" type is standard, but this can also vary. The mat should have a rubber backing, which prevents mat slippage on the floor. Foam-backed indoor-outdoor carpeting of good quality makes an excellent mat.

Instructional Procedures

1. Basic movement techniques are most important in mat work.

2. Much emphasis should be centered on body management and basic skills of locomotor and nonlocomotor movement.

3. Mats should be far enough apart to allow for free movement around them.

4. Each child should have a mat.

Sequence of Activities

Rigid adherence to the sequence presented below is not necessary, as the activities are quite flexible and demand only basic skills.

1. Command Movements. In this the child changes movements on command. Commands used are:

"Stretch": Stretch your body out in all directions as wide as possible.

"Curl": Curl into a little tight ball.

"Balance": Form some kind of a balance.

"Bridge": Make a bridge over the mat.

"Reach": Keeping one toe on the mat, reach out as far as possible along the floor in a chosen direction.

"Rock": Rock on any part of the body.

"Roll": Do some kind of a roll on the mat.

"Twist": Make a shape with a part of the body twisted.

Each of the above can be developed individually by commanding "change," with which the child makes another kind of movement or shape. Balance can be developed by changing for balance on different parts of the body or a different number of parts — one, two, three, four, or five.

2. Movements on and off the Mat. The children do different locomotor movements on and off the mat in different directions. Turns and shapes can be added. Levels are another

Balance Activities on Individual Mats

good challenge. Take the weight on the hands going across the mat.

3. Movements over the Mat. This is similar to No. 2 except that the child goes completely over the mat each time.

4. Movements around the Mat. Locomotor movements around the mat are done both clockwise and counterclockwise. Do movements around the mat keeping hands on the mat. Do the same but keep the feet on the mat.

5. Using Mats as a Base. Stretch and reach in different directions to show how big the space is. Do combination movements away from and back to the mat, such as, for example, two jumps and two hops, or six steps and two jumps.

6. Mat Games or Fun Activity. Each child is seated on his mat. On signal, each child arises and jumps over as many different mats as he can. On the next signal, each child takes a seat on the nearest mat. The last child to get seated can be designated or pay a penalty. The game can also be played by eliminating one or two mats and thus having one or two children left without a home base. This is done by the teacher standing on a mat or by turning over mats and putting them out of the game. To control roughness, make a rule that the first child to touch a mat gets to sit on it.

BALANCE BOARDS

Balance boards are small devices on which the child tries to stand and keep the board in balance. Generally, they have either a circular or square platform about 15" wide and a rounded bottom to provide the challenge for balance. A rubber pad should protect the floor. The activities are somewhat limited, consisting of maintaining balance with a variety of challenges.

Sequence of Activities

1. Secure a balanced position on the board. Change position of arms.

2. Secure balance and gradually lower the body to touch the board.

3. Change from a two-foot to a one-foot balance. Change from one foot to the other.

4. Add manipulative items such as wands to balance, hoops for hooping, beanbags and balls for tossing. Toss to self or toss to partner.

BOUNDING BOARDS

Bounding boards provide a unique type of movement similar to that of a child bouncing on a trampoline. They can be constructed easily from a piece of ¾" plywood, size 2' by 6'. The board is supported on pieces of 4" x 4" lumber, which are padded with carpet to protect the floor. The plywood must be a quality product with few knots. Marine plywood, though expensive, is the best (see appendix).

Two children can work on one board, with the performer moving forward to leave the board and return back to place. Emphasis should be on lightness, height, and relaxation during the bounding. Bounding for the most part should be done in the center of the board. The activity is for younger children only.

Balancing on Different Balance Boards

Bouncing on Bounding Boards

Sequence of Activities

1. Bound in the center; two feet, one foot.

2. Bound in the center, using turns and different arm positions. Add hand clapping.

3. Move across the board, using jumping and hopping. Return. Add turns and hand clapping.

4. Bound with numbered foot combinations, alternating two, three, or four hops on one foot and then changing to the other. These are called twoseys, threeseys, and fourseys.

5. To the previous skills, add forward and backward leg extensions, and leg changes sideward.

6. Use different numbers of hops when alternating, such as hopping once on the right foot and twice on the left. Use other combinations as 2-3, 2-4, etc.

7. Add rope jumping with slow time and fast time. Use hoops.

GYM SCOOTERS

Gym scooters make excellent devices for developmental activity if properly used. The minimum number for a class should be one scooter for each two children. However, if the scooters are used only for relays, four to six will suffice.

Two rules are important in the use of scooters. The first is that the children are not to stand on them as they would on skate boards. The second rule is that scooters, with or without passengers, are not to be used as missiles.

Scooters can be used by children individually or with partners. When used individually, many variations are possible by combining the method of propulsion and the method of supporting the body. The child may propel the scooter with his feet, hands, or both. His body position may be kneeling, sitting, prone, supine, or even sideways. His weight may be wholly or partially supported on the scooter. Variation in space factors, particularly direction, add to the interest.

On a Gym Scooter

When working with a partner, one child rides and the other pushes. The rider's weight may be wholly or partially supported on the scooter. If only partially on the scooter, the remainder of the weight is supported by the partner.

Basic movement methodology is applicable to scooter work, but care should be exercised so that it is a developmental period and not just a fun session.

Scooters are excellent for relays, and many games can be adapted to their use.

Stunts and Tumbling

THE STUNTS AND TUMBLING PROGRAM

The stunts and tumbling program is an important inclusion in the child's overall physical education experiences and can make significant contribution toward the achievement of physical education goals. Such personal characteristics as dedication and perseverance toward a goal can be furthered, since stunts are seldom mastered quickly or in a few attempts. Since much of the work is individual, the child faces his own challenge and has the opportunity to develop resourcefulness, self-confidence, and courage. On the other hand, foolhardiness and disregard for safety must be avoided.

Social interplay is provided by the various partner and group stunts requiring cooperative effort. Social attributes of tolerance, helpfulness, courtesy, and appreciation for the ability of others grow out of the lessons when the methodology is educationally sound. Further group consciousness develops from increased concern for one's own safety and that of others. Each child needs to apply proper spotting techniques and to be ready to aid others in the execution of stunts.

When a child masters a challenging stunt, his satisfaction, pride of achievement, and sense of accomplishment contribute to a gain in self-respect and improvement in his self-image.

Physical Values

Important physical values can emerge from an instructionally sound program of stunts and tumbling. Exercise in good body management can be provided, fulfilling the objective of offering opportunities for a child to manage his body effectively in a variety of situations. Coordination, flexibility, and agility can be enhanced.

The opportunity to practice control of balance is present in many stunt activities and particularly featured in some. The suggested program includes challenges for all three aspects of balance — static, dynamic, and rotational. In addition, visual control of balance can be eliminated occasionally by having the children close their eyes during balance stunts, thus centering demands on other balance controls.

The raw physical demands of held positions and stunt execution contribute to the development of strength and power of many diverse parts of the body. The many stunts which demand support by the arms, wholly or in part, provide needed development for the often weak musculature of the arm-shoulder girdle region. Basically, stunts and tumbling activities contribute to all areas of physical fitness.

Educational Values

Educationally, stunts and tumbling can provide many sound learning situations. Creative and exploratory activity should be a part of the learning experiences. Basic movement principles with appropriate problem-solving techniques give breadth to the children's responses. Variety of response should be emphasized by applying time, flow, space, quality, and body factors. The teacher needs to wring the maximum variety of response out of each activity.

Stunts and tumbling activities offer a wonderful opportunity for children to acquire fundamental concepts, such as those of right and left, near and far, wide and narrow, up and down, forward and backward, as well as introducing new terminology into their daily lives.

Quality in Movement

Attention must be given to developing quality in movement, which should be relative to the children's abilities, the character of the activity, and the objectives of the lesson. Emphasis should be placed on "doing things as well as we can," and "giving it a good try." Controlled movement rather than speed is essential. Such movement qualities as lightness and sureness, coordination, rhythmic movement, and other body management factors should be relevant teaching points. Principles of good body mechanics should be incorporated where applicable.

Children should develop a sense of achievement and give some attention to form, but concentration on form should not be an overriding consideration. The stunt should first be taught in its simple, basic, mechanical form. Later the tips and points which dress it up can be introduced. Too much emphasis on technical details and refinements at the beginning can destroy the satisfaction of self-achievement. The lower the grade level, the less emphasis there should be on technical details. Much of the emphasis at the primary level should be centered on just doing the basic stunt.

Coaching hints such as "Head up"; "Point your toes"; "Keep your knees straight"; "Arch your back"; "Legs together," etc., will emphasize the important technical points in the stunt being practiced at the time.

PROGRESSION AND GRADE LEVEL PLACEMENT

Progression is the soul of learning experiences in the stunts and tumbling program, and in this manual the activities in this program are allocated in progression within grades. It is essential that the order of those stunts which lead from one grade to another be reasonably maintained. Adherence to grade level placement is secondary to this principle. Teachers may wish to include activities from a higher grade level to provide more challenge. This would be more likely to be true in the case of the physical education specialist, who has more depth in this area than the classroom teacher. If on the other hand children come with little or no experience in these activities, the teacher should start them off with activities specified for a lower grade level.

Standard Tumbling Stunts

The essentials of a stunts and tumbling program consist in the standard tumbling activities, such as rolls, stands, springs, and related stunts commonly accepted as basic to such a program. The suggested progression of these *basic* gymnastic type activities is presented in the following chart. Descriptions of the stunts are found in the programs at the indicated grade levels.

Sequence and Grade Level Chart

Kindergarten
Forward Roll
Back Roller
Side Roll

First Grade
Forward Roll
Backward Roll (Hand Clasp Position)

Second Grade
Forward Roll Practice
Climb Up
Three Point Tip-Up
Backward Curl
Backward Roll (Regular)

Third Grade
Forward Roll Variations
Frog Handstand
Headstand

Fourth Grade
Forward Roll Combinations
Backward Roll Combinations
Knee Jump to Standing
Headstand Variations

Fifth Grade

Forward and Backward Roll Combinations
Back Extension
Neck Spring
Handstand
Cartwheel
Shoulder Roll
Jump Through
Eskimo Roll

Sixth Grade

Forward and Backward Roll Combinations
Headstand Variations
Headspring
Dive Forward Roll
Handstand
Forearm Headstand
Forearm Stand
Elbow Balance

Kindergarten and Primary Level Program

The kindergarten and primary program relies on simple stunts with good developmental possibilities, with a gradual introduction to those tumbling stunts which are classed as lead-up or preliminary to more advanced stunts. Stunts requiring exceptional body control, critical balancing, or the need for substantial strength should be left for higher grades. The program of stunts and tumbling in the lower grades should include the following:

1. A variety of simple stunts involving gross body movements, opportunity for creative expression, control of balance, and directional concepts.

2. A progressive introduction to the basic tumbling stunts such as the forward and backward rolls and basic stands.

3. Introductory work with a partner in couple stunts.

Intermediate Level Program

The intermediate level program is built upon the activities and progressions from the primary program. More emphasis is placed on the standard tumbling stunts, with the accompanying need for appropriate spotting techniques. While in the primary level most stunts can be performed with a greater degree of choice, the intermediate level presents a somewhat different aspect. More conformance to the stunt pattern or design is desired. The stunts make higher demands on strength, control, form, agility, balance, and flexibility.

While many of the stunts on the lower level can at least be done in some fashion, the teacher will find on the intermediate level certain stunts which will be too much challenge for some of the children. An attempt is made to arrange stunts for the upper grades so that the list includes stunts everyone can do, stunts which are somewhat of a challenge, and more difficult stunts which the less skillful will find quite challenging. The range of stunts provides something for all levels of ability in any grade level. For the intermediate level the program includes:

1. Basic tumbling stunts, with emphasis on progression

2. Stunts demanding critical balance

3. Stunts demanding considerable flexibility

4. Partner support stunts

5. Miscellaneous stunts demanding agility or strength

6. A program of simple pyramids

PRESENTING ACTIVITIES

Steps in presenting activities in the daily lesson plan for stunts and tumbling should include the following considerations:

1. Provide warm-up activity as needed.

2. Consider appropriate physical fitness development activity.

3. Arrange children in suitable formation for teaching.

4. Review previously learned materials and practice lead-up activities to the stunts to be presented.

5. Present the new activity with appropriate description and demonstration.

6. Provide opportunity for practice and improvement of performance.

7. Establish basis for variety through appropriate movement methodology.

8. Evaluate progress and, as needed, repeat directions. Bring in stress points, and work toward refining and perfecting performance.

Warm-up Activity

The need for warm-up activity would depend upon the nature of the day's program. Generally, this should include stretching and loosening type movements. A routine such as this can be followed:

1. **Position:** Wide straddle, feet about 3′ apart, with toes pointed ahead. **Action:** Bend, stretch, and twist in various directions, touching the floor front, back, and sides with little bending of the knees.

2. **Position:** Long sitting, with legs extended and feet about 3′ apart. **Action:** With knees reasonably straight, bend forward bringing elbows to or near the floor. Repeat, bringing chin to or near each knee in turn. Bring elbow to opposite knee. Twist and look backward.

This source holds that if the stunts and tumbling program will make these demands, then the fitness routines can be omitted. Analysis of the projected activities in the day's program will determine this. However, fitness qualities are most effectively developed through a *progressive* program of fitness activities designed for this purpose and not as concomitant values from the activity program.

Approaches for Teaching Stunts and Tumbling

A number of different approaches are avail-

Long Sitting Stretch Position

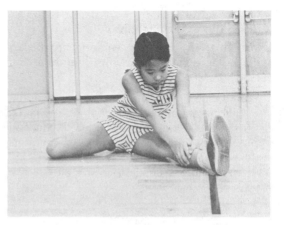

Hurdle Stretch Position

3. **Position:** Hurdle position on floor, i.e., one leg extended forward and the other under the body in a bent-knee position with the toe pointed backward. The position resembles that of a hurdler going over a hurdle. **Action:** Bring the body forward and the chin down toward the knee. Repeat the movement with the legs reversed.

A simple, previously-learned stunt sometimes provides a satisfactory warm-up activity. **Forward** and **Backward Rolls,** singly or in combination, prepare children for the activity which is to follow.

Developmental Activity

For the stunts and tumbling program, some teachers prefer to omit a formal fitness developmental period, holding to the premise that the program of activities will make sufficient fitness demands on the children and therefore fitness routines are not needed for this unit.

able for organizing a class in stunts and tumbling. The arrangement of the children will depend upon the stunts selected and whether or not mats are required. Priorities should be established in this order.

1. All children working and performing at the same time. This can be done readily for stunts which do not require mats by having the children scatter and perform. Where mats are needed, this becomes a problem, as few schools have sufficient mats to allow all children to perform at the same time. With all children active at the same time, some instructional problems are created for the teacher as he must make a total assessment of class quickly and is limited to the amount of help and coaching he can give to individual children.

2. Children working across the mats sideways. This plan increases the number of children who can work at one time on a mat. On

6' mats, two children can work at a time. On 8' mats, three can work crosswise. Two children can also perform on opposite ends of the mat when engaged in various kinds of stands, with the safety consideration of avoiding falls into each other.

3. Modified squad method. When working lengthwise on mat stunts, children should be divided into at least six groups and preferably eight. If the normal class organization is based on four squads, an alternate grouping of children needs to be established when using six groups. If eight mats are present, each squad can be assigned to two mats. No group should contain more than four to six children.

Formations for Teaching

Formations which have value in organizing a class for conducting stunts and tumbling instruction follow.

Squad Line Formation. Mats are placed in a line with the squads lined up behind the mats. Each child takes a turn and goes to the end of his line with the others moving up. An alternative method is for the child to perform and then return to his position. The children can be seated.

Squad File Formation. By positioning the mats so the children will approach the mats from the ends, a file formation can be arranged. The teacher is in front, and the children perform toward him. As soon as a child has completed his turn, he goes to the end of his line.

A weakness of this formation is that at times some children may be hidden from the teacher by other children, posing problems of control.

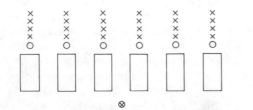

Semicircular Formation. The squad file formation can be changed readily to a semicircular arrangement. This focuses attention on the teacher, who is in the center. Groups are separated more than in the squad file formation.

(Note use for each mat the same as the previous illustration.)

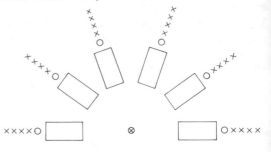

Hollow Rectangle. The squads perform on the sides of a hollow rectangle. The advantage of this formation is that the children can watch each other. It has the disadvantage that if the teacher is in the center, some portion of the class will be behind his back.

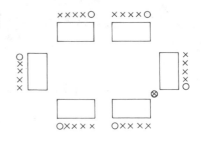

U-Shaped Formation. The mats are formed in the shape of a U. The formation has good visual control possibilities for the teacher, and the children are able to see what their classmates are doing.

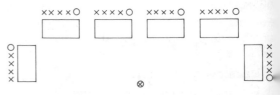

Double Row Formation. In this formation three groups form a row on one side and three on the other. The teacher is never far from any group. Children can view each other.

Demonstration Mat. If sufficient mats are available, one mat may be placed in an appropriate central position, so that little movement of the children is necessary to view the demonstration. The mat should be exclusively for demonstration.

Group Work

The teacher may sometimes wish to utilize groups or squads, each working on a different activity. Careful planning is necessary to ensure that the procedure is a learning experience and not just free play. Since it is not practical to stop the entire class for direction, the teacher must circulate from one group to another offering encouragement, comments, help, and suggestions as the activity unfolds. The problem becomes further complicated if the teacher feels his presence is needed at a station where critical supervision is indicated due to the complexity of the stunt or for safety purposes.

Group work has value where a particular type of equipment is in short supply. It has further value in a problem-solving approach with less emphasis on conforming to a particular pattern. If children can be stimulated to explore and solve problems, educational value is high. Group leadership is important. A work format must be specified at each station, which can then be supervised by the group leader.

The time factor is sometimes a problem. Generally, groups rotate on signal. However, some stations absorb the children's attention longer than others. Some groups may have already completed their chores and be ready to move on while others are not yet finished. The work format at each station must be sufficient to engage the children for the time period.

Return Activities

Return activities are discussed on page 165. They have a place in the stunts and tumbling program and work best in the lesson activities, where children perform lengthwise down the mat. Each child should turn in a designated direction (right or left) at the end of the mat and use that pathway for his return task. A popular return activity is to make use of a "magic number." Instructions for the return are given in this way: "Today, our magic number for return activity is five." For example, children may solve this problem by doing three jumps and two hops on the way back, or they may do four push-ups and one frog jump.

Return Activities. Children are doing a forward roll on the mats and doing an animal walk back to place as return activity.

Review

Review of the learning experiences from the previous lesson or lessons is important in maintaining good continuity. Points of difficulty from previous lessons should be brought out and solved. Variety beyond that which was previously secured can be developed. Quality of performance should be given consideration. "What was good?" and "How can we make our performance better?" should be key questions. It is possible that much of the new lesson could be devoted to the review and improvement of previously presented experiences. It is pointless to go on to a new lesson and leave activities in which reasonable results have not been secured. Caution should be used not to drive the activities "into the ground." One can return to them at a later date.

Description and Demonstration

The teacher can describe and demonstrate simultaneously. While the teacher may wish to demonstrate some stunts, the children love to help and can provide effective demonstration. In presenting a stunt, the following pattern should prove helpful:

1. **The Significance of the Name.** Most of the stunts have a characteristic name, and this should be a consideration in the teaching. If the stunt is of an imitative type, the animal or character represented should be described and discussed.

2. **The Stunt Description.** Stunts can be approached from the following analysis and taught in steps.

The Starting Position. Most stunts have a definite starting position. To perform properly, the child should understand what position he is to assume as the first step in doing a stunt.

The Execution. Based on the starting position, the key movements for good performance in the stunt should be stressed. Such other factors as how far to travel, how long to balance, and how many times a movement should be done should be clarified to the student.

The Finishing Position. In some stunts a definite finishing position or act is a part of the stunt. In balancing stunts, for example, it is important that the child return to standing or other position without losing balance or moving feet.

X**Safety Considerations.** Each child is entitled to know the inherent dangers of any stunt or tumbling activity. The safety rules to be followed and the duties of the spotters or helpers should be a part of the instruction.

3. **The Demonstration.** As the teacher describes the stunt, a student can demonstrate under the teacher's direction. If the stunt is one that is similar to or based upon a previously learned stunt, the description should be brief as possible. There may be little need for demonstration in such cases. For primary children the stunts are varied and can take many forms. The teacher should look for children to demonstrate unique and interesting variations of the stunt.

Care should be used in selecting children to demonstrate. Be sure the child is capable of the task. Generally, the task can be described and children can be asked to volunteer. Favoritism should be avoided, but it is difficult to escape using the more capable class members.

Three levels of demonstration are recognized: (1) provide minimal demonstration in the form of the starting position and let the children progress from this point; (2) go through the entire stunt slowly, step by step explaining what is involved; (3) execute the stunt normally as it would be done by the students. Since children need to analyze and solve problems, too much demonstration defeats this purpose.

Explanation and demonstration should cover only one or two points. Do not try to demonstrate too far in advance. Show the points necessary to get the activity underway. Add further details and refinements as the instruction progresses.

Demonstrations also have a place later in the sequence of instruction. Demonstration partway through the instruction can show successful execution of something that others do not understand or with which they are having difficulty. Demonstrations at the end of unit can show what has been achieved. Each squad or group can demonstrate its achievements in turn.

Providing Opportunity for Practice and Improvement

The character of each stunt will determine the amount of practice needed and the number of times it should be performed. The teacher should analyze a stunt to the point where he can verbalize the various small points necessary for good performance. Such directions as "Point your toes forward," "Tuck your chin down," and "Fingers spread wide" are examples of cues for successful performance.

A reasonable standard of performance should be a part of the teaching. The teacher must answer the child's question, "Did I do it?" Some stunts are on a pass-fail basis, while others can be evaluated in quality terms. A child needs standards that are both a challenge and attainable. The instruction must make clear to the child what is involved in the performance criterion of the stunt so that he knows whether or not he is within these bounds.

Quality in movement should be stressed throughout, but early emphasis should be on *doing the stunt.* Caution should be exercised in giving the child too many directions and details at the beginning which will only tend to confuse him. Directions added a few at a time stimulate the child to continued practice and improvement.

Many of the stunts require a position to be held for a short time. At first, have the child merely do the stunt. Later, have him hold for three and then five seconds. Extend this to a longer period, if indicated.

Practice and repetition are essential in establishing effective movement patterns. Often a teacher will leave an activity too soon to allow for needed progress. The following system is suggested where children take turns.

Whenever explanations and demonstrations are completed and the children begin practice, each child in a group should go through the stunt at least twice. When each child in the group has had two turns at an activity, the group remains in formation awaiting the next instructions. If this system is to function properly, groups need to be of relatively the same size and move at about the same speed. A teacher can ascertain in a glance if the children are ready for the next instructions. This avoids the necessity of whistle blowing to clear the mats.

How closely should children follow one another on the mat? A child should start his routine when the child ahead is just leaving the mat.

Securing Variety of Response

Variety of movement can be secured in two general ways. The first is to make use of the suggestions for variety incorporated in the stunt descriptions. The second is to use basic movement principles to establish problems, limitations, and suggestions which will stimulate the children to extended experiences.

The utilization of movement factors described in basic movement methodology (page 127) is of high importance. The activity potential of any one stunt can be extended by use of time factors, body factors, space factors, flow, and expressive factors.

Since most stunts have a starting position, an execution routine, and a finishing position, one or more of these could be varied to stimulate variety of movement and provide exploratory activity. For example, to secure variety in the forward roll, a child could begin with a rabbit jump, execute the forward roll with arms folded across the chest, and finish with a jump and half-turn.

Laterality is a factor that must be emphasized. The motor portion of the body is bilateral and should be so regarded. In practice, the children's attention will need to be called to using the other side or member of the body. Where appropriate, a directive is included in stunt descriptions. The concept of directionality should be established in children so that they approach performance of stunts with the principle of right and left usage without waiting to be so instructed. If a balancing stunt is done on one foot, then the next time it should be tried on the other. If a roll is made to the right, a comparable roll should be made to the left. A teacher may wish to develop the stunt thoroughly on one side before making the changes to the other side, but the change should be made.

SAFETY CONSIDERATIONS

Safety is a foremost consideration in the program of stunts and tumbling. The inherent hazards of an activity and how to avoid them must be included in the instructional procedures. Spotting techniques are particularly needed in the intermediate level program. Only a few kindergarten and primary stunts are hazardous enough to require spotting techniques for safety purposes.

Spotting

As the complexity of the activities is increased, more attention must be given to spotting. The purpose of the spotter is to assist the performer, help receive the weight, and prevent a hazardous fall. The first two can be anticipated and included in the instruction, as the stunt will determine what assistance can be given and where the spotter should aid in receiving the weight. Saving the performer from a fall is more difficult, as it cannot be anticipated.

In assisting, the spotter should take a firm hold on the performer and position himself in relation to the direction of the stunt, as he may need to move with the performer as he executes the stunt. The spotter must be careful to assist, but not to provide too much help which becomes a hindrance. The spotters should avoid "wrestling" the performer into position.

In stunts where the body is inverted, spotting is an important consideration. In the case of such stunts as the headstand and the handstand, it is important to control the child's movement so he returns to the floor in the same direction from which he got into position for the stunt.

Receiving the weight of a performer is needed only infrequently in the elementary school program. This is used in activities where the child goes through the air in some kind of a jumping or vaulting stunt, some assistance being given to help cushion his return to the floor. In the case of the cautious child, this type of help will enable him to do the stunt and get the "feel" of it. Later, as he becomes more sure of himself, he will dispense with the help.

Each stunt should be analyzed from a safety aspect and a trained spotter should be assigned routinely. It is important that spotters know both the stunt and the spotting techniques. Sufficient time must be allotted for teaching correct spotting techniques.

Children should ask others to spot when learning a new stunt. They should be willing, in turn, to assist in spotting as needed.

Other Safety Considerations

1. Emphasis should be placed on how to fall. Children should be taught to roll out of a stunt when balance is lost. In the headstand and handstand, children should try to return to the floor in the direction from which they started. The return is facilitated by bending both at the waist and at the knees.

2. Pockets should be emptied and lockets, glasses, watches, and other articles of this nature removed. A special depository for these articles should be provided, or, better yet, they should be left in the classroom.

3. No practice periods should be conducted without the presence of a teacher or proper supervisor.

4. Fatigue and overstrain in young children should be guarded against.

5. Children should be encouraged but not forced to try stunts. Care should be taken not to use peer pressure to stimulate participation.

6. Control is a basic element of the stunts and tumbling program. Children should learn to use controlled movements. Speed is secondary, and in some cases even undesirable.

ADDITIONAL CONSIDERATIONS IN METHODOLOGY
Instructional Emphasis

1. While some stunts do not require mats, it is well to include stunts requiring mats in every lesson. Children like to perform on mats, and rolling stunts using mats are vital.

2. In selecting students for demonstration, be sure the student understands and can perform reasonably correctly.

3. If a class embarks on a program of stunts and tumbling without previous experience, go back a grade or two in suggested activities and work up to the present grade level slowly.

4. Many couple stunts work well only if partners are of about the same size. However, if the stunt is of the partner-support type, then the support child should be strong enough to hold the weight of the other. This usually means a larger and stronger child on the bottom providing the support.

5. When a characteristic name is attached to a stunt, this designation should be exploited in the instruction. Time taken out briefly to

stress the characteristics and movements associated with the name will bear dividends in more effective and imaginative movements.

6. The instruction should include, in addition to safety considerations, the points to be stressed which are critical to performance. Be sure the performer understands the stress points before proceeding.

7. No two children will perform or do stunts alike. Respect individual differences and allow for different levels of success.

8. While some emphasis on form and control should be established in the lower grades, children on the intermediate level should be made more conscious of the need to refine and perfect performance. This, however, should be within the capacity of the children.

9. It is important to relate new activities to those learned previously. A good practice is to review the lead-up stunt for an activity.

10. Horseplay and ridicule have no place in a program of stunts and tumbling. See that the children have fun, but also that they respect the efforts of their classmates.

11. Proper gym shoes are a help in the program. However, children can tumble in bare feet if a change of shoes is not available.

12. When a stunt calls for a position to be held for a number of counts, use a standard counting system like "one thousand and one, one thousand and two," or "monkey one, monkey two," etc.

13. Where children are asked to reach out or place objects a distance along the floor, distances can be specified by having the children count boards on the floor away from a line or base position. Generally, start should be made at a modest distance so all can achieve success, with appropriate increases to follow. In *Balance Touch* (page 200), for example, the teacher can specify that the beanbag should be placed a certain number of board widths away from a line. Distances can then be varied by increasing the number of boards between the line and the object.

14. At times, the teacher can have children work in pairs with one child performing and the second providing a critique.

15. In using small hand apparatus (wands, hoops, etc.) with stunts, it is best to have one item for each child. If this is not possible, a minimum of two pieces is needed for each group so that the child next in line does not have to wait for the return of the needed object. One person, generally the leader of the group, should be designated to secure and return hand apparatus.

16. In planning a series of stunts, the position at the completion of one stunt determines what the next stunt can be. The child must anticipate so he can finish one stunt with the appropriate position that will allow him to go naturally and smoothly into the next stunt.

17. There should be little shifting of mats during the course of instruction. In arranging a sequence of stunts for a day's lesson, it is well to put the mat stunts together.

18. Occasional soft background music contributes to a pleasant atmosphere, but it should be low enough in volume so as not to interfere with the instruction. Long play records or tapes are excellent, as little attention is needed for the music sources.

19. The beat of a drum or tom-tom can be utilized to direct controlled movements. Children change position in small increments as guided by a beat. In *Lowering the Boom* (page 202), for example, children can lower themselves a little each time the drum sounds.

Start-and-Expand Technique

The Start-and-Expand technique should be applied to stunts where feasible. Take the example of teaching a simple *Heel Click* (page 201). The instructor can begin by saying, "Let's see all of you jump high into the air and click your heels together before you come down." (The Start) "Now, to do the stunt properly, you should jump into the air, click your heels, and land with your feet apart with a nice bent-knee action to absorb the shock." (Expansion) Further expansion can be adding quarter or half turns before landing, clapping hands overhead while clicking heels, and clicking heels twice before landing.

The start is made so simple that all children can experience some measure of success.. The instruction then expands to other elements of the stunt, adding variations and movement factors, and refining as indicated.

Social Factors

1. For mixed groups proper attire is essential to eliminate a modesty problem. On days when stunts are scheduled girls can change

to pedalpushers, slacks, or play suits. The best solution, however, is to have all children change to a gymnasium type uniform.

2. Children should have fun *with* their friends in these types of activities, but they should not be allowed to laugh *at* an inept child.

3. Social goals that should be stressed for the children are cooperating with a partner, a small group, the entire class, and the teacher. Showing consideration in taking turns is important.

4. Children should be taught to have respect for equipment and to care for it. Mats should be lifted clear of the ground and not dragged when being moved.

Basic Mechanical Principles

Certain simple mechanical and kinesiological principles should be established as the foundation of an effective program. If children can build upon these basic principles, instruction is facilitated.

1. Momentum needs to be developed and applied, particularly for rolls. Tucking, starting from a higher point, preliminary raising of the arms, are examples of devices to increase momentum.

2. The center of weight must be positioned over the center of support in balance stunts, particularly the inverted stands.

3. In certain stunts, like the neckspring and the headspring, the hips should be projected upward and forward to raise the center of gravity for better execution.

4. In stunts where the body is wholly or partially supported by the hands, proper positioning of the hands is essential for better performance. Fingers should be spread and pointed forward. The pads of the fingers apply pressure for a good basis of support. This hand position should generally be employed unless there is a specific reason to depart from it.

Stunt Check-Off Systems

Some teachers find value in establishing a check-off system to keep track of the students' progress. Two systems are suggested. The first simply checks those stunts the student has completed. The second differentiates between a stunt done well and one that meets minimum requirements. In the latter system, the teacher can make a diagonal line (/) for a stunt meeting minimum requirements and cross that line with another, making an "X," for a stunt done well. The lists of the stunts with the children's names by squads can be posted on the bulletin board or kept on squad cards for convenient use in the stunt lesson.

A glance at the cards will enable the teacher to know what stunts need to be reviewed and practiced. An analysis of this type makes a better educational experience for the children. However, care must be taken that the "check-off" system does not take too much teaching-learning time.

Some cautions need to be observed in using these systems. The lists should not result in peer pressure on students. Also, the student's sense of achievement may be distorted in that he becomes interested only in getting stunts marked on the list.

Wave or Ripple Effect

An interesting movement and sequence pattern can be injected into the instruction with the use of wave or ripple effects. These should be used only after reasonable mastery of the movements.

A squad makes a suitable size group to carry out the wave effect. The children in the group form a line alongside a series of mats laid lengthwise. A formation would look like this.

The wave effect can go in either direction, but generally moves from right to left (for performers). The child on the right begins a stunt, followed in turn by each successive child in the line. The stunt movement appears to move along the line like a wave. The timing must be constant for the time interval, when each child in succession follows the child to his right.

The wave effect is an excellent culmination of a unit or series of lessons. It also has good value in demonstrations for PTAs and other groups.

Types of activities which lend themselves well to this are:

1. Push-ups, Sit-ups, Curl-ups.
2. Forward Roll, Backward Curl, Backward Roll.
3. Drops or Falls — Knee Drop, Forward Drop, Dead Man Fall.
4. Tip-Up (Frog Handstand), Headstand.
5. Full Arch.

The Wave Effect Employing the Dead Man's Fall

KINDERGARTEN PROGRAM

The kindergarten program makes good use of simple stunts which can be subject to many interpretations. The scope of the movements should include bilateral, unilateral, and cross-lateral experiences. Laterality should also be stressed with attention to corresponding parts of the body. Balance is an important quality to be developed with stunt activities. Establishing good directional concepts is an important inclusion in the instruction. The child should be able to distinguish readily and easily such concepts as right and left, near and far, up and down, forward and backward, and wide and narrow.

Most of the stunts listed under the first grade program are quite appropriate for kindergarten children and should be utilized. In particular, the various kinds of walks and imitative movements provide important movement challenges for kindergarten children. Little emphasis should be placed on the so-called standard tumbling events.

It is also important that the movement factors from basic movement methodology (page 127), be given thorough development. The teacher should be able to select a basic movement or stunt and secure good depth and variety of response by judicious use of time, space, force, body, and expressive elements of movement. In addition, opportunity for creative exploratory responses should be included.

ACTIVITIES FOR THE KINDERGARTEN

Simple Balance Stunts
Head Touch
Side Roll
Forward Roll
Back Roller
Directional Walk
Line Walking
Alligator
Fluttering Leaf
Elevator
Cross-Legged Stand
Walking in Place
Kangaroo
See-saw (Partner Stunt)

SIMPLE BALANCE STUNTS

The child should begin to learn the concept of balance stunts, i.e., that the position should be held for a specified length of time without undue movement or loss of balance *and* a recovery must be made to the original position. Hold for 3 and 5 seconds. Also perform with the eyes closed.

One Leg Balance

Begin with lifting one leg from the floor. Later, bring the knee up. Arms should be free at first; then proceed to specified positions such as folded across the chest, on hips, on the head, or behind the back.

Double Knee Balance

Kneel on both knees, with the feet pointed to the rear. Lift the feet from the ground and balance on the knees. Vary the position of the arms.

Allow the children to experiment with different positions for balance.

HEAD TOUCH

Kneel on a mat with both knees, with the feet pointed backwards. Arms are outstretched backwards for balance. Lean forward slowly and touch the forehead to the mat. Recover to position. Vary the arm position.

SIDE ROLL

Start on hands and knees with the side selected for the roll toward the direction of the roll. By dropping the shoulder and tucking both the elbow and knee under, roll over completely on the shoulders and hips, coming again to the hands and knees position. Momentum is needed to return to the original position. Children should practice rolling back and forth from one hand-and-knee position to another.

FORWARD ROLL

Introduce the forward roll here as described on page 200 of first grade stunts.

BACK ROLLER

Practice in backward rolling should begin in kindergarten. Start in a crouched position on toes, knees together, with hands resting lightly on the floor. Roll backward and attempt to keep up a rhythmic backward-forward rolling motion.

Back Roller

Directional Walk

DIRECTIONAL WALK

Stand with side toward the desired direction, arms at sides. Take a sidestep in the desired direction (right or left), simultaneously lifting the arm and pointing in the direction of movement. At the same time, turn head in the direction of movement and sound off the direction. Complete the sidestep by closing with the other foot, dropping the arm to the side, and turning the head back to normal position. The movements should be definite and forceful, the directional command should be called out crisply. After a number of sidesteps in one direction, reverse.

The walk serves to reinforce the concept of right and left.

LINE WALKING

Use a line on the floor, a chalked line, or a board. Children walk forward and backward on the line, as follows:

1. Regular steps.
2. Follow steps. The front foot moves forward and the back foot moves up. One foot always leads.
3. Heel and toe. Take regular steps, but on each step bring the heel against the toe.
4. Hopping on the line. Change to the other foot.

ALLIGATOR

Lie face down on the floor with the elbows bent. Move along the floor alligator fashion keeping the hands close to the body and the feet pointed out.

First, stress unilateral movements, i.e., right arm and leg moving together. Then, change to

Alligator

cross-lateral movements, with the right arm moving with the left leg and vice versa.

FLUTTERING LEAF

Keeping the feet in place and the body relaxed, flutter to the ground slowly just as a falling leaf would do in the fall. The arms can swing back and forth loosely to accentuate the fluttering movements.

ELEVATOR

With the arms out level to the sides, pretend to be an elevator going down. Lower the body a little at a time, by bending the knees, keeping the upper body erect and eyes forward. Go into a deep-knee bend. Return to position. Add a body twist to the downward movement.

CROSS-LEGGED STAND

Sit with the legs crossed and the body partially bent forward. Six commands are now given:

1. "Touch the right foot with the right hand."
2. "Touch the left foot with the right hand."
3. "Touch the right foot with the left hand."
4. "Touch the left foot with the left hand."
5. "Touch both feet with the hands."
6. "Touch the feet with crossed hands."

The commands should be given in varied sequences. The child must interpret that his right foot is on the left side and vice versa.

If this seems too difficult, have the child start with the feet in normal position (uncrossed).

Variation: The stunt can be done as partner activity. One child gives the commands and the other responds as directed.

WALKING IN PLACE

Pretend to walk vigorously by using the same movements as in walking, but not making any progress. This is done by shifting the feet back and forth. Exaggerated arm movement should be made. Children can gain or lose a little ground. Two children can "walk" alongside each other with the first one going ahead and then the other.

KANGAROO

The arms are carried close to the chest with the palms facing forward. A beanbag is placed between the knees. Move in different directions employing small jumps without losing the beanbag.

SEESAW (PARTNER STUNT)

Two children face each other and join hands. One child stoops down. The seesaw moves up and down now, with one child stooping while the other rises. The children can recite the words to this version of "Seesaw, Margery Daw" as they move:

Seesaw, Margery Daw,
Maw and Paw, like a saw,
Seesaw, Margery Daw

Variation: Have the rising child jump into the air at the end of the rise.

Additional Activities

The teacher should make good use of first grade activities. The most appropriate first grade activities are the various locomotor and balance stunts.

FIRST GRADE PROGRAM

The first grade program consists primarily of simple, imitative walks and movements plus selected balance stunts and rolls. Balance stunts use the erect position. The *Forward Roll* is practiced, but its refinement is left to later grades. The *Back Roller* and backward roll from a hand-clasped position show the children some of the possibilities in these kinds of movements.

The teacher should be concerned with the creative aspects of the activities as well as performance standards. Children in this grade level tend to do stunts in different ways because of different interpretations.

The establishment of good directional concepts and the basic understanding of common movement terminology should have a prominent place in the instruction. The "why" of activity should be answered for the children.

ACTIVITIES FOR THE FIRST GRADE

Puppy Dog Run
Bear Walk
Rabbit Jump
Jump Turns
Elephant Walk
Head Balance

Tightrope Walk
Bouncing Ball
Gorilla Walk
One-Legged Balance Stands
Lame Dog Walk
Cricket Walk
Rising Sun
Forward Roll
Balance Touch
Heel Click
Seal Crawl
Crab Walk
Back Roller
Rolling Log
Lowering the Boom
Turn Over
Thread the Needle
Backward Roll — Hand Clasped Position
Wring the Dishrag

PUPPY DOG RUN

Place hands on the floor, bending the arms and legs slightly. Walk and run like a happy puppy. The teacher should see that the youngsters look ahead. By keeping the head up in good position, the neck muscles are strengthened.

Puppy Dog Run

Variations:

1. Children may also use the same position to imitate a cat. Walk softly, stretch at times like a cat. Be smooth and deliberate.

2. **Monkey Run.** Turn the hands so the fingers point in (toward each other).

3. Go sidewards, backwards, etc. Turn around in place.

BEAR WALK

Bend forward and touch the ground with both hands. Travel forward slowly by moving the hand and foot on the *same side together,* i.e., the right hand and foot are moved together, and then the left hand and foot. Make deliberate movements. This movement is classified as unilateral, as the arm and leg on the same side move together.

Variation: Lift the free foot and arm high while the support is on the other side.

RABBIT JUMP

Crouch to the floor with the knees apart. The arms are between the knees with the hands placed on the floor ahead of the feet. Move forward by reaching out first with both hands and then bringing both feet up to the hands. Eyes should look ahead.

Emphasize to the children that this is called a jump rather than a hop because both feet move at once. Note that the jump is a bilateral movement.

Variations: Try with the knees kept together and the arms on the outside. Try alternating the knees together and apart on successive jumps. Go over a low hurdle or through a hoop.

Experiment with taking considerable weight on the hands before the feet move forward. This can be aided by raising the seat higher in the air when the hands move forward.

JUMP TURNS

Jump turns reinforce directional concepts. Use quarter and half turns, right and left. Arms should be kept along the sides of the body. Stress landing lightly without a second movement.

Number concepts can be utilized. The teacher calls out the number as a preparatory command and then says, "Move." Number signals are: one — left quarter turn, two — right quarter turn, three — left half turn, and four — right half turn. Give the children a moment after the number is called before moving.

Variation: Have the arms outstretched to the sides.

ELEPHANT WALK

"The elephant's walk is steady and slow.
His trunk like a pendulum swings to
and fro."

Bend well forward, clasping the hands together to form a trunk. The end of the trunk should swing close to the ground. Walk in a slow, deliberate, dignified manner, keeping the legs straight and swinging the trunk from side to side. Stop and throw water over the back with the trunk .

"But when there are children with
peanuts around
He swings it up and he swings it down."

Follow with appropriate movements.

Elephant Walk

Variation: Arrange children in pairs, one as the mahout (elephant keeper) and the other as the elephant. The mahout walks to the side and a little to the front of the elephant, with one hand touching the elephant's shoulder. The mahout leads the elephant around during the first two lines of the poem, then during the last two lines he releases his touch, walks to a spot in front of the elephant, and "tosses" him a peanut when the trunk is swept up. He returns to the elephant's side and the action is repeated.

HEAD BALANCE

Place a beanbag, block, or book on the child's head. Have him walk, stoop, turn around, sit down, get up, etc.

The object should be balanced so that the upper body is in good posture. Use hands out to the side for balance. Later, vary the position of the arms — folded across the chest, placed behind the back, or down at the sides.

Structure problems by having the children link together a series of movements.

Head Balance

TIGHTROPE WALK ✓

In the Tightrope Walk, children should give good play to the imagination. Set the stage by discussing what a circus performer on the wire might do. Have the children select a line, board, or chalked line on the floor for the "wire." They can pretend to be on the high wire, doing various tasks with exaggerated loss and control of balance. Add such tasks as jumping rope, juggling balls, or riding a bicycle on the wire. Some may "hold" a parasol or a balancing pole while performing.

BOUNCING BALL

Toss a *lively* utility ball into the air and let the children watch how it bounces, lower and lower, until it finally comes to rest on the floor. From a bent-knee position, with the upper body erect, each child imitates a ball by beginning with a high "bounce" and gradually lowering the height of the jump to simulate a ball coming to rest.

Bouncing Ball

Variations: Have the children do this as a partner stunt with one partner serving as the bouncer and the other as the ball. Reverse positions. Try having one partner dribble the "ball" in various positions.

Toss the ball into the air and have the children move with the ball as it bounces lower and lower.

GORILLA WALK ✓

Bend knees and carry the trunk forward. Arms hang at the side. As the child walks forward, he should touch his fingers to the ground.

Gorilla Walk

Variation: Let the children stop and beat on their chests like a gorilla. Also, bounce up and down on all fours with hands and feet touching the floor simultaneously.

ONE-LEGGED BALANCE STANDS

Each balance stunt should be done with different arm positions. Begin first with the arms out to the side and then have them folded across the chest. Have the children devise other arm positions.

Each stunt can be held first for 3 seconds and then for 5 seconds. Later, eyes should be closed during the count. The child should recover to original position without loss of balance or excessive movement. Stunts should be repeated using the other leg.

Kimbo Stand. With the left foot kept flat on the ground, cross the right leg over the left to a position where the foot is pointed partially down and the toe is touching the ground. Hold this position for a specified count and return to standing position.

Knee Lift Balance. From a standing position, lift one knee up so the thigh is parallel to the ground with toe pointed down. Hold. Return to starting position.

Knee Lift Balance

Stork Stand. From a standing position, shift all the weight to one foot. The other foot is placed so that the sole of the foot is against the calf of the standing leg. Hold. Recover to standing position.

LAME DOG WALK

Walk on both hands and one foot. The other foot is held in the air as if injured. Walk a distance and change feet. Eyes should be forward. Also move backwards, in other combinations. See if the children can move with an "injured" front leg.

CRICKET WALK ✓

Squat. Spread the knees. Put the arms between the knees and grasp the outside of the ankles with the hands. In this position, walk forward or backward. Chirp like a cricket. Turn around right and left.

See what happens if both feet are moved at once!

RISING SUN

Lie on back. Using only the arms for balance, rise to a standing position.

Variation: Have the children fold arms over the chest. Experiment with different positions of the feet. Feet can be crossed, spread wide, both to one side, etc.

FORWARD ROLL

Stand facing forward with the feet apart. Squat and place the hands on the mat, shoulder width apart with the elbows against the inside of the thighs. Tuck the chin to the chest and make a rounded back. A push-off with the hands and feet provides the force for the roll. The child should carry the weight on his hands with the elbows bearing the weight of the

Forward Roll Position. Note the position of the elbows on the insides of the thighs.

thighs. By keeping the elbows against the thighs and assuming weight there, the force of the roll is easily transferred to the rounded back. The child should try to roll forward to his feet. Later, try with the knees together and no weight on the elbows.

Kneeling alongside the child, the instructor can help by placing one hand on the back of the child's head and the other under the thigh for a push, finishing the assist with an upward lift on the back of the neck.

Spotting the Forward Roll. One hand is on the back of the head and one is under the thigh.

BALANCE TOUCH

Balance Touch

An object (eraser, block, or beanbag) is placed a yard away from a line. Balancing on one foot, the child reaches out with the other foot, touches the object, and recovers to the starting position. He does not place weight on the object but merely touches it. Reach sidewards, backwards.

Variation: Try at various distances. On a gymnasium floor, count the number of boards to establish the distance for the touch.

HEEL CLICK

Stand with feet slightly apart. Jump up and click heels, coming down with feet apart. Try with a quarter-turn right and left.

Variations:

1. Have the child clap hands overhead as he clicks his heels.

2. Another variation is to have the child join hands with one or more children. A signal is needed. The children can count, "One, Two, THREE," jumping on the third count.

3. Some may be able to click the heels twice before landing. Landing should be with the feet apart.

4. Begin with a cross step to the side, and then click heels. Try both right and left.

SEAL CRAWL

The child is in a front-leaning (push-up) position, the weight supported on straightened arms and toes. Keeping the body straight, he walks forward using his hands for propelling force and dragging his feet.

Watch to see the body is straight and the head is up.

Seal Crawl

Variation: Let the child crawl forward a short distance and then roll over on his back clapping his hands like a seal, with appropriate seal grunts.

CRAB WALK

Squat down and reach back putting both hands on the floor without sitting down. With head, neck, and body level and in a straight line, walk forward, backward, and sideward.

Children have a tendency to lower the hips. See that the body is kept in a straight line.

Crab Walk

Variations:

1. As each step is taken with a hand, the other hand can slap the chest or seat.

2. Move the hand and foot on the same side simultaneously (unilateral movement).

3. Try balancing on one leg and opposite hand. Hold for 5 seconds.

BACK ROLLER

This stunt is a lead-up to the regular *Backward Roll.* Begin in a crouched position, knees together, and hands resting lightly on the floor. Roll backwards, securing momentum by bringing the knees to the chest and clasping them with the arms. Roll back and forth rhyth-

mically. On the backward movement, the roll should go well back on the neck and head. Try to roll forward to original position. Where children have difficulty in rolling back to original position, have them cross the legs and roll to a crossed-leg standing position.

ROLLING LOG

Lie on back with arms stretched overhead. Roll sideways the length of the mat. The next time roll with the hands pointed toward the other side of the mat. To roll in a straight line, keep the feet slightly apart.

Rolling Log

Variation: Alternately curl and stretch while rolling.

LOWERING THE BOOM

Start in push-up position (front leaning rest position). Lower the body slowly to the floor. The movement should be controlled so that the body remains rigid.

Variations:

1. Have the children pause halfway down.

2. Have them come down in stages inch by inch. Be sure they understand the concept of an inch as a measure of distance.

3. Call this a "flat tire." Children let themselves down slowly to the accompaniment of noise simulating air escaping from a punctured tire. See how they react to a "blowout," initiated by an appropriate noise.

TURN OVER

From a front leaning rest position (as in *Lowering the Boom*), turn over so that the back is to the floor. The body should not touch the floor. Continue the turn until the original position is assumed. Reverse the direction. Turn back and forth several times.

The body should be kept straight and rigid throughout the turn.

THREAD THE NEEDLE ✓

Thread the Needle

Touch the fingertips together in front of the body. Step through with one foot at a time without the tips losing contact. Step back to original position. Now lock the fingers in front of the body and repeat the stunt. Finally, see if children can step through the clasped hands without touching the hands.

BACKWARD ROLL — HAND CLASPED POSITION

Teachers can have good success teaching the backward roll by beginning with this approach. The child clasps his fingers behind the neck, with the elbows held out to the

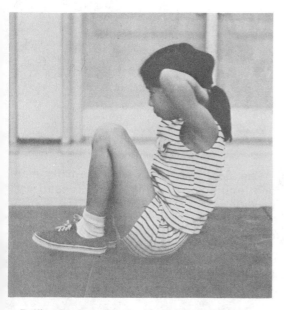

Rolling Backward in the Hand Clasped Position

sides. From a crouched position, he sits down rapidly, bringing his knees to his chest for a tuck to secure momentum. He rolls completely over backwards taking much of the weight on his elbows. In this method, the neck is protected and the pressure is taken by the elbows.

Remind the children to keep their elbows back and out to the sides to gain maximum support and assure minimal neck strain.

WRING THE DISHRAG (COUPLE STUNT)

Two children face each other and join hands. Raise one pair of arms (right for one and left for the other) and turn under that pair of arms, continuing a full turn until back to original position. Care must be taken to avoid bumping heads.

Wring the Dishrag

Variation: Try the stunt at a lower level using a crouched position.

SECOND GRADE PROGRAM

Begin with a review of the kindergarten and first grade stunts. Continued practice should be held in the *Forward Roll*. The *Backward Curl* and the regular *Backward Roll* are significant inclusions in this grade level. Additional balance stunts expand the practice opportunities for this quality.

Children of this age group are more amenable to coaching as compared to previous levels and some attention to performance factors can be stressed. However, their span of interest is short, and performance factors should be introduced as opportunities arise.

ACTIVITIES FOR THE SECOND GRADE

Forward Roll Review and Practice
Frog Jump
Seal Crawl Variations
Heel Slap
Pogo Stick
Wicket Walk
Top
Measuring Worm
Leg Balances
Turk Stand
Climb Up
Three Point Tip-Up
Push-Up
Crazy Walk
Backward Curl
Backward Roll — Regular
Seat Circle
Hand and Knee Balance
Single Knee Balance

FORWARD ROLL REVIEW AND PRACTICE

Review the *Forward Roll* (first grade). Spot and assist as necessary. Work on getting the children to come out of the roll to their feet. Grasping knees at the end of the roll is of help.

Variations:

1. Roll to the feet with the ankles crossed.
2. Some children can try to roll with the knees together.

FROG JUMP

From a squatting position, with the hands placed on the floor slightly in front of the feet, jump forward a short distance, lighting on the hands and feet simultaneously. Note the difference between this stunt and the *Rabbit Jump* (first grade).

Emphasis eventually should be on both height and distance. The hands and arms should absorb part of the landing impact.

SEAL CRAWL VARIATIONS

Review the *Seal Crawl* (first grade). Include the following variations:

1. Crawl with the fingers pointed in different directions — out and in.
2. **Reverse Seal Crawl.** Turn over and attempt the crawl dragging the heels.
3. **Elbow Crawl.** Assume the original position but with the weight on the elbows. Crawl forward on the elbows.

Elbow Crawl

The *Seal Crawl* can also be made more challenging by using the crossed-arm position.

HEEL SLAP

From an erect position with hands at the sides, jump into the air and slap both heels with the hands.

Variations: Use a one, two, three rhythm with small preliminary jumps on *one* and *two*. Make quarter or half turns in the air. During a jump, slap the heels twice before landing.

POGO STICK

Pretend to be a pogo stick by keeping a stiff body and jumping on the toes. Hold the hands in front as if grasping the stick. Progress in various directions.

Stress upward propelling action by the ankles and toes with the body kept stiff, particularly at the knee joint.

Pogo Stick

Wicket Walk

WICKET WALK

Children bend over and touch the floor with their weight *evenly* distributed on hands and feet. By keeping the knees straight, a wicket can be formed. Walk the wicket forward, backward, and sideward. Keep arms and legs as near vertical as possible.

Be sure the knees are kept reasonably straight, as the stunt loses much of its flexibility values if the knees are bent too much.

The stunt gets its name because the child's position resembles a wicket in a croquet game.

A common error in the execution of this stunt is to keep the hands positioned too far forward of the feet.

TOP

From a standing position with arms at the sides, have children try jumping, turning to face the opposite direction, turning three-quarters of the way around, and making a full turn facing the original direction. Number concepts can be stressed in having the children do half, three-quarter, and full turns.

Successful execution of the stunt should call for the child to land in good balance with hands near the sides. No movement of the feet should occur after landing.

Children should turn right and left.

Variation: Fold arms across chest.

MEASURING WORM

From a front-leaning rest position, keeping the knees stiff, bring up the feet as close as possible to the hands by inching forward with the feet. Regain position by inching forward with the hands. Emphasize keeping the knees straight, with necessary bending occurring at the hips.

LEG BALANCES

Backward. With the knee straight, extend one leg forward with the toe pointed so that it is level to the floor. Balance on the other leg for 5 seconds. Use arms out to the side for balance. Lean back as far as possible. The bend should be far enough back so the eyes are looking at the ceiling.

Forward. Extend the leg backward until it is parallel to the floor. Keeping eyes forward and arms out to the side bend forward, balancing on the other leg. Hold for 5 seconds without moving.

Forward Leg Balance

Side. Stand on the left foot with enough side bend to the left so the right (top) side of the body is parallel to the floor. Put the right arm alongside the head in a line with the rest of the body. Reverse, using the right leg for support. (Support may be needed momentarily to get into position.)

TURK STAND

Stand with feet apart and arms folded in front. Pivot on the balls of *both* feet and face the opposite direction. The legs are now crossed. Sit down in this position. Reverse the process. Get up without using the hands for aid, and uncross the legs with a pivot to face original direction.

Very little change should occur in the position of the feet.

CLIMB UP

Get down on a mat on hands and knees, with the hands placed about shoulder width apart and the fingers spread and pointed forward. Place the head forward of the hands so the head and the hands form a triangle on the mat. Walk the body weight forward so most of it rests on the hands and head. Climb the knees to the top of the elbows. This stunt is lead-up to the *Headstand* (third grade).

Variation: Raise the knees off the elbows.

THREE POINT TIP-UP

The Three Point Tip-Up ends up in the same general position as the *Climb-Up,* but with the elbows on the inside of the thighs. Squat down on the mat, placing the hands flat, fingers pointing forward, with the elbows inside and pressed against the inner part of the lower thighs. Lean forward, slowly transferring the weight of the body to the bent elbows and hands until the forehead touches the mat. Return to starting position.

This stunt also provides a background for the headstand and for the handstand given at later grades.

Some children may have better success by turning the fingers in slightly, causing the elbows to point out more, offering better support to the thigh contact.

PUSH-UP

From a front leaning rest position, lower the body and push-up back to original position. Be sure that the only movement is in the arms with the body kept rigid and straight.

Variation: Stop halfway down and halfway up. Go up and down by inches.

Note: Since the *Push-Up* is used in many exercises and testing programs, it is important that the children learn proper execution early.

CRAZY WALK

The child makes progress forward in an erect position by bringing one foot behind *and* around the other to gain a little ground each time. Set up a specified distance and see which children can cover this with the least number of steps.

Crazy Walk

Variation: Reverse the movements and go backwards. This means bringing the foot in front and around to gain distance in back.

BACKWARD CURL

This stunt has three stages.

1. Begin in a sitting position with the knees drawn up to the chest and the chin tucked down. The arms are placed out to the sides as the shoulders make contact with the mat. Roll backwards until the weight is on the shoulders and the feet and legs come back over the head so that the toes touch the mat. Roll back to starting position.

2. Same action except the hands are placed alongside the head on the mat as the child rolls back. The fingers are pointed in the direction of the roll with the palms down on the mat. A good direction to the children is "Point your thumbs toward your ears and keep your elbows reasonably close to the body."

3. The third stage is similar to #2 except that the child starts in a crouched position on his feet. He is in a deep-knee bend position with his back toward the direction of the roll. He secures momentum by sitting down quickly, bringing his knees to his chest.

The teacher has to recognize that this, like the *Back Roller,* is a lead-up to the backward roll. The hand pressure is an important item to be stressed. Teach the children to push hard against the floor to take the pressure from the back of the neck.

Variations:

1. Touch the knees behind the head instead of the toes.

2. Another interesting challenge can be made using a beanbag. Have the child keep a beanbag between his feet and deposit it behind his head, returning to position. Next, curl back and pick up the beanbag, returning it to original position.

3. A more difficult backward curl, which some children may be able to do, starts with the child sitting with legs crossed and the hands grasping the feet. Roll backwards, touching the floor overhead with the feet. Return to position.

BACKWARD ROLL—REGULAR

Start with the back to the direction of the roll in the same squat position as in the forward roll. Push off with the hands quickly, sit down, and start rolling over on the back.

The knees should be brought to the chest.

so the body is tucked and momentum is increased. Quickly bring the hands up over the shoulders, palms up, fingers pointed backward. Continue rolling backward with the knees close to the chest. The hands will now touch the mat at about the same time as the head. It is vitally important at this point to push hard with the hands. Continue to roll over the top of the head and push off the mat until ready to stand.

Proper hand position can be emphasized by telling the children to point their thumbs toward their ears, and to spread their fingers for better push-off control.

Spotting

Care must be taken never to push a child from the hip, forcing him to roll over. This puts undue pressure on the back of the neck.

The proper method of aiding the child who has difficulty with the stunt is as follows. The spotter stands in a straddle position with his near foot alongside at about the spot where the performer's hands and head will make contact with the mat. His other foot is one stride in the direction of the roll. The critical point is for the spotter to lift the hips just as the head and hands of the performer make contact with the mat. This is accomplished by taking the back hand and reaching across to the far hip of the performer, getting under the near hip with the near hand. The lift is applied on the front of the hips just below the beltline. The object is to relieve the pressure on the neck.

SEAT CIRCLE

Sit on the floor, knees bent and hands braced behind. Lift the feet off the floor and push with the hands so the body spins in a circle on the seat as a pivot. Spin right and left.

Seat Circle

HAND AND KNEE BALANCE

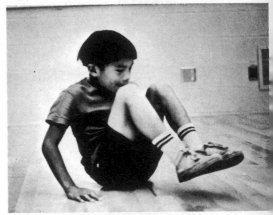

Spotting the Backward Roll. The lift is at the hips of the roller. Lift, but do not force the child over.

Hand and Knee Balance

Get down on all fours, with support on the hands and knees, supporting also on the feet with the toes pointed backward. Lift one hand and the opposite leg from the floor and balance on the other hand and knee. Keep the foot from touching during the hold. Reverse hand and knee positions.

SINGLE KNEE BALANCE

Single Knee Balance

Similar to the previous stunt, except that the balance is made on one knee (and leg), with the arms outstretched to sides. Reverse positions.

THIRD GRADE PROGRAM

In the third grade, in comparison to the K-2 program, more emphasis on form and quality of performance is centered in stunt execution. More couple and group stunts make their appearance in the third grade program.

Among individual stunts, the *Headstand* is an important addition to the tumbling area. Stunts such as the *Frog Handstand* and the *Mule Kick* give the children experience in taking the weight totally on the hands.

ACTIVITIES FOR THE THIRD GRADE

Forward Roll
Forward Roll Variations
Backward Roll Practice
Frog Handstand (Tip-Up)
Heel Stand
Russian Dance
Squat Thrust
Walrus Walk
The Reach Under
Stiff Man Bend
Coffee Grinder
Mule Kick
One Leg Balance Reverse
Curl-up
Tummy Balance
Hip Walk
Scooter
Double Lame Dog
Long Bridge
The Turtle
Headstand
Partner Hopping (Couple Stunt)
Twister (Couple Stunt)
Partner Pull-up (Couple Stunt)
Double Top (Couple Stunt)
Chinese Get-up (Couple or Group Stunt)

FORWARD ROLL

Hands are on the mat, shoulder width apart, with the fingers pointed forward. The knees are *between* the arms. From this position, push off with the feet and rock forward on the hands. Just as you feel yourself falling off balance, tuck the head down between the arms with chin on chest. The back of the head touches the mat and the weight is then borne by the rounded back. Grasp the shins and pull yourself onto your feet. Those who have trouble should put the hands between the knees and the elbows against the thighs.

FORWARD ROLL VARIATIONS

During the roll the performer can cross his legs and come to his feet in this position. The legs can be uncrossed with a pivot which will face him in the direction from which he came. He can then roll back to position.

BACKWARD ROLL PRACTICE

Continue practice with the backward roll. Spot as needed. Practice the backward roll both with the hands clasped behind the neck (first grade) and in the regular manner.

FROG HANDSTAND (Tip-up)

The stunt follows the same directions as the *Three-point Tip-up* (second grade). Squat

Frog Handstand

down on the mat, placing the hands flat, fingers pointing forward, with the elbows inside and pressed against the inner part of the knees. Lean forward using the leverage of the elbows against the knees and balance on the hands. Hold for five seconds. Return to position.

The head does not touch the mat at any time. Hands may be turned in slightly if this makes better contact between the elbows and the insides of the thigh.

HEEL STAND

Begin in a full squat position with the arms dangling at the sides. Jump upward to full leg extension with the weight on both heels, flinging the arms out diagonally. Hold momentarily and return to position. Several movements can be done rhythmically in succession.

RUSSIAN DANCE

Squat down on one heel with the other foot extended forward with the weight on its heel. With the back straight and the arms extended forward, rapidly change the position of the feet.

Russian Dance

Variations:

1. Try with the arms folded high in front.
2. Try with one foot out to the side and change to the side each time.

SQUAT THRUST

While the squat thrust later is used as an exercise, the act of completing the cycle successfully is classified as a stunt. The stunt is done in four definite movements. Starting from the position of attention, on count *one* the child squats down on the floor placing the hands flat (shoulder width) on the floor with the elbows inside the knees. On count *two*, the feet and legs are thrust back so that the body is perfectly straight from head to toe in push-up position. On count *three*, the child returns to squat position, and on the *last* count returns to the position of attention.

Girls should do three in 10 seconds and boys four in the same amount of time.

First teach proper positioning during each

of the four phases. Then stress the rhythmic nature of the movements. Music may be added.

WALRUS WALK

Similar to the *Seal Crawl* (first grade). Begin with a front leaning rest position with fingers pointed outward. Make progress by moving both hands forward at the same time. Some children may be able to clap hands as they take each step.

Before giving this stunt, review the *Seal Crawl* and variations.

Variation: Move sideways so the upper part of the body describes an arc while the feet hold position.

THE REACH UNDER

Take a position with the feet pointed ahead and spaced about 2' apart, toes against a line or board of the floor. Place a beanbag two boards in front of and midway between the feet. Without changing the position of the feet, reach one hand behind and between the legs and pick up the beanbag. Pick up with the other hand. Move the beanbag a board out at a time and repeat.

Variation: Allow the heels to be lifted from the floor.

STIFF MAN BEND

Take a standing position with the feet about shoulder width apart and pointed forward. Place a beanbag 6" behind the left heel. Grasp the right toe with the right hand, thumb on top. Without bending the knees, reach the

Stiff Man Bend

left hand outside the left leg and pick up the beanbag without releasing the toe hold of the right hand. Increase the distance slowly. Reverse positions.

COFFEE GRINDER

Put one hand on the floor and extend the body with that side to the floor in a side leaning position. The child walks around his hand making a complete circle while keeping his body straight.

The stunt should be done slowly with con-

Coffee Grinder

trolled movements. The straight body alignment should remain constant throughout the complete circle movement.

MULE KICK

Stoop down and place the hands on the floor in front of the feet. The arms are the front legs of the mule. Kick out with the hind legs while the weight is momentarily supported by the front legs. Taking the weight on the hands is important.

The stunt can be taught in two stages. First, practice taking the weight momentarily on the hands. Next, add the kick.

Variation: Make two kicks before the feet return to the ground.

ONE LEG BALANCE REVERSE

Assume a forward balance position. In this, the body leans forward, the arms are out to the sides, the weight is on one leg with the other leg extended behind. In a quick movement, swing the free leg down to give mo-

mentum to change to the same forward balance position facing in the *opposite* direction (180 degree turn). No unnecessary movement of the supporting foot should be made after the turn is complete. The swinging foot should not touch the floor.

CURL-UP

Two children work together with one child holding the other's feet. The performer lies on his back with the legs extended and feet 1' apart. The knees are up so an angle of 90 degrees is formed at the knee joint. The feet are flat (soles down) on the floor. The hands, with the fingers interlaced, are behind the lower part of the head.

The child curls up, alternating touching the right and left elbows to the opposite knees. One touch is made on each curl-up.

Boys should be able to complete 15 curl-ups while girls should be able to do at least 10.

Be sure the child returns the head completely to the floor each time. No rest should be allowed as the curl-ups must be continuous. The child may move at his own pace, however.

See page 63 for description of the *Curl-up*.

TUMMY BALANCE

Tummy Balance

The child lies prone on the floor with arms outstretched to the sides, palms down. He raises arms, head, chest, and legs from the floor, balancing on his tummy. Knees should be kept straight.

HIP WALK

The child sits in the same position as in the *Scooter,* but the arms are in thrust position with the hand making a partial fist. The child makes forward progress by alternate leg movements. The arm-leg coordination should be cross-lateral.

THE SCOOTER

The *Scooter* is an excellent movement for abdominal development. The child is on the floor in extended sitting position with arms folded in front of the chest but held chin high. To scoot, he pulls his seat toward his heels, using heel pressure and lifting the seat slightly. He then extends his legs forward again, and repeats the process.

DOUBLE LAME DOG

Support the body on a hand and leg (same side). Move forward in this position, maintaining balance. The distance should be short (5'-10') as this is strenuous.

Double Lame Dog

Four leg-arm combinations should be employed. Cross-lateral movements of right arm-left leg and left arm-right leg should be varied with unilateral movements of right arm-right leg and left arm-left leg.

Variation: Keep the free arm on the hip.

LONG BRIDGE

Begin in a crouched position with the hands on the floor, knees between the arms. Push the hands forward a little at a time until you are in an extended push-up position. Return to position.

Challenge children to extend out as far forward as they can and still retain the support.

Variations: Begin with a forward movement and then change to sideward movement, establishing as wide a spread as possible. Another variation is to work from a crossed hands position.

THE TURTLE

Turtle

With the feet apart and the hands widely spread, the body is in a wide push-up position about halfway up from the floor (elbows somewhat bent). From this position, move in various directions, keeping the plane of the body always about the same distance from the floor. Movements of the hands and feet should occur only in small increments.

THE HEADSTAND

Two approaches are suggested for the *Headstand.* The first is to relate the *Headstand* to the *Climb Up* and the second is to go directly into a *Headstand* using a kick-up to achieve the inverted position. With either method it is essential that the triangle position of the hands and head be maintained as diagrammed.

In this position, the hands are placed about shoulder width apart, with the fingers pointed forward, spread, and slightly cupped. The head is positioned on the mat about 10" to 12" forward of the hands, with the weight taken on the forward part of the head, near the hairline.

In the final inverted position, the feet should be together with the legs straight and toes pointed. The back is arched, with the weight evenly distributed among the hands and forward part of the head.

The safest way to come down from the inverted position is to return to the mat in the direction which was used in going up. Recovery is helped by bending at both the waist and at the knees. If the child overbalances and falls forward, he should tuck the head under and go into a forward roll.

Both methods of recovery from the inverted position should be included in the instructional sequences early in the presentation.

BASING THE HEADSTAND ON THE CLIMB-UP

A spotter is stationed directly in front of the performer and steadies him as needed. However, if the spotter cannot control the performer, he must be alert to move out of the way if the latter goes into a forward roll coming out of the inverted position.

The child takes the inverted position of the *Climb-Up* (page 206) and slowly moves his feet upward to the *Headstand* position, steadied by the spotter only as needed. The spotter can first apply support to the hips and then transfer to the ankles as the *Climb-Up* position is lengthened into a *Headstand*.

HEADSTAND — KICK-UP METHOD

The goal of the kick-up method is to establish a pattern which can be related to other inverted stunts, as well as serving for the *Headstand*. Keeping the weight on the forward part of the head and maintaining the triangle base, walk the feet forward until the hips are high over the body, somewhat similar to the *Climb-Up* position. Keep one foot on the mat with the knee of that leg bent and the other leg somewhat extended backward. Kick the back leg up to the inverted position, following quickly with a push by the other leg, thus bringing the two legs together in the inverted position. The timing is a quick one-two movement.

When learning, children should work in units of three students. One child attempts the stunt with a spotter on either side. Positions are rotated. Each spotter kneels, placing his near hand under the shoulder of the performer. The performer now "walks" his weight above his head and kicks up to position. The spotter on each side supports by grasping the leg.

Spotting

Teaching Points:

The triangle formed by the hands and the head is important, as well as the weight centered on the forward part of the head. The majority of the troubles which occur while doing the headstand come from incorrect head-hand relationship. The correct placement can be ensured by making sure the head is placed the length of the performer's forearm from knees, and the hands placed at the knees.

Do not let children stay too long in the inverted position or hold contests to see who can stand on his head the longest.

Most of the responsibility for getting into the inverted position shou'd rest on the performer. Spotters may help some, but should avoid "wrestling up" the performer.

PARTNER HOPPING (Couple Stunt)

Children coordinate hopping movements for short distances and in different directions. Three combinations are suggested:

1. Stand facing each other. Extend the left leg forward to be grasped at the ankle by the partner. Each then hops on his right leg.

2. Stand back to back. Lift the leg back-

ward (bend knee) and have the partner grasp the ankle. Hop as before.

3. Stand side by side with inside arms around each other's waist. Lift the inside foot from the floor and make progress by hopping on the outside foot.

If either partner begins to fall, the other should release the leg immediately. Vary by moving in different directions and patterns. Reverse feet positions.

TWISTER (Couple Stunt)

Partners face and grasp right hands as if shaking hands. #1 swings his right leg over the head of #2 and turns around, taking a straddle position over his own arm. #2

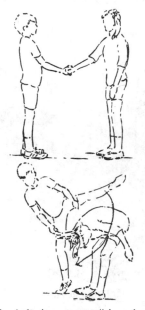

swings his left *leg* over #1, who has bent over, and the partners are now back to back. #1 now continues with his left leg and faces in the original direction. #2 swings his right leg over back to the original face to face position.

Partners need to duck to avoid being kicked by each other's feet as the legs are swung over.

Variation: The stunt can be introduced by grasping a wand instead of holding hands.

PARTNER PULL-UP (Couple Stunt)

Partners sit down facing each other in a bent-knee position with the heels on the floor

Partner Hopping

and the toes touching. Pulling cooperatively, both come to a standing position. Return to the floor.

DOUBLE TOP (Couple Stunt)

Double Top

Face partner and join hands. Experiment to see which type of grip works best. With straight arms, lean away from each other and at the same time move toes close to partner's. Spin around slowly in either direction, taking tiny steps. Increase speed.

Variation: Use a stooped position.

CHINESE GET-UP
(Couple or Group Stunt)

Two children sit back to back and lock arms. From this position both try to stand by pushing against each other's back. Sit down again. If the feet are sliding, do the stunt on a mat.

Variations:

1. Try the stunt with three or four children.
2. From a halfway down position, move like a spider.

FOURTH GRADE PROGRAM

The fourth grade program continues emphasis on the forward and back rolls with variations and combinations. Partner support stunts are introduced. Flops or falls are another addition. More emphasis should be placed on form and "dressing up" the stunt.

ACTIVITIES FOR THE FOURTH GRADE

Forward Roll Combinations
Backward Roll Combinations
Headstand Practice and Variations
Knee Walk
Knee Jump to Standing
Drops (Falls)
    Knee Drop
    Forward Drop
    Dead Man Fall
Knee Dip
Leg Dip
Stoop and Stretch
Tanglefoot
Squat Jumps
Egg Roll
Balance Jump
Toe Touch Nose
Seat Balance
Toe Tug Walk
Face to Knee Touch
Finger Touch
Leapfrog
Toe Toucher
Wheelbarrow (Couple Stunt)
Wheelbarrow Lifting (Couple Stunt)
Miscellaneous Wheelbarrow Stunts
Camel Lift and Walk

Dump the Wheelbarrow
Dromedary Walk (Couple Stunt)
Centipede (Couple or Group Stunt)
Double Wheelbarrow (Group Stunt)
Partner Support Stunts
    Double Bear
    Table
    Statue
    Lighthouse
    Hip-Shoulder Stand
Movement Exploration

FORWARD ROLL COMBINATIONS

The forward roll should be reviewed with increased emphasis on proper form. Combinations that can be introduced are:

1. Forward roll to standing position.
2. Forward roll preceded by a short run.
3. Two forward rolls in succession.
4. Leapfrog and forward roll.
5. Forward roll to a vertical jump in the air and repeat.
6. *Rabbit Jump* and forward roll.
7. Hold the toes while rolling.
8. Forward roll through a hoop.

BACKWARD ROLL COMBINATIONS

The backward roll technique should be reviewed. Continued emphasis on the push-off by the hands has to be made. Combinations to be taught are:

1. Backward roll to standing position. Correst use of the hands must be emphasized. A strong push by the hands is necessary to provide enough momentum to land on the feet.
2. Two backward rolls in succession.
3. *Crab Walk* into a backward roll.
4. Children can add a jump into the air at the completion of the roll combination.

HEADSTAND PRACTICE AND VARIATIONS

Continue work on the *Headstand.* Stress correct body arch and proper foot position. Spot as needed.

Variations:

1. Clap hands and recover. The weight must be shifted momentarily to the head for the clap. Some children will be able to clap the hands twice before recovery.
2. Employ different variations of leg positions, such as the split sideward, split forward and backward, bent knees, etc.

3. Holding a utility ball between the legs, go into the *Headstand,* retaining control of the ball.

Headstand Variation

KNEE WALK

Knee Walk

Kneel at the end of the mat. Reach back and hold both feet up from the floor. Walk the mat on the knees. Walk forward, backward, and sideward. Turn around at the center of the mat and continue.

KNEE JUMP TO STANDING

The starting position is kneeling with seat touching the heels and toes pointing backward (shoelaces against the floor). Jump to

a standing position with a vigorous upward swing of the arms. It is easier to jump from a smooth floor than from a mat, as the toes slide more readily on the floor. If a child has difficulty, allow him to come to a standing position with the feet well spread.

Variation: Jump to a standing position, and at the same time face the side direction with a quarter turn in the air. This is a jump and turn in the air in one quick motion. Try a half turn.

Drops (Falls)

A number of drops or falls can challenge children to good body control. Mats should be used. The forward fall impact should be absorbed with the hands and the arms. During the fall, the body should maintain a straight line position. Look to see that there is no change in any of the body angles, particularly at the knees and waist.

KNEE DROP

Kneel on a mat, with the body upright. Pick the feet off the floor and fall forward, breaking the fall with the hands and arms.

FORWARD DROP

From a forward balance position on one leg with the other leg extended backward, the arms extended forward and up, lean for-

ward slowly, bringing the arms toward the floor. Continue to drop forward slowly until overbalanced and let the hands and arms absorb the shock to break the fall. Head is up and the extended leg to the rear is raised high, with the knee joint maintained reasonably straight. Repeat changing position of the legs.

DEAD MAN FALL

The idea of the stunt is to fall forward from an erect position to a down push-up position. A slight bend at the waist is permissible, but the knees should be kept straight, and there should be no forward movement by the feet.

KNEE DIP

Grasp the right instep behind the back with the left hand, balancing on the left foot. With the other arm out for balance, lower and touch the floor with the bent knee. Regain balance. During the learning stages, the teacher can place a book under the knee

being lowered, making an easier stunt. Try with the other leg.

If there is difficulty, another child can support from behind.

Variation: Hold the right foot with the right hand and vice versa.

LEG DIP '

Extend both hands and one leg forward, balancing on the other leg. Lower body to heel seat and return without losing the balance or touching the floor with any part of the body. Try with the other foot.

Another child can assist from the back by applying upward pressure to the elbows.

STOOP AND STRETCH '

Stoop and Stretch

Hold a beanbag with *both* hands. Stand with the heels against a line and feet about shoulder width apart. Keeping the knees straight, reach between the legs with the beanbag, *placing* it as far back as possible. Reach back and pick it up with both hands.

Variations:

1. Bend at the knees, using more of a squatting position during the reach.

2. Use a piece of chalk instead of a beanbag. Reach back and make a mark on the floor. Try writing a number, drawing a small circle or other figure.

TANGLEFOOT /

Stand with the heels together and the toes pointed out. Bend the trunk forward, extend both arms down between the knees and around behind the ankles. Bring the hands around the outside of the ankles from behind and touch the fingers to each other, holding for a 5 second count.

Tanglefoot

Variation: Instead of touching, clasp the fingers in front of the ankles. Hold this position in good balance for 5 seconds without releasing the handclasp.

SQUAT JUMPS

Take a three-quarter squat position with the trunk erect and one foot slightly ahead of the other so that the heel of the front foot is even with the toe of the back foot. Hands are placed palms down on top of the head. Spring

into the air and change the relative position of the feet. Make 5, 10, and 15 changes, clearing the floor by 4". Children should avoid going down to a full squat position. The knees are completely straightened on each jump.

EGG ROLL

In a sitting position, assume the same clasped hands position as in *Tanglefoot*. Roll sideways over one shoulder, then to the back, followed by the other shoulder, and back up to the sitting position. The movements are repeated in turn to make a full

circle back to place. The secret is a vigorous sideward movement to secure initial momentum. If mats are used, two should be placed side by side to cover the extent of the roll. Some children can do this stunt better from a crossed ankle position.

BALANCE JUMP

With the hands and arms out to the side and the body parallel to the ground, one leg is extended behind and the weight is balanced on the other leg. Quickly change bal-

ance to the other foot, resuming the initial position with the feet exchanged. Be sure that the body is maintained parallel to the ground during the change of legs. Try with the hands outstretched forward.

Balance Jump — Starting Position

TOE TOUCH NOSE

From a sitting position on the floor, try to touch the toe of either foot to the nose with the help of both hands. More flexible youngsters will even be able to bring the foot on top of the head or behind the neck. While this is a flexibility exercise, caution should be used in forcing the leg too far. Do first with one foot and then the other.

Variation: Perform from a standing position. Begin from an erect position with the feet together. Touch the toe to the nose and return the foot to its original position without losing balance.

Try the standing version with the eyes closed.

SEAT BALANCE

Sit on the floor holding the ankles in front with the elbows inside the knees. The feet are flat on the floor, and the knees are bent approximately at a right angle. Raise the legs so that the knees are straight with the toes pointed, and balance on the seat for 5 seconds.

Variation: Make small turns of the body using the seat as a pivot point.

TOE TUG WALK

Bend over and grasp the toes with the thumb on top. Knees are bent slightly and the eyes are forward. Walk forward without losing the grip on the toes. Walk backward and sideward to provide more challenge. Also, walk in various geometric patterns like a circle, triangle, or square. This stunt can be introduced in an easier version by having the

Toe Tug Walk

children grasp the ankles, thumbs to the insides, and perform the desired movements.

Variation: Try doing the walk with the right hand grasping the left foot and vice versa.

FACE TO KNEE TOUCH

Begin in a standing position with feet together. Placing hands on the hips, balance on one foot with the other leg extended backward. Bend the trunk forward and touch the knee of the supporting leg with the forehead.

Recover to original standing position. Teachers can begin by having the children use their arms away from their sides for balance and then later stipulate the hands-on-hips position.

In learning stages, an assist can be given from behind by supporting the leg that is extended backward.

FINGER TOUCH

Put the right hand behind you with the index finger straight and pointed down. Grasp the right wrist with the left hand. From an erect position with the feet about 6" apart, squat down and touch the floor with the index

finger. Regain erect position without losing balance. In learning the stunt, the teacher can use a book or corner of a mat to decrease the distance, making the touch easier.

Avoid tilting the body to one side to get the finger to touch.

LEAPFROG

A "back" is formed by one student so that a leaper with a running start can lay his hands flat on the back at the shoulders and vault over him. Backs are formed in these following progressive heights:

Low Back. The child crouches down on his knees, curling into a tight ball with his head tucked well down.

Medium Back. From a standing position, the child reaches down the outside of his legs and grasps the ankles. His feet should be reasonably spread, and the knees bent. He should assume a stable position so he can absorb the shock of the leaper.

High Back. The child stands stiff-legged, bends over, and braces his arms against his knees. His feet should be well spread, his head down, and his body braced to absorb the vault.

High, Medium, and Low Leap Frog Positions

Leapfrog is a traditional physical education activity, but the movement is actually a jump and vault pattern. The take-off must be made with both feet. At the height of the jump, the chest and head must be held erect to avoid a forward fall. Emphasize a forceful jump to achieve height, coordinated with light hand pressure to vault over the back. Landing should be done lightly with a bent-knee action under good control.

Variations:

1. Work in pairs where the children alternate in leaping and forming backs as they progress around the room.

2. Have more than one back for a series of jumps.

3. Using the medium back as described above, vault from the side rather than from the front. Legs of the vaulter must be well spread and the back must keep his head well tucked down.

4. Combine with a *Forward Roll* on a mat following the *Leapfrog*.

TOE TOUCHER (Partner Stunt)

Partners lie on backs with heads near each other and feet in opposite directions. They grasp each other, using a hand-wrist grip, and bring up their legs (both partners) so that the toes touch. Keep high on the shoulders and touch the feet high.

Partners should be of about the same height. Strive to attain the high shoulder position, as this is the point of most difficulty.

Toe Toucher

Variation: One partner carries a beanbag, ball or other article between his feet. The article is transferred to the other partner, who lowers it to the floor.

WHEELBARROW (Couple Stunt)

One partner gets down on his hands with his feet extended to the rear, legs apart. The other partner (the pusher) grasps his legs halfway between the ankles and the knees. The wheelbarrow walks forward on his hands, supported by the pusher.

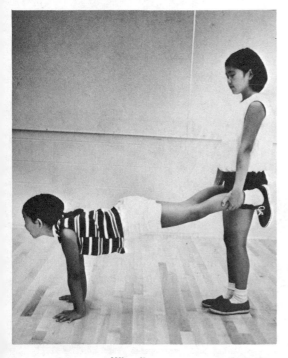

Wheelbarrow

Children have a tendency to grasp the feet too low. The pusher must not push too fast. The wheelbarrow should have his head up and look forward.

WHEELBARROW LIFTING (Couple Stunt)

Partners assume the wheelbarrow position as described. The pusher lifts his partner's legs up as high as he can without changing his hand position. He should be able to lift so that the angle of the body of the lower child with the floor is about 45 degrees.

Variation: The pusher brings the legs up to the previous level as described, changes his hand grip to a pushing position, and continues to raise the lower child toward a handstand position. The lower child should keep his arms straight and the head well up against the back of the neck.

Wheelbarrow Lifting

Miscellaneous Wheelbarrow Stunts

CAMEL LIFT AND WALK

The wheelbarrow raises his seat as high as he can, forming a camel. He can lower or he can walk in the raised position.

DUMP THE WHEELBARROW

Walk the wheelbarrow over to a mat. The lower child ducks his head (chin to the chest), raises his seat (bend at the waist), and exits from the stunt with a front roll. A little push and lift with the feet can be given by the pusher.

DROMEDARY WALK (Couple Stunt)

The first child (support) gets down on hands and knees. The second (top) child sits on him, facing to the rear, and fixes his own legs around the chest of support. The top child leans forward (for him) so he can grasp the back of the support's ankles. Arms are reasonably extended. The support takes the weight off the knees and walks forward with the top child's help.

Dromedary Walk

CENTIPEDE (Couple or Group Stunt)

The support player should be the stronger and larger individual. He gets down on his hands and knees. The top player faces the same direction, placing his hands about 2' in front of those of the support player. Now he places his legs and body on top of the support. The feet are on top and not hooked under. The centipede walks with the top player using hands only, and the support player using both hands and feet. The support child should gather his legs well under him while walking and should thus be off his knees.

Centipede Walk

Variation: More than two can do this stunt. After getting in position, the players should keep step by calling right and left out loud.

DOUBLE WHEELBARROW (Group Stunt)

This stunt is usually done by three children, but can be done by one or two more. Two children assume about the same position as in the previous stunt *(Centipede)* except that the under child has his legs extended to the

Double Wheelbarrow

rear, feet apart. The third child stands between the legs of the under child, reaches down, and picks up the legs of the lower child, forming the Double Wheelbarrow. The Double Wheelbarrow moves forward with right and left arms moving together.

Partner Support Stunts

Several considerations are important in the conduct of partner support stunts. The lower child (support) should keep his body as level as possible. This means widening his hand base so his shoulders can be more nearly level with his hips. The support performer must be strong enough to handle the support chores. Spotters are needed, particularly where the top position involves a final erect or inverted pose. Avoid stepping on the small of the lower child's back.

In the *Lighthouse* and the *Hip-Shoulder Stand,* the top performer can remove his shoes, which makes the standing position more comfortable for the support. The top child when he holds the final pose should fix his gaze forward at a spot level with his eyes and relax as much as he can while still maintaining the position.

1. DOUBLE BEAR

Double Bear

Bottom man is down on his hands and knees. Top man assumes the same position directly above with hands on shoulders and knees on the hips of the bottom man. Touch up the final position by holding heads up and backs straight.

2. TABLE

Bottom performer assumes crab position (base). Top performer straddles base, facing to the rear, and positions his hands on base's shoulders, fingers pointing toward the feet. His feet are now placed on top of the base's knees, forming one crab position on top of another. As the final touch the heads are positioned so that the eyes look up toward the ceiling and the seats lifted so the backs are straight.

3. STATUE

First child gets down in crab position. The second child straddles one foot (either) facing the child in crab position. With the help of a third person, he mounts each knee of the base child in turn so that he is standing erect. Hold for a few seconds.

Partners should be facing each other. Do not have the top child mount with his back toward the base child. Spotters are important here and should not be eliminated until the stunt is mastered.

Table

Statue

4. THE LIGHTHOUSE

Support is down on hands and knees. Top man completes the figure by standing on *the shoulders* of the support facing the same direction. He stands erect with hands out to the sides.

Lighthouse

Variation: Have the support turn around in a small circle with the partner keeping his standing balance.

5. HIP-SHOULDER STAND

Support is on his hands and knees, with his hands positioned out somewhat so his back is level. Top man faces to the side and steps up, first with one foot on support's hips, following with the other on his shoulders. A spotter should stand on the opposite side and aid in mounting. Care must be taken to avoid stepping on the small of the back.

6. MOVEMENT EXPLORATION

There are many different ways that children can support each other. It is suggested that a portion of the time be given to having the children devise various ways of supporting a partner.

Hip Shoulder Stand

FIFTH GRADE PROGRAM

The teacher should review all stunts from the previous grade. The repetition is valuable because many of the fifth grade activities have their basis in the simpler stunts performed in the fourth grade.

The children at this stage should be quite skillful in doing both the *Forward* and *Backward Rolls*. Additional routines are added. The *Shoulder Roll, Cartwheel,* and *Eskimo Roll* continue the mat-type activities. Improvement in the *Headstand* should be expected. The *Handstand* is an important introduction. The following stunts make up the suggested fifth grade program:

ACTIVITIES IN THE FIFTH GRADE

Forward and Backward Roll Combinations
Headstand Review and Variations
Neckspring
Handstand
Cartwheel
Push-up Variations

Turn-Over and Flip-Flop
Wall Walk-Up
Wall Arch
Skier's Sit
Shoulder Roll
Fish Hawk Dive
Curl-Up Practice
Walrus Slap
Rocking Horse
Heel Click (Side)
Double Scooter (Couple Stunt)
Walk Through
Jump Through
Circular Rope Skip
Eskimo Roll (Double Roll)
Back Lay Out (Partner Balance Stunt)
Front Sit (Partner Balance Stunt)
Flying Dutchman (Partner Balance Stunt)
Tandem Bicycle (Group Stunt)
Circle High Jump (Group Stunt)
Stick Carries (Group Stunt)
Two-Way Wheelbarrow (Group Stunt)

FORWARD AND BACKWARD ROLL COMBINATIONS

Combinations from the fourth grade should be reviewed. The following routines can be added:

1. *Alternating Forward and Backward Rolls.* Begin the combination with a forward roll, coming to the standing position with the feet crossed, pivoting the body to uncross the feet, thus bringing the back in the line of direction for a backward roll.

2. *Back Extension.* Carry the backward roll to the point where the feet are above the head and slightly over. Push off vigorously with the hands and shoot the feet into the air, landing on the feet.

3. A number of variations and different body positions can be added to the rolls. Holding toes, heels, ankles, or a wand can be incorporated. Utilizing different arm positions such as out to the sides, or folded across the chest gives variety. Use a wide straddle position for both the front and back rolls.

Try stiff leg sitdowns leading into the back roll.

HEADSTAND REVIEW AND VARIATIONS

Review the various aspects of the *Headstand,* using the single spotter technique as needed. Vary with different leg positions. Add the following:

1. Develop a two-foot recovery. After the stand has been held, recover by bending at the waist and knees, pushing off with the hands, and landing on the feet back to where you started.

NECKSPRING

The stunt is related to the backward curl. The performer goes into a backward curl position with the feet kept over the head. The feet are brought sharply forward toward the mat. As the shoulders come off the mat, the arms are extended with good push-off by the hands; and there is an upward snap to standing position. The neckspring can be followed by a forward roll.

Spotting: Kneel alongside the child. Place one hand under the back and the other under the *near* shoulder blade. Attention must be given to preventing a backward fall In case of improper lunging by the performer. The lower hand under the back acts as a pivot,

while a good lift is given by the hand under the shoulder.

Spotting the Neckspring

HANDSTAND

The first two phases of the *Handstand* are introduced in the fifth grade. Initially, the *Handstand* should be done with the aid of two spotters (double spotting). The second method is to perform the stunt with one spotter, employing knee pressure as a part of the spotting technique. To do the stunt, place hands on the mat, shoulder width apart, fingers spread, slightly cupped and pointed straight ahead. Keeping one leg straight, walk up close with the other leg to elevate the hips. The arms are straight and the shoulders well forward of the hands. Kick up with the straight leg and push off with the

bent leg. With the back arched, the shoulders are brought back to a point directly over the hands.

Double Spotting

Spotters should be stationed on either side of the performer. The back should be arched and the head up. It is important that the spotter on each side have a firm grip beneath the shoulders of the performer. The other hand of each spotter can assist the lift by upward pressure on the thigh. The performer walks his hips forward until they are over his hands.

Double Spotting for the Handstand, 1st stage. Note the hand support under the shoulders.

Double Spotting for the Handstand, 2nd stage.

He kicks up with one foot, pushes off with the other, and raises that leg to join the other in the inverted position. The rhythm is a one-two count.

Single Spotting (Knee Pressure)

Spotter takes a stride position, with the forward knee somewhat bent. The performer kneels on one knee, with his shoulder against the spotter's leg. The weight is transferred over the hands, and the body goes into the handstand position with one-two kick-up. Spotter catches the legs and holds the performer in an inverted position.

Single Spotting for the Handstand, 1st stage. Performer's shoulder is against spotter's leg.

Single Spotting for Handstand, 2nd stage. Note knee. pressure against performer's shoulder.

Alternate Spotting for the Handstand (Double Spotting)

Two children are used to spot a third. The first child sits on a mat with legs out straight in a wide V. The *Handstand* is done between his legs. He catches the performer at the sides of the waist. The second spotter stands directly behind the seated spotter and catches the performer's ankles. The performer must keep elbows straight, head up, back arched to avoid falling toward the spotter.

Alternate Spotting for the Handstand

CARTWHEEL

Begin with the legs and arms spread, with the left side toward the direction of wheeling. For a preliminary movement (windup), swing the left arm up and keep the right arm at the side. Now throw the weight smoothly to the left side, bringing the right arm up and the left arm down so that the hand takes a position about 2′ from the left leg. The right arm now comes down to the mat, and the right leg follows upward.

Just before the right hand touches the floor, there is a push-off with the left foot to give momentum to the roll. Swing both legs up and over the head. The right foot touches first, followed by the left. As the left foot ap-

proaches, a good push is given with the right hand to return the individual to standing position. It is important to keep the head up throughout the stunt.

The entire body in the stunt must be in the same plane throughout the stunt, and feet must pass directly overhead.

In teaching the cartwheel to children who are having difficulty, concentrate on taking the weight of the body on the hands in succession. The children need to get the feel of the weight support, and then can concentrate next on getting the body into proper position.

Spotting: A spotter stands behind the performer and moves with him. He grasps the performer at the waist with a crossed-arm position. This position allows the arms to become uncrossed as the performer wheels and is given assistance.

PUSH-UP VARIATIONS

Begin the development of push-up variations by reviewing proper push-up techniques. Stress that the only movement is in the arm and that the body should come close to, but not touch, the floor. The following variations can be explored. The order can be changed.

1. Monkey Push-up. Point fingers toward each other. Next, bring the hands close enough so the fingertips touch.

2. Circle-O Push-up. Thumbs and forefingers form a Circle-O.

3. Fingertip Push-up. Get up high on the fingertips.

4. Different Finger Combinations. Do a push-up using four, three, two fingers.

5. Extended Push-up. Extend the position of the hands progressively forward or to the sides.

6. Crossed Push-ups. Cross the arms. Cross the legs. Cross both.

7. One-Legged Push-ups. Lift one leg from the floor.

8. One-Handed Push-up. Use only one hand with the other outstretched or on the hips.

9. Exploratory Approach. Opportunity should be given to see what other types of push-ups or combinations the students can create.

TURN-OVER AND FLIP-FLOP

From a front leaning rest (push-up) position, the object is to turn completely over using only the arms and hands. The remainder of the body is kept straight. The feet, particularly, must be stiffened.

Lift one hand, depending upon the way the turn is to be made, and at the same time turn the body so the back is to the floor. The lifted hand returns quickly to the floor for support. The weight is now on the hands and heels. Continue with the other hand and complete the turn. Return by reversing the direction and making a complete turn back the other way.

Flip-Flop: Do a flip-flop by propelling the body into the air and reversing the body position as in the *Turn-Over.* Flip back. The stunt should be done on a mat.

WALL WALK-UP

From a push-up position with feet against a wall, walk up the wall backwards to a handstand position. Walk down again.

WALL ARCH

Take a position with the shoulders against a wall and the feet about 2′ out. Place the hands against the wall, employing the position used in the backward roll. Without moving the feet, work the hands downward, to give the body an arch shape. Recover to position.

SKIER'S SIT

The skier's sit is an isometric type of activity which is excellent for developing the knee extensor muscles. The child assumes a sitting position against a wall so that his thighs are level with the floor and there is a right angle at the knee joint. His body position is the same as if he were sitting in a chair; but, of

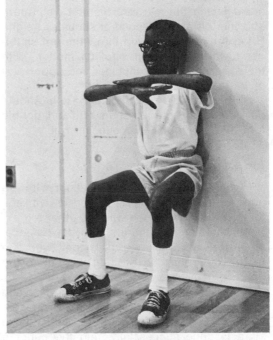

Skier's Sit

course, there is no chair. The arms are folded across the chest. The feet should be flat on the floor and the legs straight up and down. Children should try to sit for 30 seconds, 45 seconds, and 1 minute. This exercise is done by skiers to develop support muscles used in skiing.

Variation: Support the body on one leg, with the other extended forward.

SHOULDER ROLL

The *Shoulder Roll* is a basic safety device to prevent injury from tripping and falling. Rolling and "taking the fall" lessens the chances of injury.

The *Shoulder Roll* is essentially a *Forward Roll* with the head turned to one side. The point of impact is on the back of one shoulder and the finish is back to a standing position.

For a left *Shoulder Roll,* the child should stand facing the mat with his feet well apart, and the left arm extended at shoulder height. Bring the arm down and throw the left shoulder toward the mat in a rolling motion, with the roll made on the shoulder and upper part of the back.

Both right and left Shoulder Rolls should be practiced. Later, a short run and double foot take-off should precede the roll.

FISH HAWK DIVE

Place a folded paper on the floor with the edge up so that it can be picked up with the teeth. Kneel on one leg with the other leg extended behind and the arms out for balance. Lean forward, pick up the paper with the teeth, and return to position without losing balance.

Begin the stunt using an 8½-by-11" piece of paper folded lengthwise. It may be necessary to have someone hold the paper. If the stunt is done successfully, fold the paper a second time so a lower target is presented.

CURL-UP PRACTICE

The child is on his back with the feet apart, flat on the floor. The knees are bent at approximately a right angle. The stunt can be done two ways.

1. With the arms folded in front of the chest, curl-ups are done so the folded arms touch the knees each time.

2. The hands, with fingers interlaced, are grasped behind the lower part of the head. The left elbow touches the right knee on the first curl-up and the right elbow the left knee on the next.

Boys should do from 15 to 20 while the girls should do 10 to 15. Gradually increase the number during the year. Done properly and regularly, this exercise has good values in the maintenance of proper posture.

WALRUS SLAP

Review the *Seal Crawl* and the *Walrus Walk* (page 211) from previous grades. From the same position (front leaning rest), push the body up in the air by quick force of the arms, clap the hands together, and recover to position.

Variations:

1. Try clapping the hands more than once.
2. Move forward while clapping the hands.
3. Reverse *Walrus Walk.* Turn over and do a *Walrus Walk* while facing the ceiling. Clapping the hands is quite difficult in this position, and should be attempted only by the more skilled.

ROCKING HORSE

The child is face down on a mat with the arms extended overhead, palms down. With the back arched, rock back and forth. Some children may need to have someone start them rocking.

Variation: The stunt can be done by reaching back and grasping the insteps with the hands. The body arch is more difficult to maintain with this position.

HEEL CLICK (Side)

Balance on one foot with the other out to the side. Hop on the supporting foot, click heels, and return to balance. Try with the other foot. Insist on good balance.

The child should recover to the one-foot

balance position without excessive foot movement.

Variations:

1. The stunt can also be done moving. Take a short lead step with the right foot. Follow with a cross step with the left and then a hop on the left foot. During the hop, click the heels together. To hop on the right foot, reverse the above directions.

2. See how high the children can jump into the air before clicking heels.

3. Combine right and left clicks.

DOUBLE SCOOTER (Couple Stunt)

Double Scooter

First review the *Scooter,* page 213.

This stunt should be done by two children of about the same size. The children sit facing each other, sitting on each other's feet. With arms joined, they scoot forward or backward with cooperative movements. When one child moves his seat, the other child should help by lifting with his feet. Progress is made by alternately flexing and extending the knees and hips.

WALK THROUGH

From a front leaning rest position, walk the feet through the hands using tiny steps until the body is fully extended with the back to the floor. Reverse the body to original position. Hands stay in contact with the floor throughout.

JUMP THROUGH

This is related to the previous stunt except that instead of walking through, jump the feet through with one motion. Reverse with a jump and return to original position. The hands must push sharply off the floor so that the body is high enough from the floor to allow the legs to jump under.

The child may find it easier to swing a little to the side with one leg, going under the lifted hand. This is indicated in the following diagram, where the youngster swings a little to one side.

CIRCULAR ROPE SKIP

Circular Rope Skip

Crouch down in a three-quarter knee bend, holding a folded skipping rope in one hand. Swing the rope under the feet in circular fashion, jumping it each time. Reverse the direction of the rope. Work from both right and left sides with either a counterclockwise or clockwise turn of the rope .

ESKIMO ROLL (Double Roll)

This is one of the older stunts and a favorite of many youngsters. The stunt is done with two children who are designated as #1 and #2. #1 lies on the mat with feet in the direction of the roll. #2 takes a position with his feet on either side of #1's head. #1 reaches back and grasps #2's ankles with the thumbs on the inside. #1 raises his feet so #2 can similarly grasp his ankles.

#2 propels his hunched body forward, while #1 sits up and takes the position origi-nally held by #2. Positions are now reversed. The roll continues. Be sure that the top man hunches well and ducks his head to cushion the roll on the back of the neck and shoulders. Also, when the top man propels himself forward, his bent arms should momentarily take his weight. It is important that the underneath man keep his knees in a bent knee position.

Variation: Roll backward after reaching the end of the mat. To begin a reverse roll, the top man sits backward and pulls vigorously on the legs of the bottom man.

BACK LAYOUT (Partner Balance Stunt)

Back Layout

The under, or support, partner lies on his back with arms outstretched, palms down, for support. His legs are raised and his feet posi-tioned as if pushing up the ceiling. He bends his knees and his partner lies back, resting the small of his back on support's soles. Thus the top partner is balanced in a layout posi-tion with his arms out to the sides for balance and his body in a slight curve. The support partner can reach up and give support to the top's arms to provide better stability. A spot-ter should aid in positioning the top partner.

FRONT SIT (Partner Balance Stunt)

Front Sit

The support gets down in the same position as for the *Back Layout*. The top partner strad-dles the support, facing so that support and top partner are looking at each other. The top partner backs up to sit on the support's feet.

As the support raises the top partner in a seated position, the top partner extends his legs forward so that the support can reach up and support them to stabilize the seated position.

FLYING DUTCHMAN
(Partner Balance Stunt)

Flying Dutchman

The under, or support, person takes a position as in the *Back Layout*. The top person takes a position facing the support, grasping his hands, and at the same time bending over his feet. The top person now is raised from the floor by extending his knees, arching his back, and resting on the feet of the support person. He can release his grip and put his arms out level to the side in a flying position. A little experimentation will determine the best spot for the foot support.

TANDEM BICYCLE (Group Stunt)

Tandem Bicycle

As with a tandem bicycle, the stunt can be done with two or more players. A bicycle is formed by the first player with back against a wall in bent-knee position as if sitting. The second player backs up and sits down lightly on the knees. Other children may be added in the same fashion. The hands are around the waist of the player immediately in front for support. Forward progress is made by moving the feet on the same side together.

CIRCLE HIGH JUMP (Group Stunt)

Children are in circles of three, each circle having children of about equal height. Hands are joined and one child tries to jump over the opposite pair of joined hands. Each circle to be completely successful must have each child jump forward over the opposite pair of joined hands. Jumping backward is not recommended.

Circle High Jump

To reach good height in jumping, an upward lift of the joined hands is necessary. The jumper may try two small preliminary jumps before exploding into the jump over the joined hands.

Variation: Precede the jump with a short run by the group. A signal needs to be sounded so all will know when the jump is to occur during the run.

STICK CARRIES (Group Stunt)

Stick Carry

Children are in groups of three, with each group having a sturdy broom handle about 4' long. Using movement exploration techniques, two of the children are to carry the third with the broom handle. The child carried may be partially supported on or completely off the ground. Children should be of similar weight. Exchange positions. It is better to use special sticks for this purpose as ordinary wands may break.

TWO-WAY WHEELBARROW (Group Stunt)

Two Way Wheelbarrow

Review the various *Wheelbarrow* activities in the fourth grade (page 223). Add the *Double Wheelbarrow*, a stunt done by three children. In essence, one child is holding two wheelbarrows, one in front of him and one behind him. He secures the front position first in a normal wheelbarrow position. The child behind in wheelbarrow position secures his position by placing his ankles over the already established hand position of the holder.

SIXTH GRADE PROGRAM

Continued practice should be held in the rolls, the *Cartwheel*, the *Headstand*, the *Handstand*, and the *Neckspring.* It is important to review many of the Fifth Grade stunts. The sixth grade program adds a number of stunts which are quite challenging. The *Dive Forward Roll*, the *Headspring*, the *Forearm Headstand*, the *Forearm Stand*, the *Front Seat Support*, and the *Elbow Balance* provide sufficient breadth for even the most skilled. Teachers should recognize that at the sixth grade level it will be difficult for all students to accomplish everything listed. Particular attention must be paid to the lead-up stunts for any of the gymnastic type activities. There is less emphasis on exploration and more on execution, conformity, and form.

ACTIVITIES FOR THE SIXTH GRADE

Forward and Backward Roll Variations
Movement Sequences
Headstand Variations
Headspring
Long Reach
High Dive
The Bouncer
Wrestler's Bridge
Toe Jump
V-Up
Dive Forward Roll
Handstand
Partner Rising Sun
The Pretzel
Jackknife
Heel and Toe Spring
Forearm Headstand
Forearm stand
Single Leg Circle
Front Seat Support
Elbow Balance
Three Man Roll (Triple Roll)
Dead Man Lift
Injured Man Carry

Partner Support Stunts
   Knee and Shoulder Balance
   Press
   All Fours Support
   The Angel
   Side Stand
Merry-Go-Round

FORWARD AND BACKWARD ROLL VARIATIONS

Putting together different combinations of rolls should be stressed with emphasis on choice, exploration, and self-discovery. Variations can be instituted using different kinds of approaches, execution acts, and finishes.

FORWARD ROLL VARIATIONS

1. Hold toes, heels, ankles, or a wand.
2. With hands crossed, roll as in (1) above.
3. Roll with hands on knees or a ball between the knees.
4. Roll with the arms at sides, folded across the chest, or in other positions.
5. Finish with a walkout by ending the roll with one leg extended forward to walk out of the stunt. Or, finish on one knee.
6. Start with a standing broad jump, a jump over a low object, or some other jumping, hopping, or leaping movement.
7. Place low jumping box or bench under mat and roll from and to the higher elevations.
8. Place a bench or jumping box on or before the mat and work out various possibilities with these pieces of equipment.
9. Roll from a wide-straddle position (feet as wide apart sideways as possible), holding on to ankles.
10. Press forward from a front leaning rest position and go into the roll.

BACKWARD ROLL VARIATIONS

1. Begin with a stiff leg sitdown and go into the roll.
2. Push off into a backward extension, lighting on the feet.
3. Roll to a finish on one foot only.
4. Roll with hands and arms in various positions — out to the sides, clasped behind the neck, etc.

5. Roll with a ball between the knees.
6. Walk backward with a crab movement and then roll.
7. Combine forward and backward rolls.

MOVEMENT SEQUENCES

Set up problems so that the child can use and put together in sequence the stunts he has learned and other movements. Some problems that can be structured are:

1. Specify the number, kinds of stunts and movements to be done, and the sequence to be followed. For example, tell the child to do a balance stunt, a locomotor movement, and a rolling stunt.
2. Mats can be arranged so that these become the key for the movement problems to be solved. Arrange the mats in some prescribed order such as two or three in succession, in a "U" shape (three or four mats) or a hollow square formation. There should be some space between mats depending on the conditions as stated in the problem. The problem could be set up like this: "On the first mat, do a forward roll variation, then a movement to the next mat on all fours. On the second mat do some kind of a balance stunt, and then proceed to the next mat with a jumping or hopping movement. On the third mat you have a choice of activity." The problem could also be stated in more general terms, having the children do a different stunt or variation on each mat and a different movement between mats.
3. Have children work with a partner and work out a series of partner stunts. This can be done with two children of equal size and strength so they can alternate as support for stunts, or it might be two children of different sizes where the larger child would provide the support for the smaller. A third child may act as a spotter to take care of safety factors. After the children have practiced for a period of time, each partnership can demonstrate the routines which have been developed.

HEADSTAND VARIATIONS

Practice the movement from a Headstand into a forward roll to feet. Do the Headstand with a beanbag or ball between the ankles.

HEADSPRING

With forehead and hands on the mat and the legs straight, the performer leans forward until he is almost overbalanced. As the weight begins to overbalance, the feet are raised sharply and snapped forward, coupled with a push of the hands. As the feet begin to touch, the body is snapped forward to a bent-knee position. The performer keeps his balance and rises to a standing position.

Spotters can kneel on either side, giving a lift under the shoulders as the performer snaps to a standing position. A slight run may be needed to get proper momentum.

Some instructors like to introduce this going over a rolled-up mat, providing more height for the turn. ·

LONG REACH

Place a beanbag 3′ or 4′ in front of a line. Keeping toes behind the line, lean forward on one hand and reach out with the other hand to touch the beanbag. The recovery to the original position must be made with one quick motion. In this, the supporting hand comes off

Long Reach

the floor in one clean movement. Increase the distance of the bag from the line.

Variations: A piece of chalk can be used to make a mark to record a more precise distance.

Since the distance the child can reach is dependent upon his height, measure how far he can reach beyond his height. With the child lying on the floor, make a mark on the floor and make a mark at his heels and at the top of his head.

Now see how far he can reach in relation to his height, while still keeping his feet behind the restraining line.

HIGH DIVE

High Dive

Fold a piece of paper that can be picked up by the teeth. Using the arms for balance and standing on one foot only, try to pick up the paper with the teeth. If this seems too difficult, shorten the distance to the paper by elevating it on a box or book.

Begin with a regular sheet of notepaper folded lengthwise; it may need to be steadied by another child.

THE BOUNCER

Start in push-up position. Bounce up and down with both the hands and the feet leaving the ground at the same time. Try clapping while doing this. Move in various directions.

WRESTLER'S BRIDGE

Lie on the mat, bringing up the feet so that they are flat on the mat. Push up with the body and arch the neck so that the support is on the feet and head.

Wrestler's Bridge

Variations:

1. Pass a ball around the body, or toss it from side to side.

2. Place hands back on floor with the thumbs near the ears, and raise the body to a full arch, lifting the head from the floor.

3. Reverse the body position, still keeping the hands away from the floor.

4. Do a Headstand and fall forward to a *Wrestler's Bridge.* During the fall, the knees are bent for landing on the soles of the feet. After falling into the bridge position, the hands can be removed from the support position.

TOE JUMP

Toe Jump

Hold the left toe with the right hand. Jump the right foot through without losing the grip on the toe. Jump back again. Try with the other foot.

V-UP

V-Up

The child is on his back with the arms overhead and extended. Keeping the knees straight and the feet pointed, the legs and upper body are brought up at the same time to form a "V." The entire weight is balanced on the seat and should be held for 5 counts.

This exercise, like the *Curl-up,* is excellent for the development of the abdominal muscles.

Variation: Those who have trouble may employ an easier version of the stunt by placing the hands in back on the floor for support.

DIVE FORWARD ROLL

The stunt is similar to the regular forward roll except that the roll is preceded by a run and short dive. The child should take a short run and take off with both feet so that he is already partially turning in the air as his hands come down to cushion the fall. The head

should be tucked under and the roll is made on the back of the neck and shoulders.

The teacher should avoid contests to see how far a student can dive. The stunt described is actually only an elongated forward roll during which the player is off the ground for a short period of time.

Dives over objects or other students should be used with caution and reserved only for the more skilled.

HANDSTAND

The Handstand can be developed by taking it through these stages:

1. Double spotting (fifth grade).
2. Single spotting, knee support (fifth grade).
3. Single spotting, catch ankles.
4. *Handstand* against a wall.
5. Free *Handstand*.
6. Walking on hands.
7. Stunts against a wall.
8. Other stunts.

The first two stages of the *Handstand,* presented in the fifth grade program (page 228) should be reviewed. Progression can then follow this order.

Single Spotting (without knee support)

Performers should begin to use the extended starting position. The performer and spotter face each other 4' or 5' apart. The performer lifts both arms and the left leg upward as a preliminary move with the weight shifted to the right leg. The lifted arms and leg come down forcefully to the ground, with the weight shifted in succession to the left leg and then to the arms. The right leg is kicked backward and upward to establish initial momentum, quickly followed by the left leg. The downward thrust of the arms, coupled with the upward thrust of the legs, inverts the body to the handstand position. The hands should have been placed about 2' in front of the spotter, who reaches forward and catches

Single Spotting

the performer's ankles as they come up in the handstand position.

Handstand Against a Wall

Mats should be used. It is better in the beginning to place the hands too close to the wall than to have them too far from it. The extended starting position is used. Some performers may have better success in bending the knees so that the flat of the foot is against the wall. The straight arm and arched back, head-up positions must be maintained to prevent collapse into the wall.

Free-Standing Handstand

The performer should learn to turn the body when he feels he is falling, and land on his feet. Spotters can be used to prevent an awkward fall. The hands may need to move to help control the balance.

Walking on Hands

Hand walking should generally be in a forward direction. Some may find it more comfortable to walk with knees slightly bent for balance. Walking can first be done with

Handstand Against the Wall

potter supporting. This support should be minimal.

Stunts Against a Wall

A number of challenging activities can be done from the Handstand position against a wall. The first is to turn the body in a complete circle, maintaining foot contact with the wall throughout. Another stunt is to shift the support to one hand, holding it for a short period of time. A stunt demanding considerable arm strength is to perform an inverted push-up. The body is lowered by bending the elbows and then returned to Handstand position with a straightening of the elbows (push-up).

Other Stunts

Do a Handstand to a single spotter. Turn in circle with the spotter providing support. From a Handstand position with a single spotter, have the performer hand walk forward until his hands are on the toes of the spotter. Cooperative walking can be done with the performer maintaining his support on the spotter's toes.

PARTNER RISING SUN

Partner Rising Sun

Partners lie face down on the floor with heads together and feet in opposite directions. A volleyball, basketball, or ball of similar size is held between their heads. Working together, they stand up and return to position retaining control of the ball without touching the ball with the hands.

A slightly deflated ball works best. Some caution is necessary to prevent bumping heads if the ball is suddenly squeezed out.

THE PRETZEL

Pretzel

Girls do better than boys in this stunt. The object of the stunt is to touch the back of the head with the toes by raising the head and trunk and bringing the feet to the back of the head. The stunt should be done in two levels. First, challenge the child to bring his toes near enough to his head so the distance can be measured by another child with a handspan (thumb-little finger distance when spread). If this distance is met, then try touching one or both feet to the back of the head.

JACKKNIFE

Stand erect with the hands out level to the front and a little to the side. Jump up and

Jackknife

bring the feet up to touch the hands quickly. Vary by starting with a short run. Be sure that the feet come up to the hands rather than the hands moving down to touch the feet. Do several *Jackknives* in succession. The take-off must be with both feet and good height must be reached.

HEEL AND TOE SPRING

The heels are against a line. The object of the stunt is to jump backwards over the line while bent over and grasping the toes. Lean

forward slightly to allow for impetus and then jump backward over the line. Try jumping forward to original position. To be successful, the grasp on the toes should be retained.

Introduce the stunt by having the children grasp their ankles when making the jumps. This is less difficult.

FOREARM HEADSTAND

The stunt is similar to a *Headstand* except for the way the supporting base is formed. Take a kneeling position, with both elbows on the mat and the forepart of the head in the cupped hands. From this position, support the body in an inverted upright position. Spotters are needed on either side of the performer.

Variation: A second way to arrange the hand position for support is to have the hands on the floor with the palms down. A rest is made for the head by the thumbs and forefingers forming a small circle. The remainder of the fingers are spread and the elbows are out so that the base is a triangle formed by the hands and elbows. Spot in front.

Forearm Headstand

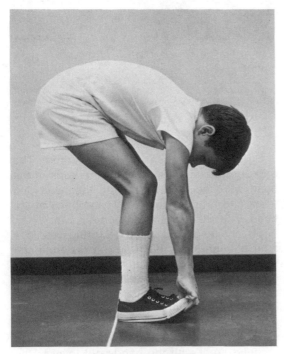

Heel and Toe Spring

FOREARM STAND

Forearm Stand

Place the forearms down on the mat with the palms down and the elbows out, forming a triangle base. Do an elbow stand so that the forearms and hands support the weight of the inverted body. Stress getting the center of gravity over the support base. There is more body curve in this stunt as compared with the head and hand stands. Spot if needed.

SINGLE LEG CIRCLE

Assume a squatting position with both hands on the floor, left knee between the arms, and the right leg extended to the side. Swing the right leg forward and under the lifted right arm, under the left leg and arm, and back

to starting position. Several circles should be made in succession. Reverse position and try with the left leg.

FRONT SEAT SUPPORT

Front Seat Support

Sit on the floor with the legs together and forward. The hands are placed flat on the floor, fingers pointed forward, somewhat between the hips and the knees. The stunt is in two stages.

1. Push down so the hips come off the floor with the weight supported on the hands and heels.

2. Support the entire weight of the body on the hands for 3 to 5 seconds. Assistance can be given with slight support under the heels to get into position.

ELBOW BALANCE

Elbow Balance

The object of this stunt is to balance the body face down horizontally on the two hands with the elbows supporting the body in the hip area. To get into position, support the arched body with the toes and forehead. Work the forearms underneath the body for support with the fingers spread and pointed to the back. Try to support the body completely on the hands for 3 seconds, with the elbows providing the leverage under the body. Assist by slight support under the toes.

THREE MAN ROLL (Triple Roll)

Practice and review the *Side Roll* (page 194). Three children get down on their hands and knees on a mat with heads all in the same direction to one of the sides. The performers are about 4' apart.

The performers are numbered 1, 2, and 3, with the #1 child in the center. The action always starts with the center child. #2 is on the right and #3 on the left. #1 starts rolling toward and under #2, who projects himself upward and over the player underneath him. #2 is now in the center and rolls toward #3,

who projects himself upward and over #2. #3, in the center, rolls toward and under #1 who, after clearing #3, is now back in the center. Thus, each performer in the center rolls toward and under the outside performer. The children should be taught that just as soon as they roll to the outside, they must get ready immediately to go over the oncoming child from the center. There is little time for delay. The upward projection of the body to allow the rolling child to go under is important.

DEAD MAN LIFT

One child lies on his back on the floor with body stiff and arms at the side. Two helpers

Dead Man Lift

stand, one on either side of the "dead man" with hands at the back of his neck and fingers touching. Working together, they lift the dead man in his rigid body position to standing position.

INJURED MAN CARRY

The "injured" child is lying on the ground on his back. Six children, three on each side, kneel down to lift him up. The injured child must maintain a stiff position. The lifters work

Injured Man Carry

their hands, palms upward, under him forming a human stretcher, and lift him up. They walk a short distance and set the injured person down carefully.

Partner Support Stunts

Basic instructions for partner support stunts (page 224) should be reviewed.

Knee and Shoulder Balance

KNEE AND SHOULDER BALANCE

The support partner is on his back, knees well up and feet flat on the floor. He puts his hands out ready to support the shoulders of the top man, who takes a position in front of the support's knees, on which he places his hands. He leans forward so his shoulders are supported by the hands of the bottom partner, and kicks up to a hand and shoulder stand.

Spotters are needed on either side of the pair. If the top man begins to fall, the support partner should maintain the support under his shoulders so that he will light on his feet. Key points for the top partner are to keep his arms straight and his head up so he can look directly into the support partner's eyes.

PRESS

The bottom partner lies on his back with knees bent and feet flat on the floor. The top

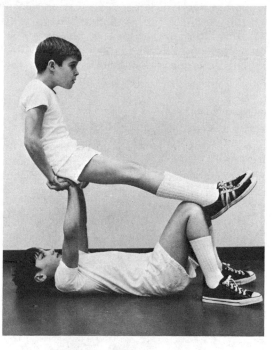

Press

partner takes a straddle position over the bottom partner. Both performers now join hands with each other. The top partner sits on the joined hands, supported by the bottom partner, and rests his legs across the bottom partner's knees. Both performers need to keep elbows straight. Hold for a specified time.

3. ALL FOURS SUPPORT

The bottom performer lies on his back with legs apart and knees up. His hands are positioned close to his shoulders with the palms up. The top performer stands on these hands and leans forward, placing his hands on the

support performer's knees. The support raises the top performer up by lifting him up with his arms. The top performer is now in an all fours position, with his feet supported by the bottom performer's extended arms and his hands supported on the bottom performer's knees.

4. THE ANGEL

The Angel is formed by the top performer standing erect on the support's knees with his arms level out to the side. The bottom performer takes hold of the top's thighs and

Angel

leans back to place the figure in balance. Hold for 5 seconds.

To get into this position, the top performer stands in front of the support partner. Support squats down and places his head between the legs of the top performer. Support raises up so that top is sitting on his shoulders. As the top performer proceeds to take his position on support's knees, support must lean well back for balance, removing his head

from between the top performer's legs. Children will need to experiment with each other to determine the best way to achieve the final position.

5. SIDE STAND

Support gets down on hands and knees to form a rigid base. Top performer stands to the side, hooks his hands, palms up, well underneath the chest and waist. He leans across, steadying with his hands, kicking up to an inverted stand. Spotters are needed on the far side.

Side Stand

Variation: The top performer instead of hooking his hands underneath supports himself by grasping the bottom performer's arm and leg.

MERRY-GO-ROUND

Eight children are needed to form the Merry-Go-Round. Four children form a circle with joined hands, using a wrist grip. Each of the remaining children drapes himself over figures presented are composed of three performers, four and five performers can be combined into similar formations.

Selected Pyramids

A pyramid is composed of a center group and two side groups, usually similar to give balance and symmetry to the entire group. Pyramid building is an excellent squad activity. The class can also be divided into larger groups, each with a leader.

Each group or squad is given the task of assembling a pyramid. After a period of practice, the groups can exhibit their pyramid. The teacher can circulate from group to group, giving help as needed.

Should the teacher wish to use pyramids for demonstration purposes, whistle signals or spoken commands can use the following pattern. Children should be at attention along a line or at the edge of the mats (if used).

Signal 1. All base performers get in position and top performers move to place.

Signal 2. All top performers mount and get into position.

Signal 3. Hands are out to the sides or up for the finishing touch. This signal is used to show the pyramid in all of its glory.

Signal 4. Pyramid is disassembled and children move to line and stand at attention.

Children should not do pyramids unless the appropriate basic balance skills have been mastered. Stunts using only one performer or pairs should also be considered in pyramid building.

Merry-Go-Round

pair of joined hands in the following fashion, to become a rider. The rider stretches out his body, face up, toward the center of the circle, with his weight on his heels. He leans back on a pair of joined hands and connects his hands *behind* the circle of standing children with the hands of the riders on either side of him. Thus, there are two sets of joined hands, the first circle or Merry-Go-Round and the four riders.

Movement of the Merry-Go-Round is counterclockwise. The circle children providing the support use side steps. The riders keep pace with small steps taken with their heels.

Try with ten or twelve children.

PYRAMIDS

Pyramids are pleasurable activities for children and provide a use for many of the skills and abilities learned in the stunts and tumbling program. The emphasis in this section is on smaller pyramid groups. A larger pyramid can be formed by utilizing three of the smaller groups. Pyramids provide opportunity for movement exploration, as the variety of figures that can be made are endless. While the

16

Relays

Relays have an important place in the program of physical education. Not only do they offer fun and enjoyment, but when properly conducted they provide good values in fitness, skills, and social objectives. Children learn to cooperate with others in the interest of winning, to conform to rules and regulations, and to use skills in situations of stress and competition. However, if rules are not enforced and the child finds that he can get by without obeying them, he is learning that he can win by cheating.

The various components of fitness can be promoted through careful selection of the movements and distances for each relay. Little equipment is needed, and relays can be selected and varied to meet almost any situation. Relays which demand strength, balance, agility, speed, and coordination have good values for physical fitness.

Relays can be combined with the teaching of skills. After skills have been taught and practiced sufficiently, they can be incorporated into relays. Children need to have mastered skills sufficiently before they enter relay competitions, otherwise they forget to perform the skills correctly in the haste to win.

In this presentation relays begin in the second grade as the individualistic characteristics of the younger children do not lend themselves well to organized team efforts. However, some preliminary work can be done in the kindergarten and first grade.

Relay formations are presented in the discussion of movement on pages 75-76.

Relays require a few special items for operation, such as blocks, pie plates, and standing pegs, which are used only for this purpose. These can be kept in a small wire or metal basket.

TYPES OF RELAYS

Three types can be identified according to the participation of the players:

Regular Relays. In this type each player completes his chore when it is his turn and then retires from action.

Revolving Relays. In a revolving relay, each player participates both when it is his turn and also as a part of the relay task. An example of this is found in a ball-handling relay in which each player handles the ball on each turn as in *Arch Ball* or *Corner Fly* relay.

Modified Relays. These are number-calling relays. They are not true relays in the sense of one player completing a chore and tagging off the next player. However, they have their place in the program, providing opportunity for alertness and quick reaction when one's number is called.

INSTRUCTIONAL PROCEDURES

1. Place from four to eight players on a team. Too many on a team drags out the race and the children lose interest.

2. If the teams have uneven numbers, either some players on the smaller teams should run twice, or a rotation system should be set up by which the extra players wait out in turn.

3. Be definite regarding the starting point, the turning point, and the finishing act. In some races, crossing the line may be the finishing act. In others the captain may be required to hold up the ball while the rest of the players are in a specified formation. A definite finishing act prevents arguments with regard to the determination of the winner.

4. In many relays, particularly of the revolving type, it helps to keep things straight if the last player or runner has some kind of identification. Armbands of crepe paper, hats, pinnies, or colored shirts provide good identification. This keeps the teacher informed of the progress of the race and allows him to anticipate the finish. The teacher can line himself with the finish line so he can make a judgment of the winner.

5. Appoint a captain for each team. Let him arrange the order, be responsible for the application of the rules, and help keep things under control.

6. Be careful of putting too much emphasis on winning. Too much pressure makes the skilled resent being on teams with those who are less able to perform.

7. Demonstrate a relay just enough so that each team understands the procedures. This can entail a simple demonstration by one individual or having the entire team practice the routine. If the new relay does not seem to be started properly, stop the group and review the instructions.

8. Any dropped or mishandled ball must be retrieved by the person dropping it. It must be started by him in the proper sequence at the point where it was dropped.

9. Distances need to be modified when restricted movements are used, such as the *Puppy Dog Run,* the *Crab Walk,* and others where the physical demands are heavy. When hopping is used, a change to the other foot should be made halfway through the race.

10. Make some rules about the handling of supplies. Have a central source, and appoint one person from each team to secure and return equipment.

11. A block, beanbag, traffic cone, Indian club, chair, standard, or other definite marker should be used for a turning point. A definite turning point is better than just having the children run to a line and back.

12. Infractions should be penalized. It is good social learning for the children to experience the situation where they must conform to rules or be assessed with a penalty. A team could be disqualified, points deducted, or other penalties imposed. Impartiality should be the rule. All teams and players should be on an equal basis.

13. For modified relays, the teacher should make up a card with a list of numbers to ensure that all numbers will be called without the need to stop the activity to make this determination.

SELECTED RELAYS

Relays should be selected in keeping with the children's previous experience in stunts and skills. Relays have a universal appeal to children, and this makes it difficult to pinpoint various relays to different grades. However, allocation is desirable so that the children, having followed the progression of relays in this guide, will have experienced a varied and interesting program and secured good fitness values.

KINDERGARTEN AND FIRST GRADE APPROACH

While relays, as such, are a little beyond the capacity of most kindergarten and first grade children, some experiences of handling beanbags and yarn balls in relay sequence are of value. Place the children in a line (side by side) formation and have them pass the articles down to the end, or arrange them in a circle formation and have them pass the beanbag around the circle. The object of the activity is to pass well and not drop the article. Some attention can be given to seeing which group can do it first, but this should not be the goal. The objective should be learning to participate in this kind of activity and to cooperate with others.

Another way to develop relay concepts is to place the squads or teams in a squad file formation and then proceed as follows:

1. The first child (head of the file) in each

team moves toward and around a given turning point a short distance away and is asked to return to his place and stand quietly. The first child to complete this action successfully wins a point for his team.

2. The child is asked to go to the rear of the line and the next child has his turn.

3. The next step would be for the child to move directly without delay to the rear of the line after he has completed his turn and stand quietly. Learning to go around the designated side of the turning point and returning up the correct aisle for safety purposes can be conceptualized.

SECOND GRADE RELAYS

LANE RELAYS

With one player at a time running around a turning point and back, many different relays using the basic locomotor skills can be scheduled. Running, walking (forward and backward), hopping, skipping, galloping, sliding, and jumping are movements that can be used in relays.

BEANBAG PASS OR BALL PASS RELAY

Supplies: Beanbag or ball for each team.

Formation: Lane with players facing to the side.

The player on the right starts the beanbag or ball, which is passed from one player to the next down the line. When it gets to the end of the line, the race is over. Be sure each player handles the bag or ball. Rotate.

CIRCLE PASS RELAY

Supplies: Ball for each team.

Formation: Each team forms a separate circle of the same size. At first the circle should be small enough so that the players can hand the ball to each other. Later, as skill increases, the circles can be enlarged.

The leader of each group starts the ball around the circle by handing. As soon as the ball gets back to the leader, the entire team sits down. The first team to be seated in good formation wins.

BOUNCE BALL RELAY

Supplies: Ball that will bounce for each team.

Formation: Lane.

A circle is drawn 10' to 15' in front of each team. The first player runs to the circle, bounces the ball once, runs back to his team, and *gives* the ball to the second player, who repeats the same routine. Each player has a turn, and the team having the last man carry his ball back over the finish line wins. To vary, have the players bounce the ball more than once.

BOWL RELAY

Supplies: Ball for each team.

Formation: Lane.

The player at the head of each team has a ball. A line is drawn 15' to 20' in front of each team. The first player runs to the line, turns, and rolls the ball back to the second player. The second player must wait behind the starting line to catch the ball and then repeats the pattern of the first player. The race is over when the last player has received the ball and carried it over the forward line.

THIRD GRADE RELAYS

LANE RELAYS

Using lane formation and a turning point, lane relays should employ running, walking, and other locomotor movements. In addition, relays can use the animal imitations explained in the stunts and tumbling program. The following are excellent for lane relays:

Puppy Dog	Crab Walk
Bear Walk	Seal Crawl
Rabbit Jump	Pogo Stick
Lame Dog Walk	Measuring Worm

PARTNER RELAYS

Supplies: None.

Formation: Lane formation of partners.

Children run with partners (inside hands joined) just like a single runner. Use running, walking, skipping, hopping, and galloping. Sliding can be used to make an interesting relay. Children face each other with both hands joined (as partners) and slide one way to a turning point, sliding back to starting point leading with the other side.

CROSS OVER RELAY

Supplies: Ball for each team.

Formation: Lane.

Review *Bowl Relay* from the second grade. This relay is similar. Two lines are drawn about 15' apart. The teams are in lane formation behind one of the lines. The player in front has a ball. On signal, each player with a ball runs to the next line and tosses the ball back to the one at the head of the line, who runs forward and repeats the throw. The race is over when the last player in line catches the ball and runs forward across the forward line.

SNOWBALL RELAY

Supplies: None.

Formation: Lane.

Teams are in lane formation, but the lanes must be from 10' to 15' apart. The first player runs forward, around the turning point, and back to his team, where he takes the next player by the hand. He repeats the trip with the second player in tow. When the two reach the team again, the second player takes the hand of the third one in line. The trip is repeated and so on until, on the last trip, the entire team will run around the turning point and finish over the starting line.

Variation: There is a variation of this race called *Locomotive.* The second player hooks on the engine (first player), and in turn each of the players hooks on until the entire team forms a train.

PASS THE BUCK RELAY

Supplies: None.

Formation: Lane with teams facing sideways.

Players are facing sideways with lanes about 5' apart. All players of a team are linked by joining hands. The leader is on the right of each team. On signal, the leader "passes the buck" to the next player (by squeezing his hand), who in turn passes the squeeze to the next and so on down the line. The end player, when he receives the "buck," runs across the front of his team and becomes the new leader. He starts the squeeze, which is passed down the line. Each player, in turn, comes around to the end of the line with the original leader finally returning to his original position.

Variation: Instead of "passing the buck," teams could pass a beanbag, Indian club, or ball.

STOOP AND STRETCH RELAY

Supplies: Beanbag for each team.

Formation: Lane.

The players stand in lane formation about 2' apart. The player in front has a beanbag which he reaches over his head and drops. Using *both* hands, the second player picks the bag up, reaches over his head, and drops it behind him. The bag continues down the line until the last player picks it up. He comes to the front of the line and starts the bag back down the line. Each player in turn comes to the front, and the relay is over when the team has returned to its original position.

BENCH RELAYS

Formation: Lane. A balance beam bench or ordinary bench is in front of each two teams.

Procedure: Several interesting races can be run using benches. The following are suggested:

1. Run forward, jump over the bench, jump back again, return, and tag off.

2. Each team has a beanbag. Run to the bench, pass the beanbag underneath, and return to the team, giving the beanbag to the next player, who repeats the run.

3. Each team has a beanbag which is placed about 3' in front of the bench. The first player runs forward, picks up the beanbag and jumps over the bench carrying the bag with him. He drops it on the far side of the bench. He then jumps back over the bench and tags off. The next runner jumps over the

bench, picks up the bag, jumps back over the bench with the bag, and places the bag on the floor near original position. The players alternate carrying the bag over and bringing it to the near side.

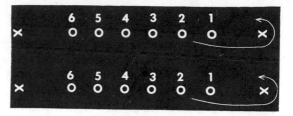

FOURTH GRADE RELAYS

LANE OR SHUTTLE RELAYS

1. Fundamental Movements. Running forward or backward, hopping forward and backward, jumping.

2. Stunt Movements. *Puppy Dog Run, Rabbit Jump, Crab.*

3. Simple Soccer skill, dribbling.
bling.

4. Variety Movements. Walking on heels, walking heel and toe, alternate double gallops, etc.

GYM SCOOTER RELAYS

Formation: Lane or shuttle. Each team has a gym scooter.

Procedure: If lane formation is used, a definite turning point around which the scooter is to go is needed. Scooters lend themselves to a wide variety of movements, both individually and with a partner. However, scooters should not be used as skate boards, employing a standing position.

Some suggestions for individual movements are:

Seated, propelling with the hands or the feet.

Kneeling, propelling with the hands.

Face down, moving in alligator or swimming fashion.

In working with doubles, the system can be employed where one partner pushes or pulls the other on the scooter to the turning point, where a change is made of rider and pusher. The other system is to have the child supplying the moving force become the next rider at the return to the team restraining line, where the next relay member becomes the pusher.

ATTENTION RELAY

Formation: Players of each team are facing forward in lane formation about arm's dis-

tance apart. The distance between teams should be about 10'. Two turning points should be placed for each team. One is 10' in front and the other 10' behind each team.

Procedure: Players on each team are numbered consecutively from front to rear. The teacher calls "Attention." All come to the position of attention. The teacher calls out a number. The player on each team holding this number steps to the right, runs around the front and the back marker, and returns to place. The first team to have all members of the team at attention, including the returning runner, wins a point.

Teaching Suggestion: The numbers should not be called in consecutive order, but all members should be called. Be sure there is enough distance between teams so the runners will not collide in the spaces between teams.

Variations:

1. Use different means of locomotion.

2. Organize the teams by pairs and have two run at a time, holding inside hands.

3. *Under the Arch.* The leader calls two consecutive numbers, for example, 3 and 4. Immediately, #3 and #4 on each team face each other and form an arch by raising both hands. The players in front of the arch (#1 and #2) run forward, go around the front marker, run to the back marker, around it, and then back to place, passing under the arch. The players behind the arch run under the arch first, run around the front marker, around the back marker, and back to place. When all have returned to place, the arch players drop hands and resume position. The first team to be at attention is the winner.

Note that the running is always forward at the start. Each player follows the person ahead of him, keeping in place. Each goes around the front marker, around the back marker, and back to place. At the appropriate time, while taking this path, the players pass under the arch.

ARCH BALL RELAY

Formation: Lane, with the player at the head of each team holding a ball.

Procedure: Each head player, using both hands, hands the ball over his head to the next person and so on down the line. The end man, on receiving the ball, runs to the head of the line, and the race continues as he passes the ball over his head. Each player has a turn at the head of the line, and when the original head returns with the ball to his place at the head of the line, the race is over.

Teaching Suggestion: Each player must handle the ball with both hands.

CARRY AND FETCH RELAY

Formation: Lane, with a circle 20" in diameter 30' in front of each team.

Procedure: Each team has a beanbag or block of wood. The first runner carries the object to the circle, runs back, and tags off. The next runner fetches the object back and hands it to the third runner, who carries it forward to the circle. The relay continues until each player has either "carried" or "fetched" the object.

CORNER FLY (Spry) RELAY

Formation: Leader and line.

Procedure: The players are in a line, facing the leader, who has a ball which he passes to and receives from each player beginning with the player on *his* left, with the exception of the last player (on his right). When

this player receives the ball, he calls out "Corner Fly." He runs forward and takes the spot of the leader, who takes a place in the line to the left. In the meantime, all players adjust positions, moving over one place to fill the spot vacated by the new leader. The relay continues with each player becoming the leader in turn. When the original leader returns to his spot with the ball, the relay is over.

FIVE IN A ROW RELAY

Formation: Lane. A line is drawn about 20' in front of the teams.

Procedure: The front player of each team has five beanbags or blocks. On signal the front player hops forward and places the five objects, one at a time, reasonably spaced, with the last object placed over the line. He changes the hopping foot and returns hopping over each object until he reaches the farthest one. He changes his hopping foot and hops back, picking up the objects one at a time. He hands the objects to the third player, who puts out the objects again. Each player in turn either distributes or gathers the objects.

Teaching Suggestion: The objects should be spaced with the last object placed beyond the line. The last is important because it determines how far each player will need to hop. Note that the only means of locomotion is hopping.

FIFTH GRADE RELAYS

LANE AND SHUTTLE RELAYS

1, Fundamental Movements. Continue with various locomotor movements. Use various combinations. Hop sideward, jump, slide.

2. Stunt Movements. *Lame Dog, Seal, Crab* sideward and backward, *Goofy Walk, Toe Tug Walk, Measuring Worm.*

GYM SCOOTER RELAYS

Formation: Lane or shuttle. Each team has a gym scooter.

Procedure: Continue the scooter relays from the fourth grade. Add partner relays such as:

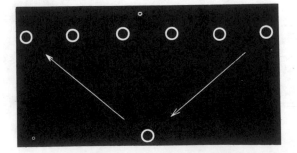

Rider kneeling, partner pushing or pulling.

Rider in seat balance, partner pushing or pulling on the feet of the rider.

Rider doing a tummy balance, partner pushing on the feet.

CHARIOT

Formation: Lane.

Procedure: Three children run as a single unit. Two of them stand side by side with inside hands joined, forming the "chariot." The "driver" stands behind and grasps the outside hands of the "chariot." Two or more chariots form a relay team. In front of each team is a turning point, around which the chariot must travel on its leg of the race. The chariot whose turn is next starts when the prior chariot crosses the original starting line. Running lanes must be spaced far enough apart to avoid collisions, as chariots demand considerable space while running.

KANGAROO

Formation: Lane or shuttle.

Procedure: The first player jumps forward with a ball between his knees held there by pressure. He goes the distance and then gives the ball to the next player. A beanbag can be used instead of a ball. Distance should be about 10 yards.

INDIAN CLUB RELAYS

Formation: Lane.

Procedure: There are a number of relays that can be run using Indian clubs.

1. *All Up, All Down.* Three Indian clubs are set in a small circle about 20' in front of each team. The first player runs forward and puts the Indian clubs down. The second runner goes forward and sets the clubs up one at a time, using only one hand. The clubs must stand. The next player puts them down, and so on.

2. Draw a short (24") line about 20' in front of each team. An Indian club is standing on one side of the line. Each player must run forward and stand the Indian club on the other side of the line, using one hand only.

3. Two adjacent circles are drawn about 20' in front of each team. Three Indian clubs are standing in one of the circles. Each runner in turn runs forward and, using one hand only, moves the clubs one at a time so they will stand in the other circle. The next player moves the clubs back one at a time to the original circle.

4. *Roll and Set.* Each team has a mat and an Indian club. The mat is placed lengthwise in front of the team, and the club is on the floor near the edge of the mat nearest to the team. The starting mark is about 5' from the edge of the mat. The first player runs toward the mat, picking up the club. With the club carried in his hand, he does a forward roll and sets the club beyond the far edge. He runs back and tags off the next player. This player runs to the club, picks it up, does a forward roll on the way back, and sets the club in the original spot. The players alternate in this fashion until all have run. The club must stand each time, or the player must return and make it stand.

OVER AND UNDER

Formation: Lane formation.

Procedure: Each player at the head of the line has a ball. The front player passes the ball over his head with both hands to the player behind him. This player passes the ball between his legs to the next player. The ball alternates over and under down the line. Each back player runs to the front and starts the over and under passing. When the team has returned to original position, it is through.

Variation: Instead of over and under, the ball can be passed right and left down the line.

PASS AND SQUAT

Formation: Lane with one player (#1) about 10' in front of his team.

Procedure: #1 has a ball. He throws it to #2, who returns the ball to #1, #2 squats down as soon as he has returned the ball to #1 so the throw can now be made to #3. When the last person in line receives the ball, he does not return it but carries it forward, straddling the members of his team including #1, who has taken a place at the head of the file. The player carrying the ball forward now acts as the passer and receiver. The race is over for a team when the original #1 player receives the ball in the back position and straddles the players back to his original position.

RESCUE RELAY

Formation: Lane with the first runner at a line about 30' in front of his team.

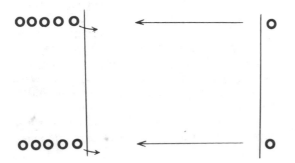

Procedure: The runner who is in front of his team runs back to the team, takes the first player in line by the hand, and "rescues" him to the 30' line. The player who has just been rescued, runs back and gets the next player, and so on until the last player has been conducted to the line.

Variation: The first player who runs back to begin the rescue routine can use either of the following carries to transport the next player. The players should be lined up in decreasing order according to their ability to carry. Generally, the player in front should be the biggest or strongest, and the weights of the others should be decreasingly lighter, with the smallest being carried last.

1. *Piggyback Carry*

The rider jumps up on the back of the carrier, who locks his arms under the rider's knees. The rider should be as high as possible.

2. *Fireman's Carry* (Not recommended for girls).

The rider takes a wide stride position with his right arm out somewhat to the side. The "Fireman" grasps the rider's right wrist with

his own left hand and, crouching down, puts his right arm through the rider's legs until his shoulder makes contact in the lower abdominal region of the rider. He then turns toward the rider's leg and picks up the rider across the back of his shoulders, retaining the hold of the rider's arm with the left hand. The rider should be high on the shoulder, and the lifting movement should be primarily with the legs.

Teaching Suggestion: The carries must be practiced before putting them into relays. Also, the child doing the carrying must release his hold on the rider immediately if he should begin to fall.

THREE SPOT RELAY

Formation: Lane. Three parallel lines are drawn in front of the teams at distances of 15', 30', and 45'.

Procedure. The three parallel lines in front of the teams provide three spots for each team. Each player is given three tasks to perform, one at each spot. He then runs back and tags off the next player who repeats the performance. Suggestions for tasks are:

Prone (face down on the floor).

Back (lie on back on floor).

Obeisance (touch forehead to floor).

Nose and Toe (touch toe to nose from sitting position).

Do a specified number of hops, jumps, push-ups, sit-ups, etc.

Perform a designated stunt such as the *Coffee Grinder, Knee Dip,* etc.

Rope Jumping with specified turns.

Teaching Suggestions: It must be made clear that the runner must perform according to the designated directions at each spot. He must complete the performance before moving to the next spot. Many other task ideas can be used. An excellent idea is to have the winning team select the requirements for the next race.

BEANBAG LEG PASS RELAY

Formation: Lane. Each member of the team is on his back, his arms out to the side, an his feet and legs perpendicular to the ground. The first player has a beanbag by his feet.

Procedure: The first player picks up the beanbag between his feet and passes it back over his head to the next player who takes it with his feet, and passes it on. Teams are not permitted the use of hands, as the beanbags must be handled entirely by the feet. The relay is over when the last person places the beanbag on the floor behind him. A little experimentation will determine the distance each player should be positioned from the next in order to pass the beanbag efficiently.

ESKIMO RELAY

Formation: Lane. Each team has two squares of cardboard about 2′ by 2′. Players race two at a time.

Procedure: The cardboards represent cakes of ice, and the task is to use the cardboards as stepping stones. One player is the stepper, and one handles the cardboards. The stepper may not touch the floor. There are two ways this can be operated in lane formation. The first is to have the cardboard player handle the cardboards to a turning point and then exchange places. The second is to operate on a crossover basis where the cardboard player conveys the stepper to the distant mark, and then brings the cardboards back. The cardboards are given to the next player at the head of the line, and the old cardboard player becomes the new stepper to be conveyed across.

Variation: The race can be run in shuttle formation with the children working in pairs. The children should go both ways (a second trip) during the race so that the stepper and cardboard handler exchange places.

SIXTH GRADE RELAYS

The sixth grade program should review and utilize the relays from the previous grades. In addition, the following have value.

LANE RELAYS

1. Continue with running, hopping, and jumping relays. Add *Sore-Toe,* where a player holds his left foot in front of him with his right hand. At the turning point, the right foot is held with the left hand.

2. Obstacles. Put three or four obstacles in a row in front of each team with the obstacles spaced evenly. Players weave in and out of obstacles in a figure eight fashion. Use with basketball and soccer dribbling techniques.

3. Continue with the various stunt races requiring the use of both hands and feet.

4. *Wheelbarrow Race.* One person walks on his hands while his partner holds him by the *knees,* wheeling him down to a mark. Change positions for the return.

5. *Piggyback Carry* and *Fireman's Carry.* These are described under the fifth grade relays. Be sure partners are about the same size. Have one partner carry the other to a turning point, and then reverse the positions for the return trip.

6. *Sedan Carry.* Three children run at one time, two to carry and one to ride. To form a seat for the carry, two children face each other. Each grasps his own left wrist with his right hand. The open hand now grasps the partner's wrist. The person carried sits on the seat and puts his hands around the necks of the carriers.

7. Different Movements. Each runner uses a different locomotor movement when he runs.

GYM SCOOTER RELAYS

Formation: Lane or shuttle. Each team has a scooter.

Procedure: Continue the scooter relays from the previous grades, adding challenges and more demanding movements. Add the scooter wheelbarrow race to the partner relays.

AROUND THE BASES

Formation: Four bases are laid out like a baseball diamond. Two teams compete at a time, lined up at opposite bases on the inside of the diamond.

Procedure: The lead-off player for each team makes one complete circuit of the bases, followed by each player in turn.

Variation: The same type of relay can be

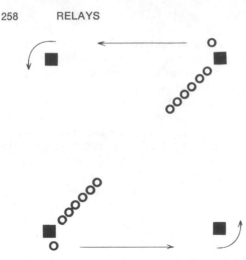

run indoors using chairs or Indian clubs at the four corners. Further variation can be made by requiring the children to run more than one lap or circuit on a turn.

CIRCULAR ATTENTION

Formation: Two teams form a circle facing counterclockwise, each occupying one-half the circle. The players of each team are numbered consecutively.

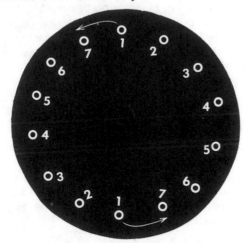

Procedure: The teacher calls the group to attention. Then, a number is called. The children holding this number (one on each team) immediately run forward (counterclockwise) around the circle and back to place, standing at attention. The first to get back at attention scores a point for his team. Call numbers until all have run.

Variation: *Circle Leapfrog.* All players are crouched down on their knees with their fore-

heads supported in cupped hands on the floor, facing counterclockwise. When a number is called, the runner straddles or leapfrogs all the children around the circle and back to place, resuming the original position. Scoring is the same as in *Circular Attention.*

HIP HIKING RELAY

Formation: Shuttle relay with the halves about 10′ apart.

Procedure: Children take a position sitting on the floor with the legs forward, the weight of the legs on the heels, and the knees bent at about 90 degrees. The arms are crossed in front and held out at shoulder level. Progress is made by reaching out with the heels and then bringing the seat forward. The first child of one shuttle line hikes forward to the other shuttle half, tagging off a child who hikes back.

Teaching Suggestions: Hip Hiking Relay has good posture values in the development of the pelvic region. However, it is a strenuous exercise and children should not hike too far during early stages.

JACK RABBIT RELAY (Jump Stick Relay)

Formation: Lane. Each runner carries a broomstick or wand 3½′ to 4′ long. A turning point is established about 30′ in front of each lane.

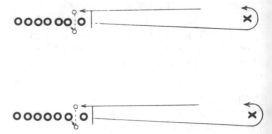

Procedure: Each player carries the broomstick and rounds the turning point from the right side. The race starts with the first player in line running forward around the turning point and back to the head of the line. In the meantime, the next player takes a short step to the right and gets ready to help with the stick. The runner with the stick is now returning on the left side and shifts the stick to his left hand. The second player reaches out his right hand and takes the other end of the stick at the head of the line. The stick is now carried under the others who must jump up to let the stick go past. When the stick has passed under all the players, the original player releases his grip and remains at the end of the line. The second runner runs around the turning point, and the next player in line helps him with the stick, becoming the next runner when the stick has gone under all the jumpers. Each player repeats until all have run.

Teaching Suggestion: If the children are unfamiliar with the relay, some practice is needed. When the children carry the stick back under the jumpers, it should be quite close to the ground.

PONY EXPRESS (Carrying the Mail)

Formation: Lane, with a turning point 20′ in front of each lane.

Procedure: The smallest child of each team is the "mail." The "mail" is carried piggyback by each runner in turn around the turning point and back to the starting line. The race begins with the "mail" in horse and rider position on the first runner. After the runner finishes his lap, the "mail" is transferred to the next runner without touching the ground. The race is over when the last runner has carried the "mail" back across the finish line.

Teaching Suggestion: The carry should be made high on the back. When the transfer of the "mail" is made, the two runners concerned should stand side by side to make the transfer.

POTATO TYPE RELAYS

Formation: Lane, with a small box about one foot square placed 5′ in front of each lane. Four twelve-inch circles are drawn at intervals of 5′ beyond the box. This makes the last circle 25′ from the starting point. Four blocks or beanbags are needed for each team.

Procedure: To start, the blocks for each team are placed in the box in front of it. The first runner goes to the box, takes a single block, and puts it in one of the circles. He returns to the box each time and places the blocks

one at a time in the circles. When the four blocks are in the circles, he tags off the second runner. This runner brings the blocks back to the box one at a time and tags off the third runner, who returns the blocks to the circles, and so on.

![Diagram showing two rows with five circles, a box, and dots at intervals]

Variation: The race can be run using Indian clubs. Instead of using a box, draw a circle large enough to contain four Indian clubs.

Teaching Suggestions: The use of the box to receive the blocks makes a definite target for the blocks to be placed. When the blocks are returned to the circles, some regulation must be made regarding the placement. The blocks should be considered placed only if they are inside or touching a line. Blocks outside need to be replaced. Paper plates can be used instead of circles drawn on the floor.

PRONE RELAYS

Formation: Players are lying face down on the floor in a circle with their heads toward the center of the circle and hands joined.

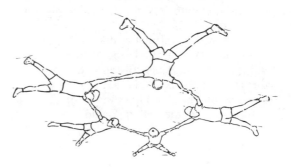

Procedure: Players on each team are numbered consecutively. When a number is called, the player with that number runs around or over the players on his team and back to place in prone lying position with hands rejoined. The first player back scores a point for his team. Play for a definite score or until all numbers have been called.

Variations:

1. *Human Hurdle.* Each team forms a small circle sitting with backs to the center of the circle. Otherwise, procedure is the same.

2. *Cyclone.* This is a team race and the team getting back to the original place first is the winner. At the starting signal, the #1 player gets up and starts around the group. Immediately after #1 passes him, the second player follows. The third player follows just as soon as #1 and #2 have passed him. The remainder of the players follow in the same manner. When #1 gets back to his place, he takes his original position. Each player in turn goes around until he gets back to his original place.

Note that the last player cannot move until all the other players have gone by him. Only then does he start his trip around the circle. When he gets back to place, the race is over. This race can be done from the original prone position or from the sitting position.

STRADDLE BALL RELAY

Formation: Lane.

Procedure: Players stand with a wide straddle, forming an alley between their legs. The player at the head of each team has a ball. He bends over, rolls the ball between their legs, and sends it down the alley to

the last man. The last player in line takes the ball between his legs, and sends the ball to the head of the line, and the routine is repeated in turn by each player. The team which rotates back to orginal position first wins.

Variation: This relay can be combined with basketball shooting drills. The teams are lined up facing a basket. Instead of the back man merely moving to the front of his team, he dribbles to the basket before proceeding to the head of his team. Many interesting combinations of scoring can be used in this relay.

TADPOLE RELAY

Formation: One team forms a circle facing in and has a ball. Another team is in lane formation with the head of the lane 10' from the circle.

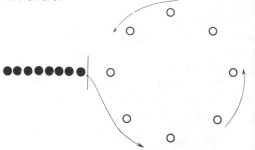

Procedure: The objective of the game is to see how many times the ball can make complete circuits of the circle by passing to each player while the other team completes a relay. The other team is in lane formation facing the circle and lined up behind a line 10' from the circle. Each player in turn runs around the outside of the circle and tags off the next runner until all have run. In the meantime, the ball is being passed around the circle on the inside. Each time the ball makes a complete circuit, the circle players count the number loudly. After the relay has been completed and the count established, the teams trade places and the relay is repeated. The team making the highest number of circuits by passing is the winner. The relay gets its name because the formation resembles a tadpole.

Variation: Vary with different types of passes and different methods of locomotion by the running team.

17

Combative Activities

Combatives are a "natural" for the program, as children love to pit strength and wits against fellow students. The cultural foundations for such activities as wrestling, boxing, judo, and fencing lie deep in our social structure. Combatives, we feel, should begin in the fourth grade and continue through the school years.

Contests can be between individuals or groups. Most of the emphasis in the program will be on individual competition, but some group activity is included.

The more rugged, struggling types of combatives are more attractive to boys than to girls. One suggestion for handling this problem is to keep the rougher types of combatives to a minimum when a mixed class is participating. Another is to schedule different types of combatives for boys and girls. Boys and girls may intermingle in tug-of-war group contests, but in most combatives separation by sex is desirable. The same activities can be scheduled, but with girls competing against girls and boys against boys.

The individual tug-of-war rope is excellent for isometric activities. Suggested isometric activities with ropes are placed at the end of this chapter. It is recommended that a few isometric exercises be practiced each time the children use tug-of-war ropes. In addition to isometrics, a few resistive movements are suggested.

INSTRUCTIONAL PROCEDURES

1. Contest instructions should be explicit as needed. The starting position should be defined so that both contestants begin from an equal, neutral position, neither having an unfair initial advantage. This concept is carried into the contest rules of how each attempts to overcome the other. What constitutes a win must be defined, including the number of trials.

2. Equate competition. When contestants of somewhat equal ability are matched, contests become more interesting because of the uncertainty of the outcome. Matching should be such that all children can win at least part of the time.

3. Sportsmanship should be stressed. Children should be encouraged to find all possible strategies and maneuvers to gain success, but only in the framework of the rules and fair means.

4. Safety factors are a greater consideration in group contests than in individual combat. Good supervision and a quick whistle are needed. Children should learn to freeze when the whistle is blown, as a child may be down in a dangerous position.

In tug-of-war contests, either individual or team, no one should suddenly let go of the rope to send the children at the other end of the rope sprawling backwards.

5. Contests can be conducted en masse on signal by the teacher, or more flexibility can be incorporated into class activity by allowing children to start contests on their own.

6. Laterality is a factor. Contests should be done with the right side (arm or leg), the left side, and the neutral position (both arms or both legs).

7. Body position can be varied. Children can utilize standing, crouching, sitting, and lying positions for the same contest.

8. Work out a system of rotation, so that a contestant will have more than one evenly matched opponent.

FORMATIONS FOR CONDUCTING COMBATIVE ACTIVITIES

Because of their nature combative activities need special consideration when arranging children for participation. Except in the first suggested formation, the emphasis is on some kind of rotation.

By Pairs. Children are paired up with a person of comparable ability. Direction can be by signal or at will of the contestants. This formation keeps everyone active and is more informal than those which follow.

Groups of Threes. The children are divided into groups of threes. In any three, two players compete against each other, and the third child acts as the referee. Opponents are changed and another child referees. One more change completes a round.

Winner-Loser Eliminations by Groups of Fours. Four evenly matched contestants are grouped together. In each activity they are matched by pairs with the winners competing against each other and the losers for third place. To save time, in the next combative activity each individual should compete against the partner with whom he just finished. Winners again compete against winners and losers against losers.

Double Line by Teams. Two teams of four to five on each team compete against each other. The teams are in lines facing each other. Each child pairs off with an opponent facing him. After competing against an opponent, the children in one of the teams rotate in the following manner: The child on the left moves behind his team and takes a new position on the right side of his team's line. All other members of his team move down one place to the left to face a new opponent. The members of the other team maintain their positions.

Double Circle by Teams. One team forms a large circle with the members facing the center of the circle. The members of the other team pair off against this team on the inside, in effect forming another circle. After each bout, the contestants move to the next opponent on the left. One of the circles can remain stationary, with the other moving to the left to find new partners.

ACTIVITIES BY GRADE LEVEL

Fourth Grade

HAND WRESTLE

Starting Position: Contestants place right foot against right foot and grasp right hands in a handshake grip. The left foot is firmly implanted to the rear for support.

Action: Each contestant tries to force the other by hand and arm pressure to move either foot.

Variations:

1. Stand left foot against left foot and contest with the left hands.

2. Each contestant stands balanced on his right foot. Clasp right hands. A player loses if his right foot is moved or his back foot touches the ground. Try with the left foot and left hand.

TUG-OF-WAR (Individual)

The basic piece of equipment needed for the individual tug-of-war contests is a rope 5' or so long including a loop on each end. To make the rope, cut a piece of rope 10' long. Heavy sash cord is good. Use two pieces of garden hose each about 24" long to line the loops. Thread the rope through the piece of hose and then tie the loop securely. The hose provides a reasonably good hand hold.

Starting Position: Two opponents face each other across a line.

Action: The first child to pull the other across the line wins.

Variations: Use various ways of pulling.

1. Right hand only, left hand only, both hands.

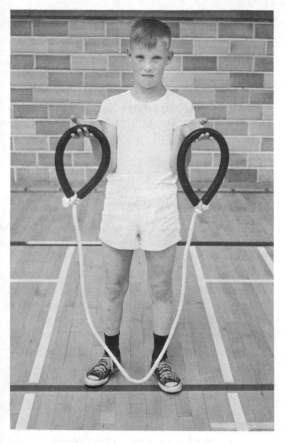

The Individual Tug-of-War Rope

2. Grasp with the right hand with the body supported on three points, the left hand and the feet. Change hands.

3. Pull with backs toward each other, with the rope between the legs.

Teaching Suggestion: If the distance to be pulled (over the line) seems not to be far enough, two parallel lines can be drawn from 8′ to 10′ apart. The contestants begin between the lines and attempt to pull the opponent out of the area between the lines.

TOUCH KNEES

Starting Position: On feet facing each other.

Action: The object is to touch one of the opponent's knees without having one's own knee touched in turn. Allow 5 touches to determine victory.

Variation: See who can step on the other's toes first.

ROOSTER FIGHT

Starting Position: Players stoop down and clasp hands behind the knees.

Action: The object is to upset the other player or make him lose his hand hold.

Variation: Squat down and hold the heels with the hands. Player loses if he is upset or his hands come loose from his heels.

ROOSTER FIGHT (Group Contest)

Starting Position: Rooster position as described in the previous contest. The children can be divided into two or more teams or the group can be on an individual basis to see which child can be the last one left.

Action: Place children around the edges of an area sufficient to contain the group. On signal, the children come forward and compete team against team or as individuals.

Fifth Grade

TUG-OF-WAR (Individual)

Repeat the tug-of-war stunts from the Fourth Grade. Add the following:

Pulling on Three Points

Pulling in Crab Position

1. Opponents are face down on all fours with the feet toward each other. Hook the loops around one foot of each opponent. The force is provided with both hands and the foot that is on the floor for each contestant.

2. Opponents in crab position. The rope is pulled by hooking a foot through the loop.

BREAKDOWN

Starting Position: Both opponents are in front leaning rest position facing each other. This is the push-up position.

Action: The object is to break down the other's position with the use of a hand by pushing or dislodging the support, and still maintain one's own position.

ELBOW WRESTLE

Starting Position: Lying on the floor or sitting at a table facing each other. Right hands are clasped with elbows held against each other.

Action: The object is to force the other's arm down while keeping elbows together.

Variation: Change to a position using left arms.

INDIAN WRESTLE (Leg Wrestle)

Starting Position: Two opponents lie on their backs on the floor or mat with heads in opposite directions, trunks close, and near arms locked at the elbows.

Action: Three counts are given. On each count each player lifts the leg nearest the opponent to a vertical position. On the third count, he hooks his opponent's leg near the foot with his heel and attempts to roll him over backward.

Variation: Use right and left legs in turn.

CATCH AND PULL TUG-OF-WAR
(Group Contest)

Starting Position: Two teams face each other across a line.

Action: The object is to catch hold of and pull any opponent across the line. When a player is pulled across the line, he waits back of the opponent's team until time is called. The team capturing the most players wins.

Variation: Have those pulled across the line join the other team. This keeps the children in the game but sometimes makes the players careless.

Teaching Suggestions: Pulling by catching hold of clothing or hair is not permitted. Penalty is disqualification. Players may cross the line to pull only if they are securely held by a teammate or chain of players.

Sixth Grade

TUG-OF-WAR

Review and use the individual tug-of-war contests from the Fourth and Fifth Grade. Add the following.

1. *Peg Pick-up.* Instead of having opponents pull each other across a line, put a peg (Indian club) behind each opponent at a suitable distance. Each one then tries to pull the other toward his own peg so he can pick it up.

2. *Four Corner Peg Pick-up.* Tie two individual ropes together at the center of each so that four loops are now available for pulling. Put four pegs in the form of a square and let four children contest to see who can pick up his peg.

3. *Doubles.* Have two children pull against two. The loops should be big enough so that both can secure handholds on them. Use right hands only, left hands only, etc.

4. *Japanese Tug-of-War.* Two children take hold of a rope, each with both hands on a loop. The children are positioned close enough together so that there is some slack in the rope. A third party grasps the rope to make a 6″ bend at the center. The contestants pull the rope so that there is no slack. On the signal "go" the third party drops the loop and the opponents try to pull the other off balance. To move a foot is to lose.

Teaching Suggestion: The individual tug-of-war rope offers good possibilities in movement exploration. Let the children try to devise other ways than those mentioned by which they can pull against each other.

SHOULDER SHOVE

Starting Position: On one foot with the other foot held by the opposite hand.

Action: Each contestant tries to knock or bump the other off balance so that he will let go of the leg.

Variations:

1. Have each child stand on one foot and fold arms. The aim is to knock the other player off balance so the uplifted foot will touch the ground.

2. Using a 6′ or 8′ circle, see which player can force the other out of the circle.

3. Use the kangaroo theme where each contestant must carry a volleyball between his legs at the knees. The object is to get him to lose control of the ball.

SHOULDER SHOVE (Group Contest)

Starting Position: Children may compete by teams or as individuals in a group contest. Have each take a position at the edges of the defined area.

Action: Any player losing his hand hold or touching the uplifted foot is eliminated. The team or individual lasting the longest wins.

Teaching Suggestion: Children may bump others from the front or side but not from the back on penalty of elimination.

Variation: *King of the Circle.* Draw a circle large enough to accommodate the group. Using the shoulder shove position, the children try to shove each other out of the circle or make others lose their shoulder shove positions. A quick whistle is needed to stop the action in case any player is down on the ground. The fallen players should be removed before the game is continued. No player may contact another from behind.

KING OF THE MAT

Starting Position: All players are on hands and knees on the edge of a large mat.

Action: Each player is trying to make another player touch any part of his body to the floor outside the mat.

Cautions: The activity can become rough and needs good supervision. Watch for unfair tactics. Players should keep on hands and knees. Boys and girls should not compete together.

Variation: The children can be divided into teams and compete team against team.

Teaching Suggestion: The game works best if the mat is a single one and not a combination of two or more mats. Smaller mats grouped together must be kept together if they are to be of use.

STICK WRESTLE

Starting Position: Two players face each other grasping a broomstick between them. Be sure the grips are fair, with each child having an outside hand.

Action: By twisting and applying pressure on the stick, either player tries to get the other to relinquish his grip.

Variations:

1. *Basketball Wrestle.* Use a basketball instead of a stick. Be sure each has the same grasp advantage at the start.

2. Have both players squat down while holding onto the stick. The object is to take away the stick or upset the opponent.

CHINESE PULL-UP

Starting Position: Opponents sit on the floor facing each other with knees straight and the soles of the feet against the opponent's soles. Each bends forward until he can grasp a broomstick between them.

Action: By a straight pull only, the object is to pull the other player forward or make him release his grip on the stick.

ROPE TUG-OF-WAR

Starting Position: Two equal teams face each other on opposite ends of a rope. A piece of tape marks the center of the rope. Two parallel lines are drawn about 10′ apart. At the start, the center marker is midway between the lines.

Action: Each team tries to pull the center marker over its near line.

Teaching Suggestions: The rope should be long enough to accommodate the children without crowding. It should be at least ¾″ in diameter. Never permit a child to wrap the rope around his hands, arms, or body in any manner.

Variations: Changes in the contest can be made by having the children in different positions for pulling. The following positions are suggested.

1. Pulling with the rope overhead. The teams have their backs toward each other.

2. Pulling with one hand on the ground.

3. Pulling from a seated position, with feet braced on floor.

ADDITIONAL ACTIVITIES WITH INDIVIDUAL TUG-OF-WAR ROPES

In working with individual tug-of-war ropes, three additional uses of the rope are suggested:

HAWAIIAN TUG-OF-WAR (Game)

Playing Area: Gymnasium playground. Two parallel lines are drawn about 20' apart.

Players: The game is between two people, but as many pairs as are in a class can play.

Supplies: An individual tug-of-war rope for each pair.

An individual tug-of-war rope is laid on the floor at right angles to and midway between the two parallel lines. The two children playing position themselves so each is standing about 1' from and facing one of the loops of the rope. This means that they are in position to pick up the rope and pull against each other on signal.

Hawaiian Tug-of-War

The object of the game is to pull the other child so you can touch the line behind you. The magic word is "hula." This signals for both children to pick up the rope and begin to pull. They must not reach down and pick up the rope unless "hula" is called. The teacher can use such commands as "go," "begin," and others trying to deceive the children.

ISOMETRIC ACTIVITIES WITH ROPES

The children should follow good isometric exercise principles, exerting sufficient force (near maximum), holding for 8 to 10 seconds, and stabilizing the base so that the selected part of the body can be exercised. Limbs should be bent about halfway, although it is preferable to use several joint angles.

As in other activities, grips can be varied. The upper grip (palms away) and the lower grip (palms toward performer) are utilized. Occasionally, a mixed grip with one hand in upper position and one hand in lower position can be used.

The force is a controlled pull, not a tug. The partner should not be forced to move his position. Much of the exercise is centered on the hands and arms, but other parts of the body come in by bracing. In the suggested exercises, partners work together. The position is the same for both partners. The exercises could also be done by one person, with the other end of the rope attached firmly to some part of the building. One or more basic activities are suggested for each position, and the teacher and children can devise others. Laterality must be kept in mind so that the right and the left sides of the body will receive equal treatment.

Standing with Sides Toward Each Other

1. Lower grip. Flexed arm pull, elbow at right angles.

2. Upper grip. Extended arm at 45 degrees from side. Pull toward side.

3. Lower grip. Arm extended completely overhead. Pull overhead.

Lower Grip, Flexed Arm Isometric

4. Loop around ankle. Feet are apart. Pull with near foot.

Partners Facing, Standing

1. Lower grip. Flexed arm pull, one hand and two hands.
2. Upper grip. Arm extended at side or down. Pull toward the rear.
3. Upper grip. Pull both hands straight toward chest.
4. Upper grip. Arms above head. Pull backwards.

Partners Facing, Seated

1. Repeat activities itemized above.
2. Hook on with both feet. Pull with both feet.

Partners on Stomach, Facing

1. Upper grip. Pull directly toward chest.

2. Lower grip. Flexed arm pull.

Partners in Prone Position, Feet Toward Each Other

1. Hook around one ankle. With knee joint at a right angle, pull.
2. Try with both feet together.

RESISTIVE EXERCISES

Using mostly the standing positions suggested for isometrics, work out resistive exercises in the following manner. One child pulls and makes progress with 8 steps. The other child then pulls him back for 8 counts. The addition of music makes this an interesting activity for children. The child being pulled out must provide the right amount of resistance to make the puller work reasonably hard.

18

Game-Type Activities

Every boy and girl in the public schools should have a chance to engage in a variety of games which are the collective heritage of centuries of children. The games have good recreational values, provide fitness values, and provide a necessary outlet for natural exuberance.

Some important objectives of a good games program for children are:

1. To provide a vigorous large-muscle activity with developmental potential, resulting in good muscular development and control.

2. To develop ability to run, maneuver, dodge, start, and stop.

3. To learn to manage and control one's body under stress.

4. To foster mental alertness in reacting strategically to the game situation.

5. To be able to understand and follow rules and directions.

6. To learn to play with others in a socially sound manner without bickering, quarreling, and fighting.

7. To encourage fair play and sportsmanship.

8. To understand self and others better.

The greatest values for physical fitness in the games program are inherent in those activities in which many children are active at once and must strain and "put out" good physical effort. Some games are useful, how-ever, in providing a period of lesser activity following a more strenuous activity. Games which make lesser demands on children are those in which there is a runner and a chaser while the remainder of the children have little part in the play.

Each game should be analyzed from the standpoint of whether or not it requires a skill which the children should practice before playing the game. If practice is indicated, the teacher selects the appropriate drills and brings the children up to the point of necessary skill to play the game pleasurably. Drills and the acquisition of necessary skills become more meaningful when the children see their purpose.

The games for kindergarten through second grade do not require a high degree of skill, and the lesser skilled children have an opportunity to excel. The third grade presents a different picture. While many of the games are of the so-called low-organized type, a number are introduced which represent the first lead-up activities in the program. A lead-up game is defined as one which introduces a skill, strategy, or part of a sport. By the time the children finish the sixth grade, they should have played regular or modified versions of basketball, softball, soccer, volleyball, and flag football (boys). Leading up to these sport-type games are simplified activities which employ one or two skills or portions from the sport. *Circle Kick Ball* is a good example of the principle of a lead-up activity. The children form a circle, and the ball is kicked back and forth until it goes between or through one of the players. The players learn to kick, trap, and defend. The concentration is on these skills.

Games for the intermediate grades are included in two sections in this book. This chapter presents tag-type and general games which do not fall under any of the sports type activities. The lead-up activities to basketball, football, volleyball, soccer, softball, and track are found with the discussions of each sport.

The intermediate grades should make use of all the primary games which are suitable or can be adapted to the intermediate program. Children in the intermediate grades enjoy and play many of the games which are introduced earlier, particularly in the third grade.

INTRODUCING VARIATIONS

The introduction of variations is an important instructional device which the games leader can use effectively. You can see the children's faces light up when the instructor says, "Let's try playing the game *this* way" and introduces an interesting variation. Variations can revive interest when it lags and can help the teacher to extract more "mileage" from an activity.

The following are effective devices which can be used to vary activities:

1. Change the distance to be run by shortening or lengthening it. For example, in *Circle Chase,* instead of having the runners go once around, double the distance.

2. Vary the runner's route. This is particularly helpful in circle games.

3. Change the method of locomotion. Use hopping, walking, skipping, galloping, etc., instead of running.

4. Play the game with partners. Have two children join inside hands and act as a single person.

5. Change the method of tagging. Limit where on the body a player may be tagged or with which hand he may be tagged.

6. Change the formation. For example, in *Circle Soccer,* make a square.

7. Vary the boundaries. Make the formation larger or smaller.

8. Include penalties. A person who is caught a number of times (say, three) has to undergo a penalty.

9. Increase the number of key men, taggers, or runners. This gets the game moving a little faster.

10. Use other helps or hindrances. In *Cat and Rat,* players may raise or lower arms, depending on whether the cat or the rat is coming through.

11. In tag or chase games, call out "Reverse." This means that the chaser now becomes the runner and the runner the chaser. Also, this can be used to change the direction of a ball around a circle.

12. Change the method or means of scoring. Make goals larger or smaller.

SAFETY SUGGESTIONS FOR GAMES

Because of the competitive spirit aroused, games have some built-in hazards which must be anticipated and for which safety considerations need to be established.

Slipping and Falling. Emphasis should be placed on the importance of running properly and practice in turning and changing direction properly. The playing area should be kept free of dangerous objects. The teacher should make certain that all players are aware of hazardous conditions of the playing area, such as slickness, holes, or loose pebbles.

Collisions and Tripping. Stress the need for all players to be alert. Goal games, where the children are divided and begin to run through each other from opposite goals, are collision-prone. If there is more than one chaser or catcher the danger is multiplied. The group should be scattered to avoid collisions. If players are running in opposite directions, they should pass each other to the right. Children should be taught to tag by touching, not shoving, and the teacher should insist that tagging be done properly.

Hitting Each Other with Wands, Beanbags, or Balls. Proper use of supplies should be taught.

Playing Dodgeball Games Safely. Dodgeball games for children provide much enjoyment and competition. Some controls are necessary, however. Glasses should be removed whenever possible. A soft, slightly deflated volleyball or rubber playground ball should be used. Avoid a basketball or heavy ball which may punish the players. Hits should be made below the waist or at least below the shoulders. A penalty should be imposed on any throw that hits a player on the head. Restraining lines, if carefully marked and observed, will prevent the thrower from getting too close to the targets. Good direction will prevent vicious throwing and ganging up on certain individuals. A better game results when teams are balanced and one or two players do not monopolize the throwing.

Maintaining Control. Participants should be coached to stop immediately when the whistle blows. A child may be down or some other safety hazard may need attention. The whistle should be used mainly for stopping the action. Start action with a verbal command.

Spatial Factors. Sufficient room for the games should be established. Colliding with fences and walls during running and chase games is an ever-present danger. Establish boundaries far enough from these and other obstacles to preserve safety. If separate groups of children are playing games, keep them far enough apart so they will not overrun each other.

MAINTAINING BALANCE IN GAMES

Balance between offense and defense or success and failure in games is important. In the tag or capture type game, there should be good opportunity to remain "safe" and still provide a strong challenge of being caught. This means that the teacher should look carefully at the basic rules concerning boundaries and other restraints. The distance to be run to a base, or between goal lines, can be lengthened or shortened as indicated.

Balance in games involving teams is important. The sides should be reasonably equated so that one side does not annihilate the other. If there is no chance of winning, children can hardly be expected to give it a good try. Rotate positions so that one or two very skilled

children will not dominate the game. On the other hand, take measures to see that the team does not lose continually because of the presence of a low-skilled or inept child, creating resentment against that child.

PRACTICAL SUGGESTIONS FOR CONDUCTING GAMES

1. The principal ingredient of successful games leadership is a vigorous, snappy approach. A hustling attitude combined with a spirit of enthusiasm will do much toward producing the desired results.

2. Know the game well before attempting to teach it. This means identifying the safety hazards, anticipating the difficulties, and adapting the game to the group and the situation.

3. Carry on much of the explanation in the classroom, so the youngsters have maximum activity on the playground.

4. Complete all preparations before starting to introduce the game. Draw lines and boundaries, and have supplies ready for distribution.

5. Put the group in formation with all possible speed. Be careful of too formal methods of organization. Use a modified "close" formation for explanations and then allow the children to fall back to game positions to start the activity.

6. Every unit or group should have a leader or someone in charge. Use these people to secure needed equipment for the game.

7. Where mingling of teams can cause confusion, identify a team with pinnies, crepe armbands, colored shoulder loops, or similar devices.

8. For maximum participation, divide the class into a number of groups as determined by the character of the activity. Many games play best with ten to fifteen players.

9. When explaining the game, talk briefly and to the point. Tell what is to be done and what is to be avoided. Demonstrate or diagram as needed. Students should be comfortable during explanations.

10. To clear up hazy points, ask for questions and then reply so all can hear. If desir-

able, repeat the question before supplying the answer.

11. Do not attempt to cover all rule infractions prior to participation. Cover enough to get the game underway and fill in with additional rules as needed. Minor faults can be corrected during the course of the game.

12. Sometimes it is well to have a trial period so children can understand the game before playing "for real." Children resent losing a point or getting caught if they feel this is due to their lack of understanding of the game.

13. Enforce the rules impartially once they have been established. Discuss the reasons for the rules with the children.

14. Where lines and limits are important, establish them definitely so that there is no question when a child is out of bounds or beyond the limits. Make clear and enforce the penalty for an infraction.

15. Suggestions for better performance and coaching hints should be a part of the instructional procedures in games. "Lean forward a little for a faster start," or "Give with your knees when you want to stop," are examples of appropriate comments by the teacher.

16. Play with the class occasionally. They like to have the teacher play with them. Do not dominate the play, however.

17. Watch the game carefully for a decrease of interest. Kill or change the game before it dies a natural death. Sometimes the teacher can stop a game even at the height of interest, and children will look forward with anticipation to the activity at a later time.

18. Stress social learning in game experiences. Allow children to call infractions or hits on themselves. Insist on respect for decisions by officials, particularly in judgment calls.

19. Be sure everyone has had a turn whenever this is practicable. Have children identify themselves by raising their hands or by the use of some other device to show that they have not had a turn.

20. Avoid overemphasis on competition. Centering too much attention on winning makes the skilled resent being on the same team with the less skilled.

21. Arrange for full participation. Rotate with a planned system or use the "sideline" players as officials or equipment monitors.

22. Most games can be modified to meet the equipment and supplies available. Some games, however, are best played with the equipment and supplies designed for them.

23. Help and encourage the losing side, but avoid biased officiating to aid the losing side. We want our children to be good losers but not "easy" losers.

24. Watch for fatigue, especially in a chaser who is unable to catch a runner. Make a change with another child as chaser.

25. Be careful of the poor citizenship situation where some child is made the "goat" or butt of jokes. Psychological hurt or trauma may be deep and permanent. The possibility of physical hurt or punishment must not be ruled out. The slow, heavy child, who cannot move readily, is at a disadvantage in dodgeball games and other activities demanding mobility.

26. While games which eliminate children in the course of play have a place in the program, these should be used with caution. Elimination should not be carried down to the "bitter end." It is better to play the game so a minor portion of the children are eliminated and then declare the remainder the winners.

27. In number-calling type games, where children compete against each other in some specified task, all teams can be given points for successful performance so that any disqualification results in loss of the possible place points, even for last place.

EXPLORATION WITH GAMES

Children should have opportunity to make up or design games of their own origin. The teacher should set the problem by specifying what is available to them in the nature of space, equipment, and number of participants. For example, the space could be designated as a 20' square or two parallel lines 30' apart. The game could be created without any equipment, or the children could be given a ball (any size) with which to work.

The teacher should divide the class into small enough groups so each child is able to make a contribution. If a group is large, there is difficulty in resolving differences of opinion. Unless there is a specific reason, not more than three or four children should be assigned to a group. The groups can also be given different game problems to solve with respect to size of space, the equipment, and other details.

After a period of time, the groups should present the games they have originated. Discussion can be held with regard to value and possible changes that might make the game better. This is an excellent learning experience and prepares children for their own free time play.

THE GAMES PROGRAM FOR KINDERGARTEN

The games program for the kindergarten level features mostly individual and creative play. Little emphasis is centered on team play or on games which demand a scoring system. The games are simple, easily taught, and not demanding in special skills. Beanbags are used in some of the activity, but ball games are not particularly appropriate for this level.

Dramatic elements are present in many of the games, and others help establish number concepts and symbol recognition. Games based on stories or poems are popular with this level.

In addition to the games presented in this section, the teacher should make use of first grade games and also those presented in Chapter 21, Story Games and Dramatic Play.

Kindergarten Games

- Blind Man's Buff
- Colors
- Fireman
  Kneeling Tag
- Magic Fountain
- Marching Ponies
  Mother, May I?
- Popcorn
- The Scarecrow and the Crows
  Statues
- Tommy Tucker's Land

BLIND MAN'S BUFF

Playing Area: Playground, gymnasium, classroom.

Players: 8-10.

Supplies: 1 blindfold for each game.

Blind Man's Buff is one of the old, traditional games. One child is blindfolded and stands in the center of a small circle formed by the other children. Another child is chosen to be inside the circle, and the Blind Man tries to catch him. As his quarry dodges him the Blind Man calls out "Where are you?" whereupon the other must respond immediately by making a sound like that of a baby chick, "Cheep, cheep!"

When the Blind Man has caught the other player, he tries to identify him by feeling his face, arms, and clothes. Identification does not affect the outcome of the game, but simply adds to the fun. Two other children are chosen to replace the first two players.

Circles should be kept small, otherwise catching is difficult and protracted. The blindfold should be adequate, as the game is spoiled if the child can see under it.

Variation: The circle children can make a buzzing sound (Z-z-z-z-z-z), which becomes louder as the Blind Man nears his quarry.

COLORS

Playing Area: Playground, gymnasium, classroom.

Players: Entire class.

Supplies: Colored paper or colored construction paper cut into circles, squares, or triangles as markers.

Five or six different colored markers should be used, with a number of children having the same color. The children are seated in a circle. Each places his marker in front of him.

The teacher calls out one of the colors, upon which all having that color run counterclockwise around the circle and back to place. The first one seated upright and motionless is declared the winner. Different kinds of locomotor movements can be specified, such as skipping, galloping, walking etc.

After a period of play, leave the markers on the floor and have the children move one place to the left.

Variations:

1. Use shapes, instead of colors. Use a circle, triangle, square, rectangle, star, diamond.

2. Use numbers.

Note: Many other articles or categories such as animals, birds, fishes, etc., can be used. The game has value in teaching elements of identification and recognition.

FIREMAN

Playing Area: Playground, gymnasium, classroom.

Players: Entire class.

Supplies: None.

A "Fire Chief" is appointed. He runs around the outside of a circle of children and taps a number of them on the back, saying "Fireman" each time. After making his round of the circle the Chief goes to the center. When he says, "Fire," the "Firemen" run counterclockwise around the circle and back to place. The one who returns first and is able to stand in place motionless is declared the winner and the new Chief.

The Chief can use other words in an attempt to fool the Firemen, but they run only on the word, "Fire." This merely provides a fun aspect, as there is no penalty for a false start. To add to the gaiety, the circle children can sound the siren as the Firemen run.

KNEELING TAG

Playing Area: Playground, gymnasium.

Players: Entire class.

Supplies: None.

Two or more children are "It." They attempt to tag the other children, who can be safe by kneeling on one knee. The child tagged changes places with "It."

The teacher should specify which knee is to be used. This should be changed partway through the game. The game can be played progressively with the children tagged joining the taggers, but it cannot be played until all children are tagged because of its safe position feature. Play until about one-half the children are tagged and then reorganize.

Children need to be encouraged to dare a little, as no one will be caught if he kneels

all the time. Players kneeling on the wrong knee are not safe.

Variation: Color concepts can be stressed by selecting a color for safety. This is more appropriate for a gymnasium where lines of different colors are already on the floor, but contruction paper in different colors can be taped to the floor as safe bases. Markers of this type are not likely to survive long, however.

THE MAGIC FOUNTAIN

Playing Area: Playground, gymnasium, classroom.

Players: Entire class.

Supplies: Pictures of animals, a box, and a stool or table.

A supply of animal pictures (10-15), is placed in a box on a stool or table to one side. This is the magic fountain. The children are seated in a circle on the floor. Four to five children are selected by the teacher; one of them is designated to draw out a picture from the magic fountain. He shows the picture to the rest of his group, but keeps it hidden from the remainder of the children in the circle.

As soon as all the chosen children have seen the picture, they return to the circle area and imitate the animal they saw in the picture. When the circle players guess the animals, the animal imitators return to the circle formation and another group of players is chosen.

Children who wish to guess what animal is being imitated should raise hands for recognition.

MARCHING PONIES

Playing Area: Playground, gymnasium, classroom.

Players: Entire class.

Supplies: None.

One child is the "Ringmaster" and crouches in the center of a circle of "Ponies" formed by the other children. Two goal lines on opposite sides of the circle are established as safe areas. The Ponies march around the circle in step, counting consecutively as they step. At a predetermined number (which has been whispered to the

Ringmaster by the teacher) the Ringmaster jumps from his crouched position and attempts to tag the others before they can reach the safety lines. Anyone tagged must join the Ringmaster in the center, helping him catch the next time.

The game should be reorganized after six to eight children have been caught. Those left in the circle are declared the winners.

Variation: Ponies must gallop to the safe area.

MOTHER, MAY I?

Playing Area: Playground, gymnasium.

Players: 8-10.

Supplies: None.

A starting and finishing line are established about 40′ apart. In a gymnasium, the game can proceed sideways across the floor. One child is "It" and stands between the two lines. The remainder of the children stand on the starting line. The object of the game is to reach the finish line first.

"It" tells one of the players how many steps he can take and what kind. The player must ask, "Mother, may I?" and await the answer before he moves. If he fails to ask the question, he goes back to the starting line. Even if the question is asked, "It" may say, "No."

The steps should be varied to provide different kinds of movements. Steps such as baby steps, scissors steps, giant steps, hopping steps, bunny steps (jumps), and others are appropriate for the game. The first to the finish line is "It" for the next game.

POPCORN

Playing Area: Playground, gymnasium, classroom.

Players: Entire class, divided into two groups.

Supplies: None.

The children should be given a short preliminary explanation of how popcorn pops in response to the heat applied. One-half the children are designated as "popcorn" and crouch down in the center of the circle formed by the rest of the children. The circle children are indicators of the heat cycle. One of them should be designated the leader,

whose actions will serve as a guide to the other children. The circle children, who are also crouched down, gradually rise to a standing position, extend their arms overhead and shake them vigorously to indicate high heat. In the meantime the "popcorn" in the center begins to pop. This should begin at a slow pace and increase in speed and height as the heat is applied. In the final stages the children are popping up rapidly.

Change groups and repeat.

THE SCARECROW AND THE CROWS

Playing Area: Playground, gymnasium, classroom.

Players: Entire class.

Supplies: None.

The children form a large circle to represent the garden, which the Scarecrow is guarding. Six Crows scatter on the outside of the circle. The Scarecrow assumes a characteristic pose inside the circle. The circle children raise their joined hands and let the Crows run through into the garden, where they pretend to eat. The Scarecrow tries to tag one of the Crows, and the circle children help the Crows by raising their joined hands, allowing them to leave the circle, but try to hinder the Scarecrow. If the Scarecrow runs out of the circle all the Crows immediately run into the garden and start to nibble at the vegetables, while the circle children hinder the Scarecrow's reentry.

When the Scarecrow has caught one or two Crows (the teacher can decide), a new group of children are selected to be Scarecrow and Crows. If after a reasonable period of time the Scarecrow has failed to catch any Crows a change should be made.

STATUES

Playing Area: Playground, gymnasium.

Players: Entire class, organized by pairs.

Supplies: None.

Children are paired off around the area One child is the swinger and the other the statue. The swinger takes the statue by one or two hands and swings it around in a small circle. The teacher voices a directive such as "pretty," "funny," "happy," "animal" or some

8

other descriptive term. The swingers immediately release the statues and sit down on the floor. The statues take a pose in keeping with the directive. The teacher or a committee of children can determine which children are making the best statues. The object is to hold the position without moving.

After the winners have been determined, the partners reverse positions. Children should be cautioned that the swinging helps to position the statues, but must be controlled.

TOMMY TUCKER'S LAND

Playing Area: Playground, gymnasium, classroom.

Players: 8-10.

Supplies: About 10 beanbags for each game.

One child is "Tommy Tucker" and stands in the center of a 15' square, within which the beanbags are scattered. Tommy is guarding his land and the treasure. The other children chant:

> I'm on Tommy Tucker's land
> Picking up gold and silver

The children attempt to pick up as much of the treasure as they can while avoiding being tagged by Tommy. Any child who is tagged must bring back his treasure and retire from the game. The game is over when there is only one child left or all the beanbags have been successfully filched. The teacher may wish to call a halt to the game earlier if it reaches a stalemate. In this case, the child with the most treasure becomes the new Tommy.

Variation: This game can be played with a restraining line, but there must be boundaries to limit movement.

THE GAMES PROGRAM FOR THE FIRST GRADE

The games for the first grade can be divided into two categories; running and tag games, and ball games. Few team activities are included, as at this level children are quite individualistic, and team play is beyond their capacities. The ball games should require only the simple skills of throwing and catching.

First Grade Games

Review Kindergarten Games
Animal Tag
• Back-to-Back
Cat and Rat
•Charlie Over the Water
•Circus Master
Gallop Tag
Midnight
•Old Man (Old Lady)
One, Two, Button My Shoe
Squirrel in the Trees
Tag Games — Simple
•Where's My Partner?
•Ball Passing
•Ball Toss
•Call Ball
Teacher Ball (Leader Ball)

ANIMAL TAG

Playing Area: Playground, gymnasium. Two parallel lines are drawn about 40' apart.

Players: Entire class.

Supplies: None.

The children are divided into two groups, each of which takes position on one of the lines. The children of Group 1 get together with their leader and decide what animal they wish to imitate. Having selected the animal, they move over to within 5' or so of the other line. Here they imitate the animal and Group 2 tries to guess the animal correctly. If they guess correctly, they chase Group 1 back to its line, trying to tag as many as possible. Those caught must go over to the other team.

Group 2 now selects an animal and the roles are reversed. However, If the guessing team cannot guess the animal, the performing team gets another try.

To avoid confusion, have the children raise hands to take turns naming the animal. Otherwise, there will be many false chases.

If the children have trouble guessing, then have the leader of the performing team give the initial of the animal.

BACK-TO-BACK

Playing Area: Playground, gymnasium, classroom.

Players: Entire class.
Supplies: None.

The number of children should be uneven. If the number is even, the teacher can play. On signal, each child stands back-to-back with another child. One child will be without a partner. This child can clap his hands for the next signal, and all children change partners with the extra player seeking a partner.

Variation: Considerably more activity can be secured by putting in an extra command. After the children are in partner formation back-to-back, the teacher can say, "'Everybody — run!" (or skip, hop, jump, slide, etc.) Other commands can be given, such as, "Walk like an elephant." The children move around the room in the prescribed manner. When the whistle is blown, they immediately find a partner and stand back-to-back.

CAT AND RAT

Playing Area: Gymnasium, playground.

Players: 10 to 20.

Supplies: None.

All children except two form a circle with hands joined. One of the extra players is the "Cat" and the other is the "Rat." The Rat is on the inside of the circle, and the Cat is outside. The following dialogue takes place:
"I am the Cat."
"I am the Rat."
"I can catch the Rat."
"Oh no, you can't"
Whereupon the Cat chases the Rat in and out of the circle. The circle players raise their arms to help the Rat, and lower them again to hinder the Cat. When the Cat catches the Rat or after a period of time if the Rat is not caught, the two children can select two others to take their places.

Variation: Instead of having the children raise and lower their hands to aid or hinder the runners, the teacher can call out, "High windows," or "Low windows." The circle players raise and lower their hands only on these signals.

CHARLIE OVER THE WATER

Playing Area: Playground, gymnasium, classroom.

Players: 15 to 20.

Supplies: None.

The children are in circle formation with hands joined. One or more extra children are in the center, depending on the number of children in the circle. The one in the center is "Charlie." The circle children skip around the circle to the following chant:
Charlie over the water, Charlie over the sea,
Charlie caught a bluebird, but can't catch *me!*
On the word "me" all circle children drop hands, stoop, and touch the ground with both hands. The center players try to tag the circle players before they stoop. Any player tagged changes places with the center player. The game then continues.

Children should be held to retaining their balance while stooping. If they fall, they can be tagged.

The following chant can be used if a girl is in the center:
Sally over the river, Sally over the sea, etc.
Other positions can be stipulated instead of stooping. Balancing on one foot, crab position, push-up position, and others can be used.

CIRCUS MASTER

Playing Area: Playground, gymnasium, classroom.

Players: 10 to 40.

Supplies: None.

One child, the "Circus Master," is in the center of the circle formed by the other children. He stands in the center, pretends he has a whip, and gets ready to have the animals perform. He gives a direction like the following: "We are going to walk as elephants do, like this!" He then demonstrates in a small circle how he wishes the children to perform. He commands, "Elephants ready — WALK." The children imitate an elephant walking around the large circle while the Circus Master performs in a small circle in the center. When ready, the Circus Master calls "Halt." He takes a place in the circle, and another child comes forward to the center.

A prearranged order for Circus Masters can be established; this is excellent for young children, as they can be prepared with a particular animal imitation. However, interest would die long before all the children could be in the center. Make arrangements for other children to be in the center when the game is played at a later date.

GALLOP TAG

Playing Area: Playground, gymnasium.

Players: 12 to 20.

Supplies: None.

Children are in circle formation, facing in. One child walks around the outside and tags another child on the back. Immediately, he gallops around the circle in either direction with the child who was tagged chasing him, also at a gallop. If the player in the lead gets around to the vacated spot before being tagged, he joins the circle. If he is tagged, he must try again with another child.

Variations:

1. The children can run or skip.

2. *Slap Jack.* Have the child tagged run in the *opposite* direction. The child who gets back to the vacant place first gets to keep the place. The other child tags again for another run.

3. *Run for Your Supper.* The children stand with clasped hands. The runner goes in either direction, tags a pair of clasped hands, and says, "Run for your supper." The two children whose hands have been tagged run in opposite directions, with the one getting back first keeping the place. The original runner after tagging the clasped hands merely steps into the circle, leaving only one space for which the two runners compete. Having the two runners, when they meet on the opposite side of the circle, bow to each other or shake hands before continuing the run back to place makes the game more enjoyable.

4. *Duck, Duck, Goose.* All children are seated cross-legged. The runner goes in either direction around the circle, tapping each child *lightly* on the head. As he does this he says, "Duck." When he wishes, he changes the word to "Goose," and that child then arises quickly and chases him around the circle back to the vacant place. If the runner gets back safely, the chaser is the new runner. If

the runner is tagged, then he must take another try as runner.

Cautions: These types of games should be played as resting activities and as such have a place in the curriculum. They are fun, but are low in developmental values. Also, there must be rapid action to keep things moving. Make a rule that the runners may travel only partway around a circle before choosing a chaser.

MIDNIGHT

Playing Area: Playground.

Players: 6 to 15.

Supplies: None.

A safety line is established about 40′ from a den in which one player is standing as the "Fox." The others stand behind the safety line and move forward slowly, asking, "Mr. Fox, what time is it?" The Fox answers in various fashions such as "Bed time," "Pretty late," "Three-thirty," and so on. He continues to draw the players toward him. At some point, he answers the question of time with "Midnight," and chases the others back to the safety line. Any player caught joins the Fox in his den and helps him catch others. However, no player in the den can leave until the Fox calls out "Midnight."

OLD MAN (OLD LADY)

Playing Area: Playground, gymnasium, classroom.

Players: Entire class.

Supplies: None.

A line is drawn through the middle of the area. Any convenient line can be used. Half the children are on one side and half on the other. The children hold hands with a partner across the center line. There must be an odd person, the teacher or another child. The teacher gives a signal for the children to move as directed on their side of the line. They can be directed to run, hop, skip, etc. At a whistle, the children run to the center line, and each reaches across to join hands with a child from the opposite group. The one left out is the "Old Man" (if a boy) or the "Old Lady" (if a girl). Children may reach over, but not cross the line. The odd person should alternate sides so that the Old Man can be on the other side at times.

The game can also be done to music with the players rushing to the center line to find partners when the rhythm stops.

ONE, TWO, BUTTON MY SHOE

Playground Area: Playground, gymnasium. Two parallel lines are drawn about 50' apart.

Players: Entire class.

Supplies: None.

One child is the leader and stands to one side. The remainder of the children are behind one of the lines. The leader says "Ready." The following dialogue takes place between the leader and the children:

Children	Leader's Response
One, two	Button my shoe
Three, four	Close the door
Five, six	Pick up sticks
Seven, eight	Run, or you'll be *late!*

The children carry on the above conversation with the leader and are toeing the line ready to run. When the word "late" is given by the leader, the children run to the other line and return. The first child across the original line is the winner and becomes the new leader.

The leader can give the last response in any timing he wishes by pausing or dragging out the words. No child is to leave before the "late."

A variation is to have the children pantomime the leader's directions.

SQUIRREL IN THE TREES

Playing Area: Playground, gymnasium.

Players: 15 to 35.

Supplies: None.

A tree is formed by two players facing each other with hands held or on each other's shoulders. A "Squirrel" is in the center of each tree, and one or two extra Squirrels are outside. A signal to change is given. All Squirrels move out of their trees to another, and the extra players try to find trees. Only one Squirrel is allowed in a tree.

To form a system of rotation, as each Squirrel moves into a tree, he changes places with one of the two players forming the tree.

TAG GAMES — Simple

Playing Area: Playground with established boundaries, gymnasium.

Players: Any number.

Supplies: None.

Tag is played in many different ways. Children are scattered about the area. One child is "It" and chases others to tag one of them. When he does, he says, "You're IT." The new "It" chases other children. Different tag games are listed:

1. Being safe through touching a specified object or color. Touching wood, iron, the floor, or a specified color can make a runner safe.

2. Seeking safety by a particular action or pose. Some actions used to become safe are:
   Stoop — touch both hands to the ground.
   Stork — stand on one foot (the other cannot touch).
   Turtle — be on one's back, feet pointed toward the ceiling.
   Hindoo — make an obeisance with forehead to the ground.
   Nose and toe — nose must be touched by the toe.
   Back to back — stand back-to-back with any other child.

3. *Locomotive Tag* — "It" specifies how the children shall move. "It" also must use the same kind of movement, i.e., skip, hop, jump, etc.

4. *Frozen Tag* — two children are "It." The rest are scattered over the area. When caught they are "frozen" and must keep both feet in place. Any free player can tag a "frozen" player and release him. The object of the taggers is to freeze all the players.

WHERE'S MY PARTNER?

Playing Area: Playground, gymnasium, classroom.

Players: Entire class.

Supplies: None.

Children are arranged in a double circle by couples, with partners facing. The inside circle has one more player than the outside. When the signal is given, the circles skip to the right. This means that they are skipping in opposite directions. When the command "Halt" is given, the circles face each other to find partners. The player left without a partner is in the "Mush Pot."

Children can gallop, walk, run, or hop instead of skipping. Reverse circles.

Variation: The game can also be played with music. When the music stops, the players seek partners.

BALL PASSING

Playing Area: Playground, gymnasium, classroom.

Players: Entire class, divided into two or more circles.

Supplies: 5 to 6 different kinds of balls for each circle.

The basis of this game is the child's love of handling objects. Not over 15 children should be in any one circle. Two or more teams combine to form a circle. The children need not be in any particular order.

The teacher starts a ball around the circle; the ball is passed from player to player in the same direction. The teacher introduces more balls until five or six are moving around in the circle at the same time in the same direction. If a child drops a ball, he must retrieve it, and a point is scored against his team. After a period of time, a whistle is blown, and the points against each team are totaled. The team with the lowest score wins.

In the absence of sufficient balls for passing, bean bags, large blocks, or softballs can be substituted.

BALL TOSS

Playing Area: Playground, gymnasium, classroom.

Players: Groups of 6 to 8.

Supplies: A ball or beanbag for each group.

The children form a circle with one in the center. The center player throws the ball to each child in turn around the circle. The ball is returned to the center player each time. The object of the game is to make good throws

and catches completely around the circle. After each child has had a turn in the center, the teacher can ask each circle to total the number of center players that were able to complete their throws without any errors.

Good form should be stressed.

CALL BALL

Playing Area: Playground, gymnasium, classroom.

Players: 6 to 8 in each circle.

Supplies: A large playground ball or volleyball.

The children form a circle with one in the center. The center child has a ball. He throws the ball into the air, at the same time calling out the name of one of the circle children. This child runs forward and tries to catch the ball *before* it bounces. If successful, he becomes the center player. If not, the center player throws again. If there are many in the circle, the game moves quite slowly for the children. Other versions are:

1. Give the children numbers with more than one child having the same number. This makes the catching competitive.

2. Use colors or animals with more than one child assigned to the same color or animal.

3. Move the children back and have them catch the ball on first bounce.

4. *Catch the Cane.* Instead of tossing a ball into the air, balance a wand on one end of the floor. The child whose number is called tries to catch the cane before it hits the ground. A little experimentation will determine how far back the circle should be from the cane.

TEACHER BALL (Leader Ball)

Playing Area: Playground, gymnasium.

Players: 6 to 8.

Supplies: Volleyball or rubber playground ball.

One child is the "Teacher" or leader and stands about 10' in front of the others who are lined up facing him. The object of the game is to move up to the Teacher's spot by not making any bad throws or missing catches.

The Teacher throws to each child in turn, beginning with the child on his left, who must catch and return the ball to him. Any child making a throwing or catching error goes to the foot of the line, on the Teacher's right. Those in the line move up, filling the vacated space.

If the Teacher makes a mistake, he goes to the foot of the line, and the child at the head of the line becomes the new Teacher.

The Teacher scores a point for himself if he remains in position for three rounds (3 throws to each child). He takes his position at the foot of the line, and another child becomes the Teacher.

This game should be used only after the children have practiced throwing and catching skills. It can be worked in as a part of the skill teaching program.

Variation: Provide specific methods of throwing and catching like, "Catch with the right hand only" or "Catch with one hand; don't let the ball touch your body."

THE GAMES PROGRAM FOR THE SECOND GRADE

The games program is quite similar to that of the first grade. The second grade teacher should make use of all games presented in the first grade. Particularly, the simple ball games of the first grade have good values and should be included as a regular part of the second grade program.

Second Grade Games
Review First Grade Games
Animal Chase
Automobiles
• Caged Lion
• Cat and Mice
Charlie Over the Water — Ball Version
Flowers and Wind
• Forest Ranger
Hill Dill
• Hot Potatoes
Hound and Rabbit
• Hunter
• I Can Do What You Can!
• In the Creek
Last Couple Out
Leap the Brook
May I Chase You?
• Mouse Trap
Red Light

Stop and Start
Two Deep
• Circle Straddle Ball
Exchange Dodgeball
Roll Dodgeball
Straddle Bowling

ANIMAL CHASE

Playing Area: Playground. Two goals are marked out 50' apart. Halfway between the lines and off to one side, a square represents the zoo.

Players: Entire class.

Supplies: None.

One child is the animal hunter and stands in the center of the area. All children are stationed on one of the two goal lines. Each player is secretly given the name of an animal, several players having the same animal designation.

The hunter calls out the name of an animal. If no one has this name, he continues different names until he hits upon one that a player has. The players run to the opposite goal line and return. As soon as the runners start, the hunter must return to his zoo (to get his gun), return to the center area, and try to tag a runner. Generally, the runners can get to the other goal line without difficulty. On the return trip, they must dodge the hunter to return to the other animals.

Any animals caught are taken to the zoo and sit until all have run. If there are quite a number of children playing the game, the number of times the hunter can chase before getting a replacement may be limited.

AUTOMOBILES

Playing Area: Playground, gymnasium.

Players: Entire class.

Supplies: Each child has a "steering wheel."

Each child is to be a driver of an automobile and needs a "steering wheel." This can be a hoop, deck tennis ring, or something the child has made out of cardboard. The teacher has three flash cards, colored red, green, and yellow respectively. These are the traffic control colors.

The children drive around the area, steering various paths, responding as the teacher raises the cards aloft one at a time. The children follow the traffic directions: red — stop, green — go, and yellow — caution.

An ambulance station and a fire station can be established with appropriate "cars." When one of these comes forward with the characteristic siren noise (made by the driver), all other "cars" pull over to the side of the road and wait until the ambulance or fire engine has gone by.

Teaching Suggestion: Have the children use the proper hand signals for making turns, slowing down, and stopping.

CAGED LION

Playing Area: Classroom or gymnasium. A ten-foot square is drawn.

Players: 10 to 20.

Supplies: None.

One child is selected to be the "Lion" and takes a position on his hands and knees inside the ten-foot square. Other players tantalize the Lion by standing in the cage area or running through it. The Lion tries to tag any of the children. Any child who is tagged by the Lion trades places with him.

Variation: *The King's Land.* The forbidden area, consisting of a twenty-foot square, is known as the King's Land. A warden is appointed who tries to catch (tag) anyone who is on the King's Land. If successful, he is released, and the tagged player becomes the new warden.

CAT AND MICE

Playing Area: Playground, gymnasium, classroom.

Players: 10 to 30.

Supplies: None.

The children form a large circle. One child is chosen to be the Cat and three others are the Mice. The Mice cannot leave the circle. On signal, the Cat chases the Mice inside the circle. As they are caught, they join the circle. The last Mouse caught becomes the Cat for the next round. The teacher should start at one point in the circle and go round the circle selecting Mice so that each child gets a chance to be in the center.

CHARLIE OVER THE WATER
— Ball Version

Playing Area: Playground, gymnasium.

Players: 8 to 12.

Supplies: 1 volleyball or playground ball.

The children are in circle formation with hands joined. One child, "Charlie," is in the center of the circle holding a ball in his hands. The children skip around the circle to the following chant:

> Charlie over the water,
> Charlie over the sea,
> Charlie caught a bluebird,
> but can't catch ME!

On the word "me" the children drop hands and scatter. On the same signal, Charlie tosses the ball into the air. He then catches it and shouts, "Stop!" All children stop immediately and must not move their feet. Charlie rolls the ball in an attempt to hit one of the children. If he hits a child, that child becomes "Charlie," and if Charlie misses, he must remain as "Charlie," and the game is repeated. However, if he misses twice, he should pick another child.

If a girl is in the center, the chant should go: Sally over the river, Sally over the sea, etc.

FLOWERS AND WIND

Playing Area: Two parallel lines are drawn long enough to accommodate the children. The lines are about 30' apart.

Players: 10 to 30.

Supplies: None.

The children are divided into two equal groups, one is the "Wind" and the other the "Flowers." Each of the teams takes a position on one of the lines facing the other. The Flowers secretly select the name of a common flower. When ready, they walk over to the other line and stand about 3' away from the Wind. The players on the Wind begin to call out, trying to guess the flower chosen. When the chosen flower has been guessed, the Flowers take off and run to their goal line, chased by the players of the other team.

Any player caught must join the other side. The roles are reversed, and the other team chooses a flower.

If one side has trouble guessing, then give

the first letter, the color or the size of the flower.

the first letter, the color, or the size of the flower.

FOREST RANGER

Playing Area: Playground, gymnasium, classroom.

Players: Entire class.

Supplies: None.

One-half of the children form a circle facing in. These are the trees. The other half of the children are the "Forest Rangers" and stand behind the trees. An extra child, the "Forest Lookout," is in the center. The Forest Lookout starts the game with the command, "Fire in the forest. *Run, run, run!*" Immediately, the Forest Rangers run around the outside of the circle to the right (counterclockwise). After a few moments, the Lookout steps in *front* of one of the trees. This is the signal for each of the Rangers to step in *front* of a tree. One player is left out, and he now becomes the new Forest Lookout. The trees become Rangers and vice versa. Each time the game is played, the circle must be moved out somewhat, as the formation narrows when the Rangers step in front of the trees.

HILL DILL

Playing Area: Playground. Two parallel lines are drawn about 50' apart.

Players: 10 to 50.

Supplies: None.

One player is chosen to be "It" and stands in the center. The other children stand on one of the parallel lines. The center player calls, "Hill Dill! Come over the hill!" The children run across the open space to the other line while the one in the center tries to tag them. Anyone caught helps "It" in the center. The last man caught is in the center for the next game.

Once the children cross over to the other line they must await the next call.

HOT POTATOES

Playing Area: Gymnasium, playground, or classroom.

Players: 8-12 in each group.

Supplies: 6 balls, 6 beanbags.

Children are seated in a small circle close enough together so that objects can be handed from one to another around the circle. Balls and/or beanbags are passed around the circle, a few being introduced at a time. The object of the game is to pass the balls or beanbags rapidly so no one gets "stuck" with more than one object at a time. If he does, the game is stopped, and he moves back and waits. After three are out of the circle, the game starts over.

Start the game with two or three objects and gradually add objects until someone has more than one at a time.

Variation: Reverse the direction of passing on signal.

HOUND AND RABBIT

Playing Area: Playground, gymnasium.

Players: 15 to 30.

Supplies: None.

Players are scattered around the area in groups of three. Two of the three make a tree by facing each other and putting hands on each other's shoulders. The third child, who takes the part of a rabbit, stands between them. An extra "Rabbit" is outside and is chased by a "Hound." The Hound chases the odd Rabbit, who takes refuge in any tree. No tree may hold more than one rabbit, so the other child must leave and look for another tree. When the Hound catches the Rabbit they exchange places and the game continues.

A rotation system should be used whenever a Rabbit enters a tree. The three in any one group should rotate so that the entering Rabbit becomes a part of the tree, and one of the children making up the tree becomes the Rabbit.

THE HUNTER

Playing Area: Playground, gymnasium, classroom.

Players: Entire class.

Supplies: Individual markers are needed for the children. In the classroom, the seat can be used for home.

A leader, the "Hunter," walks around the room in any manner he wishes. He begins the game with the question, "Who wants to hunt ducks (bears, lions, rabbits)?" The players volunteering fall in line behind him and start on the hunt. The Hunter can go through various creeping and hunting motions. When he is ready, he shouts, "Bang!" All run for a marker or a seat, including the Hunter. The first one back to a marker or seat is chosen as leader for the next game.

To make the game interesting, the leader should take quite a few children on the hunt. Be sure that all get a chance to hunt.

Variation: A novel method of making leader changes is to have one place (seat or marker) designated as the leader for the next time. This is chosen only after the Hunter takes the occupant out. The teacher can make this selection, the location of which is unknown to the runners.

I CAN DO WHAT YOU CAN!

Playing Area: Playground, gymnasium, classroom.

Players: Not more than 6 or 7 in a group. Any number of groups can play.

Supplies: Usually none. The game can be played with each child using the same piece of equipment, such as a ball, wand, beanbag, etc.

This is primarily a "follow-the-leader" type of game. Each group works independently of the others. Each group forms a semicircle with the leader in front. The leader starts any type of activity he wishes, and the other children attempt to make the same moves along with him. After a brief period, the teacher blows the whistle, and another leader takes his place in front of the group.

This works well with selected pieces of hand apparatus, provided each child in the group has the same type of equipment. Tossing, throwing, catching, bouncing, wand stunts, and beanbag tricks are some activities which are easily adapted to the game. Caution children not to demand outlandish or silly performances from the group.

IN THE CREEK

Playing Area: Playground, gymnasium, classroom.

Players: Entire class.

Supplies: None.

A creek is formed by drawing two parallel lines 2' to 3' apart, depending upon the ability of the children. The lines should be long enough to accommodate the children comfortably with enough room for each to jump. If necessary, two or three sets of lines can be drawn.

The children line up on one of the banks, all facing the creek and facing the same direction. The object of the game is to make the children commit an error in the jumping.

The teacher or leader gives one of two directions:

"In the creek."

"On the bank."

Children now on the bank jump into the creek or over to the other bank depending upon the command. When they jump on the bank, they immediately turn around and get ready for the next command.

If children are in the creek and the command "In the creek" is repeated, they must not move.

Errors are committed when a child steps on a line, makes a wrong jump, or moves when he should remain still.

Children who make a mistake can be sent down to another game or eliminated. The first is the better suggestion, as this keeps them in activity.

After a period of time, the original directions may not challenge the children. Different combinations can be set up. "In the creek" means to jump and land with both feet. "On the bank" one way would be a leap. "On the bank" the other way would be a hop. Also, false commands can be given, such as "In the ocean," or "In the lake." No one is to move on these commands under penalty of elimination.

It is a good plan to keep things moving fast with crisp commands. Children should be charged with judging their own errors.

LAST COUPLE OUT

Playing Area: Playground, gymnasium.

Players: 10 to 15.

Supplies: None.

Players are lined up by couples in a column formation with an "It" standing at the head of the column. He has his back to the column. He calls, "Last couple out!" The object of the game is to have the last couple separate and rejoin beyond the place where "It" is standing without being tagged by him. If "It" tags either of the two, that person becomes "It." The old "It" joins the remaining player as his partner, and the pair go to the head of the line.

If the couple is able to join hands without being tagged, they take places at the head of the column, and "It" takes a try at the next couple.

"It" is not permitted to look back and cannot start his chase until the separated couple comes up even with him on both sides.

Variation: The game can be played by partners who have inside hands joined.

LEAP THE BROOK

Playing Area: Gymnasium or other flat surface.

Players: Entire class.

Supplies: None.

A brook is marked off on the floor for a distance of about 30'. For the first 10' it is 3' wide, for the second 10' 4' wide, and for the last 10' the width becomes 5'.

The children form a single file and jump over the narrowest part of the brook. They should be encouraged to do this several times, using different styles of jumping and leaping.

Stress landing as lightly as possible on the balls of the feet in a bent-knee position.

After they have satisfactorily negotiated the narrow part, the children move up to the next width, and so on.

Teachers should remember that fitness values are only in repeated effort. Good form should be stressed throughout the game.

The selection of the distances is arbitrary, and they may be changed if they seem unsuitable for any particular group of children.

Variation: Use different means of crossing the brook — leaping, jumping, hopping. Also, specify the kinds of turns to be made — right or left; quarter, half, three-quarter or full turns.

Have the children use different body shapes, arm positions, etc.

MAY I CHASE YOU?

Playing Area: Playground.

Players: 10 to 30.

Supplies: None.

The class stands behind a line long enough to accommodate all. The runner stands about 5' in front of the line. One child in the line asks, "May I chase you?" The runner replies, "Yes, if you are wearing - - -." He can name a color, an article of clothing, or a combination of the two. All who qualify immediately chase the runner until one tags him. This person becomes "It."

The children will think of other ways to identify those who may run.

MOUSE TRAP

Playing Area: Playground, gymnasium, classroom.

Players: 20 to 40.

Supplies: None.

Half of the children form a circle with hands joined, facing the center. The other children are on the outside of the circle. Three signals are given for the game. These can be given by word cues, or whistle.

The circle players represent the mouse trap, and the outer players are the mice.

Signal 1. The "Mice" skip around the circle playing happily.

Signal 2. The trap is opened, that is, the circle players raise their joined hands to form arches. The Mice run in and out of the trap.

Signal 3. The trap snaps shut (the arms come down). All Mice caught join the circle.

The game is repeated until all or most of the Mice are caught. The players exchange places, and the game begins anew. Do not allow the children to run in and out using adjacent openings.

RED LIGHT

Playing Area: An area 60' to 100' across with goal toward which the players move.

Players: Entire class.

Supplies: None.

The object of the game is to be able to move across the area successfully without getting caught. One player is the leader and stands on the goal line. He counts very rapidly from one to ten while he has his back to the players. He quickly adds the words "Red Light" to the counting and turns around. In the meantime, the players have been moving across the area during the counting and must freeze on the words "Red Light." Any player caught moving after "Red Light" must return to the starting position. The first player across the area wins and is the leader for the next game.

After the leader has sent back all who were caught, he turns his back again to begin his count. The players may move when his back is turned. However, he may turn around quickly and catch any movement. Once he starts his counting he cannot turn around until he has called "Red Light."

Variations:

1. Instead of counting, the leader (with his back turned) can clap his hands five times, turning around to catch movement on the fifth clap.

2. Another excellent variation of the game is to have the leader face the oncoming players. He calls out "Green Light" for them to move and "Red Light" for them to stop. He can call other colors and the players should not move.

3. Different types of locomotion can be worked in. The leader names the type of movement (i.e., hop, crawl, etc.) before turning his back to the group.

STOP AND START

Playing Area: Playground.

Players: Any number can play.

Supplies: None.

The children are in the center of the playground, scattered enough so each has room to maneuver. The teacher or leader stands a little to one side and gives directions. He points in a direction and calls "Gallop." Any other locomotor movement can be used. Suddenly, he calls "Stop." All children must stop immediately without further movement. Any-

one moving can be sent over to the side to another group.

TWO DEEP

Playing Area: Playground, gymnasium.

Players: 15 to 20.

Supplies: None.

All children except two form a circle standing about fingertip distance apart and facing the center. A runner and chaser stand on the outside. The chaser tries to catch the runner, who can save himself by stopping in front of any player. This player now becomes the runner and must avoid being caught. When the chaser tags the runner, the positions change immediately, and the runner becomes the chaser.

Encourage the children to make changes often. If there seems to be too much running, make a rule that a child may travel only halfway around the circle before he must make a change.

Since this game is a lead-up to *Three Deep,* it should be learned reasonably well.

CIRCLE STRADDLE BALL

Playing Area: Playground, gymnasium, classroom.

Players: 10 to 15.

Supplies: 2 volleyballs or rubber playground balls.

Children are in circle formation, facing in. Each stands in wide straddle step with the side of his foot against the neighbor's. The hands are on the knees.

Two balls are used. The object of the game is to throw one of the balls between the legs of any player before he can get his hands down and stop it. Each time the ball goes between the legs of an individual, a point is scored against him. The players having the least points against them are the winners.

Be sure the children catch and roll the ball rather than bat it. Children must keep their hands on their knees until a ball is thrown at them.

After practice, the following variations should be played.

Variation: One child is in the center with a ball and is "It." The other children are in the same formation as above. One ball is used. The center player tries to roll the ball through the legs of any child he chooses. He should mask his intent, using feints and changes of direction. Any child allowing the ball to go through his legs becomes "It." All players start with hands on knees until the ball is thrown.

EXCHANGE DODGEBALL

Playing Area: Playground, gymnasium.

Players: 12 to 20.

Supplies: Volleyball or rubber playground ball.

Children form a circle with one child, "It," in the center. The children are numbered off by fours or fives in such a way that there are three or four children who have the same number. The center player also has a number which he uses when he is not "It."

The center player has a ball which he places at his feet. He calls a number, picks up the ball, and tries to hit one of the children who are exchanging places. When a number is called, all children with that number exchange places. The center player remains "It" until he can hit one of the children below the waist.

Variation: Use animal names instead of numbers.

ROLL DODGEBALL

Playing Area: Playground, gymnasium.

Players: 20 to 30, divided into two teams.

Supplies: 2 volleyballs or rubber playground balls.

Half of the children form a circle and the other half are in the center. Two balls are given to the circle players. The circle players roll the balls at the feet and shoes of the center players, trying to hit them. The center players move around to dodge the balls. When a center player is hit, he leaves the circle.

After a period of time or when all the children have been hit, the teams trade places. If a specified time limit is used, the team having the fewest hits wins. Or, the team which puts out all the opponents in the shortest space of time wins.

Variation: Center players are down on hands and feet. Only one ball is used, otherwise the game is the same. Do not play too long in this position as this is quite strenuous.

Teaching Suggestion: Be sure to have practice in rolling a ball first. Balls which stop in the center are "dead" and must be taken back to the circle before being put into play. It is best to have the player who recovers a ball roll it to one of his teammates rather than to have him return to his place with the ball.

STRADDLE BOWLING

Playing Area: Playground, gymnasium.

Players: 4 to 6.

Supplies: Volleyball or rubber playground ball.

Children may compete within a group, or teams can compete against each other. One child is the bowling target and stands in straddle position with his feet wide enough apart so the ball can pass through easily. Another child is the ball chaser and stands behind him.

A foul line is drawn 15' to 25' away from the target, depending upon the ability of the children. The bowlers line up behind this line for turns.

Children can be given one chance or a number of tries. To score a point, the ball must go between the legs of the target. When the children on the throwing line have bowled two of them relieve the target and chaser.

Variations:

1. Scoring can be changed to allow 2 points if the ball goes through the legs and 1 point if it hits a leg.

2. Other targets can be used. A box lying on its side with the opening pointed toward the bowler forms a good target. Two or three Indian clubs at each station make excellent targets. Scoring could be varied to suit the target.

3. *Bowling One Step.* For groups of squad size or smaller, each of the players in turn gets a chance to roll at an Indian club or bowling pin. A minimum distance is set up short enough so most bowlers can hit the pin (10' to 15'). The player keeps rolling until he misses. The object is to take a step back

ward each time the pin is knocked down. The winner is the one who has moved the farthest back.

Children should be cautioned that accuracy, not speed, is the goal. Also, the players should experiment with different spin effects to curve the ball.

THE GAMES PROGRAM FOR THE THIRD GRADE

Compared with the first two grades, the games program undergoes a definite change in the third grade. The chase and tag games become more complex and demand more maneuvering. Introductory lead-up games make an appearance. The interests of the children are turning toward games which have a sports slant. Kicking, throwing, catching, batting, and other sports skills are beginning to mature. Outside sports influences like the Little League program add force to the sports interests.

Third Grade Games

Review Second Grade Games
Bronco Tag
Busy Bee
Couple Tag
Cross Over
Crows and Cranes
Eagle and the Sparrows
Flying Dutchman
Fly Trap
Follow Me
Frog in the Sea
Galloping Lizzie
Jump the Shot
Poison Circle
Right Face, Left Face (Maze Tag)
Steal the Treasure
Three Deep
Through the Tunnel Race
Triple Change
Weathervane
Balance Dodgeball
Bat Ball
Beanbag Target Toss
Bounce Ball
Circle Team Dodgeball
Club Guard
Competitive Circle Contests
Newcomb

One Step
Toss Target Ball
Circle Kick Ball* (page 431)
End Ball* (page 408)

*These are lead-up games and descriptions are found on the pages indicated among the sports outlines.

BRONCO TAG

Playing Area: Playground, gymnasium.

Players: 15 to 30.

Supplies: None.

One child is a runner and another the chaser. The remainder of the children are divided into groups of three. Each group of three forms a bronco by standing one behind the other with the last two grasping the waist of the player in front. The front player is the head, and the player on the end is the tail. The runner tries to hook on to the tail of any bronco. The head of that bronco now becomes the runner.

The chaser pursues the runner who tries to avoid being caught by hooking to a bronco. The chaser now has to pursue the new runner. If tagged, the roles are reversed, and the runner becomes the chaser.

The game is more interesting if the children change places rapidly.

BUSY BEE

Playing Area: Playground, gymnasium, classroom.

Players: Entire class.

Supplies: None.

Half the children form a large circle facing in and are designated as the stationary players. The other children seek partners from this group, and each stands in front of one of the stationary players. An extra child is in the center and is the "Busy Bee."

The Bee calls out directions which are followed by the children:

"Back to back."
"Face to face."
"Shake hands."
"Kneel on one knee," (or both).
"Hop on one foot."

The center child then calls out "Busy Bee." Stationary players stand still, and all inner circle players seek another partner while the center player also tries to get a partner. The child without a partner becomes the Busy Bee.

Children should be thinking of the different movements they might have the class do if they should become the Busy Bee. In changing partners, children should be required to select a partner other than the stationary player next to them.

After a period of time, rotate the active and stationary players. Also, vary by using different methods of locomotion.

Variations:

1. Select a definite number of changes — ten for example. All children who have not repeated any partner during the ten exchanges and who have not been "caught" as the Busy Bee are declared the winners.

2. Instead of having the children stand back-to-back, have them lock elbows and sit down as in the *Chinese Get-up.* After they sit down and are declared "safe," they can get up and the game proceeds as described above.

COUPLE TAG

Playing Area: Playground, gymnasium. Two goal lines are established about 50' apart.

Players: Any number.

Supplies: None.

Children run by pairs with inside hands joined. All pairs, except one, line up on one of the goal lines. A pair is in the center and is "It."

The pair in the center calls, "Come," and the children run to the other goal line, keeping hands joined. The pair in the center tries to tag any pair using *only* the joined hands. As soon as a couple is caught, it helps the center couple. The game continues until all are caught. The last couple caught is "It" for the next game.

CROSS OVER

Playing Area: Playground with two parallel goal lines about 40' apart.

Players: 15 to 20.

Supplies: None.

Divide the players in two groups; each group stands on one of the goal lines. A catcher is in the center between the two lines. He faces one of the lines and calls out the name of one of the players. This player immediately calls out the name of a player in the other line. These two players try to change goal lines while the catcher tries to tag one of them. Any player tagged becomes the catcher for the next call.

If there are more than twenty children, it is best to divide the group into two games. Since only two children run at a time, the game can drag with a large group as chances to run will not occur frequently. Watch out for favoritism among the children.

Variation: With a larger group, this game can be played by partners. In calling out names, it would be necessary to call only one of the partners. Tagging would be done by the free hands with the inside hands kept joined. No tagging would count if the catchers separated, and a pair running across the area would be counted as caught if they were unable to keep together.

CROWS AND CRANES

Playing Area: Playground, gymnasium. Two goals are drawn about 50' apart.

Players: Any number.

Supplies: None.

Children are divided into two groups, the "Crows" and the "Cranes." The groups face each other at the center of the area about 5' apart. The leader calls out either "Crows" or "Cranes" using a "Kr-r-r-r-r" sound at the start of either word to mask the result.

If "Crows" is the call, the Crows chase the Cranes to the goal. If "Cranes" is given, then the Cranes chase. Any child caught goes over to the other side. The team which has the most players when the game ends is the winner.

Variations:

1. Have the children stand back-to-back in the center about a foot apart.

2. The game can be played with the two sides designated as "Black" and "White." A piece of plywood painted black on one side and white on the other can be thrown into the

air between the teams instead of having any-one give calls. If black comes up, the black team choses, and vice versa.

3. The game can also be played as "Blue, Black, and Baloney." On the commands "Blue" and "Black," the game proceeds as described above. On the command "Baloney" no one is to move. The caller should be sure to sound the "BI-I-I-I" before ending with one of the three commands.

4. Another variation of the game is to have a leader tell a story using as many words beginning with "cr" as possible. The players run only when the words "Crows" or "Cranes" are spoken. Words which can be incorporated into a story are crazy, crunch, crust, crown, crude, crowd, crouch, cross, croak, critter, etc. Each time one of these words is spoken the beginning of the word is lengthened with the cr-r-r-r sound. No one may move on any of the words except Crows or Cranes.

EAGLE AND THE SPARROWS

Playing Area: Playground with two parallel lines drawn about 50' apart. A circle representing the eagle's nest is drawn in the center.

Players: Entire class.

Supplies: None.

One player is the "Eagle" and is down on one knee in his nest. The other players circle around him flying like sparrows, until the Eagle suddenly gets up and chases the "Sparrows" to either line. Any Sparrow caught joins the Eagle and helps him catch others. However, no center player can chase until the Eagle starts first.

If the group is large, begin with two or three Eagles in the center.

Variation: All Sparrows must take three hops before they can start running.

FLYING DUTCHMAN

Playing Area: Playground or gymnasium.

Players: 20 to 30.

Supplies: None.

The children are in a circle with hands joined. Two children with hands joined are the runners. The runners go around the out-side of the circle and tag a pair of joined hands. Immediately, the runners continue around the circle while the tagged pair runs around in the other direction. The first pair back to the vacated spot gets to keep the spot, and the other pair becomes the runners. Be sure to establish rules for passing when the couples go by each other on the way around. Couples should keep to the right in passing.

Variations:

1. The runners reverse their direction immediately when tagging.

2. The game can be played by groups of threes instead of couples. The tag is made on the back of any one person, who with the persons on each side of him makes it a group of three. Groups should keep hands clasped or be disqualified.

FLY TRAP

Playing Area: Playground, gymnasium.

Players: Entire class.

Supplies: None.

One-half the class is scattered around the playing area sitting on the floor in tailor (cross-legged) fashion. These children form the trap. The other children are the "Flies" and buzz in and around the seated children. When a whistle is blown, the Flies must freeze at the spot. If any of the trappers can reach the Flies that fly is seated at his location and becomes a trapper.

The game continues until all the Flies have been caught. Some realism is given to the game if the Flies make buzzing sounds and move with their arms out as wings.

A little experience with the game will enable the teacher to determine how far apart to place the seated children. In tagging, the children must keep their seats on the ground.

After all the Flies have been caught, the children trade places.

Change the method of locomotion occasionally.

FOLLOW ME

Playing Area: Playground, gymnasium.

Players: 8 to 30.

Follow me   8-30 players

Supplies: A marker for each child. Squares of cardboard or plywood can be used.

Children are arranged roughly in a circle, each standing or sitting with one foot on his marker. An extra player is the "Guide." He moves about the circle pointing at different players and asking them to "follow me." Each player as chosen falls in behind the Guide. The Guide now takes his group on a tour with the members of the group performing just as the Guide does. The Guide may hop, skip, do stunts, or perform other movements and the children following him must do likewise. At the signal "Home" all run for places at the markers. One child will be without a marker. This child chooses another Guide.

It is not a good idea to make the last child the new leader, as this will cause some children to lag and try to be last. In our version, he gets to choose a new leader. One way to overcome the tendency to lag would be to make the first one back the leader or have a special leader marker. The first one to this marker becomes the new leader.

A penalty can be imposed on the one who doesn't find a marker.

FROG IN THE SEA

Playing Area: Any small area indoors or outdoors.

Players: 6 to 8 in each game.

Supplies: None.

One player is the "Frog" and sits down tailor fashion (crossed legs). The others mill about him trying to touch him, but at the same time, keeping out of his reach. They can call, "Frog in the sea, can't catch me." The Frog must stay in his sitting position and try to tag those tantalizing him. Anyone tagged exchanges places with the Frog.

Care should be taken so that the children do not punish the Frog unnecessarily.

Variations:

1. The Frog may not tag anyone until the teacher says, "Jump Frog."

2. The game proceeds as originally described. When the teacher says, "Jump Frog," the Frog can project himself in any direction with a jump. He is permitted to tag both during the original part of the game and at the jump.

GALLOPING LIZZIE

Playing Area: Playground.

Players: 10 to 15.

Supplies: Beanbag.

This is a version of the game of *Tag*. One player is "It" and has a beanbag. The other players are scattered on the playground. The player with the beanbag runs after the others and attempts to hit one with the beanbag below the shoulders. This person becomes "It" and the game continues. Be sure that "It" must throw the bag and not merely touch another person with it.

Variation: The game can be played by children in pairs. In this case, a pair of children become "It" with one of the players handling the beanbag. A specific kind of a toss can be specified — overhand, underhand, left hand.

JUMP THE SHOT

Playing Area: Playground, gymnasium.

Players: 10 to 20.

Supplies: A jump-the-shot rope.

The players stand in circle formation. One player with a long rope stands in the center. A soft object is tied to the free end of the rope to give it some weight. An old, deflated ball makes a good weight.

The center player turns the rope under the feet of the circle players, who must jump over it. Anyone who touches the rope with his feet is eliminated and must stand back from the circle. Re-form the circle after three or four children are eliminated.

The center player should be cautioned to keep the rope along the ground. The speed can be varied. A good way to turn the rope is to sit cross-legged and turn the rope over the head.

POISON CIRCLE

Playing Area: Playground, gymnasium.

Players: 8 to 12 in each circle.

Supplies: Volleyball or rubber playground ball.

Players form a circle with hands joined with good solid grips. Inside the circle of players, another circle is drawn on the floor with chalk. This should be a foot or two smaller than the circle of children. The ball is placed in the center of this area.

At a signal, the circle pulls and pushes trying to force a child to step into the inner circle. When this occurs, everyone yells, "Poison," and the children scatter. The one who stepped in the circle quickly picks up the ball and tries to hit one of the other children below the waist. He must throw from within the circle. If he hits a child, it is a "dud" against the child. If he misses, it is a "dud" against the thrower. Anyone with three "duds" pays a penalty.

RIGHT FACE, LEFT FACE (Maze Tag)

Playing Area: Playground, gymnasium.

Players: 25 to 35.

Supplies: None.

Children stand in straight rows both from front to rear and side to side. A runner and a chaser are picked. The children all face the same way and join hands with the players on each side. The chaser tries to tag the runner going up and down the rows, but not breaking through or under the arms. The teacher can help the runner by calling "right face" or "left face" at the proper time. At this command, the children drop hands, face the new direction, and again grasp hands with those who are now on each side. New passages are now available to the runner and chaser. When the runner is caught or the children become tired, a new runner and chaser are chosen.

Variations:

1. Directions can be used instead of the facing commands. The teacher can call out, "North, South, East, or West."

2. The original game from which the game above was taken is called "Streets and Alleys." In this version, the teacher calls out, "Streets" and the children face in one direction. The call "Alleys" causes them to face at right angles.

3. The command "Air Raid" can be given, which means that the children drop to their knees and make themselves into a small ball, tucking their heads and seat down.

STEAL THE TREASURE

Playing Area: Playground, gymnasium, classroom.

Players: 8 to 12.

Supplies: 1 Indian club.

A playing area twenty feet square is outlined with a small circle in the center. An Indian club is the treasure and is placed in the circle. A "Guard" is set to protect the treasure. Players now enter the square and try to steal the treasure without getting caught. The Guard tries to tag them. Anyone tagged must retire from the circle and wait for the next game. The player who gets the treasure is the next Guard. If getting the treasure seems too easy, make a rule requiring the child to carry the treasure to the boundaries of the square.

Bear and Keeper. This game is similar in action. Instead of a treasure a "Bear" is seated cross-legged on the ground and is protected by his "Keeper." Anyone who touches the Bear without being tagged becomes the new Keeper, with the present Keeper becoming the bear. A rougher version of this game played by boys is that the Bear stands crouched over and the boys try to swat him on the seat without getting tagged.

THREE DEEP

Playing Area: Playground, gymnasium.

Players: 20 to 30.

Supplies: None.

A runner and chaser are chosen. One-half of the remaining children form a circle, facing in. Each of the other children stands behind one of the circle players, forming a double circle formation with all facing in.

The chaser tries to tag the runner, who can escape by taking a position in front of any pair of players. This forms a three-deep combination, from which the game gets its name. The outer player of the three now is the runner. When the chaser tags the runner, the positions are reversed.

The game becomes more interesting if frequent changes are made. It may be well to limit running to halfway round the circle. In no case should the runner leave the immediate circle area.

Variation: The teacher may call out, "Reverse," which means that the positions of the runner and chaser are reversed.

THROUGH THE TUNNEL RACE

Playing Area: Playground, gymnasium, classroom.

Players: 6 to 8 on each team. Many teams can compete.

Supplies: None.

Teams compete against each other and are lined up in relay (lane) formation. The players spread their legs in straddle position, and the last man of each line crawls through the legs. The other players follow in turn until the team is back in original order. As soon as a player has crawled through the tunnel, he stands up so the player coming through next can go through his legs. The team that gets back in original order first wins.

TRIPLE CHANGE

Playing Area: Playground, gymnasium.

Players: 15 to 30.

Supplies: None.

Players form a large circle, facing in. Three children stand in the center. Those forming the circle and those in the center are numbered off by threes. The players in the center take turns, each calling out his own number. When a number is called, all those with that number change places. The one in the center *with this number* tries to find a place. The child without a place goes to the center and waits until the other center players have had their turns.

Variation: The teacher could call out the numbers, not necessarily in order, to add an element of suspense to the game.

WEATHERVANE

Playing Area: Playground, gymnasium, classroom.

Players: Entire class.

Supplies: None.

Children stand alongside their desks or are scattered throughout the area. A leader stands at the front of the class and gives the directions. He calls out the four main compass directions — North, South, East, and West. The children jump in place making the necessary turn in the air to face the called direction. This could involve a quarter, half, or three-quarter turn. If the direction is called which the children are facing, then each child jumps in the air with no turn. All turns should be in the same direction for a period of time to avoid confusion.

A child can sit down after a stipulated number of errors. An alternate method would be for each child to keep track of the number of errors he made.

Variations: After the children become skillful in turning, a number of variations could be used.

1. A full turn could be required when a direction is repeated.

2. Right and left turning could be alternated.

BALANCE DODGEBALL

Playing Area: Playground or gymnasium.

Players: Entire class.

Supplies: A ball for each child who is "It."

Children are scattered over the area. One or more children have a ball and are "It." Children are safe from being hit if they are balanced on one foot. This means that one foot must be off the ground, and the other foot which supports the weight must not be moved on penalty of being hit. Hits should be made below the shoulders. Anyone legally hit becomes "It."

Teaching Suggestion: To avoid having "It" stand by a child waiting for him to lose his balance or touch a foot to the ground, have the child count rapidly up to ten. "It" must then leave him and seek another child.

Variation: Footsie Dodgeball. To be safe from being hit, the child must have both feet off the ground at the time of being hit.

BAT BALL

Playing Area: A serving line is drawn across one end of a field which is approximately 70' by 70'. A 3' by 3' base is drawn in the center of the playing field about 50' from the serving line.

Players: Two teams, 8 to 15 on each team.

Supplies: Volley or similar ball.

One team is scattered out in the playing area. The other team is behind the serving line with one player up at bat. The batter puts the ball in play by batting it with his hand into the playing area. The ball must land in the playing area or be touched by a member of the fielding team to be counted as a fair ball. As soon as the ball is hit, the batter runs to the base and back across the serving line. In the meantime, the fielding team fields the ball and attempts to hit the runner below the shoulders.

Scoring: The batter scores a run each time a fair ball is hit and he touches the base and gets across the serving line before being hit by the ball. He also scores a run if the fielding team commits a foul.

Out: The batter is out if the ball is caught on a fly. Two consecutive foul balls also put the batter out. The batter is out if hit by a thrown ball in the field of play.

Fouls: Fielders, in recovering the ball and attempting to hit the batter, may not run with the ball. The ball must be passed from fielder to fielder until thrown at the batter. A pass may not be returned to the fielder from whom it was received.

BEANBAG TARGET TOSS

Playing Area: Classroom, gymnasium. Three concentric circles are drawn on the floor with radii of 10″, 20″, and 30″.

Players: 2 to 6 for each target.

Supplies: 5 beanbags, blocks of wood, or round, smooth stones.

Players, in turn, toss the five beanbags in sequence toward the target. A throwing line should be established 10′ to 15′ from the target; the distance depends upon the children's skill.

Scoring:

Center area — 15 points
Middle area — 10 points
Outer area — 5 points
Any bag touching a line — 3 points

To score in an area the bag must be completely in the area and not touching a line. If the bag touches a line, it scores 3 points.

Each child is given 5 throws and the score is determined from the final position of the 5 bags.

Variations:

1. Two children can compete against each other alternating single throws until each has taken the allotted five. The score of each is noted. For a second turn, the child scoring the highest from the previous effort throws first.

2. Outside, players can use flat stones on a hard surface.

BOUNCE BALL

Playing Area: A rectangular court 40′ by 60′ divided into two halves by a center line. Each half is 30′ by 40′.

Players: Two teams, 8 to 15 players on each.

Supplies: 2 volleyballs or rubber playground balls of about the same size.

Each team occupies one of the halves and is given a volleyball. One or two players from each team should be assigned as ball chasers to retrieve balls behind their own end lines.

The object of the game is to bounce or roll the ball over the opponent's end line. A ball thrown across the line on a fly does not count.

Two scorers are needed, one at each end line. Players can move wherever they wish in their own areas but cannot cross the center line. After the starting signal, the balls are thrown back and forth at will.

Variation: Use a row of benches across the center line. Throws must go over the benches and bounce in the area to score.

CIRCLE TEAM DODGEBALL

Playing Area: Playground, gymnasium.

Players: 20 to 40.

Supplies: Volleyball or rubber playground ball.

The children are divided into two teams, one of which forms a large circle. The other team grouped together is in the center of the circle. One of the circle players has the ball.

When the starting signal is given, the circle players try to hit the center players with the ball. Any center player hit below the shoulders is eliminated and leaves the circle. Scoring can be done in several ways.

1. Establish a throwing time of one minute. Count the number of center players remaining.

2. Play until all center players have been eliminated. Score is determined by the number of seconds it takes to eliminate the players.

3. Allow a throwing time of one minute. Do not eliminate any center players but give one point to the circle players for each successful hit.

4. Limit the number of throws a team can take. After the specified number of throws, count the remaining center players.

The teams trade places and the scores are compared to determine the winner.

CLUB GUARD

Playing Area: Gymnasium, outdoor smooth surface.

Players: 8 to 10 in each game.

Supplies: Indian club, volleyball.

A circle about 15′ in diameter is drawn. Inside this circle at the center, an 18″ circle is drawn. The Indian club is put in the center of the small circle. One child guards the club. The other children are back of the larger circle which is the restraining line for them. This circle should be definite.

The circle players throw the ball at the club and try to knock it down. The guard tries to block the throws with his legs or body. He must, however, stay out of the smaller inner circle.

The outer circle players pass the ball around rapidly so one of the players can get an opening to throw, as the guard needs to maneuver to protect the club. Whoever knocks down the club becomes the new guard.

If the guard steps in the inner circle, he loses his place to whoever has the ball at that time.

A small circle cut from plywood or similar material makes a definite circle so that it is known when the guard steps inside. A hoop can be used.

Variation: Set up more than one club to be guarded.

COMPETITIVE CIRCLE CONTESTS

Playing Area: Playground, gymnasium.

Players: Two teams, 10 to 15 on each.

Supplies: 2 volleyballs or rubber playground balls, 2 Indian clubs.

Two teams can compete against each other in the form of independent circles. The circles should be of the same size, and lines can be drawn on the floor to assure this. The players of each team are numbered consecutively so that there is a player in each circle with a corresponding number.

These numbered players go to the center of the opponent's circle in turn and compete for their teams against the circle of opponents.

To begin, the #1 players go to the opponent's circle. Three different contests are suggested, using the above arrangement as the basis.

Individual Dodgeball. The circle players throw at the center players, who represent the other team. The circle which hits the center player first wins a point.

Club Guard. In this contest, the center player guards an Indian club as in *Club Guard.* Whichever circle knocks down the club first wins a point.

Touch Ball. The circle players pass the ball from one to another while the center players try to touch it. Whichever center player touches the ball first wins a point for his team.

After the #1 players have competed, they return to their own team circle and the #2s go to the opponent's circles. This is continued until all players have competed. The team with the most points wins.

NEWCOMB

Playing Area: Volleyball Court.

Players: Two teams, 8 to 10 on each.

Supplies: Volleyball.

Each team occupies one side of the court. The children may be positioned in two or three lines of players, depending upon the number of children and the size of the court. There is no rotation system, and service is informal.

The object of the game is for one team to throw the ball underhanded over the net in such a way that it will not be caught. The game starts with a member of one team throwing the ball into the opposite court. The ball is thrown back and forth until an error is committed. Each time a team commits an error, a point is scored for the opposite team. Errors are: (1) failure to catch a ball, (2) not throwing the ball across the net successfully, and (3) throwing the ball so it falls out-of-bounds on the other side of the net. The first team reaching a score of 15 is the winner.

There is no formal rotation, but the teacher can change the lines from front to back at times. The child nearest to the ball which touched the floor or went out-of-bounds starts the play with a throw. The ball may be passed from one player to another before it is thrown across the net.

Variation: Use more than one ball.

ONE STEP

Playing Area: Playground.

Players: 2. Any number of pairs can compete against each other depending upon the space available.

Supplies: Ball or beanbag.

The game is excellent for practicing throwing and catching skills. Two children stand facing each other about 3' apart. One has a ball or beanbag. The object of the game is to throw or toss the ball in the stipulated manner so that the partner can catch it *without moving his feet* from their position on the floor. When the throw is completed successfully, the thrower takes one step backward. He awaits the throw from his partner. Limits can be established back to which the partners step, or the two children who can move to the greatest distance apart as compared to other couples are the winners. Variables to provide interest and challenge are (1) the type of throw, (2) the type of catching, and (3) the kind of a step. Throwing can be underhand, overhand, two-handed, under one leg, around the back, etc. Catching can be two-handed, left hand, right hand, to the side, etc. The step can be a giant step, a tiny step, a hop, a jump, or some similar designation.

When either child misses, moves his feet, or fails to follow directions, the partners move forward and start over. A line of children facing each other make a satisfactory formation for having a number of pairs compete at the same time.

TOSS TARGET BALL

Playing Area: Playground with sufficient clear space.

Players: 10 to 15.

Supplies: A ball for each child plus a basketball for the center player.

Each child stands in a circle and has a small ball (tennis or sponge) suitable for throwing. One child stands in the center with a basketball. The center player tosses the basketball straight up about 15' to 20'. Children throw at the basketball and try to hit it while it is up in the air. Children should be cautioned to throw at the target when it is at its zenith. A child that hits the ball scores a point for himself.

Variation: Divide the group into teams, each designated by a number or color (if various colored balls are available). The teacher calls a number or color, and only that team throws, scoring a point for each hit. The teacher can call the numbers in order or at random to provide the element of suspense. All should have an equal number of turns.

GAMES FOR INTERMEDIATE LEVEL CHILDREN

In contrast to games for the lower grades, the activities for the intermediate level are more difficult to allocate with precision to a specific grade level. In many cases this involves an arbitrary decision, based on both judgment and choice. However, it is felt that the allocation of games to grade levels is important as this assures the children of new experiences for each school year.

The intermediate program should make good use of all appropriate games from the lower grades which can be utilized for the older children. Modifications of the game with respect to rules and boundaries allow use on many levels, even in junior and senior high school programs.

Intermediate games presented here should be supplemented by the lead-up games found in the following sections.

Other activities are found in the section on individual and dual activities, chapter 20.

The Games Program for the 4 Fourth Grade

Review Third Grade Games
Addition Tag
Alaska Baseball
Box Ball
Cageball Kick-Over
Circle Chase
Circle One-Step
Four Square
Hand Hockey
Hook On
Islands
Jump the Shot Variations
Loop Touch
Loose Caboose
March Attack
O'Grady Says
Running Dodgeball
Squad Tag
Trades
Trees
Whistle Mixer

ADDITION TAG

Playing Area: Playground.
Players: Entire class.
Supplies: None.

The object of the game is to catch all the children by tagging. Two couples are "It" and each stands with inside hands joined. These are the taggers. The other children run individually. The couples move around the playground trying to tag with the free hands. Anyone tagged joins the couple, making a trio. The three now chase until they catch a fourth. Once a fourth person is caught, the four divide and form two couples, adding another set of taggers to the game. This continues until all the children are tagged.

Some limitation of area should be established, enough to enable the couples to catch the runners. If the children are scattered to distant parts of a playground, the game moves slowly and is fatiguing. A legal tag is made only if the couples or groups of three keep their hands joined.

· The game can be used as an introductory activity as all children are active.

ALASKA BASEBALL

Playing Area: Playground.
Players: Entire class.
Supplies: Volleyball or soccer.

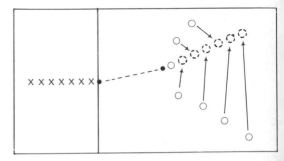

The players are organized into two teams, one of which is at bat and the other in the field. A straight line provides the only out-of-bounds, and the team at bat is behind this line at about the middle. The other team is scattered in the fair territory.

One player propels the ball by either batting (as in volleyball) or kicking a stationary soccer ball. His teammates are in a close file just behind him. As soon as he sends the ball into the playing area, he starts to run around his own team. Each time the runner passes the head of the file, the team gives a loud count.

There are no outs. The first fielder to get the ball stands still and starts to pass the ball back over his head to the nearest teammate who moves directly behind him to receive the ball. The remainder of the team in the field must run to the ball and form a file behind it. The ball is passed back overhead with each player handling the ball until the last player in line has a firm grip on it. He shouts, "Stop." At this signal, a count is made of the number of times the batter ran around his own team. In order to score a little more sharply, a half count should be made. Allow five batters to bat and then change the teams. This is better than allowing one entire team to bat before changing to the field as the players in the field get quite tired from too many consecutive runs.

Variation: Set up regular bases. Have the batter run the bases instead of scoring as indicated. Scoring can be in terms of a home run made or not, or the batter can continue around the bases, getting a point for each base.

BOX BALL

Playing Area: Playground, gymnasium.

Players: Four teams, 6 to 10 on each team.

Supplies: A sturdy box, 2' by 2' and about 12" deep. One volleyball or similar type for each team.

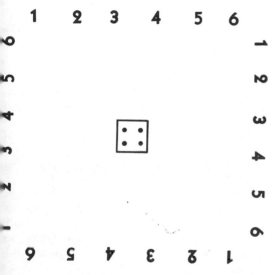

Any number of teams can play the game, but four makes a convenient number. Each team occupies one side of a hollow square at an equal distance from the center. Each team is facing inward and is numbered off consecutively from right to left. The teams should be of even numbers.

A box containing as many balls as there are teams is put in the center. The instructor calls a number, and the player from each team who has this number runs forward to the box and takes a ball. He now runs to the head of his line and takes the place of #1. In the meantime, the players in his line have moved to the left just enough to fill in the space left

by the runner. Upon reaching the head of the line, the runner passes the ball to #1 and so on down the line to the end man. The last man runs forward and returns the ball to the box. The first team to return the ball to the box scores 1 point.

The runner must not pass the ball down the line until he takes his place at the head. The ball must be caught and passed by each man. Failure to conform to each of these rules results in disqualification.

The runner now stays at the head of the line. He retains his number, but it is not important to maintain the line in consecutive number sequence.

CAGEBALL KICK-OVER

Playing Area: Playground (grassy area), gymnasium.

Players: Two teams, 7 to 10 on each team.

Supplies: A cageball — 18", 24", or 30" size.

The two teams sit facing each other with their legs outstretched and the soles of the feet about 3' apart. Each player supports his weight on his hands, which are placed slightly back of him, while maintaining the sitting position.

The teacher rolls the cageball between the two teams. The object of the game is to kick the ball over the other team. After a point is scored, the teacher rolls the ball into play again. A system of rotation can be used whereby, when a point is scored, the player on the left side of the line takes a place on the right side, moving all the other players one position to the left.

If the ball is kicked out at either end, no score results, and the ball is put into play again by the teacher.

Variation: Allow the children to use their hands to stop the ball from going over them.

CIRCLE CHASE

Playing Area: Playground, gymnasium.

Players: 20 to 40.

Supplies: None.

The group is arranged in the circle, standing elbow distance apart, and facing the center. Depending upon the size of the group count off by threes, fours, or fives around the circle. The teacher calls out a number. All players with this number start running around the circle. Players try to catch and tag the player ahead. Those tagged drop out of the game, while those not tagged make one lap around the circle and back to place. Players should try both to tag and keep from being tagged.

After all numbers have been called, the remaining players re-form the circle and count off to get new numbers. The game is then repeated until a designated number remains.

The game is interesting and competitive, but has the basic weakness that those who are eliminated, the slower children, probably need the running the most. It is best to get them back into the game as soon as practical.

Variation: Instead of having each player run around once, let him run around two or three times before stopping at his position.

CIRCLE ONE-STEP

Playing Area: Playground.

Players: Not more than 5 or 6 in a group.

Supplies: A ball for each group.

The teacher should review and play *One-Step,* a game for the third grade. For *Circle One-Step,* the children form a circle facing in so that with arms outstretched to the side, the hands can touch. One child is designated as the leader. The leader throws the ball around the circle either right or left consecutively. After each person in order handles the ball successfully (throwing and catching), the ball is back to the leader. Each child now takes a step back, enlarging the circle. This action is repeated until one of the children makes an error. Errors are made by dropping the ball, not throwing properly, or moving the feet more than a half step in any direction while catching.

Different kinds of throws can be designated or each child must throw in the fashion of the leader. The kind of a step back can be specified as a "giant step," "a tiny step," or something similar.

Teachers should recognize that the circles could become quite large and may need a limitation. If a group's circle reaches the maximum size specified they score one point and start over. The groups should be scattered widely over the available playground space so the circles will not interfere with each other.

FOUR SQUARE

Playing Area: Usually outside on a hard surface, according to the following diagram.

Players: 4 players play the game, but others are in line for a turn.

Supplies: Playground ball or volleyball.

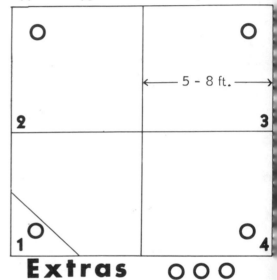

The squares are numbered 1, 2, 3, and 4. A service line is drawn diagonally across the far corner of square #1. The player in the #1 square must stay behind this line when he serves. The serve always starts from the #1 square.

The ball is served by dropping it and serving it underhanded from the bounce. If the serve hits a line, the server is out. The server can hit the ball to any of the other three courts. The player receiving the ball must keep it in play by striking the ball after it has bounced once in his square. He directs it to any other square with an underhand hit. Play continues until one player fails to return the ball or commits a fault.

The following are faults:

1. Hitting the ball sidearm or overhand.

2. Ball landing on a line between the squares. (Ball landing on an outer boundary is considered good.)

3. Stepping in another square to play the ball.

4. Catching or carrying a return volley.

5. Allowing ball to touch any part of the body except the hands.

When a player misses or commits a fault, he goes to the end of the waiting line and all players move up. The player at the head of the waiting line moves into square #4.

Variations:

1. A two-foot circle into which the ball cannot be hit without scoring an error can be drawn at the center of the area.

2. The game can be changed by varying the method of propelling the ball. The leader sets the means. The ball can be hit with the partially closed fist, the back of the hand, or the elbow. Also, the foot or the knee can be used to return the ball. Call out "fisties, elbows, footsies, or kneesies" to set the pattern.

3. *Chain Spelling.* The server names a word, and each player in returning the ball must spell the correct letter in proper rotation.

HAND HOCKEY

Playing Area: Field, about 100' by 100'.

Players: Two teams composed of 12 to 15 each.

Supplies: Soccer or volleyball.

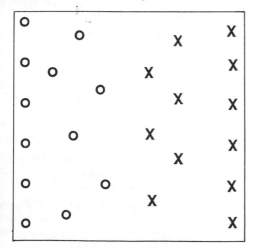

One-half the players of each team are guards and are stationed on the goal line they are defending. The other half of the players on each team are active players and are scat-tered throughout the playing area.

The object of the game is to bat or push the ball with either hand so that it crosses the goal line the other team is defending. Players may move the ball as in hockey, but may not throw, hoist, or kick it. The defensive goal line players are limited to one step into the playing field when playing the ball.

The ball is put in play by rolling it into the field of players at about the center. After a goal has been scored or after a definite time period, guards become active players, and vice versa.

If out-of-bounds, the ball goes to the opposite team and is put in play by rolling it from the sidelines into the playing area. If the ball becomes entrapped among players, play is stopped and the ball is put into play again by a roll from the referee.

Players must play the ball and not resort to rough tactics. A player who is called for unnecessary roughness or illegally handling the ball must go to the sidelines (as in hockey) and remain in the penalty area until the players change positions.

Players should scatter and attempt to pass to each other rather than bunch around the ball.

Variation: Scooter Hockey. The game is played in the same way as described except that the active players from each team in the center are on gym scooters. The position one takes on the gym scooter can be specified or it can be free choice. If specified, some positions which can be used are kneeling, seated, or using a tummy balance.

HOOK ON

Playing Area: Playground, gymnasium.

Players: 15 to 30.

Supplies: None.

One child is a chaser and another a runner. The remainder of the children are scattered by pairs around the area. They stand with inside hands joined and outside hands on hips, making a loop to which the runner can hook on.

Whenever the tagger catches the runner, the positions are reversed. To get away the runner hooks on with his arm to any pair. This makes three in a line, and the child on the other end of the line becomes the runner.

Teaching Suggestion: Do not let the runner go too far without hooking to one of the pairs. The fun comes from a constant change of partners.

ISLANDS

Playing Area: Gymnasium, hard top surface outside.

Players: Entire class.

Supplies: None.

With chalk, a number of patterns of "Islands" are laid out on the floor in the following fashion.

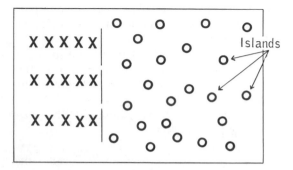

The object of the game is for the children to step, jump, or hop from "Island" to "Island" without error. Errors occur by stepping on a line or outside of an Island. Islands can be of different sizes and in different arrangements, depending upon the ability of the children. Courses can be laid out under two plans. The first would be to establish courses in order of increasing difficulty. The children would move to a more difficult course after completing one successfully. The other plan would be to make each course reasonably easy at the start and increase the difficulty as the course progresses. Children can leap, jump, or hop from Island to Island.

It would be well for the teacher to review and play *Leap the Brook,* a game in the second grade list, before introducing *Islands.*

JUMP THE SHOT VARIATIONS

Playing Area: Playground, gymnasium, classroom.

Players: 10-30.

Supplies: A jump-the-shot rope.

Review the *Jump the Shot* as described in the Third Grade Games.

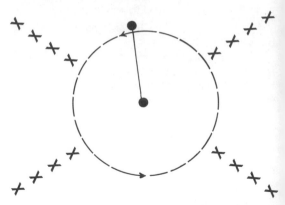

Variations: Squads line up in the following fashion in spoke formation.

Each member is given a definite number of jumps (3, 4, or 5). The next squad member in line must come in immediately without missing a turn of the rope. A player scores a point for his squad when he comes in *on time,* jumps the prescribed number of turns, and exits successfully. The squad with the most points wins.

Try with couples. Couples must join inside hands and stand side by side when jumping.

LOOP TOUCH

Playing Area: Playground, gymnasium. Three parallel lines are drawn 15' apart.

Players: 2 players work together. As many pairs can play as there is room to run.

Supplies: None.

The activity is played on an area which has three parallel lines across the length, forming two outside lines and a center line. Partners form a team and compete against other pairs.

The partners are divided, each standing on an outside line, facing each other ready to run. On the starting signal, the partners run to the center line, grasp right hands, run around each other (right hand loop), and run back and touch the outside line. Without stopping, they run back to the center, meet and make a left-hand loop, and run back for another touch. Continuing — they meet again in the center, make a two-hand loop, and back to the outside line for a touch. Once again, they run to the center, join hands, raising the joined hands above the head for a finishing act.

The first pair to finish wins. The children need to be reminded that each time they return to the outside line, they must touch it with a foot. Failure to do so results in disqualification.

Variations: Other stunts could be done in the center such as:

1. Leapfrog.

2. Crawl through the other's legs.

3. Do a specified number of sit-ups with partner holding the legs.

LOOSE CABOOSE

Playing Area: Playground, gymnasium.

Players: 12 to 30.

Supplies: None.

One child is designated as the "Loose Caboose" and tries to hook on to a train. Trains are formed by three or four children standing in a column formation with each child placing his hands on the waist of the child immediately in front of him. The trains, by twisting and turning, endeavor to keep the Caboose from hooking on to the back. Should this happen, the front child in the train becomes the new Caboose. Each train should attempt to keep together and not break apart. If the number of children is twenty or more, or there seems to be difficulty in hooking the Caboose to the end of a train, there should be two Cabooses.

MARCH ATTACK

Playing Area: Playground, gymnasium. Two parallel lines are drawn about 60' apart.

Players: 15 to 40, divided between two teams.

Supplies: None.

One team takes a position on one of the lines with their backs to the area. These are the chasers. The other team is on the other line facing the area. This is the marching team.

The marching team moves forward on signal, marching in good order toward the chasers. When they get reasonably close, a whistle or other signal is given and the marchers turn and run back to their line, chased by

the other team. If any of the marchers are caught before reaching their line, they change to the other team. The game is repeated with the roles of marcher and chaser exchanged.

O'GRADY SAYS

Playing Area: Playground, gymnasium, classroom.

Players: Entire class.

Supplies: None.

This game is borrowed from the U. S. Army. Different facing directions are given like "right face," "left face," and "about face." Also, calling to attention and standing at ease can be used. A leader stands in front and calls out the various commands. The players are to follow *only* if the command is preceded by "O'Grady says." Any one moving at the wrong time is eliminated and should sit down.

Additional commands involving other movements can be used. To be effective, the commands must be given rapidly.

RUNNING DODGEBALL

Playing Area: Playground, gymnasium. Two parallel lines are drawn about 40' apart to form a gauntlet. The gauntlet is about 60' in length.

Players: Two teams, 10 to 15 on each team.

Supplies: 4 volley or rubber balls suitable for dodgeball.

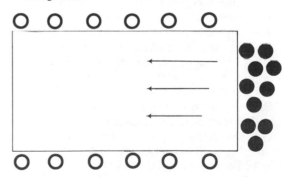

Team A does the throwing and Team B runs the gauntlet. Team A's players are divided with half on one side of the gauntlet and half on the other. Four volleyballs are split between them.

Team B's players line up at one end of the gauntlet. They are to run through the gauntlet between members of Team A without getting hit. In moving through, they can run separately or all together.

The throwing team may recover the volleyballs lying in the running area, but must return to the sides before throwing. After a count is made of the successful runners, the teams trade places and the game is repeated.

Variations:

1. Instead of having the team run once across, designate that the players are to run across and immediately start back. They score a point only if they make the round trip without being hit.

2. A good active game can be played by having the ball rolled instead of thrown. This causes the players to jump high into the air to avoid being hit.

SQUAD TAG

Playing Area: Playground, gymnasium.

Players: Entire class.

Supplies: Pinnies or markers for a squad. Stopwatch.

This is a straight tag game with the entire squad acting as taggers. The object is to see which squad can tag the remainder of the class members in the shortest time. The tagging squad should be marked.

The tagging squad stands in a football huddle formation in the center of the area. Heads are down and hands are joined in the huddle. The remainder of the class is scattered as they wish throughout the area. On signal, the tagging squad scatters and tags the other class members. When a class member is tagged, he stoops in place and remains there. Time is taken when the last member is tagged. Each squad gets a turn.

Children need to be cautioned to watch for collisions, as there is much chasing and dodging in different directions. Definite boundaries need to be established.

TRADES

Playing Area: Playground, gymnasium, classroom. Two parallel lines are drawn 60' apart.

Players: Entire class.

Supplies: None.

The class is divided into two teams of equal numbers, each of which has a goal line. Team B, the chasers, remains behind its goal line. Team A approaches from its goal line marching to the following dialogue:

Team A "Here we come."
Team B "Where from?"
Team A "New Orleans."
Team B "What's your trade?"
Team A "Lemonade."
Team B "Show us some."

Team A moves up close to Team B's goal line and proceeds to act out the motions of an activity, occupation, or specific task, which they have chosen previously. The members of Team B make as many guesses as necessary to guess what the pantomime represents. Team A gives the initials of the activity to help. A correct guess means that Team A must run back to its goal line chased by Team B. Any member caught must join Team B. The game is repeated with the roles reversed. The team ending with the greater number of players is the winner.

Teaching Hint: If one team has trouble guessing, the other players should provide hints. Also, teams should be encouraged to have a number of activities chosen so that little time is consumed in the huddle choosing the next activity to be guessed.

TREES

Playing Area: Playground, gymnasium. Two parallel lines are drawn 60' apart.

Players: Entire class.

Supplies: None.

All players except "It" are on one side of the area. On the signal "Trees," the players run to the other side of the court. "It" tries to catch as many as possible. Any player tagged by "It" becomes a tree and must stop where he was tagged and keep both feet in place. He cannot move his feet, but can tag any of the runners who come close enough. "It" continues to chase the players as they cross on signal until all but one are caught. This player becomes the tagger ("It") for the next game.

To speed things up, two taggers may be chosen. Also, the taggers should have reasonable ability to catch the others, or the game will move slowly. Children cross from side to side only on signal "Trees."

WHISTLE MIXER

Playing Area: Playground, gymnasium, classroom.

Players: Any number.

Supplies: Whistle.

Children are scattered throughout the area. To begin, they walk around in any direction they wish. The teacher blows a whistle a number of times in succession with short, sharp blasts. Whatever the number of blasts, the children form small circles with the number in the circle equal to the number established by the whistle signal. Thus, if there are four blasts, the children form circles of four — no more, no less. Any children left out are eliminated. Also, if a circle is formed with more than the specified number, the entire circle is eliminated.

After the circles have been formed and the eliminated children have been moved to the sidelines, the teacher calls, "Walk" and the game continues. In walking, the children should move in different directions.

Variation: A fine version of this game can be done with the aid of a tom-tom. Different beats of the tom-tom would indicate various locomotor movements — skipping, galloping, slow walk, normal walk, running. The whistle would still be used to set the number to be in each circle.

The Games Program for the Fifth Grade ⟩

Review Fourth Grade Games
Battle Dodgeball
Bombardment
Bronco Dodgeball
Circle Hook On
Circle Tug-of-War
Four Team Grab Ball
Jolly Ball
Mickey Mouse
Number Tug-of-War
Scooter Kick Ball
Sunday
Third Man
Touchdown
Two Square
Whistle Ball

BATTLE DODGEBALL

Playing Area: Playground, gymnasium.

Players: Two teams, 10 to 15 on each team.

Supplies: 2 volleyballs or rubber playground balls.

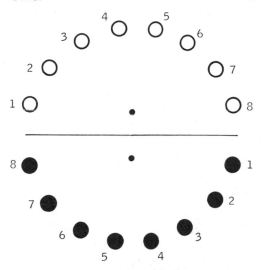

The teams form one circle, each occupying one-half the circle. Players on each team are numbered consecutively. For any one number, there is a player on each team. Two volleyballs are placed about 5' apart in the center of the circle, one on each side of a center line which separates the teams from each other.

The teacher calls out the number he chooses. The two players with that number run forward; each picks up a ball and tries to hit the other with it. Players on the sides of the circle may retrieve balls and throw them to their teammate in the center. However, each competing player must stay in his half of the circle.

The winning player scores a point for his team. Play for a certain number of points or until each player has had a turn.

Variation: Call two numbers, which means that two compete against two. Compete until one or both are hit.

BOMBARDMENT (Indian Clubs)

Playing Area: Gymnasium.

Players: Two teams, 10 to 15 on each team.

Supplies: 12 Indian clubs for each team. 4 volley or rubber playground balls.

A line is drawn across the center of the floor from wall to wall. This divides the floor into two courts, each of which is occupied by one team. Another line is drawn 25' from the center line in each court. This is the club line. Each team sets their Indian clubs on this line. These should be spaced. Each team is given two of the balls.

The object of the game is to knock over the other team's clubs. Players throw the balls back and forth but cannot cross the center line. Whenever a club is knocked over by a ball or accidentally by a player, the club is removed. The team with the most clubs standing is declared the winner.

Out-of-bounds balls can be recovered but must be thrown from the court.

Variation: Instead of removing the clubs, they can be reset. Two scorers, one for each club line, are needed for this version.

BRONCO DODGEBALL

Playing Area: Playground, gymnasium.
Players: 15 to 20.
Supplies: Volleyball or rubber playground ball.

One-half the children form a circle about 10 yards across. These are the throwers. The other children are in the center and form a bronco, made by the children standing in file formation, each with hands placed on the hips of the child immediately in front. The object of the game is to hit the rear member of the bronco with the ball. This is the only child who may be legally hit. The bronco moves around, protected by the child at the head of the file. He, however, is not permitted to use his hands.

As soon as the child at the rear of the bronco is hit, he leaves the circle, and the next child on the end becomes the target. If the bronco breaks during the maneuvering, all children to the rear of the break are eliminated. Exchange the circle and bronco players.

Five or six children may be as many as can conveniently maneuver as a bronco. Have two broncos in the center if the group is large. Stress quick passing and throwing, as this is the key to reducing the number in the bronco.

CIRCLE HOOK-ON

Playing Area: Playground, gymnasium, classroom.
Players: 4.
Supplies: None.

This is a game of one child against the other three, who form a small circle with joined hands. The object of the game is for the lone child to tag a designated child in the circle. The other two children in the circle by dodging and maneuvering around attempt to keep the tagger away from the third member of the circle. The circle players may maneuver and circle in any direction they wish, but must not release hand grips. The tagger in attempting to touch the protected circle player must go around the outside of the circle. He is not permitted to go underneath or through the joined hands of the circle players.

Variations:

1. Use a piece of cloth, handkerchief, or "flag" tucked in the belt in back of the child opposite. The fourth child tries to pull the "flag" from the belt.

2. Instead of tagging, the chaser tries to hook on the child being protected.

Teaching Hints: Watch for roughness by the two in the circle protecting the third. The game works better if the children are of about equal ability physically. Allow a period of time and rotate if the chaser is not successful. In any case, the children should rotate so that each has a chance to be the tagger.

Circle Hook-On—The teacher plays with the children

CIRCLE TUG-OF-WAR

Playing Area: Playground, gymnasium.

Players: 10 to 15 in each circle.

Supplies: 12 to 15 Indian clubs.

The object of the tug-of-war is to have the other players break a grip or knock over a club. A circle is formed by the players, who join hands with good grips. In the center of the circle, the Indian clubs are placed in a scattered formation. After the starting signal, the players pull or push to eliminate other players. Both players who break a grip are eliminated or any player who knocks over a club in the struggle is out. After about half are eliminated, re-form the circle and start anew.

Variation: The game can also be played with the players facing out. With their backs to the center, they have more trouble dodging the Indian clubs.

FOUR TEAM GRAB BALL

Playing Area: Playground, gymnasium.

Players: Four teams, 6 to 8 on each.

Supplies: 4 balls of approximately the same size. The balls should be of different colors or marked so they can be told apart.

A line is drawn 30′ to 50′ from a wall. Behind this line and facing the wall, the teams are in file formation. A wall or fence is necessary to limit the length of the throws, but a limiting line can be used.

The player at the head of each file has a ball. At a signal, each player throws or rolls the ball in the direction of the wall. The object of the game is to recover a ball (not your own) and return first to the line. The child first back with another ball scores 2 points for his team. The second scores 1 point. No points are given for third and fourth place. If it happens that the child brings back the ball which he threw, his team loses one point. After the children run back to the line, they take places at the end of the file; and the game is repeated with four new players.

There is less confusion if the teams are permanently assigned a ball. To start each throw, then, the balls must be returned to the respective teams. However, if there is considerable difference in the performance of the balls,

then the team should throw the ball which was returned by its player.

The children will learn very quickly that the advantage lies in keeping the ball as close as possible to the fence or wall since the other players have to run farther.

JOLLY BALL

Playing Area: Playground, gymnasium.

Players: 20 to 30.

Supplies: Cageball 24″ or larger; or a push-ball 36″ to 48″.

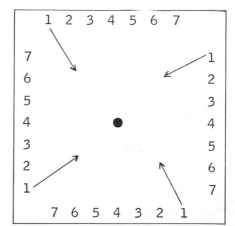

Four teams are organized, each of which forms one side of a hollow square. The children are sitting down facing in with hands braced behind them. On each team, the children are numbered consecutively from one to as far as needed. Each child waits until his number is called. The four active players (one from each team) move forward in crab position and try to kick the cageball over the heads of any one of the three opposing teams. The players on the teams can also kick the ball. Ordinarily, the hands are not to be used, but this could be allowed among less skilled children and in the learning stages of the game.

A point is scored against a team that allows the ball to go over its line. A ball that goes out at the corner between teams is dead and must be replayed. When a point is scored, the active children retire back to their teams; and another number is called. This game is quite strenuous for the active players in the center, and time should be called after a reasonable length of time if no score develops.

Variation: The game can also be played by allowing two children at a time from each team to be active.

MICKEY MOUSE

Playing Area: Playground, gymnasium, classroom.
Players: Entire class.
Supplies: 4 Indian clubs.

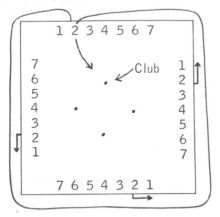

A hollow square, about 10 yards on each side, is formed by four teams, each of which occupies one side facing in. The teams should be even in numbers. Each team is numbered consecutively from right to left. This means that there is one person on each team with the same number. The children are seated cross-legged.

A number is called by the teacher. The four children with this number run to the right all the way around the square and through their *own* vacated space toward the center of the square. Near the center in front of each team stands an Indian club. The first child to put the Indian club down on the floor is the winner. The clubs should be at an equal distance in front of the teams and far enough away from each other to avoid collisions in the center.

Scoring is kept by the words, "Mickey Mouse." The player who puts the club down first gets to write two letters of the name. The player who is second gets to put down one letter. The lettering can be done in a space in front of each team, where the name would be reasonably protected from the runners. The first team to complete the name is the winner.

In number games of this type, the numbers are not called in order. The teacher should keep some kind of a tally to assure that each number is called.

Variation: Instead of having the group seated, have each one take a prone position, ready to do a push-up. The teacher gives a preliminary command, such as "ready." Each child comes up to a push-up position. The teacher then calls the number. The children not running then return to the prone position on the floor. In this manner, each time a number is called, each child will do a push-up.

NUMBER TUG-OF-WAR

Playing Area: Playground, gymnasium, classroom. Two parallel lines are drawn about 20' apart.
Players: 10 to 16.
Supplies: Individual tug-of-war rope.

The game is between teams, each of which lines up behind one of the lines. The players on each team are numbered consecutively. There is a player on each team designated by the same number. In the center between the two lines, lying crosswise, is an individual tug-of-war rope.

The teacher calls out any number, and the two players with that number rush out to the rope. If either can get back to his side without the other getting a hold on the rope, he wins. Otherwise, if both can secure holds on the rope, then a tug-of-war contest ensues. The winner is the player who is able to touch his base line with his foot.

Variation: Call out two numbers or set up the original game so that two children on each side have the same number. The tug-of-war then is two against two. This will accommodate more children in the game.

SCOOTER KICK BALL

Playing Area: Gymnasium, Basketball Court.

Players: 20-30, divided into 2 teams.

Supplies: Cageball, gym scooters for active players.

Players on each team are divided into active players (on scooters) and goal defenders. The active players are seated on the scooters, and the goal defenders are seated on the goal line with feet extended. The object of the game is to kick the cageball over the goal line defended by the opposite team. The players are positioned as follows.

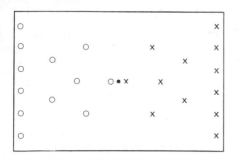

The game is started with a face-off of two opposite players on scooters at the center of the court. This position is also used after a goal is scored. The active players on scooters may propel the ball only with their feet. Touching the ball with the hands in an attempt to stop or propel the ball is a foul and results in a free kick by the opposition at the spot of the foul. A player may use his head or body to stop or propel the ball.

The players defending the goal are seated on the goal line. One of two rules can apply to their defense. The first rule is to limit their defense by applying the same rule as for scooter players — not permitting use of the hands to stop the ball. The feet, body, and head may be used.

If scoring seems too easy, then permit the defenders to use their hands. Defenders should be restricted to the seated position at the goal line and not permitted to enter the field of play to propel or stop the ball.

If the sidelines are close to the walls of the gymnasium, there is little need to call out-of-bounds balls as the ball can rebound from the wall.

The number of scooters will determine the number of active players. The game works well if one-half the players from each team are in the center on scooters and the other half as goal defenders. After a goal or stipulated period of time, active players and goal defenders exchange places. The teacher may wish to have girls against girls as active players with the boys as defenders, and then reverse their positions.

Some consideration for glasses should be made as the ball moves quite suddenly, and glasses might be broken. One other problem arises with the active player who falls off his scooter. He should be required to seat himself on his scooter before he can be eligible to propel the ball.

Variation: If there are enough scooters so that each child in the game can have one, the game can be played under much the same rules as in soccer. A more restricted goal (perhaps one-half of the end line) can be set up with standards. A goalie can defend this area. All other players are active and can move to any spot on the floor.

Caution must be exercised so that the floor space is sufficient to allow for some freedom to play the game. Putting too many active players in a relatively small space will cause a jamming up of the players.

SUNDAY

Playing Area: Two parallel lines are drawn about 50' apart.

Players: Entire class.

Supplies: None.

One player is "It" and stands in the center of the area between the two lines. All other children are on one of the two lines. The object is to cross to the other line without being tagged or making a false start.

Players stand with the front foot on the line. They must run across immediately when "It" calls out, "Sunday." Anyone who doesn't come immediately is considered caught. "It" may call out other days of the week to confuse the runners. No player may make a start if another day of the week is called. What "making a start" is must be defined. At the beginning, define it as a player moving either foot. Later, when the children get better at the game, a forward movement of the body can make one "caught."

"It" must be careful to pronounce "Monday" in such a way that it cannot be confused with "Sunday." If trouble develops here, eliminate "Monday" from the signals for the false start.

THIRD MAN

Playing Area: Playground, gymnasium.

Players: 20 to 35.

Supplies: None.

The game, *Three Deep,* should be reviewed and played. In *Third Man,* the players are scattered by pairs in the area. Each pair stand facing each other, with enough room so that the runner may come and stand between them.

A runner and a chaser are chosen. The chaser tries to tag the runner, who can escape and become safe by taking a position *between* the two players of any couple. In doing so, he faces either of the two. The person to whom he turns his back is the "Third Man" and becomes the runner. When the chaser tags the runner, the positions are reversed.

The game becomes more interesting if frequent changes are made. No one should be permitted to run very far without making a change. A runner is not permitted to run between a couple without stopping, as this causes confusion. The runner must not leave the immediate area of the players. Watch for favoritism in making exchanges.

Variation: The teacher can blow a whistle or call out "Reverse," which means the positions of the runner and chaser are changed.

TOUCHDOWN

Playing Area: Playground, gymnasium. Two parallel lines are needed about 60' apart.

Players: Two teams, 10 to 15 on each team.

Supplies: Small object which can be concealed in the hand.

Two teams face each other, each standing on one of the parallel lines. One team goes into a huddle and the members decide which player is to carry an object to the opponent's goal line. The team moves out of the huddle and takes a position like a football team. On the charge signal, "Hike," the players run toward the opponent's goal line, each player holding his hands as if he were carrying the object. On the charge signal, the opponents also run forward and tag the players. When a player is tagged, he must immediately stop and open both hands to show whether or not he has the object.

If the player carrying the object can reach the goal line without being tagged, he calls "Touchdown," and scores six points for his team. The team scoring retains possession of the object and gets another try. If the player carrying the object is tagged in the center area, the object is given to the other team. They go into a huddle and try to run it across the field and score.

TWO SQUARE

Playing Area: Generally outside on a hard surface according to the *Four Square* diagram (see page 298).

Players: Two players, but others may be in line for a turn.

Supplies: Playground or volleyball.

The basic rules are the same as for *Four Square,* except that only two players are involved and two squares are used. If there are players waiting for a turn, the active player who misses or fouls can be eliminated as in *Four Square.* If only two players wish to play, a score can be kept.

In *Two Square,* the ball must be served from behind the base line.

WHISTLE BALL

Playing Area: Playground, gymnasium, classroom.

Players: Groups of 6 to 8.

Supplies: A ball for each group.

A group of not more than eight children stand in a circle formation. A ball is passed rapidly back and forth among them in any order. The object is to stay in the game the longest. Children sit down in place if:

1. They have the ball when the whistle blows. (The teacher should set a predetermined time period, at the end of which a whistle is blown. This can be anywhere from 5 to 20 seconds, with the time periods varied.)

2. A child makes a bad throw or fails to catch a good throw.

3. A player returns the ball directly to the person from whom he received it.

When the game gets down to two or three players, the time limits should be short.

Teaching Suggestions: One way to control the time periods is to appoint a child as timer, giving him a list of the time periods, a whistle, and a stop watch. The timer should be cautioned not to give any advance indication when he will blow the stop signal. If an automatic timer can be secured, this enhances the game.

The Games Program for the Sixth Grade

Review Fifth Grade Games
Beater Goes Round
Cageball Target Throw
Chain Tag
Fox and Geese
Jump the Shot Variations
• Low Bridge
Odd and Even
One Base Dodgeball
Over the Wall
Pin Dodgeball
Prisoner's Base
Scatter Dodgeball
Spud

BEATER GOES ROUND

Playing Area: Playground, gymnasium.

Players: 10 to 15.

Supplies: Knotted towel.

All players, except one, stand in a circle facing counterclockwise with their hands behind them. The extra player walks around the circle in line of direction and puts the knotted towel into a player's hands. This player immediately starts hitting the player in front of him, who runs around the circle with the striker after him. The player who gave the towel steps into the circle at one of the empty places. The new player with the towel now continues the game.

Some control is necessary in this game. Children should be hit across the seat and not over the head and shoulders. Also, see that no child is repeatedly punished. No beater should be permitted to give the towel back to the player from whom he received it. Some question the appropriateness of the game for girls or mixed groups.

CAGEBALL TARGET THROW

Playing Area: Gymnasium with a space about the size of a small basketball court.

Players: Two teams, 5 to 15 on each team.

Supplies: 1 cageball (18", 24", or 30"), 12 to 15 balls of various sizes.

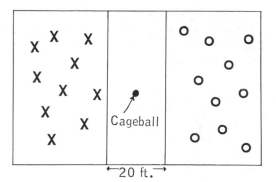

An area about 20′ wide is across the center of the playing area, with a cageball in the center. The object of the game is to throw the smaller balls against the cageball, forcing it across the line in front of the other team. Players may come up to the line to throw, but may not throw while inside the cageball area. However, a player may enter the area to recover a ball. No one is to touch the cageball at any time, nor may the cageball be pushed by a ball in the hands of a player.

If the cageball seems to roll too easily, it should be deflated slightly. The throwing balls can be of almost any size — soccers, volleyballs, playground balls, etc.

Variation: Have two rovers in the center area, one from each team, to retrieve balls. These players cannot block throws or prevent a ball from hitting the target, but are there merely to retrieve balls for their teams.

CHAIN TAG

Playing Area: Playground with two parallel lines about 50' apart.

Players: 20 to 40.

Supplies: None.

This game is essentially like other goal-exchange games except in the manner that players can be caught. In this case, the center is occupied by three players who form a chain with joined hands. The free hands on either side of the chain do the tagging.

The players in the center call, "Come," and the other children cross from one line to another. The "Chain" tries to tag any of the runners. Any one caught joins the Chain. When the Chain becomes too large, it should be divided into several smaller Chains.

Variation: Catch of Fish. In this game, Chain catches the children by surrounding them like a fish net. The runners cannot run under or through the links of the Net.

FOX AND GEESE

Playing Area: Playground, gymnasium.

Players: 15 to 30.

Supplies: A handkerchief, strip of cloth, or other flag; one for each file.

One player is the "Fox," and the remainder of the players are divided into groups of four or five. At the head of each group is a "Gander," and the rest of the group are "Geese." The Geese line up in file behind the Gander and each firmly grasps the waist of the player in front. The last player in the file has a handkerchief tucked in his belt at the back.

The Fox attempts to get the handkerchief, while the Gander tries to protect his Geese. If the Fox gets the handkerchief, the Gander of that file becomes the new Fox. The old Fox joins the group as rear player and puts the handkerchief in his belt at the back.

If the file breaks in moving around, this is considered the same as if the handkerchief were pulled.

JUMP THE SHOT VARIATIONS

The sixth grade teacher should emphasize the *Jump the Shot* routines and variations as listed in the Fourth-Grade Program. The following should be added to the activity routines.

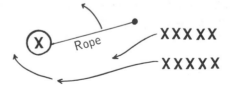

Two squads are in file formation and face the rope turner.

1. Each player runs clockwise (against the turn of the rope), jumping the rope as often as necessary to return to the squad.

2. Each player runs counterclockwise in the same direction as the rope is turning and tries to run around the circle before the rope can catch up with him. If this happens, he must jump to allow the rope to go under him. The best time for a player to start is just after the rope has passed him.

3. Try some of the stunts where the hands and feet are on the ground, and see if the players can have the rope pass under them. The *Rabbit Jump,* push-up position, *Lame Dog,* and others offer possibilities.

LOW BRIDGE

Playing Area: Gymnasium, classroom.

Players: 5-10.

Supplies: Wand, low standards.

This game is popular in many lands and some players develop a fine degree of skill in the task required. The object of the game is to move under a bar supported like a high jump bar without dislodging the bar or touching the ground with the hands or body. The bar should be started high enough so all children can go under it successfully. Each child is to get three tries to go under the bar. If he fails, he is eliminated and acts as an official for the event.

Blocks could be used together with different sized boxes to support the wand. Some kind of a system is needed so that the wand can be lowered a little at a time for each repetition of the event. The wand is lowered after all children have gone under or have had three misses. Two miniature standards similar to the type used for the high jump make the event precise and easy to administer.

ODD AND EVEN

Playing Area: Playground, gymnasium. Two parallel lines about 40′ apart.

Players: 10 to 40 with the players divided into two groups (teams).

Supplies: A cubical box numbered like a dice.

A box 6″ by 6″ with large numbers painted on the sides, the numbers running 1 through 6.

The two groups face each other about 5′ apart in the center between the two parallel lines. One group is the "Odds" and the other is the "Evens." The box is rolled between the two lines of players. If an odd number comes up (1, 3, 5) then the Odds team chases the Evens to the line back of the Evens team. If an even number (2, 4, 6) comes up, the chase is the other way.

Those caught before reaching their home line can be handled in one of two ways:

1. Any player caught joins the other side. This has a tendency in some cases to make the players careless. The team with the most players at the end of the time period wins.

2. They are eliminated and stand back of their line until the game is declared over. The team with the most players left wins.

Variation: The game can also be played as *Black and White.* A card with black on one side and white on another is substituted for the large dice. One team is designated as the white team and the other as the black.

ONE BASE DODGEBALL

Playing Area: Playground, gymnasium. A home line is drawn at one end of the playing space. A base or standard is placed about 50′ in front of the home line.

Players: Two teams, 8 to 15 on each team.

Supplies: Base (or standard), volleyball or playground ball.

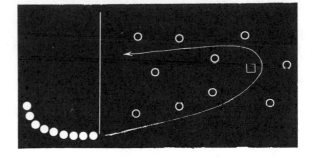

One team is scattered out in the fielding area. The boundaries of this area are determined by the number of children. The other team is lined up in single file behind the home line. Two children are running at a time.

The object of the game for the fielding team is to hit the players with the ball. They try to round the base and head back for the home line without being hit. The game is continuous, meaning that as soon as a running team player is hit or crosses the home line, another player starts immediately.

The fielding team may not run with the ball but must pass it from player to player, trying to hit one of the runners.

The running team scores a point for each player who successfully runs around the base and back to the home line.

To start the game, the running team has two players ready at the right side of the home line. The others on the team are in line waiting for a turn. The teacher throws the ball anywhere in the field, and the first two runners start toward the base. They must run around the base from the right side. After all have run, the teams exchange places. The team scoring the most runs wins.

Teaching Suggestions: Players on the fielding team should make short passes to a person close to a runner so that the runner can be hit. They must be alert because two children are running at a time.

The next player on the running team must watch carefully so that he can start the instant that one of the two preceding runners is back safely or has been hit.

OVER THE WALL

Playing Area: Playground.

Players: Entire class.

OVER THE WIND / Entire class

Supplies: None.

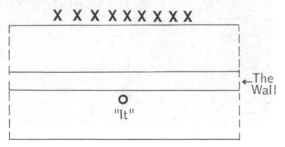

Two parallel goal lines are drawn about 60' apart. Two additional parallel lines about 3' apart are laid out parallel to the goal lines in the middle of the game area. This is the "Wall." Side limits have to be established.

One player is "It" and stands on or behind the Wall. All other players are behind one of the goal lines. "It" calls, "Over the Wall." All players must then run across the Wall to the other goal line. "It" tries to tag any player he can, who, if caught, helps him catch the others. Players are also considered caught if they step on the Wall. They must clear it with a leap or jump and cannot step on it anywhere including the lines. After crossing over to the other side safely, players must wait for the next call, "Over the Wall."

The game can be made more difficult by increasing the width of the Wall. "It" can step on or run through the Wall at will.

PIN DODGEBALL

Playing Area: Gymnasium.

Players: Entire class.

Supplies: 2 volleyballs, 6 Indian clubs.

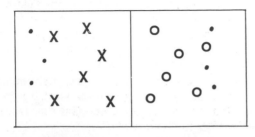

Two teams of equal numbers play the game. Each team is given one volleyball and three Indian clubs. A court 30' x 60' or larger with a center line is needed. The size of the court would depend upon the number of children in the game. The object of the game is to eliminate all players on the opposing team or to knock down their Indian clubs. The volleyballs are used to throw at the opposing team members or to knock down the clubs. Each team stays in its half of the court.

A player is eliminated if:

1. He is hit *on the fly* by a ball he does not catch.

2. He steps over the center line to throw or retrieve a ball. Any opposing team member hit under these circumstances is not eliminated.

3. He attempts to block a thrown ball with a ball in his hand, and the thrown ball touches him in any manner. A player can legally block a thrown ball with a ball held in his hand.

A foul is called if a player holds a ball longer than 10 seconds without throwing at the opposing team. The ball is immediately given to the opposing team.

Players who are eliminated should move to the sidelines and sit down, so that it can be clearly determined who is still active.

The Indian clubs are put any place in the team area as desired. Players may guard the clubs, but must not touch them. When a club is knocked down, it is removed immediately from the game. If a club is knocked down unintentionally by a member of the defending team, the club is counted as "down."

A player can be "saved" if the ball hits him and is caught by a teammate before it touches the ground.

A referee should take his position at the side of the court near the center line. When a foul is called for holding the ball over 10 seconds, play stops, and the ball is rolled to the offended team.

The game is won whenever all players from one team have been eliminated or all three clubs on one side have been knocked down.

PRISONER'S BASE

Playing Area: A rectangular area marked off as in the diagram. The size of the area would depend somewhat upon the number playing.

Players: 2 teams with 5 to 15 on each side. Each team has a captain.

Supplies: None.

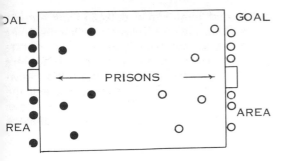

To win the game, a team must have one of its players enter the opponent's goal area without being tagged, or one team must capture all players from the opposing team. The basic rule of the game is that any player may be tagged only by an opponent who has left his own goal area *after* the player who is tagged. The game is started by players moving into the neutral area to entice the other team to chase them. Other players await their chances to tag an opponent who has left his goal line earlier. Each player tries to tag an opponent to make him a prisoner and, in turn, tries to avoid being tagged.

Players may return to their own goal line as often as they wish in order to become eligible to tag an opponent. Prisoner and tagger return without penalty to the tagger's prison.

A prisoner must keep one foot in the prison and can stretch forward as far as he is able to make rescue easier. To be rescued, a prisoner must be tagged by his own teammate who has been able to reach him without being tagged. The rescued and the rescuer return to their own goal line without the penalty of being tagged. Both are now active players.

If more than one prisoner is captured, they may form a chain by holding hands, last prisoner caught acting as anchor and keeping one foot in the prison. Only the first prisoner at the end of the chain can be released.

The captain directs his team strategy as some players guard the goal, others guard the prisoners, and another group acts as taggers.

Any player who crosses a side line to avoid being tagged is considered a prisoner.

Variation: A popular version of this game is called *Stealing Sticks.* The game is played in the same manner, except that ten sticks or Indian clubs are added. These are divided with five going to each team. Any player crossing

the opponent's goal area without being tagged is eligible to take home one stick. The game continues until one side has lost its sticks. If the play is ended before either side has possession of all the sticks, the team with the most sticks wins.

SCATTER DODGEBALL

Playing Area: Playground or gymnasium. If outside, definite boundaries should be set.

Players: Any number can play.

Supplies: 2 or 3 volleyballs or rubber balls suitable for dodgeball.

The children are scattered throughout the area. The teacher rolls the two balls into the playing area. Anyone may pick up a ball and throw it at anyone else. If a person is hit or the ball in his hand is struck with a ball, he goes to the side line. If he has a ball in his hand, he should drop it immediately and not attempt to throw. If two children throw at each other and both are hit, both are eliminated.

No player may have possession of all volleyballs. The ball must be actually thrown, as touching another player while the ball is held in the hand does not put the player out.

Children should be cautioned not to punish others unnecessarily with hard hits. Throws should be below the waist whenever possible, and a throw hitting the head puts the thrower out of the game.

SPUD

Playing Area: Playground.

Players: 8 to 12.

Supplies: Rubber playground ball (6″-8½″) or volleyball.

Players are numbered consecutively and stand in a small circle. One player is in the center, holding the ball. He tosses the ball straight up moderately high, at the same time calling the number of one of the other players. All players scatter immediately, except the player whose number was called. He goes to the center of the circle, catches the ball, and immediately calls, "Stop." All players stop at once in place and must not move their feet from the fixed position. The player with the ball takes three steps in any direction, selecting a player whom he wishes to hit. He throws the ball at this player, trying to hit him. If he misses, he gets a point (dud) against him. If he hits a player or the player moves his feet, the player gets one point against him. The player against whom the point was scored throws up the ball for the next game. When a player gets a stipulated number of points (3 or 4), he is out of the game or he can pay a penalty.

Teaching Suggestion: Some control must be made on the toss of the ball into the air. It should be of moderate height and go straight up and down. There should also be some control over the order of the numbers to avoid favoritism or collusion. If there is a problem, make a rule that a number may not be called more than twice during the course of a game. When one or two are eliminated, re-form the game. If the throwing is too successful, make a rule that the children must keep only one foot in place, or decrease or shorten the number of steps taken after catching.

Variations:

1. Use a fleece ball instead of the playground or volleyball. With a fleece ball, do not allow any steps by the thrower.

2. Keep one foot in place after the stop.

19

Rhythmic Activities

Rhythmic movement should be a part of each child's school experience. Children have a natural love for rhythmic movement and for using the body in expressive movement. Such movement is both a need and a delight. Not only are dance activities a tool for self-expression, but inherent in rhythmics are excellent possibilities for physical development. Progress toward the perfection of simple skills is enhanced by the accompaniment of rhythm.

Through gross body movements and loco-motor patterns, children gain better appreciation and understanding of the use of their bodies. Several other important objectives grow out of the program of rhythmics. Certainly, it is an important goal for each child to be able to keep time — to be able to move in keeping with the rhythm. An appreciation of the place that rhythmic activity has in our lives is another important immediate goal. This probably will be gained in proportion to the pleasure and satisfaction which children derive from dance activities.

Important attitudes and social learnings can be promoted through a well-conducted program of dance activities. To be at ease with the opposite sex, to learn social graces, and to make common elements of courtesy a practice are important goals of rhythmic program. Couple dances offer excellent opportunity to achieve these goals. Soon the children will be taking part in social functions sponsored by the school in which the ability to participate successfully in rhythmic activities is important.

Developmental possibilities for fitness are high in a well-conducted rhythmic program, particularly in the types of activities stressed on the primary level. Vigorous movements and gross body activities make up many of the rhythms for primary children. Rhythmic activities offer a maximum of participation for children, as an entire class or a good portion of it can be active at one time. Once the children have been stimulated by the desire for imitation and self-expression, their movement experience can produce good fitness values.

Movement expression through rhythm offers good opportunities for incidental and direct teaching in body mechanics and posture. The proper carriage of the body and the most efficient ways of moving should be included in the teaching of rhythmics. With the encouragement of an appropriate rhythm, children acccept postural coaching and correction naturally as a part of the teaching procedure.

RHYTHMIC ACCOMPANIMENT

The rhythmic accompaniment should be of good quality, since it must stimulate the child to movement. The following are some of the sources which can supply suitable rhythmic background for movement.

The first is the tom-tom or dance drum. Good commercial varieties of both instruments

315

are available at nominal cost. A resonant drumbeat seems to have a stimulating effect on the children. Reasonably satisfactory substitutes can be made from simple materials. For example, a sheet of rubber, plastic, or parchment can be stretched tightly enough over both ends of a #10 tin can with top and bottom removed to produce an acceptable beat.

A second source of accompaniment is the record player, for which specialized record sets are on the market for a variety of activities. Basic and other rhythmic sets are available from many sources.* The record sets are excellent, containing a number of short selections on regular and long-play discs. Each selection for basic skills is identified with the type of movement for which it was designed. In addition, many standard records for specific dance steps, marches, folk dances, foxtrots, and modern combo selections serve a variety of purposes. In fact, any record with good accent and rhythm can be utilized somewhere in the rhythmic program.

The teacher should build up a personal collection of records so that eventually he will be familiar with them and able to derive maximum benefit from his own record assortment. Kindergarten and primary teachers should possess personal record sets for basic skills and creative expression. Odd lot used records can sometimes be secured inexpensively at rummage sales.

The record player should be of good quality with a variable speed control. It should be adaptable to a range of record types (33, 45, or 78 rpm). Some protection against needle bounce is needed. Either it must have built-in protection or it should be cushioned on foam rubber pads. The volume must be sufficient to carry the music over the competition of the activity's noise. It should also have an input for a microphone.

A third source of rhythmic accompaniment, the tape recorder, adds another important tool, as music can be recorded on tape in an infinite number of ways, the simplest of which is the straightforward recording of music. With a little practice, directions can be recorded along with the music as desired. The tape recorder is particularly valuable in special-

*See appendix for list of record sources.

ized routines where a number of abrupt changes of music are required, as in exercises to music or continuity exercises. No delay of action, as in changing records on a record player, is encountered. The tape recorder has the disadvantage that the tempo cannot be adjusted, as with most recorders little or no variation in tempo is possible once the music has been recorded on the tape.

The piano is the fourth source of accompaniment. It offers excellent possibilities but does demand a reasonable degree of skill, or the program will suffer. It has the further drawback that if the teacher plays and follows the printed music, it is difficult for him to observe the children's progress. It is also difficult to provide demonstration and offer individual coaching help when one is playing the piano.

A fifth source is the use of songs, poems, spoken phrases, and other vocal forms. The children can express themselves to a poem recited in a rhythmic manner. With singing games, the children can learn the music and the words, and the activity can proceed using only the children's voices.

Several other instruments or devices for providing rhythmic accompaniment merit mention. The tambourine plays a useful role in the rhythmic program, as it can be used to provide two different types of percussion accompaniment. Shaking it gives a metallic ringing type of noise, while striking it with the knuckles or on the elbow produces a drumlike sound. The metallic sound can stimulate the children to one kind of movement, and the drumlike beat to a contrasting movement.

Another simple percussion device can be made by using two 12″ sticks about the thickness of a broom handle. Blocks, coconut shells, and tin can rattles are examples of other useful sound makers.

Because the wealth of fine recordings of well-selected rhythms and music presently available can provide a good basis for a broad program of rhythmics, some teachers rely on recordings entirely. The use of percussion instruments provides the teacher with a measure of variety and class control not possible with a recording. It should be remembered that there will be times when the record player or tape recorder is not operating or is not available, and so other means of providing the rhythmic background will need to be supplied.

At times, it is desirable to have the children operate or provide the rhythmic background. While it is of value for children to have this experience, a poor rhythmic accompaniment can nullify much of the effectiveness of a good rhythmic lesson. Children with training can do a creditable job handling the record player. Providing proper accompaniment with a drum or other percussion instrument demands a reasonable degree of skill which comes from practice and perhaps some innate skill.

CHARACTERISTICS OF RHYTHMIC BACKGROUND

Music has essential characteristics which the children should recognize, understand, and appreciate. These characteristics are also present in varying degrees in other types of rhythmic accompaniment.

The teacher should make use of proper terminology when discussing characteristics of a piece of music. The following terms should be employed.

Tempo. Generally, tempo is the speed of the music. Tempo can be constant, show a gradual increase (acceleration), or show a decrease (deceleration).

Beat. This is underlying rhythmic quality of the music. The beat can be even or uneven. Music with a pronounced beat is easier for the children to follow.

Meter. Meter refers to the manner in which beats are put together to form a measure of music. Common meters used in rhythmics are 2/4, 3/4, 4/4, and 6/8.

Accent. The notes or beats which carry the heavier emphasis define accent, usually given to the first underlying beat of such measure. Accent is generally expressed by a heavier movement.

Intensity. The force of the music can be loud, soft, light, or heavy.

Mood. Mood is related somewhat to intensity, but carries the concept deeper into human feelings. Music can interpret many human moods, such as feeling cheerful, sad, happy, gay, warlike, fearful, stately, and others.

Phrase. A phrase is a natural grouping of measures. In most cases, the group of measures will total eight underlying beats or counts.

Patterns. Phrases of music are put together into rhythmic patterns. Children should recognize when the music pattern repeats or changes to another pattern.

THE PROGRAM OF RHYTHMIC ACTIVITIES

An advantage, and also somewhat of a problem, in the program of rhythmic activities is the unlimited amount of suitable activities and approaches that can be presented to elementary school children. It is in the rhythmic area that sometimes the preferences of the teacher govern the choice of content. Some teachers feel, for example, that it is important to emphasize creative and expressive activities on all grade levels, K-6. Another teacher, a member of a square dance club, may center his program on that type of dancing. These are questionable educational approaches. The problem is that there is so much valuable material in rhythmics that it cannot all be covered during the limited time available for this area. So, choices must be made.

The various types of rhythmic activities should be balanced in the program. The chart which follows shows a broad rhythmic program for the elementary grades in which the activities are allocated according to grade level.

An examination of the chart reveals that the program for grades K-2 emphasizes fundamental rhythms, creative rhythms, and singing games, with lesser attention to folk dances in the lower two grades. As the program moves into the third grade, singing games begin to fade, rope jumping and musical games enter the picture, as well as simple folk dances. Mixers appear to a limited extent in the third grade.

The program among grades 4-6 is similar, except for square dancing. The latter activity is given some attention in the fifth grade with lead-up types of dances and is stressed in the sixth grade. For the intermediate level, folk dances, mixers, and rope jumping make up the bulk of the program, with some inclusion of musical games and fundamental rhythm activities of the manipulative type.

Rhythmic Activity Types — Grade Level Placement

Activity Type	Grade Level						
	K	1	2	3	4	5	6
Fundamental Rhythms	X	X	X	X	S	S	S*
Creative Rhythms — Identification	X	X	X	X			
Creative Rhythms — Dramatization	X	X	X	X			
Singing Games	X	X	X				
Folk Dances	S	S	X	X	X	X	X
Mixers				S	X	X	X
Square Dancing						S	X
Rope Jumping to Music			S	S	X	X	X
Musical Games			S	S	S	S	S

*Key: x means the activity is an integral part of that grade level.
s means the activity is given only minor emphasis.

Another type of analysis can be made to note the progression of basic and specific dance steps as they are introduced into the program. Dances employing these steps appear in each of the respective grade level programs.

Kindergarten. Basic Locomotor Movements

First Grade. Basic Locomotor Movements

Second Grade. Basic Locomotor Movements

Third Grade. Basic Locomotor Movements, Sliding, Draw Steps, Bleking Step, Step Hops

Fourth Grade. Two-Step, Indian Steps, Marching, Rope Jumping Steps

Fifth Grade. Schottische, Polka, Tinikling Steps, Two-Step Pivot

Sixth Grade. Waltz, Square Dance, Varsouvienne.

It should be stressed that the dance steps as presented are given instructional treatment at the appropriate levels. They may be, and usually are, employed at succeeding grade levels. The dances suggested for each grade level provide for the utilization of the dance steps allocated to that level in a suitable activity. Descriptions of these dance steps and appropriate instructional procedures are included with the presentation of the dances for each grade level.

FUNDAMENTAL RHYTHMS

The fundamental rhythm program sets the basis for rhythmic movement in all forms of dance activities. Essentially, it is Basic Movement using the medium of rhythm. It centers on basic skills — locomotor, nonlocomotor, and manipulative, with the most attention given to locomotor skills. Fundamental rhythms have an important place in the primary grades and some of the more suitable activities should be extended upward into the intermediate level.

The general purpose of a program of fundamental rhythms is to provide a variety of basic movement experiences so that the child can move effectively and efficiently and develop a sense of rhythm in connection with these movements. While the creative aspects of fundamental rhythms are important, it is necessary first to establish a vocabulary of movement competencies for each child so that he has a basis on which to create.

The skills in a fundamental rhythm program are important not only in providing background in creative dance, but also in setting the basis for the more precise dance skills of folk, social, and square dances, which follow later in school programs. The basic skills are also related to effective movement in all forms of living and, in particular, to the activities of the physical education program.

The following fundamental movement patterns are basic to the program of fundamental rhythms.

Locomotor Movements

Even Types. Walking, running, hopping, leaping, jumping, draw steps, and such variations as marching, trotting, stamping, and twirling.

Uneven Types. Skipping, galloping, sliding

Nonlocomotor Movements

Simple Movements. Bending, swaying, twisting, swinging, raising, lowering, circling, and rotating various parts of the body.

Mimetics. Striking, lifting, throwing, pushing, pulling, hammering, and other common tasks.

Object Handling

Ball skills. Other objects such as hoops, wands, and even chairs can be used.

Methodology

In practice, the program depends much upon the teacher to initiate and guide the simple patterns. It is important that the rhythms be conducted in an atmosphere of fun and enjoyment. Furthermore, the accompaniment should be suitable and proper for the movements to be experienced.

The element of creativity must not be stifled in a program of fundamental movements. The instruction can be directed toward a specific movement (like walking), and a reasonable range of acceptability can be established. In other words, we are practicing walking, but we can walk in many different ways.

Teachers who may feel awkward and insecure in developing rhythmic programs with a strong creative approach will find the fundamental rhythms a good starting point. Combining the child's love of rhythmic movement with the basic movements which he enjoys can be the beginning of a refreshing and stimulating experience.

The approach to fundamental rhythms should be a mixture of direct and indirect teaching. For many of the movements there is a "standard" or "preferred" technique. For example, there is a correct way to walk, and children should recognize and learn the correct fundamentals. Within the framework of good technique, a variety of movement experiences should be elicited.

The following pattern represents an effective approach the teacher may take in teaching a basic movement skill.

1. With the children comfortable, let them listen to the music. Discuss with them the elements of tempo, beat, meter, accent, and other characteristics of music. As the children listen for phrasing, they become aware of any special changes or effects which are present in the music. Active listening is important as differentiated from merely hearing. Good listening techniques are developed only with practice.

2. To gain a sense of the beat, the children may clap hands to the rhythm. Other simple rhythmic movements done with the hands, arms, legs, or feet help get the feel of the rhythm.

3. Discuss the important qualities and key factors of the movement. What are the important considerations in doing the movement? What are the things which must be observed?

4. The children now move about the room, using the selected basic movement or combination of movements. Movement patterns in the early stages of teaching may need to be somewhat controlled; but as soon as possible, movement should be free, informal, and in every direction instead of around the room in a circular direction.

5. Increasing variety and combinations should be encouraged to reinforce the learning potential. Children should be encouraged to experiment with directional changes and other combinations. Often the teacher can call a halt and have one of the children demonstrate a novel and interesting movement variation which he has employed.

6. During and after the lesson, discussions can be held with the children with regard to "What are we doing that is good, and how can we improve on our movement?" "What different kinds of things can be done to the rhythm?"

It is well to have a child handle the record player. For this the child needs some training. A system of signals for good control is also needed. This frees the teacher for other instruction.

Creative Approach to Fundamental Rhythms

In a lesson emphasizing the creative aspects of fundamental rhythmics, the approach differs from one emphasizing specialized patterns. The purpose of the creative approach to fundamental learning is to have the child gain an interpretation or impression from the selected rhythm and then move creatively as he chooses, using basic skills.

As in the previous approach, the child listens to the music and also gains a sense of the beat by clapping or other simple movements.

After discussing with the children the characteristics of the music, the children are encouraged to select the kinds of movements that the music suggests to them. Movement then is free and unstructured. Extension of movement experiences with variety and different combinations is now possible.

Ideas to Utilize Different Movement Fundamentals

In exploring the range of ideas using movement, the following suggestions should be of value. The resourceful and imaginative teacher, with the aid of the children, can make use of these ideas and others to make up interesting lessons in movement.

An effective and interesting method of stimulating variation is to have the children change movement patterns or combinations with the completion of a phrase of music (8 counts or beats). The music provides the cue for changes, and the children must think ahead to plan the new patterns.

The concept of laterality must be stressed. Movements performed with one side of the body should be done with the other. Directions should be reversed to include the opposite way of moving.

Rhythm Variations

The factors discussed previously (page 127) for securing a variety of response in basic movement can be utilized in the program of fundamental rhythms.

The rhythm can be varied with different tempos. In most instances, early instruction or experience is presented to a slower tempo, which is increased after the movement patterns are learned. The music selected can be changed to provide a variety of tempo, mood, and quality.

In working with fundamental rhythmic patterns, a good rhythmic beat pattern is basic. The tom-tom is especially valuable in working with children in basic rhythm teaching, providing an easy way to vary the tempo, accents, and other characteristics of the basic beat. Stops and starts, changes to different rhythms, and many other innovations are possible with skillful handling of the tom-tom. Combinations of different rhythms can be put together easily and effectively with a tom-tom or drum.

Intensity or force of the music can be changed, giving rise to different modes of response, resulting in movements which can be light or heavy, strong or weak.

Space factors such as direction, level, and different floor patterns add variation. Floor patterns can reinforce learning concepts as children recognize and employ circles, squares, figure eights, etc.

The use of different parts of the body singly or in various combinations is important in establishing variety. The different positions of the arms and legs provide many ways of moving. One can perform high on the toes, with toes in or out, on the heels, with stiff knees, kicking high in front or to the rear, with knees brought up high, in a crouched position, and in many other positions.

Arms can swing at the sides or be held stiff, be held out in front or overhead. Arms can move in circles or in different patterns, and in other poses. The body can be bent forward, backward, sideward, and it can be twisted, or turned. By combining different positions of the arms, legs, and body, the children can assume many interesting variations of position.

Working with a Partner or a Group

A child may work with a partner or as a member of a group. Be sure that the tasks or directions are appropriate and that sufficient practice and mastery has been accomplished before partner or group work is instituted.

Fundamental Locomotor Movements

In the sections which follow, movement fundamentals are analyzed, and some ideas are presented based on a particular locomotor movement or combination of movements.

Walking. In walking, one is always in contact with the ground or floor, and the feet move alternately. This means that the stepping foot must be placed on the ground before the other foot is lifted for its step. Marching is a more military, precise type of walk, accompanied with lifted knees and swinging arms.

The weight of the body is transferred from the heel to the ball of the foot and then to the toes for the push-off for the next step. The toes are pointing straight ahead with the arms swinging freely from the shoulder in opposition to the feet. The body is erect and the eyes are focused straight ahead at eye level. Legs are swung from the hips with the knees bent only enough to clear the foot from the ground.

Some ways that walking can be used as an activity are:

1. Walk forward one phrase (8 counts) and change directions. Continue to change at the end of each phrase.

2. Use high steps during one phrase and low steps during the next.

3. Walk forward for one phrase and sidewards during the next. The side step can be a draw step or it can be of the grapevine type. To do a grapevine step to the left, lead with the left foot with a step directly to the side. The right foot crosses *behind* the left and then in front on the next step with that foot. The pattern is a step left, cross right (behind), step left, cross right (in front), and so on.

4. Find a partner, face each other and join hands. Pull your partner by walking backwards as he resists somewhat (8 counts). Reverse roles. Try using pushing action by walking forward (8 counts) as partner resists when he moves backward. Reverse roles.

5. Walk slowly and gradually increase the tempo. Begin fast and decrease.

6. Walk in various directions while clapping hands alternately in front and behind. Try clapping hands under the thighs at each step or clap hands above the head.

7. Walk forward four steps, turn completely around in four steps. Repeat.

8. While walking, bring up the knees and slap with the hands on each step.

9. On any one phrase take four fast steps (one count to each step) and two slow steps (two counts to each step).

10. Walk on heels, toes, or with a heavy tramp.

11. Walk with a smooth gliding step or walk silently.

12. Gradually lower the body while walking (going downstairs) and raise yourself again (going upstairs).

13. Use a waltz with good beat and walk to it accenting the first beat of each measure. Add a sway of the body to the first beat of the measure.

14. Walk high on tiptoes, rocking back and forth.

Running. Running, as contrasted to walking, is to move more rapidly in such a manner that for a brief moment both feet are off the ground. Running varies from trotting, a slow run, to sprinting, a fast run for speed.

Running should be done lightly on the toes. It should be a controlled run and not a dash for speed. Children may cover some ground on the run or they can run in place.

Running should be done with a slight body lean. The knees are bent and lifted. The arms swing back and forth from the shoulders with a bend at the elbows.

Many of the suggested movements for walking are equally applicable to running patterns. Some additional suggestions are listed:

1. Walk during a phrase of music and then run for an equal length of time.

2. Run in different directions, turning at times.

3. Left the knees as high as possible while running.

4. Run and touch different spots on the floor or on the wall.

Skipping. Skipping is actually a series of step-hops done with alternate feet. To teach a child to skip, ask him to take a step with one foot and then take a small hop on the same foot. He now takes a step with the other foot and a hop on that foot. Skipping should be done on the balls of the feet with the arms swinging to shoulder height in opposition to the feet.

Almost all of the combinations suggested for walking and running are useful for skipping movements. Combinations of skipping, walking, and running can be devised in many different fashions.

Hopping. In hopping, the body is sent up and down by one foot. The body lean, the other foot, and the arms serve to balance the movement. Hopping on one foot should not be sustained too long. Children should change to the other foot after a short period

Some variations and combinations for hopping include:

1. Hop like a bouncing ball. Hop very high,

gradually reducing the height. The procedure can be reversed.

2. Hop along a line, crossing back and forth over the line each time.

3. Draw a small circle (about 18" across) on the floor. Hop across, in and out of the circle.

4. Hop in different figures like a circle, triangle, square, etc.

5. Trace out numbers by hopping. Try writing short words by hopping.

6. Alternate big and little hops. Form other combinations.

7. Hop on one foot a specific number of times and change to the other foot.

8. Turn around hopping in place.

Jumping. Jumping, as the term is used in fundamental movements, means to take off with both feet and land on *both* feet. The arms aid in the jump with an upswing, and the movement of the body helps lift the weight along with the force of the feet. A jumper lands lightly on the balls of his feet with his knees bent.

The suggestions listed for hopping can be applied to jumping. In addition, the teacher can devise other movement patterns such as these:

1. Jump with the body stiff and arms held at the sides.

2. Jump and turn in the air. Quarter, half, and even full turns can be done to rhythm. Work gradually into full turns.

3. Combine jumping in combination with hopping, walking, running, and skipping.

4. Increase and decrease the speed of jumping.

5. Land with feet apart or crossed. Alternate feet forward and back.

Leaping. Leaping is an elongated step designed to cover distance or to go over a low obstacle. Leaping is usually combined with running, as a series of leaps is difficult to maintain. It can be included in a running sequence, using the music phrase as the cue. An excellent piece to use for leaping is "Pop Goes the Weasel." The youngsters can take a leap on the "Pop" part of the piece.

Sliding. Sliding is done usually to the side. It is a one-count movement with the leading foot stepping out to the side and the other foot following quickly. A novel way to use slid-

ing is to head in a direction with a definite number of slides and then do a half-turn in the air and continue the slide leading with the other foot but retaining the original direction.

Galloping. Galloping is similar to sliding, but the progress of the individual is in a forward direction. One foot leads, and the other is brought up rapidly to it. The hands can be in a position as if holding a horse's reins. Since later in the rhythmic program the gallop is used to teach the polka, it is important that the children learn to change the leading foot. The leading foot can be changed after a series of eight gallops with the same foot leading. Later, the changes can be reduced to four gallops and finally to two gallops. These changes have value in perceptual-motor training.

Draw Step. The draw step is a two-count movement to either side. A step is made directly to the side and on the second count the other foot is drawn up to it. The cue is made by "left (or right), close; left, close; left close"; etc.

Nonlocomotor Movements

Nonlocomotor movements include those movements that the body is able to execute while the feet remain in place. They provide for dramatic and expressive movement and involve movements by the arms, legs, head, or torso, singly or in combination. Specific movements used in this portion of the rhythmic program include swinging, circling, rotating, twisting, lowering, raising, bending, extension, flexion, and combinations of the movements. These can be used strictly as nonlocomotor movements or in combination with locomotor movement. Large, free, unhampered movements to the full range of flexibility are a goal. Instruction can range from specific movements to creative opportunity of free choice.

Object-Handling Rhythms

A fruitful area for primary children is found in the application of rhythm to ball skills. Hoops, wands, and chairs are occasionally used in movement to rhythm. To get full value from such activities, each child should have an object of his own with which to work.

While the school normally has volleyballs, soccer balls, and rubber playground balls, these can be supplemented by small balls of various types, provided that they have a lively bounce.

Ball Skills. The following ball skills lend themselves well to rhythm:

1. Bounce and catch. Bounce a number of times and then catch. Various combinations. Combine with various locomotor movements.

2. Throw against a wall and catch. Volley against a wall.

3. Bounce continuously (dribble).

    Dribble in place.

    Dribble under the legs. Also, dribble behind the individual.

    Dribble and move. Form circles, triangles, and other patterns. Dribble forward, backward, sideward, stop and go.

    Dribble using different locomotor movements—hopping, jumping, sliding, and skipping.

4. Volley continuously in rhythm, using the hands, elbows, head, knees, etc. Add locomotor movements.

5. Work with a partner or in groups passing a ball or balls from one to another in rhythm. Vary with bounce passes.

For bounce and catch skills, a little experimentation by the teacher with various selections will uncover suitable music. A number of firms now produce music especially made for various bouncing, dribbling, and catching skills. The sets of records for fundamental rhythms usually have numbers adaptable for various skills using balls.

Dribbling skills with rhythm are particularly appropriate for intermediate children. The tie-up of a basketball skill with rhythm tends to make the rhythmic program more attractive to boys.

A selected polka with a definite beat makes a suitable selection for dribbling. If the record player has a variable speed control, a finer adjustment can be made coordinating the tempo of the record with the dribbling skills.

The record, "Pop Goes the Weasel," provides a fine rhythmic background for partner work. One child can dribble and work creatively in any manner he wishes until the music comes to the "Pop" part of the chorus, which is the signal for passing the ball to his partner, who repeats the performance. The children should be encouraged to move in different directions with a variety of locomotor movements while dribbling and to move back toward the partner when the music is approaching the signal for the ball exchange.

Other Activities

Danish ball rhythms also interest children. These routines are done employing a special type of ball and include swinging, turning, and twisting movements to music while retaining control of the ball. Many interesting routines are possible but are too lengthy and difficult of description to be included here.

Rope jumping skills are manipulative activities, but are given special attention (page 376) because of their uniqueness to the rhythmic program.

Hoops and wands are sometimes included in rhythmic routines, generally in nonlocomotor activities. Swinging, lifting, and other movements of a graceful type can be combined into sequence routines. Some type of waltz music provides a suitable background for the movements.

Some teachers have worked out sequence routines of rhythmic movement utilizing chairs. Swinging, lifting, and lowering movements predominate, with the chairs moved somewhat in the style of weight-training activities. A swinging type of waltz music or a "dreamy" fox-trot makes suitable accompaniment for these activities. The movement provides resistive types of activities contributing to arm and shoulder girdle development. Chair activities are more appropriate to the upper grades.

CREATIVE RHYTHMS — IDENTIFICATION

In an identification rhythm, the child expresses himself by trying to "be something." The child in his own mind takes on the identity, for example, of a soldier, giant, horse, elephant, train, or other familiar character, creature, or object. He proceeds to interpret this identity with expressive movements to the accompaniment of a suitable rhythm.

There are many sources of subjects for interpretations through these rhythms. Some of the following will be found useful:

1. Animals — elephants, ducks, seals, chickens, dogs, rabbits, lions, and other animals.

2. People — soldiers, Indians, firemen, sailors, various kinds of workers, forest rangers, cowboys, etc.

3. Play Objects — seesaws, swings, rowboats, balls, various toys, and many common articles with which the children play.

4. Make-Believe World — giants, dwarfs, midgets, gnomes, witches, trolls, dragons, pixies, and fairies, among others.

5. Machines — trains, planes, jets, rockets, automobiles, bicycles, motorcycles, tractors, elevators, etc.

6. The Circus — clowns, various trained animals, trapeze artists, tight and slack wire performers, jugglers, acrobats, and bands.

7. Nature — fluttering leaves, grain, flowers, rain, snow, clouds, wind, tornado, hurricane, and others.

Instructional Procedures

An atmosphere of creative freedom must be a part of each lesson. Encourage children to explore, interpret, and express themselves in varied and original movement as they react to the rhythm. They need to "lose themselves" in the interpretation by assuming the identity of what they are imitating.

While there are variations, three general approaches can be used:

1. The first is to begin with a rhythm and let each child decide what he would like to be, based on the character of the rhythm. The approach is, "What does this rhythm make you think of?" The children may be many things and move in many different ways.

2. A second approach is to select a piece of music and have the children listen and choose what they are to imitate. All children would be imitating the same character, object, or thing. Within the selection each child would have the privilege of creating as he wished. If the choice were a giant, the child would interpret his concept of the giant.

3. The third approach to creative identification is to have the children choose a character or object with which they wish to be identified and then look for a suitable rhythm in keeping with the choice. From sets of records where bands are labeled for various imitations, an appropriate band could be selected. Or, the children could listen and experiment with several choices before making a final selection.

Some questions which can be posed to the children are:

"What does the music make us think of?"

"What does the music tell us to do?"

"How can we move with the music and our selected interpretation?"

Listening is important as the children must get the mood of the music. To be effective the music must be appropriate for the identity to be assumed, otherwise movement becomes artificial. In pantomiming the selected identity, the child should keep his movements in time with the rhythm.

There are many specialized recordings which provide excellent musical background for identification rhythms. Although designated for a particular identity, the selections can be adapted for other characterizations.

CREATIVE RHYTHMS — DRAMATIZATION

Both identification and dramatization rhythms have in common the basic purpose that the child should react creatively and rhythmically to the selected rhythm. However, the approach differs. In an identification rhythm, the child should listen to the music, determine its quality and characteristics, and then act creatively in assuming the identity of his selection.

In a dramatic rhythm, the children act out an idea, a familiar event, or an ordinary procedure. This could be based on a story, an idea, a poem, an emotion, or a song. It could take almost any form. A variety of rhythmic background can accompany the unfolding of the story. Recordings, a piano selection, percussion rhythms, or even a rhythm band can be used. A teacher or a student reader can provide the verbal background and directions for the drama, but the story can unfold without this.

A second method would be to begin with a piece of music, generally a recording, and develop an idea to fit the music. The piece of music selected should have sufficient changes of tempo and pattern to provide different kinds and quality of background. A general idea or plan of action can be selected and fitted to the music. An idea like "Going to the Fair" may be selected. A recording is chosen which is adaptable. The children can devise a script in keeping with the idea and following the music.

A third opportunity in a dramatic rhythm is for children to express moods or feelings. A piece of music is played, generally a recording, and the children discuss its qualities and how it makes them feel. Children can and will interpret the music differently, however. Moods which can be expressed are being happy, gay, sad, brave, fearful, cheerful, angry, solemn, silly, stately, sleepy, funny, cautious, bold, and nonchalant.

The teacher aids in setting the stage, and the children carry the activity to its point of fulfillment in the event or story selected. The teacher should avoid setting preconceived standards for the children and attempting to hold to these. An idea may be expanded in many directions, and success in the activity can be judged by the degree to which the children have been able to interpret freely and creatively.

An example of how an idea can be exploited for a rhythmic lesson of creativity is "The Wind and the Leaves." One or more children are chosen to be the "Wind," and the remainder of the children are the "Leaves." Two kinds of rhythm are needed. The first indicates the blowing of the Wind. The second rhythm is quieter and stimulates the Leaves to flutter to the ground after the wind has stopped. Thus, the story divides itself into two parts, each of which offers many possibilities of creativity.

Rhythm 1. Fast, high, shrill — indicating the blowing of the Wind. The intensity and the tempo would illustrate the speed and force of the wind.

Rhythm 2. Slow, measured, light beat to match the Leaves fluttering in the still air and finally coming to rest at various positions on the ground.

During the first rhythm, the children representing the Wind can show how they would represent a heavy blow. While this is going on, the Leaves show what they feel it means to be blown about.

During the second rhythm, the Wind is still and the Leaves are fluttering to the ground.

Other characterizations could be added. "Street Sweepers" could come along and sweep the Leaves up.

Other ideas useful for dramatic rhythms are:

1. Building a house, garage, or other project.

2. Making a snowman. Throwing snowballs. Going skiing.

3. Flying a kite. Going hunting or fishing. Going camping.

4. Acting out stories which include Indians, cowboys, firemen, engineers.

5. Interpreting familiar stories like the Sleeping Beauty, The Three Bears, Little Red Riding Hood, and others.

6. Building from household task ideas like chopping wood, picking fruit, mowing the lawn, cleaning the yard.

7. Celebrating holidays like Halloween, Fourth of July, Thanksgiving, Christmas.

8. Ideas using the seasons — spring, summer, fall, winter.

9. Sports activities. Playing football, basketball, baseball, track and field, swimming, tennis, golf, and others.

Two other ideas may be of help. One teacher had success with her class by devising a game called "Guess What." The class was divided into groups, and each was given the task to act out an idea using percussion accompaniment. Each group put on its performance before the others, and at the completion the other groups guessed what the interpretation was. Be sure that the interpretations are not too long.

Another idea of value in dramatic rhythms is to use a tape recorder. In this way, bits of music and other accompaniment can be put together as desired. This procedure allows for the story or idea to be structured with its own individually designed rhythmic background.

CREATIVE RHYTHMS IN THE INTERMEDIATE GRADES

While children at this level have generally outgrown those activities in which they imitate animals and objects, some creative activities appropriate to the intermediate grades are desirable. Rhythms involving basic skills can be valuable learning experiences for these children, based on a creative approach. The movements should be vigorous and challenging so that there is good acceptance by the more skilled, particularly the boys.

The children can be given problem-solving activities involving the use of various locomotor movements, changes in direction, changes to other types of activity, and the like.

An example of activity of this kind is the change of movement on alternate phrases of a piece of music. For the first phrase (8 counts) the child moves in a straight line either walking (slow rhythm) or running (rapid rhythm). During the second phrase (8 counts), he changes his movement according to the type of problem set up. The directions could allow him to make any kind of movement so long as he stays in his own space, and they might call for a movement where the hands are placed on the floor. Thus, he alternates between the locomotor movement and a movement within the limitation of the problem.

The use of the tom-tom is recommended. A skillful teacher can vary the tempo, signal movement changes, and provide a variety of interesting activity. The teacher can pound out a beat, with the boys and girls moving according to the rhythm provided. Some variety can be added by the following devices: (1) upon a single loud beat, each student abruptly changes direction, or turns around, or jumps into the air, or leaps into the air; (2) a very quick, heavy double beat is given, signaling the children to stop in place without any movement, or fall to the floor; (3) various changes in beat patterns and accents can be given, with the children following the pattern with movement.

Some caution should be exercised in utilizing creative activities of a dramatic and expressive nature in the upper grades. The acceptance by intermediate boys has been marginal at the best. At a time when children are looking forward to becoming more adult, activities of this nature *seem to them* like turning the clock backwards. With the abundance of suitable rhythmic materials for intermediate children, a repeat of these experiences of the primary grades, even if upgraded, would seem poor utilization of instructional time.

SINGING GAMES

A singing game is described as a dance where the children sing verses, and the verses give direction to the movement. Usually there is considerable latitude in the resultant movement patterns as the children follow and interpret the action picture of the words. A singing game is usually an interpretation of an old story, fable, or some kind of a task.

Instructional Procedures

In presenting a singing game, the following steps provide a logical sequence of progression. Seat the children on the floor.

Background. Tell something about the singing game, discussing its nature and meaning. Set the stage so the children can make an appropriate interpretation.

Analyzing the Music. Have the children listen critically to the music and analyze with respect to tempo, mood, rhythmic qualities, and major parts. They can clap to the beat.

Learning the Verses. Writing the verses on a blackboard or on a poster card speeds learning and saves time. It is generally better to learn one verse at a time and put this into action before proceeding with the others, but if the verses are learned in the classroom before the activity period, then all should be learned. Sometimes the music teacher and the physical education teacher can cooperate. The children can learn the music and the verses during the music period and add the action during the activity period.

Adding the Action. Arrange the children in formation quickly and proceed with the action. Encourage creative interpretation as determined by the framework of the singing game. Begin with the largest workable part of the activity which the children can handle at one time. After this is learned, add other increments.

In most cases there will be little need to practice a step pattern to be used in the activity, as most singing games involve only simple basic steps, which are subject to individual interpretation.

Including Variations. The teacher should be alert to possible variations, which may be suggested by the children.

Other Suggestions. The source of music must be loud enough for the children to hear as they sing, otherwise the singing will be out of time with the music. After the children learn the verses and can sing reasonably well, the music source may not be necessary, as the children's singing can carry the activity.

In singing games where a key figure is the center of attention, several children may assume the part, spreading the attention and involving more children. In activities where children select partners during the course of the action, boys should select girls and vice versa.

FOLK DANCE AND OTHER DANCE ACTIVITIES

A folk dance is defined as a traditional dance of a given people. In this form, a definite pattern of dance routine is usually specified and followed. In the original form little variation from the traditional dance pattern was permitted, but in physical education practice the elementary school program utilizes many variations and departures.

Few, if any, of the folk dances for kindergarten and primary children involve special dance steps. Rather, the simple fundamental locomotor movements are the basis for the dances. The more specialized steps such as the two-step, polka, schottische, waltz, and others are a part of the intermediate level program.

A first consideration in teaching folk dance is whether or not the basic step important to a dance is known well enough to serve as the basis of the dance. If instruction is indicated, this can be handled one of two ways. The first way is to teach the step separately prior to learning the dance of which it is a part. The second way is to teach the dance in its normal sequence, giving specific instruction on each step as it comes up. The first way is generally more efficient, as the children can concentrate on one element, the step, at a time. The mastery of the step does not become a stumbling block for the dance, as the dance will not be introduced until sufficient skill has been acquired in the step. In some instances, the step can be learned one day and incorporated in the dance during the next class session. Children experiencing difficulty can be helped between classes and can be encouraged to practice at home.

Introducing New Steps

The ability level of the group and the degree of difficulty of the dance step concerned will influence the manner in which the instruction proceeds. Several approaches may be necessary to assure that everyone has acquired sufficient skill in the step. The following considerations are important:

Analysis of the Step. Explain and discuss the characteristics of the rhythm, the accents, and the foot pattern in relation to the rhythm.

a. Listen to the music.

b. Clap hands or tap feet to the rhythm. Emphasize the accents with a heavier clap or tap.

c. Use the blackboard to illustrate the relationship of the step to the music.

d. Demonstrate the step.

Selection of Formation. Select the formation most suitable for teaching. Progression can follow this pattern with regard to formation:

a. *Scattered around the room.* This is the simplest of arrangements. Children can concentrate on their own movements without the worry of coordinating with a partner or group.

b. *Line or lines.* A series of lines can be formed. Children move in this formation.

c. *Single circle.* No partners.

d. *Double circle.* With a partner.

Position of the Dancers. In general, one practices first individually and later with a partner. When starting with a partner, the side-by-side position can be assumed and finally the closed position, if this is the ultimate goal. Another approach to reaching the closed dance position is to have the partners face each other, but at arm's length determined by joined hands.

Method of Presentation. The sequence of presentation can be repeated as often as indicated as the dancers move from individual instruction to working with a partner.

a. Use a walk-through, talk-through approach without music. Let the dancers move slowly (by the numbers) as the instructor puts them through the step.

b. Increase the practice speed, still without music.

c. Practice with the music. The tempo can be slowed so that it approximates the practice speed.

d. Apply the step to a simple sequence.

The relation of cues to the accompaniment is important. Cues mean verbal directions, given as the step is done. The tempo of the cues should be increased to approximate the tempo of the music. It is confusing to children to practice a dance with cues given at one speed and find that they need to adjust the speed of their dancing to a different tempo when the music is introduced. Music should be at a slow and comfortable learning tempo, which can be increased gradually.

Movement Patterns. Steps should usually be done in place first, followed with forward, backward, or other movements. Half-turns and full turns round out the movement possibilities.

Introducing a New Dance

Most dances are taught by the whole-part-whole method, wherein the largest whole part of the dance which the children can grasp at one time is taught. Much of the procedure in teaching a new step is applicable to a folk dance, but with modifications. The following steps are presented with the assumption that a new step has been learned, and we are now ready to proceed with the dance itself.

1. With the children sitting informally or in the formation for the dance, tell them about the dance and its characteristics.

2. Have the children listen to and analyze music for accents, phrases, or changes.

3. Singly or with partners (as indicated), have the children walk through as much of the dance as they can absorb. Practice without and then with the music, using a slowed tempo until enough has been learned to proceed to the next part. Provide at this point only the basics needed for the dance, as too many details and refinements tend to cause confusion.

4. A technique of value in the whole-part-whole method of presentation is to have the children learn one-half of a two-part dance or one-third of a three-part dance and put this to music. When the music comes to the part the children do not know, have them stand and listen, awaiting the repetition of the portion they have learned. Listening to the music during the unknown part of the piece emphasizes the changes, and fixes the relationship of the parts to the whole in the children's minds.

5. Teach the remaining portions of the dance and put the whole together, beginning at a slow tempo, then gradually increasing this to the normal tempo of the dance.

7. Add such refinements as partner changes (if a mixer), needed points of technique, and other details.

8. Change partners and repeat the dance

Suggestions for Teaching Dance Activities

1. Progression is important in teaching rhythmic activities. It is sound instructional procedure to progress from the simple to the more complex, from a slowed to a normal tempo, from solo to partner activity, from the familiar to the unfamiliar, and from a simple to the stipulated partner position.

2. In the lower grades, the teacher need not be too concerned with strict mechanics. Children should be held to reasonable standards for their age. Too high standards breed frustration and kill some of the enjoyment in the activity.

3. Time is saved if a monitor can be sent into the dance room or area to warm up the record player before the other children come in. Third graders are quite capable of handling this chore. When the class comes in, the activity can proceed without undue delay. Newer record players with transistors need little warm-up, but should be made ready.

4. The teacher can be freed for better instructional duty if a child handles the record player. Have definite signals for starting and stopping the music. Normally music should be stopped at the completion of a full pattern.

5. The teacher should have definite starting and stopping signals for the dancers, such as "Ready and begin," "Ready — Now" and "Stop." The signal for the dancers to begin should be given on the musical phrase just prior to the beginning of a full pattern. The phrase is usually 8 beats in length, and the starting signals can be given on the fifth and seventh beats of the phrase in the following manner:

```
BEATS                    ↓        ↓
  1    2    3    4    5    6    7
                    "Ready and begin"
                    "Ready  —  Now!"
```

6. The proportion of activity to rest periods should be well-balanced. The children can be seated on the floor to analyze and discuss the dance, the music, or the movements.

7. The steps and the dance should be repeated often enough so that the movements and the dance are reasonably learned. Too much repetition or emphasis on mastery may cause the children to react negatively.

8. Get the group in formation as quickly as possible. Children are able to grasp an understanding of the dance or step more easily if they are in the formation used for the activity.

9. Individual help is to be given as needed, but do not hold the class to the pace of the slow learner. Assign some of the more able as partners.

10. Stress the enjoyment which comes from knowing a dance and being able to do it well. As an instructor, know the dance, have the instructional sequences thought out beforehand, and have appropriate music ready.

11. Conduct activities as informally as possible, but retain control of the group.

12. Stress a good social environment. Folk dance instruction offers good opportunity for healthful boy-girl relationships and implementation of good standards of courtesy.

13. Change partners often and make frequent use of mixers. This makes for better sociability, adds interest, and gives all an equal opportunity to have good dancing partners.

14. Stress postural points for proper carriage and efficient movement.

Arranging for Partners

Some teachers believe in having the boys choose girl partners, but this should be used with caution if it will cause embarrassment or distress to those chosen last. Other methods can be used which will avoid the problem of some children being looked over and overlooked.

1. Down the center by twos. The boys are on the right side of the room and girls on the left, both facing the same direction towards one end of the room. All march forward to the end of the room, turn toward each other, march down the center by twos, and then into circle formation.

2. Boys join hands in a circle formation and each girl steps behind a boy.

3. Boys stand in a circle facing counterclockwise while the girls form a circle around them facing clockwise. Both circles move in the direction they are facing and stop on signal. The boy takes the girl nearest him as his partner.

4. For square dances, take the first four couples from any of the previous formations to form a set. Continue until all sets are formed.

5. Squad exchange. Two squads can be assigned to establish partners. The boys in one squad are paired off with the girls in the other. The squad leaders can supervise this chore.

6. Drawing partners. The names of all girls can be put into a box and the boys draw names from the box to determine partners. For variety, the names can be drawn in the classroom and the boy escorts his partner to the activity area. This process should be carried out without ostentation and in a dignified manner.

7. Girls' choice. Occasionally allow the girls to select partners.

Partners should be changed with regularity. Changing can be done formally by having the boys move forward one or more places in a circle formation to take a new partner. Mixers are an important activity for this purpose in the program.

Both boys and girls should accept partners with grace and courtesy. Allow them to discuss and help set their own standards in this area. It is important to help them to be at ease with the opposite sex.

If the class is unbalanced and several members of one sex are left over after partners are chosen, find some way to include them in the activity by rotation. In some cases girls can dance with girls, but it is better not to have boys dancing with each other.

Formations for Singing Games and Folk Dances

The formations illustrated below cover almost all of the singing games and dances. The teacher should be able to verbalize the formation, and the children should be able to take their places in formations without confusion. The formations are listed under single circle, double circle, or other categories.

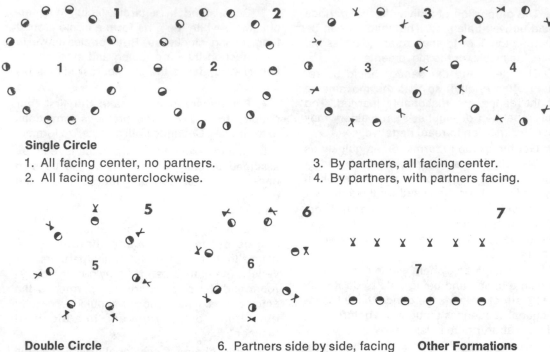

Single Circle

1. All facing center, no partners.
2. All facing counterclockwise.
3. By partners, all facing center.
4. By partners, with partners facing.

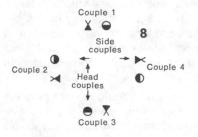

Double Circle

5. Partners facing each other.

6. Partners side by side, facing counterclockwise.

Other Formations

7. Longways Set.

Couple 1

Side couples

Couple 2   Head couples   Couple 4

Couple 3

8

8. Square Dance Formation.

Dance Positions

In most dance positions, where the girl clasps the boy's hand, the boy holds his hands palms up and the girl joins the grip with a palms down position. The following dance positions for partners are common to many dances.

Partners Facing Position. Partners are facing. The boy extends his hands forward with palms up and the elbows slightly bent. The girl places her hands in the boy's hands.

Side-by-Side Position. Partners stand side by side, boys usually to the left of the girl. The boy offers his partner his right hand, held

Partners Facing Position

above waist level, palms up. The girl places her left hand in the upraised hand.

Closed Position. This is the social dance position. The boy faces the girl, holding her right hand in his left hand out to the side about shoulder level with the elbows bent. His right hand is on the girl's back just below her left shoulder blade. Her left arm rests lightly on the top of his right arm with her left hand on his shoulder.

Open Position. From the closed position, the boy turns to his left and the girl to her right, with the arms remaining about the same. Both are now facing in the same direction and are side by side.

Varsouvienne Position. Boy and girl stand side by side, facing the same direction. The boy holds the girl's left hand with his left hand in front. She brings her right hand directly back over her right shoulder, and the boy reaches behind her back at shoulder height and grasps this hand with his right.

Peasant Position. Also called the waist-shoulder position. Partners face each other, and the boy places his hands on the girl's waist. The girl places her hands on the boy's shoulders.

Skater's Position. This is the crossed-arm position where the dancers stand side by side, facing the same direction, with the right hand held by the right, and the left by the left.

Program Suggestions

1. Material should be selected to interest and challenge the children. It should be part of an overall curriculum which shows progression from grade to grade.

2. Make frequent use of mixers. This creates better sociability, adds interest, and gives all an equal opportunity to have good dancing partners.

3. The following can be a guide for a rhythmic lesson in folk dance.

Minutes

5   Introductory Dance.
        Generally, a dance the children know and enjoy. Or, it could be rope jumping to music.

5–10   Review of material from previous class. A dance that needs practice and refinement.

Side-by-Side Position

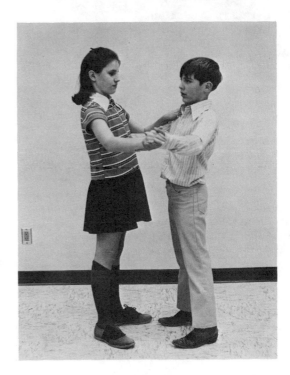

Closed Position

Open Position

Varsouvienne Position

Time would vary according to how much review is needed.

10–15   Presentation of new material.

5–10   Older dances already mastered with emphasis on enjoyment.

A musical game or other type of game could be played.

Vary the program with different types of dances rather than all of one type, unless the period is quite short.

4. At times, have a choice dance.

5. On occasion, finish up the period with a musical game (pages 375-6) or a favorite game.

KINDERGARTEN

The kindergarten list is made up primarily of singing games. The list of suggested activities is not extensive, as the kindergarten program should make good use of the activities listed under the first grade. Some of the dances are individual, and some require partners. The movements demand only the simplest kind of locomotor steps. The following are suggested rhythms for kindergarten, for which the required skill is specified:

Dances	Skills
Farmer in the Dell	Walking
Baa Baa Blacksheep	Stamping, Walking
Twinkle, Twinkle, Little Star	Tiptoe Steps
Mulberry Bush	Walking or Skipping
Bluebird	Walking
Let Your Feet Go Tap, Tap, Tap	Skipping
Ten Little Indians	Indian Dancing
Pease Porridge Hot	Turning in a Circle
Touch your Shoulders	Body Identification

FARMER IN THE DELL

Records: Victor 21618 and 45-5066 (Album E 87)
Folkraft 1182

Formation: Children are in single circle with hands joined and facing the center. One child is chosen to be the farmer and stands inside the circle.

Verses:

1. The farmer in the dell
   The farmer in the dell
   Heigh-ho! the dairy-O!
   The farmer in the dell
2. The farmer takes a wife
3. The wife takes a child
4. The child takes a nurse
5. The nurse takes a dog
6. The dog takes a cat
7. The cat takes a rat
8. The rat takes the cheese
9. The cheese stands alone

Directions:

Verse 1. The circle players walk to the left with hands joined while the Farmer is deciding on a child to be selected for his "wife."

Verse 2. The Farmer chooses another child who is led to the center and becomes his wife. The child selected joins hands with him, and they walk around the inside of the circle in the opposite direction from that of the big circle.

Verses 3 to 8. Each child selected in turn joins the center group.

Verse 9. All children in the center with the exception of the child who is the "cheese" return to the outside circle. The circle stops and the children face the center clapping hands during this verse.

Suggestions: The game should be repeated until all children have had an opportunity to be in the center.

Variations:

1. Several farmers may be chosen to start. When the outer circle gets smaller, the children can no longer join hands.

2. Verse 8 can be: "The cat chases the rat." During this, the Cat does chase the Rat in and out of the circle with the children raising and lowering their joined hands to help the Rat and hinder the Cat. If the Cat catches the Rat, he gets to be the Farmer for the next game. If not, the Rat becomes the Farmer. The Rat must be caught during the singing of the verse.

Peasant Position

Skaters Position

BAA BAA BLACKSHEEP

Records: Folkraft 1191
         Russell 700A
         Victor E-83

Formation: Single circle, all facing center.

Verse:

Baa Baa Blacksheep, have you any wool?
Yes sir, yes sir, three bags full.
One for my master and one for my dame,
And one for the little boy who lives down the
     lane.

Directions:

Line 1. Stamp three times, shake forefinger three times.

Line 2. Nod head twice and hold up three fingers.

Line 3. Bow to the person on the right and then to the left.

Line 4. Hold one finger up high and walk around in a tiny circle, again facing the center.

TWINKLE, TWINKLE, LITTLE STAR

Record: Childcraft EP-C4

Formation: Children are in a single circle, facing in.

Verse:

Twinkle, twinkle, little star.
How I wonder what you are.
Up above the world so high
Like a diamond in the sky.
Twinkle, twinkle, little star.
How I wonder what you are.

Directions: Children are in a large enough circle so that they can come forward seven short steps without crowding.

Line 1. Children have arms extended overhead and fingers extended and moving. Each child takes seven tiptoe steps toward the center of the circle.

Line 2. Continue with seven tiptoe steps in place making a full turn around.

Line 3. Each child makes a circle with his arms and hands, rocking back and forth.

Line 4. All form a diamond with the fingers in front of the face.

Line 5. With the arms overhead and the fingers extended, move backward to original place with seven tiptoe steps.

Line 6. Turn in place with seven tiptoe steps.

MULBERRY BUSH

Records: Victor 20806, 45-5065;
         Columbia 90037-V;
         Folkraft 1183

Formation: Single circle, facing center, hands joined.

Chorus:

Here we go round the mulberry bush,
The mulberry bush, the mulberry bush,
Here we go round the mulberry bush,
So early in the morning.

Verses:

1. This is the way we wash our clothes,
    Wash our clothes, wash our clothes,
    This is the way we wash our clothes
    So early Monday morning

2. This is the way we iron our clothes,
    (Tuesday morning)

3. This is the way we mend our clothes,
    (Wednesday morning)

4. This is the way we sweep our floor,
    (Thursday morning)

5. This is the way we scrub our floor,
    (Friday morning)

6. This is the way we make a cake,
    (Saturday morning)

7. This is the way we go to church,
    (Sunday morning).

Directions: The singing game begins with the chorus, which is also sung after each verse. As each chorus is sung, the children skip (or walk) to the right. On the words "so early in the morning" each child drops hands and makes a complete turn in place.

During the verses, the children pantomime the actions suggested by the words. Encourage the children to use large and vigorous movements.

BLUEBIRD

Record: Folkraft 1180.

Formation: Single circle, hands joined and facing the center. One child stands outside the circle and is the "Bluebird."

Verse:

Bluebird, bluebird, through my window,
Bluebird, bluebird, through my window,
Bluebird, bluebird, through my window,
Hi diddle dum dum dee.

Chorus:
   Take a little boy (girl) and tap him (her) on
     the shoulder
               (repeat twice more)
   Hi diddle dum dum dee.

Directions: During the verse all circle children lift joined hands high, forming arches,
under which the "Bluebird" weaves in and
out. At the completion of the verse the Bluebird should stand directly behind one of the
circle players. During the chorus, the Bluebird
taps the child in front of him lightly on the
shoulders with both hands. This child then
becomes the new Bluebird with the old Bluebird keeping his hands on his shoulders, forming a train. As the chorus is sung, the Bluebird
train moves around the various directions in
the center area of the circle. When the verse
is sung again, the train moves in and out of the
arches. Continue the action until seven or
eight children form the train. Return the train
children to the circle formation and begin
anew with a new Bluebird.

LET YOUR FEET GO TAP, TAP, TAP

Record: Folkraft 1184.

Formation: Double circle, partners facing.

Verse:
   Let your feet go tap, tap, tap,
   Let your hands go clap, clap, clap,
   Let your finger beckon me,
   Come, dear partner, dance with me.

Chorus
   Tra, la, la, la, la, la, la, etc.

Directions:

   Line 1. Tap foot three times.

   Line 2. Clap hands three times.

   Line 3. Beckon and bow to partner.

   Line 4. Join inside hands and face counterclockwise.

   Chorus. All sing and skip counterclockwise.

   Note: This can be sung to "Merrily We Roll
Along," with a little adjustment for line 2.

TEN LITTLE INDIANS

Record: Folkraft 1197.

Formation: Children are in a circle. Ten children are selected and numbered consecutively from 1 to 10, but remain in the circle.

Sequence: The piece is played four times to
   allow a complete sequence of the dance.

1. One little, two little, three little Indians,
   Four little, five little, six little Indians,
   Seven little, eight little, nine little Indians,
   Ten little Indian Braves (Squaws).

   During this verse, the Indians as num-
      bered go from the circle to the center
      when their number is mentioned in the
      singing, while the remainder of the
      circle children clap lightly.

2. During the second repetition of the music, the Indians in the center do an
   Indian dance, each in his own way.

3. The verse under #1 is again sung, but
   this time the Indians in the center return to the circle when their numbers
   are sung.

4. During the last rendition of the piece, all
   children dance as Indians, moving in
   any direction they wish, not retaining
   the circle formation.

   The dance is repeated with another
   set of Indians.

PEASE PORRIDGE HOT

Record: Folkraft 1190.

Formation: Double circle, partners facing.

Verse:
   Pease porridge hot
   Pease porridge cold
   Pease porridge in a pot
   Nine days old!
   Some like it hot,
   Some like it cold,
   Some like it in a pot,
   Nine days old!

   Directions: The dance is in two parts. The
first is a patty-cake rhythm, done while the
children sing the above verse. During the second part, the children dance with a circular
movement.

Part I
   Line 1. Clap own hands to thighs, clap own
hands together, clap own hands to partner's
hands.
   Line 2. Repeat action of line 1.
   Line 3. Clap hands to thighs, clap own hands
together, clap right hand against partner's
right, clap own hands together.

Line 4. Clap left hand to partner's left, clap own hands together, clap both hands against partner's hands.

Lines 5-8. Repeat lines 1-4.

Part II

Join both hands with partner and skip around in a small, turning circle counterclockwise for the first four lines, ending with the word "old!" Reverse direction and skip clockwise for the remainder of the verse. Move one step to the left for a new partner.

TOUCH YOUR SHOULDERS

Music: Verses are sung to the tune of "Mary Had a Little Lamb."

Formation: None needed, but children can be in any arrangement.

Verses:

1. Touch your shoulders and your knees.
   Touch your shoulders and your knees.
   Touch your shoulders and your knees.
   Make your feet go stamp, stamp, stamp.
2. Touch your elbows and your toes, etc.
   Make your hands go clap, clap, clap.
3. Touch your ankles, reach up high, etc.
   Shake yourself up in the sky.
4. Touch your hips and touch your heels, etc.

   Jump up high; one, two, three.

Directions: The verses are self-explanatory in describing the action. Children use both hands in touching. Additional verses can be devised by the children using body parts not previously mentioned and a different finishing line.

FIRST GRADE

The first grade singing games and folk dances are introductory in nature and involve simple formations and uncomplicated changes. The movements are primarily walking, skipping, and running. Only a few of the dances are done with partners, so the problem of getting the boys and girls paired off as partners is not important. Most of the activities are quite flexible in nature, and the children can interpret the words and music in various ways.

The rhythmic activities listed under the kindergarten program should be added to the list of suggested activities.

Dances	Skills
The Farmer in the Wheat	Skipping
London Bridge	Walking
The Muffin Man	Skipping
Oats, Peas, Beans, and Barley Grow	Walking, skipping
Looby Loo	Skipping
Pussy Cat	Walking, draw step, jumping
The Thread Follows the Needle	Walking
I See You	Skipping, two-handed swing
Sing a Song of Sixpence	Walking
Dance of Greeting	Running, bowing
Hickory Dickory Dock	Running
Chimes of Dunkirk	Sliding

THE FARMER IN THE WHEAT

Records: Victor 21618 and 45-5066. Folkraft 1182.

Formation: Single circle, facing center. Three children — the Farmer, the Sun, and the Rain — stand in the center.

Verses:

1. The farmer in the wheat.
   The farmer in the wheat.
   Heigh-ho the dairy-o,
   The farmer in the wheat.
2. The farmer sows his wheat, etc.
3. He covers them with dirt, etc.
4. The sun begins to shine, etc.
5. The rain begins to fall, etc.
6. The wheat begins to grow, etc.
7. The farmer cuts his grain, etc.
8. The farmer stacks his grain, etc.
9. They all begin to dance, etc.

Directions:

Verse 1. Children in the circle walk to the left with hands joined.

Verse 2. The Farmer skips around the inside of the circle counterclockwise and sows his wheat, while the children continue to walk.

Verse 3. The children stop, drop hands, and

face the center. The Farmer skips around the circle, tapping each child on the head; as he is touched, the child sinks down to the ground, becoming a wheat stalk.

Verse 4. The Sun skips around spreading sunshine.

Verse 5. The Rain skips around showering the wheat.

Verse 6. Children rise slowly and jerkily to a standing position with arms overhead to simulate the heads of wheat.

Verse 7. The Farmer skips around the inside of the circle and cuts the grain. Each child falls to the ground.

Verse 8. The Farmer skips around the group, arranging children by pairs to lean against each other to form stacks.

Verse 9. Paired children, inside hands joined, skip counterclockwise around the circle. The Farmer, Sun, and Rain form a small circle and skip clockwise.

LONDON BRIDGE

Records: Victor 20806.

Formation: Single circle moving either clockwise or counterclockwise. Two children are chosen to form the bridge. They face and join hands, holding them high in the air representing a bridge ready to fall.

Verses:
1. London Bridge is falling down,
   Falling down, falling down.
   London Bridge is falling down,
     My fair lady.
2. Build it up with iron bars, etc.
3. Iron bars will rust away, etc.
4. Build it up with gold and silver, etc.
5. Gold and silver I have not, etc.
6. Build it up with pins and needles, etc.
7. Pins and needles rust and bend, etc.
8. Build it up with penny loaves, etc.
9. Penny loaves will tumble down, etc.
10. Here's a prisoner I have got, etc.
11. What's the prisoner done to you? etc.
12. Stole my watch and bracelet too, etc.
13. What'll you take to set him free? etc.
14. One hundred pounds will set him free, etc.
15. One hundred pounds we don't have, etc.
16. Then off to prison he (or she) must go, etc.

Directions: All children pass under the bridge in a single line. When the words "My fair lady" are sung, the bridge falls and the child caught is a prisoner. He or she must choose either gold or silver and must stand behind the side of the bridge which represents his choice. No one must know which side is gold or silver until after he has made his choice as a prisoner. When all have been caught, the game ends with a tug-of-war.

Variation: Using more bridges will speed up the game.

THE MUFFIN MAN

Record: Folkraft 1188.

Formation: Children are in a single circle, facing the center with hands joined. One child, the Muffin Man, is in the center.

Verses:
1. Oh, do you know the muffin man,
   The muffin man, the muffin man?
   Oh, do you know the muffin man,
   Who lives in Drury Lane?
2. Oh, yes we know the muffin man, etc.
3. Four of us know the muffin man, etc.
4. Eight of us know the muffin man, etc.
5. Sixteen of us know the muffin man, etc.
6. All of us know the muffin man, etc.

Directions:

Verse 1. The children in the circle stand still and sing, while the Muffin Man skips around the circle. He chooses a partner by skipping in place in front of him. On the last line of the verse, "Who lives in Drury Lane," the Muffin Man and his partner go to the center.

Verse 2. The action is the same except two children now skip around in the circle and choose two partners.

Verse 3. The action is repeated with four skipping and four partners being chosen.

The verses continue until all children have been chosen. When all have been chosen, the last verse is sung while the children skip around the room.

OATS, PEAS, BEANS, AND BARLEY GROW

Records: Victor 20214. Folkraft 1182.

Formation: Single circle with a "farmer" in the center.

Verses:

1. Oats, peas, beans, and barley grow,
   Oats, peas, beans, and barley grow.
   Do you and I, or anyone know, how
   Oats, peas, beans, and barley grow?
2. First, the farmer sows the seed,
   Then he stands and takes his ease,
   He stamps his foot and claps his hands
   And turns around to view his lands.
3. Waiting for a partner,
   Waiting for a partner,
   Open the ring and choose one in
   While we all gaily dance and sing.
4. Now you're married, you must obey
   You must be kind in all you say
   You must be kind, you must be good,
   And keep your wife in kindling wood.

Directions:

Verse 1. The children walk clockwise around the farmer.

Verse 2. All stand in place and follow the actions suggested by the words of the verse.

Verse 3. Circle players again move clockwise while the Farmer chooses a partner, which should be done before the end of the verse.

Verse 4. Everyone skips during this verse. The circle continues in the same direction it has been while the Farmer and his partner (wife) skip in the opposite direction.

LOOBY LOO

Records: Victor 20214. Russell 702. Folkraft 1102, 1184. Columbia 10008D.

Formation: Single circle, all facing center with hands joined.

Chorus: A chorus is repeated before each verse. During the chorus all children skip around the circle to the left.
   Here we dance looby loo
   Here we dance looby light
   Here we dance looby loo
   All on a Saturday night.

Verses:

1. I put my right hand in
   I take my right hand out
   I give my right hand a shake, shake, shake,
   And turn myself about.
2. I put my left hand in, etc.

3. I put my right foot in, etc.
4. I put my left foot in, etc.
5. I put my head way in, etc.
6. I put my whole self in, etc.

Directions: On the verse part of the dance, the children stand still facing the center and follow the directions of the words. On the words "And turn myself about," they make a complete turn in place and get ready to skip around the circle.

The movements should be definite and vigorous. On the last verse, the child jumps forward and then backwards, shakes himself vigorously, and then turns about.

PUSSY CAT

Record: Russell 700B.

Formation: Single circle, all facing center with hands joined. One player, the "Pussy Cat," is in the center. If desired, more than one Pussy Cat can be in the center.

Verse:
   Pussy Cat, Pussy Cat, where have you been?
   I've been to London to visit the Queen!
   Pussy Cat, Pussy Cat, what did you there?
   I frightened a mouse from under her chair!

Chorus: The chorus is a repeat of the same music, but the children sing tra la, la, la, etc., instead of the words.

Directions:

Line 1. Sung by the circle children as they walk counterclockwise around the circle.

Line 2. Sung by the Cat as the children reverse the direction and walk around the other way.

Line 3. Sung by the children as they drop hands, walk toward the center, and shake a finger at the Cat.

Line 4. Sung by the Cat who on the last word "chair" jumps high into the air, and the others pretend fright and run back to the circle.

Chorus:

Line 1. Children take two draw steps (one to each measure) to the right followed by four stamps.

Line 2. Repeat to the left.

Line 3. Four steps (one to each measure) to the center.

Line 4. Three steps backward in the same tempo as line 3, followed by a jump.

A draw step is made by stepping directly to the side and bringing the other foot in a closing movement. It is a step with one foot and a close with the other.

Variation: Have more than one Pussy Cat in the circle or have a number of smaller circles, each with a Pussy Cat.

THE THREAD FOLLOWS THE NEEDLE

Records: RCA Victor 22760 (Album E87). Pioneer 3015.

Formation: A single line of about eight children is formed. Hands are joined and each child is numbered consecutively.

Verse:

The thread follows the needle
The thread follows the needle
In and out the needle goes
As mother mends the children's clothes.

Directions: The first child (#1) is the needle and leads the children, forming stitches until the entire line has been sewn. When the music starts, the needle leads the line under the raised arms of the last two children (#7 and 8). When the line has passed under their arms, they turn and face the opposite direction, letting their arms cross in front of them. This forms the stitch.

The leader now repeats the movement and passes under the next pair of raised arms (#6 and 7). Number 6 is now added to the stitch when he reverses his direction. This is repeated until the entire line has been stitched, with the leader turning under his own arm to complete the last stitch.

To "rip" the stitch, children raise their arms overhead and turn back to original positions. The game can be repeated with a new leader.

SEE YOU

Records: Victor 20432. Russell 726. Folkraft 1197.

Formation: The boys and girls stand in two longways sets as follows.

(1)	x	x	x	x	x	x	x	boys
(2)	o	o	o	o	o	o	o	girls
(3)	x	x	x	x	x	x	x	boys
(4)	o	o	o	o	o	o	o	girls

Lines 1 and 2 are facing lines 3 and 4. The space between the two middle lines (2 and 3) should be from 10' to 12'.

Lines 1 and 4 are the active players. Each active player's partner is directly in front of him and stands with hands on hips.

Verse:

I see you, I see you
Tra, la, la, la, la, la.
I see you, I see you
Tra, la, la, la, la, la.

Chorus:

Tra, la, la, etc.
Tra, la, la, etc.

Directions:

Verse:

Line 1. On the first "I see you" each active player looks over partner's left shoulder in peekaboo fashion. On the second "I see you" active player looks over partner's right shoulder in same peekaboo fashion.

Line 2. Tempo is doubled and active players make three fast peekaboo movements, left, right, left.

Line 3. Repeat the action of line 1, except the first peekaboo is made to the right.

Line 4. Repeat the action of line 2, except the movements are right, left, right.

Chorus:

Line 1. All children clap on the first note ("tra") and the active players, passing to the left of their partners, meet in the center with a two-handed swing, skipping around once in a circle, clockwise.

Line 2. All children clap again ("tra") and each active player now faces his own partner, skipping around with him once in a circle, clockwise.

Partners have now changed places with the active players, and the entire pattern is repeated with a new set of players in the active roles.

SING A SONG OF SIXPENCE

Records: Folkraft 1180. Victor 22760. Russell 700.

Formation: Players are in circle formation facing the center. Six to eight players are crouched in the center as blackbirds.

Verses:

1. Sing a song of sixpence, a pocket full
   of rye,
   Four and twenty blackbirds, baked in a
   pie,
   When the pie was opened the birds began to sing,
   Wasn't that a dainty dish to set before
   the king?
2. The king was in his counting house,
   counting out his money,
   The queen was in the pantry, eating bread
   and honey,
   The maid was in the garden, hanging out
   the clothes,
   And down came a blackbird and snipped
   off her nose!

Directions:

Verse 1:

Line 1. Players walk around in a circle.

Line 2. Circle players walk with shortened
steps toward the center of the circle with arms
outstretched forward.

Line 3. Players walk backward with arms
now up. The blackbirds in the center fly
around.

Line 4. Circle players kneel as if presenting
a dish (blackbirds continue to fly around).

Verse 2:

Line 1, 2, and 3. Pantomime action of words,
counting out money, eating, and hanging up
clothes.

Line 4. Each blackbird snips off the nose of
a circle player who now becomes a blackbird
for the next game.

DANCE OF GREETING

Records: Victor 45-6183, 20432. Folkraft 1187.
Russell 726.

Formation: Single circle, all facing center.
Each boy stands to the left of his partner.

Measures:

1	All clap, clap, and bow to partner (girl curtsies).
2	Repeat but turn back to partner and bow to neighbor.
3	Stamp right, stamp left.
4	Each player turns around in four running steps.
5–8	Repeat action of measures 1–4.

9–12	All join hands and run to the left for four measures (16 counts).
13–16	Repeat action of measures 9–12 with light running steps in the opposite direction.

Variation: Instead of using a light running
step, use a light slide.

HICKORY DICKORY DOCK

Record: Victor 22760.

Formation: Children are in a double circle
partners facing.

Verse:

Hickory Dickory Dock, tick tock,
The mouse ran up the clock, tick tock.
The clock struck one, the mouse ran down.
Hickory, Dickory, Dock, tick tock.

Directions:

Line 1. Stretch arms overhead and bend the
body from side to side like a pendulum, finish
with two stamps on "tick, tock."

Line 2. Repeat action of line 1.

Line 3. Clap hands on "one." Join hands
with partner and run to the right in a little
circle.

Line 4. Repeat the pendulum swing with the
two stamps.

CHIMES OF DUNKIRK

Records: Victor 45-6176, 17327. Folkraft 1188.
Columbia A-3016.

Formation: A single circle with boys and girls
alternating. Partners face each other. Hands
are on own hips.

Measures:

1–2	All stamp lightly left, right, left.
3–4	Clap hands overhead, swaying back and forth.
5–8	Join hands with partner and make one complete turn in place clockwise.
9–16	All join hands in a single circle facing the center and slide to the left (slides).

SECOND GRADE

The second grade includes many activities
similar to those taught in the first grade. In
addition, there is more emphasis on partner
type dances and change of partners. The

dance patterns tend to become more definite, and more folk dances are included. The movements are still confined primarily to the simple locomotor types with additional and varied emphasis in more complicated formations.

Dances	Skills
Down the Mississippi	Bending, scooter movements
Did You Ever See a Lassie	Walking
Go Round and Round the Village	Walking
Shoemaker's Dance	Skipping
Jolly Is the Miller	Marching
Shoo Fly	Walking, skipping
Ach Ja	Walking, sliding
A Hunting We Will Go	Sliding, skipping
How D'ye Do, My Partner	Bowing, skipping
Rig-a-jig-jig	Walking, skipping
Broom Dance	Marching, skipping
The Popcorn Man	Jumping, skipping

DOWN THE MISSISSIPPI

Records: To the tune "Here We Go Round the Mulberry Bush." Victor 20806, 45-5065, Columbia 90037-V, Folkraft 1183.

Formation: None. Children can be scattered or in a circle as desired. Each child is seated on the floor with his legs together and extended forward.

Verses:
1. This is the way we row our boat, row our boat, row our boat,
   This is the way we row our boat,
   Down the Mississippi!
2. This is the way we glide along, etc.
3. This is the way we rock the boat, etc.
4. This is the way we turn around, etc.
5. This is the way we float for home, etc.
6. This is the way we spell Mississippi, spell Mississippi, spell Mississippi.
   This is the way we spell Mississippi,
   M-I-S-S-I-S-S-I-P-P-I   WOW!

Directions:
Verse 1. Each child rows his boat in time to the music.
Verse 2. Each child folds his arms across his chest and bends forward and backward.

Verse 3. Each child, with arms outstretched to the side, bends from side to side.

Verse 4. Each child by rowing with one "paddle" only, turns on his side completely around in stages.

Verse 5. Each child folds his arms across his chest and moves in any direction he wishes using scooter movements. Reach out with the heels and pull the seat up to the heels.

Verse 6. Children sing the first three lines (no action) and then sound out (spell) Mississippi in staccato fashion.

(May they never misspell Mississippi!)

DID YOU EVER SEE A LASSIE

Records: Victor 45-5066, 21618, Folkraft 1183, Columbia 10008D.

Formation: Children are in a single circle, facing half left with hands joined. One child is in the center.

Verse:
Did you ever see a lassie, a lassie, a lassie?
Did you ever see a lassie do this way
   and that?
Do this way and that way, and this way and
   that way.
Did you ever see a lassie do this way
   and that?

Directions:
Measures:

1–8   Children with hands joined walk to the left in a circle. Since this is fast waltz time, there should be one step to each measure. The child in the center gets ready to demonstrate some type of movement.

9–16   All stop and follow the movement suggested by the child in the center.

As the verse starts over, the center child selects another to do some action in the center and changes places with him.

The word "laddie" should be substituted if the center person is a boy.

GO ROUND AND ROUND THE VILLAGE

Record: Folkraft 1191.

Formation: Single circle, hands joined. Several extra players stand outside, scattered around the circle.

Verses:

1. Go round and round the village,
   Go round and round the village,
   Go round and round the village,
   As we have done before.
2. Go in and out the windows, etc.
3. Now stand and face your partner, etc.
4. Now follow me to London, etc.

Directions:

Verse 1: Circle players move to the right and the extra players on the outside go the other way. All skip.

Verse 2: Circle players stop and lift joined hands, forming the windows. Extra players go in and out the windows, finishing inside the circle.

Verse 3: Extra players select partners by standing in front of them. Should select opposite sex.

Verse 4: The extra players and partners now skip around the inside of the circle while the outside circle skips the opposite way.

Variations:

1. All chosen players can continue and repeat the game until the entire circle has been chosen.

2. An excellent way is to have the boys in the circle and the girls as extra players. In this way, everyone will select and be selected as a partner. Reverse and put the girls in the circle and leave the boys as the extras.

SHOEMAKER'S DANCE

Records: Victor 20450, 45-6171, Russell 750, Folkraft 1187, Columbia A-3038.

Formation: Double circle, partners facing, boys on the inside.

Verse:

See the cobbler wind his thread,
Snip, snap, tap, tap, tap.
That's the way he earns his bread,
Snip, snap, tap, tap, tap.

Chorus:

So the cobbler blithe and gay,
Works from morn to close of day,
At his shoes he pegs away,
Whistling cheerily his lay.

Directions:

Measures:

1–2   Clenched fists are held in front about

chest high. On "see the cobbler" one fist is rolled forward over the other three times. On "wind his thread" roll the fists over each other backwards three times.

3   Fingers of the right hand form a scissors and make two cuts on "snip snap."

4   Double up fists and hammer one on top the other three times.

5–8   Same action, except finish up with three slaps instead of hammering fists.

Chorus: Partners join inside hands, outside hands on hips. All skip to the left around the room. Near the end of the chorus, all slow down and face each other. All children take one step to the left to secure a new partner.

JOLLY IS THE MILLER

Records: Victor 45-5067 or 20214, E-87, Folkraft 1192, American Play Party 1185.

Formation: Double circle, partners with joined inside hands facing counterclockwise. Boys are on the inside. A "Miller" is in the center of the circle.

Verse:

Jolly is the Miller who lives by the mill;
The wheel goes round with a right good will;
One hand on the hopper and the other on the sack;
The right steps forward and the left steps back.

Chorus: The children march counterclockwise with inside hands joined. During the second line when the "wheel goes round" the dancers should make their outside arms go in a circle to form a wheel. Children change partners at the words "right steps forward and the left steps back." The Miller then has a chance to get a partner. The child left without a partner becomes the Miller.

SHOO FLY

Records: Folkraft 1102, 1185; Decca 18222

Formation: All are in a circle with hands joined facing in. Boy stands with his girl on right.

Verse:

Shoo fly, don't bother me,
Shoo fly, don't bother me,
Shoo fly, don't bother me,

I belong to Company G.
I feel, I feel, I feel like a morning star,
I feel, I feel, I feel like a morning star.

Directions: The dance is in two parts and finishes with a change of partners.

Measures:

1–2   Walk forward four steps toward the center of the circle swinging arms back and forth.

3–4   Walk four steps backward to place with arms swinging.

5–8   Repeat all of above.

9–16 Each boy turns to the girl on his right, takes hold of both hands and skips around in a small circle, finishing so this girl will be on his left when the circle is re-formed. His new partner is on his right.

      The dance is repeated with new partners.

Variation: For the second part of the dance the following is an interesting substitute for the two-handed swing.

Designate one couple to form an arch by lifting joined hands. This couple now moves forward toward the center of the circle. The couple on the opposite side moves forward, under the arch, drawing the circle after it. When all have passed through the arch, the couple forming the arch turn under their own joined hands. The dancers now move forward to form a circle with everyone facing out. The dance is repeated with all facing out.

To return the circle to face in again, the same couple again makes an arch and the lead couple backs through the arch, drawing the circle after them. The arch couple turn under their own arms.

In this version, there is no change of partners.

ACH JA

Record: Evans, Child Rhythms, VII.

Formation: Double circle, partners facing counterclockwise, boys on the inside.

Verse:

When my father and my mother take the children to the fair,
Ach Ja! Ach Ja!

Oh, they have but little money, but it's little that they care,
Ach Ja! Ach Ja!
Tra la la, tra la la, tra la la la la la la
Tra la la, tra la la, tra la la la la la la
Ach Ja! Ach Ja!

Directions:

Measures:

1–2   Partners walk eight steps in line of direction.

3   Partners drop hands and bow to each other.

4   Each boy now bows to the girl on his left, who returns the bow.

5–8   Measures 1–4 are repeated.

9–10 Partners face each other, join hands and take four slides in line of direction (counterclockwise).

11–12 Four slides are taken clockwise.

13   Partners bow to each other.

14   Boy bows to girl on his left, who returns the bow. To start the next dance, the boy moves quickly toward this girl, who is his next partner.

A HUNTING WE WILL GO

Records: Folkraft 1191, Victor 45-5064, 22759.

Formation: Longways set with the children in two lines facing each other, boys in one line and girls in the other.

Verse:

Oh, a-hunting we will go,
A-hunting we will go,
We'll catch a fox and put him in a box
And then we'll let him go!

Chorus:

Tra, la, la, la, la, la, la, etc.

Directions: Everyone sings.

Lines 1 and 2. Head couple with hands joined slides between the two lines to the foot of the set (8 counts).

Lines 3 and 4. Head couple slides to original position (8 counts).

Chorus. Couples join hands and skip in a circle to the left following the head couple. When the head couple reaches the place formerly occupied by the last couple in the line (foot couple), they form an arch under which the other couples skip. A new couple is now the head couple and the dance is repeated until each couple has had a chance to be at the head.

Variation:

1. On the chorus, the head couple separates, and each leads his own line down the outside to the foot of the set. The head couple meets at the foot and forms an arch for the other couples. The other dancers meet two by two and skip under the arch back to place.

2. The first two couples slide down the center and back on lines 1, 2, 3, and 4. Otherwise the dance is the same.

HOW D'YE DO, MY PARTNER

Records: Victor 21685, Folkraft 1190.

Formation: Double circle, partners facing, boys on the inside.

Verse:
How d'ye do, my partner?
How d'ye do today?
Will you dance in the circle?
I will show you the way.

Directions:
Measures:

1–2   Boys bow to their partners.

3–4   Girls curtsy.

5–6   Boys offer right hand to girl, who takes it with her right hand. Both turn to face counterclockwise.

7–8   Couples join left hands and are now in a skater's position. They get ready to skip when the music changes.

9–16   Partners skip counterclockwise in the circle slowing down on measure 15. On measure 16 the girls stop and the boys move ahead to secure a new partner.

RIG-A-JIG-JIG

Record: Ruth Evans, Childhood Rhythms, Series VI, Folkraft 1199.

Formation: Single circle, all facing center, boys and girls alternating. One child is in the center.

Verse:
As I was walking down the street,
Heigh-ho, heigh-ho, heigh-ho, heigh-ho,

A pretty girl I chanced to meet,
Heigh-ho, heigh-ho, heigh-ho.

Chorus:
Rig-a-jig-jig, and away we go,
away we go, away we go.
Rig-a-jig-jig, and away we go,
Heigh-ho, heigh-ho, heigh-ho.

Directions: While all sing, the center player walks around the inside of the circle until the words "a pretty girl" and then stands in front of a partner. Girls choose boys and vice versa. He then bows to her on the last line of the verse.

He takes her hands in skater's position and on the chorus they skip around the inside of the circle while the circle players clap hands in time.

The dance is repeated with the partners separating and choosing new partners until all have been chosen.

On the second time the verse is sung the words "a nice young man" or "a handsome man" can be substituted for "a pretty girl."

Variation: The dance can be done by alternating boys and girls and using the appropriate verses. Select four or five boys to begin in the center. They choose partners and after the skip return to the circle. The girls continue the dance choosing five more boys, and so on.

BROOM DANCE

Record: Victor 20448.

Formation: Double circle, partners facing counterclockwise with boys on the inside. An extra boy with a broom is in the center.

Verse:
One, two, three, four, five, six, seven,
Where's my partner, nine, ten, eleven?
In Berlin, in Stettin,
There's the place to find him (her) in.

Chorus:
Tra la la, etc.
(repeats the music)

Directions: The record has three changes of music and then a pause. The verse is sung during the first change and repeated during the second change. The chorus is the third change. During the verse, which is repeated, all march counterclockwise. The boy in the center hands the broom to another boy and takes his place in the inner line. The boy with the broom in turn hands the broom to another inner line member and takes his place, and so on. The one who has the broom after the two verses are sung (on the word "in") takes the broom to the center. He then pretends to sweep while the others skip with inside hands joined. If there are extra girls, the dance can be done with the girls exchanging the broom by making the direction of the march clockwise.

Variation I: The first verse is sung during the first music change and the children march as in the original dance. During the second music change, the following routine is done. Note that in this routine the broom may be exchanged only when the boys move to a new partner.

Routine for the second music change.

Measures:

1–2 Beginning with the outside foot, take seven steps forward and pause on the eighth.

3–4 Beginning with the inside foot, take seven steps backward and pause as before.

5 Beginning on the outside foot, take three steps away and pause.

6 Beginning with the inside foot, take three steps in and pause.

7–8 Swing once around in place with a right elbow swing. As the boy comes back to place, he moves forward to the next girl. During the exchange of partners, the broom man gives the broom to another boy and takes his place.

Variation II: This routine is used during the first change of the music.

Boys and girls form separate lines facing each other about 20' apart. The broom man is in the center. The teacher holds the broom to one side.

Measures:

1–2 Lines advance toward each other with seven steps.

3–4 Lines retreat with seven steps.

5–6 Lines again advance seven steps.

7–8 Lines retreat seven steps until the word "in!" All, including the broom man, rush for a partner and get ready to march around the room. The player left goes to the center to become the new broom man. The new broom man now takes the broom from the teacher, and the dance proceeds in the second and third changes of the music as in the original dance. Note that the broom should not be given to the broom man until after the first music change.

THE POPCORN MAN

Record: Folkraft 1180 (The Muffin Man)

Formation: Children are in a single circle, facing the center with hands at sides. One child, the Popcorn Man, stands in front of another child of opposite sex.

Verses:

1. Oh, have you seen the Popcorn Man,
   The Popcorn Man, the Popcorn Man?
   Oh, have you seen the Popcorn Man,
   Who lives on - - - Street?

2. Oh, yes, we've seen the Popcorn Man,
   The Popcorn Man, the Popcorn Man.
   Oh, yes, we've seen the Popcorn Man,
   Who lives on - - - Street

Directions:

Verse 1. The children stand still and clap hands lightly with the exception of the Popcorn Man and his partner. These two join hands and jump lightly in place keeping time to the music.

Verse 2. The Popcorn Man and his partner now skip around the inside of the circle individually, and near the end of the verse each stands in front of a child, thus choosing new partners.

Verse 1 is now repeated with two sets of partners doing the jumping. During the repetition of Verse 2, four children now skip around the inside of the circle and choose partners. This continues until all the children are chosen.

Boys should choose girls, and girls should choose boys for partners. The children should choose the name of a street which they would like to put into the verses.

THIRD GRADE

In the third grade most of the emphasis shifts to the folk dance. Simple locomotor skills are still the basis of the movement patterns. Continued emphasis is on the simple skills, with more attention to sliding and draw steps. The formations tend to be more of the partner type with partner changes included in many of the dances. Some basic formations are introduced which are later used in more advanced dances in the intermediate grade.

Most of the steps used in the dances — draw steps, sliding, and skipping — have been previously described and employed in dances. To these are added the step-hop and the Bleking step. To do the step-hop, the child takes a short step with one foot and then hops on that foot. He then takes a step with the other foot and hops on it. A description of the Bleking step is found in the dance directions for the Bleking dance.

Dances	Skills
Paw Paw Patch	Skipping
Yankee Doodle	Marching, turning
Three Blind Mice	Skipping
Jump Jim Joe	Jumping, running, draw steps
Carrousel	Draw steps, sliding
Children's Polka	Draw steps, running
Bleking	Bleking step, step-hops
Crested Hen	Step-hops, turning under
Hansel and Gretel	Bleking step, skipping
Gustaf's Skoal	Walking, skipping, turning
Csebogar	Skipping, sliding, draw steps, elbow swing

Rope Jumping to Music (see page 376)

PAW PAW PATCH

Records: Victor 45-5066, Folkraft 1181, Honor Your Partner 103.

Formation: Children are in a longways set of five or six couples; boys are in one line and the girls are in another on the boys' right, all facing forward.

Verse:

1. Where, Oh where is sweet little Nellie,
   Where, Oh where is sweet little Nellie,
   Where, Oh where is sweet little Nellie,
   Way down yonder in the paw paw patch.
2. Come on, boys, let's go find her, etc.
3. Pickin' up paw paws, puttin' in your basket, etc.

Description:

Verse 1. Girl at the head of her line turns to her right and skips around the entire group and back to place. All others remain in place, clap, and sing.

Verse 2. The first girl turns to her right again and follows the same path as in verse 1. This time she is followed by the entire line of boys who beckon to each other.

Verse 3. Partners join inside hands, and skip around in a circle to the right following the head couple. When the head couple is at the foot of the line, they make an arch under which the other couples skip back to original formation, with a new head couple.

The entire dance is repeated until each couple has had a chance to be the head couple.

Instead of using the name "Nellie," the name of the girl at the head of the line can be sung.

Variation: The dance can be arranged to feature the boys instead of the girls. In verse 1, substitute the name of "Freddie" for "Nellie." In verse 2, change to "Come on, girls, let's go find him." The action is changed as follows:

Verse 1. Boy at the head of the line turns to his left and skips around the group.

Verse 2. The boy turns again to the left, followed by the entire line of girls.

Verse 3. Partners turn to the left.

YANKEE DOODLE

Records: Victor 22760. Victor 45-5064.

Formation: Children are in sets of threes. The sets are a line of three with a boy in the center, holding to a girl on either side of him. The sets are facing counterclockwise in a large circle formation.

Verse:

Yankee Doodle came to town
Riding on a pony,
Stuck a feather in his hat
And called it macaroni.

Chorus:
>   Yankee Doodle keep it up,
>   Yankee Doodle dandy;
>   Mind the music and the step,
>   And with the girls be handy.

Description: On the verse, the dancers march around the circle with knees up high like prancing ponies. Arms are swung back and forth.

On the first two lines of the chorus, the center dancer of each set takes the dancer on his right by the right hand and they walk (or skip) around each other. On the next two lines, he does the same with the left-hand dancer but using the left hand. When the center dancer (boy) comes back to his place in the line of threes, he moves forward to the set ahead of him and the dance repeats.

THREE BLIND MICE

Record: None.

Formation: Children are in a hollow square formation facing the inside of the square with six to eight on each side of the square. Each of the sides performs independently in turn as one part of the four-part round.

Verse (all sing):
> Three blind mice,
> Three blind mice,
> See how they run,
> See how they run,
> They all ran after the farmer's wife
> Who cut off their tails with a carving knife
> Did you ever see such a sight in your life, as
> Three blind mice

Description: Sides of the square are numbered 1, 2, 3, and 4. Each acts as one part of the round and begins in turn. All perform the same movements when their turn comes up as part of the round.
Line 1. Clap hands three times.
Line 2. Stamp the floor three times.
Line 3. Four skips forward.
Line 4. Four skips backwards to place.
Line 5. Turn in place with four light steps.
Line 6. Face the center, raising one hand above the other, and make a cutting motion.
Line 7. Put both hands over the ears with a rocking motion sideways.
Line 8. Clap hands three times.
Sing through twice. Do not overlap the lines

at the corners or there will be crowding when the children skip forward.

JUMP JIM JOE

Record: Folkraft 1180.

Formation: Double circle, partners facing. Boys are on the inside. Both hands are joined.

Verse:
> Jump, jump, and jump, Jim Joe,
> Take a little twirl and away we go,
> Slide, slide, and stamp just so — and
> Take another partner and jump, Jim Joe

Description:
Line 1. Two slow and then three fast jumps in place.

Line 2. Partners run around each other clockwise in a small circle in place and return to position.

Line 3. With hands on hips each person moves to his left with two draw steps (step left, close right, step left, close right), followed by three stamps. Each person has a new partner.

Line 4. Join hands with the new partner and run around each other back to place, finishing the turn with three light jumps on the words, "Jump, Jim Joe."

CARROUSEL

Records: Victor 45-6179, Folkraft 1183.

Formation: Children are in a double circle, all facing inward. The inner circle, representing the merry-go-round, joins hands. The outer players, representing the riders, place hands on the hips of the partner in front of them.

Verse:
> Little children, sweet and gay, carrousel is running. It will run to evening,
> Little ones a nickel, big ones a dime,
> Hurry up, get a mate, or you'll surely be too late.

Chorus:
> Ha, ha, ha, happy are we,
> Anderson and Peterson and Henderson and me,
> Ha, ha, ha, happy are we,
> Anderson and Peterson and Henderson and me.

Description: During the verse, the children take slow draw steps (step, close) to the left. This is done by taking a step to the side with the left foot and closing with the right on count 2. This gets the merry-go-round underway slowly. Four slow stamps replace the draw steps when the words, "Hurry *up,* get a mate, or you'll *surely* be too *late.*" A stamp is made on each of the italicized words. The circle now has come to a halt.

During the chorus, the tempo is increased, and the movement is changed to a fast slide. Be sure to have the children take short, light slides.

All sing during the dance.

CHILDREN'S POLKA (KINDERPOLKA)

Records: Victor 45-6179, 2042, Russell 750, Folkraft 1187.

Formation: Single circle, partners facing. Hands are joined and extended sideways.

Although this dance is called a polka, it does not use the polka step.

Measures:

1–2   Take two draw steps to the center — step, close, step, close. Finish with three light stamps.

3–4   Repeat, moving away from the center.

5–8   Repeat measures 1–4.

9–10   Clap thighs with the hands and then the hands together in slow tempo. Clap hands to partner's hands in three fast claps.

11–12 Repeat 9–10.

13   Extend the right foot forward on the heel, place the right elbow in left hand, and shake the forefinger three times at partner.

14   Repeat, extending the left foot and using the left forefinger.

15   Turn self around in place using four running steps.

16   Face partner and stamp lightly three times.

BLEKING

Records: Victor 45-6169, 20989, Folkraft 1188.

Formation: Single circle, partners facing with both hands joined. Boys are facing counterclockwise and girls clockwise.

Part I. The Bleking Step

Measures:

1   Hop on the left foot and extend the right heel forward with the right leg straight. At the same time thrust the right hand forward. Hop on the right foot, reversing the arm action and extending the left foot to rest on the heel.

2   Repeat the action with three quick changes — left, right, left.

3–4 Beginning on the right foot, repeat the movements of measures 1 and 2.

5–8 Repeat measures 1–4.

Part II. The Windmills

Partners now extend their joined hands sideways shoulder high.

Measures:

9–16 Partners turn in place with a repeated step-hop. At the same time, the arms move up and down like a windmill. The turning is done clockwise with the boy starting on his right foot and the girl with her left. At the completion of the step-hops (16) the partners should be in the original places ready for Part I again.

Variations: Change original position to double circle, partners facing, the boys with backs to the center.

Part I. As above.

Part II. All face counterclockwise, partners with inside hands joined. Partners do the basic schottische of "step, step, step, hop" throughout Part II.

CRESTED HEN

Records: Victor 45-6176, 21619, Methodist M-108, Folkraft 1159, 1194.

Formation: Children are in sets of three, two girls and one boy. Groups are scattered around the room.

Part I

Measures:

1–8 Dancers in each set form a circle. Starting with a stamp with the left foot, each set circles to the left using step-hops.

1–8 (repeated). Dancers reverse direction, beginning again with a stamp with the left foot and following with step-hops. The change of direction should be vigorous and definite with the left foot crossing over the right in changing the direction.

Part II

During this part, the dancers use the step-hop continuously in making the pattern figures. The girls release their hands to break the circle and stand on each side of the boy.

Measures:

9–10 The girl on the right with four step-hops dances under the arch formed by the other girl and the boy.

11–12 The boy turns under his own left arm with four step-hops, forming again the line of threes.

13–16 The girl on the left now repeats the pattern, going under the arch formed by the other two. The boy turns under his right arm to unravel the line.

As soon as Part II is completed, dancers again join hands in a small circle. The entire dance is repeated.

HANSEL AND GRETEL

Records: Victor 45-6182, Folkcraft 1193.

Formation: Double circle, partners facing with boys on the inside.

Part I

Measures:

1–2 Boys bow and girls curtsy.

3–4 Take partner's hands in crossed arm position, right hand to right hand and left to left.

5–6 Jump and extend the right heel forward. Repeat with the left heel.

7–8 Leaning away from partner, turn around in a small circle with seven light fast steps.

Part II

9–16 Take sixteen skips with partner around the circle with inside hands joined.

Part III

Measures:

17 Face partner, hands on hips.

18 Stamp right, left, right.

19 Stand still facing partner, hands on hips.

20 Clap hands three times.

21–22 Join hands, crossed hands position. Jump and extend the right heel then the left.

23–24 Turn with partner in a small circle using seven light steps.

Part IV

This repeats Part III except that in measure 18 nod head three times instead of stamping. In measure 20, snap fingers three times instead of clapping. Hold hands about shoulder high when snapping.

Variation: The dance can be made a mixer by having the dancers, when they finish turning around in a small circle, move directly to the left to get a new partner. Thus there would be changes of partners at the finish of the partner turn for Part I, III, and IV. The inside circle of boys would be moving counterclockwise on the change while the outer circle would be moving clockwise.

GUSTAF'S SKOAL

Records: Methodist M-108, Victor 45-6170, 20988, Folkraft 1175, Linden 701, RCA Victor EPA-4135.

Formation: Similar to a square dance set of four couples, each facing the center. Boy is to the left of his partner. Couples join inside hands and outside hands are on the hips. Two of the couples facing each other are designated as the "head couples." The other two couples, also facing each other are the "side couples."

The dance is in two parts. During Part I, the music is slow and stately. The dancers perform with great dignity. Part II is light and represents fun and dancing.

Part I

Measures:

1–2 Head couples holding inside hands walk forward three steps and bow to the opposite couple.

3–4 Head couples take three steps backward to place and bow to each other. During all of this the side couples hold their places.

5–8 Side couples perform the same movements while head couples hold places.

1–8 Dancers repeat entire figure.

Part II

9–12   Side couples raise joined hands, forming an arch. Head couples skip to the center where they meet opposite partners. Each, after dropping his own partner's hand, takes the hand of the dancer facing him and skips under the nearest arch. After going under the arch, drop hands and head back to home spot to original partner.

13–16   Clap hands smartly on the first note of measure 13 while skipping. Skip toward partner, take both hands and skip once around in place.

9–16   (repeated). Head couples form the arches and the side couples repeat the pattern just finished by the head couples.

Variation: During the first part of Part I where the dancers take three steps and bow, a shout of "Skoal" at the same time raising the right fist about head high as a salute can be substituted for the bow. The word "Skoal" means a toast.

CSEBOGAR

Records: Victor 45-6182, 20992, Kismet 141, Methodist M-101.

Formation: Single circle with partners. Girls are on the right; all are facing center with hands joined.

Part I

Measures:

1–4   Take seven slides to the left.

5–8   Seven slides to the right.

9–12   Take four skips to the center and four backwards to place.

13–16   Hook elbows with partner and turn around twice in place skipping.

Part II

Partners are now facing each other with hands joined in a single circle.

Measures:

17–20   Holding both hands of the partner, take four draw steps (step, close) toward the center of the circle.

21–24   Four draw steps back to place.

25–26   Toward the center of the circle with two draw steps.

27–28   Two draw steps back to place.

29–32   Hook elbows and repeat the elbow swing, finishing up with a shout facing the center of the circle in the original formation.

Variation: Instead of the elbow turn, partners may use the Hungarian Turn. Partners stand side by side and put the right arm around the partner's waist. The left arm is held out to the side, elbow bent with the hand pointing up, and the palm facing the dancer.

FOURTH GRADE

Basic Dance Steps

Two-step, marching

Suggested Dances

Bingo
American Indian Dances
Glow Worm Mixer
Grand March
Tunnel Under
Shoemaker's Dance — Two-step Version
Tantoli
Little Brown Jug
Norwegian Mountain March
Oh Susanna
Pop Goes the Weasel
Virginia Reel
Circle Virginia Reel
Five-Foot-Two Mixer
Green Sleeves
Rope Jumping (see page 376)

Learning the Two-Step. The forward two-step can be taught simply by moving forward on the cue "step, close, step" starting on the left foot and alternating thereafter.

The "close" step is made by bringing the toe of the closing foot to a point even with the instep of the other foot. All steps are almost glides, a kind of shuffle step.

Begin the instruction in a single circle and have all dancers begin the two-step on the left foot, moving counterclockwise. Next, arrange children by couples in a circle formation, boys on the inside, all facing counterclockwise. Repeat the instruction, with both partners beginning on the left foot. Next, practice the two-step with partners, with the boy beginning on his left foot and the girl starting on her right. The next progression is to have them move "face to face" and "back to back"

BINGO

Records: Victor 45-6172 or 41-6172, Folkraft 1189.

Formation: Double circle, partners side by side, facing counterclockwise, inside hands joined, boy on the inside.

Bingo is a favorite of young people. The singing must be brisk and loud. The dance is in three parts.

Part I

Partners walk counterclockwise around the circle, singing

"A big black dog sat on the back porch
   and Bingo was his name.

A big black dog sat on the back porch
   and Bingo was his name."

Part II

All join hands to form a single circle, girls on partners' right. They sing (spelling out) as follows with these action.

"B-I-N-G-O   All take 4 steps into the center
 B-I-N-G-O   All take 4 steps backward
 B-I-N-G-O   All take 4 steps forward again
 And Bingo   Take 4 steps backward, drop
   was his   hands and face partner
   name."

Part III

Shake right hands with partner, calling out "B" on the first heavy note. All walk forward, passing partner, to meet oncoming person with a left handshake, calling out "I" on the next chord. Continue to the third person with a right handshake, sounding out the "N." Pass on to the fourth person, giving with a left handshake and a "G." Instead of a handshake to the fifth person, face each other, raise arms high above the head, shake all over, and sound out a long drawn out "O." The fifth person is the new partner and the dance is repeated.

AMERICAN INDIAN DANCES

Most tribal civilizations included dance as an important part of their living. This is especially true of the American Indian. Dances were done in preparation for war, in harvest and other kinds of celebrations; in animal pantomimes like the buffalo and eagle dances; and in religious ceremonies. In many cases the dance routines were quite precise, while in other cases there was little conformity. Many different types of steps are used in the many American Indian tribal dances. To introduce these dances, five of these steps are presented. Body positions in the dances should be exaggerated with much bending, twisting, and turning, and grotesque movements. Arms generally dangle. A tom-tom provides the rhythmic background.

The Shuffle. This is a light one-count movement where the pressure is on the balls of the feet, with the feet dragging on the floor. The dancers shuffle forward, backward, turn around, move in various directions.

The Toe-Heel Step. This is a two-count movement which is done from a crouched position at moderate rhythm. On the first part of the step the foot comes down on the toes with the heel kept high in the air. On the second count, the heel is dropped to the ground.

The Heel-Toe Step. This step is similar to the toe-heel, except that the weight first is on the heel (count 1), and then the toe is brought down (count 2).

The Three-in-One Step. Four counts are needed to complete this step. With the weight completely on the left foot, the right toe is touched out to the side (count 1), moved forward (count 2), and further forward (count 3). Each of these are taps with no weight placed on the tapping foot. On the fourth count, a step forward is taken with the right foot. The weight is now on the right foot, and the step is repeated with the left foot. The cue is "tap, tap, tap, step."

The War Dance. The War Dance is done to a fast beat and can be either a fast step-hop or a double bounce. The latter is in the nature of two flat-footed bounces on each foot alternating. It is fast and vigorous and accompanied with exaggerated body movements. Extreme facial contortions are a part of the war dance.

No attempt is made to put the steps together in a sequence. This could be a movement problem for children, using these steps as well as others. Decide on the type of dance and let the children establish the routines together with the basic beats.

GLOW WORM MIXER

Records: Folkraft E1158, Imperial 1044, MacGregor 310.

Formation: Double circle by partners, all facing counterclockwise. Partners have inside hands joined and boys are on the left.

The dance is done in 16 steps and is best described in terms of four patterns of 4 steps each.

Steps:	Action:
4	1. Four walking steps forward.
4	2. Face partner and back away 4 steps. Steps should be short.
4	3. Boy changes partner by walking 4 steps to the girl of the couple ahead of him. The girl of that couple moves forward to meet him.
4	4. Join right elbows with the girl and make a four-step turn. At the end of the turn, release elbows immediately, join inside hands, and get ready to repeat the dance.

Variation: This can be made a get-acquainted activity. Change #4 of the above to the following: 4. Meet the girl, stop, shake hands, and say, "How do you do?"

GRAND MARCH

Record: Any good march or square dance record with about the same tempo.

Formation: Girls on left side of the room, facing the end. Boys on the right side, facing the same direction (end). This is the foot of the hall. The teacher or caller stands at the other end of the room, the head of the hall.

Call:	Action:
1. Down the center by twos.	1. Lines march forward to the foot of the hall, turn the corner, meet at the center of the foot of hall, and march in couples toward the caller with inside hands joined. The girls' line should be on the proper side so that when the couples come down the center, the boy is on the girl's left. Odd couples are #1, 3, 5, etc. Even couples are #2, 4, 6, etc.
2. Twos left and right.	2. Odd couples go left and even couples right around the room and meet at the foot of the hall.
3. Down the center by fours.	3. Couples walk down the center, four abreast. When they approach the caller —
4. Separate by twos.	4. Odd couples go left, and even couples right. They meet again at the foot.
5. Form arches.	5. Instead of coming down the center, the odd couples form arches and the even couples tunnel under. Each continues around the sides of the hall to meet at the head.
6. Other couples arch.	6. The even couples arch and the odd couples tunnel under. Each continues around the sides of the room to the foot.
7. Over and under.	7. The first odd couple arches over the first even couple and then ducks under the second even couple's arch. Each couple goes over the first couple and under the next. Continue around to the head of the hall.
8. Pass right through.	8. As the lines come toward each other, they mesh and pass through each other in the following fashion. All drop handholds. Each girl walks between the boy and girl of the opposite couple. Continue to the foot of the hall.

Call:	Action:
9. Down the center by fours.	9. Down the center four abreast.
10. Fours left and right.	10. The first four go left around the room and the second four right. Fours meet at the foot.
11. Down the center by eights.	11. Eight abreast down the center.
12. Grapevine.	12. All persons join hands in each line and keep them joined. The leader takes either end of the first line and starts around the room with the line trailing. The other lines hook on and form one long line.
13. Wind it up.	13. The leader winds up the group in a spiral formation like a clock spring. The leader makes the circles smaller and smaller until he is in the center.
14. Reverse (unwind).	14. The leader turns and faces in the opposite direction and walks between the lines of the winding dancers. He unwinds the line and leads it around the room.
15. Everybody swing.	15. After the line is unwound, everybody swings.

TUNNEL UNDER

Record: Any good march or square dance record.

This is an informal, fun activity which is thoroughly enjoyed by the children. It can be used for entering or leaving the room at the beginning or finish of a rhythmic lesson. The children are in a column of partners with the girl on the right of the boy and inside hands joined. To begin — the boy and girl in the lead couple face each other and form an arch by both hands joined overhead. The next couple goes under the arch and immediately forms a second arch. The remainder of the couples in turn go through the tunnel and form arches. Just as soon as the last couple passes under, the original lead couple follows through the tunnel. The teacher should direct the tunnel so that it forms turns and corners, ending at the selected point. If the children are leaving the room, the tunnel can head eventually in the direction of the door. As the couples reach the door, they pass directly out without forming any more arches.

The tunnel can be unraveled at any time by having the lead couple, after passing under the tunnel, walk forward with the other couples following.

SHOEMAKER'S DANCE (Two-Step Version)

Record: Victor 45-6171 or 20450.

Formation: Double circle, partners facing, boys on the inside.

Measures:	Action:
1–2	Arms are held shoulder high with fists clenched. Quickly rotate the fists around each other three times and then reverse direction.
3	Cut the thread with scissors. "Snip, snap."
4	With hands in a fist, tap one on top the other three times.
5–8	Repeat measures 1–4.
9–16	Partners join inside hands, face counterclockwise, and two-step around the circle, beginning with the outside foot.

TANTOLI

Record: Victor 45-6183

Formation: Double circle, girl on right of partner in open social dance position. Boy puts his right arm around the girl's waist, and the girl's left hand is on the boy's right shoulder. Outside hands are on hips.

Part I:

Measures:	Directions:	Action:
1–2	Heel and toe. Step, close, step.	Tilt body backward and place left heel (right for girls) forward on floor with toe pointing up. Tilt body forward and place the left toe (right for girls) backward on the floor. Do a two-step (step, close, step).
3–4	Heel and toe. Step, close, step.	Repeat starting with the other foot.
5–8	Repeat measures 1–4.	

Part II:

9–12	Step-hop.	With inside hands joined, partners take 8 step-hops forward, swinging arms back and forth.
13–16	Turn away.	The boys turn to the inside (left), making a small circle with 8 step-hops to the girl behind them for a new partner. The girls turn to the outside (right) and step-hop one turn in place, awaiting a new partner.

Part II can be done with a polka or two-step.

LITTLE BROWN JUG

Records: Columbia 52007, Folkraft F1304A, Columbia 36021, Imperial 1213

Formation: Double circle, partners facing with boys on the inside. Partners join hands shoulder high. Directions are given for the boys; girls use the opposite foot.

Measures:	Action:
1–4	Boys touch left toe to the side and then bring the foot back beside the right foot. Repeat. Three slides to the left and close.
5–8	Repeat to the opposite direction leading with the right foot. The three slides bring the dancers back to original position.
9–12	All clap hands to thighs three times. Clap partner's left hand three times. Clap partner's right hand three times. Partners clap both hands three times.
13–14	Partners hook right elbows and skip around until the boy faces the next girl, the one who *was* on his right in the original formation.
15–16	Boy hooks left elbow with this girl who is his new partner. He skips completely around her with a left elbow swing, back to the center of the circle and all get ready to repeat the dance.

Teaching Suggestion: When the boy hooks right elbow, he has only to make about a three-quarter turn until he faces the girl who is to be his new partner.

NORWEGIAN MOUNTAIN MARCH

Records: Victor 45-6173, 20151; Folkcraft 1177

Formation: Sets of threes, one boy and two girls. The boy stands in front with the two girls behind him forming a triangle. The girls join inside hands and the boy reaches back to take the girls' outside hands. The dance portrays a guide leading two climbers up a mountain.

The basic step of the dance is a fast waltz run with the first beat of each measure accented, and the bodies of the dancers should sway to the music. Throughout the dance the dancers keep their hands joined.

Measures:	Directions:	Action:
1–8	Waltz run.	Run forward 24 steps, bending with and accenting the first note of each measure, beginning with the left foot.
9–16	Waltz run.	Repeat action of measure 1–8.
17–18	Boy under.	The boy moves backward under the girls' raised arms for 6 steps.
19–20	Left girl under.	The girl on the boy's left takes 6 steps to cross in front of the boy and go under his raised *right* arm.
21–22	Right girl turn.	The girl on the right with 6 steps turns under the boy's right arm.
23–24	Boy turn.	The boy turns under his own right arm. The dancers should be in the original triangle.
25–32		A repeat of measures 17 to 24 is made except that the right girl goes under the boy's left arm, followed by the left girl turning under the same left arm. The boy turns under this arm to unwind the group.

Teaching Suggestion: Time must be taken to practice the turns. It may be a good plan to have a demonstration group.

OH SUSANNA

Records: Victor 45-6178, 20638; Folkraft 1186; Decca 18222; Imperial 1080, 1146.

Formation: Couples in a single circle facing the center with the boy on the left of the girl; all hands are joined.

Measures:	Directions:	Action:
1–4	Slide left.	All take 8 slides to the left.
5–8	Slide right.	All take 8 slides to the right.
9–12	To the center and back.	Four skips to the center and 4 skips back.
13–16	Grand right and left.	Partners face, touch right hands, walk past each other right shoulder to right shoulder and give a left to the next. Continue grand right and left until the music changes. Pick the next girl for partner.
17–24	Promenade.	Promenade or two-step around the circle.

The dancers should promenade until the verse portion of the piece begins again for a repeat of the dance.

During the grand right and left, if a dancer does not secure a partner, he or she should come to the center of the circle. After finding a partner, the couple joins the promenade.

POP GOES THE WEASEL

Records: Victor 45-6180, 20151; RCA Victor LPM-1623; Folkraft 1329; Folk Dancer MH 1501; Columbia A3078.

Formation: Double circle, couples facing. In each set of two couples, #1 couple is facing clockwise and #2 counterclockwise.

Measures:	Action:
1–4	Couples walk or skip 4 steps forward and then 4 backwards.
5–6	Each set of two couples joins hands and skips clockwise one full turn, returning to position.
7–8	#1 couple lifts joined hands and #2 couple skips under to move forward (counterclockwise) to meet the next #1 couple.
	Repeat as long as desired.

Variation:

Formation: Dancers are in sets of threes, all facing counterclockwise. Each forms a triangle with one child in front and the other two with joined hands forming the base of the triangle. The front dancer reaches back and holds the outside hands of the other two dancers. The groups of three are in a large circle formation.

Measures:	Action:
1–6	Dancers skip around the circle for the first six measures.
7–8	On the "Pop goes the weasel," the two back dancers raise their joined hands and the front dancer backs up underneath to the next set. This set, in the meantime, has "popped" its front dancer back to the set behind it.

VIRGINIA REEL

Record: Any good reel. Methodist M104; Imperial 1092; Folkraft 1141, 1249; Columbia A-3079.

Formation: Six couples in a longways set of two lines, facing each other, boys in one line and girls in the other. The boy on the left of his line and the girl across from him are the head couple.

During the first part of the dance, all perform the same movements.

Measures:	Calls:	Action:
1–4	All go forward and back.	Take 3 steps forward, curtsy or bow. Take 3 steps back and close.
5–8	Right hands around.	Move forward to partner, join right hands, turn once in place, and return to position. Use forearm grasp.
9–12	Left hands around.	Repeat the action with the left hands joined.
13–16	Both hands around.	Partners join both hands and turn once in clockwise direction and back to place.
17–20	Dos-a-dos your partner.	Partners pass each other right shoulder then back to back, and move backwards to place.
21–24	All go forward and back.	Same as measures 1–4.
25–32	Head couple sashay.	Head couple with hands joined slides 8 slides down to the foot of the set and 8 slides back to position.
33–64	Head couple reel.	The head couple begins the reel with linked right elbows and turns 1½ times. The boy is now facing the next girl and his partner is facing the next boy. The head couple now each link left elbows with the person facing them and turn once in place. Head couple meets again in the center and turns once with a right elbow swing. The next dancers down the line are turned with a left elbow swing and then back to the center for another right elbow turn. Thus, the head couple progresses down the line, turning each dancer in order. After the head couple has turned the last dancers they meet with a right elbow swing but turn only halfway round and sashay back to the head of the set.
65–96	Everybody march.	All couples face toward the head of the set, with the head couple in front. The head girl turns to her right and the head boy to his left, and each goes behind the line of dancers followed by the other dancers. When the head couple reaches the foot of the set, they join hands and make an arch, under which all other couples pass. The head couple is now at the foot of the set and the dance is repeated with a new head couple.

The dance can be repeated until each couple has had a chance to be the head couple.

CIRCLE VIRGINIA REEL

Variation: A simpler dance using some of the same principles can be done in a circle formation.

Formation: Double circle, boys on the inside with partners facing.

Action: The dancers follow the calls given, and after a series of patterns, change partners by having the boy move to the next girl to his left. The calls can come in any order and the change of partner is made with "On to the next." The following calls work effectively:

Forward and back.	Dos-a-dos your partner.
Right hand swing.	Right elbow swing.
Left hand swing.	Left elbow swing.
Both hands swing.	Swing your partner.

FIVE-FOOT-TWO MIXER

Record: Ed Durlacher Album, Series III, Record 301, Honor Your Partner Album

Formation: Couples are in a double circle formation, facing counterclockwise, boys on the inside holding partner in a skater's position.

Measures:	Directions:	Action:
1–2	Two-steps.	Take 2 two-steps in line of direction, beginning on the left foot for *both* boy and girl.
3–4	Walk.	Four walking steps.
5–6	Two-steps.	Two two-steps in line of direction.
7–8	Walk and turn.	The girl turns in with 4 walking steps, while the boy walks forward 4 steps. The left-hand grip is dropped and the right-hand grip is retained. A single circle is now formed with the men facing out and the girls facing in.
9–10	Balance forward and balance back.	Each does a two-step forward and a two-step balance back.
11–12	Walk around your partner.	Drop neighbor's left hand, continue grip with partner's right hand, walk 4 steps to make a half circle to face the opposite direction. A new single circle is now formed with the boy facing in and the girl facing out. This maneuver amounts simply to the partners exchanging places.
13–14	Balance forward and balance back.	All do a two-step forward and a two-step balance back.
15–16	Walk with a new partner.	Drop right-hand grip (with partner), keep hold of new partner with left hand, and use the 4 steps to walk into skater's position with the new partner. Everyone is now in the original formation, but with a new partner.

GREEN SLEEVES

Record: Victor 45-6175, Honor Your Partner Album #13

Formation: Couples are in circle formation, all facing counterclockwise. Boys are on the inside and inside hands are joined. Couples are numbered #1 and #2. Two couples form a set.

Measures:	Directions:	Action:
1–8	Walk.	Walk forward for 16 steps.
9–12	Right-hand star.	Each member of couple #1 turns individually to face the couple behind them. All join right hands and circle clockwise (star) for 8 steps.

Measures:	Directions:	Action:
13–16	Left-hand star.	Reverse and form a left-hand star. Circle counterclockwise. This should bring couple #1 back to place and they face in original position (counterclockwise).
17–20	Over and under.	Couple #2 arches and couple #1 backs under 4 steps while couple #2 moves forward 4 steps. Couple #1 now arches and couple #2 backs under — 4 steps for each.
21–24	Over and under.	Repeat measures 17–20.

FIFTH GRADE

Basic Dance Steps

Schottische, Step Swing, Polka, Two-Step Pivot

Suggested Dances

Schottische
Schottische Mixer
Horse and Buggy Schottische
Ace of Diamonds
Heel and Toe Polka
Klappdans
Come Let Us Be Joyful
Seven Jumps
Sicilian Circle
Tinikling
La Raspa
Narcissus
Rope Jumping (see page 376)

Learning the Two-step Turn. Begin with the students in a number of lines with enough space between to maneuver. Begin by teaching a quarter turn first. To help the students, have them watch the wall they are facing. They should face in turn the north, east, south, and west walls. The cue is a "left, close, pivot," and a "right, close, pivot." Next, do this with partners, first with both hands joined in front, and later in social dance position.

Learning the Schottische. The schottische is actually a light run. The cue is "step, step, step, hop; step, step, step, hop; step-hop, step-hop, step-hop, step-hop." A full pattern of the schottische, then, is 3 steps and a hop, repeated; followed by 4 step-hops. Boy starts on the left foot and partner on opposite foot. The step can be learned first in a single circle and later practiced by couples in a double circle formation.

Learning the Polka Step. The polka step can be broken down into four movements; (1) step forward left; (2) close the right foot to the left, bringing up the toe even with the left instep; (3) step forward left; and (4) hop on the left. The next series begins on the right foot.

Several methods can be used to learn the polka.

1. Step-by-Step Rhythm Approach. Analyzing the step very slowly, have class walk through the steps together in even rhythm. Cue is "step, close, step, hop." Gradually adapt the rhythm until there is a quick hop and a slower step, close step. Accelerate the tempo to normal polka time and add the music.

2. Two-step Approach. Beginning with the left foot, two-step with the music, moving forward in line of direction in a single circle. Gradually accelerate the tempo to a fast two-step and take smaller steps. Without stopping, change to a polka rhythm by following each two-step with a hop. Use a polka record for the two-step, but slow it down considerably to start.

3. The Gallop Approach. Form the students in lines of 6 to 8 on one end of the room. Have them cross the floor by taking 8 gallops on the left and then 8 on the right. Repeat several times. Emphasize that in order to change from a left gallop to a right (and vice versa), a hop is needed. Repeat the gallops across the room alternating 4 at a time. Repeat later alternating 2 on each side. This is the polka step.

4. The polka movement can be also taught based on skipping. If children skip twice on the same side and alternate these movements, they are doing the polka.

5. By Partners. After the polka step has been learned by one of the four methods, the step should be practiced by partners in a double circle formation, boys on the inside and all facing counterclockwise with inside hands joined. Boys begin with the left foot and girls with the right.

SCHOTTISCHE

Record: Victor 26-0017 or any good schottische.

Formation: The dance is done by couples facing line of direction (counterclockwise). The boy is on the girl's left and inside hands are joined.

There are many variations of the schottische based upon the basic pattern of the schottische step. The pattern can be divided into Part I and Part II.

Measures: **Action:**

Part I

1–2   Partners start with the outside feet and run lightly forward 3 steps and hop on the outside foot.

3–4   Beginning with the inside foot, run forward 3 steps and hop with the inside foot.

Part II

5–8   Four step-hops are taken beginning with the outside feet. A number of different movement patterns may be done while the 4 step-hops are taken.

    1. Drop hands, turn away from each other on the 4 step-hops to rejoin hands again in original position.

    2. Turn in peasant position, clockwise direction.

    3. Join both hands and "dishrag" (turn under the joined hands).

    4. Boy kneels and girl takes the step-hops around him counterclockwise.

SCHOTTISCHE MIXER

Formation: Double circle by partners, all facing counterclockwise. Boys are on the left of the girls. Inside hands are joined.

Action: Two full patterns of the schottische step are done with each exchange of partners.

    Part I — 4 measures. All run forward 3 steps and hop. Repeat.
             4 measures. All do 4 step-hops moving forward.

    Part II — 4 measures. All run forward 3 steps and hop. Repeat.
              4 measures.

    Boy turns in a small circle to the inside on the 4 step-hops to circle to the girl immediately behind him. This is his new partner.

    Girl turns to the outside (right) in a small circle *in place* on the 4 step-hops and looks for the boy circling to her from the couple ahead.

HORSE AND BUGGY SCHOTTISCHE

Record: Any good schottische. MacGregor 400; Imperial 1046.

Formation: Couples are in sets of fours in a double circle, all facing counterclockwise. Couples join hands and give the outside hands to the other couple.

Action:

    Part I — All run forward step, step, step, hop; step, step, step, hop.

    Part II — During the 4 step-hops, one of two movement patterns can be done:

    1. The lead couple drops inside hands and step-hops around the outside of the back couple, who move forward during the step-hops. The lead couple now joins hands behind the other couple and the positions are reversed.

    2. The lead couple continues to hold hands and move backward under the upraised hands of the back couple, who untwist by turning away from each other.

    3. Alternate 1 and 2.

ACE OF DIAMONDS

Records: Victor 45-6169, 20989; Folkraft 1176; Methodist M-102.

Formation: Couples are in a double circle, partners facing with boys on the inside of the circle. Girls, with hands on hips, are facing the center.

Measures:	Action:
1–4	Clap hands once, hook right arms with partners, and walk around partner clockwise for 6 steps.
5–8	Clap hands once, hook left elbows, and walk around partner for 6 steps in counterclockwise direction. Partners should now be back to original places.
9–12	With arms folded high, all take 4 slow step-hops toward the center. The boy moves backward and begins with the left foot while the girl moves forward. The step is made on the first beat of the measure and the hop on the second.
13–16	Four step-hops back to place.
17–24	Join inside hands and polka counterclockwise around the circle.

Variation: For measures 9-16, Bleking type step. Partners should hop on the left foot and thrust the right heel forward. Hop on the right and put the left heel forward. Three more changes are made rapidly. The rhythm is slow, slow, fast, fast, fast. Repeat.

HEEL AND TOE POLKA

Records: Old Timer 8005, MacGregor 400.

Formation: Double circle, all facing counterclockwise. Boys are on the inside, and partners have inside hands joined.

Directions are for the boy. Girl uses opposite foot.

Measures:	Directions:	Action:
1–2	Heel-toe, step-close-step.	With weight on the inside foot, extend the outside heel forward on the floor. On "toe," bring the toe alongside the instep. Weight is still on the inside foot. Step left, right, left.
3–4	Heel-toe, step-close-step.	With weight on the outside foot, repeat the measures 1-2 beginning with the inside heel and toe. Step right, left, right.
5–6	Heel-toe, step-close-step.	Repeat measures 1-2.
7–8	Heel-toe, step-close-step.	Repeat measures 3-4.
9–16	With inside hands joined and partners side by side, do 8 two-steps in line of direction.

Variations:

1. The dance can be done as a couple dance in social dance position. During the 8 two-steps, the dancers can do two-step turns.

2. The polka step can be substituted for the two-step.

3. Heel and Toe Polka Mixer. A mixer can be made out of the dance in the following manner. The entire dance is done as illustrated above (Measures 1-16). During the next repetition of the dance, measures 1-8 are not changed. During measures 9-16, the dancers change partners by the boys turning in a small circle to the left to the girl behind them, while the girl turns to her right in a small circle returning to her position. She looks for the boy coming from the couple ahead of her.

KLAPPDANS

Records: Victor 45-6171, Folkraft 1175.

Formation: Double circle, all facing counterclockwise. Boys on the inside. Inside hands are joined and the other hand is on the hip.

Measures: **Action:**

1–8   Beginning with the outside foot, partners polka around the circle.

9–16   All do the heel and toe polka, leaning back on the "heel" and forward on the "toe."

17–20   Partners face each other and bow. Clap hands 3 times. Repeat.

21–22   Clap partner's right hand, own hands, partner's left hand, and own hands.

23   Each makes a complete turn *in place* to the left, striking right hand against right hand in turning, which is a pivot on the left foot.

24   Stamp 3 times.

25–32   Repeat measures 17-24.
      A mixer can be made out of the dance by having the dancers on measures 23 and 24 progress one partner to the left while whirling. There would be two changes of partners for each complete pattern of the dance.

COME LET US BE JOYFUL

Records: Victor 45-6177, Folkraft 1195.

Formation: A set is composed of two lines of three facing each other. Sets are in a circle formation. Each line of three has hands joined.

Measures: **Action:**

1–2   All walk forward and bow — 3 steps and a bow.

3–4   Walk backward 3 steps and close (bring feet together).

5–8   Repeat measures 1-4.

9–10   Center dancer in each set hooks right elbow with partner on the right hand and turns her in place by walking around her.

11–12   Hooks left elbow with the other partner and turns her in place.

13–16   Repeats measures 9-12.

17–20   All walk forward 3 steps and bow, walk backward 3 steps and close.

21–24   Both lines advance again but instead of bowing and retiring, move through (right shoulders pass each other) to the oncoming group of three to form a new set.

   The dance is repeated.

SEVEN JUMPS

Records: Methodist M-108, Victor 45-6172, Victor 21617.

Formation: Single circle with hands joined.

   There are seven jumps to the dance. Each jump is preceded by the following:

Measures: **Action:**

1–8   The circle moves to the right with 7 step-hops, one to each measure. On the eighth measure, all jump high in the air and reverse direction.

9–16   Circle to the left with 7 step-hops. Stop on measure 16 and face the center.

First Jump

17   All drop hands, place on hips, and lift the right knee upward, toe pointed downward.

18   Stamp right foot to the ground on the first note and join hands on the second note.

Second Jump

1–18	Repeat measures 1-18, except do not join hands.
19	Lift left knee, stamp, and join hands.

Third Jump

1–19	Repeat measures 1-19. Do not join hands.
20	Put right toe backward and kneel on right knee. Stand, join hands.

Fourth Jump

1–20	Repeat measures 1-20. Do not join hands.
21	Kneel on left knee. Stand, join hands.

Fifth Jump

1–21	Repeat measures 1-21. Do not join hands.
22	Put right elbow to floor with cheek on fist. Stand, join hands.

Sixth Jump

1–22	Repeat measures 1-22. Do not join hands.
23	Put left elbow to floor with cheek on fist. Stand, join hands.

Seventh Jump

24	Repeat measures 1-23. Do not join hands.
	Forehead on floor. Stand, join hands.

Finale

1–16	Repeat measures 1-16.

SICILIAN CIRCLE

Records: Methodist 104, Columbia 52007 (Little Brown Jug), Folkraft 1115, Folkraft 1242 (with calls).

Formation: Couples are in sets of two couples, one of which is facing clockwise and the other counterclockwise. The sets are in circle formation.

Measures:	Directions:	Action:
1–4	Go forward and back.	Couples with inside hands joined move forward (4 steps) toward the opposite couple and return.
5–8	Circle four hands round.	Couples circle once around clockwise.
9–12	Right and left through.	Couples give right hands to the person opposite and pass the person opposite. Couples join inside hands and turn in place to the left so that they face each other.
13–16	Right and left back.	Couples repeat and return to original position.
17–20	Ladies chain.	Girls cross to opposite places by giving each other the right hand as they start and dropping hands as they pass each other. They give left hands to the opposite boy, who takes the hand with his right. The couple then turns around in place.
21–24	Chain right back.	Repeat, chaining back to original partner.
25–28	Go forward and back.	Repeat measures 1-4.
29–32	Go forward and pass through.	Couples walk forward toward opposite couple, drop hands, and pass through. The girl walks through between the two members of the opposite couple.

Each couple walks forward after passing through to meet an oncoming couple, forming a new set. The dance is repeated.

TINIKLING (Philippine Islands)

Record: RCA Victor LPM-1619.

Formation: Sets of fours scattered around the room. Each set has two strikers and two dancers.

Dance Description:

Two 8′ bamboo poles and two crossbars on which the poles rest are needed for the dance. One striker kneels at one end of the poles, the other at the other end, both holding the end of a

A Tinikling Set

pole in each hand. The music is in waltz meter, ¾ time, with an accent on the first beat. The strikers slide and strike the poles together on count 1. On the other two beats of the waltz measure, the poles are opened about 15″ apart, lifted an inch or so, and tapped twice on the crossbars in time with counts 2 and 3. The rhythm is "Close, tap, tap" and is continued throughout the dance.

Basically, the dance requires that a step be done *outside* the poles on the close (count 1) and two steps done *inside* the poles (counts 2 and 3) when the poles are tapped on the crossbars. Many step combinations can be devised.

The basic tinikling step should be practiced until it is mastered. The step is done singly, although both dancers are performing. Each dancer takes a position at an opposite end and on opposite sides so that his right side is to the bamboo poles. This means that each dancer is on the left side of the poles with respect to his position.

Count 1. Step slightly forward with the left foot.

Count 2. Step with the right between the poles.

Count 3. Step with the left between the poles.

Count 4. Step with the right outside to the right (for him).

Count 5. Step with the left between the poles.

Count 6. Step with the right between the poles.

Count 7. Step with the left outside to original position.

The initial step (count 1) is used only to get the dance underway. The last step (count 7) to original position is actually the beginning of a new series (7, 8, 9 — 10, 11, 12).

The dancer may go from side to side, or he may return to the side from which he entered. He may also straddle the poles during the close.

The dance may be done singly with the two dancers moving in opposite directions from side to side, or they may enter from and leave toward the same sides. Dancers can do the same step patterns, or may do different movements. The dancers may dance as partners moving side by side with inside hands joined, or they can face each other and have both hands joined.

Teaching Suggestions:

Steps should be practiced first with the poles stationary or by using lines drawn on the floor. Wands or jump ropes can be used as stationary objects over which to practice.

Since the dance is popular and lots of fun, there should be a number of sets of equipment so many children can be active.

LA RASPA

Records: Imperial 1084, Folkraft 1190, World of Fun M106, Columbia 38185.

Formation: A partner dance, with couples scattered around the room.

Measures:	Action:
1–4	Partners face in opposite directions standing left shoulder to left shoulder. Boy clasps his hands behind his back, girl holds skirt. Do one Bleking step, beginning with the right.
5–8	Couples now face the other way, with right shoulder to right shoulder. Do one Bleking step, beginning with the left.

Measures:	Action:
9–16	Repeat measures 1-8.
17–20	Hook right elbows, turning with 8 running steps. Clap hands on the eighth step.
21–24	Hook left elbows and repeat in the reverse direction.
25–32	Repeat measures 17-24.

NARCISSUS

Record: Windsor 7601.

Formation: Couples in a double circle. Boys have their backs to the center of the circle and have both hands joined with the girls, who are facing them.
Directions are for the boys; girls use the opposite foot.

Directions:

1. Step left, close right, step left, close right.   Two draw steps to the boy's left.
2. Slide, slide, slide, dip.   Continue in the same direction with 3 slides and a dip.
3. Step right, close left, step right, close left.   Repeat #1 beginning to the right.
4. Slide, slide, slide, dip.   Continue to the right with 3 slides and a dip.
5. Step left, swing, step right, swing.   Step left, swing right across, step right, swing left across.
6. Step left, swing, step right, swing.   Repeat #5 and immediately take girl in social dance position.
7. Four two-steps in social dance position turning twice (two full turns) clockwise while keeping relative position in the circle with the couple progressing in a counterclockwise direction.

Variation: For #7, have the dancers retain the two-handed grip and during the 4 two-steps make one complete turn (a quarter turn for each two-step).

Variation for Mixer: A change of partners can be made during the 4 two-steps (#7). The boy hooks right elbow with his partner and takes 2 two-steps around her clockwise. Instead of returning to his own place, he takes the remaining 2 two-steps to move in position in front of the girl who originally was on his right. This is his new partner and the dance is repeated.

SIXTH GRADE

Dance activities for the sixth grade introduce three important new elements. These are the waltz, varsouvienne, and square dancing. This, in turn, means that more emphasis is placed on individual couple dances. The teacher must be more concerned with the change of partners because, in some dances, the children are in a scattered formation, and the usual technique of having each partner move forward so many places may need to be modified. One simple solution is to have the nearest couples exchange partners, with the stipulation that no one should dance a second time with the same partner.

Introductory material for square dancing is found in many of the dances already presented. While not actually having the dancers in a square dance set, many of the basic square dance maneuvers are used in previous dances. A dance like the *Sicilian Circle* employs many of the skills needed in square dancing.

Dance Steps

Waltz, Square Dancing, Varsouvienne.

Suggested Dances

Rye Waltz

Little Man in a Fix

Spanish Circle

Badger Gavotte

Lili Marlene

Brown-Eyed Mary Mixer

Varsouvienne

Varsouvienne Mixer

Teton Mountain Stomp (Mixer)

Square Dances

    Oh Johnny, Oh

    My Little Girl

    Hot Time

Rope Jumping (see page 376)

Learning the Waltz. The waltz consists of three walking steps to a measure, one long (on the first count) and two short. The first count should always be emphasized. This gives the waltz its characteristic "swing." The waltz is generally written with two measures coming together. One measure is heavy and the other light. The boy should start on the heavy beat with his left foot. The progression of teaching the waltz is:

    The rhythm

    The waltz balance

    The waltz box

    The waltz turn

1. *The Rhythm.*

Have the class clap hands accenting the first beat of each measure. Work out combinations where half the class claps the first beat and the other half the second and third beats of each measure. Let them tap with their feet.

Put the class in circle formation with all facing in and holding hands. Have them step in place with an accent on the first beat of each measure. Start with the left foot. In the learning stages, both boys and girls follow the same directions. The cue is "Step, step, step; *step,* step, step."

2. *The Waltz Balance.*

After the dancers have learned to identify the first beat and have gotten the feel of waltz music, the waltz balance can be introduced. Retain the circle formation for this instruction. The balance is performed forward and backward first.

Step forward (count 1) with the left foot, close with the right foot alongside the left (count 2), and step in place (count 3) with the left foot. Step backward with the right foot (count 1), close with the left foot (count 2), and step in place with the right foot (count 3). Later the students will step very lightly on the third count or simply balance during this count.

The balance should be practiced to the side. The movement is step left (to the side), close right, step left in place. Step right (to the side), close left, and step right in place.

The patterns of the waltz balance should be done with partners. Both hands are joined, partners facing, and boys on the inside. The boy steps forward with his left foot while the girl steps backward right. The next progression is to perform the balance in social dance position. After some practice in the circle formation, the couples can be on their own around the room for practice.

3. *The Waltz Box.*

The waltz box is the soul of waltz dancing

and makes waltzing a pleasure. The box pattern should first be learned individually and then practiced either in a line formation or in a large single circle. A 6-count sequence, comprising two waltz measures of 3 counts each, is executed to complete the box, with the boy stepping either forward or backward on the first count. The forward movement is the accepted basis for learning the box.

Moving as individuals, all dancers step directly forward on the left foot, with a sliding step. On the second count, the next movement is forward and to the right with the right foot. On the third count the left foot closes to the right. The movements for the first three counts are as follows:

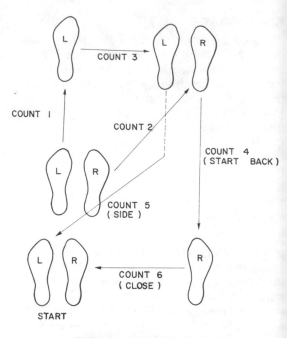

Waltz Box Steps (6 counts)

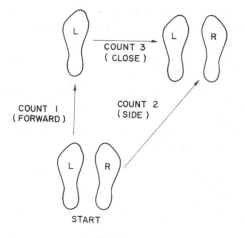

Waltz Step (3 counts)

The next three movements reverse direction and laterality. The fourth count of the sequence directs the right foot to move directly backward. The left foot moves backward and out. On the sixth count, the right foot closes to the left, at which point the dancer has returned to original position. This is a diagram of the entire sequence. The cue is: "forward, side close; back, side close."

Next the box should be practiced with a partner in extended arm position. Partners face each other and reach out and join hands. Following this, the pattern of the box should be practiced in social dance position.

The forward step movement should be practiced until it has been reasonably mastered before the initial backward step is introduced. When the students are on their own

dancing with partners, they can practice informal turns before proceeding to the formal waltz turn.

4. *The Waltz Turn.*

When teaching the waltz turn, it is a pivot (left), step (right), close (left); pivot (right), step (left), close (right). To pivot the boy turns his *leading* foot to the outside, if the step is forward.

At first the children should make quarter turns. They can check this by facing each wall in turn in a clockwise direction. Later, a complete turn is made in six counts (two measures).

The turn should be practiced individually and then with a partner. It is important to master the clockwise turn also, since many of the dances call for this turn. The dancers should learn to make progression around the room in the line of direction (counterclockwise) while the couples themselves are turning clockwise. This is accomplished more easily if the boy will take the initial backward step in the line of direction.

Square Dancing. Introductory square dancing is fun and a challenge for youngsters because of the adult slant of the activity. In many cases the children have come in contact with the activity because the parents belong to square dance clubs or have been square dancers.

The teacher is sometimes concerned about being able to call square dance figures. The skill of calling does take practice and study, but in some instances the youngsters can call successfully. However, the fun of square dancing begins with a good, solid caller.

Singing calls, however, present a slightly different approach. Children can learn the music and the words together with the movements. The entire group can sing while dancing or one or more children can provide the singing call.

Innumerable square dance records with calls are on the market and the teacher should have a variety of simple dances. Some records duplicate the music on the two sides. One side presents the music with calls, and the other without the calls.

The basic skills should be a challenge but not a chore to the children. It needs to be emphasized that square dancing is continued throughout the junior high school program, and that the sixth grade work is only an introduction.

Teaching Suggestions

1. Teach youngsters to listen to the call. It is equally important that they know what the call means. Youngsters are to have fun but must be quiet enough to hear the call.

2. Generally, the caller will explain the figures, have the children walk through the patterns, and then call the figure.

3. It is important to follow the directions of the caller and not to move too soon. Children should be ready for the call and move at the proper time.

4. The teacher should remember that there are many different ways of doing different turns, swings, hand positions, etc., and as many opinions on how they should be done. Settle on good principles and stick with them.

5. If a set is confused, the dancers should return to home positions (for each couple) and try to pick up from that point. Otherwise the choice is to wait until the dance is over or a new sequence has started.

6. Change partners at times through the dancing. Have each boy move one place to his right and take a new partner. Another way is to have the girls (or boys) keep positions, and the partners change to another set.

7. The shuffle step should be used rather than a skipping or running step beginners usually tend to use. The shuffle step makes a smoother and more graceful dance, has better carry-over values for dancing, and conserves energy. The shuffle step is a quick walk or about a half-glide in time to the music. It is done by reaching out with the toes in a gliding motion. The body should be in good posture and not be bouncing up and down on each step.

The Square Dance Formation. Each couple is numbered around the set in a counterclockwise direction. It is important to have the couples know their positions. The couple with their backs to the music is generally couple #1 or the head couple. The couple to the right is #2, etc. While the head couple is #1, the term "head couples" includes both #1 and #3. In some dances, couples #2 and #4 are the side couples. (See page 330.)

With respect to any one boy (gent), the following terms are used:

Partner: the girl at his side.

Corner Lady: the girl on the boy's left.

Righthand Lady: the girl in the couple to the boy's right.

Opposite or Opposite Lady: the girl directly across the set.

Other terms that are used are:

Home: the original or starting position.

Active or Leading Couple: the couple leading or visiting the other couples for different figures.

Square Dance Figures

Honor your partner — partners bow to each other.

Allemande left — face your corner, grasp left hand with your corner, walk around your corner, and return to your partner. Generally, the next figure is a right and left grand.

Right and left grand — facing your partner, touch right hands with partner, walk past your partner, and touch left hands with the next person in the ring, and so on down the line. This causes the boys to go in one direction around the circle and the girls in the other, alternately touching right and left hands until partners meet. The girl reverses direction by turning under uplifted joined right hands, and the couple promenades home.

Promenade — walk side by side with your partner with the right hand joined to the right hand and left to left in a crossed-arm (skater's) position. Walk around once to home position.

Swing your partner (or corner) — the boy and girl stand side by side with right hip against right hip. The dancers are in social dance position, except that the boy's right arm is more around to the side than in back at the shoulder blade. The dancers walk around each other until they return to starting position.

Right and left through (and back) — two couples pass through each other, girls to the inside, touching right hands passing through. After passing through, the boy takes the girl's left hand in his left, puts his right hand around her waist, and turns her in place so that the couples are again facing each other. On "right and left back" the figure is repeated, and the couples return to place.

Dos-a-dos your partner (or corner) — walk around your partner passing right shoulder to right shoulder. Return to place by partner.

Ladies chain — from a position with two couples facing each other, the ladies cross over to the opposite gent, touching right hands as they pass each other. When they reach the opposite boy, they join left hands with him. At the same time the gent places his right arm around the lady's waist, and turns her once around to face the other couple. On "chain right back" the ladies cross back to partners in a similar figure.

All around your lefthand lady, see-saw your pretty little taw — boy does a dos-a-dos with his corner girl, and then passes around his partner left shoulder to left shoulder.

Do-pass-so — give the left hand to your partner and walk around your partner. Release your partner and, with right hands joined, walk around your corner. Return to partner, take left hand in left hand, and turn her in place with the arm around the waist. The turning movement is similar to the figure used in "Right and left through" and "Ladies chain."

Circle right (or left) — all eight join hands and circle. You can add "Into the center with a great big yell." The circle is usually broken up with a swing at home base.

Other calls — there are many other calls which can be used. The figures presented are basic and provide enough material for sixth grade square dancing. However, there will be other sequences which are needed for special dances. These can be learned as the dance is learned.

RYE WALTZ

Records: MacGregor 298, Old Timer 8009, Imperial 1044, Folk Dancer 3012.

Formation: Couples in closed position, forming a circle with the boy's back to the center of the circle.

Directions are for the boys; girls use opposite foot.

Part I. The Slide.

1. Point left toe to side (count 1) and return to the instep of the other foot (count 2). Repeat (counts 3 and 4).

2. Take 3 slides to the boy's left and dip (counts 5, 6, 7, and 8). The dip is made by placing the right toe behind the left foot.

3. Repeat #1 using the right foot for pointing.

4. Repeat #2 but sliding to the right. (Some records repeat 1-4).

Part II. The Waltz

5. Starting with the boy stepping *backward* on the left foot, waltz for 16 measures, turning clockwise.

6. At the end of the waltz, some records repeat II. This means that the couple waltzes until the music changes, doing then 3 slides to the left and a dip.

LITTLE MAN IN A FIX

Records: Michael Herman 1053, Folk Dancer MH1054.

Formation: Two couples form a set; sets are scattered out on the floor. The two boys lock or hook left elbows, having right arms around the girls' waists. The girl places her left hand on the boy's shoulder and her free hand on the hip.

Measures:	Action:
1–8	Turn in place counterclockwise using 24 little running steps (3 to a measure).
9–16	Without stopping, boys grasp left hands, and each takes the left hand of the partner in his right hand. The object now is to form a "wheel." The boys raise joined hands, forming an arch under which the girls pass right shoulder to right shoulder. After they pass under, the girls turn left, face each other, and join hands over the boys' joined left hands. The wheel continues to turn left to complete a total of 24 running steps.
17–20	Boys release left hands, and girls release joined right hands, separating the couples. The boy of each couple now stands on the left of the girl, with inside hands joined. Each couple does 4 Tyrolean Waltz steps. The Tyrolean Waltz step leads off with the outside foot into a side-by-side waltz step. On the first measure (1-2-3), the joined hands are swung forward. On the second measure, leading off with the inside foot, a second waltz step is done side-by-side with the hands swinging backward. This completes 2 waltz steps, one to a measure. The next 2 waltz steps are similar.
21–24	In regular social dance position, waltz four measures with partner.
25–32	Repeat measures 17–24.

The music starts anew, and each couple seeks another couple to form a set. There should be an extra couple, whose man is the "Little Man in a Fix," as he was not able to link up with another couple to form a set. The extra couple stands by itself until the Tyrolean Waltzes are danced, at which time they join the others on the floor.

SPANISH CIRCLE (Waltz Mixer)

Record: MacGregor 633

Formation: Double circle, couples facing. A set is formed by two couples, one of which is facing counterclockwise and the other clockwise.

The dance involves a new figure in the waltz. The girls turn under the lifted arms. Practice can be done in the regular formation of the dance.

Measures:	Action:
1–2	Partners are side by side with inside hands joined. Couples balance forward and back, swinging arms forward and back. Start with the outside foot.
3–4	With 2 waltz steps, exchange partners. On the first waltz, which is forward, the inside hands are swung forward. Hands are released immediately, and the boy takes the opposite girl's left hand in his right, and she turns under the upraised arms to a new position alongside him. Couples are now facing inside and outside of the circle.
5–8	Repeat action of measures 1–4. Couples have now progressed one-half the distance around the circle. Note that the boy progresses clockwise and the girl counterclockwise.
9–16	Repeat measures 1–8. Couples are back in home position.
17–24	All join right hands, forming a star formation and do 4 waltz steps, turning clockwise. Release right hands, face in opposite direction, forming a star formation with the left hand. Do 4 waltz steps back to position, turning counterclockwise.

Measures:	Action:
25–28	The boys do a side balance and back to place. Repeat. The girls join right hands and balance forward and back. They waltz past each other (right shoulder to right shoulder) to exchange places. This is done by dropping hands and turning around to the *left* and backing into place. Each boy has a new partner.
29–32	Boys join inside hands with a new partner and balance forward and back. During the two waltzes, couples pass through each other to form a new set with the oncoming couple.

Variation:

25–32	In closed dance position, with the boy taking his lead step in the direction he was facing at the start, the two couples waltz around each other and back to place, moving around to the right. Continue around to the right and forward to meet the oncoming couple, forming a new set.

BADGER GAVOTTE

Records: MacGregor 610, Folkraft 1094.

Formation: The dance is by couples. Couples are arranged in a circle in open position, with inside hands joined and facing counterclockwise.
Directions are for the boys. Girls use the opposite foot.

Measures:	Directions:	Action:
1–4	Walk-2-3-4, slide, slide, slide, dip.	Beginning with the left foot, walk forward 4 steps, face and join hands, and take 3 slides and dip. Touch the right toe behind the left foot for the dip.
5–8	Walk-2-3-4, slide, slide, slide, dip.	Change hands, walk in the reverse direction starting with the right foot. Repeat the 4 steps, the 3 slides, and dip to the clockwise direction.
9–12	Two-step.	In closed dance position, do 4 two-steps, moving in line of direction but circling clockwise.
13–14	Pivot, pivot, pivot, pivot.	Boy turns girl clockwise using 4 pivots, beginning with the left foot.
15–16	Turn your girl and bow.	Boy stands in place for 2 counts, turning the girl under his right hand arched with the girl's left. She turns in place and then steps back with the right and curtsies, while the boy bows.

Dance is repeated.

LILI MARLENE

Records: Western Jubilee 725, MacGregor 310.

Formation: Couples in circle formation, facing counterclockwise. Inside hands are joined.
Directions are for the boys. Girls use the opposite foot.

Measures:	Directions:	Action:
1–4	Walk-2-3-4, slide, slide, slide, close.	Starting with the left foot, walk forward 4 steps, turn and face partner, join both hands, take 3 slides in line of direction and close.
5–8	Walk-2-3-4, slide, slide, slide, close.	Repeat measures 1–4, but start with the right foot and travel in the opposite direction.
9–12	Step swing, step swing.	Still with joined hands, step to the left and swing the right foot across the left. Step to the right and swing the left across. Repeat right and left.

Measures:	Directions:	Action:
13–16	1-2-3-turn, 1-2-3-turn	Facing counterclockwise with inside hands joined, take 3 steps in line of direction beginning with the left foot and pivot on the third count with the right foot pointed clockwise on the fourth count. Repeat, beginning with the right foot and turning (pivot) on the right foot. Couples should now be facing line of direction with inside hands joined.
17–20	Two-step.	Take 4 two-steps forward.
21–24	Two-step away.	Drop inside hands; and on 4 two-steps, circle away from partner. Boy makes a larger circle to the girl behind him. Girl circles back to place, meeting the boy from the couple ahead.

BROWN-EYED MARY MIXER

Records: Little Brown Jug. Columbia 52007, Old Timer 8051.

Formation: Couples facing counterclockwise, boys on the inside. Right hands and left hands are joined in crossed-arms position (skaters). Directions are opposite for the girl.

Measures:	Directions:	Action:
1–4	Two-step left and two-step right, walk-2-3-4.	Do a two-step left and a two-step right and take 4 walking steps forward.
5–8	Repeat measures 1–4.	
9–10	Turn your partner with the right.	Boy takes girl's right hand with his right and walks around this girl to face the girl behind him.
11–12	Now your corner with your left.	Turns girl behind him with the left.
13–14	Turn your partner all the way around.	Turns own partner with the right going all the way around.
15–16	And pick up the forward lady.	Boy steps up one place to the girl ahead of him who is his new partner.

VARSOUVIENNE

Records: MacGregor 398, Old Timer 8077; Folkraft 1034, 1165.

Formation: Couples in varsouvienne position. Directions are the same for both partners.

Measures:	Action:
1	Bend left knee and bring left foot in front of right leg on the up-beat. Step forward with the left and close with the right, taking the weight on the right foot.
2	Repeat measure 1.
3–4	Cross left foot over right instep, then step in place with the left foot. Step with the right foot to the right (behind partner), step forward with the left (alongside partner), and point right toe forward. The girl in the meantime does the same steps but almost in place moving slightly to her left. The girl is now on the left side of the boy still in varsouvienne position.
5–8	Repeat measures 1–4 beginning with the crossing of the right foot.
9–10	Cross left, step left, step right, step left, point right. Retaining only the left-hand grip, the boy does the stepping in place while the girl rolls out to the left away from the boy.
11–12	Cross right, step right, step left, step right, point left. Still retaining the left hands,

Measures:	Action:
	the girl turns under the boy's lifted left hand and walks back into the varsouvienne position.
13–16	Repeat measures 9-12.

VARSOUVIENNE MIXER

Record: Same as previous dance.

Formation: Couples are in circle formation all facing counterclockwise in varsouvienne position.

Measures:	Action:
1–12	The first 12 measures are the same as the previous dance.
13–14	The girl rolls to the center with the cross, step, step, step, point. Left hands are still held.
15–16	The girl walks to the boy of the couple behind her, crossing in front of him to varsouvienne position. They both finish with the left foot pointed.

Teaching Suggestion: The girl should look behind her to see who her next partner will be.

TETON MOUNTAIN STOMP (Mixer)

Records: Windsor 7615; Western Jubilee 725.

Formation: Double circle, partners facing with both hands joined. Boys are on the inside of the circle. Directions are described for the boys. The girls use the opposite feet.

Measures:	Directions:	Action:
1–4	Left, right, left, stamp. Right, left, right, stamp.	Step left, close right, step left, stamp right. Repeat, beginning with the right foot.
5–6	Left, stamp, right, stamp.	Step left, stamp right, step right, stamp left.
7–8	Walk — turn.	Both face line of direction, join inside hands and walk 4 steps. On the last step, the boy turns around.
9–10	Walk — turn.	The boy backs 4 steps while the girl moves forward 4 steps. Both are moving counterclockwise, the girl facing and the boy with his back to line of direction. Both turn around on the last step. The girl now has her back to line of direction.
11–12	Walk.	Each takes 4 steps *forward.* The boy walks in line of direction, but the girl is now walking clockwise. Each skips one person and meets the next for a new partner.
13–16	Two-step, two-step, walk.	Both face counterclockwise with inside hands joined. They take 2 two-steps, beginning on the outside foot and then 4 steps in line of direction.

Variation: For measures 13–16.

When the boy meets his new partner, he swings her for 8 counts (twice around).

OH JOHNNY, OH

Records: Folkraft 1037, Old Timer 8041, 8043, Decca 954, MacGregor 652.

Formation: Square dance set of four couples.

Call (all sing):	Action:
1. All join hands and you circle the ring.	1. Circle of eight moving left.
2. Stop where you are and you give her a swing.	2. Swing your partner.

Call (all sing):	Action:
3. And now you swing that girl behind you.	3. Swing the corner lady (on man's left).
4. Now swing your own if you have time and then you'll find an —	4. Swing your partner.
5. Allemande left on your corners all	5. Turn the corner lady with the left hand.
6. And dos-a-dos your own	6. Pass right shoulders and move back to back around partner.
7. And all promenade with the sweet corner maid singing, "Oh Johnny, Oh Johnny, Oh!"	7. Promenade with new (corner) lady.

The dance is repeated three more times until original partners are together again.

Variation: The dance can be done in a circle formation with couples facing counterclockwise, girls on the right. The corner girl is the one from the couple immediately in back.

Teaching Suggestion: In the circle formation, couples should swing around only once.

MY LITTLE GIRL

Record: Folkraft 1036.

Formation: Square dance set of four couples. The caller sings the call.

Call:	Action:
1. First couple promenade the outside around the outside of the ring.	1. The first couple promenades around the outside of the set while the other couples move into the center.
2. Head ladies chain right down the center and they chain right back again.	2. Ladies #1 and #3 chain and chain right back.
3. Head ladies chain the right-hand couple and they chain right back again.	3. Ladies #1 and #3 chain and chain back with the right hand ladies.
4. Head ladies chain the left-hand couple and they chain right back again.	4. Chain with the left hand ladies.
5. Now it's all the way around your left-hand lady — Oh Boy! What a baby!	5. The four boys move around their corner girls, returning to position.
6. See saw your pretty little taw — Prettiest girl I ever saw.	6. Move around behind partners and return to position.
7. Allemande with your left hand — A right to your honey and a right and left grand.	7. Self-explanatory.
8. Deedle — I, Deedle — I, Deedle — I, Do — You meet your gal and promenade.	8. Self-explanatory.
9. And listen while I roar — You swing your honey till she feels funny — She's the gal that you adore.	9. Promenade back to position and all swing.

The dance is repeated three times with the second, third, and fourth couples promenading. For couples #2 and #4, the word "side" for "head" in lines 2, 3, and 4.

HOT TIME

Record: Folkraft 1037, Windsor 7115.

Formation: Square dance set of four couples.

This is a singing call and everyone should sing. Much of the action is self-explanatory.

Call:	Action:
Introduction	
All join hands and circle left the ring.	Circle left.

Call:

Stop where you are and everybody swing.
Promenade that girl all around the ring.
There'll be a hot time in the old town tonight.

Action:

All swing.
All promenade.

The Figure

First couple out and circle four hands 'round.

First couple goes to couple on the right and circle four.

Pick up two and circle six hands 'round.

Take second couple to third and circle.

Pick two more and circle eight hands 'round.

All three couples move to the fourth and circle.

There'll be a hot time in the old town tonight, my baby!

Circle eight.

Allemande left with the lady on the left.

Break and do a left allemande. Pass by partner (right shoulders) to next lady.

Allemande right with the lady on the right,

Allemande right is the opposite of allemande left and is done with the right hand.

Allemande left with the lady on the left

Again pass partner by without touching, to corner lady.

And a grand old right and left around the town.

Self-explanatory.

When you meet your honey, it's dos-a-dos around,

At the end of the grand right and left, partners go back to back.

Take her in your arms and swing her round and round.

All swing.

Promenade home, you promenade the town—

All promenade.

There'll be a hot time in the old town tonight, my baby!

Continue to promenade.

Repeat three more times with the second, third, and fourth couples leading out. Do not repeat the introduction.

Finale

All join hands and circle left the floor.

Circle left.

Swing her 'round and 'round, just like you did before.

All swing.

Because that's all, there isn't any more.

Continue swinging.

There'll be a hot time in the old town tonight.

Additional Square Dances

For additional dances to round out the program, the following are suggested:

Take a Little Peek
Birdie in the Cage — 7 Hands Round
Forward Six and Fall Back Six
Dive for the Oyster
Red River Valley
Star by the Right
Divide that Ring

These and others are available from a number of sources in the form of single records or in albums. In addition, the square dance patterns and steps, previously described in this chapter, are on records with simple "walk-through" instructions. Square dance records may be secured with or without calls.

The following sources, among others, have excellent material in square dance records and albums suitable for the elementary school program.

Educational Record Albums	David McKay Co. 119 West 40th Street New York, N. Y. 10018
Honor Your Partner Records	Educational Activities, Inc. Freeport, N. Y. 11520
Square Dance Records	Teaching Aids Service 31 Union Square W. New York, N. Y. 10003

GAMES USING RHYTHMIC BACKGROUND

A number of interesting games can be played using music as a part of the game. Most of them are simple in principle and are based on the idea of movement changes when the music changes or stops. Some of them are similar to the old, old game of Musical Chairs.

CIRCLE STOOP

Children are in a single circle facing counterclockwise. A march or similar music can be used or the game can be played to the beat of a tom-tom. The children march in good posture until the music is stopped. As soon as the child no longer hears the music or beat of the tom-tom, he stoops and touches both hands to the ground without losing balance. The last child to touch both hands to the ground successfully pays a penalty by going into the mush-pot (center of the circle) or being eliminated. Children should march in good posture and anyone stooping, even partially, before the music is stopped should be penalized. The duration of the music should be varied, and the children should not be able to observe the stopping process if a record player is used.

Variations:

1. Employ different locomotor movements like skipping, hopping, or galloping while using suitable music.

2. Use different positions for stopping instead of stooping. Positions like the push-up, crab, lame dog, balance on one foot, or touch with one hand and one foot add to the interest and fun.

PARTNER STOOP

The game follows the same basic principle of stooping as in Circle Stoop but is done with partners. The group forms a double circle with partners facing counterclockwise, boys on the inside. When the music starts, all march in line of direction. After a short period of marching, a signal (whistle) is given, and the inside circle (boys) turns around and marches the other way — clockwise. Partners are now separated. When the music is stopped, the outer circle (girls) stands still, and the boys *walk* to rejoin their partners. As soon as a boy reaches his partner, they join inside hands and stoop without losing balance. The last couple to stoop goes to the center of the circle and waits out the next round.

Variation: The game can be played with groups of three instead of partners. The game begins with the groups of three marching abreast holding hands and facing counterclockwise. On the signal, the outside players of the threes continue marching in the same direction. The middle players of the threes stop and stand still. The inside players reverse direction and march clockwise. When the music stops, the groups of three attempt to reunite at the spot where the middle player stopped. The last three to join hands and stoop are put into the center for the next round.

FOLLOW ME

The game has its basis in the phrasing of the music. The children are in circle formation facing in with a leader in the center. The leader performs a series of movements of his choice, either locomotor or nonlocomotor, for the duration of one phrase of music (8 beats). The children imitate his movements during the next phrase. The leader takes over for another set of movements, and the children imitate during the next phase following. After a few changes, the leader picks another child to take his place.

Variations:

1. A popular way to play this game is to have the children follow the leader as he performs. This means changing movement as the leader changes and performing as the leader does, with everyone keeping with the rhythm. A change is made as soon as the leader falters or loses his patterns or ideas.

2. The game can be done with partners. One partner performs during one phrase, and the other partner imitates his movements during the next phrase. The teacher can decide which couple is making the most vivid and imaginative movements and is doing the best job of following the partner's movements.

FREEZE

Children are scattered around the room. When the music is started, they move around the room guided by the character of the music. They walk, run, jump, or use other locomotor movements dependent upon the selected music or beat. When the music is stopped, they freeze and do not move. Any child caught moving after the cessation of the rhythm pays a penalty.

A tom-tom or piano provides a fine base for this game as the rhythmic beat can be varied easily and the rhythm can be stopped at any time. In the absence of a tom-tom or drum, two sticks or Indian clubs can be knocked together to provide the beat.

Variations:

1. Specify the level at which the child must freeze.

2. Have the child fall to the ground or go into one of the different positions like the push-up, crab, lame dog, a balance, or some other defined position.

RIGHT ANGLE

A tom-tom can be used to provide the rhythm for this activity. Some of the basic rhythm records also have suitable music. The children change direction at right angles on each heavy beat or change of music. The object of the game is to make the right angle changes on signal and not bump into other children.

ARCHES

The game is similar to *London Bridge.* Arches are placed around the playing area. To form an arch, two players stand facing one another with hands joined. When the music starts, the players move in a circle, passing under the arch. Suddenly, the music stops and the arches come down by dropping the hands. All players caught in an arch immediately pair off together to form other arches, keeping in a general circle formation. If a "caught" player does not have a partner, he should wait in the center of the circle until one is available. The last players caught (or left) form arches for the next game.

The arches should be warned not to bring down their hands and arms too forcefully, so that the children passing under them will not be pummeled. Also, children with glasses need consideration in the process of catching as when the arches close, glasses can be knocked to the floor. Glasses should be removed, or children with glasses can begin as part of the arches.

Variation: Different types of music can be used and the children can move according to the pattern of the music.

WHISTLE MARCH

A record with a brisk march is needed. The children are scattered around the room individually walking in various directions, keeping time to the music. A whistle is blown a number of times, at which signal lines are formed of that precise number, no more and no less. The lines are formed by having the children stand side by side with locked elbows. As soon as a line of the proper number is formed, it begins to march to the music counterclockwise around the room. Any children left over go to the center of the room and remain until the next signal. On the next whistle signal (single blast) the lines break up and all walk individually around the room in various directions as before.

Teaching Hint: It may be well to make a rule that children may not lock elbows with the same children with whom they formed the previous line.

ROPE JUMPING TO MUSIC*

Rope jumping is an excellent complete body activity. It increases coordination, rhythm, and timing. It tones up the circulorespiratory system and increases both speed and endurance. It makes a contribution to weight control and total physical condition. It can contribute to good posture habits. It has good carry-over values.

Some people prefer to refer to the activity as rope skipping. In the material which follows, the terms are used interchangeably.

From an educational standpoint, rope jump-

*The material on rope skipping is used by permission of the Seattle Public Schools, William Haroldson, Director of Physical Education. The Seattle Public School Bulletin on Rope Skipping was based originally on terminology and steps excerpted in part from the pamphlet, *Rope Skipping Fundamentals* by Paul Smith, Physical Education Supervisor, Shoreline Public Schools, Seattle, Wash.

ng has good value in the school program. It allows a maximum amount of student activity within a minimum amount of time and space. The activities are in good progression. The teacher can begin at the student's level and develop from that point. It is inexpensive and easily taught.

It provides a creative activity that has unlimited possibilities for new material. The further the youngsters progress, the more they tend to invent steps and routines of their own. The activity is not seasonal in character.

For the teacher and administrator, it provides excellent program material for PTA meetings and other demonstrations.

Because it is a learned activity, the material is not allocated to grades. Teachers should begin the year with a review of all fundamentals and such other material as the children have mastered. The second grade, however, is probably an appropriate place where the activity should be introduced.

Records for Rope Jumping

Any record with a steady tempo of 120 to 150 beats per minute will suffice for beginning instruction. Some records that have been found to work well are:

1. PR980 Ball Bouncing and Rope Skipping, Album #12 — Durlacher.
2. Marches, Album #1 — Durlacher.
3. Waiting for the Robert E. Lee — 45 RPM, Jack Barbour — Accent Sunny Hills AC102-S.
4. Wheels and Orange Blossom Special — 45 RPM, Billy Vaughn, Dot, 45-161774.
5. Yankee Doodle — El Molino — Shoo Fly, all on Windsor School Series Record—Happy Hour Records — A-7S1, Windsor.
6. Pop Goes the Weasel is another record which is good for rope jumping. The fact that there is a verse and a chorus arrangement means that one type of jumping (slow time) could be done to the verse and another (fast time) could be done to the chorus. Folk Dancer MH1501 and Victor 45-6180 are good records.

The teacher will discover many other records and albums which will work well as the children progress and become more familiar with the various rope skipping activities.

The Rope

To determine the proper length of rope for a particular individual, stand on the center of the rope. The ends, when drawn up each side of the body, should terminate at approximately armpit height. For elementary schools all ropes may be cut in 9' lengths. Any adjusting for smaller children may be done by wrapping the rope around the hands. See page 37 for other rope sizes.

Explanation of Terminology

Most steps can be done in three different rhythms: slow time, fast time, and double time.

1. Rebound

This is simply a hop in place as the rope passes over the head. Better jumpers will only bend the knees slightly without actually leaving the floor. It is used only in slow-time jumping (explained below), and its object is to carry the rhythm between steps.

2. Slow Time

In slow-time rhythm the performer jumps over the rope, rebounds (jumps in place) as the rope passes over the head, then executes the second step, or repeats the original step a second time, on the second jump.

The performer actually jumps over the rope to every other beat of the music in slow-time rhythm. The odd beat occurs as the rope passes over the head. The rhythm is carried by the rebound.

The rope is rotating slowly (passes under the feet on every other beat) and the feet also move slowly since there is a rebound between each jump.

Slow-time rhythm — slow rope, slow feet, with a rebound.

3. Fast Time

In fast-time rhythm we have the opposite of slow time. The rope rotates in time with the music, which means twice the number of rope turns for the same time as in slow time. The rope will be turning fast (120 to 180 turns per minute, depending upon the tune's tempo), and the performer executes a step only when the rope is passing under the feet.

Fast-time rhythm — fast rope, fast feet.

4. Double Time

In double-time rhythm the rope is turned at the same speed as for slow time, but rather than taking the rebound the performer executes another step while the rope is passing over the head. A slow rope with fast feet.

Double time is the most difficult to master. When the feet are speeded up there is a tendency also to speed the rope up (which is wrong).

Double-time rhythm — slow rope, fast feet.

Progression of Rope Jumping

All explanations are given and should usually be learned first in slow-time rhythm. After the students master all the steps in the various rhythms, routines may be devised combining the different steps and rhythms.

If a student has difficulty with a step, have him go through the foot motions without the rope first.

Placing offset marks on the gym floor with a marking pen helps students keep their stations.

Begin with music almost immediately. The music tells the performer when to do the step and also helps him to keep a steady rhythm.

Place the best jumpers together in one line. They tend to help one another keep the proper rhythm.

To use rope skipping as a conditioner for other sports, use the fast-time rhythm and turn the rope at high speed for designated periods of time. One hundred eighty turns of the rope per minute (try the Can-Can) is a very fast time and is excellent for varsity sports type of conditioning.

Watch continually for different steps and tunes that will lend themselves to new routines.

Basic Steps*

Remember, most steps can be done in three different rhythms — slow time, fast time, and double time. After the youngsters have mastered these first six steps in slow time, you may wish to introduce fast and double time. The alternate foot basic step and spread legs, forward and backward, are two steps that seem to work well in introducing double time jumping.

1. Two Foot Basic Step

With feet together, jump over the rope as it passes under the feet and take a preparatory rebound while the rope is over the head.

*A color film, *Rope Skipping — Basic Steps,* featuring the system and steps in the text may be ordered from Martin Moyer Productions, 900 Federal Avenue, Seattle, Washington 98102.

2. Alternate Foot Basic Step

As the rope passes under the feet, the weight is shifted alternately from one foot to the other, raising the unweighted foot in a running position.

3. Swing Step Forward

Same as alternate foot basic step, except that the free leg swings forward. Keep knee loose and let foot swing naturally.

4. Swing Step Sideward

Same as swing step forward except free leg is swung to the side. Knee should be kept stiff.

5. Rocker Step

One leg is always forward in a walking stride position in executing the rocker step. As the rope passes under the feet the weight is shifted from the back foot to the forward foot. The rebound is taken on the forward foot while the rope is above the head. On the next turn of the rope, the weight is shifted from the forward foot to the back foot, repeating the rebound on the back foot.

6. Spread Legs, Forward and Backward

Start in a stride position as in the rocker, with weight equally distributed on both feet. As rope passes under feet, jump into the air and reverse feet position.

7. Cross Legs Sideward

As the rope passes under the feet, spread legs in a straddle position (sideward). Take rebound in this position. As the rope passes under the feet on the next turn, jump into the air and cross feet with right foot forward. Repeat with left foot forward. Continue to alternate forward foot.

8. Toe Touch Forward

As rope passes under feet, swing right foot forward. Alternate, landing on right foot and touching left toe forward.

9. Toe Touch Backward

Similar to the swing step sideward (4) except toe of free foot touches to the back at the end of the swing.

10. Shuffle Step

As rope passes under feet, push off with right foot, side stepping to the left. Land with weight on left foot and touch right toe beside left heel. Repeat in opposite direction.

11. Heel Toe

As rope passes under feet, jump with weight landing on right foot, touching left heel forward. On next turn of the rope, jump, landing on the same foot, and touch left toe beside right heel. Repeat, using opposite foot.

12. Heel Click

Do two or three swing steps sideward in preparation for the heel click. When the right foot swings sideward instead of a hop or rebound when the rope is above the head, raise the left foot to click the heel of the right foot. Repeat on the left side.

13. 3 Step Tap

As rope passes under feet, push off with right foot and land on left. While the rope is turning above the head, brush the sole of the right foot forward, then backward. As the rope passes under the feet for the second turn, push off with the left foot, landing on the right, and repeat.

14. Crossing Arms Forward

When the rope is above the head starting the downward swing, bring the right arm over the left and the left arm under the right, until the left hand is under the right armpit and the right hand is against the upper left arm. Jumping can be continued in this position or the arms can be crossed and uncrossed on alternate turns of the rope.

15. Double Turn of the Rope

Do a few basic steps in preparation for the double turn. As the rope approaches the feet, give an extremely hard flip of the rope from the wrists. Jump from 6" to 8" into the air and allow the rope to pass under the feet twice before landing.

Everything explained above can be done to fast- and double-time rhythms as explained earlier. The steps can also be done to the three rhythms while turning the rope backwards.

Going from Forward to Backward Jumping Without Stopping the Rope

1. As the rope starts downward in forward jumping, rather than allowing it to pass under the feet, the performer swings both arms to the left (or right) and makes a half turn of his body in that direction (turn facing the rope). On the next turn spread the arms and start turning in the opposite direction. This method can be used from forward to backward jumping and vice versa.

2. When the rope is directly above the head, the performer may extend both arms, causing the rope to hesitate momentarily. At the same time as he extends both arms, he makes a half-turn in either direction and continues skipping with the rope turning in an opposite direction from the start.

3. From a crossed-arm position as the rope is going above the performer's head, he may uncross the arms and turn simultaneously. This will start the rope turning and the performer skipping in the opposite direction.

Rope Jumping Routines

It is in this area that the opportunities for creative activity are endless. The teacher can select a basic piece of music with suitable rope jumping rhythm, and the children can devise routines.

The best type of music to use has a definite two-part format, which can be labeled a verse part and a chorus part. The table shows how a number of basic jumping steps can be organized using slow and fast time.

The schottische is excellent for rope jumping to music, most easily accomplished to double-time rope speed. It can serve as an effective way of learning the schottische step.

1st verse part	Two foot basic step	Slow time
Chorus	Two foot basic step	Fast time
2nd verse part	Alternate basic foot step	Slow time
Chorus	Alternate basic foot step	Fast time
3rd verse part	Swing step forward	Slow time
Chorus	Swing step forward	Fast time
4th verse part	Swing step sideward	Slow time
Chorus	Swing step sideward	Fast time

A Bleking record (see page 348) offers interesting variety for jumping. The rhythm is slow-slow: fast-fast-fast (repeated four times). The rope should be turned in keeping with the music. The chorus part allows for considerable variety of response.

Rope jumping to music offers excellent opportunity for creativity and exploratory movement, as well as contributing to the general movement potential of the child. However, rope jumping should also be done without music. The approach without music is covered in the material which follows at the beginning of the next chapter, Individual and Dual Activities.

20

Individual Rope Jumping — Without Music
Long Rope Jumping
Other Activities

Individual and Dual Activities for All Grades

Included in this section are several types of activities which are difficult to allocate to specific grade levels because allocation would in many cases depend upon previous experience. The section includes individual rope jumping without music, long rope activities, *Tetherball, Sidewalk Tennis.* and several miscellaneous activities.

INDIVIDUAL ROPE JUMPING — WITHOUT MUSIC

Rope jumping as a rhythmic activity has been presented just previously. There is some repetition in the material which follows, but the activity is now presented on an individual basis, without music. With or without music, the carry-over values are excellent, and the children should be given an opportunity to practice and learn both ways.

General Suggestions

The rope should be turned with a quick, easy motion of the hands and wrists in contrast to forceful turning by the arms. The body should be erect and relaxed, and the jumping done in a relaxed, easy motion.

The bounce of the body should be made lightly, usually on the toes, with just enough straightening of the knee joints to propel the body into the air. The clearance from the ground should be minimal and easy, enough to allow the rope to go under the feet. The ends of the rope should be held primarily with the thumb and first two fingers.

The teaching should include postural considerations. Performed properly with the body in good alignment, rope jumping can contribute important values to the maintenance of posture. In particular, the head and upper part of the body should maintain proper positioning.

Working with Children in Rope Jumping Without Music

Children should work with various speeds in rope jumping. However, fast-time jumping is more demanding and has better fitness values than the slower routines, slow-time and double-time jumping. The three routines were discussed just previously in the chapter on rhythmics.

To establish rhythm and practice new routines, the rope first can be turned to the side, using slow-time rhythm. Take both ends of the rope in one hand (usually the right) and turn the rope forward but at the side of the body. Work on the rhythm of the turn, gradually adding the bounce of the toes. The rope should slap the floor lightly on each turn. The bounce of the body is coordinated with the turn of the rope so that the feet are off the ground when the rope hits the floor.

After sufficient practice, the rope can be shifted to normal jumping position and the routine practiced in regular position.

Numerous combinations are possible in rope jumping when the following variations and approaches are considered.

1. Changes in the speed of the turn, utilizing slow time, fast time, and double time routines. Also accelerate and decelerate.

2. The use of the various steps and foot patterns described on page 378.

3. Crossed hand positions, forward and backward.

4. Going from forward to backward and return. Carry the rope to the side when making the change.

5. Double turns. The rope passes under the feet twice before the jumper lands. The jump must be higher than normal and the rope speeded up. Some may be able to do triple turns.

6. Progress forward and in other directions jumping, hopping, skipping, and using other steps.

7. Backward jumping. Most steps can be done or modified when the rope is turned backwards.

8. Partners jumping. Partner runs in and both jump as a single person.

9. See how fast one can turn the rope for 15, 30, or 60 seconds. Count the number of successful turns.

10. Try the Circular Rope Skip. See page 233 for description.

LONG ROPE JUMPING

Groups of five make a convenient group for practicing long rope skills. Two of the group are turners and the others jumpers. The children should rotate between turning and jumping. The rope should be 12' to 16' long.

INTRODUCTORY SKILLS

1. Hold the rope 6" from the ground. Children jump over, back and forth. Raise the rope a little each time. Be sure to hold the rope loosely in the hands.

2. The *Ocean Wave* is another stationary jumping activity. The turners make waves in the rope by moving the arms up and down. The children try to time it so as to jump over a low part of the "wave."

3. *Snake in the Grass.* The holders stoop down and wiggle the rope back and forth on the floor. Children try to jump over the rope and not touch it as it moves.

4. Swing the rope in a pendulum fashion. Children jump the rope as it passes under them.

5. Have the child stand in the center between the turners. Carefully turn the rope in a complete arc over the jumper's head. As the rope completes the turn, the jumper jumps over it. He immediately exits in the same direction as the rope is turned.

6. Run through the turning rope without jumping.

7. While the rope is being turned, the jumper runs in and jumps once. He runs out immediately. The rope must be coming toward the jumper (front door).

INTERMEDIATE SKILLS

1. Front Door — When the rope is turned forward toward the jumper, it is called the front door.

2. Back Door — The rope is turned away from the jumper.

3. With the line of children at a 45-degree angle, try the following:

Run in front door, out back door.

Run in front door, jump once, run out.

Run in back door, jump once, run out.

Run in front or back door, increase the number of jumps, run out.

Run in front or back door, jump any number of times, but do a quarter, half, three-quarter, and full turns in the air.

4. Hot Pepper — Turners turn the rope with increased speed with the jumper trying to keep up with the rope.

5. High Water — The rope is turned so that it is gradually higher and higher off the ground.

6. Two, three, or four children jump at a time. After some skill has been reached, children in combination can run in, jump a specified number of times, and run out keeping hands joined all the time.

7. Circling with two, three, or four at a time. Start as a small circle, run in and jump in a circle. Keep the circle moving in one direction. Run out as a circle.

8. Have the rope held at high jumping height. Practice high jumping skills — scissors, western roll, modified western (belly) roll. Jump for form and not for height. Be sure the rope is held loosely. If mats are available, these are a help.

9. Bounce a ball while jumping. Toss a ball back and forth to a partner standing outside the turning rope. Toss a ball back and forth to a partner as you jump.

10. The jumper jumps with an individual rope while jumping under the long rope. Both ropes should be turned the same way. Later the long rope can be turned in the opposite direction.

TWO ROPES

1. Double Dutch — Two ropes are turned alternately; rope near the jumper is turned front door; rope away from jumper is turned back door.

2. Double Irish — Two ropes are turned alternately, the reverse of Double Dutch.

3. Egg Beater — Two large ropes are turned at right angles simultaneously with four turners.

4. Fence Jumping — Two ropes are held motionless about 2' apart, parallel to each other and each about 12" above the ground. Have the players jump or hop in and out of the ropes in various combinations. The children can devise many different methods.

5. Try two rope combinations with the jumper using an individual rope. Jumper must jump fast time with the individual rope.

FORMATION JUMPING

Four to six long ropes with turners can be placed in various patterns with tasks specified for the ropes. Ropes can be turned in the same direction (front door or back door), or the turning directions can be mixed. Suggested formations are the following:

FITNESS ROUTINE WITH ROPES

Four children are in column formation holding the rope on one side of the body with the hand on that side. There are three signals for changes in the maneuver. On the first signal, the four children run in column formation (as in follow the leader) holding the rope on one side (right or left). The leader takes them in various directions. On the second signal, the rope is shifted overhead quickly to the other side, and the running continues. The third signal causes the four to stop and form a jumping group. The two on the outside (front and rear) become the turners, and the two in the center perform as jumpers. On the next signal, the routine is repeated except that the jumpers now take the front and rear positions with the rope so that they will become turners on the next jumping.

RHYMES

As the jumpers become proficient, they can make use of many familiar rhymes which are used for long ropes. For example —

1. Teddy Bear, Teddy Bear, turn around
   Teddy Bear, Teddy Bear, touch the ground
   Teddy Bear, Teddy Bear, show your shoe
   Teddy Bear, Teddy Bear, you better skidoo.
   or
   Teddy Bear, Teddy Bear, say your prayers
   Teddy Bear, Teddy Bear, go upstairs
   Teddy Bear, Teddy Bear, turn out the light
   Teddy Bear, Teddy Bear, say good night.

Spoke

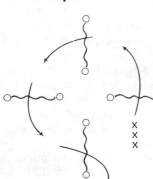

Zigzag

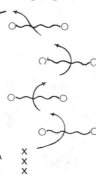

Line

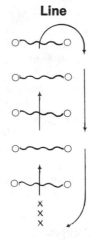

2. For counting a definite number of turns —
   Bulldog, poodle, bow wow wow
   How many doggies have we now?
   One, two, three, etc.

                   or

   Lady, lady, at the gate
   Eating cherries from a plate.
   How many cherries did she eat?
   One, two, three, etc.

The rope is turned a specified number of turns, after which the jumper exits from the jumping.

3. For Red Hot Pepper —
   Mabel, Mabel, Set the table
   Bring the plates if you are able
   Don't forget the salt and
       Red Hot Pepper!

On the words "Red Hot Pepper" the rope is turned as fast as possible until the jumper misses.

OTHER ACTIVITIES

TETHERBALL

Tetherball is a popular game and is a natural where space is limited. The equipment consists of a pole and a tetherball attached to the pole by a length of rope. Pole assemblies outside are generally put in permanently with a concrete installation.

Two to four players can participate, but the game is generally played by two children.

The first server is picked by lot. One player stands on each side of the pole. Server puts ball in play by tossing it in the air and hitting it in the direction he chooses. The opponent must not strike the ball on the first swing around the pole. On the second time around the pole, he hits the ball back in the opposite direction. As the ball is hit back and forth, each player tries to hit the ball so that the rope winds completely around the pole in the direction in which he has been hitting the ball. The game is won by the player who succeeds in doing this or whose opponent forfeits the game by making any of the following fouls:

1. Hitting ball with any part of the body other than the hands or forearms.

2. Catching or holding the ball during play.

3. Touching the pole.

4. Hitting the rope with the forearm or hands.

5. Throwing the ball.

6. Winding the ball around the pole below the 5′ mark.

After the opening game, winner of the previous game serves. Winning four games wins the set.

SIDEWALK TENNIS

Playing Area: On any sidewalk, four cement squares in a row can be used. Areas can be drawn on the gymnasium floor or other surfaced area.

Players: 2.

Supplies: Tennis ball or other rubber ball which bounces well. Paddles can be used.

SIDEWALK TENNIS

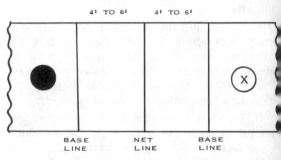

The game is between two players, one in each court. The object is for the server to serve the ball over the net line into the other court. The server must bounce the ball behind the base line and hit the ball underhanded into the opponent's court. The receiver must let the ball bounce and then return it with the open palm. Points are scored only by the server. If he fails to make a good serve or a good return, he loses the serve. Points are scored when the receiver fails to make a good return.

It is a foul and loss of serve if the server steps over the base line when serving. It is out of bounds if the ball at any time lights beyond the base line. Any ball lighting on a line bordering a court is considered to have landed in that court.

The first player scoring eleven points wins provided he is two points ahead. If either player does not have a two point advantage when his score totals eleven, the game continues until one player is two points ahead.

Variation: The game can be played as doubles. Partners alternate on returns.

STEP TARGET

Playing Area: Set of porch steps with a sidewalk in front and a restraining line 8' to 10' back from the steps marked on the sidewalk.

Players: Only one can play at a time, but there can be other children waiting turns.

Supplies: Sponge, rubber, or tennis ball.

A child stands back of the restraining line with the ball. He throws the ball against the steps in such a manner that he can catch it on the fly or first bounce. He continues to throw and score as long as he catches the returns on the fly or on the first bounce. When he misses, the next child takes the turn.

Scoring is done as follows:

100 points	Catching ball hitting the stair *edge*
10 points	Catching any other ball on the fly
5 points	Catching any ball on first bounce

First player to reach the score of 500 is the winner.

HOPSCOTCH

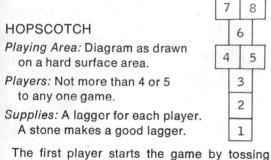

Playing Area: Diagram as drawn on a hard surface area.

Players: Not more than 4 or 5 to any one game.

Supplies: A lagger for each player. A stone makes a good lagger.

The first player starts the game by tossing his lagger into the first (#1) box. He then hops *over* the first box into the second box. He then hops into box #3 on the same foot. The general rule is to hop on one foot in the single boxes and both feet (one in each) into the double boxes. When he reaches boxes #7-8, he turns around completely in place with a jump exchange of the feet into the opposite boxes. He hops back with a jump into boxes #4-5. When he reaches box #2, he reaches over and picks up his lagger, hops into box #1 and out. He now tosses his lagger into box #2 and repeats the routine. He con-

tinues into the other boxes with his lagger until he has covered all eight. Certain rules are basic.

1. The player may not hop into the box where his lagger is tossed. He picks up the lagger on the way back by stopping in the box immediately in front. After he has picked up the lagger, he can hop into the box.

2. A player loses his turn if his lagger fails to be tossed into the correct box or rests on a line.

3. Stepping on a line, missing a box, falling, or stepping into a box where the lagger rests are fouls and stop the turn at that point.

4. After a player has gone completely through the boxes (through the "eighties"), he may write his name in any box, and no one but that player may step in that box. The player whose name is in the most boxes wins.

There are innumerable forms of hopscotch and each area has its favorites. Hopscotch formations take the forms of simple lines of boxes, crosses, squares, snail, and other varied figures. It is truly an international game, played in almost every country.

KICK SHUFFLE

Playing Area: Diagram as illustrated on a hard surface.

Players: 2–4.

Supplies: 3 kicking blocks (2" x 4" x 4").

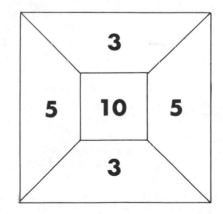

The target can be laid out permanently with paint or temporarily with chalk. The blocks are made from regular 2" x 4" lumber. They should be cut a little short of 4" in order to match the width of the lumber.

The first player stands at a kicking line drawn about 15′ from the front of the target. He stands at the line with the forward foot, and with the other slides or kicks the blocks, one at a time, at the court. He scores the points as listed if the block rests in a particular space. If the block is on a line *between* two spaces, he scores the lower figure. If the block stops on an outside line, it scores nothing.

The game can be played by two or three players who take turns at a target. With larger numbers or using partners, it would be better to lay out a court with two targets, one at each end, similar to shuffle board courts.

Other diagrams could be arranged.

O'LEARY

O'Leary is an individual contest played with each child having a small ball or it can be played with a number of children taking turns when a player makes an error. The child chants the following to the tune of "Ten Little Indians": "1-2-3 O'Leary, 4-5-6 O'Leary, 7-8-9 O'Leary, 10 O'Leary, Postman." He bats the ball with the open hand to the ground (as in basketball dribbling), keeping time to the counting. On the word "O'Leary" he gives a harder bounce and performs a stipulated task. This means that the task is repeated four times during the course of one routine.

On the word "Postman" the child catches the ball. The tasks can vary, but should have the same established order for each game. The following progression is suggested for the game with each task being done on the word "O'Leary."

1. Swing the right leg outward over the ball.

2. Swing the left leg outward over the ball.

3. Swing the right leg inward over the ball.

4. Swing the left leg inward over the ball.

5. Grasp hands together forming a circle with the arms. Ball passes through arms from below.

6. Same as 5, ball passes through from above.

7. Form a circle with the forefingers and thumbs. The ball passes upward through the circle.

8. Same as 7, but ball passes downward through the hands.

9. Alternate 1 and 2 on each "O'Leary."

10. Alternate 3 and 4.

11. Alternate 5 and 6.

12. Alternate 7 and 8.

13. Do 1, 2, 3, and 4 in order.

14. Do 5, 6, 7, and 8 in order.

15. Finish with a complete turn around on each "O'Leary."

21

Story Games and Dramatic Play

Stories
Dramatic Play with Poems
Other Experiences as a Basis for
Dramatic Play

Story games and dramatic play have a part in the program of physical education for the primary grades, particularly the first and second grades. The children love to interpret stories with gross body movements and dramatic movement patterns.

Story plays and creative rhythms provide similar experiences except that in the first case the children interpret the unfolding of the story in movement rather than take cues from the rhythm. However, story plays too can be conducted with the aid of rhythm.

A story play should provide a variety of creative opportunities, be a satisfying experience, allow freedom of response, and encourage all to participate at a level of ability, regardless of the quality of performance. The activity should be conducted informally in such a way that it will allow children to investigate the range of body movement and give way to free response within the limits of the story. Story plays can give opportunity for each child to achieve status and find his place among his classmates.

Story games are so labeled because the children regard it as a game to match the words of the story with movement patterns. However, there should be no competition, nor should there be any elimination of children who do not achieve a certain standard or routine.

A skillful leader can do an effective piece of work in story games with comparatively simple materials. The old, familiar stories offer excellent material for stories. Then, too, many poems can be utilized as a basis for movement experiences. The leader should be able to draw out ideas from child and adult worlds.

Formations should be informal, with the children scattered or in a loose circle. All should be able to see and hear the leader. It is important that a good story basis be set for the stories, so probably the teacher would need to do the relating. However, if children are capable, they can be utilized.

STORIES

Children love to act out and dramatize many of the old, familiar stories. No doubt, both the children and the teacher have favorites. Some may be in the following list:

The Three Bears
The Three Pigs
Black Beauty
Cinderella
Rumpelstiltskin
The Shoemaker and the Elves
The Pied Piper
Mother Goose Stories
Henny Penny
The Sleeping Beauty
The Town Musicians
Peter Pan

The list is only a starting point, but is given

to illustrate the kinds of stories that have possibilities.

Stories may need to be adapted and rewritten, using only the main points of the story to direct the movement.

As an illustration, the story, "Jack the Giant Killer" is given with the story in the left hand column and the suggested actions on right. It should be emphasized that the actions grow out of the discussions with the children with respect to the best way *they feel* the story should be interpreted.

JACK THE GIANT KILLER

Once upon a time a giant, called Caramaran, lived on top of a mountain in a cave. He was a very wicked giant so the king of the country offered a large reward to the person who would kill the giant. So Jack, a country boy, decided he would try his luck.

1. One morning Jack took a shovel and pick and started toward the mountain. He hurried, as he wished to climb the mountain before dark.

1. Picking up pick and shovel and running around in a circle.

2. Jack finally reached the foot of the mountain and started to climb up.

2. Walking around in a circle with high knee movements.

3. He came to a place where he had to use his hands to help him climb.

3. Climbing with motions using hands and arms.

4. Just as it grew dark, Jack reached the top of the mountain. When he was sure the giant was asleep in his bed, he took his pick and began to dig a hole outside the cave entrance.

4. Vigorous digging movement with trunk twisting, standing with feet apart.

5. After he had loosened the dirt with his pick, Jack took the shovel and threw the dirt up on all sides of the hole.

5. Vigorous shoveling movement, first right, then left, throwing the dirt in various directions.

6. Then Jack covered up the hole with some long straws and sticks he picked up.

6. Forward, downward bending, picking up straws, twisting alternately left and right.

7. After this was done, Jack waited until morning, when he called loudly and wakened the giant, who strode angrily out of the cave. As he was very tall, he took big steps.

7. Arms overhead, stretching up tall, walking around in a circle on tiptoes.

8. The giant was so very angry he didn't look where he was going and walked right into the hole Jack had made. Down he fell and was killed.

8. Stooping quickly as if falling.

9. Then Jack filled up the hole with the dirt he had taken out.

9. Forward, downward movements, pushing dirt into hole, moving around in a circle, and doing the same thing over again.

10. Jack went into the cave, got the giant's treasure, and ran home to tell his mother about it.

10. Running around circle in the opposite direction, carrying the treasure.

11. When he got home he was so excited and tired he was all out of breath. Ever after this Jack was called the Giant Killer.

11. Deep breathing.

DRAMATIC PLAY WITH POEMS

The field of poetry can be exploited to its fullest for source material for dramatic play. Mother Goose Rhymes are particularly suited for activity, and there are many others. Poetry has some advantages over stories because of the use of catchy phrasing, rhyming, and the "feeling" that is in much of it.

Poems have an appeal particularly for kindergarten and first grade children. Some examples of poems together with suggested actions follow.

THE GIANT

The Words	Action
1. Once a giant came a-wandering	Children wander around the room in a swaggering, giant type of step and movement.
2. Late at night when the world was still	Children become quiet and put a finger up to the lip to indicate silence.
3. Seeking a stool to sit on	Giant swaggers around looking for a place to sit.
4. He climbed on a little, green hill.	All children perform climbing movements to get to the top of the hill.
5. "Giant, Giant! I am under you,	Children crouch down and pretend that they are stepped upon.
6. Move or this is the last of me."	Children try to push the giant away.
7. But the giant answered, "Thank you,	Children walk around surveying the countryside.
8. I like it here, don't you see."	Giant swaggers around with thumbs under armpits.

GIANTS AND DWARFS

The Words	Action
1. Let us all be little men,	Walk around like dwarfs, with body in a hunched position and arms and legs bent.
2. Dwarfs so gay and tiny, then,	Continue walking. Be gay.
3. Let us stand up straight and tall	Walk on tiptoes, arms stretched upward.
4. We'll be giants, one and all.	Continue walking, occasionally turning around.

PAT-A-CAKE

Each child has a partner, partners facing.

The Words	Action
1. Pat-a-cake, pat-a-cake, baker's man,	Clap own hands, clap hands to partner. Repeat. Shake forefinger at partner three times.
2. Bake me a cake as fast as you can,	Stir the cake fast and vigorously.
3. Pat it, and mold it, and mark it with a "T,"	Follow words with patting, molding, and putting a "T" on top of the cake.
4. And bring it safely home to baby and me.	Walk around in good balance carefully so the cake will not be dropped.

Children find another partner during the walking and the poem is repeated.

HIPPITY HOP

Each child has a partner; inside hands are joined.

The Words	Action
1. Hippity hop to the barber shop,	Partners skip around the room.
2. To buy a stick of candy.	Stop. Face partner. Reach in pocket for money, holding up one finger.
3. One for you and one for me,	Point to partner, point to self.
4. And one for cousin Andy.	Join inside hands and skip around the room.

RIPE APPLES

The Words	Action
1. Lovely ripe apples on branches so high,	With arms stretched upward, children sway back and forth.
2. I cannot reach them, way up in the sky.	Reach up high with one arm at a time.
3. I stretch up so tall, and I jump this way.	On tiptoes, stretch upward. Then jump upward to pick an apple.
4. I know when I've picked them, I'll eat them today.	Pretend to eat, raising hands alternately to mouth.
5. I'll sit down and rest, and eat them some more.	Sit down cross-legged and continue to eat.
6. "Um-m-m. Aren't they good?"	Shake heads, rub tummy while repeating in unison the last line.

WALLABY KANGAROO

The Words	Action
1. Wallaby, wallaby, kangaroo,	Children have hands in front of shoulders to represent paws of the kangaroo. Look around from right to left but do not move.
2. How do you jump the way you do?	
3. I'm sure if I tried for a year and a day,	Jump around like a kangaroo.
4. I'd never be able to jump that way.	Continue to jump like a kangaroo.

THE WIND

The Wind is a more complicated poem and necessitates a little preparation. The children should be seated to hear the poem, discuss its contents, and plan appropriate responses. Different responses should be expected, dependent upon how each child interprets the poem. To stimulate an adequate response, the poem should be read with feeling.

I saw you toss the kites on high
And blow the birds about the sky:
And all around I heard you pass,
Like ladies' skirts across the grass.
    Oh Wind, a-blowing all day long
    Oh Wind, that sings so loud a song.

I saw the different things you did
But always you yourself you hid,
I felt you push, I heard you call,
I could not see yourself at all.
    Oh Wind, a-blowing all day long
    Oh Wind, that sings so loud a song.

Oh you that are so strong and cold,
Oh blower, are you young or old?
Are you a beast of field and tree
Or just a stronger child than me?
    Oh Wind, a-blowing all day long
    Oh Wind, that sings so loud a song.

First Verse:	**Action**
1. Wind blowing very hard.	1. a. Tossing up kites, holding the string, and skipping around the circle while the kites are in flight. b. Pulling the kites in hand over hand.
2. Birds being buffeted around in air.	2. Little running steps with arms stretched sideways and swaying movements side to side in imitation of birds.
Second Verse:	
3. "I saw the different things you did." Blowing poplar trees.	3. With the arms stretched overhead the children imitate tall poplar trees; they then alternate vigorous side bending with forward, downward bending.
4. Blowing a paper sack around.	4. Representation of empty paper sack, crouching on floor, then jumping up as high as possible, moving into the center of the circle.
5. "I heard you call."	5. Long drawn out calls in imitation of the wind.
Third Verse:	
6. The wind is so strong and cold that the children have to stop play and get warm.	6. a. Jumping on toes with feet placed sideways and clapping of hands overhead and on thighs. b. Clapping arms around body.
7. Still the wind blows on.	7. Deep breathing.

It might be necessary to explain in this day and age how skirts used to billow!

OTHER EXPERIENCES AS A BASIS FOR DRAMATIC PLAY

Many everyday experiences from the childhood and adult world can form the basis for much dramatic play. The children can help the teacher plan the story to guide the play. A simple idea like the *Railroad Train* can be a good basis. It could be developed in the following fashion.

RAILROAD TRAIN

Each child is given the name of a part of a freight train. Several trains may be formed. The teacher tells a story in which the various parts of the train are mentioned in the telling. Several children are the engines, and the story usually begins with this portion of the train. After the story unfolds, the children form in line, one behind the other in the order named. After the trains have been assembled and all "cars" are on the train, the story continues by describing a train trip. The route is described in detail, with the train going slowly up and down grades, around curves, stopping at stations, and finishing up with a wreck. It is also possible to assemble the trains by having each of the parts of the train on "side tracks" and the train backing up to hook on the "cars."

Some attention should be given to the story, as the imagination of the teller is very important. Also, children can make suggestions for the train ride.

It is apparent that there is no dearth of material or ideas. Imagination plays a big part in widening the scope of dramatic play.

For another illustration of how an idea can be expanded, let us take the children on an imaginary hike.

THE HIKE

The Words

1. Today we are going on a hike. What are some of the things we need to take?
2. We are going to roll our packs into a nice, neat bundle. Put down your tarp first, next arrange your blankets, and put the rest of your things in. Now let's roll the pack and tie it up.
3. Off we go.

4. Time to rest.
5. Off again.
6. Make blazes so we can find our way back. Make trail markers.
7. Here we are. Pick out a good spot for the tent and put it up.
8. We need lots of wood for the campfire. Will you see what you can find?
9. Build the fire and broil the steaks.
10. Bugle call for "turning in."

Action

1. Children will suggest various articles which should be included.
2. Children lay out packs, roll, and tie.

3. Children march two by two around the room carrying packs.
4. All remove packs and sit down.
5. Resume marching.
6. Children make blazes in various manners. Arrange stones for markers.
7. Cut stakes and poles. Drive stakes and put up tents. Arrange beds.
8. Children go out and drag in logs and wood. Some cutting may be needed.
9. As directed.
10. Children go to one side, brush their teeth, wash up, and then turn in. They crawl in tent, cover themselves carefully, and go to sleep.

It should be noted that integration with other subject fields is possible. Conservation practices can be stressed. Safety in the woods can be emphasized.

Some suggestions of how other ideas can be used follow.

Playing

In the leaves
In the snow, making a snowman, sledding
Riding a bicycle, wagon, tricycle, kiddie car, or other vehicle
On the playground
Flying a kite

Going to

A circus
A zoo
A toy shop
The farm

Doing Common Things Like

Washing and hanging up clothes
Washing dishes
Trimming a Christmas tree
Pitching hay
Sowing grain
Making a garden
Shaking and beating rugs
Cutting grain

Pretending to Be

An animal — bear, deer, squirrel, giraffe, elephant, pony, etc.
An imaginary creature — giant, witch, dwarf, troll, etc.
An official or worker — conductor, policeman, engineer, etc.

Having Fun at

Paddling a canoe, rowing a boat
Playing baseball, football, track, basketball, etc.
Skiing, ice skating, roller skating, water skiing.
Swimming, using different strokes

Celebrating

Holidays — Christmas, Halloween, Thanksgiving, Fourth of July
Seasons — Fall, winter, spring, summer

Industries, Professions like

Lumbering
Fishing
Construction
Road Building

22

Classroom and Limited Area Activities

One of the most difficult problems confronting physical education teachers is how to conduct a program when adverse weather forces the activity inside and the gymnasium facilities are not adequate to handle the load. When no appropriate gymnasium facility is available, it may be necessary to use classroom and other limited spaces, such as the hall or cafeteria. The indoor situation can be broken down into four categories:

The Relaxation Period

This is designed to provide a break in the day's routine, and in a sense it is like recess. It is a kind of safety valve which allows the children to let off steam, but it can also be used to enrich their experiences while it offers them relaxation. Since it is in addition to regular physical education experiences, the relaxation period should provide different activities from those of the regular program. This period is usually short, not more than ten minutes or so.

The Occasional Classroom
Physical Education Lesson

This is an emergency situation, when the physical education lesson must be taught in the classroom or related facility because the usual facility is not available, and for this reason it is the most difficult type to plan. The program emphasis has to be shifted, as the usual rugged, active program of the gymna-sium or playground is not suitable for the classroom conditions.

The Split Gymnasium-Classroom Program

Where facilities are available but not adequate for a daily program the classes held in regular physical education facilities have to be supplemented by classroom physical education. For example, in a school where twenty classrooms share one gymnasium a particular classroom is scheduled only twice a week for regular physical education. This can be supplemented by lessons in the classroom to meet the weekly time requirement.

Planning must include both aspects, the regular and the classroom programs. The more rugged activities and instructional emphasis on skills are centered in the regular physical education program. To the classroom are allocated those activity areas which are suitable for limited spaces.

Indoor Classroom Physical Education

In this situation, no suitable gymnasium facilities are present at all, and so all physical education which cannot be conducted on the playground must be carried on in the classroom, or no program is possible. Planning for this situation must include two programs, one for the playground and one for the classroom. The classroom program should be in sequential lessons, which means that the lesson order is established and followed consecutively as the indoor program days materialize.

GUIDES FOR CONDUCTING CLASSROOM AND LIMITED SPACE ACTIVITIES

The following considerations are presented which have relevance in degree to one or more of the situations previously described for conducting activities in a classroom situation.

The Noise Problem

The noise problem must be solved. Several suggestions are offered. The children have to recognize that the activity is a privilege and their cooperation is essential. They must keep their exuberance under control to the point that the class activity does not interfere with other classes. Another solution would be for the same section of the school to have physical education periods at the same time. If all classes in the same part of the building are playing at the same time, there is little disturbance with each other. This would also be true if one class were directly above the other. The noise, particularly from shuffling and moving feet, would seriously interfere with a recitation, lecture, or study period.

Equipment and Supplies

If there is to be an appreciable amount of classroom physical education, a separate set of equipment and supplies from that used in the regular physical education program is needed. A supply cart which contains most of the normal items needed is an efficient answer. It can be rolled directly into the classroom and saves sending monitors to a central point to carry in needed items.

Equipment carts containing balance beams (portable), light folding mats, balance boards, individual mats, and other equipment are also time-savers. Tumbling mats should be the light, folded variety, which can be handled by the children with ease.

Each classroom should also have a special collection of games, targets, manipulative objects, and other special items for indoor play. Many of the items can be constructed by the children.

Only supplies that will not damage should be used. Small sacks stuffed with excelsior, fleece balls, beanbags, yarn balls, sewn rolled-up sox, balloons, and articles of this nature can be used with little danger to the facilities.

Preparing the Facilities

If the classroom desks and chairs are moveable, flexibility is present to provide space for a variety of activities. Equipment can be pushed together to permit circle activities and rhythms. Chairs and desks can be pushed to one side to form an open space. If mats, balance beams, or benches are to be used, several wider aisles can be made by pushing adjacent rows together.

Instruction should be given in how to prepare desks for moving. All personal items must be put away; desk tops should be cleared, and books and other things stacked underneath so they will not fall out when the desks are moved. Items and projections which might cause tripping or damage should be placed in safe positions.

Windows should be opened and the temperature lowered, which may involve an adjustment of the thermostat.

If the desks and chairs are fixed, then space is more limited. The aisles as established should be used. As much space as possible should be cleared.

Halls have a low priority for use. The noise permeates the entire building, and the activity interferes with the passage of students.

Program Suggestions

Too many teachers look for special classroom activities when the necessity to use the room for physical education occurs. Some end up with a program of trivial games, which only provide entertainment and relief from tension. Granted, they do play a part in the program, but their importance is minor compared to that of other activities.

The activities of the regular physical education program should be carefully examined to determine which can be utilized and which can be modified for the classroom program. Stunts and tumbling, certain pieces of apparatus (moveable), selected manipulative equipment, rhythmic activities, and movement experiences should be considered.

Six tumbling mats (4' x 7') can be positioned in the available space. Four balance beams fit easily in the regular aisles or can be placed in the spaces available. Benches can be used in the classroom, but present a problem in getting them in and out of the area.

Target activities with beanbags, yarn balls,

and regular rubber playground balls can be used. Targets can be placed at the end of the rows. Balls can be rolled or bounced. Ring toss games also contribute to skills.

Rhythmic activities are excellent for classroom work. The formations depend upon the size of the room and whether or not the desks are moveable. Nonlocomotor creative rhythms and ball bouncing rhythms are valuable.

Relays, particularly the modified (number calling) type, have a place in classroom activities. Many can be modified for the classroom environment. Regular rows can be used with the last child performing first with the leader positioned at the head of the row. Fast walking should be substituted for running.

Movement experiences are also an important inclusion. Traffic patterns are important for locomotor movements. Story plays and poems also have a place in the picture. These should require only limited locomotor movement.

Fitness activities can be adapted to classroom work. Many exercises are quite appropriate for this. Isometric exercises without equipment and with wands are readily done in the classroom. Partner isometrics consume little space. Jumping and hopping in place cause few spatial problems.

Many of the regular physical education games can be adapted for the space available. In addition, other activities, identified as classroom type games, should be included. These vary from reasonably active games to quiet games.

This source questions a heavy emphasis and reliance on social recreation and intellectual games. Movement is the key to physical education, and the games should induce movement and/or provide an opportunity to practice skills.

Other Considerations

Children should accept responsibility to a considerable degree for their own conduct. They should realize and accept the limitations of classroom physical education.

Small group play has a place in classroom activity. A number of groups scattered around the room may be involved in different activities.

Rules, strategies, and techniques of sports activities can sometimes be covered in indoor sessions. Good visual aids are also invaluable.

As many children as possible should engage in activity at one time, since activity is the key to physical education. Some system of rotation should be established to ensure that all children have a proportionate share of the activity time.

Watch for overheating. Have the children remove excess clothing. Allow them to wear gym shoes, depending on the activity.

Stress safety. Caution players about colliding with chairs and desks. If the aisles are used for activity, tell the children to keep their feet well under their desks to avoid tripping players.

SUGGESTED CLASSROOM ACTIVITIES

ADD AND SUBTRACT

Playing Area: Classroom.

Players: 2–4.

Supplies: 2 rubber heels or blocks of wood for each player. One is marked with a plus sign and one with a minus sign. Different colored beanbags could be used.

Lay out a nine-square diagram with each square 12″ wide. The squares are numbered 1 through 9. Each player tosses two rubber heels (or beanbags) toward the target on the floor, one at a time. He adds the score made by the plus throw and subtracts the score of the minus throw. Scores are determined where the heel rests on the target. If the heel rests on a line between two squares, the higher value is taken. Any throws falling completely outside the target area are scored minus 5.

The game adapts itself well to the classroom, as a target can be drawn at the front of each aisle.

AROUND THE ROW

Formation: Row in a classroom.

Players: Whatever number there is in a row.

Supplies: None.

The game is played by rows with an extra player for each row. The children form a row plus the extra player on the command "March" and walk around the row. At a signal they stop marching and attempt to get a seat. One player is left out. The game continues to the next row using the player left out as the extra.

BALLOON VOLLEYBALL

Formation: A rope is stretched across the middle of the classroom.

Players: Entire class.

Supplies: 2 balloons. Extras should be availabe as there is breakage.

This is an informal game with the children trying to bat the ball back and forth across the rope. Two balloons should be used at once to provide good action. Several variations are possible.

1. All children standing. Rope should be stretched just over their reach.

2. All children sitting on the floor. Rope about 3′ from the floor.

3. Children in seats that cannot be moved. Rope should be about 5′ high.

In each case, a system of rotation should be set up. Scoring is done when a side fails to control a balloon and allows it to touch the floor or a wall. The balloon can be batted as often as possible.

Variation: If a small marble or button is put *inside* the balloon, the balloon will take an erratic path, adding to the interest.

BASKETBALL BOUNCE

Formation: Individual or by team formation.

Players: 2 to 6 for each basket.

Supplies: Basketball, volleyball, or other rubber ball. Wastepaper basket.

Each player on his turn stands behind a line which is 5′ to 10′ from a wastepaper basket. Five chances are allowed to bounce the ball on the floor in such a fashion that it goes in the basket. Score 5 points for each successful "basket."

BEANBAG PITCH

Playing Area: Classroom.

Players: 2 to 6 for each target.

Supplies: Beanbags and a small box for target for each team.

A target box is placed at the head of each row. A pitch line is drawn 10′ to 15′ back of the target. Each player takes a specified number of pitches at the box. Scores are taken for each player, and the team with the highest score wins.

BICYCLE RACE

Playing Area: Classroom.

Players: One-half the class.

Supplies: The desks are needed.

Alternate rows perform at a time. The children stand in the aisle between two rows of desks. Each child places one hand on his own desk and one on the desk next to him. Upon the signal, "Go," each child imitates riding a bicycle with his legs, while supported by his hands. The child who rides the longest without touching the floor with his feet is the winner for his row. Winners can compete later for the champion bicycle rider of the room.

BOILER BURST

Playing Area: Classroom, playground.

Players: Entire class.

Supplies: None.

The seats are arranged so that there will be one less seat than players. The extra player stands at the front of the class and begins a story. At a dramatic moment, he says, "And the boiler burst!" The children exchange seats, and the narrator tries to secure a seat. If he is successful, another child replaces him. The new narrator may develop his own story or continue that begun by his predecessor.

The game can be adapted to an outdoor situation by having markers for each child. To make the game more vigorous, the children could be required to run to a turning point and back. The child who does not secure a marker is the new story teller.

BOWLING

Formation: File by rows.

Players: 2–6.

Supplies: Bowling pin or pins. Balls for rolling.

Many bowling games are possible in the classroom, using the aisles as the "alley." Various kinds of balls can be used for rolling. The target can be a single pin or group of pins.

Competition can be between individuals in a row or between rows.

CAT AND MICE (Classroom Game)

Playing Area: Classroom, playground.

Players: 5–20.

Supplies: None.

This is an excellent activity in the classroom. One player is designated as the "Cat," sits at the front desk (teacher's), and puts his head down on his hands on the desk so he cannot see. The remainder of the children are the "Mice." One Mouse from each row comes to the front, stealthily approaches the desk, and scratches on the desk. When he is ready, the Cat gets up from his chair and chases the Mice back to their seats. Any child caught joins the Cat at the desk and helps catch the others. The game is over when each of the children has had a chance to approach the desk.

CHAIR QUOITS
Formation: File.
Players: 2–6.
Supplies: Chair for each group; 5 deck tennis rungs or rope rings.

A line is established about 10' from a chair turned upside down so that the legs are pointed toward the thrower. Each throws the 5 rings for the following scores.

Ringer on back legs . . . . 10 points
Ringer on front legs . . . . 5 points

Make a score sheet and keep score for several rounds.

Variation: Fruit jar rings can be used with the chair or with other targets.

CHANGE SEATS
Playing Area: Classroom.
Players: Entire class.
Supplies: None.

All seats should be occupied, removed, or books put on them to indicate that they are not to be used. The teacher gives the commands "Change left, Change right, Change front," or "Change back." One or more children are "It" and do not have seats.

At each command, the children move *one seat* in the direction of the call. The children who are "It" try to move into any seat they can. When the command "Change front," is given, the child in the front seat must turn and move to the rear seat of his row. Similarly, those on the outside rows on "Change left," or "Change right," must move around to the other side of the room to get their proper seats.

It needs to be emphasized that on command each child is to move to the designated seat in keeping with the command. If he is in error, one of the players who is "It" takes his seat.

If the game seems to become too boisterous, the children should be made to walk.

DO THIS, DO THAT
Playing Area: Playground, gymnasium, classroom.
Players: Entire class.
Supplies: None.

One child is the leader and performs various movements, which are accompanied by either "Do this," or "Do that." All players must execute the movements which are accompanied by "Do this." If the directions are "Do that," no one is to move. Those who move at the wrong time are eliminated and sit down in place.

Play until a portion is eliminated and re-form the game with another leader, selected from the children not caught.

FLOOR PING PONG
Formation: Regular table tennis court marked off on the floor.
Players: 2 to 4.
Supplies: Table tennis ball; a paddle for each player.

Play as in regular table tennis. Games should be short (10 points), so many children can be accommodated. A makeshift net can be set up with blocks and a wand.

GERONIMO
Formation: Children seated in regular classroom arrangement.
Players: Entire class.
Supplies: None.

One child is the leader and walks among the children seated in the classroom. He suddenly points to a child and says, "Geronimo." This child must immediately put both hands to his ears. The child directly behind him must put both hands on top of his head. The children on either side must cover the ear next to "Geronimo" with the opposite hand. Play with duds as penalties. Three duds is out.

The game can be made harder with more intricate movement tasks. Change the movement of the child on either side to holding the near ear with the opposite hand and holding the nose with the other hand.

HUNTER, GUN, RABBIT

Playing Area: Classroom.
Players: Entire class.
Supplies: None.

The children are divided into two teams, which line up facing each other. They can be sitting or standing. Each team has a captain.

Each team privately decides on one of the following three imitations:

Hunter — bring hands up to the eyes and pretend to be looking through binoculars.

Gun — bring hands and arms up to a shooting position and pretend to shoot.

Rabbit — put hands in back of head with fingers pointed up. Move hands back and forth like moving rabbit ears.

A signal "Go" is given, and each team pantomimes its choice. To score, the following priorities have been set up.

1. If one side is the hunter and the other the gun, the hunter wins as the hunter shoots the gun.

2. If one team selects the gun and the other imitates a rabbit, the gun wins as the gun overcomes the rabbit.

3. If one side is the rabbit and the other the hunter, the rabbit wins as it can run away from the hunter.

4. If both teams have the same selection, no point is scored.

The first team scoring ten points wins.

IMITATION

Formation: Children scattered around the room. The leader is in front.
Players: Entire class.
Supplies: Record player, records.

The game is based on the music phrase length of 8 counts. The leader performs for 8 counts with any kind of movement he wishes. For the next 8 counts, the children imitate his movements in the same sequence. The leader sets another round of movements and the children imitate.

After a period of imitation, the leader selects another child to be in front as leader.

LOST CHILDREN

Playing Area: Classroom.
Players: Entire class.
Supplies: None.

One child is chosen to be the policeman (or policewoman) and leaves the room. The other children walk around the room. The teacher or leader calls the policeman in and says, "The children are lost. Will you please take them home safely?"

The policeman then takes each child to his seat. The players stay where they are until the policeman seats them. Success for the policeman is determined by the number of children he can seat correctly. He is not permitted to look in the desks or in books for clues to correct seating.

OVERHEAD RELAY

Playing Area: Classroom.
Players: Each row in a classroom forms a team.
Supplies: Beanbag, eraser, or similar object for each team.

The first person in each row has the object to be passed on his desk in front of him. At the signal to pass, he claps his hands, picks up the object, and passes it overhead to the child behind him. This child places the object on the desk, claps his hands, and passes overhead. When the last child in the row receives the object, he runs forward to the head of the row, using the aisle to his right. *After* he has passed by, each child, using the *same* aisle, moves back one seat. The child who has come to the front now sits down in the first seat, places the object on the desk, claps his hands, and passes overhead.

This continues until the children are back in their original seats and the object is on the front desk. The first row done wins.

PUT HANDS

Formation: Students are standing or seated. They can be scattered around the room.
Players: Entire class.
Supplies: None.

One child is the leader and stands in front

of the class. He gives certain directions verbally and tries to confuse the class by doing something else. He can say, "Put your hands on top of your head." He might put his own hands on top of his shoulders. Those who are in error have a point scored against them. Directions he can give, to which he should make other movements, are:

"Put your hands on—shoulders, toes, knees, head, chest, etc."

"Reach out to the — side, front, back, high."

"Put your right hand (or left) on your shoulder, behind your back, etc."

After a short time, the leader should be changed.

SIMON SAYS

Playing Area: Classroom.

Players: Entire class.

Supplies: None.

One player is selected to be "Simon" and stands in front of the class. He gives a variety of commands like, "Stand up," "Clap your hands," "Turn around," and others. He may or may not precede a command by the words, "Simon says." No one is to move unless the command is preceded by these words. Those who move at the wrong time are eliminated and must sit out the game.

The leader gives commands rapidly, changing to different movements. He tries to confuse the class by doing all movements himself.

Variation: *Birds Fly.* In this game, the children hold their hands and arms out as if to fly. The leader calls out commands like "Dogs fly," "Birds fly," and "Horses fly." Each time he makes a flying motion as he calls out. The children should move their arms only when the creature is one that can fly. Otherwise, they are eliminated.

SNAP

Formation: Children seated in a circle.

Players: 10–15.

Supplies: None.

This is a rhythm game involving a three-count rhythm. The children must practice the rhythm well before the game can be successful. The action is as follows:

Count 1	Slap knees
Count 2	Clap hands
Count 3	Snap fingers

Each child in the circle has a number. The leader calls a number on the third count (snap fingers). The player whose number was called then calls another when he snaps his fingers. The object of the game is to keep the precise rhythm and keep the numbers called back and forth across the circle.

Errors:

Breaking the rhythm.

Not calling another number after yours has been called.

Calling when your number has not been called.

Calling a number of a player who has been eliminated.

Players are eliminated after they have made three errors. The number of an eliminated player is dead and cannot be called.

TEN, TEN, DOUBLE TEN

Playing Area: Classroom.

Players: Entire class.

Supplies: Small object.

All the children except one leave the classroom. The child left in the room places the object in some place visible but not too easily found. The children come back into the room. As soon as a child sees the object, he continues searching for another moment so as not to give away the position. He calls out, "Ten, ten, double ten, forty-five, fifteen, buckskin six" and sits down in his seat. The child who found the object first gets to place it for the next game. The child who was last finding it, or any who did not, must remain in their seats for the next turn.

WHERE, OH WHERE

Playing Area: Classroom.

Players: Entire class.

Supplies: Spool or other small object which can be hidden in a closed hand.

The children are seated in regular seats or can be in a circle formation seated on the floor. One child is chosen to be "It" and turns his back to the group while hiding his eyes.

The object is passed among the children from hand to hand until a signal is given. "It" turns around and attempts to guess who has the object. He gets three guesses. All children, including the one who has the object, do various movements and stunts to confuse the guesser. The object must be held in the hand, however. If the guess is correct, the child with the object becomes the new guesser. If not, "It" tries again. If a child misses on three turns in a row, he should choose another child to be "It."

If the number is large, two children can be "It," thus doubling the chances of guessing as each should be allowed three guesses.

WHO'S LEADING

Formation: Children are in a circle formation either sitting in chairs or on the floor. They can be standing, but this gets fatiguing.

Players: Entire class.

Supplies: None.

One child is "It." He steps away from the circle and covers his eyes. The teacher points to one child who is the "Leader." The Leader starts any motion he chooses with his hands, feet, body, etc. All children follow the movements as he does them. The child who is "It" watches the group as they change from one motion to another to try to determine who is leading. Players should cover up for the leader, who also tries to confuse "It" by looking at other players.

"It" gets three guesses. If not successful, he chooses another child to be "It." If he guesses correctly, he gets another turn (limit of 3 turns).

ZOO

Playing Area: Classroom.

Players: Entire class.

Supplies: None.

Seven children are chosen to stand in front of the class and one of them is selected as the leader. The leader directs each of the other six children to choose his favorite animal, and then places them in line, saying the name of the animal as he does so.

On signal 1 the six children, performing in the order in which they were just announced by the leader, imitate the animal they have chosen. Ten to fifteen seconds should be allowed for this.

On signal 2 the rest of the children stand, wave their arms, jump or hop in place, turning round if they wish, and then sit down, close their eyes, cover them with their hands, and put their heads down on the desks.

The leader now arranges the six "animals" in a different order. When this has been done the seated children return to sitting position. Another signal is given, and the animals perform once again for a short period.

Once this has been completed, any seated child can volunteer to place the six children in their original positions, naming the animal in each case. If this child succeeds in placing the animals in their original stand position and calling them by their chosen name he may become an animal in the zoo and choose a name for himself. He then takes his place among the animals, and the game continues until twelve or some other designated number are in the zoo.

Other categories such as flowers, Mother Goose, play characters, and so on can be used.

OTHER GAMES

The teacher should examine the sections on games, both primary and intermediate, for activities of possible use.

Integration
with
Other Subjects

Art
Geography
Health and Safety
History
Language Arts
Music
Number Concepts — Mathematics
Projects

Many physical education experiences and learning situations provide opportunity for the use of and combination with other subject areas for the purpose of broadening the learning environment. Conversely, other subject areas can be of use in broadening and enriching the physical education program.

Even in the unit-of-work study program, physical education should be considered for its contributions. Take the example of the class which is studying the Oregon Trail as its unit of work. Combining with the geographical, historical, home economics, health, music, and social study approaches, the unit can also study the recreational life of the pioneers. Games and dances used by the Trail youngsters as well as Indian games and dances can be a part of the study.

The opportunities for integrating physical education activities with other subject media are numerous and limited only by the ingenuity of the teacher and the interests of the children. Some suggestions about the ways in which physical education can relate to and complement other subject areas are presented. These introduce the topic and provide some examples. Many other integrations can be devised.

ART

Children like to make things for their own programs. Posters, decorations, and costumes bring together art and physical education areas. Others are:

1. Art work for games — toss games, clown faces, etc.

2. Bulletin boards and displays — offer numerous possibilities.

3. Drawing action figures related to different activities.

4. Making costumes for demonstrations.

5. Making charts of field or game areas with player positions.

6. Making programs for demonstrations.

GEOGRAPHY

Since the origins of physical education materials are diverse and scattered, geographical associations provide the classroom teacher with another outlet for learning experiences. Is it possible to find clues for the play and sports habits of people in their location, terrain, and other geographical factors? Some areas of study are:

1. Climate in different areas — how this affects the play habits of the people.

2. Games of different countries — how others play.

3. Folk Dances — origins, characteristics of the country, and of the people.

4. Students from other countries explaining their play habits and games.

HEALTH AND SAFETY

It is difficult to separate health and safety from physical education. Physical education should be carried on in a healthful and safe atmosphere. Many opportunities for incidental teaching of health concepts arise. Safety considerations for each activity are important in the planning. Other examples are:

1. Fitness concepts — knowledge of basic understandings, the development of fitness, and its relationship to the health of the individual.

2. Exercise and health — the part exercise plays in our health.

3. Safety campaigns — playground and gymnasium safety.

4. Recreation and health — the importance of recreation in our living.

5. Learning the why and wherefore of physical examinations.

6. Studying the mechanics of posture.

7. Learning the part nutrition, rest, and body care can play in daily living.

8. Checking and inspecting equipment and facilities for safety standards.

HISTORY

Physical education is rich in historical background. Practically all activities have a historical aspect with regard to origin and background. Many of today's activities have a traditional basis. The historical aspects of physical education offer many possibilities for historical study and should be developed. Appreciations and favorable attitudes can be furthered if children understand the background of an activity. Some suggestions for incorporating history are:

1. The origins of activities — events like the discus throw, shot-put, and the pole vault are performed now only because of the tradition behind them. The origins of such games as baseball, basketball, and American football are equally interesting.

2. Dances — ethnic background, historical period emphasis, meanings.

3. Fitness of other peoples — the ancient Greek, Persian, and Roman civilizations. Modern emphasis on fitness — the U.S.S.R. and other countries.

4. The Ancient and Modern Olympics — the ancient games and how the modern games came into being.

5. Knighthood and the tournaments.

LANGUAGE ARTS

Physical education materials make useful subjects for written and oral expression. The world of sports and games provides many examples of outstanding individuals who can serve as topics for presentations. Additional suggestions follow.

1. Reading — children can read game descriptions, rules, and related materials.

2. Writing — biographies, summaries of game programs.

3. Oral expression — pupil demonstrations, explanations, speaking at evaluation sessions.

4. Spelling — new words in the coming physical education lesson, difficult sports terms.

5. Creative expression — working out story plays for the story periods.

6. Word origins — study of physical education terminology. Terms like gymnasium, calisthenics, and exercise have special origins.

7. Explanation of games or directions for an activity.

8. Announcing at demonstrations.

9. Writing sports stories.

MUSIC

Rhythm is an integral part of physical education, and much of the program features both music and rhythm. Musical training should not be isolated from physical education. The two areas overlap and should blend in the children's experiences. Examples of combining musical and physical education are:

1. Understanding rhythm — learning the characteristics of the music and rhythm while physical education provides the interpretation through movement.

2. Learning singing games — the words and music can be taught by the music teacher and the movement patterns taught later in the physical education class.

3. Learning about music — learning the

names of different musical selections, becoming familiar with the heritage of music.

4. Working out rope jumping routines to a selected piece of music.

NUMBER CONCEPTS — MATHEMATICS

Concepts of numbers can be strengthened. Practical application of the processes of addition, subtraction, division, multiplication, percentage computation, and measurement can be demonstrated through selected physical education procedures. Ways in which number concepts can be related to physical education are:

1. Measuring performance—distance, time, height.

2. Working out averages — from tests and other measured performances.

3. Working with percentages — batting, team standings, other comparisons.

4. Geometric principles — layout of fields and areas.

5. The metric system — comparison of European records (metric system) and American performances. Measurements taken with metric system.

6. Number perception — in games where numbers are called for signals, different combinations could be used. For example, instead of calling out "8," the teacher could say, "36 divided by 3 minus 4."

PROJECTS

Class projects in physical education or related areas form excellent educational opportunities. The teacher and the children should plan together. Many ideas can be found for these projects. Playdays form an excellent area. A playday could be organized with one or more classes in the same school, with a class in another school, or just among the children of the class itself. Demonstrations and exhibitions for parents are fruitful projects. A convocation program or demonstration in the gymnasium before other children merits consideration.

Other projects could be a study of games of other lands, the Olympic Games, a sport, or other physical education activity. Another suggestion is to have a rhythmic party, inviting another class.

The program can be planned, invitations written, committees formed, and all the necessary details arranged.

The enterprising teacher will think of many other ideas which can be used as projects for the children. The project could be on a yearly basis or could be one for each season.

Basketball Activities

An activity as popular as basketball needs little motivation. The fundamentals of the game are to be stressed in physical education classes with emphasis on lead-up activities. Additional opportunity for playing should be provided in a broad intramural program.

Basketball in the elementary schools should not be regarded as a proving ground for future high school stars. It should be an instructional program with the basic purpose the overall development of *all* children. Ball handling skills should be developed slowly and should be an outgrowth of the instruction in basic skills on the primary level. In the primary grades, the children learn the elements of catching, bouncing, passing, and dribbling many kinds of balls. Later, in the intermediate grades, shooting, offensive and defensive play, and rules are added to this base. The suggested program begins in the third grade, and the program for this grade is included in the plan of progression which follows.

EMPHASIS—DIFFERENT GRADE LEVELS

Third Grade

Little actual basketball playing is done in the third grade. Concentration should be on the simple basic skills of passing, catching, shooting, and dribbling. The lead-up game, *End Ball*, permits the youngsters to use their basic skills in a game where the children are more or less stationary.

Fourth Grade

The fourth grade adds to the basic skills ac-

quired in the third grade. The improvement of the skills and the addition of the lay-up shot, more dribbling skills, and different passes are emphasized in this grade. *Captain Ball* adds the elements of simple defense, jump balls, and critical passing. Basic rules covering traveling and dribbling violations should be taught.

Fifth Grade

In the fifth grade, different kinds of basketball games are introduced. Shooting games, such as *Around the Key* and *Twenty-One,* are popular. *Sideline Basketball* and *Captain Basketball* provide new experiences for the children. Continued practice on all the basic skills previously introduced is necessary for good progression. More basketball skills are added to the already growing group. Selected rules necessary to play the simple version of basketball should be covered.

Sixth Grade

The sixth grade should continue practice on all skills. Shooting games from the other grades can be continued, and the game of *In the Pot* can be added. *Basketball Snatch Ball* and *One Goal Basketball* give opportunity to use skills which have been acquired. Regular basketball with its formations, line-up, and other details should be covered so that the children can be ready to participate in basketball played as a regular game. Officiating should be taught because it is of value to have children officiate for their scrimmages or games.

GRADE	THIRD	FOURTH	FIFTH	SIXTH

Skills	Passing
	   Chest or Push
	   Baseball
	   Bounce
		Passing
		   Underhand
		   One-hand
		   Two-hand
			Passing
			   One hand
			     push
			   All passes to
			     moving tar-
			     gets
				Passing
				   Two-hand
				     overhead
				   Long passes

	Catching
	   Above waist
	   Below waist
			Catching
			   While moving	

	Shooting
	   Two-hand
	     chest
		Shooting
		   Two-hand
		     chest
		   Lay-up, right
		     and left
			Shooting
			   One-hand
			     push
			   Free throws
				Shooting
				   One-hand jump

	Dribbling
	   Standing and
	     moving
		Dribbling
		   Down and
		     back
		   Right and left
		     hands
			Dribbling
			   Figure eight
			   Pivoting
				Dribbling
				   Practice with
				     eyes closed

			Guarding	Stopping
				   Parallel stop
				   Stride Stop
				   Three-man
				     weave

Knowledges	Rules
	   Dribbling
		Rules
		   Violations
		   Dribbling
		   Traveling
		   Out of bounds
			Rules
			   Held ball
			   Personal fouls
			   Holding
			   Hacking
			   Charging
			   Blocking
			   Pushing
			   etc.
				Rules
				   Conducting the
				     game
				   Officiating

Activities	End Ball	Birdie in the
		   Cage
		Captain Ball
			Captain Basket-
			   ball
			Sideline
			   Basketball
			Twenty One
			Around The Key
				Flag Dribble
				One Goal Basket-
				   ball
				Five Passes
				Basketball Snatch
				   Ball
				In The Pot
				Three on Three

Skill Tests		Dribble	Figure Eight
			   Dribble
			Wall Test
				Figure Eight
				   Dribble
				Baskets per
				   Minute
				Free Throws

PRACTICAL SUGGESTIONS

1. Many basketball skills, particularly on the third grade level, do not stipulate the use of basketballs. Other balls such as volley, playground, and rubber balls can be used successfully.

2. The junior size basketball should be used for the elementary school program.

3. If practical, the baskets should be lowered to 9' as compared with the high school height of 10'.

4. The program should concentrate on skills with many drills. Basketball offers endless possibilities, and drills should be utilized to give variety and breadth to the instructional program.

5. In the sixth grade, the girls can play against the girls on one end of the floor, and the boys can occupy the other end.

6. Each child should have an opportunity to practice all the skills. This is not possible when a considerable portion of the class time is devoted to playing the game.

SKILLS IN BASKETBALL

The basic skills in basketball to be covered in the elementary school class program in physical education can be divided into passing, catching, shooting, dribbling, and game skills.

Passing

Chest or Two-Hand Push Pass. The feet may be in an even position or one may be slightly ahead of the other. The ball is held at chest level with the fingers spread slightly above the center of the ball. The elbows are comfortably bent, and the delivery is made with a snap of the wrists. As the arms are extended, the fingers and wrists release the ball. A step is taken in the direction of the throw, or the weight shifts from rear to front foot.

Baseball or One-Hand Pass. Stand with the side toward the direction of the throw. The ball is brought back with both hands to a point over the shoulder or at the side of the head. The ball is now thrown like a softball, using the hand and wrist of the throwing arm for good follow-through.

Bounce Pass. Either of the previous two passes described can be adapted to make a bounce pass. The object is to throw the ball to a teammate on first bounce so the ball comes up to the outstretched hands. It should rebound waist high by hitting the floor 4' to 5' from the receiver. Do not bounce the ball at the receiver's feet.

Underhand Pass. For the two-hand underhand pass, the ball should be held in both hands near one hip with the elbows bent. The delivery is made with a snap of the wrists and follow-through with the elbows. A step is taken in the direction of the throw.

For the one-hand underhand pass, the ball is brought back with both hands (one in front and propelling hand behind) and thrown like an underhand toss in softball.

One-Hand Push Pass. One hand is placed in front and one in back of the ball. The pass is made with the wrist and fingers of the pushing hand. A step is taken with the left foot if the right hand propels the ball, and vice versa. The pass later becomes the one-hand set shot, using about the same technique.

Two-Hand Overhead Pass. This pass is used when there is a height advantage. Player stands in short stride position (one foot slightly ahead of the other). The ball is held overhead with both hands with the fingers slightly back of the ball. The action is mostly in the wrist and fingers. The ball should go on a level path and be received high.

Catching

A player should move to meet a basketball when catching it. The fingers should be relaxed and spread. To receive a high pass, the thumbs are together, and the little fingers meet for one caught low. For passes received at waist level, the hands are in a parallel position. A little "give" with the hands and arms to absorb the recoil is important.

Dribbling

The wrist and hand furnish most of the force for the dribble. The dribble is a push with the partially cupped hand. The hand should "feel" the ball coming back up just before pushing for the next dribble. The ball should not be batted.

Shooting

Children should start with the two-hand set shot. Later, they can be introduced to the more popular one-hand variety.

Push Shot. The feet may be together or one

foot ahead with the knees slightly bent. The hands are placed behind the ball and a little to the side. The wrist action should start when the ball is at eye level. There should be good follow-through.

Lay-Up Shot. From the right side, the shot should be timed so that it can be made taking off the left foot. Carry the ball in both hands until just before shooting. Aim at a spot on the backboard, shooting with the fingertips, arm extended. The shooting hand should be behind, not under, the ball.

One-Hand Push Shot. The shot begins much like the one-hand push pass, except that the ball is aimed above the basket. The ball is held in front of the body in front of the right shoulder. Dip the right hand slightly and put plenty of wrist and finger flick into the shot.

One-Hand Jump Shot. The ball is held above the head with the left hand in front and the right hand back and under the ball. At the height of a jump, the ball is released by a push of the right hand with good use of fingers and wrist motion. The ball is guided with the pads of the fingertips.

Defense

The player, with his knees slightly bent and the feet comfortably spread, should face his opponent. The weight should be evenly distributed on both feet to allow for movement in any direction. A defensive player should stand about 3' from his opponent and wave one hand to distract or block passes and shots. Movement sidewards is done with a sliding motion. A defensive player should be loose and able to move quickly, so as not to be caught flatfooted.

Stopping

To stop quickly, the weight of the body should be dropped to lower the center of gravity, and the feet applied as brakes. In the parallel stop, the body turns sideward, and the feet act together as brakes. The stride stop comes from a forward movement and is done on a one-two count. The stopping begins with one foot hitting the ground with braking action, and the other is firmly planted *ahead* on the second count. The knees are bent, and the body center of gravity is lowered. From a stride stop, the movement can become a pivot by picking up the front foot and carrying it

to the rear and at the same time fading to the rear.

DRILLS IN BASKETBALL

With so many different skills which can be put into various combinations, the possibilities of basketball drills are endless. Some of the more common drills are given.

Passing and Catching

Many standard skill formations can be used, particularly the two-line, circle, circle and leader, line and leader, shuttle turnback, and the regular shuttle. With only five players in a circle formation, a star drill is particularly effective. Players pass to every other player, and the path of the ball in a full round forms a star.

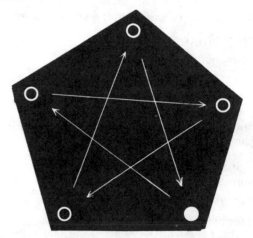

The star drill adapts itself well to a ball passing relay.

Another valuable drill is the three-man weave. This drill needs sufficient explanation and must be practiced. It should be remembered that the player in the center always starts the drill. The drill has two other key points. The first to remember is that "you always go behind the player to whom you threw the ball." The second is that "just as soon as you go behind and around the player, head diagonally across the floor until you receive the ball." The pass from the center man can start to either side.

Dribbling

Dribbling drills feature moving to a point and back and also weaving in and around objects. The shuttle formation makes an excellent drill for dribbling.

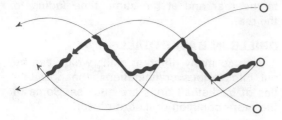

Three Man Weave

SHUTTLE DRIBBLING DRILL

Formation: Shuttle.

Players: 6 to 8.

Supplies: Basketball.

Player from one line dribbles up to the other line, passes or hands the ball, and then continues to the back of that line. The next player dribbles the ball back to the starting point.

FILE DRIBBLING DRILL

Formation: File.

Players: 4 to 8.

Supplies: Basketball.

Dribble down to a line and back. Player can dribble right-handed going down and left-handed coming back.

DRIBBLE AND PIVOT DRILL

Formation: File.

Players: 4 to 8.

Supplies: Basketball.

The player at the head of the line dribbles forward to a prescribed point, stops, pivots to face the file, and passes to the next player, who repeats. First player goes to the end of his file.

FIGURE EIGHT DRILL

Formation: File.

Players: 4 to 8.

Supplies: Basketball, 3 obstacles (chairs, Indian clubs, etc.)

Players dribble in and around the obstacles. Be sure that the player changes dribbling hands each time so that his body is between the ball and the obstacle, which represents an opponent.

Variation: Have the dribbler circle each obstacle once and go to the next, which he circles in the other direction, using the other hand for dribbling.

SHOOTING

Shooting drills should be practiced from both a stationary and a moving position.

LAY-UP DRILL

Formation: Double file.

Players: 6 to 16.

Supplies: Basketball.

One file retrieves the ball and passes to the player coming in for a lay-up shot. Players change to the end of the other file each time. The drill can also be varied by the retrieving team passing the ball back to the head of the other file, from which point the player dribbles in for the shot. Change sides and approach the basket from the other side.

FILE AND LEADER

Formation: File and leader.

Players: 6 to 8.

Supplies: Basketball.

The player at the head of the line passes the ball to the leader and then:

1. Runs by him on either side receiving a return pass for a lay-up shot.

2. Stops at a point in front or to the side of the leader and receives a return pass for a set shot.

SET SHOT FORMATION

Formation: Semicircle and leader.

Players: 4 to 8.

Supplies: Basketball.

Players scatter in a semicircle with the leader acting as the retriever. He passes to each player in succession who takes his shot. Players should start from a close distance and work back. Two, and even three, squads can practice on one basket. Rotate shooting areas after a period of practice. Each child should have a chance at the leader's position.

BASKETBALL ACTIVITIES
Third Grade
END BALL

Players on each team are divided into three groups: forwards, guards, and end men. The object is for a forward to throw successfully to one of his end zone players.

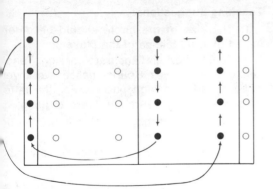

Playing Area: A court 20' by 40' Is divided in half by a center line. End zones are marked 3' wide, completely across the court at each end.

Players: 9 to 12 on each team.

Supplies: Basketball or 10" rubber playground ball.

The players from each team are positioned as follows. The end zone players take a position in one of the end zones. Their forwards and guards then occupy the half of the court farthest from this end zone. The forwards are near the center line, and the guards are back near the end zone of that half.

The ball is put in play with a center jump between the two tallest opposite forwards. When a team gets the ball, the forwards try to throw over the heads of the opposing team to an end zone player. To score, the ball must be caught by an end zone player with *both* feet inside the zone. No dribbling or moving with the ball is permitted by any player.

Fouls: Fouls result in loss of the ball to the other team. Fouls are:

1. Holding a ball more than five seconds.
2. Stepping over the end line or stepping over the center line into the opponent's territory.
3. Walking (travel) with the ball.
4. Pushing or holding another player.

Out of Bounds: The ball belongs to the team that did not cause it to go out of bounds. The nearest player retrieves the ball out at the sideline and returns it to the guard of the proper team.

Teaching Suggestions: Encourage fast, accurate passing. Players in the end zones must practice jumping high to catch and still land with both feet inside the end zone area.

A system of rotation is desirable. Each time a score is made, players on that team can rotate one person. (See diagram.)

Variations:

1. A game which carries the progression one step farther is *Free Throw End Ball.* In keeping with the rules, the end zone player scores one point when he catches the ball. He is allotted one free throw, which gives him the chance to score an additional point.

2. **Corner Ball.** This differs from *End Ball* only in that the scoring zone is located in the corners. A 3' by 3' square is drawn in each corner which imposes the limitation that only two players from each team are in position to receive the ball, one in each corner on the respective end of the playing area. Otherwise, the play is the same is in *End Ball.*

Fourth Grade
BIRDIE IN THE CAGE
Formation: Circle with one player in the center.

Players: 8 to 15.

Supplies: Soccer ball, Basketball, Volleyball.

The object of the game is for the center player to try to touch the ball. The ball is passed from player to player in the circle, and the center player attempts to touch the ball on one of these passes. The player who threw the ball that was touched takes the place in the center. Also, in case of a bad pass resulting in the ball leaving the circle area, the player whose fault caused the error changes to the center of the ring.

Teaching Suggestions: The ball should move promptly and rapidly. Passes to a neighboring player should not be allowed. If there is difficulty in touching the ball, a second center player may join the first.

Play can be limited to a specific type of pass, such as bounce, two-hand, etc.

CAPTAIN BALL
A team is composed of a captain, three forwards, and three guards. The guards throw the ball into the forwards, who attempt to throw the ball to their captain.

Playing Area: 30' x 60'. Three 2' circles are laid out in the shape of a triangle with a fourth circle (for the captain) in the center of the triangle. Hoops make excellent circles.

Players: 7 on each side.

Supplies: Basketball.

The captain and the three forwards are each assigned to respective circles and must always keep one foot inside the circle. Guarding these four circle players are three guards.

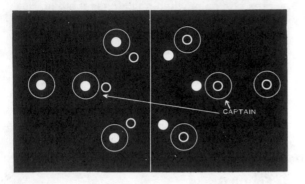

The game is started by a jump at the center line by two guards from opposing teams. The guards can rove in their half of the court but must not enter the circles of the opposing players. The ball is put in play by a center jump after each score.

As soon as a guard gets the ball, he throws it to one of his forwards who must maneuver to be open. The forward now tries to throw it to the other forwards or into the captain. Scoring is as follows:

> 2 points — all three forwards handle the ball, and it is then passed to the captain.
> 1 point — the ball is passed to the captain but has not been handled by all forwards.

Fouls:

1. Stepping over the center line, or stepping into circle by guard.

2. Traveling, running, or kicking the ball.

Penalty: Free throw. Ball is given to one of the forwards who is unguarded and gets a throw to the guarded captain. If successful, scores one point. If not successful, ball is in play.

Out of Bounds: As in basketball. Ball is awarded to the team (guard) which did not cause the ball to go out.

Out of the Circle: If a forward or captain catches a ball with *both* feet out of his circle, the ball is taken out of bounds by the opposing guard.

Teaching Suggestions:

1. The size of the circle should be determined by the abilities of the players.

2. Teach short and accurate passing. Teach faking with the eyes. Bounce passes work well when mixed with high passes. For the latter pass, the circle players can learn to jump.

3. Rotate the turns at center jump among the guards.

4. Use hoops or circular pieces of plywood for the circles.

Variations: Play with four guards instead of three. This makes it more difficult for the forwards to move the ball.

Fifth Grade

CAPTAIN BASKETBALL

Captain Basketball is nearer to the game of basketball than *Captain Ball*. *Captain Ball* has limited movements of the forwards because of the circle restrictions. *Captain Basketball* brings in more natural passing and guarding situations, similar to those found in the basketball scrimmage.

Playing Area: Basketball court with center line. A captain's area is laid out by drawing a line between the two foul restraining lines 4' out from the end line. The captain must keep one foot in this area.

Players: 6 or 8 on each team.

Supplies: Basketball.

The game is played much the same as basketball. A throw by one of the forwards into the captain scores two points. A free throw scores one point.

A team normally is composed of three forwards, one captain, and four guards. The captain must keep one foot in his area under the basket.

The game is started with a jump ball, after which the players advance the ball as in basketball. However, none may cross the center line. Thus, the guards must bring the ball up to the center line and throw it to one of their forwards. The forwards maneuver and attempt to pass successfully into the captain.

Fouls: As in basketball. Stepping over the center line or a guard stepping into the captain's area draws a free throw.

Free Throw. The ball is given to a forward

at the free throw line. He is unguarded and has five seconds to pass successfully to his captain, who is guarded by one player. The ball is in play if the free throw is unsuccessful.

Teaching Suggestions:

1. The game provides a good opportunity to learn both rules and techniques of basketball.

2. While players are required to remain in their own half of the court, they should be taught to move freely in that area.

3. Stress short, quick passes, as long passes are not effective.

4. Stress proper guarding techniques.

5. If only 6 play on each team, the team has 3 guards, 2 forwards, and the captain.

SIDELINE BASKETBALL

Playing Area: Basketball court.

Players: Class is divided into two teams, each team lining up on one side of the court facing the other.

Supplies: Basketball.

The game can be played by three or four active players from each team. The remainder of the team stand on the sideline and catch and pass the ball to the active players. They may not shoot, nor may they enter the playing floor.

Active players play regular basketball except that they may pass and receive the ball from the sideline players. The game starts with the active players of each team occupying one of the end lines. When the whistle blows, the teacher passes the ball to one of the active players (usually to the team that did not score), and regular basketball is played until one team scores or three minutes have elapsed. When either occurs, the active players take places in the line on the left side of their line and three new active players come out from the right. All other players move down three places.

No official out-of-bounds on the sides is called. The players on that side of the floor simply recover the ball and put it in play by a pass to an active player without delay or waiting for a signal. Free throws are awarded when a player is fouled.

Sideline players may not pass to each other but must pass back to an active player. Sideline players should be well spaced along the side.

TWENTY-ONE

Playing Area: One end of a basketball court.

Players: 3 to 8 in each game, with a number of games played on one end of the floor. Players are in file formation.

Supplies: Basketball.

Each child is permitted a long shot (from a specified distance) and a follow-up shot. The long shot, if made, counts two points and the short shot one. The follow-up shot must be made from the spot where the ball is recovered from the first shot. The normal one-two step rhythm is permitted on the short shot from the place where the ball was recovered.

The first player scoring a total of 21 is the winner. If the ball misses the backboard and basket altogether on the first shot, the second shot must be taken from the corner.

Variations:

1. For a simpler game, allow dribbling before the second shot.

2. A player continues to shoot as long as he makes every shot. This means if he makes *both* the long and short shot, he goes back out to the original position for a third shot. All made shots count, and he continues until he misses.

3. The game works very well as team competition with each player contributing his total to the team score.

4. Various combinations and types of shots may be used.

AROUND THE KEY

Playing Area: One end of a basketball floor.

Players: 3 to 8 players.

Supplies: Basketball.

Spots are arranged for shooting as indicated in the diagram. A player begins at the first spot and continues to shoot as long as he makes the shot. When he misses, he has two choices. The first is to wait for his next turn and continue from the place where he missed. The second is to "risk it," which means that he gets another shot from where he missed. If he makes this, he continues. If he misses, he starts over from the beginning on his next turn.

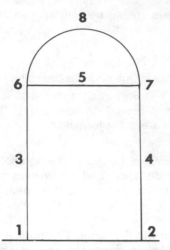

The winner is the one who completes the key first or who has made the farthest progress.

In the beginning, it is well to give each child two shots from each spot.

Variations:

1. Each child shoots from each spot until he makes the basket. A limit of three shots from any one spot should be set. The child finishing the round of nine spots with the lowest number is the winner.

2. The order of the spots can be changed. A player can start on one side of the key and continue back along the line, around the free throw circle, and back down the other side.

Sixth Grade

FLAG DRIBBLE

Playing Area: One end of a basketball floor or a hard surface area outside with boundaries.

Players: 4 to 8

Supplies: Each player has a basketball and a flag tucked in the belt at the back.

To play this game, children must have reasonable skill in dribbling. The object of the game is to eliminate the other players, while avoiding being eliminated. A player is eliminated if he loses control of his ball, if his flag is pulled, or if he goes out-of-bounds. Keeping control of the ball by dribbling is interpreted to mean continuous dribbling without missing a bounce. A double dribble (both hands) is regarded as loss of control.

The game starts with the players scattered around the playing area near the sidelines. Each has a ball. The extra players wait outside the area. On signal, each player begins to dribble in the area. While keeping control of his own dribble and staying in bounds, he attempts to pull a flag from any other player's back. He also can knock aside any other player's ball, thus eliminating him. As soon as the game in progress is down to one player, he is declared the winner. There are times when two players will lose control of their basketballs at about the same time. In this case, both are eliminated.

Variation: If it is impractical to use flags, as it may be in the case of girls, the game can be played without this feature. The objective becomes only to knock aside or deflect the other basketballs, while retaining control of one's own ball.

ONE GOAL BASKETBALL

Playing Area: An area with one basketball goal.

Players: Two teams, 2 to 4 on each.

Supplies: Basketball.

If a gymnasium has as many as four basketball goals, many children can be kept active with this game. If only two goals are present, a system of rotation can be worked out.

The game is played with the regular rules with the following exceptions:

1. The game begins with a jump at the free throw mark with the centers facing the side lines.

2. When a defensive player recovers the ball, either from the backboard or on an interception, the ball must be taken out beyond the foul line circle before offensive play is started and an attempt at a goal can be made.

3. After a basket is made, the ball is taken in the same fashion away from the basket to the center of the floor where the other team starts offensive play.

4. Regular free throw shooting can be observed after a foul, or some use the rule that the offended team takes the ball out-of-bounds.

5. If an offensive player is tied up in a jump ball, he loses the ball to the other team.

Variation: A system of rotation can be instituted wherein the team that scores a basket "holds" the floor, and the losing team must retire in favor of a waiting team. For more experienced players, a score of three or more points can be required for eliminating the opponents.

FIVE PASSES

Playing Area: One-half a basketball floor.

Players: Two teams, 4 to 5 on each team.

Supplies: Basketball, colored shirts or markers.

The object of the game is to complete five consecutive passes, which scores a point. On one basketball floor, two games can go on at the same time, one in each half.

The game is started with a jump ball at the free throw line. The teams observe regular basketball rules in ball handling, traveling, and fouling. Five consecutive passes must be made by a team, which counts out aloud as the passes are completed.

The ball must not be passed back to the person from whom it was received.

No dribbling is allowed. If for any reason the ball is fumbled and recovered, or improperly passed, a new count is started. After a successful score, the ball can be thrown up again at a center jump at the free throw line. A foul gives a free throw which can score a point. Teams should be well marked to avoid confusion.

Variations:

1. After each successful point (five passes), the team is awarded a free throw which can score an additional point.

2. After a team has scored a point, the ball can be given to the other team out of bounds to start play again.

3. Passes must be made so all players handle the ball.

BASKETBALL SNATCH BALL

Playing Area: Basketball court.

Players: Two teams, 6 to 15 on each team.

Supplies: 2 basketballs, 2 hoops.

Each team occupies one side of a basketball floor. The players on each team are numbered consecutively, and must stand in this order. The two balls are laid in two hoops, placed one on each side of the center line. When the teacher calls a number, the player from each team whose number was called runs to the ball, dribbles it to the basket on his right, and tries to make the basket. As soon as the basket is made, he dribbles back and places the ball on the spot where he picked it up. The first player to return the ball after making a basket scores a point for his team. The teacher should use some system of keeping track of the numbers so all children will have a turn. Numbers can be called in any order.

Variation: Players can run by pairs with two players from each team assigned the same number. In this case the ball must be passed between the paired players at least three times before a shot can be taken. Three passes are required before the ball is returned to its spot.

IN THE POT

Playing Area: Basket and adjacent area.

Players: 4 to 12 in each game. A number of games can be played on one basket.

Supplies: Basketball.

This is a shooting game with emphasis on accuracy. A player is allowed a long and a short shot. If he makes *either* shot, he adds points to the pot. A long shot counts two points, and a short shot adds one to the pot. A player who misses *both* shots takes out whatever points are in the pot, and these are scored against him. When he has accumulated ten points against him, he is eliminated and must drop out until the winner is determined.

No dribbling is allowed. The short shot must be taken at the spot where the ball was recovered from the backboard, and each player may take this shot with the one-two rhythm. If the first shot touches neither the backboard nor the basket, the short shot is taken from the corner of the floor.

Each player keeps his own score of points against him, and the group playing keeps track of the points in the pot. If there are more points in the pot than are needed to eliminate a player, only sufficient points for the elimination are taken out. The remainder are left in the pot for the next shooter that misses.

THREE ON THREE

Playing Area: One-half of a basketball court.

Players: Teams of three, 3 to 5 teams.

Supplies: Basketball.

An offensive team of three stands just forward of the center line facing the basket. The center player has a basketball. Another team of three is on defense and awaits the offensive team in the area near the foul line.

The remaining teams await their turns and stand beyond the end line.

Regular basketball rules are used. At a signal, the offensive team advances to score. A scrimmage is over when a score is made, or the ball is recovered by the defense. In either case, the defensive team moves to the center of the floor and becomes the offensive unit. A waiting team comes out on the floor and gets ready for defense. The old offensive team goes to the rear of the line of waiting players. Each team should keep its own score.

By using only one-half the floor, two games can be carried on at the same time.

Variations:

1. If the offensive team scores, it remains on the floor and the defensive team drops off in favor of the next team. If the defense recovers the ball, the offensive team rotates off the floor.

2. If a team makes a foul (by one of the players), that team rotates off the floor in favor of the next team.

BASKETBALL TESTS

The tests in basketball cover dribbling, passing, shooting, and free throws. For timing, a stopwatch is needed.

Straight Dribble. A marker is placed 15 yards down the floor from the starting point. The dribbler must dribble around the marker and back to the starting position. Allow 3 trials, take best time.

Figure Eight Dribble. Three obstacles (Indian clubs, bases, etc.) are placed 5 yards apart and 5 yards from the starting point. The player must dribble in and out of the markers in the path of a figure eight. Allow 3 trials, take best time.

Wall Pass Test. A player stands 5' from a smooth wall. He is given 30 seconds to make as many catches as he can from throws or passes against the wall. Balls must be caught on the fly. Generally, the two-hand or chest pass is used in this test.

Baskets Per Minute. A player stands near the basket in any position that he wishes. On the signal he shoots and continues shooting for a period of 1 minute. His score is the number of baskets he made during the time period.

Free Throws. Score is kept of the number of free throws made from a specified number of tries. Players should be allowed three or four warm-up tries.

THE GAME OF BASKETBALL

For elementary school children, the game of basketball is similar to the official game played in the junior and senior high schools, but has modifications in keeping with the capacities of the children. The following represents the basic rules which apply to the game for elementary children. There are fewer and fewer differences between the game for boys and that for girls.

Teams. A team for boys is made up of five players, composed of two guards, one center, and two forwards. It is recommended that this player format also apply to girls, even if the present American rules specify differently. The trend is toward the five-player game for girls, and it is predicted that girls' rules will shortly legalize this to conform with rules used in most other parts of the world.

Timing: The game is divided into four quarters; each is 6 minutes in length.

Officials. The game is under the control of a referee and an umpire, both of whom have an equal right to call violations and fouls. They work on opposite sides of the floor and are assisted by a timer and a scorer.

Putting the Ball in Play. Each quarter is started with a jump ball at the center circle. Throughout the game, the jump ball is used when the ball is tied up between two players, or when it is uncertain who caused an out-of-bounds ball to go out.

After each successful basket or free throw, the ball is put in play at the end of the court under the basket by the team against whom the score was made.

Violations. The penalty for a violation is the award of the ball to the opponents at a near out-of-bounds point. The following are violations:

1. Traveling — taking more than one step with the ball without passing, dribbling, or shooting. Sometimes called walking or steps.

2. Stepping out-of-bounds or causing the ball to go out-of-bounds.

3. Taking more than 10 seconds to cross the center line from the back to the front court.

Once in the forward court, the ball may not be returned to the back court by the team in control.

4. Double dribble — a second series of dribbling without another player handling the ball, palming (not clearly batting) the ball, or dribbling the ball with both hands at once.

5. Stepping on or over a restraining line during a jump ball or free throw.

6. Kicking the ball intentionally.

7. Remaining more than 3 seconds in the area under the offensive basket, bounded by the two sides of the free throw lane, the free throw line, and the end of the court.

Personal Fouls. Personal fouls are holding, pushing, hacking (striking), tripping, charging, blocking, and unnecessary roughness.

When a foul is called, the person who was fouled receives one free throw. If he was fouled in the act of shooting (basket missed), he receives two shots. If the basket is made, the score counts and one free throw is awarded.

Technical Fouls. Technical fouls include failure of substitutes to report to the proper officials, delay of game, and unsportsmanlike conduct.

Disqualification. A player who has five personal fouls called against him is out of the game and must go to the sidelines. Disqualification can result from extreme unsportsmanlike conduct or a vicious personal foul.

Scoring. A basket from the field scores 2 points and a free throw one point. The team that is ahead at the end of the game is declared the winner. If the score is tied, an overtime period of 2 minutes is played. If the score is still tied after this period, the next team to score (1 or 2 points) is declared the winner.

Substitutes. Substitutes must report to the official scorer and await a signal from the referee or umpire before entering the game. The scorer will sound his signal at a time when the ball is not in play so that the official on the floor can signal for the player to enter the game.

Football
Type
Activities

Touch and flag football are modifications of the game of American Football. A ball carrier is considered down in *Touch Football* when he is touched with one hand. Some rules call for a two-handed touch, while others require a player to wear one or two flags which the opponents must seize in order to down the ball carrier (hence the name, *Flag Football).* The shape of the ball makes the skills of ball handling more difficult than with a soccer or volleyball. This, in turn, means that the teacher must spend sufficient time in football skills if the children are to enjoy the activity.

Flag Football has advantages over *Touch Football* in that the ball carrier is not stopped by a touch but must lose his flag. This means that there can be more twisting and dodging, making the game more interesting and challenging. In addition, there is little argument over whether or not the ball carrier was downed.

EMPHASIS ON DIFFERENT GRADE LEVELS

Fourth Grade. Passing, centering, and catching should comprise the fourth grade program. Most of the time should be spent on skills. The two lead-up games of *Keep Away* and *Football End Ball* make use of the skills listed.

GRADE	FOURTH	FIFTH	SIXTH
Skills	Passing Centering Catching	Stance Pass Receiving Punting	Blocking Carrying the ball Running and dodging Ball exchange Lateral passing
Knowledges			Football rules Plays and formations
Tests	Passing for distance Centering	Punting for distance Passing for distance	Passing for accuracy Passing for distance
Activities	Keep Away Football End Ball	Kick Over Fourth Down	Football Boxball Flag Football Pass Ball

Fifth Grade. The fifth grade should review the skills of the fourth grade level. The emphasis then shifts to passing skills with moving receivers in football drills. Punting and kicking games are introduced.

Sixth Grade. More specialized skills like blocking, carrying the ball, ball exchanges, and football agility skills feature the lead-up work for the game of *Flag Football.*

PRACTICAL SUGGESTIONS

To insure better play in football-type activities, the following suggestions are made.

1. Children should have a chance to practice all skills. In drills, which give opportunity to a number of skills, a system of rotation should be organized so players shift positions automatically and practice all skills.

2. Roughness and unfair play must be controlled by strict enforcement of the rules and good supervision.

3. The junior size football should be used in the elementary grades.

4. Girls, too, like to handle footballs and should have a chance to practice skills. *Football End Ball* is an excellent game for girls to make use of passing and catching.

5. Play should be organized so that when the boys play *Flag Football,* the girls can be playing *Football End Ball,* soccer, or speedball.

6. Drills should be carried out with attention to proper stance and approximating game conditions. Boys should line up in proper stance when going out for passes.

7. Football-type games should be organized so that the play is not dominated by one or two individuals.

FOOTBALL SKILLS

Passing. Skillful forward passing is needed in *Flag Football* and the lead-up games; this is a potent weapon. The ball should be gripped lightly behind the middle with the fingers on the lace. The thumb and fingers should be relaxed. The left foot should be placed so it points in the direction of the pass, and the body is turned sidewards, when throwing right-handed. The ball is raised with two hands up and over the right shoulder. The ball is delivered directly forward with an over-hand movement of the right arm, with the index finger pointing toward the line of flight.

Lateral Passing. Lateral passing is pitching the ball underhanded to a teammate. The ball must be tossed sideward or backward. The ball should be tossed with an easy motion, and no attempt should be made to make it spiral like a forward pass.

Catching. The receiver should keep his eyes on the ball and catch it in his hands with a slight giving movement. As soon as the ball is caught, it should be tucked in carrying position. The little fingers should be together for most catches.

Carrying the Ball. The ball should be carried with the arm on the outside, and the end of the ball into the notch formed by the elbow and arm. The fingers add support to the carry.

Centering. Player takes a position with his feet well spread and toes pointed straight ahead. His knees are bent, and he should be close enough to the ball to reach it with a slight stretch. The right hand takes about the same grip that would be used for passing. The other hand is on the side near the back and merely acts as a guide. Center passing for the T-formation is with one hand, however. The other arm rests on the inside of the thigh.

Stance. The three-point stance is the one most generally used in *Flag Football.* Feet are about shoulder width apart, toes pointing straight ahead, with the toe of one foot even with the heel of the other. The hand on the side of the foot that is back is used for support, resting the knuckles on the ground. The player should look straight ahead and always take the same stance irrespective of the direction he is to move.

Some players prefer the parallel stance wherein the feet, instead of being in the heel and toe position, are lined up even. In this case, either hand can be placed down for support.

Blocking. In blocking in *Flag Football,* the blocker must stay on his feet. The block should be more of an obstruction than a take-out. He should set with his shoulder against the opponent's shoulder or upper body. Making contact from any direction from the rear not only is a foul, but can cause injury.

Ball Exchanges. Children love to work plays where the ball is exchanged from one player to another (a reverse) or even with two exchanges (double reverse). The object is to start the play in one direction and then give the ball to another player heading in the opposite direction. The ball can be handed backwards or forwards. The player with the ball always makes the exchange with the inside hand, the one nearest the receiving player. The ball is held with both hands until the receiver is about 6′ away. The ball is then shifted to the hand on that side with the elbow bent, partially away from the body. The receiver comes toward the exchange man with his near arm with bent elbow carried in front of his chest with the palm down. The other arm has the palm up and is carried about waist high. As the ball is given (not tossed) to the receiver, he clamps down on the ball to secure it. Then, as quickly as he can, he changes it to normal carrying position.

A fake reverse can be run where the ball carrier fakes the change and keeps the ball.

Punting. Punting should be first practiced with a soccer or rubber playground ball of that size. The kicker should stand with the feet slightly apart, the knees flexed with the kicking foot slightly forward. The fingers should be extended in the direction of the center. The eyes should be on the ball from the time it is centered until it is kicked. The kicker should actually see his foot kick the ball. After the ball is received, the kicker should take a short step with his kicking foot. A second step is taken with the other foot. The kicking leg is swung forward, and at the impact the knee is straightened to provide maximum force. The toes are pointed, and the long axis of the ball makes contact high and on the outside of the instep. The leg should follow through well after the kick.

FLAG FOOTBALL DRILLS

Drill in flag football skills can be organized for a single skill or a combination of skills. Another consideration that is important is the rotation of players during drills so that each child will have an opportunity to practice all skills. A sufficient supply of footballs is a necessity to any efficient drill period in football skills.

BALL CARRYING

Formation: Regular zone flag football field with 20 yard interval lines.
Players: 6 to 12.
Supplies: Football, flags for each player.

The ball carrier stands on the goal line ready to run. Three defensive players await him at 20 yard intervals, each one stationed on a zone line facing the ball carrier. Each defender is assigned to the zone he faces and must down the ball carrier by pulling a flag while the carrier is still in the zone. The ball carrier runs and dodges trying to get by each defender in turn without having any of the flags pulled. If one flag is pulled, the runner continues. If both flags are pulled, the last defender uses a two-hand touch to down the ball carrier. After the runner has completed his run, he goes to the end of the defender line and rotates to the defending position.

BALL EXCHANGE

Formation: Shuttle with the halves about 15 yards apart.
Players: 10 to 20.
Supplies: Football.

The two halves of the shuttle face each other across the 15 yard distance. A player at the head of one of the files has a ball and carries it over to the other file, where he makes an exchange with the front player of that file. The ball is carried back and forth between the shuttle files. The receiving player should not start until the ball carrier is almost up to him. A player, after handing the ball to the front player of the other file, continues around and joins that file.

CENTERING

Drill 1.

Formation: Shuttle turnback, 5 yards between halves of the shuttle.
Players: 6 to 8 in each drill.
Supplies: Football.

The ball is centered back and forth between the two parts of the shuttle. As soon as a player takes his turn, he goes to the end of *his* line.

Drill 2.

Formation: Semicircle and leader.
Players: 6 to 8.
Supplies: Football.

The leader centers the ball to each player in turn; they pass or center the ball back. After one complete round, the leader rotates to one end of the line, and a new leader repeats the routine.

COMBINATION

Formation: Regular offensive formation with passer, center, end, and ball chaser.
Players: 4 to 10.
Supplies: Football.

Passing, centering, and receiving skills are combined into one drill. Each player, as soon as he has taken his turn, rotates to the next spot. A minimum of four players is needed. The four positions are:

Center — centers the ball to the passer.
Passer — passes the ball to the end.
End — receives the pass.
Ball Chaser — retrieves the ball if missed by the receiver (end), or takes a pass from the end (if he caught the ball) and carries the ball to the center spot which is his next assignment.

The rotation follows the path of the ball. This means that the rotation system moves from center to passer to end to ball chaser to center. Extra players should be stationed behind the passer for turns.

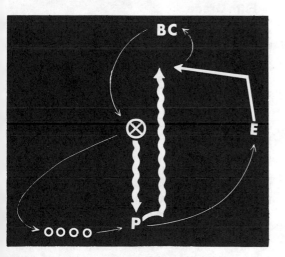

KICKING

Formation: Shuttle turnback, with the two parts kicking distance apart.
Players: 6 to 8 in each drill.
Supplies: Football.

The emphasis is on kicking skills, but the skill of catching a kicked ball should be practiced. The two halves of the shuttle formation face each other and kick back and forth. Centering the ball can be added to the drill.

ONE-ON-ONE DEFENSIVE DRILL

Formation: Center, passer, end, defender.
Players: 8 to 10.

The drill is as old as football itself. A defensive player stands about 8 yards back awaiting an approaching end. The passer tries to complete the pass to the end while the defender tries to stop or intercept the ball. Have one defender practice against all the players and then change defenders.

Variation: Have two ends and two defenders. Passer throws to the end that appears to be the most unguarded.

PASSING AND CATCHING

Formations: Passing and catching can be organized through many different drills, such as line and leader, file and leader, shuttle turnback, double line formation, and others.
Players: 6 to 8.
Supplies: Football.

The formation will dictate the pattern and rotation of players.

PUNT RETURN

Formation: A center, kicker, two lines of ends, and receivers.
Players: 10 to 20.
Supplies: Football, flags for each player.

The object of the drill is for the receiver to catch a punted ball and return it to the line of scrimmage while two ends attempt to pull a flag or make a tag.

Two ends are ready to run downfield. The center centers the ball to the kicker, who punts the ball downfield to the punt receiver. The ends cannot cross the line of scrimmage until the ball is kicked. Each end makes two trips downfield as a "tackler" before rotating to the punt receiver position.

A good punter is necessary for this drill. Only selected children with the degree of skill to punt the ball far enough downfield should be permitted to kick. It is also important that the ends wait until the ball is kicked, or they will be downfield too soon to give the receiver a fair chance to make a return run.

STANCE

Formation: Squads in extended file formation.
Players: 6 to 8 in each file.
Supplies: None.

The first person in each file performs and when finished with his chores goes to the end of his file. On the command "Ready," the first person in each file assumes a football stance. The teacher can correct and make observations. On the command "Hip," the players charge forward for about five yards. The new players at the head of the line get ready.

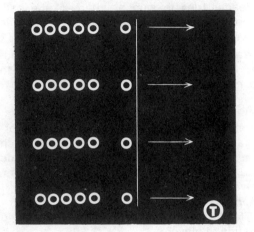

ACTIVITIES
Fourth Grade

FOOTBALL END BALL

The only difference between this game and *Basketball End Ball* is that a football is used. Distances children are to throw from the forwards to the end men should be governed by the children's capacity. See page 408 for a description of *End Ball*.

KEEP AWAY

Playing Area: Football field or large play space.
Players: Two teams, 8 to 12 on each side.
Supplies: Football, pinnies, colored shirts, or crepe identification marks.

The object of the game is for one team to retain possession of the ball as long as possible, keeping it from the other team. Teams should be marked so that the players can distinguish opponents.

The same body contact rules that govern basketball should be enforced. The defensive team trying to recover the ball may play the ball, but the players are not permitted to push, shove, hold, or otherwise interfere physically with an opponent. Players scatter and one team attempts to retain possession of the ball by passing to teammates. No player can take more than five steps with the ball under penalty of loss to the other team.

Variations:

1. A certain number of *consecutive* successful passes could score a point. Begin with five passes, and if this proves too easy, raise the number. The five passes should be to five different players.

2. The captain can start the passing and if every player on a team handles the ball, a score is made when the captain again has the ball in his possession. Players could handle the ball more than once, but no point could be scored until each member of the team has handled the ball, and it is returned to the captain.

Watch out for roughness. A quick whistle is needed to avoid pile-ups. If there is too much roughness, award the ball to the other team when it hits the ground. Otherwise, the ball should be in play.

Fifth Grade

KICK OVER

Playing Area: Football field with a ten-yard end zone.
Players: 6 to 10 on each team.
Supplies: Football.

Teams are scattered on opposite ends of the field. The object is to punt the ball over the other team's goal line. If the ball is caught in the end zone, no score results. If the ball is kicked beyond the end zone on the fly, a score is made regardless whether or not the ball was caught. A ball kicked *into* the end zone on the fly and not caught also scores a goal.

Play is started by one team with a punt from a point 20' to 30' in front of the goal line it is defending. On a punt, if the ball is not caught, the team must kick from the spot of recovery. If the ball is caught, three long strides are allowed to advance the ball for a kick. Players should be numbered and kick in rotation.

Variation: Scoring can be made only by a drop kick across the goal line.

Teaching Suggestion: The player whose turn it is to kick should move fast to the area from which the ball is to be kicked.

FOURTH DOWN

Playing Area: Football field (use only one-half) or equivalent space.
Players: Two teams, 6 to 12 on each team.
Supplies: Football.

Every play is a fourth down, which means that the play must score or the team loses the ball. No kicking is permitted, and players may pass any time from any spot in any direction. This means that there can be a series of passes on any play either from behind or beyond the line of scrimmage.

The teams line up in an offensive football formation. The ball is put in play by centering. The back receiving the ball can either run or pass to any of his teammates. The one receiving the ball has the same privilege.

To start the game, the ball is placed in the center of the field and the team that wins the toss has the chance to put the ball into play. After each touchdown, the ball is brought to the center of the field, and the team against which the score was made puts the ball into play.

To down a runner or pass receiver, a two-handed touch above the waist is made. The back first receiving the ball from the center has immunity against tagging provided he does not try to run. All defensive players must stay 10' away from him unless he runs. The referee should wait a reasonable length of time for the back to pass or run, and if he holds the ball beyond that, the referee shall call out "Ten Seconds." The back must now throw or run within 10 seconds, or the defensive players can tag him.

The defensive players scatter to cover the receivers. They can use a man-to-man defense with each player covering an offensive man or employ a zone defense.

Since the team with the ball loses possession after each play, rules for determining where the ball is to be placed when the other team takes possession are needed.

If a player is tagged with two hands above the waist, the ball goes to the other team at this spot.

If an incomplete pass is made from *behind* the line of scrimmage, the ball is given to the other team at the spot where the ball was put into play.

Should an incomplete pass be made by a player while *beyond* the line of scrimmage, the ball is brought to the spot from which it was thrown.

Variation:

1. The game could be called *Third Down* and two downs would be allowed to score.

Teaching Suggestions:

1. The team in possession should be encouraged to pass as soon as practical, as children become tired from running around to become free for a pass.

2. The defensive team can score by intercepting a pass. Since passes can be made at any time, upon interception, the player should look down the field for a pass to one of his teammates.

Sixth Grade

FOOTBALL BOX BALL

Playing Area: Football field 50 yards long. Five yards beyond each goal is a 6' by 6' square which is the box.
Players: Two teams, 8 to 16 on each.
Supplies: Football, team colors.

The teams should be marked so that they can be distinguished. The object of the game is similar to *End Ball* in that the team tries to make a successful pass to the captain in the box.

To begin the play, players are onside, which means that they are on opposite ends of the field. One team, losing the toss, kicks off from their own ten-yard line to the other team. The game now becomes a kind of a keep-away with either team trying to secure and retain possession of the ball until a successful pass can be made to the captain in the box. The captain must catch the ball on the fly and still stay with both feet in the box. This scores a touchdown.

Rules: A player may run sidewards or backwards when in possession of the ball. He may not run forward but is allowed his momentum (two steps) if receiving or intercepting a ball. Penalty for illegal forward movement while in possession of the ball — loss of ball to opponents, who take the ball out-of-bounds.

The captain is allowed the opportunity of only three attempts or to score one goal. If either occurs, another player is rotated to the box.

On any pass or attempt to get the ball to the captain, the team loses the ball. If a touchdown (successful pass) is made, the team brings the ball back to its ten-yard line and kicks off to the other team. If the attempt is not successful, the ball is given out-of-bounds on the end line to the other team.

Any out-of-bounds is put in play by the team which did not cause the ball to go out-of-bounds. No team can score from a throw-in from out-of-bounds.

In case of a tie ball, a jump ball is called at the spot. The players face off in a jump ball as in basketball.

Players must play the ball and not the individual. For unnecessary roughness, the player is sidelined until a pass is thrown to the other team's captain. Ball is awarded to the offended team out-of-bounds.

On the kickoff, all players must be onside, that is, behind the ball when it is kicked. Penalty is loss of ball to the other team out-of-bounds at the center line. After the kickoff, players may move to any part of the field.

On the kickoff the ball must travel 10 yards, and then it can be recovered by either team. A kickoff outside or over the end line is treated as any other out-of-bounds.

A ball hitting the ground remains in play as long as it is inbounds. Players may not bat or kick a free ball. Penalty is loss of ball to the other team out-of-bounds.

Falling on the ball means loss of ball to the other team.

FLAG FOOTBALL (MODIFIED)

Flag Football is an important modification of the game of football. Many versions of flag and touch football exist and are used successfully. *Flag Football* can be played with one or two flags. The flag is a length of cloth which is hung from the belt of each player. A ball carrier is considered down when a defensive player grasps and removes the flag from his belt. In the single flag game, the flag is hung from the back. In the two-flag version, each player has two flags which are hung from the sides at the waist. Sometimes it is difficult for a player to reach around the ball carrier and remove the one flag hung in the back. This leads to a rougher type of game. With two flags, the defensive player has a choice of pulling either flag to stop the play.

Playing Area: A field 30 by 60 yards marked off in 20 yard intervals with lines parallel to the goal line. This divides the field into three zones.

If there is sufficient room, end zones of 10 yards can be marked off, defining the area behind the goal in which passes can be caught.

Numbers: 6 to 9 on a team. If 6 or 7 are on a team, four men are required to be on the line of scrimmage. For 8 or 9 players, five offensive men must be on the line.

Supplies: Football, two flags for each player. Flags should be about 3" wide and 24" long.

Timing: The game shall consist of two halves. A total of 25 plays shall make up each half. All plays count in the 25 except the try for one point after a touchdown and a kickoff out-of-bounds.

Scoring: Touchdown — 6 points. Point after touchdown — 1 point. Safety — 2 points. A point after touchdown is made from a distance of 3' from the goal line. One play (pass or run) is allowed for the extra point.

Kickoff: The game is started with a kickoff. The team winning the toss has the option of selecting the goal it wishes to defend or choosing to kick or receive. The loser of the toss takes the option not exercised by the first team.

The kickoff is from the goal line, and all players on the kicking team must be onside. The kick must cross the first zone line or it does not count as a play. A kick that is kicked out-of-bounds (not touched by the receiving team) must be kicked over. A second consecutive kick out-of-bounds gives the ball to the receiving team in the center of the field. The kickoff may not be recovered by the kicking team unless caught and fumbled by the receivers.

Downs and Yardage: The field is divided into three twenty-yard zones. A team has four downs to move the ball into the next zone or lose the ball. For example, a team that secures the ball in the center has four downs to move the ball into the next zone or score. I the ball is legally advanced into the last zone, then the team has four downs to score. A ball on the line between zones is considered in the more forward zone.

Time-Outs: Time outs are permitted only for injuries or when called by the officials for any reason.

Substitutions: Unlimited substitutions are permitted. Each must report to the official.

Forward Pass: All forward passes must be thrown from behind the line of scrimmage. All players on the field are eligible to receive or intercept passes.

Huddle: The team in possession of the ball usually huddles to make up the play. After any play, the team has 30 seconds to put the ball into play after the referee gives the in play signal.

Blocking: Blocking is done with the arms close to the body. Blocking must be done from the front or side, and blockers must stay on their feet.

Tackling: A player is down if one of his flags has been pulled. The ball carrier must make an attempt to avoid the defensive player and is not permitted to run over or through the defensive player. The tackler must play the flags and not the ball carrier. Good officiating is needed as defensive players may attempt to hold or grasp the ball carrier until they can remove one of the flags.

Punting: All punts must be announced. Neither team can cross the line of scrimmage until the ball is kicked. Kick receivers may run or use a lateral pass. They cannot make a forward pass after receiving a kick.

Fumbles: All fumbles are dead at the spot of the fumble. The first player who touches the ball on the ground is deemed to have recovered the fumble. When the ball is centered to a back, he must gain definite possession of the ball before a fumble can be called. He is allowed to pick up a bad pass from the center or a ball of which he did not have possession.

Touchback: Any ball kicked over the goal line is ruled a touchback and is brought out to the twenty-yard line to be put in play by the receiving team. A pass intercepted behind the goal line can be a touchback if the player does not run it out. It is a touchback even if he is tagged behind his own goal line.

Safety: A safety occurs when the team *defending* a goal line causes the ball to go back over the goal line by fumbling, running, or being caught during a scrimmage play behind its own goal line.

Penalties:

Loss of five yards

Off side.

Delay of game (too long in huddle).

Failure of substitute to report.

Passing from spot not behind line of scrimmage (also loss of down).

Stiff arming by ball carrier or not avoiding a defensive player.

Failure to announce intention to punt.

Shortening the flag in the belt. Playing without flags in proper position.

Faking the ball by the center (he must center the pass on the first motion).

Loss of fifteen yards

Holding, illegal tackling.

Illegal blocking.

Unsportsmanlike conduct (can be disqualification).

PASS BALL

Pass Ball is a more open game than *Flag Football*. The game is similar to *Flag Football* with these differences:

1. The ball may be passed at any time. This means that it can be thrown at any time beyond the line of scrimmage, during an interception, during a kickoff, or during a received kick.

2. Four downs are given to score a touchdown.

3. A two-handed touch on the back is used instead of pulling a flag.

4. If the ball is thrown from behind the line of scrimmage and results in an incomplete pass, the ball is down at the previous spot on the line of scrimmage. If the pass originates otherwise and is incomplete, the ball is placed at the spot from where this pass was thrown.

5. Since the ball can be passed at any time, no downfield blocking is permitted. A player may screen the ball carrier, but cannot make a block. Screening is defined as running between the ball carrier and the defense.

TESTING FOOTBALL SKILLS

Tests for football skills include the skills of centering, passing, and kicking (punting).

Centering. Each player is given 5 trials centering at a target. The target should be stationed 6 yards behind the center. Targets which can be used are:

1. An old tire suspended from the ground so that the bottom of the tire is about 2' from the ground. Scoring: For centering the ball through the tire — 2 points, for hitting the tire but not going through it — 1 point. Possible total — 10 points.

2. If a baseball pitching target is used in the softball program, the device is quite suitable also for a centering target. Scoring is the same as with the tire target.

3. A 2' by 3' piece of plywood is needed. This is held by a player at the target line in front of his body with the upper edge even with the shoulders. The target is held stationary and is not to be moved during the centering. Scoring: For hitting the target — 1 point. Possible total — 5 points.

Other targets can be devised.

Passing for Accuracy. Suspend a tire about shoulder height so that it is fairly stable. The tire can be suspended from goal posts or by the use of volleyball standards. Each player is given five throws from a minimum distance of 15 yards. As skill increases, increase the distance.

Scoring: for throwing through the tire — 2 points, for hitting the tire but not passing through — 1 point. Possible total — 10 points.

Passing for Distance. Each player is allotted three passes to determine how far he can throw a football. The longest throw is measured to the nearest foot. It is important to reserve the test for a relatively calm day as the wind can be quite a factor (for or against) in the test.

The passes should be made on a field marked off in 5 yard intervals. Markers made from tongue depressers mark the first pass distance. If a later throw is longer, the marker moves to that point. With markers, the members of a squad can complete the passing turns before measuring, which can then be done at one time for all members of a squad.

Kicking for Distance. Punting, place kicking, and drop kicking can be measured for distance with similar techniques described for passing for distance.

FLAG FOOTBALL FORMATIONS

The following formations are based upon a 9 player team, with 4 backs and 5 linemen. The formations would necessarily vary if the number on each team were decreased. A variety of formations can be presented to the children, making a varied and more interesting game. Backfield formations can be right or left. Only the formation to the right is presented.

Key: Center   X   Back   B
     End   E   Lineman   O

Offensive Line Formations

Balanced (tight ends)
E   O   X   O   E

Unbalanced Right (tight ends)
E   X   O   O   E

Line Over Right (tight end)
X   E   O   O   E

Right End Out (can be one or both)
E   O   X   O   (5 YD)   E

Right End Wide (can be one or both)
E   O   X   O   (15 YD)   E

Right End Wide, Left End Out (can be reversed)
E   (5 YD)   O   X   O   (15 YD)   E

Spread (3 to 5 yards between each lineman)
E   O   X   O   E

Offensive Formations

It should be noted that the formations diagrammed can be combined with any of the offensive line formations. For purposes of clarity, a balanced line with tight ends is used for all formations. However, a variety of line formations can be used with each of the backfield formations.

Single Wing

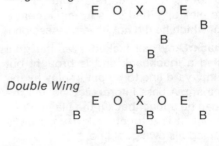

Double Wing

Punt

```
      E  O  X  O  E
         B     B
               B

               B
```

Flanker Right

```
      E  O  X  O  E
               B
            B           B
            B
```

Wing Right, Flanker Left

```
      E  O  X  O  E
                  B
   B           B
            B
```

Wing Right, Flanker Right

```
      E  O  X  O  E
                 B        B
            B
         B
```

T Formation (regular)

```
      E  O  X  O  E
            B
         B  B  B
```

Wing T

```
      E  O  X  O  E
               B           B
            B  B
```

Spread

```
      E  O   X  O  E
   B              B        B
               B
```

Pass Patterns

The following pass patterns may be run by the individual pass catcher, whether he is a lineman or a back. They are particularly valuable to use in practice where the pass receiver will inform the passer of his pattern.

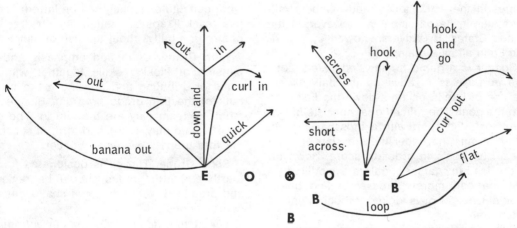

26

Soccer

Emphasis on Each Grade Level
Practical Suggestions
Basic Soccer Rules for Lead-Up Games
Soccer Skills
Drills for Soccer Skills
Activities
Tests for Soccer Skills

Soccer football is one of the most popular games in the world today, and numbers millions among its participants. However, in the United States, it is overshadowed by American Football as a fall sport.

Soccer is a game for the "educated feet." The purpose is to advance the ball without the use of hands or arms down the field and into the goal. The official goal consists of two goal posts 24' apart with a crossbar 8' high. The ball must go under the crossbar and between the posts in order to score. However, in the lead-up games, goals are modified so that the ball merely crosses a line below shoulder height or is kicked through a line of defenders.

Success in soccer depends upon how well individual skills are coordinated in team play. Good soccer also stresses position play rather than groups of individuals dashing about chasing a ball.

Soccer rates high in its contributions to fitness and offers many opportunities to develop social and emotional qualities.

EMPHASIS ON EACH GRADE LEVEL

Fourth Grade: Preliminary to the fourth grade, the children should have played *Circle Kick Ball* and had some experience in kicking skills on an elementary level. *Circle Kick Ball* is to be reviewed. Fourth grade material stresses kicking primarily and its use in simple lead-up games. Simple rules regarding touching the ball with the hands or arms and what constitutes fouling can be introduced on this level. Traps are taught so children can control the ball without the use of hands.

Fifth Grade. Continued emphasis and expansion of kicking skills together with the skills of dribbling and passing make up the bulk of the fifth grade program. Simple elements of team play are brought in. The children should play a modified form of soccer in the fifth grade, seven-man soccer.

Sixth Grade. The skills designated for the fourth and fifth grades should be reviewed and practiced, with additional challenges and combinations.

The sixth grade children can be *introduced* to regular soccer, but the regular game is not suitable for class work. Since it requires 22 players, rarely will there be this number of boys or girls present in a particular class so that such a game can be played. The seven-player game is a much better substitute as it brings out vigorous action for all players. A unit of study on soccer as an international game is of value, as few American children realize how important this game is in the lives of the people of other lands. The game is gaining in popularity in the United States.

PRACTICAL SUGGESTIONS

1. Planning soccer experiences is based on the recognition that the skills of soccer

must be developed. Few children have opportunities for soccer skills. In addition, the skill of controlling the ball with the feet comes slowly, and sufficient drills together with suitable lead-up activities in progression are important.

2. Soccer, with its attack and defense, can be a rough game. Rough play like pushing, shoving, kicking, and tripping must be controlled. Rules need to be strictly enforced. Good execution of skills leading to good ball control will help eliminate knots of players. Attention to proper heading, volleying, and kicking skills will help eliminate injuries from contacting the ball. Players need to be alert for kicked balls as these may strike players in the face or head unexpectedly. Girls should be taught to fold arms across the chest when stopping the ball. Glasses should be removed when possible or glass guards provided.

3. While some skills are such that separation of sexes may not be necessary, soccer game play is the type of activity which boys should not engage in competitively with or against girls. The game can become quite vigorous, active, and rough, with much contact.

This separation requires separate competitive soccer activities. Where there is a normal balance of boys and girls in a class of 30 or so, two separate games of seven-player soccer fits into the class pattern very well. With smaller numbers of either boys or girls, teams with a lesser number on the side can be utilized.

4. Children need to be watched carefully for fatigue, as soccer is a vigorous game. The teacher should use methods of rotation to help rest players.

5. If soccer is played indoors or on a hard surface, the ball can be deflated enough so it will be confined to the ground. It is difficult for children to keep a lively, bouncing ball in control on a hard surface.

6. Scoring can be modified for children in keeping with their capacities. Scoring must be a challenge but should be neither too easy nor too difficult. To avoid arguments, when the ball is to be kicked through a line of children, the height should be limited to shoulder level or below. This tends to emphasize an important soccer principle of control of the ball on the ground.

GRADE	FOURTH	FIFTH	SIXTH
Skills	Instep Kick Side of Foot Kick Toe Kick Toe Trap Foot Trap	Heel Kick Outside Foot Kick Dribbling Knee Trap Passing	Kicking Goals Kickoff (Place Kick) Punt Volleying Heading
Knowledges	Simple Rules	Ball Control and Passing	The Game of Soccer Team Play and Rules
Activities	Soccer Touch Ball Circle Kick Ball (Review) Circle Soccer Soccer Dodgeball Diagonal Soccer Sideline Soccer Soccer Snatch Ball	Pin Kick Ball Dribble Call Ball Line Soccer Three Line Soccer Modified Soccer (7-Man)	Modified Soccer (7-Man) Zone Soccer (Coed) Regulation Soccer Modified Speed Ball
Tests	Toe Trap Accuracy Kick (Stationary Position)	Dribbling Trapping (3 Types) Accuracy Kick	Dribbling Punt Place Kick Penalty Kick Accuracy Kick

BASIC SOCCER RULES FOR LEAD-UP GAMES

Since lead-up games contain the basic elements of soccer, the rules should show good similarity in many of the activities. There will be variations for the individual games, but the following represent general rules that have a wide application.

1. The ball may not be deliberately played with the hands, forearms, or arms. Mere incidental touch should be disregarded. If the arms are in contact with the body and are used only to block or stop the ball from this position, there is no violation. The free kick is the normal penalty for a touch violation. The ball is placed on the ground with defenders not closer than a specified distance (10', for example), depending on the game. A goal cannot be scored from a free kick of this type. The ball must not be kicked before the referee signals. In some games where the free kick is not practical a score can be awarded for an illegal touch.

2. The goalkeeper is exempt from the illegal touch rule. He may handle the ball *within his own area* by catching, batting, or deflecting with his hands. He may not be charged by the opponents and while holding the ball is limited to four steps by official rules. In elementary school play, the teacher should insist that the goalkeeper get rid of the ball immediately by throwing or kicking. This removes the temptation to play or rough up the goalie. In some lead-up games, a number of students may have privileges of the goalie in handling the ball. The rules need to be clear, and the ball handling should be done within a specified area.

3. For serious fouls like tripping, striking, kicking, holding, or pushing an opponent, a direct free kick is awarded. A goal *may be* scored from such a kick. In soccer, if the team commits one of these fouls within its own penalty area (defensive), a penalty kick should be awarded. Only the goalkeeper may defend against this kick, which is from 12 yards out. All other players must be outside the penalty area until the ball is kicked. In lead-up games, consideration should be given to penalty-type fouls. These would be committed in a limited area by the defensive team near the goal it is defending. A kick can be awarded or a goal can be scored for the attacking team for the foul.

4. The ball is out of play, and the whistle should blow when the ball crosses any of the boundaries, a goal is scored, or a foul is called. When a team last touches or causes the ball to go out-of-bounds on the sides, the other team is awarded the ball. The ball is put in play with an overhead throw-in by both hands.

5. If the ball is caused to go over the end line *by the attacking side,* the defending team receives a kick from any point desired near the end of line of that half of the field. If the defense last touched the ball going over the end line, then the attacking team is awarded a corner kick. The ball is taken to the corner on the side where the ball went over the end line, and a direct free kick is executed. The ball may score from this kick.

6. The game is started by a kickoff with both teams onside. In lead-up games, the kickoff can be used, or the ball can be dropped for a free ball. In some games, the teacher may find it advisable simply to award the ball for a free kick in the back court to the team not making the score.

7. Playing time in lead-up games can be by quarters or by reaching a predetermined score. In a regular soccer game, the play is by halves.

8. If the ball is trapped or ensnarled among a number of players or someone has fallen, a quick whistle is needed. The ball can be put in play by dropping it between players of opposite teams. It can also be rolled in for a start under these conditions.

9. While the offside rule is of little value in elementary play, the children should understand the rule and the reasons for the rule. Its purpose is to prevent the "cheap" goal where a player on offense waits near the goal to take a pass behind the defenders and score easily against the goalkeeper. While there are a number of details to the concept of offside, essentially a player on offense ahead of the ball must have two players between him and the goal. One of these players naturally is the goalkeeper. The offside rule does not apply when the player receives the ball directly from an attempted goal kick, an opponent, a throw-in, or a corner kick.

SOCCER SKILLS

Soccer is a game based on kicking, so it is important that the students learn to control the ball with the feet. Practice must be intense enough to develop foot-eye coordination.

The basic kick for soccer is the instep kick, used for long distances and for scoring. It also allows the player to kick the ball in the air (volleying) or from a bounce.

Two other kicks are important. These are the kicks done with the inside and outside of the foot, respectively. These are for ball control, primarily for passing.

Three other kicks are listed and included in the drills. They are the heel kick, the toe kick, and the soccer punt. In strict soccer circles, neither the heel kick or the toe kick hold any weight. Many American boys are used to the toe kick, as this is the one used for the football kickoff and place kick. Not too much time should be spent on the soccer punt, as this is a move restricted to the goalie only.

Kicking should stress driving the ball for distance, passing, and scoring. The emphasis should be on accuracy. Kicking is also used for volleying, defined as redirecting a ball in air flight before it hits the ground. Volleying is also done in regular soccer deflecting the ball with other parts of the body, including the head. However, on the elementary level heading should be used with caution.

Dribbling, the purpose of which is to maintain control of the ball by self, is done with a series of short kicks.

Trapping is defined as stopping the ball with a part of the body. Trapping is done with the sole of the foot (toe), the inside of the foot, or one or both knees. Its purpose is to secure control of a ball coming toward a player either on the ground or through the air. Not much stress in the elementary school play is placed on trapping an air flight ball, which is done with a thigh or total body trap.

Basic Soccer Kicks

Instep Kick. The kicker approaches the ball from a 45° angle from the left, if he is a right-footed kicker. In the kick, the top of the instep meets the ball as in punting a football. It is necessary to approach from the side and kick with a moderate sideswing, or the toe will drive into and make contact with the surface. On the step into the ball, the left foot is placed close beside the ball, taking the weight of the body for the kick. With the body in a somewhat forward lean, the kicking foot makes contact with the ball with the instep. The power comes from the knee by snapping the bent leg forward. The eye is on the ball, which is contacted with the instep. The child must kick through the ball with good follow-through.

Inside Foot Kick. Contact is made with the inside of the foot. The kick is used for passing or goal kicking. The knee is slightly bent, and the leg is swung from the hip. The kick is used for short distances only. The toe should be held down during the kick.

Outside Foot Kick. This kick is used for only short distances and for passing or maneuvering the ball. Contact is made with the outside of the foot.

Other Soccer Kicks

Heel Kick. The heel kick has value for a short pass to a teammate behind the player. Player steps slightly ahead of the ball and with a short snappy punch of the heel propels the ball backwards.

Toe Kick (Kickoff). The toe kick is not considered to be as accurate as other kicks, but has some use in kicking off and driving the ball for distance. The technique is different from the instep kick in that the ball is approached directly from behind. The step made with the nonkicking foot should be to a point slightly back of the ball. The kicking toe is kept up, with the foot at right angles with the leg. The force is from the snap of the knee with good follow-through.

Punt. Used by the goalkeeper only, the punt can be done stationary or on the run. The ball is held by both hands at waist height in front of the body. In the stationary position, the kicking foot is forward. A short step is taken with the kicking foot and then a full step on the other leg. With the knee bent, the kicking foot swings forward and upward. As contact is made with the ball at the instep, the knee straightens and additional power is secured from the other leg through a coordinated rising on the toes or hop.

Trapping

In the elementary school, three types of trapping should be taught. Relaxation and "giving" with the ball are important in all traps.

1. *Sole of the Foot Trap.* This is the simplest of all traps and involves stopping a rolling ball by putting the sole of the foot on the ball and holding it to the ground.

2. *Foot Trap.* Using the inside of the foot and giving with the ball, the motion of the ball is stopped by the inside of the foot.

3. *Knee Trap.* The knee trap can stop both a rolling and a bouncing ball. The ball is smothered with one or both knees. Usually both knees are used.

Dribbling. Dribbling is to move the ball with a series of taps or pushes to cover ground and still retain control of the ball. The best contact point is the inside of the big toe. Both the inside and outside of the foot at times can be used to move the ball.

Volleying. The change of the direction of a ball on the fly is called volleying. This can be done by stiffening a part of the body so the ball will rebound in the desired direction. Volleying can be done with the instep, knee, thigh, hip, or shoulder.

Heading. Heading is a special kind of volleying in which the direction of flight is changed by making an impact with the head. The neck muscles can be used to aid in the blow. The eye must be kept on the ball until the moment of impact which is made at the top of the forehead at the hairline.

DRILLS FOR SOCCER SKILLS

The drills for soccer consist of emphasis on kicking, volleying, trapping, passing, dribbling, and scoring. Some of the drills concern themselves with only one skill, but the majority offer opportunity to practice a variety of skills.

Circle. The circle formation can be used for kicking, passing, and trapping. The ball may be kicked back and forth across the circle or may be passed from player to player in a circular direction. Trapping may be included in the skills.

Circle and Leader. The circle and leader formation lends itself well to the development of soccer skills. The use of the leader in the center allows for more controlled skill practice. The leader passes and receives the ball from each circle player in turn. After completing a round to all the players, the leader takes his place in the circle, and another child becomes the leader.

Two Line Drill. Two lines of three to four children face each other across a ten-yard distance. Players practice kicking, passing, and trapping in this formation. The ball is kicked back and forth in a sequential pattern to include each child.

Shuttle Turnback. The two halves of a shuttle formation face each other about 10 yards apart. The first player in the file kicks to the first person of the other file, who traps the ball and then prepares for his kick. After kicking, the player goes to the end of *his* file.

Shuttle Dribbling. Dribbling, passing, and trapping can be practiced in the regular shuttle drill. The first player dribbles to the other file. The ball continues to be dribbled back and forth in turn. Each dribbler joins the rear of the file toward which he dribbled.

The player can dribble part way toward the other file and, when about 5 yards away, pass to the head of the other file.

Three-Man Shuttle Dribble Drill. Three players make up this drill and are positioned in this fashion.

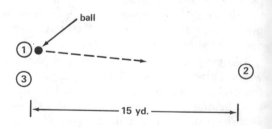

#1 has the ball and dribbles to #2, who dribbles the ball back to #3. The drill can be conducted several ways. The first is to dribble the entire distance. A second way would be to dribble a portion of the distance and then pass the ball to the end man. Also, obstacles can be placed so it is necessary to dribble in and out of each obstacle.

Circular Dribbling. The players form a large

circle standing about 3 yards apart and facing in. One player starts dribbling the ball around the circle, alternating going outside the first player and inside the next in a weaving pattern. After a player completes the round of the circle, he passes to the player ahead of him who continues the drill. Eight players in a circle make a nice number for this drill.

The drill can be used as a relay but considerable control is needed to assure that the path of the ball has been accurate and complete in the weaving movement.

File (lane) Formation Drills. Each team is in a relay formation to practice the skills. A standard or base should be placed about 15' in front of the file. The following patterns of drills illustrate some of the possibilities from this formation.

1. Player dribbles forward, around the base, and back to the file.

2. Player dribbles forward, around the base, and from this point passes back to the head of the file.

3. Use three obstacles, 4 yards apart. Player dribbles in and out of the obstacles in a weaving motion, forming a figure-eight pattern.

Passing Drill. A double shuttle formation is used for this drill, which is the equivalent of two teams alongside each other in shuttle formation. The shuttle halves are about 25 to 30 yards apart.

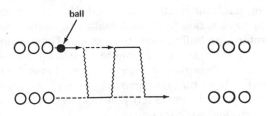

ball

Two players, one from each file, move at a time. One player has the soccer ball. A short dribble is taken forward and then the ball is passed to the other player moving forward with him. The second player takes a short dribble forward and passes the ball back. This continues until they reach the other files, where two players repeat the maneuver, re-turning the ball to its original starting place. The ball is shuttled back and forth by two players at a time.

Heading and Volleying. Two drills are suggested for volleying, with 4 to 6 players in a drill formation.

1. *Circle and Leader.* The leader in the center tosses the ball to each in turn for practicing heading or volleying. This is a drill for control and for developing good form.

2. *Circle Formation.* After the children have some practice in volleying and heading, they can volley or head the ball in a circle formation trying to keep it up continuously.

Goal Kicking. Three stages are suggested for goal kicking drills.

1. A file of players is stationed about 40' in front of the goal. A ball chaser awaits behind the goal. Each file player in turn dribbles forward about 10' to 15' and attempts to score a goal. Use different kinds of kicks.

2. A goalie guards the goal while another child is the ball chaser. Each file player in turn advances with the ball and tries to outwit the goalie and score a goal.

3. Three-on-two drills emphasize the need for accurate passing and kicking. Two players are on defense and three offensive players advance with the ball. The object for the three is to advance and score a goal.

Relays. Almost all soccer drills can be organized as relays. Caution is urged to introduce relays only after the children have mastered the skills sufficiently to have reasonable control of the path of the soccer ball. Insistence on procedure in soccer relays is important. The ball should always be under good control, and a relay should finish with the ball in the possession of the team, not just kicked through or past some line. Touching the ball with the hands or arms should mean disqualification.

ACTIVITIES
Third Grade

CIRCLE KICK BALL

Formation: Circle.
Players: 10–20.
Supplies: Soccer or 10" playground ball.

Players kick the ball (with the side of the

foot) back and forth inside of the circle. The object is to kick the ball out of the circle *underneath* shoulder level of the circle players. A point is scored against each of the players where the ball left the circle. Any player kicking the ball *over* shoulder level gets a point against him. A variation is to eliminate the offending players instead of scoring points against them.

Fourth Grade

SOCCER TOUCH BALL

Formation: Circle with player in center.
Players: 8–10.
Supplies: Soccer ball.

Players are spaced around a circle about 10 yards in diameter. The object of the game is to keep the player in the center from touching the ball. The ball is passed back and forth as in soccer. If the center player touches the ball with a foot, the person who kicked the ball goes to the center. Also, if there is an error (a missed ball), the person responsible for the error exchanges with one in the center.

CIRCLE SOCCER

Formation: A double circle is drawn on the floor. The outer circle is 20' to 25' in diameter, and the inner circle is placed so that a 2' space is available between circles. A diameter is drawn across both circles.

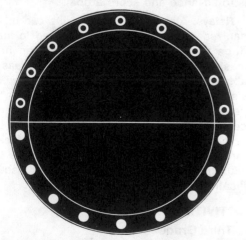

Players: 16–30 children divided into two teams.
Supplies: Soccer ball, slightly deflated.

The object of the game is to kick the ball *through* the defense of the other team. Each team occupies the space between the circles, one on each side of the diameter.

Scoring: One point is scored for the opponents if:

1. The ball is touched with the hands.

2. The ball goes through the team below the shoulder level.

3. A player steps over the inner circle when kicking.

4. The ball is kicked higher than the shoulders of the smaller of two adjacent players. A game consists of 15 points.

Dead Ball: If the ball comes to rest in the circle, any player on that side may pass the ball to a teammate. Any other ball is put into play where it left the circle. If between two players, the one on the right has the right to play the ball.

Blocking: The ball may be blocked with any part of the body except the hands and forearms.

Rotation: After each score, the players on each team rotate one place to the right.

Teaching Suggestions: Emphasize that girls are to cross arms over the chest when blocking a ball. Particularly on hard surfaces, the ball should be deflated enough to stay on the ground. Kicking with the side of the foot will also keep the ball low. Children should be encouraged to trap the ball before returning it.

Variation: The same principle of kicking through the other team as in *Circle Soccer* can be used if the two teams are lined up facing each other about 20' apart. However, two retrievers, one from each team, are needed to return the ball to their own teams. They roam the center and pass only to their own teammates. They may compete for the loose ball but cannot block or impede the ball. A rotation system after each point is needed to include the retrievers.

SOCCER DODGEBALL

Formation: One team forms a circle with the other team grouped in the center.
Players: 20–30.
Supplies: Soccer ball, slightly deflated.

This is a variation of *Team Dodgeball* (page 293), except that the ball is kicked instead of thrown at the center players. Players may not use their hands to control or retrieve the ball. A point is scored for the kicking team for each time a person in the center is hit. Hit players can be eliminated or remain to be hit again. A point is deducted from the team score for every violation by touching with the hands.

The ball should be deflated slightly and kicked with the side of the foot.

DIAGONAL SOCCER

Formation: A square about 40′ by 40′ with a diagonal line from corner to corner.
Players: 20 to 30.
Supplies: Soccer ball.

The diagonal line divides the playing area into two team halves; the members of the team line up on the sides of the square in their half. Two players are out on the floor from each team in their own half of the floor. These are the active players; the others act as line guards. The active players try to intercept passes and kick through the opposite team's line to score. When a score is made, the active players rotate to the sidelines, and two new players take their places.

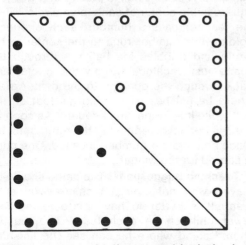

Players on the sidelines may block the ball with their bodies but cannot use their hands. The team against whom the point was scored starts the ball for the next point.

Scoring: Scoring is much the same as in *Circle Soccer* in that a point is scored for your opponents if:

1. You allow the ball to go through your line below shoulders.

2. You touch the ball illegally.

3. You kick the ball over the other team above shoulder height.

4. An active player steps over the diagonal line to retrieve or kick the ball.

Teaching Suggestions: If the class is large, enlarge the area and use 3 or 4 active players at a time.

SIDELINE SOCCER

Formation: Rectangle about 100′ by 60′.
Players: 10 to 15 on each team.
Supplies: Soccer ball.

The teams line up on the sidelines of the square with the end lines open. Three active players from each team are called for from the end of the team line. These remain active until a point is scored and then are rotated to the other end of the line.

SIDELINE SOCCER

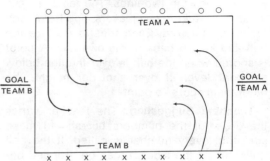

The object is to kick the ball over the end line which has no defenders. The three compete against each other, helped by the players on the sidelines. To score a ball must go over the end line at or below shoulder height and counts one point. None of the players may play the ball with the hands. The active players follow the restrictions of no pushing, holding, kicking, or other rough play. This constitutes a foul and causes a point to be awarded to the other team.

The ball must be last kicked by an active player to score. If the ball is out-of-bounds or does not score, play continues until a point is scored by the group of active players.

Play is started by the referee dropping the ball between two players from opposite teams. Out-of-bounds is given to the team on that side. This is a free kick but cannot score a goal directly from the kick. Violation of the touch rule is also a free kick at the spot of the foul.

Teaching Suggestions: When the ball is dropped the remaining players should be back protecting their goal.

Variation: If the scoring seems to be too easy, make smaller goals on each end by use of jumping or volleyball standards or other markers to narrow the scoring area.

The distance between goals can also be increased to make more playing area.

SOCCER SNATCH BALL

Formation: Two parallel lines about 30′ apart.
Players: 6 to 10 on each team.
Supplies: Soccer ball.

Each team is numbered consecutively and is back behind its line. For each number on one team there is a corresponding number on the other team.

The teacher places the ball at a spot midway between the two lines. The teacher calls a number, and the two players, one from each team, run forward. Each tries to capture the ball and kick it back to his *own* line. A point is scored when the ball is over the line below shoulder level. If over shoulder height, the other team scores a point.

Teaching Suggestion: The teacher varies the order of the numbers but should make sure that every number is called. If the ball goes out on the sides, it can be dropped between the two active players.

Fifth Grade

PIN KICKBALL

Formation: Two teams about 20 yards apart
  and facing each other.
Players: 7 to 10 on each team.
Supplies: 4 or more pins (cones, Indian clubs,
  or bowling pins), 1-2 soccer balls.

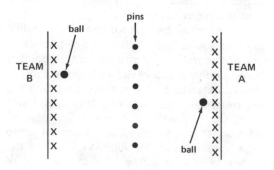

At least 4 pins are placed equidistant between the two lines of players. The object of the game is to knock over the pins with the kicked ball. Toss coin for the first kick. Kicks must be made from the line on which the teams are standing. Players should trap the ball and concentrate on accuracy. Begin with one ball and add another.

Score one point for each pin knocked over. The player who knocked down the pin sets it up again.

The type of kick can be specified or it can be left up to choice. Be careful of one or two players dominating the game. This can be controlled somewhat by having those who just scored go to either side of the line. More soccer balls can be added if the game seems slow. As accuracy improves, the distance between teams can be increased.

DRIBBLE CALL BALL

Formation: Circle formation for each team.
Players: 6–10 on each team.
Supplies: Soccer ball for each team.

The players on each team are numbered consecutively. The teams should be equal in numbers. A soccer ball is placed in a two-foot square in the center of each team circle. When the teacher calls a number, each opponent holding this number runs to the center of his circle and dribbles the ball out through the space just vacated, around the circle, and back through the opening to the center area, where he finishes by placing his foot on the ball while it is in the small square. As soon as the winner is determined, he returns to his place and another number is called. One point is scored for the winner.

Teaching Suggestions: The game should be played with not over ten children on each team. It is better to have more teams with fewer children on each team. The teacher should stand where he can see the finishing order of teams. The players could be seated in the circle, and the player whose number is called arises and competes. If the players are seated, there is less tendency to make the circle smaller. The game is over when all numbers have been called.

Variation: If as many as four teams are competing against each other, scoring can be on the basis of 3 points for first, 2 for second, and 1 for third.

LINE SOCCER

Formation: Two goal lines about 50' to 80' apart with sidelines 40' to 60' wide.

Players: 10 to 20 on each team.

Supplies: Soccer ball.

LINE SOCCER

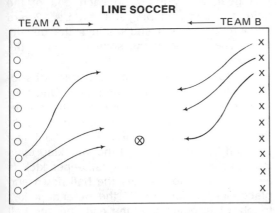

TEAM A ——→   ←—— TEAM B

Each team stands on one goal line which it is to defend. The referee stands in the center of the field holding a ball. At the whistle, two players (more if the teams are large) from the right side of each line of players run to the center and become the active players. The referee drops the ball to the ground, and the players try to kick it through the other team defending the goal line. The players in the field may advance by kicking only. The line players act as goalies and are permitted to catch the ball. The ball must be laid down immediately and either rolled or kicked. It cannot be punted or drop kicked.

Scoring: One point is scored when the ball is kicked through the opponent's goal below shoulder level. One point is also scored in case of a personal foul involving pushing, kicking, tripping, etc.

Penalties: For illegal touching by the active players, a direct free kick from a point 12 yards in front of the penalized team's goal line is given. All active players on the kicking team, except the kicker, must be to one side until the ball is kicked.

Time Limit: A time limit should be set of 2 minutes for any set of players. If no goal is scored during this time, a halt is called and players are changed.

Out of Bounds: The ball is awarded to the opponents of the team last touching it out-of-bounds. A throw in from the side line is in

order. If the ball goes over the shoulders of the defenders at the end line, any end line player may retrieve the ball and put it in play with a throw or kick.

Teaching Suggestions: *Line Soccer* should be played with the rules of soccer where possible. If boys and girls are together, girls should compete only against girls as active players. Arrange the rotation so this occurs.

Variations:

1. If there is enough space, the teams can be divided into fourths (1s, 2s, 3s, and 4s). They need not keep any particular order at the end lines but simply come out as active players when called. By the use of numbers, the teacher can put different groups against each other.

2. An offside line can be used. This is a line parallel to the goal line and 5' from the line. No offensive player can cross the offside line. The object is to keep the charging players away from the defensive line.

3. A regular goal can count two points while a goal from a direct free kick can count only one.

4. Instead of giving a score for a personal foul a penalty kick can be awarded. For illegal touching, a free kick can be awarded.

THREE LINE SOCCER

Formation: Soccer field 80' to 120' long, 60' to 100' wide. A center line bisects the field.

Number: 15 to 20 on each team.

Supplies: Soccer ball.

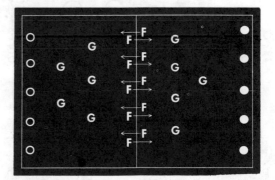

This game follows the same general rules as *Line Soccer*. Each team is divided into three equal groups who line up as Forwards, Guards, and Goalies. Whenever a point is scored or the time is called, the teams rotate positions.

The forwards stand at the center line for the kickoff and then for play move into the forward (for them) portion of the field. The guards are scattered in the back half of the field, and the goalies are on the goal line. Thus forwards compete against guards of the other team, while the goalies guard the goal.

The goalies may use their hands to defend their goal, but the other players follow regular soccer player rules.

The game is started with a kickoff at the center with all players on side. After each score, the team that did not score gets to kick off.

Penalties:

Free Kick — For illegal touch and from the spot of the foul.

Direct Free Kick — Personal foul by a team in its front court.

Penalty Kick — Personal foul by a team in its back court (defense). The ball is placed 12 yards from the goal line and only the goalies may defend.

MODIFIED SOCCER (Seven-Player Game)

Formation: Any large area 100' by 150'.

Players: 7 on each team.

Supplies: Soccer pinnies or colors to mark teams.

SEVEN-PLAYER SOCCER

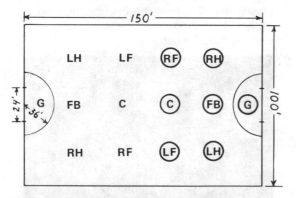

This should be the basic game for soccer play in elementary schools. It provides much more activity than the eleven-man game, where there can be considerable lack of activity when the ball is at the other end of the field.

In a physical education class, the teacher should plan one game for the girls and one

for the boys. This occupies a total of 28 children and is convenient for class instruction, provided the balance of boys and girls permits this. If not, the numbers can be reduced and the field size should be smaller.

A goal, 24' wide, is on each end of the field, marked by jumping standards. A 12-yard semicircle on each end outlines the penalty area. The center of the semicircle is at the center of the goal.

The game follows the general rules of soccer with one goalie for each side. One new feature needs to be introduced, the corner kick. This occurs when the ball goes over the end line but not through the goal last touched by the defense. If the attacking team last touched the ball, the goalkeeper kick is awarded. The goalie puts the ball down and place-kicks it forward. If the defenders last touch a ball going over the end line, the ball is taken to the nearest corner for a corner kick. This is a direct free kick, and a goal can be scored from the kick.

Most soccer rules, previously outlined, apply to this version of the game.

The forwards play in the front half of the field, and the guards are in the back half. However, neither are restricted to these areas entirely but may cross the center line without penalty.

A foul by the defense within its penalty area (semicircle) results in a penalty kick, taken from a point on the semicircle directly in front of the goal. Only the goalie is allowed to defend. The ball is in play, with the others waiting outside the penalty area.

The players are designated as center forward, outside right, outside left, right halfback, left halfback, fullback, and goalie. Position play should be emphasized.

Variation: Five-Player Soccer. The game can be played with five on a side, each team having a goalie, two forwards, and two guards. The area for play should be smaller.

Sixth Grade

MODIFIED SOCCER
(Seven-Player Soccer)

This game, introduced in the fifth grade, should be an important part of the sixth grade program.

ZONE SOCCER (Coed)

Playing Area: Soccer field 100' to 150' long, 90' to 120' wide.

Players: Two teams of 8 to a side (4 boys and 4 girls).

Supplies: Soccer ball.

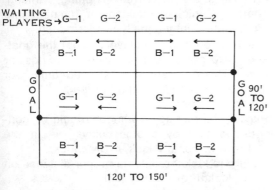

CODE: TEAM 1: BOYS, B—1; GIRLS, G—1
       TEAM 2: BOYS, B—2; GIRLS, G—2

The field is divided into six zones as illustrated, with a pair of players (one from each team), occupying each zone. At the side of the field (at the top of the diagram) extra players await turn to rotate on to the field. The occupants of any one zone are either both boys or both girls. Players must play a ball only in their zone or on a line bordering the zone. This allows for mixed participation, but boys compete against boys and girls against girls. Also, the size of the teams means that two separate games can be organized in a normal class situation utilizing 32 or more students. The game proceeds as in soccer with the following exceptions:

1. There is no goalkeeper. No players may use the arms and hands to stop or handle the ball.

2. The ball to score must go through the goal at shoulder height or below. Each goal from the field scores 2 points.

3. In addition to the other fouls normally called in soccer, a free kick is declared if a player kicks or interferes with a ball not in his zone. A goal may be scored from such a kick. A score resulting *directly* from a free kick counts 1 point. On a free kick, the defensive players in the zone where the ball is kicked must be back at least 15'. Any foul closer than 15' to the goal results in moving the ball out 15' in front of the goal with the defender positioned on the goal line.

4. Balls which go outside on the sidelines are placed in play by a throw-in by the opposite team at the point where the ball went out.

5. Balls which go over the end line, except for a deliberate kick by the defense, are put in play by a free kick by the defense 5' in front of the goal line at the point where the ball crossed the goal line. A deliberate kick over its goal line by the defense results in a free kick 15' directly in front of the goal by an offensive player.

6. Players rotate after every score or at the end of a fixed time period. A system of rotation is set up so that the sidelined players move into the adjacent zone. The players on the far side after rotating off the field go around to take the place of the original sidelined players who have just moved into the adjacent zone.

7. After a score, the ball is put in play just back of the center line by the team which did not score. A team cannot score *directly* from this kick. The ball must be passed to another player before a score can result.

REGULATION SOCCER

Players: 11 on each side, including 5 forwards, 3 halfbacks, 2 fullbacks, and 1 goalkeeper.

SOCCER FIELD

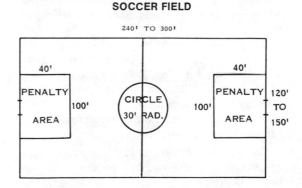

The Field:

Duties of Players:

Forwards — Advance the ball into scoring territory and attempt to score.

Halfbacks — Work both as offense and defense. Must do a great deal of running. Must back up both offense and defense.

Fullbacks — Primarily defense. Must be skilled in defensive movements.

Goalkeeper — The last line of defense. Must be agile and skillful in blocking the ball. May use hands on defense within own penalty area.

The Kickoff: On the toss of the coin, the winner gets the choice of kicking off or selecting his goal. The loser exercises the option not selected by the winner.

The ball must travel forward about 1 yard by the kicker, and he cannot touch it again until another player has kicked it. The defensive team must be 10 yards away from the kicker. After each score, the team not winning the point gets to kickoff. Both teams must be onside at the kickoff. The defensive team must stay onside and out of the center circle until the ball is kicked.

Scoring: Regular soccer rules call for scoring by counting the number of goals made.

Playing Time: Elementary school children should play not more than six-minute quarters. There should be a rest period of one minute between periods and ten minutes between halves.

Out of Bounds: When the ball goes out-of-bounds on the sides, it is put in play with a throw-in from the spot where it crossed the line. No goal may be scored nor may the thrower play the ball a second time until it has been touched by another player. All opponents are to be 10 yards back at the time of the throw.

If the ball is caused to go out-of-bounds on the end line by the attacking team, a goal kick is awarded. The ball is placed in the goal area and kicked beyond the penalty area by a defending player. He may not touch it twice in succession, and all defensive players are to be 10 yards back.

Corner Kick: If the ball is caused to go out-of-bounds over the end line by the defensive team, a corner kick shall be awarded. The ball shall be placed one yard from the corner of the field and kicked into the field of play by an attacking player. The 10 yard restriction also applies here to the defensive player.

Dropped Ball: If the ball is touched by two opponents at the same time and caused to go out-of-bounds, a drop ball shall be called.

The referee drops the ball between two opponents, who cannot kick the ball before it touches the ground. A drop ball is also called when the ball is trapped among downed players.

Fouls: Personal fouls involving unnecessary roughness are penalized. Tripping, striking, charging, holding, pushing, or jumping into an opponent intentionally are forbidden.

It is a foul for any player except the goalkeeper to handle the ball with the hands, or arms. The goalkeeper is allowed only four steps and must then get rid of the ball.

Other fouls are:

Playing the ball again when it should be contacted first by another player as in the throw-in, penalty kick, or free kick.

Failure to kick the ball the proper distance on the kickoff or penalty kick.

Goalkeeper carrying the ball more than four steps.

Kicking the ball before it hits the ground on an official drop ball.

Penalties: A penalty kick is awarded if a personal foul is committed by the defense within its own penalty area. The ball is placed 12 yards from the goal, and only the goalkeeper can be in the penalty area.

A direct free kick is awarded at the spot for a personal foul and illegal touching. This kick may score a goal.

A free kick is awarded for the other infractions listed. Another player must play the ball after the free kick in order that a goal can be scored.

Teaching Suggestions: Players should be taught to play their positions, staying on their side of the field.

Teams should wear pinnies or shirts so that the teams can be distinguished.

Teams should attempt to develop control and accuracy. The ball is better advanced by passing rather than by long kicking.

The lines should be spread to avoid crowding.

Halfbacks should take most free kicks so the forwards can be in position.

Eyeglass protectors must be worn by those with glasses.

After some skill has been acquired, the offside rule may be applied.

MODIFIED SPEEDBALL

Speedball combines the techniques of soccer and basketball. The ball may be advanced as in soccer or by passing as in basketball. Rule departures from the game of soccer are:

1. Any player may catch a kicked ball *before* it touches the ground. The ball can be advanced by passing as in basketball. As soon as the ball touches the ground, the play is as in soccer, until another kicked ball is caught in the air. A ball which bounces from the ground, even though it is in the air, cannot be caught. It is a ground ball and must be played as such.

2. A player catching the ball is allowed only two steps, or traveling is called, giving the other team the ball outside. Jump ball may be called as in basketball when the ball is tied up with two opposing players.

3. Fouls follow the same pattern as in soccer. The penalty area in speedball is a line 10 yards out from the goal line.

4. One air dribble is allowed in advancing the ball. To make an air dribble, a player throws the ball into the air ahead of himself, runs forward, and catches the ball before it hits the ground. Dribbling the ball by bouncing, as in basketball, is not permitted.

5. For violations for traveling and illegal handling of the ball, the other team is awarded the ball out of bounds for a throw-in.

Scoring:

Goal — a ball kicked through the goal as in soccer scores 2 points.

Touchdown — a ball passed over the goal line caught by a teammate scores 1 point.

TESTS FOR SOCCER SKILLS

The tests for soccer skills cover various kinds of kicks, dribbling, and trapping.

Dribbling — Figure Eight. Three obstacles or markers are arranged in line, 4 yards apart with the first positioned 4 yards from the starting line. The starting line is 4 yards wide. A stopwatch is used, and the timing is done to the nearest tenth of a second.

Three trials are given each player, with the fastest trial taken as the score. On each trial, the contestant dribbles over the figure-eight course and finishes by kicking or dribbling the ball over the 4-yard finish line, at which time the watch is stopped.

The test is best done on a grass surface, but if a hard surface must be used, the ball should be deflated somewhat so that it can be controlled.

Trapping. The formation is a file plus one. The one in front of the file is the thrower. The thrower stands 15' to 20' in front of the file and rolls the ball on the ground to the player at the head of the file. Three trials each for the toe trap, foot trap, and knee trap are given. The ball must be definitely stopped and controlled. A score of 9 points is possible, one point awarded for each successful trap.

The thrower should adopt one type of throw which is to be used for all traps and all players. If the scorer judges that the roll wasn't a proper opportunity, the trial is taken over. For the fourth grade, the only trap taught is the toe trap. Five trials can be allowed.

Soccer Punt for Distance. A football or other field, marked in gridiron fashion at 5 or 10 yard intervals, is needed. One soccer ball is needed, but if three can be used, considerable time is saved. A measuring tape (25' or 50') plus individual markers round out the supply list.

Each player is given three kicks from behind a restraining line over which he cannot cross during the kicks. One child marks the kick for distance while one or two other children act as ball chasers.

After the three kicks, the player's marker is left at the spot of his longest kick. This is determined by the point where the ball *first touches* after the kick. Measurement is taken to the nearest foot.

The squad or small group should all kick before the measurements are taken. The punt must be from a standing, not running, start.

If a child crosses the line during the kick, it is ruled a foul and counts as a trial. No measurement is taken.

Soccer Place Kick for Distance. The directions are the same for this test as for the punt for distance with two exceptions. The ball is kicked from a stationary position. It must be laid on a flat surface and not elevated by dirt, grass, or other means.

The second difference is that the child is

given credit for the entire distance of the kick including the roll. The kicking should be done to a grassy surface as the ball will roll indefinitely on a smooth, hard surface. If the surface presents a problem, the test can be limited to the distance the ball has traveled in flight.

Penalty Kick. The child faces a target area from behind a point 10 yards out where the ball has been placed. The child stands behind the ball.

The target area is formed by a rope

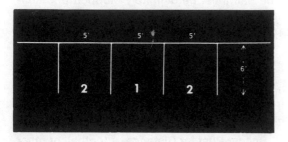

stretched tight so it will be 6' above the ground. Four ropes are dropped from this at distances 5' apart. This outlines three target areas 6' high and 5' wide. The center target area scores 1 point and the side areas 2. This is in keeping with the principle that a penalty kick should be directed away from a goalkeeper toward either corner of the goal.

Each child is allotted 5 kicks at the target. A score of 10 points is possible.

Accuracy Kick. The same target is used for this kick as for the penalty kick. However, the center area scores 2 points and the side areas 1 each. A balk line is drawn about 20' from the target. The child is back another 20' for a start. He dribbles the ball forward and must kick the ball as it is moving but before it crosses the balk line. Five trials are given and a score of 10 points is possible.

Variation: The test can also be used with a stationary kick (placekick). The kicking distance would depend upon the capacities of the group.

27

Softball

The major emphasis in softball should be on instruction and lead-up games. Children have adequate opportunity during recess, noon-hour, and other times to play the regular game. In the physical education class, too much of the softball participation is of the "choose-sides-and-let-'em-go" variety. Since youngsters are eager for and love softball, a good instruction program should make use of this drive. Softball instruction should begin in the third grade and progress through the sixth. By the time the children are in the fifth grade, they should be playing regular softball, modified for their level.

Since softball experiences vary so much, it is difficult to allocate with sureness the various skills and knowledges for a progressive program. The third grade program is outlined because it is felt that planned instruction in the game should begin on this level. It is recognized that second graders should throw and catch with softballs along with other types of balls.

EMPHASIS ON DIFFERENT GRADE LEVELS

Third Grade

Teaching the basic skills of throwing, catching, and batting is the emphasis on the third grade level. The lead-up games for the third grade are simple but provide an introduction to the game of softball. There is very little

emphasis on the pitcher and catcher. A few basic rules of the game are learned.

Fourth Grade

In the fourth grade, specific skills of pitching, infield play, base running, and batting provide the material for this portion. Proper pitching techniques in keeping with the pitching rules are important to the budding softball player.

Fifth Grade

The fifth grade student should be provided with the background to play the game of regulation softball designed for his age level. The material for instruction is pointed toward this end. An expansion of the fourth grade program is emphasized, with additional techniques useful in the regular game of softball added.

Sixth Grade

The sixth grade program adds *Tee Ball*, new pitching techniques, and double play work. Batting, throwing, catching, and infield skills are continued.

PRACTICAL SUGGESTIONS

1. Safety is of utmost importance. The following precautions should be observed.
   a. Throwing the bat is a constant danger. The members of the batting team should stand on the side opposite the batter. For a righthanded batter, the batting team

441

members should be on the first base side, and vice versa.

b. To control the batter in keeping him from throwing the bat:

(1) Have the batter touch the bat to the ground before dropping it.

GRADE	THIRD	FOURTH	FIFTH	SIXTH
Skills Throwing	Gripping the ball Overhand throw Underhand toss	Continued practice Around the bases	Throw-in from outfield Side arm throw	Continued practice

Catching
  and
Fielding
	Catching thrown
	  balls
	Catching fly balls
	Grounders
		Continued practice
		Fielding grounders
		  in infield
		Sure stop for
		  outfield
			Catching flies from
			  fungo batting
			Infield practice
				Flies and infield
				  practice

Batting	Simple skills	Fungo hitting Continued practice	Different positions at plate	Tee batting Bunting

Fielding
  positions
		Infield practice
		How to catch
			Infield positions
			Backing up other
			  players
				Double play

Base
  running
	To first base	To first base and
		  turning
		Circling the base
			Getting a good
			  start off base
			Tagging up on
			  fly ball
				Sacrifice

Pitching	Simple underhand	Application of
		  pitching rule
			Target pitching	Curve, drop,
				  slow pitches

Coaching			Coaching at bases	

Knowledges
Rules
	Strike Zone
	Foul and Fair ball
	Safe and out
		Foul Tip
		Bunt Rule
		When the batter is
		  safe or out
			Pitching Rule
			  Position
			  Illegal Pitches
			Infield Fly
			Keeping Score
			Base Running
				Review all rules
				Situation type quiz

Activities	Throw It and Run Two Pitch Softball	Two Pitch Softball (from 3rd grade) Hit and Run Kick Softball Hit the Bat	Five Hundred Batter Ball Home Run Kick Pin Softball Scrub (Work-up)	Tee Ball Twice Around Far Base Softball Hurry Baseball Three Team Softball Base Circling Contest
Tests	None	Target Throw Throw for distance	Old Woody (Strike Target) Throw for distance Circling the bases	Tee Batting Old Woody Throw for distance Circling the bases Fielding Grounders

(2) Call the batter "out" if he throws the bat.

(3) Have the batter carry the bat to first base.

(4) Have the batter change ends with the bat before dropping it.

(5) Have the batter place the bat in a 3' circle before running.

c. Sliding leads to both injury and destruction of clothing. No sliding should be permitted. Runner should be called out.

d. If a catcher stands close behind the plate while catching, he must wear a mask.

e. Colliding while running for the ball can be held to a minimum if players are taught to call for the ball and not to trespass on other players' areas.

2. Care of equipment is a responsibility of

all. The trademark of the bat should be kept up when contacting the ball in the middle of the swing. The bat should be used to bat softballs only. Hitting rocks and sticks with the bat injures the bat and lessens its effectiveness and life. The bat should be carried, not thrown, from one person to another.

3. The spoiler of many games of the softball type is the pitcher-batter duel. If this is prolonged with few hits by the batter, the remainder of the players justifiably become bored from standing around. Having a member of the batting team pitch is one method of eliminating the problem.

4. Players should rotate positions often. A good rule in physical education classes is that everyone, including the pitcher, should rotate to another position at the start of a new inning.

5. The distance between the bases has a heavy effect on the game. The distance should be lessened or increased according to the game and the capacities of the children.

6. Umpires can be appointed or the team at bat can umpire. A rule that can be followed is that the person who made the last out of the previous inning is the umpire for the coming inning. There should be instruction for all in umpiring. To expect a child to umpire properly without proper instruction is poor teaching.

7. Encourage good players to recognize and give approval to those who are less skillful. Since there are many differences in ability, an opportunity for a lesson in tolerance is present. It is important not to let an error become a tragedy to a child.

8. Each player should run out his hit, no matter how hopeless it seems.

9. Analyze each of the lead-up games for its purpose and practice the needed skills before their inclusion in the game.

10. Insist on conformance to the rules. Copies of the *Official Guide for Softball* should be available in the classroom.

11. Children must recognize that perfection in softball skills comes only through good practice sessions.

12. Teach respect for officials and acceptance of the umpire's judgment. The disreputable practice of baiting the umpire should be no part of the child's softball experiences.

BASIC RULES FOR SOFTBALL THIRD AND FOURTH GRADES

For the few lead-up games and as an introduction to softball, it is necessary to establish certain selected rules for use in the third grade. The following provides a minimum.

1. The nine players on a softball team are the catcher, pitcher, first baseman, second baseman, shortstop, third baseman, left fielder, center fielder, and right fielder. The right fielder is the outfielder nearest first base.

2. All pitching is underhand.

3. A pitch to be called a strike must be over the plate and between the knees and shoulders of the batter. A ball is a pitch which does not go through this area.

4. A foul ball is a batted ball that settles outside the foul lines between home and first or home and third. A ball that rolls over a base is a fair ball. Also, any fly ball that lands in foul territory is a foul ball.

5. No lead-off from any base is permitted in softball. The runner must keep his foot on the base until the pitcher releases the ball.

6. The batter is out if a fly ball, either foul or fair, is caught.

7. The batter is safe if he reaches first base before the fielding team can get the ball to the first baseman with the foot on the base.

8. A batter is out if he misses the ball three times. This is called striking out.

9. A run is scored if the baserunner makes the circuit of bases (first, second, third, and home) before the batting team has three outs.

BASIC RULES FOR SOFTBALL FIFTH AND SIXTH GRADES

Most sporting goods establishments have copies of the official rules available. An official rule guide should be used for rules study. However, the following represent some of the basic rules for the game. The rules listed in the section immediately preceding should be reviewed.

Playing Area. The official diamond has 60' base lines and a pitching distance of 46'. Play in the intermediate grades should be with base lines not over 45' and a pitching distance of 35' or less.

Number of Players. Nine players make up a team.

Batting Order. Players may bat in any order, although at times it is convenient in class play to have them bat according to their positions in the field. Once the batting order has been established, it may not be changed even if the player changes to another position in the field.

Pitching Rules. The pitcher must observe the following:

1. Face the batter with both feet on the pitching rubber with the ball held in front with both hands.

2. The pitcher is allowed one step toward the batter and must deliver the ball while taking that step.

3. The ball must be pitched underhanded.

4. He cannot fake a pitch nor make any motion toward the plate without delivering the ball.

5. He cannot roll or bounce the ball to the batter to keep him from hitting it.

6. No quick return before the batter is ready is allowed.

Batting. The bat must be a softball bat. The batter cannot cross to the other side of the plate when the pitcher is ready to pitch. If a player bats out of turn, he is out. A bunt foul on the third strike is out. A pitched ball that touches or hits the batter entitles the batter to first base, provided he does not strike or bunt at the ball.

Base Running. No lead-off is permitted. The runner must hold his base until the ball leaves the pitcher's hands on the penalty of being called out. On an overthrow where the ball goes into foul territory *and* out of play, runners advance one base beyond the base to which they were headed at the time of the overthrow. On an overthrow at second base by the catcher with the ball rolling into center field, the runners may advance as far as they can. To avoid being tagged on a base line, the runner is limited to a 3' distance on either side of a direct line from base to base. A runner hit by a batted ball while *off* the base is out. The batter, however, is entitled to first base. Base runners must touch all bases. If a runner fails to touch a base, it is an appeal play, which means that the fielding team must call the

oversight to the attention of the umpire, who will then (and not before) rule on the play.

Fly Ball. Any fly ball, foul or fair, when caught is out. A foul fly, however, must be over the head of the batter or it is ruled as a foul tip. A foul tip caught counts as a strike, and the ball is in play. A foul tip, then, caught on the third strike makes the batter out.

SOFTBALL SKILLS FOR THE THIRD GRADE

Overhand Throwing. The ball is held with two fingers on top, third and fourth fingers on one side, and the thumb on the other. The hand is brought back so the hand is well behind the shoulder at about that height. The left side of the body is turned in the direction of the throw, and the left arm is raised and in front of the body. The weight is on the back (right) foot with the left foot advanced with the toe touching the ground. The arm comes forward, and the ball is thrown with a downward snap of the wrist. The weight of the body is brought forward into the throw, with the weight shifting to the front foot. There should be good follow-through.

Underhand Toss. The hand and arm are brought back with the palms facing forward in a pendulum swing. The elbow is held slightly bent. The weight is mostly on the back foot. The arm comes forward almost like a bowling motion, and the ball is tossed. The weight shifts to the front foot during the toss.

Pitching. Stand with both feet facing the batter, and the ball held in front. As the ball is brought back for the toss the forward step of the left foot begins. When the toss is made, the weight is shifted to the forward (left) foot.

Catching Fly Balls. There are two methods for catching a fly ball.

1. For a low ball, the fielder keeps his little fingers together and forms a basket with his hands.

2. For a higher ball, the thumbs are together, and the ball is caught just in front of the chin.

There should be "give" with the catching hands. Care should be taken with a spinning ball to provide sufficient squeeze of the hands to stop the spinning.

Fielding Grounders. Always play the ball, don't let the ball play you. Advance on the ball. Try to catch it on a high hop or just as it hits the ground. Feet should be well apart and the eyes on the ball.

The little fingers are together and the hands are lower with a stooping motion rather than being bent over. For right handers, the left foot should be slightly ahead.

Batting (Right Handed). Stand with the left side of the body toward the pitcher with the feet spread and the weight on both feet. The body should be facing the plate. Hold the bat with the trade mark up so that the left hand (for right-handed batters) grasps the bat lower than the right. The bat is held over the right shoulder pointing both back and up. The elbows are away from the body for free swinging.

The swing begins with a hip roll and a short step forward in the direction of the pitcher. The bat is now swung level with the ground at the height of the pitch. Eyes are kept on the ball until it is hit. After the hit, there is good follow-through.

Beginning batters should use the choke grip, which is to hold the bat several inches above the small end of the bat.

Base Running. Children should be taught to run directly toward first base and run to a spot past the base. Too often, they run to first base, stop, and put a foot on it.

SOFTBALL SKILLS FOR THE FOURTH TO SIXTH GRADES

Throwing and catching should be continued from the third grade instruction. Additional points to be emphasized are:

Throwing and Catching. Step toward the target and follow through well. Begin at short range and increase distances. Practice getting the ball away quickly.

Add the sidearm throw, which is used for short distances and when there is need to throw quickly. The ball is thrown from the hand at shoulder level with a bent elbow and quick snap of the wrist.

In catching, stress relaxation and giving with the ball. Players should keep the eyes on the ball and move quickly in position in front of the path of ball. Getting the ball away fast after a catch should be emphasized.

In fielding grounders, the body should be crouched with the hands about 6" above the ground. The hands can be lowered or raised depending on the path of the ball.

Infield Practice. Infield practice should be held frequently, from the simple throwing around the bases to a full fledged practice.

Batting. Youngsters should have experience with different grips on the bat — the end, choke, and modified grips. Stress a light grip on the bat, as this relaxes the forearm muscles. The bat should be held back but not on the shoulder. The arms are away from the body. As the ball is delivered, the batter takes a short, low step forward. The hit is made with a free, full, level swing and follow-through.

Points the batter should avoid are:
Lifting the front foot high off the ground.
Stepping back with the rear foot.
Dropping the rear shoulder.
Chopping down on the ball or golfing.
Dropping the elbows.
Crouching or bending forward.
Failing to keep eyes on the ball.

Bunting. The child turns almost facing the pitcher, with his right foot alongside the home plate. As the pitcher releases the ball, the upper hand is run about halfway up the bat. Hold the bat loosely in front of the body and parallel to the ground. Just meet the ball. The ball can be directed down either first or third base lines.

The surprise or drag bunt is done without the squaring around or facing the pitcher. Hold the bat in a choke grip, and, when the pitcher lets go of the ball, run the right hand up on the bat. Direct the ball down either foul line, keeping it inside as near the line as possible.

Sure Stop for Outfield Balls. To keep the ball from going through an outfielder and allowing extra bases, a type of stop can be used which uses the body as a barrier in case the ball is missed by the hands. The fielder turns half right and lowers the left knee to the ground at the point where the ball is coming. The hands attempt to catch the rolling ball, but if missed, the body will generally stop the ball.

Baserunning. Since in softball the runner must hold the base until the pitcher releases the ball, the children should be shown a type of leaning sprint start with the left foot on the bag and the right toes digging in for a start. In running to bases, the children should run at the base and avoid circling.

Pitching. The pitcher should assume his position with both feet on the rubber and facing the batter. The ball is held with both hands in front of the body. As the arm comes forward, the child steps with his left foot. Additional speed can be had from a good stretch to rear before the throw. However, the goal at this stage is accuracy. Good follow-through and wrist action are important.

Fielding Positions. In the infield, children should be off the bases in proper fielding positions. Shifts for both the infield and outfield should be made on right- and left-handed hitters. Players should be taught to straddle the bag when receiving the ball for a tag play.

DRILLS FOR SOFTBALL SKILLS

Softball Throwing and Catching Drills

Many drills can be utilized for throwing and catching softballs. The ball can be thrown from one player to another in various formations, using normal throwing, pitching, rolling grounders, or throwing fly balls. Leader and class formations have particular value. Groups should be kept small so children will get many turns. For a normal size class, at least four softballs are needed for most drills.

The following formations are suggested.

1. Two line — 3 to 4 children in each line.

2. Around the Bases — 4 to 8. Establish a diamond using the normal base distance for the children. Throw around and across the bases. If more than one child is at a base, they take turns.

3. Shuttle turn back — 4 to 8. Each child after his turn goes to the back of the file.

4. Leader and line or semicircle — 5 to 8. The leader completes a round of the specified throwing skill and then rotates by going to the end of the line to his left (facing the others). A child from the other end of the line comes forward, and the children all move over one place.

If sufficient space is a problem, the leader and file formation can be used. Also, the lead-er may have a base in his spot to provide a target for throwing or pitching.

Batting Drill. A batter, pitcher, and catcher are in position with the remainder of the players scattered in the field. Each player is allowed a certain number of swings. The pitcher should serve the type of pitch that can be hit easily. The catcher stands back from his regular position and retrieves the balls which are missed by the batter. Not over 10 players should be in any one drill.

An order of rotation will assure each player his turn. Players can be numbered and take turns in that order.

Bunting can also be practiced with a formation of this type. However, only one or two fielders are needed for a bunting drill.

Infield Drill. The children are placed in the normal infield positions of catcher, first, second, third, and shortstop. One child acts as batter and gives directions. The play should begin with practice of throwing around the bases either way. After this, the "batter" rolls the ball to the different infielders beginning with the third baseman and continuing in turn around the infield, with each throwing to first to retire an imaginary batter-runner. Various play situations can be developed.

If the batter is skillful enough, he can hit the ball to the infielders instead of rolling the ball, making a more realistic drill. If a second softball is available, time is saved when the ball is thrown or batted past an infielder.

Pitching Drill. Groups of five or six children can practice pitching skills in these formations.

1. Semicircle and leader. The leader stands behind a base and acts as the catcher for the other children who stand in a semicircle facing him and stationed the pitching distance (35') away. Each in turn pitches to the leader.

2. Pitching, catching, umpiring. The three skills are combined into a drill, which can be done with a minimum of four players. A pitcher is in position in front of a home plate at regular pitching distance. Another player stands as the batter but does not strike at the ball. A catcher is behind the plate and an umpire behind him. Extra players line up behind the pitcher to take turns.

The pitcher should observe all legal restrictions for his position. The pitcher should pitch to a defined number of "batters," or be given a set number of pitches. The umpire observes good practice in his position and calls the balls and strikes.

Group Drill. Organization by groups is excellent for working in softball skills. Generally, four to six groups are used. Even then, there can be two units at any one station. Selected players can be in charge of each of the groups. The work formats for the groups must be specified. Here is an example of how this works:

Station 1. Batting and fielding.

Station 2. Bunting and running to first.

Station 3. Fielding grounders and throwing to first.

Station 4. Catching fly balls and relaying to the plate.

Rotation can be on signal. Enough time should be allocated at each station to accomplish the purpose of the drill. It may be that only a partial rotation will be accomplished during the first lesson and completed during the second.

ACTIVITIES

Third Grade

THROW IT AND RUN SOFTBALL

Playing Area: Softball diamond reduced in size.

Players: Two teams of 7 to 11 each. Usually 9 players are on a side.

Supplies: Softball or similar ball.

The game is played very much like softball with the following exception. With one team in the field at regular positions, the pitcher throws the ball to the "batter" who, instead of batting the ball, catches it, and immediately throws it out into the field. The ball is now treated as a batted ball, and regular softball rules prevail. However, no stealing is permitted, and the runners must hold bases until the batter throws the ball. A foul ball is out.

Variations:

1. **Under-Leg Throw.** Instead of having the batter throw directly, have him turn to the right, lift his left leg, and throw the ball under the leg into the playing field.

2. **Beat-Ball Throw.** The fielders, instead of playing regular softball rules, throw the ball

directly home to the catcher. The batter, in the meantime, runs around the bases. He gets one point for each base he touches before the catcher gets the ball and calls out, "Stop." There are no outs, and each batter gets a turn before changing sides to the field. A fly ball caught would mean no score. Similarly, a foul ball would score no points but would count as a turn at bat.

TWO-PITCH SOFTBALL

Playing Area: Softball diamond.

Players: Regular softball teams but the numbers can vary.

Supplies: Softball, bat.

This introductory game is played like regular softball with the following changes:

1. A member of the team at bat is the pitcher. Some system of rotation should be set up so every child takes a turn as pitcher.

2. The batter has only two pitches in which to hit the ball. He must hit a fair ball on either of these pitches or he is out. He can foul the first ball, but if he fouls the second he is out. There is no need to call balls or strikes.

3. The pitcher, because he is a member of the team at bat, does not field the ball. A member of the team at field acts as the fielding pitcher.

4. If the batter hits the ball, regular softball rules are followed. However, no stealing is permitted.

Variation: Three Strikes

In this game, the batter is allowed three pitches (strikes) to hit the ball. Otherwise, the game proceeds as in *Two-Pitch.*

Fourth Grade

TWO-PITCH SOFTBALL

Described in the third grade program, the game should be emphasized in the fourth grade also.

HIT AND RUN

Playing Area: Softball field, gymnasium.

Players: Two teams, 6-15 players on each team.

Supplies: Volleyball, soccer, or playground ball. Home plate and base marker.

One team is at bat and the other scattered out in the field. Out-of-bounds must be established, but the area does not need to be shaped like a baseball diamond. The batter stands at home plate with the ball. In front of him 12' away is a short line over which the ball must be hit to be in play. In the center of the field about 40' away is the base marker.

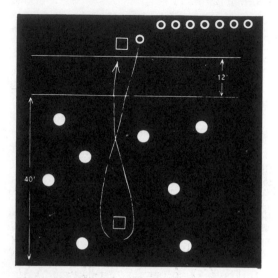

The batter bats the ball with his hands or fist so it crosses the short line and lights inside the area. He then attempts to run down the field, around the base marker, and back to home plate without being hit by the ball. The members of the other team field the ball and attempt to hit the runner. The fielder may not run or walk with the ball but may throw to a teammate closer to the runner.

A run is scored for each successful run around the marker and back to home plate without getting hit with the ball. A run is also scored if a foul is called on the fielding team for walking or running with the ball.

The batter is out if:

1. A fly ball is caught.

2. He is hit below the shoulders with the ball.

3. The ball is not hit beyond the short line.

4. The team touches home plate with the ball before the runner does. This may be used *only* when the runner stops in the field and does not continue.

The game can be played in innings of three outs each, or a change of team positions can be made after all from one team have batted.

Variations: Five Passes. The batter is out if:

1. A fly ball is caught.

2. The ball is passed among five different players of the team in the field with the last pass to a player at home plate, beating the runner to the plate. The passes must not touch the ground and must be among five different players.

Teaching Hint: The distance the batter runs around the base marker may have to be shortened or lengthened, depending upon the children's ability.

KICK SOFTBALL

Playing Area: Regular softball field with a home base 3' square.
Players: Regular softball teams but numbers can vary.
Supplies: Soccer or other ball to be kicked.

Batter stands in the kicking area three-foot square home plate. Batter kicks the ball rolled on the ground by the pitcher. The ball should be rolled only with moderate speed. An umpire calls balls and strikes. A strike is a ball which rolls over the three-foot square. A ball is one that rolls outside this area. Strikeouts and walks are called the same as in softball. The number of foul balls allowed should be limited. No base stealing is permitted.

Otherwise, the game is played as in softball.

Variations:

1. The batter kicks a stationary ball. This saves time as there is no pitching.

2. *Punch Ball.* Using a volleyball, the batter can hit a ball as in a volleyball serve, or he can punch a ball pitched by the pitcher. The latter sometimes causes some pain if the pitch is too hard.

HIT THE BAT

Playing Area: Open field for fungo batting.
Players: 3-10 children.
Supplies: Softball, bat.

Children, except the batter, are scattered in the field. The batter tosses the ball to himself and hits the ball to the fielders. The object of each fielder is to become the batter. The fielder becomes the batter if:

1. He catches three flies from the *present* batter.

2. He can hit the bat with the ball.

To become eligible to throw to the bat, the fielder must field the ball cleanly. The batter lays the bat down on the ground facing the throw so it presents the largest possible target.

If a fielder catches a fly ball, he gets ten steps toward the bat from where he caught the ball. If he catches the ball on first bounce, he gets five steps. He tries to hit the bat.

Variations:

1. If hitting the bat seems to be difficult, count a throw as successful when the ball goes directly over the bat.

2. Two balls caught on first bounce can count as one fly ball caught.

3. The batter is not put out if he can catch the ball on the fly after it rebounds from the bat after being hit by a rolling ball.

Fifth Grade

FIVE HUNDRED

Playing Area: Field big enough for fungo hitting.
Players: 3 to 12, although more can play.
Supplies: Softball, bat.

There are many versions of this old game. A batter stands on one side of the field and bats the ball out to a number of fielders who are scattered. The fielders attempt to become batter by reaching a score of 500. To do this, the fielder is granted points for the following:

Points

200 Catching a ball on the fly
100 Catching a ball on first bounce
 50 Fielding a grounder cleanly

Whenever a change of batters is made, all fielders lose their points and must start over.

Variations:

1. The fielder must total exactly 500.

2. Points are subtracted from the fielder's score if he fails to handle a ball properly. Thus, if he drops a fly ball, he loses 200 points. Similarly with the other scores.

BATTER BALL

Playing Area: Softball diamond lines as in diagram.
Players: Two teams, 8 to 12 on each.
Supplies: Softball, bat, mask.

Batter Ball involves batting and fielding but no base running. It is much like batting practice but adds the element of competition.

A line is drawn directly from first to third base. This is the balk line over which a batted ball must travel to be fielded.

Another line is drawn from a point on the foul line 3½' behind third base to a point 5' behind second base (in line with home plate). Another line connects this point with a point on the first base line 3½' behind that base. The shaded space is the infield area.

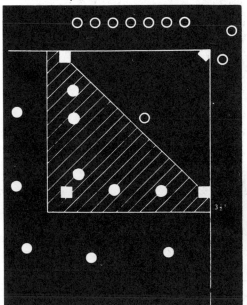

Each batter is given three pitches by a member of his own team to hit the ball into fair territory across the balk line. The pitcher may stop any ground ball he wishes before it crosses the balk line. The batter then gets another turn at bat.

Scoring:

1. Successful grounder — 1 point. The batter scores one point when an infielder fails to handle cleanly his grounder within the infield area. Only one player may field the ball. If the ball is fielded properly, the batter is out.

2. Line drive in infield area — 1 point. A ball from the bat which lands first in the infield area can be handled only on first bounce for an out. If it bounces in front of the balk line, it is classed as a grounder and can be handled on any bounce. Any line drive caught on the fly also is an out.

3. Fly ball in infield area — 1 point. Any fly ball in the infield area must be caught or the batter scores one point. The ball must be caught legally by the first person touching it.

4. Two-bagger — 2 points. Any fly ball, line drive or not, that lights fairly in the outfield area without being caught scores two points. If caught, the batter is out.

5. Home run — 3 points. Any fly ball driven over the heads of the farthest outfielder in that area scores a home run.

Three outs can constitute an inning, or all batters can be allowed one turn at bat and then change to the field.

A new set of infielders should be in place for each inning. The old set goes to the outfield. Pitchers should be limited to one inning. They take a turn at bat.

Teaching Suggestions: Many games of this type take special fields, either rectangular or a narrowed angle type. This game was selected because it uses the regular softball field with the added lines. The lines can be drawn with a stick or can be marked with regular marking.

The pitcher has to decide whether or not, he should stop the ball. If the ball goes beyond the restraining line, even though he touched it, the ball is in play.

HOME RUN

Playing Area: Softball diamond. First base only is used.
Players: 4-10.
Supplies: Softball, bat.

This game can be played with as few as four children. The needed players are a batter, catcher, pitcher, and one fielder. The other players are fielders, although some can take positions in the infield.

The batter hits a regular pitch, and on a fair ball must run to first base and back home before the ball can be returned to the catcher.

The batter is out when:

1. A fly ball, fair or foul, is caught.

2. He strikes out.

3. On a fair ball, the ball beats him back to home plate.

To keep skillful players from staying in too long at bat, a rule can be made that after a certain number of home runs, the batter automatically must take his place in the field.

A rotation (work-up) system should be set up. The batter should go to right field, move to center, and then to left field. The rotation continues through third baseman position, shortstop, second base, first base, pitcher, and catcher. The catcher becomes the next batter. Naturally the number of positions is dependent upon the number of players in the game.

If there are sufficient numbers, there can be an additional batter waiting to take his turn.

The game can actually be played with three youngsters, eliminating the catcher. With only one fielder, the pitcher covers home plate.

The first base distance should be far enough to be a challenge but close enough so a well-hit ball will score a home run. The distance would be dependent on the number playing and the capacity of the children.

Variations:

1. It is possible to play this game more like softball, allowing the batter to stop at first if another batter is up.

2. A fly ball caught by a player puts the fielder directly to bat. The batter then takes his place at the end of the rotation, and the other players rotate up to the position of the fielder who caught the ball. The rule may cause children to scramble and fight for fly balls, which is a situation not desired in softball. It should be ruled that the ball belongs to the player into whose territory it falls.

3. *Triangle Ball.* Another version of *Home Run* is *Triangle Ball.* For this game, first base and third base are brought in toward each other, narrowing the playing field. Second base is not used. Thus the game gets its name from the triangle formed by home plate and the two bases. The batter must circle first and third bases and return home before the ball reaches home plate. The game can also be played with as little as three players, with the pitcher covering home plate.

KICK PIN SOFTBALL

Playing Area: Softball diamond; 45-foot base distances; 20-foot pitching distance.
Players: Two teams, 8 to 12 on a side.

Catcher, pitcher, 3 basemen, and the rest fielders.

Supplies: 1 soccer ball, 4 Indian clubs.

The Indian clubs are placed on the outside corner of each base and in the middle of home plate. The batter kicks a ball rolled by the pitcher who aims at the Indian club on home plate. The kick must be a fair ball. The batter *circles around* the outside of the bases and finally touches home plate. In the meantime the fielders retrieve the ball and pass it successively to the basemen on first, second, third, and then home. As each baseman receives the ball, he kicks the club down and passes to the next base.

The batter is out when:

1. A pitched ball knocks down the club on home plate.

2. The ball is caught on the fly by a fielder.

3. The batter knocks over any club during his time at bat.

4. A second foul ball occurs any time at bat.

5. If the ball, in its rotation from first base to the other bases in succession, gets ahead of the runner, and the baseman kicks the club down.

The batter scores a run only on a home run, beating the ball to home plate.

The game can be played by innings with three outs, or it can be played so each player of the team at bat gets a turn before changing to the field.

Teaching Suggestions: Indian clubs stand with difficulty outside. A 3-inch square of plywood screwed to the bottom will make them stand easily.

Old bowling pins can generally be secured from the local bowling alley. The industrial arts department can aid in restoring a flat bottom for better standing.

The pitcher should use judgment in rolling the ball. The fun comes in the kick and the resultant run and not the duel between the batter and the pitcher. This can be controlled somewhat by the addition of a rule that if a certain number of balls (not hitting the club if the batters let the ball go by) are thrown, the batter gets a free kick. The kick would be a placekick with the ball placed just to the left of home plate where the batting box for the right-handed batter is located.

Variations:

1. *Hit Pin Softball* is about the same game except that instead of kicking the club, the club Is knocked over with the ball held in the hands.

2. Instead of counting home runs, a point can be given for each base rounded before the club is kicked by the baseman holding the ball. A home run scores four points under this counting system.

SCRUB (Work-Up)

Playing Area: Softball field.
Players: 7 to 15.
Supplies: Softball, bat.

The predominant feature of *Scrub* is the rotation of the players. The game is played with regular softball rules with each individual more or less playing for himself. There are at least two batters and generally three. A catcher, pitcher, and first baseman are essential. The remainder of the players assume the other positions. Whenever the batter is out, he goes to a position in right field. All other players move up one position with the catcher becoming a batter. Thus, the first baseman becomes pitcher, the pitcher moves to the catcher, and all others move up one place in a predetermined shift.

Variations:

1. If there are only two batters, then one base is sufficient. The runners use only first base and return back to home plate.

2. If a fly ball is caught, the fielder and batter exchange positions.

Sixth Grade

TEE BALL

Playing Area: Softball field.
Players: Two regular softball teams, but numbers can vary.
Supplies: Softball, bat, batting tee.

The game is an excellent variation of softball and is played under its rules with the following exceptions.

Instead of hitting a pitched ball, the batter hits the ball from a tee. The catcher places the ball on the tee. After the batter hits the ball, the play is the same as softball. With no pitching, there is no stealing. A runner stays on the base until the ball is hit by the batter.

A fielder occupies the position normally held by the pitcher. His primary duty is to field bunts and any ground balls he can reach, and to back up the positions in the field on throws as a pitcher would normally position himself.

Teams can play regular innings for three outs or change to the field after each player has had a turn at bat.

A tee can be purchased or made from radiator hose. If the tee is not adjustable, it would be better to have three different sizes available.

Tee Ball has many advantages. There are no strike-outs, every child hits the ball, there is no waiting for the pitcher-catcher duel, and there are many opportunities for fielding.

The batter should take his position far enough back of the tee so that in stepping forward to swing, the ball will be hit slightly in front of the batter.

TWICE AROUND

Playing Area: Softball infield.
Numbers: Two teams, 4 to 8 on each team.
Supplies: Softball.

Twice Around provides competition and practice for throwing around the bases and base running. It should be used only after instruction has been held in both skills.

One team is stationed in the field with at least one player near each base. As a minimum, a catcher and three basemen are needed in the field. The extra players in the field are assigned to bases so some bases, including home plate, will have two fielders. When two fielders are at a base, one takes the first throw and the other takes the second time around.

A player from the team at bat stands with one foot on home plate and ready to run to first base. His task is to make one complete circuit of the bases and tag home plate. The ball starts in the catcher's hands. At the signal "Go," he throws the ball to first base from where it is thrown to second, third, and then home. It continues for another round, which gives the game the name of "Twice Around."

The object of the game is to have the ball beat the batter back to home plate on its second round, with the batter making only one circuit.

The capacity of the children will determine the ideal base distance. The teacher should start with a 45-foot distance and then vary according to the level of the children to run, throw, and catch.

The fielders must not interfere with the runner and should stand back from the base unless catching the ball. Each fielder must throw with one foot on the base or touch the base while the ball is held in his hands. If the ball is missed at a base, it must go back to that base and be in touch before continuing.

If the batter is being put out continually, a delay in the throwing cycle can be put in by having the batter roll or throw the ball to a pitcher. The pitcher would then throw the ball to the catcher, and the twice around travel would then start.

FAR BASE SOFTBALL

Playing Area: Softball field with a far base. The far base is 3' by 6' and is located just to the first base side of second base.
Players: Regular softball teams but the number can vary.
Supplies: Softball and bat.

First and third bases are used only to determine foul balls. The batter hits the pitched ball and runs to the far base. He must reach the base before the ball or before he is tagged with the ball. He may stay there or try to return home. However, once he leaves the base, he cannot return except for a caught fly ball. Several runners may be on the far base as long as a batter is left. The batter remains at bat until he hits the ball. A limit should be placed on the number of fouls that can be hit.

Each team is allowed three outs. Outs are made by catching a fly ball, by striking out, by the ball getting to the far baseman before the runner, and by tagging the runner when off the base.

HURRY BASEBALL

Playing Area: Softball diamond. Shortened pitching distance.
Players: Two teams, 8 to 12 on each team.
Supplies: Softball, bat.

Hurry Baseball demands rapid changes from batting to fielding and vice versa. The game is like regular softball with the following exceptions:

1. The pitcher is from the team at bat. He must not interfere with or touch a batted ball on the penalty of the batter being called out.

2. The team coming to bat does not wait for the fielding team to get set. Since it has its own pitcher, the pitcher gets the ball to the batter just as quickly as the batter can grab a bat and get ready. The fielding team has to hustle to get out to their places.

3. Only one pitch is allowed to a batter. He must hit a fair ball or he is out. The pitch is made from about two-thirds of the normal pitching distance.

4. No stealing is permitted.

5. No bunting is permitted. The batter must take a full swing.

The game is good fun and provides fast activity in the fast changes that need to be made immediately when the third out has been made. Teams in the field will learn to put the next hitter as catcher, so he can immediately take his place in the batter's box when the third out is made. Batters must bat in order. Scoring follows regular softball rules.

THREE TEAM SOFTBALL

Playing Area: Softball diamond.
Players: 12 to 15, divided on 3 teams.
Supplies: Mask, ball, bat.

This version of softball works well with 12 players, a number considered too few to divide into two effective fielding teams. The players are divided into three teams. The rules of softball apply with the following exceptions.

1. One team is at bat, one team covers the infield (including the catcher), and the third team provides the outfielders and the pitcher.

2. The team at bat must bat in a definite order. This means that instances, due to the few batters on each side, could occur when the person due to bat is on a base. He must be replaced by a player not on base so he can take his turn at bat.

3. After three outs, the teams rotate, with the outfield moving to the infield, the infield taking a turn at bat, and the batters going to the outfield.

4. An inning is over when all three teams have batted.

5. The pitcher should be limited to pitching one inning only. A player may repeat as pitcher only after all members of his team have had a chance to pitch.

BASE CIRCLING CONTESTS

Playing Area: Softball diamond.
Players: 4 squads (entire class).
Supplies: None.

Children love to run around the bases, and contests employing this feature are popular with them. The contest lends itself well to a class of four squads. Each squad takes a position beyond one of the bases, far enough back so as not to interfere with the runners. Each captain can arrange his runners in any order for running that he wishes, but once arranged all must run in this order.

Scoring: 1st — 4, 2nd — 3, 3rd — 2, 4th — 1. Players must touch all bases on penalty of disqualification. Each player scores points for his team as he finishes in his heat.

The bases need to be fastened securely to avoid inequities and falls. Having bases painted on a black or hardtop surface is a solution.

Variation: If four split-second stopwatches are available, each child can be timed and other means of scoring devised.

TESTS FOR SOFTBALL SKILLS

Tests for softball skills include throwing (accuracy and distance), fielding grounders, circling the bases, and pitching.

Throw for Accuracy. A target with three concentric circles of 18", 36", and 54" is drawn on a wall. Scoring is 3, 2, and 1, respectively, for the circles.

Five throws are given to each child for a possible score of 15. Balls hitting a line score for the higher number.

Instead of the suggested target, a tire could be hung. Scoring would allow 2 points for a throw through the tire and 1 point for just hitting the tire. A maximum score of 10 points is possible with this system.

Throw for Distance. The softball throw for distance is a part of the fitness testing program recommended by this text and is found in that section in the appendix.

Fielding Grounders. A file of players is stationed behind a restraining line. A thrower is about 30′ in front of this line. Each player in turn fields five ground balls. His score is the number of balls he fields cleanly.

It is recognized that there will be inconsistencies in the throw and bounce of the ground balls served up for fielding. If the opportunity obviously was not a fair one, the child should get another opportunity.

Circling the Bases. A diamond with four bases is needed, plus a stopwatch for timing. The object is to time the runner circling the bases. Two runners can run at one time by starting from opposite corners of the diamond. Two watches are needed with this system.

Variation: The batter can bunt a pitched ball and run around the bases. The timing starts with the bunt and finishes when the batter touches home plate.

Pitching. Pitching is one of the easier skills to test in softball, and certainly is one of the most popular with children. There are two basic methods used for testing:

1. Allow a certain number of pitches at a target. Scoring is on the basis of the number of strikes which can be thrown out of a designated number of pitches.

2. Regular pitching, as if to a batter, counting balls and strikes. "Batters" would be either struck out or walked. The test score would be how many batters the child was able to strike out from a given number at bat. This could be expressed in a percentage.

A target is needed and should be 20″ wide and 36″ high. This can be devised a number of ways. It can be outlined temporarily on a wall with chalk, or a more permanent means would be to use paint. The lower portion of the target should be about 18″ above the ground or floor. The target could be constructed from plywood or wood. Some means of support or hanging would be needed.

Scoring would be based upon whether or not the pitch entered the strike zone as typified by the target. The boundaries of the target should be counted as good. The pitching distance should be normal (35′), and regular pitching rules should be observed.

Old Woody. Old Woody is the name of a pitching target which is in the form of a stand that can be moved from school to school. The target size is as outlined below. A sturdy frame holds the target and allows it to be used in most any spot. The contest is based upon the number of strikeouts a pitcher can throw to an imaginary batter. He continues pitching until he "walks" the batter. Other variations could be used.

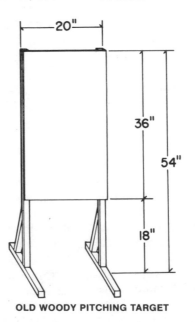

OLD WOODY PITCHING TARGET

28

Track and Field Activities

Emphasis on Different Levels
Instructional Procedures
Track and Field Events

The urge to run, jump, and hurdle is strong in both boys and girls. In an age of feminine emergence in track and field, girls should receive their share of attention. Children are motivated not only by competition, but also by the status and prestige attached to star performers. At least children should have an early opportunity to see if they have talent in track and field activities.

Competition is important, but must not be overemphasized. More attention should be given to improvement and progress toward a personal goal than toward beating fellow classmates. However, the basic emphasis of track and field, the desire to come out on top, must not be lost.

Class records and performances can be integrated into classroom work in art and number concepts. The design of tracks is an extension of this idea.

The program for the elementary grades in track and field should consist of short sprints (40 to 100 yards), running and standing long jumps, the high jump, the hop-step-and jump, and relays. Jogging and distance running should be primarily for practice and not competition. Children should learn to stride for distance to establish pace. Relays should be an important inclusion. Hurdling can be included if the equipment problem can be solved, as children enjoy these activities.

An all-school playday type of meet gives

EMPHASIS ON DIFFERENT LEVELS

Grade	Fourth	Fifth	Sixth
Skills Track	40-60 yard dashes Standing start Sprinter's start Jogging	50-80 yard dashes Sprinter's start Baton passing Relays Striding for distance Jogging	60-100 yard dashes Sprinter's start Baton passing Relays Striding for distance Jogging Hurdling
Skills Field	Long jump Standing long jump	Long jump Standing long jump High jump	Long jump Standing long jump High jump Hop, step, and jump

impetus to track and field practice, providing a goal for the competitors. The number of events should be wide to encourage broad competition. Children should be limited to two or three events, including relays. The program should include a number of relays. Competition can be based on home rooms. Holding the event on a school morning or afternoon gives status to the affair, and allows all children to participate.

Fourth Grade

The fourth grade should stress running short distances. The children should be introduced to the standing and sprint starts, the two long jumps, and jogging.

Fifth Grade

More serious efforts in the area of form begin in the fifth grade. The high jump is added to the fourth grade program and the scissors style can be used in the learning stages. Jogging should be continued.

Striding for distance should be started, as well as relay work, including baton passing. The sprinter's start should be strongly emphasized.

Sixth Grade

Hurdling is the only addition to the list of previous activities. This should be over modified hurdles and primarily for practice. In the high jump, both the regular and modified western rolls should be shown.

An effort should be made to have the youngsters develop pace in distance running. Jogging should be over longer distances up to and exceeding a mile. Relaxed, easy running should be the goal.

INSTRUCTIONAL PROCEDURES

1. Spiked running shoes should not be permitted. Many light gym or running shoes are available and are quite suitable. Spiked shoes create a safety problem and also give an unfair advantage to children whose parents can afford them. Running in bare feet is not recommended.

2. Form should be stressed at all times, but appropriate to the individual. The child should be brought to the realization that good results in track and field are due to good form and diligent practice.

3. The amount of activity, particularly distance striding, should be built up progressively. A period of conditioning should precede any competition or all-out performance.

4. Warm-up activity consisting primarily of bending and stretching exercises should precede track and field work.

5. Distance running should be under control for children of this age.

6. Pits for long and high jumping must be maintained properly. They should contain sand, sawdust mixtures, or loose dirt for long jumping. For high jumping, mats by themselves or placed over secured inner tubes or tires are satisfactory. Commercial landing platforms are excellent but expensive.

7. The metal variety of high jump crossbars is economical in the long run. A satisfactory substitute can be made from rope, with a weight on each end to keep it taut and still allow it to be displaced. In Europe, small leather bags with shot are used as weights to keep the rope level.

TRACK AND FIELD EVENTS

Sprinting Form. The body leans forward, with the arms swinging in opposition to the legs. The arms are bent at the elbows and swing from the shoulders in a forward and backward plane, not across the body. Forceful arm action aids sprinting action. The knees are lifted sharply forward and upward and brought down with a vigorous pushing motion, with a forceful push by the toes. Sprinting should be a driving and striding motion as opposed to the inefficient pulling action shown by some runners.

Running Form. In running form, as compared to sprinting techniques, the body is more erect and the motion of the arms more or less takes care of itself. Pace is an important consideration. In running, concentrate on the following:

The quality of lightness and ease.

The quality of relaxation and looseness.

Good striding action.

Slight body lean and good head position.

How the foot meets the ground will generally take care of itself. Some children like to run up on their toes, others use more of the foot.

Standing Start. The standing start should be practiced and best techniques employed, as this type of start has a variety of uses in physical education activities. Many children find it more comfortable to use this start rather than the sprint start. However, as soon as practical, children should accept and employ the sprint start for track work.

The feet in the standing start should be at a comfortable stride position, with the body weight forward in a lean and the weight on the toes. One arm can be back to give a thrust for the start.

The Norwegians use the standing start in a novel way.

Command Action

"On your mark."	Runner takes a position at the starting line with left foot forward.
"Get set."	Right hand is placed on the left knee, and the left hand is carried back for a thrust.
"Go."	Left hand comes forward, coupled with a drive by the right foot.

The advantages claimed for this start are that it forces a body lean and makes use of the forward thrust of the arm, coordinated with the step of the opposite foot.

Sprint Start. There are several different kinds of sprinter starts, but it is best to concentrate on a single type. To take the "on the mark" position, the toe of the front foot is placed from 4" to 12" behind the starting line. The thumb and first finger are placed just behind the line, with the other fingers adding support. The knee of the rear leg is placed just opposite the front foot or ankle.

For the "get set" position, the seat is raised so that it is slightly higher than the shoulders, the knee of the rear leg is raised off the ground, and the shoulders are moved forward over the hands. The weight is evenly distributed over the hands and feet.

On the "go" signal, push sharply off with both feet, with the front leg straightening, as the back leg comes forward for a step. The body should rise gradually and not "pop" up suddenly.

Baton Passing. The runner exchanges the baton from his left hand to the right hand of the runner ahead. The runner should carry the baton like a candle when passing. The receiver reaches back with his right hand with the fingers pointed down and thumb to the inside, and begins to move ahead when the coming runner is 3 to 5 yards back of him. He grasps the baton and immediately shifts it to his left hand while moving. The exchange should be made on the move with the front runner timing his start and increase of speed to the pace of the runner coming in. If the baton is dropped, it must be picked up or the team is disqualified.

An alternate way of receiving the baton is to reach back with the hand facing up. The first method is considered more suitable for sprint relays.

Standing Long Jump. In both the standing and running long jump, the measurement is made from the take-off board or line to the nearest point on the ground touched by the jumper. It is important that the children do not fall or step backward after making the jump. In the standing long jump, the performer toes the line with the feet flat on the ground and fairly close together. His arms are brought forward in a preliminary swing and then swung down and back. The jump is made with both feet as the arms are swung forcibly forward to assist in lifting the body upward and forward. While in the air, the knees should be brought upward and forward with the arms forward to sustain balance.

Long Jump. A short run is needed and should be planned so that the toes of the jumping foot will contact the board in a natural stride. The jumper takes off with one foot and should strive for height. The landing is made on both feet after the knees have been brought forward. The landing should be made in a forward direction, not sidewards.

Each contestant is given a certain number of trials (jumps). If a jumper runs into the pit or steps over the scratch line while jumping, this counts as one of the trials.

Measurement is from the scratch line to the nearest point of touch.

The pit for the long jump should be filled properly and the sharp edges covered or leveled with sand. The take-off board should be adjusted to the jumping ability of the poorer jumpers in the group. Early jumping should be done for form. Distance can come later.

The pit must be clear before the next jumper takes his turn.

Working with the High Jump. Three styles of high jumping are presented. There has been some debate regarding the desirability of teaching the scissors style. Some maintain that this is a logical and relatively easy way for the children to jump and that the technique has utilitarian value outside of track and field work, while others believe that a youngster trained to jump this way would have to change his technique if he became seriously interested in high jumping. The decision of whether or not to include the scissors style in the instructional program probably depends upon personal convictions.

High jump techniques are developed by effective practice. The bar should be at a height which offers some challenge, but allows concentration on technique rather than on height. Too much emphasis on competition for height quickly eliminates the poorer jumpers, who are the ones who need the practice the most.

High jump work should be a part of rotational group practice covering several events if only one high jump pit is available. The practice of keeping the entire class together on a single high jump facility is poor methodology. This concentrated arrangement will determine who are the best jumpers in the class, but does little else.

High Jump — Scissors Style. The high jump bar is approached from a slight angle. The take-off is by the outside leg (the one farthest from the bar). The near leg is lifted and goes over first, followed quickly by the rear leg in a looping movement. There should be a good upward kick with the front leg, together with an upward thrust of the arms. The knees should be straightened at the highest point of the jump. The landing is made on the lead foot followed by the rear foot.

High Jump — Western Roll. An approach at an angle of 45 degrees is used. The take-off is with the inside foot, with the outside foot swung forward and upward. The side of the body lies paralled to the bar in crossing the bar. The hands and take-off foot hit the ground about the same time.

High Jump — Modified Western Roll. This form is sometimes called the straddle jump because the body in crossing is face down to the bar. The take-off is the same as in the normal Western Roll. The landing is made on the swing-up foot and the hands. This jump is popularly termed the "Belly Roll."

Hop, Step, and Jump. This event is increasing in popularity, particularly because it is included in Olympic competition. A take-off board and a jumping pit are needed. The distance from the take-off board to the pit should be a distance that the poorer jumpers can make. The event begins with a run, similar to the broad jump. The take-off is with one foot, and the jumper must light on the same foot to complete the hop. He then takes a step followed by a jump. The event finishes like the long jump with a landing on both feet. The jumper must not step over the take-off board in his first hop, under penalty of fouling. Distance is measured from the front of the take-off board to the closest place where the body touches. This is usually a mark made by one of the heels, but could be a mark made by an arm or other part of the body if the jumper landed poorly and fell backwards toward the take-off board.

Jump Combinations. Different jumping combinations can be set up to challenge the children. Combinations like two or three standing long jumps, and up to five hops in succession can be used.

Relays

Two types of relays are generally included in a program of track and field for children.

Shuttle Relay. Since the children are running toward each other, one great difficulty in running relays is control of the exchange. In the excitement, the next runner may leave too early, and the tag or exchange is made ahead of the restraining line. A high jump standard can be used to prevent early exchanges by having the runner await the tag with his arm held around the standard. A difficulty with this is the provision of enough standards needed for all teams.

Circular Relays. These relays make use of the regular circular track. The baton exchange technique is important, and practice is needed for this technique.

Jogging and Pace Running

Children should get some practice in running for moderate distances in an effort to acquire some knowledge of pace. The running should be loose and relaxed. Distances up to 600 yards may be a part of the work. This prepares the student for the 600-yard run, a part of the national physical fitness test.

A fun activity is to allow children to estimate pace and time. On a circular track, stipulate a target time and have the children see how close they can come to it.

Hurdles

Hurdling is an interesting activity, but poses equipment problems. Hurdles can be assembled by using canes supported on blocks or cones. Begin with 12" heights and move to 18". Start with one hurdle and add others. Hurdles should be about 25' apart. For a 60-yard course, there will be 6 hurdles.

Children should recognize that hurdling is akin to sprinting and speed is essential. The child should go over the hurdle with the same leading foot each time.

A single or double hurdle course can be set up, primarily for practice. If there is competition, then it should be on a time basis. If regular hurdles are available, then practice on the lower temporary hurdles should precede work on regular hurdles.

A Suggested Track Facility

The presence of a track facility is a boon to the track program. Few elementary schools have the funds or space for a quarter-mile track. A shorter track facility which can be installed permanently with curbs or temporarily with marking lime is suggested. Discarded fire hose could be used to mark the curbs and could be installed each spring with spikes.

DIAGRAM OF A ⅛ MILE TRACK (220 YARDS)

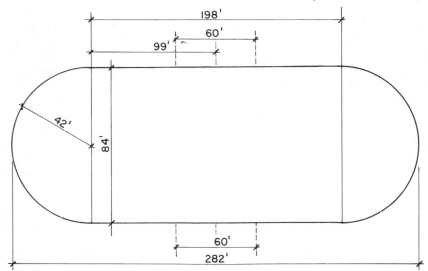

The facility is one-eighth mile in length and has a straightaway of 66 yards in length, which is ample for the 60 yard dash. It allows flexibility in relays, since relay legs of 55, 110, and 220 yards are possible.

Sixth grade classes could profit in number concepts by helping lay out the track and calculating the distances from the dimensions, thus strengthening number concepts.

Interval Training

A track of this size facilitates the interval type of training. Children should know this

technique, which consists of running at a set speed for a stipulated distance and then walking around back to the starting point. Children on the one-eighth mile track could run for 110 yards and then walk the remainder of the distance back to the starting point. This should be repeated a number of times.

Or, the child may run the entire 220 yards and then take a timed rest, after which he repeats the performance. Breathing should return to near normal before he attempts the next 220 yard chore.

Volleyball and Related Activities

Volleyball is an excellent recreational activity and is important to the program because it is one of the few sports which can be conducted coeducationally. In many gymnasiums, the lack of more than one court means playing twelve to fifteen children on a side, which provides relatively little activity for some of the children. These games are usually dominated by three or four skillful children on each side, with the others taking only a minor part. If there is only one court, then an alternate activity should be operated along with the volleyball game so that none of the teams on the court number more than six to eight children.

Volleyball cannot be played with much success unless a good basis of skills is established. There must be concentration on the skills with attention to proper technique. Hand-eye coordination in volleyball leading to good ball control comes slowly, and patience is needed.

The game of *Newcomb* has been removed from volleyball lead-up activities because of the emphasis on throwing and catching skills, which are not part of volleyball. *Newcomb* has value for children, but not as a lead-up game to volleyball. It is found on page 294.

GRADE	FOURTH	FIFTH	SIXTH
Skills	Serve — Underhanded Simple Return	Overhand Pass Forearm Pass	Overhand Serve Set Up Spiking Blocking
Knowledges	Simple Rules Rotation	Basic Game Rules	Game Strategy Additional Rules

Activities to
be stressed
	Beach Ball
	  Volleyball
	One-Bounce Volleyball
	Shower Service Ball
		Keep It Up
		Four-Square
		  Volleyball
		Wall Volley
		Cage Volleyball
		Volleyball
			Volleyball
			Three-and-Over
			  Volleyball

Testing	Simplified Serve
	  Test
		Simplified Serve
		  Test
		Wall Test
			Serve Scoring Test
			Wall Test

EMPHASIS AT EACH GRADE LEVEL

Fourth Grade

In the fourth grade, the children are introduced to the game by playing *Beach Ball Volleyball*. Where the ball is large and easily handled, it is possible to keep it going and get the feel of the game.

Serving underhanded is introduced along with simple volleying skills.

Bounce Volleyball employs the serve and uses regular rules of scoring. A system of rotation is used in the game.

Fifth Grade

Students in this grade learn to handle the high and low .passes. They are introduced to the regular game and should learn the basic rules. They should review the serve and polish up on this skill. *Keep It Up* and *Wall Volley* employ skills of passing. *Cage Volleyball* follows the scoring rules but ūses modifications. *Four-Square Volleyball* provides an interesting form of volleyball competition.

Sixth Grade

For sixth grade students, the program should add the concepts of overhand serve, set-up, spiking, and blocking. Game rules which affect these phases of the game should be covered. An introduction to elementary strategy should be a part of the instruction.

GENERAL SUGGESTIONS

For a class of about thirty students, two volleyball courts are needed. Not more than a total of 12 to 18 children can play profitably in volleyball games.

A court should be 25' by 50' with a net height of 6' to 7'. If no net is available, one can be improvised by using a rope as a substitute. A line called the center line should be drawn on the floor across the center of the court directly under the net.

Regular volleyball rules call for one chance to serve the ball over the net *without* touching the net. In learning stages, the teacher can modify the rules to allow a second chance. Another modification is to move the server forward from his base line to a point where he can serve the ball over the net successfully.

At the net, the players should stand an arm's length away for best play. Other players should play their positions rather than "ganging up" on the ball.

Rotation should be introduced in the fourth grade and used in lead-up games.

To save time, children should be taught to roll the ball to the server. Other players should let the ball roll to its destination without intercepting it.

The use of the fist to hit the ball on volleys causes poor control and interrupts the play. Both hands should be used to hit the ball. If difficulty occurs with the enforcement of this, the teacher can rule hitting with the fist a foul, causing loss of a point.

A referee should be appointed, as violations of rules occur in the heat of the game. A referee positioned near the net can call violations effectively.

The ball should be a volleyball or one of similar size and should be properly inflated. A heavy, flabby ball takes much away from the game.

BASIC RULES

Officially, six players make up a team under the rules. However, any number from six to nine make suitable teams for elementary schools.

To begin, captains toss a coin for the order of choices. The winner can choose either to serve or to take his choice of courts. Whichever option he selects, the opposing captain takes the other.

At the completion of any game, the teams change courts, and the losing side serves.

To be in position to serve, the player must have both feet behind the right one-third of the end line. He must not step on the end line during the serve. The server is in what is known as "right back" position.

Only the serving team scores. The server retains his serve, scoring consecutive points, until his side loses and is put out. Members of each team take turns serving, the sequence being determined by the plan of rotation.

Official rules allow the server only one serve to get the ball completely over the net and into the opponent's court. Even if the ball touches the net (net ball) and goes into the correct court, the serve is lost.

The lines bounding the court are considered

to be in the court. Balls landing on the lines are counted as good.

Any ball that touches or is touched by a player is considered to be "in," even though the player who touched the ball was clearly outside the boundaries at the time. He is considered to have played the ball if he touches it.

The ball must be returned over the net at least by the third volley, which means that the team has a maximum of three volleys to make a good return.

Chief violations causing loss of the point or serve are:

1. Touching the net during play.

2. Not clearly batting the ball. This is sometimes called palming or lofting the ball.

3. Reaching over the net during play.

4. Stepping *over* the center line. Contact with the line is not a violation.

A ball going into the net may be recovered and played, provided no player touches the net.

The first team to reach a score of fifteen points wins the game *provided* the team is at least two points ahead of the opponent. If not, play continues until one team secures a two point lead.

Only players in the front line may spike, but all players may block.

No player may volley the ball twice in succession.

DESCRIPTION OF SKILLS

Underhand Serve. There are many different serves in volleyball, but best results are obtained if the instruction is concentrated first on the simple, basic underhand serve. The description is for a right-handed player. Stand with the left foot forward and pointed toward the net. The ball is held in the palm of the left hand with the arm across the body so the ball may be struck with the right hand moving straight forward. The right hand forms a partial fist with the knuckles toward the ball. Swing the right hand forward in an underhanded motion striking the ball out of the left palm. The ball is not tossed into the air but remains in contact with the left palm until struck by the right hand.

An alternate method is to use the cupped hand to strike the ball.

Overhand Pass or Return. The Overhand Pass must be mastered if there is to be interesting, competitive play. Otherwise, if the ball is served and not returned well or often, the game is dull and uninteresting.

Move directly under the ball and receive it with cupped hands and fingertip control. Feet should be in an easy comfortable position with the knees bent. The cup of the fingers is made so that the thumbs and forefingers are close together and the other fingers spread. The hands are held forehead high, with the elbows out and level to the floor. The player, when he is in receiving position, looks as if he is about ready to shout upward through his cupped hands.

Contact the ball at eye level and propel it with the force of the fingers, not the palms. At the moment of contact, straighten out the legs and follow-through well with the hands and arms.

If the ball is a pass to a teammate, it should reach good height to allow for control. If the pass is a return to the other side, it can be projected forward with more force.

Forearm Pass. This technique has replaced the old underhand pass, where the ball was contacted with the hands. The body must be in good position to assure a proper volley. The player must move rapidly to the spot where the ball is descending to prepare himself for the pass.

Body position is important. The trunk leans forward and the back is straight, with about a 90 degree angle between the thigh and body. The legs are bent and the body is in a partially crouched position, with the feet shoulder-width apart.

The hands are clasped together so that the forearms are kept parallel. The clasp should be relaxed, with the type of handclasp a matter of choice. The thumbs can be kept either parallel or crossed. The arms rotate inward, and the wrists flex toward the floor. The elbow joint is locked.

The ball contact is made, if possible, from a spot between the knees. The motion should be a cushioned, controlled stroke, with the arms at times merely providing a rebound volley.

Overhand Serve. The Overhand Serve requires more practice than the Underhand, but it is considered a more effective serve. The most commonly used overhand serve is the floater, that is, sending the ball across the net in such a fashion that it has no spin.

The server stands with a slightly staggered stance, with the left foot forward (right-handed server). The knees are relaxed for comfort and ease, with the body slightly turned as governed by the position of the feet. The ball should be held with both hands at about eye level. The left hand is under the ball for support and balance, and the striking hand is on top of the ball. The position represents somewhat a one-handed shot position in basketball.

The ball is tossed lightly about 2′ to 3′ above the head so that it descends a foot or more in front of the shoulder of the striking hand. On the toss, the body weight is transferred to the back foot.

Contact is made with the ball in a motion resembling a baseball catcher's throw to second base. The arm is flexed and cocked, with the hand drawn back near the ear. The upper body rotates slightly to the right in a preparatory move.

As the ball drops, the body weight transfers to the front foot with either a short step or a slide. The striking arm snaps forward from its cocked position. To assure a floater, little follow-through of the arm is made.

Hand contact can be made in several ways; the open hand, the cupped hand with knuckle contact, and the clenched hand (fist). The wrist remains rigid in all hand contact methods. Contact with the ball should be made in the middle.

Recovery Shots. The purpose of a recovery shot is simply to save the ball from hitting the floor when it is in a difficult trajectory, and neither the overhand or forearm passes can be used. One-arm recoveries are generally used, utilizing the hand, fist, or back of the hand. Children should regard these as emergency measures and not as standard returns.

Set-Up. The name applies to a pass which sets up the ball for a possible spike. The object is to raise the ball with a soft, easy pass to a position one or two feet above the net and about one foot from the net. The set-up is generally the second pass in a series of three. An overhand pass is used for the set-up. It is important that the back line player, who has to tap to the setter, makes an accurate and easily handled pass.

Spike. Spiking is the most effective play in volleyball and, when properly done, is extremely difficult to return properly. It depends a great deal upon the ability of a teammate to set it up properly. On the elementary level, spiking should be done by jumping high into the air and striking the ball above the net, driving it into the opponent's court. It is the "kill" shot in volleyball. Experienced players may back up for a short run. However, the jump must be made straight up so as not to touch the net, and the striking hand must not go over the net.

DRILLS FOR VOLLEYBALL SKILLS

Serving, passing (overhand and forearm), setting up, and spiking are the volleyball skills for which the drills are organized.

Serving

1. *Formation:* Shuttle turnback. Four to six players are in each drill, divided between the two halves of the shuttle formation. The children serve back and forth from a short distance. The second step is to have them serve back and forth over a net, positioned about in the middle of each court. As skill increases, gradually move the service back until the serve can be made from behind the base line.

2. *Formation:* Two teams face each other from opposite sides of a volleyball court. All players serve from behind the base lines. The ball is served back and forth across the net. There should be some method of taking turns, but a rigid order is not required. Two or more volleyballs should be used in the drill.

Passing (Overhand and Forearm).

1. *Formation:* Circle with leader. Leader in the center tosses ball at proper height to each player for an overhand pass. After tossing to all players in the circle, a new leader takes the place. Repeat for forearm passes.

2. *Formation:* Circle. Players in a small circle volley back and forth without regard to any particular order, except that players should not volley back to the person from whom the ball was received.

3. *Formation:* Double line. Players stand in two lines facing each other at a distance of

about 10'. The ball is volleyed back and forth from one line to the other.

4. *Formation:* File and leader. After the players have had sufficient preliminary practice, volleying across the net is introduced. The leader stands on one side of the net with the file players in position on the other. Both the leader and the child in front of the file are about 5' from the net. The leader tosses the ball over the net to the front player of the file, who volleys the ball back over to him. This player goes to the rear of the file. The leader tosses the ball over to the next player, and so on. After one full round, the leader is changed. After volleying skill has been developed, the leader can volley the ball back, rather than catching and tossing it back.

Wall Volley

Formation: File in front of a smooth wall. A line is drawn on the wall 6½' from the floor and parallel to it.

One player from each file begins by throwing the ball above the line and attempting to keep it in play by volleying. Change after a short period.

Set-up and Spike Drill

Formation: Leader and file. The leader stands close to the net and tosses the ball up (set-up) for spiking. Each player in turn practices spiking.

A second stage of this drill is the addition of the set-up player. The ball is tossed to the set-up player, who sets up the ball for the line of spikers. Rotate the positions after the line of spikers has completed one round.

Fourth Grade

ACTIVITIES

BEACH BALL VOLLEYBALL

Playing Area: Volleyball court.
Players: Two teams, 6 to 9 each.
Supplies: A beach ball, 12"-15".

This is a simplified version of volleyball, using a beach ball instead of a regular volleyball. The players of each team are in two lines on the respective sides of the net. The ball is put in play by one player in the front line by throwing the ball into the air to himself and then hitting it over the net. Play continues until the ball touches the floor. The ball may

be volleyed any number of times before crossing the net.

A team loses a point to the other team if the ball goes over the net and hits the floor out-of-bounds without being touched by the opposing team. Otherwise, a team loses a point if it fails to return the ball over the net.

Serving is done by the front line only. When the ball hits the floor, a player in the front line of the team on that side puts the ball in play.

When either team has scored 5 points, the front and back lines of the respective teams change. When the score has reached 10 for the leading team, the lines change back. Game is 15.

Variation: The ball must go over, on or before the third volley.

ONE-BOUNCE VOLLEYBALL

Playing Area: Volleyball court.
Players: Two teams, 6 to 9 each.
Supplies: Volleyball.

The game utilizes the formations and rules of volleyball, with the exception that the ball may bounce once between hits or passes. Play begins with the regular serve as in volleyball. The served ball may be played as in volleyball or the team can allow the ball to bounce once between passes.

In the early stages of the game, there can be any number of hits and bounces, provided the ball does not bounce more than once between hits. Later, allow only three players to handle the ball before it must be returned across the net.

SHOWER SERVICE BALL

Formation: Two volleyball teams, each occupying its respective court. Players are scattered in no particular formation. A line, parallel to the net, is drawn through the middle of each court.

Players: 6 to 12 on each team.
Supplies: 3 to 6 volleyballs.

The game involves the skills of serving and catching. To start the game, the volleyballs are divided between the teams and are handled by players in the serving area. The serving area is between the base line and the line drawn through the middle of each court.

Balls may be served at any time in any order, just so the server is in the serving area (back half) of his court. Any ball that is served across the net is to be caught by any player near the ball. The person catching or retrieving a ball from the floor moves quickly to his serving area and serves. A point is scored *for* a team whenever a served ball hits the floor in the other court or is dropped by a receiver. Two scorers are needed, one for each side.

Teaching Suggestion: The line through the middle of each court should be moved back toward the base line after serving skill becomes better. Later, the game can be played without the line, with all serves made from back of the base line of each court.

Fifth Grade

KEEP IT UP

Playing Area: Playground, gymnasium.

Players: 5 to 8 players on each team.

Supplies: Volleyball for each team.

Each team forms a small circle of not more than eight players. The object of the game is to see which team can make the greatest number of volleys in a specified time or which team can sustain the ball in the air for the greatest number of consecutive volleys without error.

Directions:

1. Game is started with a volley by one of the players on the signal "Go."

2. Balls are volleyed back and forth with no specific order of turns, except that the ball cannot be returned to the player from whom it came.

3. A player may not volley a ball twice in succession.

4. Any ball touching the ground does not count and ends the count.

FOUR-SQUARE VOLLEYBALL

Playing Area: A regular volleyball court with a second net at right angles to the original net, dividing the playing area into four equal courts.

Players: 2 to 4 on each of four teams. An extra team can be "off," awaiting rotation to the #4 court.

Supplies: Volleyball.

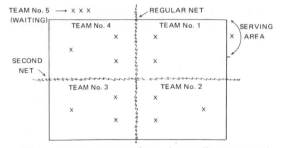

FOUR-SQUARE VOLLEYBALL

The courts are numbered as diagrammed. The object of the game is to force one of the teams to commit an error. Whenever a team makes an error, it moves down to the #4 court or "off," in case there is a waiting team. A team errs by not returning the ball to another court within the prescribed three volleys or by causing the ball to go out-of-bounds.

The ball is always put in play by a serve by a player from the #1 team, the serve being made from any point behind the end line of that team. Players rotate for each serve. The serve must be made into courts #3 or #4. Play is then like in volleyball, but the ball may be volleyed into any of the other three courts.

No score is kept. The object of the game is for the #1 team to retain its position.

WALL VOLLEY

Playing Area: For each team, an area with a smooth wall.

Players: 2 to 6 on each team. As many teams as there are areas available.

Supplies: One volleyball for each team.

Formation: The first player from each team takes his place in front of the wall and back of a line drawn 4' from the base of the wall.

Each player is given a specified time (30 seconds) to volley the ball against the wall as many times as he can, while staying behind the restraining line. A good hit is one that is made from behind the line and which hits the wall on the volley. After the time period, the second player comes forward and repeats the performance. The team score is the total of the individual members.

Variation: Each player must stop when he misses. Those with no misses continue throughout the time period.

CAGE VOLLEYBALL

Cage volleyball is a variation of regular volleyball. The ball used is a cageball, 18"-24" in diameter.

Directions:

1. In serving, toss the ball into the air, propel it with both hands.

2. Assistance may be given on the serve to get the ball over the net.

3. Any number of hits may be made in any combination or order by the players, but the ball must be clearly batted and not lofted or carried.

4. Scoring and rotation follow volleyball rules.

VOLLEYBALL

The rules for volleyball are listed in the early part of the unit (page 461). A referee should supervise the game. He generally has three calls:

1. Side out — the serving team fails to serve the ball successfully to the other court, fails to make a good return of a volley, or makes a rule violation.

2. Point — the receiving team in this case fails to make a legal return or is guilty of a rule violation.

3. Double foul — fouls are made by both teams on the same play, in which case the point is replayed. No score or side out results.

There should be some emphasis on team play. Back court players should be encouraged to pass to front court players, rather than merely batting the ball back and forth across the net.

Sixth Grade

VOLLEYBALL

There should be continued play in volleyball with increased attention to team play. The concept of offensive volleyball should be introduced with some attention to the skill of spiking. However, the emphasis on setting up and spiking should not be overriding considerations. Continued practice on the basic skills of serving and volleying should be an important part of the instruction. Closer attention to the details of good technique will make for more efficient play.

The game *Three and Over* serves to emphasize the basic offensive strategy of volleyball.

THREE-AND-OVER VOLLEYBALL

This game follows the regular rules of volleyball with the exception that the ball must be played three times before going over. The object is to establish the concept of team volleyball with the routine of pass, set-up, and spike. The team loses the serve or point if the ball is not played three times.

TESTS FOR VOLLEYBALL SKILLS

Serving and volleying are the skills to be tested in volleyball. Serving is tested in two ways, one with a simple serve, and one with an accuracy score.

Simplified Serve Test. The child to be tested stands in the normal serving position behind the end line on the right side. He is given a specific number of trials in serving. His score is the number of times he serves successfully out of his trials (10). The serve must clear the net without touching and land in the opponents' court. A ball touching a line is counted as good.

Serve Accuracy Test. A line is drawn parallel to the net through the middle of one of the courts. Each half is further subdivided into three equal areas by lines parallel to the sidelines. This makes a total of six areas, which correspond to the six positions of members of a volleyball team. The areas are numbered from 1 to 6.

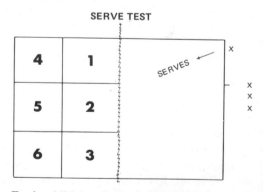

SERVE TEST

Each child is allotted one service attempt to serve the ball into each of the six areas in turn. Scoring is as follows.

2 points—serving into the designated court area.

1 point—missing the designated area but landing in an adjacent area to the target area.

0 points—failing to serve into the target or adjacent area.

Wall Test for Volleying. The player stands behind a restraining line 4' away from a wall. A line is drawn on the wall parallel to the floor and 6½' up, representing the height of the net. A player is allowed 30 seconds to make as many volleys as he can above the 6½' line, while keeping behind the restraining line. A counter is assigned to each testing station to count the successive volleys.

To start, the child makes a short toss to himself for his first volley. If time permits, more than one opportunity can be allowed, and the best count from any of the 30-second periods is his score.

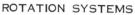

ROTATION SYSTEMS

TWO LINES

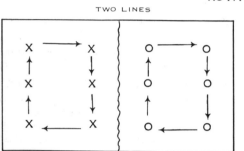

THREE LINES

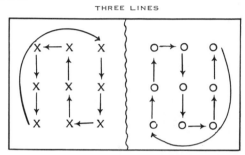

Appendix I

Physical Fitness Tests

Two types of fitness tests are suggested for the elementary level. The first is the screening test, which is designed to measure basic minimums in a quick, easily administered procedure.

The second type of test is the diagnostic test, of which two are presented. The first of these is the National Physical Fitness Test, recommended by the President's Council on Physical Fitness and Sports. It has the advantage of national approval and norms, but demands considerable time in its administration. The second test proposed is the Oregon Motor Fitness Test, which has been offered because of its simplicity and ease of administration.

A discussion of test administration and the Presidential Physical Fitness Award System rounds out the presentation.

A. A SCREENING TEST FOR IDENTIFYING THE PHYSICALLY-UNDERDEVELOPED CHILD

A screening test generally establishes basic minimums which must be met, or the child is screened out for further investigation. It is not to be regarded as a diagnostic tool, but merely as a device to identify quickly the more deficient children. In some cases, the borderline student can meet the basic physical minimums and is not so identified. However, those children with serious deficiencies can be readily identified by a screening test. The regular physical fitness test gives more detailed and relative information about fitness levels of all children, including those who are physically underdeveloped.

A feasible screening test* for identifying the physically-underdeveloped child is recommended by the President's Council on Physical Fitness. It is designed to measure basic minimums of strength, flexibility, and agility, with the three simple items which make up the test.
1. Pull-ups (arm and shoulder strength).
2. Sit-ups (flexibility and abdominal strength).
3. Squat thrusts (agility).

It is recommended that all pupils be screened at the beginning of the school year, and that those who fail any test item should be re-tested every six weeks until they pass the item failed.

Instructions for Administration of the Screening Test

Divide the class into pairs, with one pupil acting as a scorer for his partner who performs the test. After each test, results are recorded by the teacher on the record form.

The equipment needed includes a chinning bar, a stopwatch (or watch with a sweep second hand), and record forms. For the girls, the chinning bar must be adjustable to chest height. This poses some problems; but generally improvisation can be accomplished with a pipe and two step ladders, provided the pipe can be securely held. Begin with the taller girls and lower the height of the bar as needed. This keeps the adjustment of the bar for height to a minimum.

PULL-UP (Boys)

Equipment: A chinning or exercise bar of sufficient height that can be gripped.

Starting Position: Grasp the bar with palms facing forward; hang with arms and legs fully extended, with feet clearing the floor. Partner stands slightly to one side to count and keeps the body from swinging.

Action: Pull up the body until the chin is *over* the bar and lower the body back to a

*Youth Physical Fitness (Washington, D.C.; U.S. Government Printing Office, 1967) pp. 19-26.

fully extended arm position. One count is given for each completed pull-up.

To Pass: Boys must complete at least one pull-up.

Rules: The body must not swing. Neither can the knees be raised or the legs kicked as in climbing. The pull-up must be a pull and not a snap. Since only one pull-up is required, it should be done in reasonable form.

MODIFIED PULL-UP (Girls)

Equipment: Any bar adjustable in height and comfortable to grip. A piece of pipe placed between two ladders and held securely may be used.

Starting Position: Adjust height of bar to chest level. Grasp bar with palms facing out. Extend the legs under the bar, keeping the

body and knees straight. The heels are on the floor. Fully extend the arms so they form an angle of 90 degrees with the body line. The partner braces the pupil's heels to prevent slipping.

Action: Pull body up with the arms until the chest touches the bar. Lower the body until the elbows are fully extended.

To Pass: Girls must complete at least 8 modified pull-ups.

Rules: The body must be kept straight. The chest must touch the bar and the arms must be *fully* extended on each return. No resting is permitted.

SIT-UPS (Boys and Girls)

Starting Position: Pupil lies on his back with his legs extended and his feet about 1′ apart. The hands, with fingers interlaced, are grasped

behind the neck. Another pupil holds his partner's ankles and keeps his heels in contact with the floor while counting each successful sit-up.

Action: Sit up and turn the trunk to the right, touching the right knee with the left elbow. Return to starting position. Sit up and touch right elbow to left knee. Return. Each time the body is returned to the floor, one sit-up is counted.

To Pass: Boys are to do 14 sit-ups and girls 10.

Rules: Knees must be kept on the floor, and the sit-up must bring the elbow down to the knee rather than meeting with the uplifted knee. A *full* return to lying position must be made.

SQUAT THRUSTS (Boys and Girls)

Equipment: Stopwatch or sweep-second hand watch.

Starting Position: Pupils stand at attention. The test is a four-count movement.

1. Bend knees and place hands on the floor in front of the feet. Hands may be outside, inside, or in front of the knees. Note that the best support is made when the hands are placed at shoulder width apart.

2. Thrust the legs far enough back that the body is straight from the shoulders to the feet (the push-up position).

3. Return to squat position.

4. Return to erect position.

To Pass: A ten-second time limit is made during which boys must complete 4 and the girls 3 complete squat thrusts.

Rules: The pupil must return to the fully erect position of attention each time. The pupils should have had enough practice to be familiar with the movements so that the test is one of agility and not of motor educability. Since the time period is short, it is important that it be established accurately.

B. THE NATIONAL PHYSICAL FITNESS TEST

This test has been adopted by the President's Council. It affords an opportunity to compare each child with national norms and to interpret each individual test item in qualitative terms of poor, satisfactory, good, and excellent.

Careful attention to the manner in which each test item is given is important. The test can be given in three class periods.

The overall test consists of seven different test items.

1. Pull-Ups (Flexed Arm Hang for Girls)
2. Sit-Ups
3. Shuttle Run
4. Standing Broad Jump
5. Fifty-Yard Dash
6. Softball Throw for Distance
7 Six-hundred-Yard Run-Walk

A program for the test items could follow this plan:

1st Day. Pull-Ups and Flexed Arm Hang, Sit-Ups, Shuttle Run.

2nd Day. Standing Broad Jump, 50-Yard Dash, Softball Throw for Distance.

3rd Day. Six-hundred-Yard Run-Walk.

The children for the first two days' testing can be divided into three groups, each of which takes position at one of the test stations. At the conclusion of the testing for the station, the groups rotate to the next station.

Three groups can be used for the final day's testing for the 600-yard run-walk. However, there is necessity for only two groups in the administration of this test, since each runner has a scorer for himself.

PULL-UPS (Boys)

The technique for the pull-up is described in the screening test, presented on page 468.

Standards for Pull-Ups (Boys)

	Age 10	11	12	13
Excellent	8	8	9	10
Good	5	5	5	7
Satisfactory	3	3	3	4
Poor	1	1	1	2

FLEXED ARM HANG (Girls)

Equipment: A stopwatch and a sturdy bar, comfortable to grip and adjustable in height (height of the bar should be approximately the same as that of pupil being tested). A bench or chair can be used with a bar of fixed height and removed immediately when the position of hanging is assumed.

Starting Position: Two spotters, one in front and one in back, help raise the pupil's body so that the chin is above bar, elbows are flexed, and chest is close to bar. Feet must be clear of floor, and pupil must employ the overhand grip.

Action: Hold position as long as possible.

Rules:

1. Start timing as soon as the pupil is in proper position and released by spotters.

2. Stop timing when (a) pupil's chin touches bar; (b) pupil's head tilts back to keep chin over bar; (c) pupil's chin drops below bar.

3. Knees must not be raised.

4. Kicking the legs is not permitted.

Standards for Flexed Arm Hang (Girls)
(In seconds)

	Age 10	11	12	13
Excellent	31	35	30	30
Good	18	17	15	15
Satisfactory	10	10	8	9
Poor	6	5	5	5

SIT-UPS

Like the pull-ups, the sit-up is a part of the screening test and is described under that topic on page 470. Top limit for girls is 50.

Standards for the Sit-Ups

Boys

	Age 10	11	12	13
Excellent	100	100	100	100
Good	76	89	100	100
Satisfactory	50	50	59	75
Poor	34	35	42	50

Girls

	Age 10	11	12	13
Excellent	50	50	50	50
Good	50	50	50	50
Satisfactory	39	37	39	38
Poor	26	26	26	27

SHUTTLE RUN

Equipment: Two blocks of wood, 2″ x 2″ x 4″ (blackboard erasers can be used) and stopwatch. Mark two parallel lines 30′ apart. Place the blocks of wood behind one of the lines.

Starting Position: Pupil stands behind the line opposite the blocks, ready to run.

Action: On the signal, "Ready! — Go!" the pupil runs to the blocks, picks up one and *places* it behind the starting line. He does not throw or drop it. He then runs and picks up the second block and *carries* it back across the starting line.

Rules: Two time trials are allowed, with the better recorded to the nearest tenth of a second. Disqualify if the blocks are dropped or thrown.

Standards for the Shuttle Run
(In seconds to the nearest tenth)

Boys

Age	10	11	12	13
Excellent	10.0	10.0	9.8	9.5
Good	10.5	10.4	10.2	10.0
Satisfactory	11.0	10.9	10.7	10.4
Poor	11.5	11.3	11.1	10.9

Girls

Age	10	11	12	13
Excellent	10.0	10.0	10.0	10.0
Good	11.0	10.9	10.8	10.6
Satisfactory	11.5	11.4	11.3	11.1
Poor	12.0	12.0	11.9	11.8

STANDING BROAD JUMP

Equipment: Any level surface and tape measure.

Starting Position: Pupil stands ready to jump just behind the take-off line. Preparatory to jumping, the pupil should have knees flexed and should swing the arms backwards and forwards in a rhythmical motion.

Action: The jump is made with the arms swung forcefully forward and upward, taking off on the balls of the feet.

Rules: Three trials are allowed, with the best scored in feet and the nearest inch. Measure from the take-off line to the heel or the part of the body that touches nearest to the take-off line.

Standards for the Standing Broad Jump
(In feet and inches)

Boys

Age	10	11	12	13
Excellent	6-1	6-3	6-6	7-2
Good	5-7	5-9	6-1	6-7
Satisfactory	5-2	5-4	5-8	6-0
Poor	4-10	5-0	5-4	5-7

Girls

Age	10	11	12	13
Excellent	5-8	6-2	6-3	6-3
Good	5-2	5-6	5-8	5-8
Satisfactory	4-10	5-0	5-2	5-3
Poor	4-5	4-8	4-9	4-10

FIFTY-YARD DASH

Equipment: Stopwatch.

Starting Position: Pupil stands behind the starting line. The starter takes a position at the finish line with a stopwatch. He raises one hand preparatory to giving the starting signal.

Action: When the starter brings down his hand quickly and hits his thigh, the pupil leaves his mark. The time is noted and recorded.

Rules: One trial is allowed unless it is obvious that the child did not have a fair trial. Time is recorded to the nearest tenth of a second.

Standards for Fifty-Yard Dash
(In seconds to the nearest tenth)

Boys

Age	10	11	12	13
Excellent	7.0	7.0	6.8	6.5
Good	7.5	7.5	7.2	7.0
Satisfactory	8.0	7.8	7.6	7.0
Poor	8.5	8.1	8.0	7.6

Girls

Age	10	11	12	13
Excellent	7.0	7.0	7.0	7.0
Good	7.7	7.7	7.6	7.6
Satisfactory	8.2	8.1	8.0	8.0
Poor	8.8	8.5	8.4	8.4

SOFTBALL THROW FOR DISTANCE

Equipment: Softballs (3), tape measure, small metal or wooden markers.

The Field: Marked off at 5 yard intervals up to a restraining line. A football field marked in conventional fashion makes an ideal area for the test.

Starting Position: Pupil stands several feet behind the restraining line, ready to throw. The throw must not be from a run.

Action: The pupil throws the ball overhand as far as he can from behind the restraining line.

Rules: Three trials are allowed with the best trial measured to the nearest foot. The first is marked, and the mark is moved if a longer throw is made. Only an overhand throw is permitted, and the thrower cannot cross the restraining line during the throw.

Standards for the Softball Throw
(In feet)

Boys

Age	10	11	12	13
Excellent	138	151	165	195
Good	118	129	145	168
Satisfactory	102	115	129	147
Poor	91	105	115	131

Girls

	10	11	12	13
Excellent	84	95	103	111
Good	69	77	90	94
Satisfactory	54	64	70	75
Poor	46	55	59	65

600-YARD RUN-WALK

Equipment: Stopwatch, running area with starting and finishing lines to cover 600 yards. (See note.)

Starting Position: Pupils are divided into pairs. While one runs, the other stands near the timer and listens for the finishing time. The timer calls out the time on a continuous basis, until all the runners have crossed the finish line.

Action: On the signal to start, the pupil starts running the 600-yard distance. Students should be cautioned to pace themselves.

Rules: The time is recorded in minutes and seconds. Walking is permitted but the object is to cover the distance in the shortest time.

Standards for the 600-Yard Run-Walk
(In minutes and seconds)

Boys

Age	10	11	12	13
Excellent	1:58	1:59	1:52	1:46
Good	2:15	2:11	2:05	1:55
Satisfactory	2:26	2:21	2:15	2:05
Poor	2:40	2:33	2:26	2:15

Girls

Excellent	2:05	2:13	2:14	2:12
Good	2:26	2:28	2:27	2:29
Satisfactory	2:41	2:43	2:42	2:44
Poor	2:55	2:59	2:58	3:00

Note: A quarter-mile track makes a satisfactory running area. However, on a playground a small track can be laid out so the runners take two laps around it to cover the distance. If a square is laid out 75 yards on a side, two laps by each child would cover the 600 yards. A rectangle could be used with 50 yards on the shorter sides, and 100 on the longer sides.

C. THE OREGON MOTOR FITNESS TEST

The Oregon Motor Fitness Test was developed cooperatively by the University of Oregon, Oregon State University, physical educators throughout the public schools, and the Department of Education for the State of Oregon. The test is presented by permission of the Department of Education.

The test is a valuable tool for measuring physical fitness qualities because of its simplicity. It uses simple equipment and can be given to a class usually in one class period. Like most tests on the elementary level, the testing program begins in the fourth grade. The tests are different for boys and girls.

Directions for Administering the Boys' Test Battery
(Grades 4, 5, and 6)

PUSH-UPS

Starting Position: The pupil assumes a front-leaning rest position with the body supported on hand and toes. The arms are straight and at right angles to the body.

Action: The pupil dips or lowers the body so that the chest touches or nearly touches the floor, then pushes back to the starting position by straightening the arms, and repeats the procedure as many times as possible.

Rules: The chest, no other part of the body, must touch or nearly touch the floor with each dip. The arms must be completely extended with each push-up. The body must be held straight, with no bend in the hips, throughout the exercise.

Scoring: The number of times the body is

correctly pushed up. If the body sags, if the hips rise, or if the pupil does not push completely up or go completely down, no credit is given for each push-up.

STANDING BROAD JUMP

Starting Position: A take-off line is drawn on the floor or mat. At a distance that all can jump, additional lines are drawn parallel to the take-off line and 2″ apart to a point exceeding the farthest jump anticipated. The first line should be an even number of feet from the take-off line. The pupil toes the take-off line with both feet, but with feet slightly apart, prior to each jump.

Action: Taking off from both feet, the pupil jumps as far as he can. In jumping, he crouches slightly and swings the arms to aid in the jump.

Rules: The pupil must take off from both feet and land on both feet. The start must be from a stationary position.

Scoring: The distance to the nearest inch from the take-off line to the closest heel position. If the pupil falls back, he should retake the test. Record the best of three trials.

KNEE-TOUCH SIT-UPS

Starting Position: The pupil lies on his back on the floor, knees straight, feet approximately 12″ apart, with hands clasped behind head. A scorer kneels on the floor and holds the soles of the feet against his knees, pressing firmly.

OREGON MOTOR FITNESS TEST SCORE CARD—BOYS GRADES 4, 5, AND 6

NAME ....

SCHOOL ....   COUNTY ....

DATE	Month Sept. 19......			Month 19......			Month 19......			Month 19......			Month 19......			Month 19......			Month 19......			Month 19......			Month 19......		
GRADE																												
AGE																												
HEIGHT																												
WEIGHT																												
OBJECTIVE TESTS	Test Score	Rat-ing	Std. Pts.	Test Score	Rat-ing	Std. Pts.	Test Score	Rat-ing	Std. Pts.	Test Score	Rat-ing	Std. Pts.	Test Score	Rat-ing	Std. Pts.	Test Score	Rat-ing	Std. Pts.	Test Score	Rat-ing	Std. Pts.	Test Score	Rat-ing	Std. Pts.	Test Score	Rat-ing	Std. Pts.
Standing Broad Jump																												
Push-Ups																												
Sit-Ups																												
TOTAL STANDARD POINTS																												

RATING NORMS FOR BOYS GRADES 4, 5, AND 6

TEST ITEMS	Superior	Good	Fair	Poor	Inferior	Grade
Standing Broad Jump	69-Up	62- 68	52- 61	42- 51	12- 41	
Push-Ups	25-Up	18- 24	7- 17	1- 6	0	4
Sit-Ups	64-Up	47- 63	22- 46	1- 21	0	
Standing Broad Jump	73-Up	66- 72	56- 65	46- 55	16- 45	
Push-Ups	22-Up	16- 21	7- 15	1- 6	0	5
Sit-Ups	70-Up	52- 69	22- 51	2- 21	0- 1	
Standing Broad Jump	77-Up	70- 76	59- 69	49- 58	18- 48	
Push-Ups	24-Up	18- 23	9- 17	4- 8	0- 3	6
Sit-Ups	75-Up	55- 74	25- 54	1- 24	0	
TOTAL STANDARD POINTS	204-Up	180-203	144-179	112-143	111-Down	

DIRECTIONS FOR RECORDING AND SCORING TESTS

1. Record the actual test score for each item in the column marked "Test Score" on this side of the score card.
2. Using test score, check rating norms and record superior, good, fair, poor, or inferior for each test item in the rating column.
3. Find standard point score corresponding to each actual test score in the "Scoring Table" on the back of the card and record in column marked "Standard Points"
4. Add "Standard Points" for all test items and record total at bottom of card in space on line marked "Total Standard Points".
5. Using total standard points, check rating norms to determine fitness rating of superior, good, fair, poor, or inferior. Record this rating in the space provided at the bottom of the rating column.
6. Repeat the test at the end of the school year; it is recommended that a mid-year test also be given. Below-standard individuals should be tested more frequently.

SCORING TABLE
FOR BOYS GRADES 4, 5, AND 6

Std. Pts. Based on T-Score	Standing Broad Jump in Inches			Number of Push-Ups			Number of Sit-Ups		
	4th	5th	6th	4th	5th	6th	4th	5th	6th
100	97	100	106	55	43	39	131	153	158
98	95	99	104	53	41	37	127	148	153
96	93	97	102	51	40	36	123	143	147
94	91	95	100	50	39	35	118	138	142
92	90	94	98	48	37	34	114	133	137
90	88	92	97	46	36	33	110	128	132
88	86	90	95	44	34	32	106	123	127
86	85	88	93	42	33	30	102	118	122
84	83	87	91	40	32	29	97	113	117
82	81	85	90	38	30	28	93	108	112
80	80	83	88	36	29	27	89	103	107
78	78	82	86	35	27	26	85	98	102
76	76	80	84	33	26	25	81	93	97
74	74	78	83	31	25	23	76	88	92
72	73	77	81	29	23	22	72	83	87
70	71	75	79	27	22	21	68	78	81
68	69	73	77	25	21	20	64	73	76
66	68	72	75	23	19	19	60	68	71
64	66	70	74	22	18	18	56	63	66
62	64	68	72	20	16	16	51	58	61
60	63	66	70	18	15	15	47	53	56
58	61	65	68	16	13	14	43	48	51
56	59	63	67	14	12	13	39	43	46
54	57	61	65	12	11	12	35	38	41
52	56	60	63	10	9	10	30	33	36
50	54	58	61	9	8	9	26	28	31
48	52	56	60	7	6	8	22	23	26
46	51	55	58	5	5	7	18	18	21
44	49	53	56	3	4	6	14	13	16
42	47	51	54	1	2	5	9	8	11
40	46	49	53		1	3	5	4	6
38	44	48	51			2	1	1	2
36	42	46	49			1			
34	41	44	47						
32	39	43	45						
30	37	41	44						
28	35	39	42						
26	34	38	40						
24	32	36	38						
22	30	34	37						
20	29	33	35						
18	27	31	33						
16	25	29	31						
14	24	27	30						
12	22	26	28						
10	20	24	26						
8	18	22	24						
6	17	21	23						
4	15	19	21						
2	13	17	19						
1	12	16	18						

GENERAL INSTRUCTIONS TO TEACHERS

1. The motor fitness tests are to be taken by only those individuals who are physically able to participate in the regular program of physical education.
2. In no instance should pupils be permitted to perform any test more than is necessary to get one hundred points. Performance should be stopped on any test if, in the opinion of the instructor, the pupil is overtaxing himself.
3. Individuals should be acquainted with the tests in advance of the testing period and sufficient practice should be allowed for thorough understanding of the execution of the tests.
4. Time should be provided for a few minutes warm-up at the beginning of each test period.
5. All equipment and facilities necessary for the administration of the tests should be prepared before the testing period begins.
6. Establish a policy of strictly enforcing all rules and regulations in scoring and administering the test.

Action: The pupil performs the following movement as many times as possible: (a) Raise the trunk, rotating it somewhat to the left, and bend forward far enough to touch the right elbow to the left knee. (b) Lower the trunk to the floor. (c) Sit up again, but rotate the trunk to the right and touch the left elbow to the right knee. (d) Again lower the trunk to the floor.

Rules: The knees may be slightly bent as the subject sits up. The pupils must not pause during the test; the movement must be continuous either when leaning forward to touch the knee or when lowering the trunk to the floor. Bouncing from the floor is not permissible.

Scoring: One point is given for each complete movement of touching elbow to knee. No score should be counted if the subject unclasps hands from head, rests on the floor or when sitting, or keeps knees bent when lying on the back or when beginning the sit-up.

Directions for Administering the Girls' Test Battery
(Grades 4, 5, and 6)

HANGING IN ARM-FLEXED POSITION

Equipment: A horizontal bar or similar support parallel to the floor; a stopwatch, or a watch with a second hand; a stool or bench.

Starting Position: The student stands on a stool or table placing the hands shoulder-width apart, palms outward on a one-inch

---

OREGON MOTOR FITNESS TEST SCORE CARD—GIRLS GRADES 4, 5, AND 6

NAME ....

SCHOOL .... COUNTY ....

DATE	Month Sept. 19......			Month 19......			Month 19......			Month 19......			Month 19......			Month 19......			Month 19......			Month 19......			Month 19......		
GRADE																											
AGE																											
HEIGHT																											
WEIGHT																											
OBJECTIVE TESTS	Test Score	Rat- ing	Std. Pts.	Test Score	Rat- ing	Std. Pts.	Test Score	Rat- ing	Std. Pts.	Test Score	Rat- ing	Std. Pts.	Test Score	Rat- ing	Std. Pts.	Test Score	Rat- ing	Std. Pts.	Test Score	Rat- ing	Std. Pts.	Test Score	Rat- ing	Std. Pts.	Test Score	Rat- ing	Std Pts
Hanging in Arm-Flexed Position																											
Standing Broad Jump																											
Crossed-Arm Curl-Ups																											
TOTAL STANDARD POINTS																											

RATING NORMS FOR GIRLS GRADES 4, 5, AND 6

TEST ITEMS	Superior	Good	Fair	Poor	Inferior	Grade
Hanging in Arm-Flexed Position	30-Up	20- 29	5- 19	1- 4	0	
Standing Broad Jump	65-Up	58- 64	49- 57	39- 48	0- 38	4
Crossed-Arm Curl-Ups	66-Up	50- 65	26- 49	2- 25	0- 1	
Hanging in Arm-Flexed Position	31-Up	22- 30	10- 21	2- 9	0- 1	
Standing Broad Jump	75-Up	68- 74	57- 67	46- 56	0- 45	5
Crossed-Arm Curl-Ups	68-Up	52- 67	28- 51	4- 27	0- 3	
Hanging in Arm-Flexed Position	37-Up	27- 36	12- 26	1- 11	0	
Standing Broad Jump	73-Up	66- 72	55- 65	44- 54	0- 43	6
Crossed-Arm Curl-Ups	71-Up	55- 70	31- 54	1- 30	0	
TOTAL STANDARD POINTS	204-Up	180-203	144-179	112-143	111-Down	

DIRECTIONS FOR RECORDING AND SCORING TESTS

1. Record the actual test score for each item in the column marked "Test Score" on this side of the score card.
2. Using test score, check rating norms and record superior, good, fair, poor, or inferior for each test item in the rating column.
3. Find standard point score corresponding to each actual test score in the "Scoring Table" on the back of the card and record in column marked "Standard Points".
4. Add "Standard Points" for all test items and record total at bottom of card in space on line marked "Total Standard Points".
5. Using total standard points, check rating norms to determine fitness rating of superior, good, fair, poor, or inferior. Record this rating in space provided at the bottom of the rating column.
6. Repeat the test at the end of the school year; it is recommended that a mid-year test also be given. Below-standard individuals should be tested more frequently.

SCORING TABLE
FOR GIRLS GRADES 4, 5, AND 6

Std. Pts. Based on T-Score	Arm-Flexed Hang in Seconds			Standing Broad Jump in Inches			Number of Crossed-Arm Curl-Ups		
	4th	5th	6th	4th	5th	6th	4th	5th	6th
100	69	65	77	91	104	102	130	120	149
98	66	63	75	89	103	101	126	117	145
96	64	61	72	87	101	99	122	114	140
94	61	59	70	86	99	97	118	110	136
92	59	56	67	84	97	95	114	106	131
90	57	54	62	83	95	93	110	103	127
88	54	52	62	81	93	91	106	99	122
86	52	50	60	79	92	89	102	95	118
84	49	48	57	78	90	87	98	92	113
82	47	46	55	76	88	85	94	88	109
80	44	44	52	75	86	84	90	84	104
78	42	42	50	73	84	82	86	81	100
76	40	40	47	71	82	80	82	77	95
74	37	38	44	70	81	78	78	73	91
72	35	35	42	68	79	76	74	70	86
70	32	33	39	67	77	74	70	66	82
68	30	31	37	65	75	72	66	63	77
66	27	29	34	63	73	70	62	59	73
64	25	27	32	62	72	68	58	55	68
62	23	25	29	60	70	67	54	51	64
60	20	23	27	59	68	65	50	48	60
58	18	21	24	57	66	63	46	45	55
56	15	19	22	55	64	61	42	41	51
54	13	16	19	54	62	59	38	38	46
52	10	14	17	52	61	57	34	34	42
50	8	12	14	51	59	65	30	30	37
48	5	10	12	49	57	53	26	27	33
46	3	8	9	47	55	51	22	23	28
44	1	6	7	46	53	50	18	19	24
42		4	4	44	51	48	14	16	20
40		2	1	42	50	46	10	12	16
38				41	48	44	6	8	11
36				39	46	42	3	4	6
34				38	44	40	1	1	1
32				36	42	38			
30				34	41	36			
28				33	39	35			
26				31	37	33			
24				30	35	31			
22				28	33	29			
20				26	31	27			
18				25	30	25			
16				23	28	23			
14				22	26	21			
12				20	24	19			
10				18	22	18			
8				17	20	16			
6				15	19	14			
4				14	17	12			
2				12	15	10			
1				11	14	9			

GENERAL INSTRUCTIONS TO TEACHERS

1. The motor fitness tests are to be taken by only those individuals who are physically able to participate in the regular program of physical education.
2. In no instance should pupils be permitted to perform any test more than is necessary to get one hundred points. Performance should be stopped on any test if, in the opinion of the instructor, the pupil is overtaxing himself.
3. Individuals should be acquainted with the tests in advance of the testing period and sufficient practice should be allowed for thorough understanding of the execution of the tests.
4. Time should be provided for a few minutes warm-up at the beginning of each test period.
5. All equipment and facilities necessary for the administration of the tests should be prepared before the testing period begins.
6. Establish a policy of strictly enforcing all rules and regulations in scoring and administering the test.

standard horizontal bar or ladder with elbows flexed to permit chin to be level with the bar.

Action: The support is removed. The student holds her chin at the level of the bar as long as possible.

Rules: The legs should remain extended throughout.

Scoring: The number of seconds the student is able to maintain some flexion in the elbow, preventing the upper arm from straightening.

STANDING BROAD JUMP

Starting Position: A take-off line is drawn on the floor or mat. At a distance that all can jump, additional lines are drawn parallel to the take-off line and 2" apart to a point exceeding the farthest jump anticipated. The first line should be an even number of feet from the take-off line. The student toes the take-off line with both feet, but with feet slightly apart, prior to each jump.

Action: Taking off from both feet, the student jumps as far as she can. In jumping, she crouches slightly and swings the arms to aid in the jump.

Rules: The student must take off from both feet and land on both feet. The start must be from a stationary position.

Scoring: The distance to the nearest inch from the take-off line to the closest heel position. If a student falls back, she should retake the test. Record the best of three trials.

CROSSED-ARM CURL-UPS

Starting Position: The student assumes a lying position on the back with knees bent at approximately a right angle, soles of the feet flat on the floor, arms folded and held against the chest. The feet of the student tested should be held down firmly by a partner. The feet are hip-width apart.

Action: The student rises to an erect sitting position and returns to a back lying position as many times as possible without stopping.

Rules: The feet must remain on the floor throughout the test. The elbows must be kept down, and the arms are not used to help the body sit up. Bouncing from the floor is not permissible. Resting during any phase of the performance is not allowed.

Scoring: The number of times the student raises herself correctly to a sitting position.

D. TEST ADMINISTRATION

Throughout the school year, testing should be accomplished at least twice. Testing should be done at the beginning of the school year to select the low-fitness children and to point out directions the program should take. Testing at the end of the year can provide information with respect to what has been accomplished. Another testing period can be scheduled midway (January or February) to provide an indication of progress at that point.

Testing is always a problem for the individual teacher without help. It is difficult for children to supervise each other and secure reliable measurements.

This source would like to recommend a plan where the school secures the help of the PTA in the testing program. Interested parents make excellent testers. A team of parents for testing can be established on a school, group of schools, or school district basis, depending upon the situation. Where such a plan is in operation, school districts report enthusiastic support of the testing and of the entire physical education program.

The testers must first undergo orientation and training in the testing procedures. A trial run with one class or a small group will help iron out most difficulties. The testing program should be organized efficiently with good testing procedures. Each tester should have detailed instructions for each station.

If enough parents are available, it is well to have two testers at each station. One has a clip board and does the recording, while the other does the measuring.

Two systems of recording the information can be used. One is to have class lists at each station for recording. The second is for each child to have an individual record card, which he carries with him from station to station. The first method is speedier, but care must be taken to match the correct name with the performance. The class lists have to be transferred to the individual cards after the testing is over.

Some school districts are successfully using IBM cards on which to record the data. This provides a ready and easy means of analyzing the data. Laborious hand tabulation of the results is eliminated.

The test results, or at least the interpretation thereof, should be a part of the child's health records and should be included in the periodic progress report to the parent. The school report card should contain a section devoted to the physical side of the child.

Test results for a class and for the school should be interpreted in the light of national norms and in comparison with local achievement. Testing is meaningless unless the real concern is for upgrading the physical education program and raising physical levels of the children to desirable standards.

E. PRESIDENTIAL PHYSICAL FITNESS AWARDS

An award program has been established by the President's Council on Physical Fitness to give recognition to those students who demonstrate exceptional physical achievement. Boys and girls who score at or above the standards listed below in all seven events of the national test will be eligible for the Presidential Award.

Presidential Physical Fitness Award

Boys

Age	Situps	Pullups	Broad Jump	50-Yard Dash	600-Yard Run	Soft Ball Throw	Shuttle Run
10	100	6	5'8"	7.4 sec.	2 min. 12 sec.	122 ft.	10.4 sec.
11	100	6	5'10"	7.4 sec.	2 min. 8 sec.	136 ft.	10.3 sec.
12	100	6	6'2"	7.0 sec.	2 min. 2 sec.	150 ft.	10.0 sec.
13	100	8	6'9"	6.9 sec.	1 min. 53 sec.	175 ft.	9.9 sec.

Girls

Age	Situps	Flexed Arm Hang	Broad Jump	50-Yard Dash	600-Yard Run	Soft Ball Throw	Shuttle Run
10	50	21 sec.	5'4"	7.5 sec.	2 min. 20 sec.	71 ft.	10.8 sec.
11	50	20 sec.	5'8"	7.6 sec.	2 min. 24 sec.	81 ft.	10.6 sec.
12	50	19 sec.	5'9"	7.5 sec.	2 min. 24 sec.	90 ft.	10.5 sec.
13	50	18 sec.	5'10"	7.5 sec.	2 min. 25 sec.	94 ft.	10.5 sec.

The student who qualifies receives a certificate suitable for framing. Printed in gold and black, it bears the President's signature, Presidential seal, a congratulatory message, and the recipient's name. In addition, schools are required to purchase an Award emblem for each student qualifying for the honor. The emblem is designed to be worn on sweaters, jackets, and blazers.

The awards program has for its purposes: (1) to motivate boys and girls to develop and maintain a high level of physical fitness, (2) to encourage good testing programs in the schools, and (3) to stimulate improvement of health and physical education programs in our schools.

Schools desiring to participate in this awards program should write to:

Presidential Physical Fitness Awards
1201 Sixteenth Street, N.W.
Washington, D. C. 20036

Appendix II

Diagrams for Constructing Physical Education Equipment and Supplies

Diagrams are presented for constructing the following physical education materials:

1. Balls, Yarn
2. Balance Boards
3. Balance Beams (Jump Board)
4. Blocks and Cones
5. Bounding Board
6. Individual Mats
7. Individual Tug of War Ropes
8. Jumping Boxes
9. Magic Ropes (Stretch Ropes)
10. Quoits or Deck Tennis Rings
11. Plastic Markers and Ball Scoop
12. Wands

In most cases the diagrams present measurements which can be subject to variation. In some instances several designs are presented to provide choice. The selection of materials is also subject to choice.

YARN BALLS

To make a yarn ball the following materials are needed:

One skein of yarn per ball
Piece of box cardboard 5" wide and 10" or so long
Strong light cord for binding

Wrap the yarn 20 to 25 times around the 5" width of the cardboard. Slide the yarn off the cardboard and wrap it in the middle with the cord, forming a tied loop of yarn. Continue until all the yarn is used up.

Take two of the tied loops and connect (tie) them together at the centers, using several turns of the cord. This forms a bundle of two tied loops as illustrated.

Next, tie bundles together by pairs. Then, form the ball by tying the paired bundles together until all bundles are used.

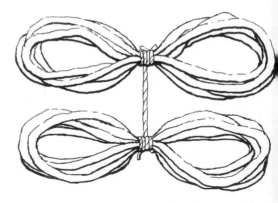

The final step is to cut and trim the formed ball. Cutting should be carefully done so that the lengths are reasonably even or considerable trimming will be needed.

The ball can be soaked in hot water or steamed to make it shrink and become more firm. Only cotton and wool yarns will shrink. Nylon and similar materials are impervious to water.

BALANCE BEAM

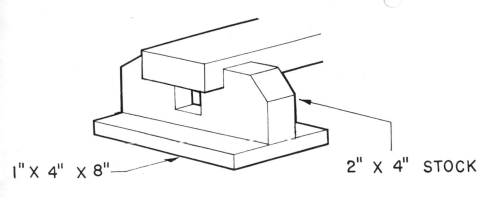

1" X 4" X 8"

2" X 4" STOCK

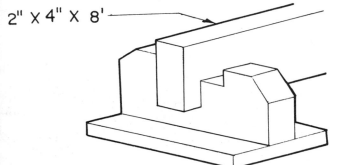

2" X 4" X 8'

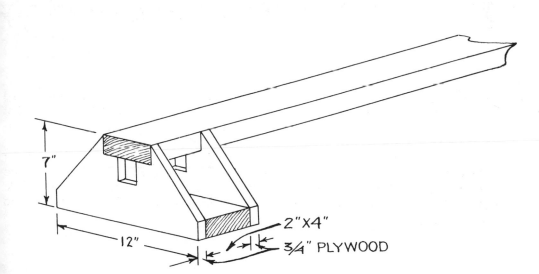

7"

12"

2"X4"

3/4" PLYWOOD

BALANCE BOARDS

1. SINGLE AXIS

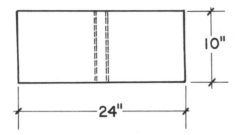

10"

24"

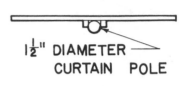

1½" DIAMETER
CURTAIN POLE

2. SQUARE TOP, SQUARE BOTTOM

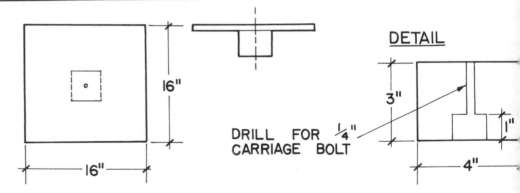

16"

16"

DETAIL

3"

1"

4"

DRILL FOR ¼"
CARRIAGE BOLT

3. CIRCULAR BOARD

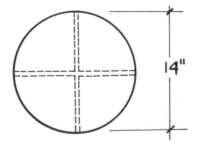

14"

3"-6"

BLOCKS AND CONES

USED TO MAKE HURDLES AND OBSTACLES

<u>BLOCKS</u>   4"X4"X12" OR 4"X4"X8"

<u>DOWN POSITION</u>

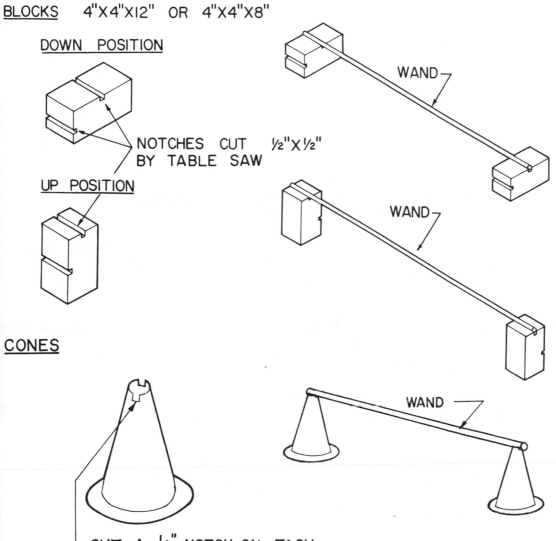

NOTCHES CUT   ½"X½"
BY TABLE SAW

<u>UP POSITION</u>

WAND

WAND

<u>CONES</u>

WAND

CUT A ½" NOTCH ON EACH
SIDE OF TOP LIP OF CONE

BOUNDING BOARD

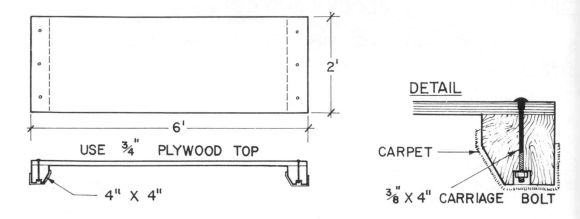

USE ¾" PLYWOOD TOP

4" X 4"

DETAIL

CARPET

⅜" X 4" CARRIAGE BOLT

HOOPS – CONSTRUCTION, SUPPORT

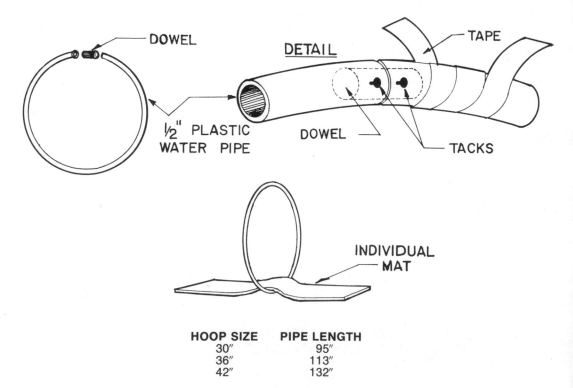

DOWEL

DETAIL

TAPE

½" PLASTIC WATER PIPE

DOWEL

TACKS

INDIVIDUAL MAT

HOOP SIZE	PIPE LENGTH
30″	95″
36″	113″
42″	132″

INDIVIDUAL TUG OF WAR ROPES

1. SINGLE

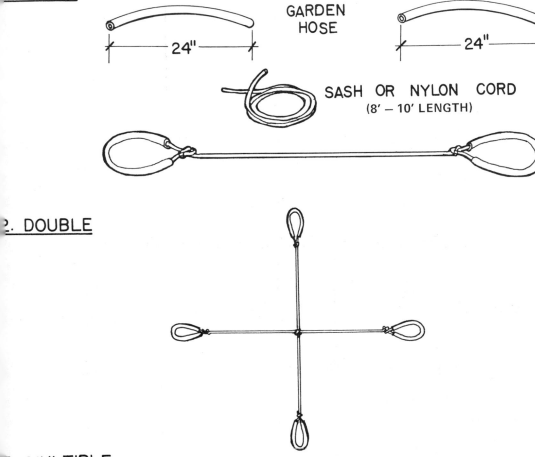

GARDEN HOSE

24"   24"

SASH OR NYLON CORD
(8' – 10' LENGTH)

2. DOUBLE

3. MULTIPLE

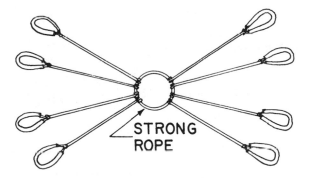

STRONG ROPE

INDIVIDUAL MATS

INDOOR — OUTDOOR CARPETING

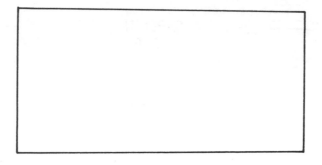

20"X 40"   OR   24" X 48"

JUMPING BOXES

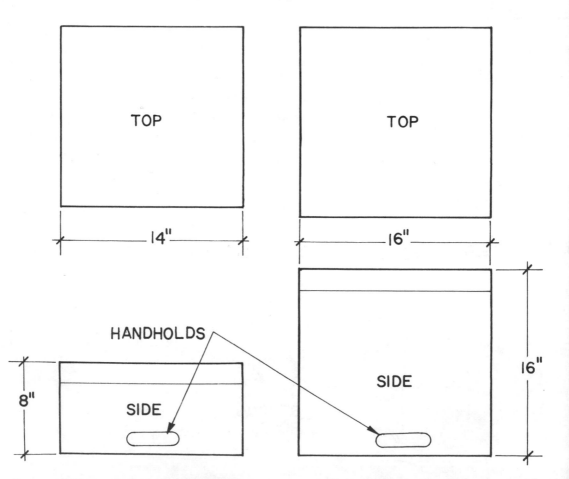

TOP

TOP

|← 14" →|

|← 16" →|

HANDHOLDS

8"

SIDE

SIDE

16"

MAGIC (STRETCH) ROPES

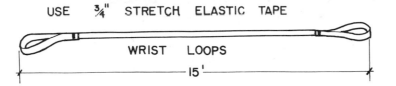

USE   ¾" STRETCH ELASTIC TAPE

WRIST LOOPS

15'

PADDLE DIAGRAM

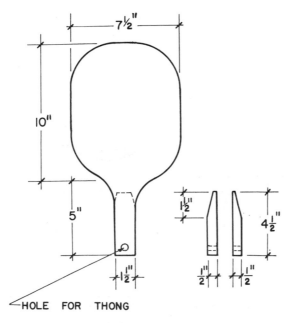

7½"

10"

5"

1½"

HOLE FOR THONG

1½"

4½"

½"   ½"

PLASTIC MARKERS AND BALL SCOOP

MARKER

SCOOP

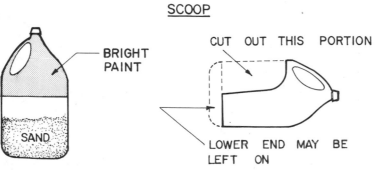

BRIGHT PAINT

SAND

CUT OUT THIS PORTION

LOWER END MAY BE LEFT ON

QUOITS OR DECK TENNIS RINGS

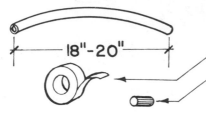

½" GARDEN HOSE

PLASTIC ELECTRICIAN'S TAPE

⅝" WOODEN DOWELL 2" LONG

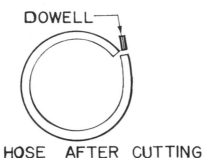

DOWELL

FINISHED RING

HOSE AFTER CUTTING

WANDS

⅝" OR ¾" DOWLING

LENGTHS: K-1 = 30",   1-3 = 36",   4 - 6 = 42"

Appendix III

Sources for Records for the Rhythmic Program in the Elementary School

The following sources, in most cases, handle a variety of records. It is suggested that you write and ask for descriptive literature. The request should include the type of rhythmic program and the grade level for which the records are intended.

Bee Cross Media Inc.
Dept. JH
36 Dogwood Glen
Rochester, N. Y. 14625

Bowmar Records
Dept. J-569
622 Rodier Dr.
Glendale, Calif. 91201

Canadian F. D. S.
Educational Recordings
605 King Street
W. Toronto, 2B, Canada

Cheviot Corporation, Dept. J-33
P. O. Box 34485
Los Angeles, Calif. 90034

Children's Music Center
5373 W. Pico Blvd.
Los Angeles, Calif. 90019

Dance Record Center
1161 Broad Street
Newark, N. J. 07114

David McKay, Inc.
750 Third Ave.
New York, N. Y. 10017

Educational Activities, Inc.
P. O. Box 392
Freeport, N. Y. 11520

Educational Recordings of America, Inc.
P. O. Box 6062
Bridgeport, Conn. 06606

Folkraft Records
1159 Broad Street
Newark, N. J. 07714

Freda Miller Records for Dance
Department J, Box 383
Northport, Long Island, N. Y. 11768

Hoctor Educational Records, Inc.
Waldwick, N. J. 07463

Herbert
1657 Broadway
New York, N. Y. 10019

Instructor Publications, Inc.
Dansville, N. Y. 14437

Kimbo Educational Records
P. O. Box 55
Deal, N. J. 07723

Leo's Advance Theatrical Co.
32 West Randolph Street
Chicago, Ill. 60601

Loshin's
215 East Eighth St.
Cincinnati, Ohio 45202

Master Record Service
708 East Garfield
Phoenix, Ariz. 85000

Merrback Records Service
P. O. Box 7308
Houston, Tex. 77000

RCA Victor Education Dept. J
155 E. 24th Street
New York, N. Y. 10010

Record Center
2581 Piedmont Road N. E.
Atlanta, Ga. 30324

Rhythms Productions Records
Dept. J., Box 34485
Los Angeles, Calif. 90034

Rhythm Record Co.
9203 Nichols Road
Oklahoma City, Okla. 73120

Russell Records
P. O. Box 3318
Ventura, Calif. 93003

Selva and Sons, Inc.
Dept. J, 1607 Broadway
New York, N. Y. 10019

Square Dance Square
P. O. Box 689
Santa Barbara, Calif. 93100

Stanley Bowmar Co., Inc.
4 Broadway
Valhalla, N. Y. 10595

Appendix IV

Bibliography and Related Materials Resource

For the user's convenience this bibliography is divided into major subject areas. Addresses of the various publishers can be obtained at most libraries and from the *Publishers' Trade List Annual* and *Books in Print*. A listing of card packets for games, rhythms, and stunts has also been included. It should be noted that in some instances titles include more than one area, however, these were classified under the area of greatest emphasis.

"AAHPER" refers to the American Association for Health, Physical Education and Recreation, 1201 Sixteenth Street, N.W., Washington, D.C. 20036.

The bibliography is organized under the following headings:

1. Curriculum in Elementary School Physical Education
2. Fitness and Exercise
3. Games and Similar Activities
4. Rhythms, Songs, and Dances
5. Stunts, Tumbling, and Apparatus
6. Health, Safety, and Posture
7. Perceptual-Motor Development
8. Card Packets for Games, Rhythms, and Stunts
9. English Books on Movement
10. Miscellaneous

1. CURRICULUM IN ELEMENTARY SCHOOL PHYSICAL EDUCATION

AAHPER. *Essentials of a Quality Elementary School Physical Education Program.* Washington, D. C., 1970.

— *Promising Practices in Elementary School Physical Education.* Washington, D. C., 1969.

— *Trends in Elementary School Physical Education.* Washington, D. C., 1970.

Anderson, Elliot, and laBerge. *Play with a Purpose.* New York: Harper & Row, 1966.

Andrews, Sauborn, and Schneider. *Physical Education for Today's Boys and Girls.* Boston: Allyn & Bacon, 1960.

Arra, Carl. *Physical Education in the Elementary School.* Cranbury, N. J.: A. S. Barnes, 1970.

Association for Childhood Education International. *Physical Education for Children's Healthful Living.* Washington, D. C.: ACEI, 1968.

Boyer, Madeline Haas. *The Teaching of Elementary School Physical Education.* New York: J. Lowell Pratt, 1965.

Brown, Margaret C., and Betty K. Sommer. *Movement Education: Its Evolution and a Modern Approach.* Reading, Mass.: Addison-Wesley, 1969.

Bucher, Charles A., and Evelyn M. Reade. *Physical Education and Health in the Elementary School.* New York: Macmillan, 1971.

Corbin, C. *Becoming Physically Educated in the Elementary School.* Philadelphia: Lea & Febiger, 1969.

Cratty, Bryant, et al. *Movement Activities, Motor Ability, and the Education of Children.* Springfield, Ill.: C. C. Thomas, 1970.

Demeter, Rose. *Hop-Run-Jump: We Exercise with Our Children.* Edited by M. Wuest and M. Moskin. New York: John Day, 1968.

Department of Education, N. S. W. *Physical Education in Primary Schools.* Sydney, N. S. W., Australia; Minister for Education, N. S. W., n. d.

Detroit Public Schools. *It's All in the Game — About Children in Play.* Detroit: The Board of Education of the City of Detroit, 1961.

Espenschade, Anna S. *Physical Education in the Elementary Schools (#27 of the Series, What Research Says to the Teacher).* Washington, D. C.: National Education Association, 1963.

Fabricius, Helen. *Physical Education for the Classroom Teacher.* Dubuque, Iowa: Wm. C. Brown, 1965.

Fait, Hollis F. *Physical Education for the Elementary School Child.* Philadelphia: Saunders, 1971.

Gilliom, Bonnie Cherp. *Basic Movement Education for Children: Rationale and Teaching Units.* Reading, Mass.: Addison-Wesley, 1970.

Glass, Henry "Buzz." *Exploring Movement.* Freeport, New York: Educational Activities, Inc., 1966.

Greene, Arthur S. *Physical Activities for Elementary Schools.* Minneapolis, Minn.: T. S. Denison, 1963.

Hackett, Layne C., and Robert G. Jenson. *A Guide to Movement Exploration.* Palo Alto, Calif.: Peek Publications, 1966.

Halsey, Elizabeth, and Lorena Porter. *Physical Education for Children, A Developmental Program.* New York: Henry Holt (Dryden Press), 1963.

Hatcher, Caro, and Hilda Mullin. *More than Words — Movement Activities for Children.* Pasadena: Parents-for-Movement Publications, 1969.

Humphrey, James H. *Child Learning Through Elementary School Physical Education.* Dubuque, Iowa: Wm. C. Brown, 1965.

Jordan, Diana. *Children and Movement.* New Rochelle, N. Y.: Sportshelf, 1968.

Kirchner, Cunningham, Worrell. *Introduction to Movement Education.* Dubuque, Iowa: Wm. C. Brown, 1970.

Kirchner, Glenn. *Physical Education for Elementary School Children.* 2d ed. Dubuque, Iowa: Wm. C. Brown, 1971.

Latchaw, Marjorie. *A Pocket Guide of Movement Activities for the Elementary School.* Englewood Cliffs, N. J.: Prentice-Hall, 1970.

Latchaw, Marjorie, and G. Egstrom. *Human Movement: With Concepts Applied to Children's Movement Activities.* Englewood Cliffs, N. J.: Prentice-Hall, 1970.

Miller, Arthur G., and Virginia Whitcomb. *Physical Education in the Elementary School Curriculum.* Englewood Cliffs, N. J.: Prentice-Hall, 1969.

Mosston, Muska. *Developmental Movement.* Columbus, Ohio: Charles E. Merrill Books, 1965.

Neilson, Van Hagen, and Comer. *Physical Education for Elementary Schools.* New York: Ronald Press, 1966.

Ontario Department of Education. *Physical Education — Junior Division.* Toronto, Ontario: Canadian Association for Health, Physical Education, and Recreation (515 Jarvis St.), 1960.

Porter, Lorena. *Movement Education for Children.* Washington, D. C.: AAHPER, 1969.

Salt, Fox, and Stevens. *Teaching Physical Education in the Elementary School.* New York: Ronald Press, 1960.

Schurr, Evelyn. *Movement Experiences for Children.* New York: Appleton-Century-Crofts, 1967.

Smalley, Jeannette. *Physical Education Activities for the Elementary School.* Palo Alto, Calif.: National Press Publications, n.d.

Society of State Directors of Health, Physical Education, and Recreation. *A Statement of Basic Beliefs.* Washington, D. C., 1964.

Spath, Martha. *Education in Play.* Kirksville, Mo.: Simpson, 1966.

Stanley, Sheila. *Physical Education: A Movement Orientation.* Scarborough, Ontario: McGraw-Hill Book Co. of Canada, 1969.

Sweeney, Robert T. *Selected Readings in Movement Education.* Reading, Mass.: Allison-Wesley, 1970.

Tillotson, Joan, et al. *A Program of Movement Education for the Plattsburgh Elementary Public Schools.* Plattsburgh, N. Y., 1969.

Vannier, Maryhelen, and Mildred Foster. *Teaching Physical Education in Elementary Schools. Philadelphia:* Saunders, 1963.

Wickstrom, Ralph L. *Fundamental Movement Patterns.* Philadelphia: Lea & Febiger, 1970.

Wiener, Jack, and John Lidstone. *Creative Movement for Children: A Dance Program for the Classroom.* New York: Van Nostrand-Reinhold, 1969.

Young, Helen L. *A Manual-Workbook of Physical Education for Elementary School Teachers.* New York: Macmillan, 1963.

2. FITNESS AND EXERCISE

Available at the AAHPER

Exercise and Fitness (Statement by the American Medical Association and the AAHPER). 1964.

Fitness Test Manual. 1965.

Your Child's Health and Fitness. (Brochure. Available in quantities.)

Your Child's Health and Fitness Filmstrip.

Also available from the AAHPER is a variety of fitness materials, including record forms, certificates, emblems, and bar patches. Write for descriptive literature.

Available from the President's Council on Physical Fitness. Write to Superintendent of Documents, U. S. Government Printing Office, Washington, D. C.

Adult Physical Fitness. 1963.

Vim (Fitness program for girls), 1964.

Vigor (Fitness program for boys), 1964.

Youth Physical Fitness. Suggested Elements of a School Centered Program, 1966.

Physical Fitness Elements in Recreation, 1963.

Bowerman, William J., and W. E. Harris. *Jogging.* New York: Grosset and Dunlap, 1967.

Nelson, Dale O. *Special Exercises for Physical Fitness.* Logan, Utah: Dept. of Health, P. E., and Rec., Utah State University, 1964.

Royal Canadian Air Force. *Exercise Plans for Physical Fitness.* New York: Pocket Books, 1962.

Wallis, Earl L., and Gene A. Logan. *Exercises for Children.* Englewood Cliffs, N. J.: Prentice-Hall, 1966.

3. GAMES AND SIMILAR ACTIVITIES

AAHPER. *After-School Games and Sports: Grades 4-5-6.* Washington, D. C., 1964.

————. *How We Do It Game Book.* Washington, D. C., 1964.

————. *ICHPER Book of Worldwide Games and Dances.* Washington, D. C., 1967.

————. *Recreational Games and Sports (Girls),* Washington, D. C., 1963.

————. *Values in Sport.* Washington, D. C., 1963.

Athletic Institute. *How to Improve Your Track and Field for Elementary School Children and Junior High School Girls.* Chicago: Athletic Institute, n.d.

Bancroft, Jessie H. *Games,* revised edition. New York: Macmillan, n.d.

Bell, R. C. *Board and Table Games from Many Civilizations.* New York: Oxford University Press, 1960.

Bentley, William G. *Indoor and Outdoor Games.* Palo Alto, Calif.: Fearon Publishers, 1966.

Borst, Evelyne. *The Book of Games for Boys and Girls: How to Lead and Play Them.* New York: Ronald Press, 1953.

Borst, Evelyne and Elmer D. Mitchell. *Social Games for Recreation.* New York: Ronald Press, 1959.

Depew, Arthur M. *The Cokesbury Game Book.* Nashville: Abingdon Press, 1960.

Donnelly, Richard J., William G. Helms, and Elmer D. Mitchell. *Active Games and Contests.* New York: Ronald Press, 1958.

Ewing, Neil. *Games, Stunts, and Exercises.* Palo Alto, Calif.: Fearon Publishers, 1964.

Frankel, Lillian and Godrey. *Games for Boys and Girls.* New York: Sterling, n.d.

Gardner, Grace H. *Games We Like to Play.* New York: Williams-Frederick Press, 1959.

Geri, Frank. *Illustrated Games, Rhythms and Stunts for Children* (Upper Elementary). Englewood Cliffs, N. J.: Prentice-Hall, 1957.

_____. *Illustrated Games and Rhythms for Children* (Primary Grades). Englewood Cliffs, N. J.: Prentice-Hall, 1955.

Harbin, E. O. *Games of Many Nations.* Nashville: Abingdon Press, 1954.

_____. *Games for Boys and Girls* (Gr. 3-5). Nashville: Abingdon Press, 1951.

Hindman, Darwin A. *Complete Book of Games and Stunts.* Englewood Cliffs, N. J.: Prentice-Hall, 1956.

_____. *Handbook of Indoor Games and Stunts.* Englewood Cliffs, N. J.: Prentice-Hall, 1955.

Hofsinde, Robert. *Indian Games and Crafts.* New York: Morrow, 1957.

Hunt, Sarah E. *Games and Sports the World Around.* New York: Ronald Press, 1964.

Kraus, Richard. *The Family Book of Games.* New York: McGraw-Hill, 1960.

_____. *Play Activities for Boys and Girls.* New York: McGraw-Hill, 1957.

Latchaw, Marjorie. *A Pocket Guide of Games and Rhythms for the Elementary School.* Englewood Cliffs, N. J.: Prentice-Hall, 1958.

Lowenfeld, Margaret. *Play in Childhood.* New York: Wiley, 1967.

Macfarlan, Allan A. *Book of American Indian Games.* New York: Association Press, 1958.

_____. *More New Games for 'Tween-Agers.* New York: Association Press, 1958.

Macfarlan, Allan and Paulette. *Fun with Brand-New Games.* New York: Association Press, 1961.

Matterson, E. M. *Play and Playthings for the Preschool Child.* Baltimore: Penguin, 1967.

Nagel, Charles. *Play Activities for Elementary Grades.* St. Louis: Mosby, 1964.

Stuart, Frances R. *Classroom Activities.* Washington, D. C.: AAHPER, 1963.

4. RHYTHMS, SONGS AND DANCES

Andrews, Gladys. *Creative Rhythmic Movement for Children.* Englewood Cliffs, N. J.: Prentice-Hall, 1954.

Ashton, Dudley. *Rhythmic Activities — Grades K-6.* Washington, D. C.: AAHPER, 1964.

Barr, Lillian J. *Motion Song for Tots.* Minneapolis: T. S. Denison, n.d.

Bley, Edgar S. *Best Singing Games for Children of All Ages.* New York: Sterling, 1959.

Boorman, Joyce. *Creative Dance in the First Three Grades.* New York: McKay, 1969.

Buttree, Julia M. *The Rhythm of the Redman in Song, Dance and Decoration.* New York: Ronald Press, 1930.

Carabo-Cone, Madeleine. *Playground as Music Teacher.* New York: Harper & Row, 1959.

Doll, Edna, and Mary Jarman Nelson. *Rhythms Today.* Morristown, N. J.: Silver, 1965.

Driver, Ann. *Music and Movement.* New York: Oxford University Press, 1936.

Duggan, Schlottman and Rutledge. *The Folk Dance Library* (five volumes). The Teaching of Folk Dance, Folk Dances of Scandinavia, European Countries, British Isles, United

States and Mexico. New York: Ronald Press, 1948.

Evans, Ruth. *40 Basic Rhythms for Children.* Putnam, Conn.: U. S. Textbook Co., 1958.

Flood, Jessie B., and Cornelia F. Putney. *Square Dance U. S. A.* Dubuque, Iowa: Wm. C. Brown, 1955.

Fox, Grace and Kathleen G. Merrill. *Folk Dancing.* New York: Ronald Press, 1957.

Harris, Pittman and Waller. *Dance-A-While.* Minneapolis: Burgess, 1964.

Heaton, A. *Fun Dances.* Dubuque, Iowa: Wm. C. Brown, 1959.

Kraus, Richard G. *Square Dances of Today and How to Teach and Call Them.* New York: Ronald Press, 1950.

Kulbitsky and Kaltman. *Teacher's Dance Handbook No. 1.* Newark, N. J.: Folkraft, 1959.

LaSalle, Dorothy. *Rhythms and Dances for Elementary Schools.* New York: Ronald Press, 1951.

Mason, Bernard S. *Dances and Stories of the American Indian.* New York: Ronald Press, 1944.

McIntosh, David S. *Singing Games and Dances.* New York: Association Press, 1957.

Metz, Louis L. *Action Songs and Rhythms for Children.* Minneapolis: T. S. Denison, 1962.

Murray, Ruth Lovell. *Dance in Elementary Education.* New York: Harper & Row, 1963.

Russell, Joan. *Creative Dance in the Primary School.* London: McDonald & Evans, Ltd., 1965.

Ryan, Grace L. *Dances of our Pioneers.* New York: Ronald Press, 1939.

Tobitt, Janet. *Red Book of Singing Games and Dances from the Americas.* Evanston, Ill.: Summy-Birchard, n.d.

_____. *Yellow Book of Singing Games and Dances From Around the World.* Evanston, Ill.: Summy-Birchard, n.d.

5. STUNTS, TUMBLING, AND APPARATUS

Bailie, Sam, and Avelyn Bailie. *Elementary School Gymnastics.* St. Louis: Atlas Athletic Equipment Co., 1969.

Baley, James A. *Gymnastics in the Schools.* Boston: Allyn and Bacon, 1965.

Bedard, Irving. *Gymnastics for Boys.* Chicago: Follett, 1962.

Drehman, Vera L. *Head Over Heels.* New York: Harper & Row, 1970.

Harris, Rich. *Introducing Gymnastics.* Napa, Calif.: Physical Education Aids, 1964.

Keeney, Charles J. *Fundamental Tumbling Skills Illustrated.* New York: Ronald Press, 1966.

O'Quinn, Garland Jr. *Gymnastics for Elementary School Children.* Dubuque, Iowa: Wm. C. Brown, 1967.

Provansnik and Zabka. *Gymnastic Activities with Hand Apparatus for Girls and Boys.* Minneapolis: Burgess, 1965.

Szypula, G. *Tumbling and Balancing for All.* Dubuque, Iowa: Wm. C. Brown, 1957.

U. S. Gymnastic Federation. *Age-Group Gymnastics Work Book.* Tucson, Ariz.: U. S. G. F. Press, 1964.

6. HEALTH, SAFETY, AND POSTURE

AAHPER. *Answers to Health Questions in Physical Education.* Washington, D. C., n.d.

_____. *Health Appraisal of School Children.* Washington, D. C., 1969.

_____. *Healthful School Environment.* Washington, D. C., 1969.

_____. *Physical Growth Chart for Boys.* Washington, D. C., 1960.

_____. *Physical Growth Chart for Girls.* Washington, D. C., 1960.

_____. *Safety Education in Physical Education for the Classroom Teacher.* Washington, D. C., 1961.

_____. *Suggested Safety Policies: Accident Prevention in Physical Education Athletics,* and Recreation. Washington, D. C., 1964.

_____. Teaching Safety in the Elementary School (Classroom Teachers Series). Washington, D. C., 1962.

Darrow, May Goodall. The Posture Problem Up To Date. New York: Vantage Press, 1959.

Davies, Evelyn A. The Elementary School Child and His Posture Patterns. New York: Appleton-Century-Crofts, 1958.

Kelley, Ellen Davis. Teaching Posture and

Body Mechanics. New York: Ronald Press, 1949.

Lowman, Charles, and Carl Haven Young. Postural Fitness: Significance and Variances. Philadelphia: Lea & Febiger, 1960.

Smith, Helen N. and Mary E. Wolverton. Health Education in the Elementary School. New York: Ronald Press, 1959.

Wells, Katherine F. Posture Exercise Handbook. New York: Ronald Press, 1963.

7. PERCEPTUAL-MOTOR DEVELOPMENT

AAHPER. Approaches to Perceptual-Motor Experiences. Washington, D. C., 1970.

_____. Motor Activity and Perceptual Development — Some Implications for Physical Educators. Washington, D. C., 1968.

_____. Perceptual - Motor Foundations: A Multidisciplinary Concern. Washington, D. C., 1969.

Braley, Konicki, and Leedy. Daily Sensorimotor Training Activities. Freeport, N. Y.: Educational Activities, Inc., 1968.

Cratty, Bryant J. Perceptual-Motor Behavior and Educational Processes. Springfield, Ill.: C. C. Thomas, 1969.

Cratty, Bryant J., and Martin, Sister M. M. Perceptual-Motor Efficiency in Children, Philadelphia: Lea & Febiger, 1969.

Delacato, Carl W. The Diagnosis and Treatment of Speech and Reading Problems. Springfield, Ill.: C. C. Thomas, 1963.

_____. The Treatment and Prevention of Reading Problems. Springfield, Ill.: C. C. Thomas, 1959.

Getman, G. N. How to Develop Your Child's

Intelligence. Luverne, Minn., 1962.

Gillingham, Anna, and Bessie W. Stillman. Remedial Training for Children with Specific Disability in Reading, Spelling, and Penmanship. 6th Edition, 1960. Distributed by Anna Gillingham, 25 Parkview Avenue, Bronxville 8, N. Y.

Godfrey, Barbara, and N. C. Kephart. Movement Patterns and Motor Education. New York: Appleton-Century-Crofts, 1969.

Kephart, Newell C. The Slow Learner in the Classroom. Columbus, Ohio: Charles E. Merrill Books, 1960.

Roach, Eugene, and Newell C. Kephart. The Purdue Perceptual-Motor Survey. Columbus, Ohio: Charles E. Merrill Books, 1966.

Rosborough, Pearl M. Physical Fitness and the Child's Reading Problem. New York: Exposition Press, 1963.

Stuart, Marion F. Neurophysiological Insights into Teaching. Palo Alto, Calif.: Pacific Books, 1963.

Van Whitsen, Betty. Perceptual Training Activities Handbook. New York: Teachers College Press, 1967.

8. CARD PACKETS FOR GAMES, RHYTHMS, AND STUNTS

Berger, H. Jean. Program Activities for Camps. Minneapolis: Burgess, 1961.

Fischer, Hugo, and Dean Shawbold. Individual and Dual Stunts. Minneapolis: Burgess, 1950.

Frederick, A. Bruce. Gymnastic Action Cards. Minneapolis: Burgess, 1965.

Harris, Jane A. File O' Fun (card file for social recreation), 2d ed. Minneapolis: Burgess, 1970.

Richardson, Hazel A. Games for the Elementary School Grades. Minneapolis: Burgess, 1951.

_____. *Games for Junior and Senior High Schools.* Minneapolis: Burgess, 1957.

Stuart, Frances R., and John S. Ludlam. *Rhythmic Activities, Series I (K-3).* Minneapolis: Burgess, 1963.

_____. *Rhythmic Activities, Series II (4-6).* Minneapolis: Burgess, 1963.

Vick, Marie, and Rosann McLaughlin Cox. *A Collection of Dances for Children.* Minneapolis: Burgess, 1970.

9. ENGLISH BOOKS ON MOVEMENT

Since much of the newer emphasis on movement has its origins in England, a selected list of English books is offered. These books may be secured from the Physical Education Association of Great Britain and Northern Ireland, which stocks all books and can provide information on other British books. The address is Ling Book Shop, 10 Nottingham Place, London, W.1, England. If only one book is desired, the author recommends the book by Bilbrough and Janes, which presents a middle-of-the-road approach of English methods.

Bilbrough, A. and P. Jones. *Physical Education in the Primary School.* London: London Press, Ltd., 1964.

Cameron, W. McD. and Peggy Pleasance. *Education in Movement.* Oxford: Basic, Blackwell, and Mott, Ltd. 1963.

Edmundson, Joseph, P. E. Teachers' *Handbook for Primary Schools.* London: Evans Brothers Limited, 1960.

Laban, Rudolph (Revised by Lisa Ullmann). *Modern Educational Dance. London:* McDonald and Evans, Ltd., 1963.

London City Council. *Educational Gymnastics.* London: London City Council, 1964.

Ministry of Education. *Physical Education in the Primary School.* Part 1, "Moving and Growing;" Part 2, "Planning the Programme." London: Her Majesty's Stationery Office, 1952.

Randall, Marjorie. *Basic Movement.* London: G. Bell and Sons, Ltd., 1963.

Sharpe, Julie M. P. E. Teachers' *Handbook for Infant Schools.* London: Evans Brothers, Ltd., 1959.

Note: The Infant School in England serves children 5 to 7 years of age. The Primary School is somewhat synonymous with our intermediate school.

10. MISCELLANEOUS

AAHPER. *Adapted Education.* Washington, D. C., 1969.

_____. *Desirable Athletic Competition for Children of Elementary School Age.* Washington, D. C., 1968.

_____. *Planning Areas and Facilities for Health, Physical Education, and Recreation.* Washington, D. C., 1965.

_____. *Preparing Teachers for a Changing Society.* Washington, D. C., 1970.

_____. *Professional Preparation of the Elementary School Education Teacher.* Washington, D. C., 1969.

Athletic Institute and AAHPER. *Equipment and Supplies for Athletics, Physical Education and Recreation.* Washington, D. C., 1960.

Bale, Robert O. *Outdoor Living.* Minneapolis: Burgess, 1961.

Bell, Virginia Lee. *Sensorimotor Learning.* Pacific Palisades, Calif.: Goodyear, 1970.

Carter, Joel W. *How To Make Athletic Equipment.* New York: Ronald Press, 1960.

Cratty, Bryant J. *Movement Behavior and Motor Learning.* Philadelphia: Lea & Febiger, 1964.

Doll, Edgar A. *Oseretsky Motor Proficiency Tests.* Minneapolis: American Guidance Services, 1946.

Hartley, Ruth E., and Robert M. Goldenson. *The Complete Book of Children's Play.* New York: T. Y. Crowell, 1957.

Hammerman, Donald R., and William M. Hammerman. *Outdoor Education: A Book of Readings.* Minneapolis: Burgess, 1968.

Holt, John. *How Children Fail.* New York: Pitman, 1964.

_____. *How Children Learn.* New York: Pitman, 1969.

Institute for the Development of Education Activities, Inc. Three Pamphlets. 1. Symposium on the Training of Teachers for Elementary Schools. 2. The British Infant School. 3. Innovations in the Elementary School. Melbourne, Fla., 1969.

Lawther, John D. *The Learning of Physical Skills.* Englewood Cliffs, N. J.: Prentice-Hall, 1968.

Milliken, Margaret, Austin Hammer, and Ernest McDonald. *Field Study Manual for Outdoor Learning.* Minneapolis: Burgess, 1968.

Sapora, Allen V., and Elmer D. Mitchell. *The Theory of Play and Recreation.* New York: Ronald Press, 1961.

Singer, Robert. *Motor Learning and Human Performance.* New York: Macmillan, 1968.

Index

GAMES

TRUNK TWISTER
IR

ROWING PACE 6#

CURL UPS 6?

JUMP THE ROPE